I ACTED FROM PRINCIPLE

T0308819

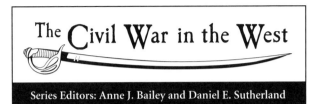

The Civil War in the West

Series Editors: Anne J. Bailey and Daniel E. Sutherland

I acted from principle

The Civil War Diary of
Dr. William M. McPheeters,
Confederate Surgeon
in the Trans-Mississippi

Edited by
CYNTHIA DEHAVEN PITCOCK
BILL J. GURLEY

THE UNIVERSITY OF ARKANSAS PRESS
Fayetteville
2002

Copyright © 2002 by The University of Arkansas Press

All rights reserved
Manufactured in the United States of America

09   08   07   06   05   5   4   3   2

Designed by Liz Lester

⊛ The paper used in this publication meets the minimum requirements
of the American National Standard for Permanence of Paper for Printed
Library Materials Z39.48-1984.

LIBRARY OF CONGRESS
CATALOGING-IN-PUBLICATION DATA

McPheeters, William M. (William Marcellus), 1815–1905.
    I acted from principle : the Civil War diary of Dr. William M.
McPheeters, confederate surgeon in the trans-Mississippi / edited
by Cynthia DeHaven Pitcock, Bill J. Gurley.
        p.   cm. — (Civil War in the West)
Includes bibliographical references and index.
ISBN 1-55728-725-2 (alk. paper)
    1. McPheeters, William M. (William Marcellus), 1815–1905—
Diaries. 2. Surgeons—Confederate States of America—Diaries.
3. United States—History—Civil War, 1861–1865—Personal
narratives, Confederate. 4. United States—History—Civil War,
1861–1865—Medical care. 5. United States—History—Civil War,
1861–1865—Social aspects. 6. Southwest, Old—History—Civil
War, 1861–1865—Personal narratives, Confederate. 7. Southwest,
Old—History—Civil War, 1861–1865—Medical care.
8. Southwest, Old—History—Civil War, 1861–1865—Social
aspects. 9. Confederate States of America. Army—Surgeons—
Biography. I. Pitcock, Cynthia DeHaven. II. Gurley, Bill J., 1959–
III. Title. IV. Series.

E625 .M35 2002
973.7′75′092—dc21   2002005330

Dedicated to the Confederate surgeons
who served in the Trans-Mississippi Department.

CONTENTS

	List of Maps and Figures	viii
	Series Editors' Preface	ix
Preface	The Diary	xi
	Acknowledgments	xv
Prologue	"A Bold Beginning," 1841–62	3
Chapter 1	The Helena Campaign, 1863	29
Chapter 2	The Womenfolk, 1863	45
Chapter 3	The Loss of Little Rock, 1863	55
Chapter 4	Winter Quarters, 1863–64	75
Chapter 5	"No Abiding Camp," Winter 1864	103
Chapter 6	Red River and Jenkins' Ferry, 1864	123
Chapter 7	A Summer's Respite, 1864	157
Chapter 8	The Grand Expedition, 1864	197
Chapter 9	Arkansas Again, 1864–65	251
Chapter 10	Banishment and Reunion, 1865	271
Chapter 11	Surrender, 1865	291
Epilogue	The Homing, 1865–1905	313
Appendix	Extant Reports	321
	Notes	335
	Index	383

MAPS AND FIGURES

MAPS

The Trans-Mississippi Theater (1863–1865)   2

McPheeters's Journey to Helena (June–August 1863)   28

Confederate Retreat from Little Rock to Winter Quarters
    (September 1863–March 1864)   74

Route of Churchill's Infantry Corps during the
    Red River Campaign (March–June 1864)   122

Price's Missouri Raid (September 1864–January 1865)   196

McPheeters's Journey to Reunite his Family
    (February 1865)   270

Surrender and Return to St. Louis (May–July 1865)   290

FIGURES

Following Page 102

William McPheeters at age forty five, 1860.

St. Louis from the Illinois side of the Mississippi River in 1854.

Julia Dent Grant, wife of Gen. Ulysses S. Grant.

Lieut. Gen. Theophilus H. Holmes.

Gen. E. Kirby Smith.

Maj. Gen. Sterling Price.

Sallie McPheeters.

A page of McPheeters' diary.

Following Page 250

Maj. Gen. Thomas J. Churchill.

Brig. Gen. James C. Tappan.

Maj. Gen. Mosby M. Parsons.

The McDowell Medical College.

Dr. William M. McPheeters, circa 1875.

Sallie McPheeters, May 10, 1899.

Planter's (House) Hotel.

SERIES EDITORS' PREFACE

The Civil War in the West has a single goal: To promote historical writing about the war in the western states and territories. It focuses most particularly on the Trans-Mississippi theater, which consisted of Missouri, Arkansas, Texas, most of Louisiana (west of the Mississippi River), Indian Territory (modern-day Oklahoma), and Arizona Territory (two-fifths of modern-day Arizona and New Mexico), but it also encompasses adjacent states, such as Kansas, Tennessee, and Mississippi, that directly influenced the Trans-Mississippi war. It is a wide swath, to be sure, but one too often ignored by historians and, consequently, too little understood and appreciated.

Topically, the series embraces all aspects of the wartime story. Military history in its many guises, from the strategies of generals to the daily lives of common soldiers, forms an important part of that story, but so too do the numerous and complex political, economic, social, and diplomatic dimensions of the war. The series also provides a variety of perspectives on these topics. Most importantly, it offers the best in modern scholarship, with thoughtful, challenging monographs. Secondly, it presents new editions of important books that have gone out of print. And thirdly, it premieres expertly edited correspondence, diaries, reminiscences, and other writings by witnesses to the war.

It is a formidable undertaking, but we believe that The Civil War in the West, by focusing on some of the least familiar dimensions of the conflict, significantly broadens our understanding of that dramatic story.

Forty-seven-year-old William Marcellus McPheeters had not counted on going to war in 1862. He was a nationally known physician, professor, medical author and editor, and public-health reformer when the Civil War began, and he had been comfortably settled in St. Louis for over twenty years. However, he was also an avowed Southerner, and the pressure on him to take an active part in the national struggle had become intense. Having consistently refused to take an oath of allegiance to the United States, he was arrested and threatened with imprisonment

more than once during the first year of the war, and an equally pro-
Confederate younger brother, who served as minister to a Presbyterian
church in St. Louis, was arrested. When Federal authorities entered
McPheeters's house and confiscated virtually all of his household goods,
he traveled to Richmond and offered his services to the Confederate
government in the spring of 1862.

He became a surgeon in the Confederate army, assigned, at his
request, to the staff of Maj. Gen. Sterling Price. For the next three years,
McPheeters was in the thick of the western war. He served for several
months in Mississippi before being assigned to Arkansas in April 1863.
He began his wartime diary two months later and maintained it
until signing his parole in June 1865. Being the first published daily
account of the Trans-Mississippi war by a Confederate medical officer,
McPheeters's diary offers a unique perspective. It records wonderful
details about the struggle to keep men alive, not only from battlefield
wounds but also from exposure, sickness, disease, and malnutrition. It
also provides intimate looks at Confederate civilians, behind the scenes
glimpses of the army's high command west of the river, and information about the treatment accorded McPheeters's family and other
Southern sympathizers in St. Louis.

The value of McPheeter's journal has been enhanced considerably
by the editorial work of Cynthia DeHaven Pitcock, an authority on
the history of medicine, and Bill J. Gurley, who combines a broad
knowledge of the military history of the Trans-Mississippi with his
nationally recognized expertise in pharmaceutical science. McPheeters
did not write his journal with an eye toward publication. Consequently,
he failed to identify many of the people and events to which he refers.
The meticulous endnotes supplied by Pitcock and Gurley, in which
they identify nearly three hundred (often obscure) individuals, have
remedied that defect, and their introduction to the diary provides a
thorough biography of McPheeters and the story behind the document.
Taken together, McPheeters, Pitcock, and Gurley have produced a riv-
eting and quite valuable account of the war in the Trans-Mississippi.

ANNE J. BAILEY
DANIEL E. SUTHERLAND
Series Co-editors

PREFACE

The Diary

William Marcellus McPheeters's story is far more than yet another account of a profoundly upright man who fought for the South during the American Civil War. The literature of this mid-nineteenth-century conflict abounds with such stories, and clearly McPheeters was one of the responsible, educated, God-fearing souls who owned no slaves and did not profit directly or indirectly from the commerce of slavery. He was not a member of the plantation-owning class.

He was a hill-country Whig born in 1815 to the family of a Presbyterian minister in Raleigh, North Carolina. One of six children, McPheeters was brought up on the rigid precepts of pioneer pragmatism and unbending Calvinism as well as the optimism widely shared in the new Republic. Both Thomas Jefferson and John Adams had espoused the Enlightenment notion of an "aristocracy of merit" designed to dislodge and replace the old world's "aristocracy of privilege," and nowhere in the new nation was this credo more passionately internalized than in the Carolinas. Those states' fiercely independent sons mistrusted big government, the federal courts, and the national bank. Their antipathy focused upon New England, for it was there that the pale ghosts of Federalism and old Tory wealth stalked the land.[1]

William McPheeters prepared himself to enter the "aristocracy of merit" by qualifying for a profession in medicine. In keeping with early lessons learned, his allegiance to God and country focused in 1860 not upon the angry sectional split of the country but upon the constitutional right of the Southern states to secede from the Union and form a new nation. McPheeters had left North Carolina to reside in St. Louis, Missouri, and had lived there twenty years by the time the war broke out. He and other Southerners were denied their civil and legal rights, publicly harassed by Federal military authorities, and eventually stripped of human rights as well, despite Pres. Abraham Lincoln's careful orders to his military forces in the fragile, potentially explosive Border States.

In a violently divided city, McPheeters was followed, arrested, threat-ened, and finally confronted with a choice of signing a loyalty oath, which severely transgressed his personal integrity, or going to a Federal prison. He decided to attempt an escape and, as the only alternative left to him, serve the Confederacy.

The diary McPheeters kept while in Confederate service offers a pair of unique features. It is the first known daily account by a Confederate medical officer in the Trans-Mississippi Department. This diary appears here in its complete and original form, not edited later, not "improved" by McPheeters himself, nor brought "up to date" by well-meaning descendants or editors. It is exactly as the doctor first wrote it. The editors have bracketed any added words that the doctor, for whatever reason, omitted in the original.

McPheeters, by his own request, served under Maj. Gen. Sterling Price and his Missouri forces west of the Mississippi River, principally in Arkansas, a state that was newly settled and still frontier. Farms there were small, family homes were modest, fortunes nascent, and slave holdings less numerous than those of Tidewater Virginia or the Mississippi Delta. The doctor's diary is an account by a medical officer of the harrowing Confederate struggle in that state. Disease, malnutrition, and shortages of all kinds stalked the "butternut boys," and McPheeters's account causes the historian's field glasses to swing to the West, where the fight was bit-ter and the sacrifice unimagined.

The second important feature of this diary is that it tells the dual story of both McPheeters's and his wife, Sallie Buchanan McPheeters. Her wartime experience included harassment by Federal military offi-cials, imprisonment in a Federal military prison in St. Louis, and ban-ishment from Missouri along with their two small children. Forced as refugees to board a riverboat, they were shipped more than four hun-dred miles downstream from St. Louis accompanied by a small band of pro-Confederate women. They were put ashore, penniless, with few possessions, exiles terrified not only by the fury of war but also by the ravages of a hundred-year flood.

The policy of banishment, widely practiced by the Union in the Border States and all Federally occupied territories, drew criticism even from the Northern press as the war neared its conclusion, but no offi-cial action or articulation of presidential moderation came to the rescue of the McPheeters family. Their personal ordeal was a trial by fire, and in its aftermath, the restoration of their lives and fortune in the same city from which they had been banished is a saga of great courage and aggressive good will. It also serves as a bellwether for the prevailing moods in the repaired Union.

The wartime diary of William Marcellus McPheeters, M.D., is part of the William McPheeters Collection at the Missouri Historical Society in St. Louis, Missouri.

ACKNOWLEDGMENTS

Transcribing and annotating the diary of Dr. William McPheeters has been a journey across the Trans-Mississippi West, through both past and present. But whether on the road or locked deep in some archive, we have been fortunate to have some savvy and patient guides.

The journey started in Missouri, and the invaluable assistance of many individuals in that state must be duly recognized. In St. Louis this includes, at the Missouri Historical Society, Martha Clevenger, Dina Young, and Ellen Thomason; at Washington University School of Medicine Library, Paul Anderson; at Washington University, Edward G. Weltin, professor emeritus; and at the St. Louis Mercantile Library, Charles E. Brown. In Columbia, we must acknowledge Fae Sotham, Laurel Boeckman, Lynn Gentzler, and Dr. James Goodrich at the State Historical Society of Missouri. In Jefferson City we are thankful for the assistance of Bob Hawkins. In Republic we appreciate the aid of Dr. Tom Sweeney of General Sweeny's Museum. And finally in Keytesville, we are especially indebted to Janet Weaver, curator of the Sterling Price Museum.

Our journey continued on to Kansas, where Carolyn Bartles of Two Trails Publishing in Shawnee Mission kindly shared her wellspring of information on Missouri's Confederates.

Other persons along the way who deserve recognition include: Steve Bounds at the Mansfield State Commemorative Area in Mansfield, Louisiana; Courtney Page at the Howard-Tilton Memorial Library at Tulane University; Major L. Wilson, professor emeritus at the University of Memphis; John Anderson at the Texas State Library and Archives Commission; and Donald Keesing of Cabin John, Maryland.

Much of our time was spent in Arkansas, where in Little Rock we owe a very special thanks to the entire research staff at the Arkansas History Commission, especially Jane Wilkerson and Russell Baker. At the University of Arkansas for Medical Sciences, we are indebted to the services of Judy Smith, Cindy Blot, Edwina Walls Mann, Margaret Johnson, Dr. Chris Hackler, and Dr. Jonathan Wolfe. We cannot overlook the encouragement of William Worthen at the Historic Arkansas

Museum. Special mention must be given to Genevieve DeHaven Emmerling for her continued support and enthusiasm throughout this journey, as well as to Bill Kerr and Meigs Brainard. In Washington we greatly appreciate the assistance given to us by the archivists and staff at the Southwest Arkansas Regional Archives. In Fayetteville we are especially grateful to Dr. Daniel Sutherland and Kevin Brock for their constructive editing of the original manuscript, and to Larry Malley, who appreciated the unique story of Dr. McPheeters and encouraged its publication.

Finally, the journey ended at home, where without the patience and encouragement of our spouses, Catherine Gurley and James A. Pitcock, this project would not have come to fruition.

BILL GURLEY AND CYNTHIA PITCOCK
Little Rock
March 4, 2002

I ACTED FROM PRINCIPLE

The Trans-Mississippi Theater (1863-1865)

"A Bold Beginning," 1841–62

Send us forth into the world to do thy will
with gladness and singleness of heart.

William McPheeters came to St. Louis, a thriving western metropolis of twenty thousand, in 1841. His formal education, just finished, was the best America could offer in preparation for the practice of medicine—graduation from the University of North Carolina at Chapel Hill, the M.D. degree from University of Pennsylvania College of Medicine in Philadelphia, and a postdoctoral year as resident physician at the famed Old Blockley Hospital.[1] He traveled by riverboat to St. Louis, arriving on October 15, 1841, at dawn, and he took a room at The Planters House, a fashionable hotel well located in the heart of the city at Fourth and Pine Streets.

McPheeters was a slender young man, just under six feet tall, with sandy hair and gray eyes, a reserved temperament, and impeccable manners from his mother's Southern home and table.[2] He was twenty-six years old. His prospects, borne of careful training and self-discipline, knew no bounds in this promising city he thoughtfully chose for its growth potential and professional opportunity. St. Louis, even at this early date, had a community of fifty prominent physicians, a medical college, and was home to the Medical Society of Missouri, then five years old.[3] McPheeters was welcomed by the society, but when he attended meetings, he found the group deeply rent by professional and personal rivalries so vicious as to all but paralyze the society. Serving as president when McPheeters arrived was a highly controversial and widely known physician, William Beaumont, but characteristically, McPheeters sidestepped all forms of controversy and was soon elected to the office of secretary. He was not inclined toward any of the organization's fiery factions, making it his business to befriend and ally himself with members of all circles and coteries; thus, in the best sense of the word, McPheeters was a friend to all. This was a temper of mind that served him well throughout his life, especially during wartime when so many men were consumed by bitterness and blame.

Eager to establish himself as a practitioner, he explored the center of the city to find a suitable location for his practice. "I took rooms," he wrote in his journal three weeks after his arrival, "at No. 45 Chestnut . . . , one for an office and one for a chamber." As he undoubtedly expected, it was slow going for several months while he waited for patients to discover him, hoping as well that his new professional contacts would pay off through referrals.[4] He sat alone in these rooms, waiting for his career to begin, but he made productive use of his time by attending lectures on medicine at the Medical Department of Kemper College. Many years later he recalled: "Prior to my arrival [in St. Louis] the celebrated Joseph Nash McDowell assisted by his friend and colleague Dr. John S. Moore established the first medical college west of the Mississippi River . . . popularly known as McDowell College. Fresh from the University of Pennsylvania and the wards of Blockly Hospital, I had the pleasure of occasionally listening to the second course of lectures in this pioneer institution."[5]

He promptly affiliated with the Presbyterian church at the corner of Eighth and Pine Streets, and there he met prominent St. Louisians who shared his social values, his faith, and his keenly developed sense of decorum. During this early period, he was introduced to the family of Lt. John Graham, USN, whose country home, Montrose, lay fourteen miles west of the city and whose origins were Southern, like his own, having come to St. Louis from Kentucky. McPheeters soon became a frequent guest in their plantation home, and he shared many Graham friendships. One friendship in particular with Pink Seldon of Lynchburg, Virginia, was especially gratifying.[6] A young doctor blessed with Tarheel good looks who resided at a fashionable hotel while waiting for his medical practice to develop did not escape the notice of fashionable St. Louis matrons. McPheeters received invitations to evening socials at elegant city residences, and in these halcyon days of his bachelorhood, he formed a network of friendships that supported and served him throughout his life, especially in 1865, when he and his family returned to the city after the war.

One important invitation came from the home of a Colonel O'Fallen, where McPheeters met Miss Julia Dent, future bride of Ulysses S. Grant. She was a highly placed young lady, attending a finishing school at the time, and the daughter of a wealthy business man and planter. Thirty years later McPheeters described his social life to an eager young reporter in St. Louis, whose newspaper articles focused upon Civil War nostalgia. "Miss Dent was a frequent guest at the elegant and hospitable suburban residence of Col. O' Fallen," McPheeters recalled. "In my frequent visits there as a young man . . . under the same roof, it was a privilege to mingle with Miss Dent and her accomplished hostesses on many festive occasions, and to lead them in the dance, and otherwise extend to them many acts of conventional gallantry—never dreaming, however, that these attentions were being bestowed on the future mistress of the White House."[7]

While still waiting for private patients to discover his medical office, McPheeters joined an effort to establish the first medical dispensary, a free clinic for the poor, west of the Mississippi River, an achievement that filled him with pride many decades later. The dispensary was privately funded, and the clinic was held in rooms at the Unitarian church that were offered by its minister, Rev. William Greenleaf Eliot. McPheeters linked his name in this undertaking with several prominent physicians of St. Louis. "This institution subsequently obtained a small annual appropriation from the city, and was kept up for a number of years . . . until the work of gratuitous attendance upon the poor by means of free public dispensaries, was taken up by the medical colleges and other interested parties."[8]

Then, at last, during the winter, McPheeters's first private patient arrived at his office door—a penniless boatman who was desperately ill. The young doctor helped him in, examined him, and in due course wrote a prescription, which the patient was too poor and too sick to take to the apothecary. McPheeters went for him, paid for it himself, and returned to the patient waiting in the office. In his journal that evening, McPheeters wrote with wry humor, "a bold beginning."[9] The patients who followed at an agonizingly slow pace often paid their medical bills by means of barter.

> *October 15, 1842.* I have now been in St. Louis one year as a practicing physician. During which time I have booked four hundred

and seven dollars and have received only thirty-eight dollars in money. Received more in furniture.[10]

Continuing his friendship with the Graham family at Montrose, McPheeters fell heir to the matchmaking skills of Mrs. Graham and her daughters when his proposal of marriage was accepted by their long-ensconced houseguest Pink Seldon. The wedding ceremony was held in the parlors of Montrose, and the bride and groom spent their honeymoon there as well. Ten months later, however, McPheeters lost his young wife to "illness owing to her confinement." He wrote these stark words in his diary with dark brevity.[11] Once again the young man, now a widower chastened by sorrow, returned with renewed intensity to his medical practice in St. Louis.

His career path took him to a new opportunity. He submitted an article to the *St. Louis Medical and Surgical Journal* in February 1844 and later that same year published two more articles, whereupon, he was invited by the editor, Dr. M. L. Linton, to join him as coeditor. For the next sixteen years, McPheeters's articles and editorials were powerfully instrumental in guiding and defining the medical profession and medical education in St. Louis and beyond.[12]

McPheeters and Linton cooperated in an effort by the medical society to organize a second medical school in St. Louis, and a plan went forward to the point that classes were advertised and faculty appointments announced. McPheeters was to teach Materia Medica and Clinical Medicine, and classes were to begin in April 1843 with a fee for instruction of forty dollars. The undertaking did not materialize at that time, but other efforts to establish a second medical school in St. Louis soon took shape under the auspices of St. Louis University, and again McPheeters was a member of the newly formed faculty. He served as professor until his resignation in 1862.

During his years as coeditor of the medical journal, McPheeters established several themes designed to raise the perception of local practitioners to larger questions of professional standards and public health. He was deeply interested in the formation of a statewide medical society. None existed when he wrote his first editorial on the subject in 1845, calling for a statewide convention.[13]

A third editor, Victor J. Fourgeaud, joined McPheeters and Linton at the *Journal*. He was a man of broad education, and during his editorial stint, he wrote articles on the history of medicine in ancient Egypt, Greece, and Rome. He was equally familiar with the medicine of contemporary Europe. With this background, he was capable of investigating diseases and deaths in St. Louis scientifically, using an empirical method as McPheeters had suggested. Anticipating the public-health movement by more than forty years, the editors agreed that Fourgeaud should conduct a study of the causes of mortality in the St. Louis area. A severe flood of the Mississippi River in 1844 had brought this to their attention. The river, for twenty years the project of the U.S. Corps of Engineers, went viciously out of control in June that year. Flooded homes were evacuated by volunteers, many citizens drowned or were unaccounted for, and the community was unprepared to meet this crisis. When the waters receded in late August, the *St. Louis Medical and Surgical Journal* reported that the city and outlying areas were "afflicted with stagnant pools, mud deposits and vegetable decomposition—this accounts for the resulting fevers."[14]

McPheeters, Linton, and Fourgeaud turned their editorial attention first to the problem of tuberculosis in St. Louis and then to the dreaded outbreaks of epidemic cholera, which annually threatened the lush river valleys of America. The editors devoted a section to a study of the water supply of the city, suggesting that lead pipes might pollute the city's drinking water. They wrote with urgent concern that a children's hospital should be established in St. Louis because, they observed, the climate of the city was particularly deadly for children. They proposed that the hospital's organization should mirror the free public-school system designed to serve the deserving poor. Unfortunately, these forward-looking editors were destined to wait for more than thirty years to see a children's hospital established in the city.[15] But in 1848 Fourgeaud left for California.

The rapid, chaotic growth of population in St. Louis was another topic of concern addressed by political and professional leaders of the city. The swell of German and Irish immigrants throughout the 1840s had helped triple the city's population since McPheeters's arrival, and by the end of the decade, St. Louis was home to nearly seventy thousand people. McPheeters saw the newcomers as a potential source of disease. One day he watched as 350 Europeans landed at the port, streaming down the gangway from the steamboat *New Uncle Sam*. This was a familiar scene in those days, when on average more than a hundred commercial steamboats tied up at the wharf. Bewildered foreigners ,"poorly nourished, filthy and poverty stricken," were crowded ashore to remain in the city.[16] He editorialized fervently against the slums in which these people were forced to live, not from the point of view of a political figure but as a medical reformer calling for drastic measures in public sanitation. St. Louis had no sewer system, he wrote, and new streets were added so rapidly to the city that no attempt was made to pave them. Alleyways were filthy. Then in January 1849 a case of dreaded cholera was reported, something of a curiosity since cholera usually struck in summer months, but the people knew that the horror of an epidemic was inevitable.

Although at least a quarter of the population, including many doctors, fled St. Louis in panic, McPheeters joined those physicians who remained in the city in their hastily organized effort to treat the rapidly increasing number of patients, most of whom were poor, recently arrived immigrants. This was his first experience with cholera, and he carefully gathered statistics for presentation in the medical journal the following year. Accurate numbers of those stricken by the outbreak and those killed were difficult to come by, but McPheeters daily checked with hospitals, newspapers, and doctors to attempt a statistical analysis. Among the remaining population, he later reported, there were 8,108 deaths due to cholera during the year-long epidemic of 1849. He described his duties: "It was like going into a continuous battle for sixty days and coming out each day with a loss of 100 killed." His two articles on epidemic cholera, which appeared in the *St. Louis Medical and Surgical Journal,* became well known in national medical literature for the next two decades as American cities, ravaged by regular outbreaks of cholera, attempted to take preventative measures to stem the deadly tide. In this regard McPheeters became something of an early public-health reformer long before there was a movement with which to identify politically. As cholera continued unabated to work its devastation into the spring of 1849, St. Louis received another deadly blow—a major fire, which broke out in the vicinity of the wharf and spread quickly to destroy almost all of the commercial district. It was a popular belief that the fire would act to purify the corrupted air that carried disease, but McPheeters refuted this theory in his articles on cholera and received harsh criticism from a local newspaper. The writer attributed his incorrect conclusions to the fact that he was a "young physician." McPheeters was then thirty-six years old.[17]

The year 1849 brought both tragedy and happiness to the doctor. He completed a formal and rather complicated courtship of Sallie Buchanan, a recognized beauty and socialite of St. Louis and the daughter of a prominent resident of the city who also had Southern connections. The Graham family of Montrose shared the Buchanan's Kentucky friendships, and it may have been in that circle that McPheeters first met Sallie, with whom he fell in love. The bridegroom described their wedding in his diary in his familiar, laconic style:

> *May 10, 1849,* I was married by the Rev. E. C. Hutchinson to Sallie Buchanan, eldest daughter of George Buchanan. The wedding took place at the Buchanan residence on 4th and St. Charles Streets from whence we soon adjourned to the Odd Fellows' Hall where a large number of friends and acquaintances was invited to meet.[18]

This wedding, one of the most important of the social season, ushered in a marriage that endured to the last day of McPheeters's life fifty-five years later. Sallie was a proud and spirited young woman, fashionably turned out with chestnut curls and expressive, wide gray eyes. Still a beauty at her golden wedding anniversary celebration, Sallie McPheeters by then had manifestly shown herself to be a woman of substance and courage, standing firm through persecution, banishment, warfare, privation, and the deaths of her two young sons.[19]

Among the professional honors enlarging McPheeters's career was his appointment in October 1848 to the professorship of pathology, anatomy, and clinical medicine in the Medical Department of St. Louis University. The following spring McPheeters was chosen to attend a nationwide meeting in Cincinnati of the American Medical Association, then in its first year. He was motivated to redouble his organizational efforts in medical circles at home. "The poor showing which Missouri made in comparison with other western states," he editorialized in the *Journal,* "was a source of mortification to those of us who were present."[20] He headed a drive to create a statewide medical society and served as presiding officer at the convention held in St. Louis for that purpose.

As McPheeters achieved the age of forty years, he was widely known and admired both professionally and socially in Missouri. Not only did he hold a professorship at St. Louis University, serve on the City Board of Health, share the editorship of the *St. Louis Medical and Surgical Journal,* and maintain a large private practice, but he was also appointed by the U.S. government to serve as the director of the Marine Hospital in St. Louis.

The decade of the 1850s seemed to hold even more promise and prosperity for McPheeters and his growing family. He joined fourteen other professors and doctors of St. Louis to found the Academy of Science. He and Sallie were highly placed in the city and maintained a wide circle of successful friends. Their richly appointed home on Olive Street was filled with Sallie's portion of the treasure from the Buchanan household.[21] The city around them grew not just in numbers but also in obvious wealth as great buildings of granite and marble were erected by the newly enriched city fathers. St. Louis had become the star city of the West. Prosperity abounded.

But beneath the superficial glitter and optimism of a nation caught up in pursuit of prosperity, deep in the bones of the body politic the first shooting pains of political disaster could be felt. The growing Republic was polarizing in a fatal tremor of social and economic tensions led by political leaders eyeing the Executive Mansion and by merchants lusting after European consumers. The old, haunting contest over slavery was the issue, "the fire bell in the night," that ignited the flame. With fervent, inflamatory rhetoric, both the North and South approached in a cavalier manner the prospect of civil war. It would be an affordable loss, the abolitionists of Boston shouted, if the end of slavery required the sacrifice of a generation of Southern whites. The Dred Scott case, originating in the Circuit Court of Missouri, worked its way to the U.S. Supreme Court, where Scott was pronounced to be property rather than a person. In every community across the country, political rhetoric grew more heated, especially in the Border States, where the citizens might be evenly divided, as in Missouri. The people of Missouri, where slavery was legal, aligned themselves on both sides of the conflict, many joining political and paramilitary groups.[22] With the Fugitive Slave Act (1850) came a flame of anger from the North toward all Southern whites, and this flame was fanned forcefully by Harriet Beecher Stowe's romantic novel of a runaway slave, *Uncle Tom's Cabin,* which could be bought across America for a dime.

For McPheeters, still a Southern Whig who (as a young man) had proudly supported Henry Clay, the anti-Southern political propaganda preached from Protestant pulpits of St. Louis was repugnant; he deeply resented the division of the city into angry factions. The German immigrants in St. Louis, for the most part, allied themselves with antislavery Unionist factions, whereas Irish immigrants allied themselves with Southern sympathizers. The McPheeters family owned no slaves in their household, unlike many wealthy St. Louisans, but hired two live-in Irish women and a German manservant. For McPheeters, the issue was never slavery. If the South elected to leave the Union by a vote of the populace, he firmly opposed the threatened use of military force by the national government against its own citizens to prevent secession. Furthermore, he considered Lincoln to be a sectional dark-horse winner pushed forward by political managers of no integrity who might proclaim the preservation of the Union but who would, without hesitation, destroy it in the process.[23]

However, neither McPheeters nor any other thoughtful person could have imagined that civil war, even the prospect of it, would destroy the very nature of the community in which he claimed a place and the sanctity of his legal and civil rights. After the election of Abraham Lincoln, as the nation was breaking apart, political hatreds and indiscriminate violence, so chaotic in a Border State, seemed to have free rein. Moreover, after martial law was declared, St. Louis divided into two armed camps, and violence became commonplace on city streets.[24]

The winter of 1861–62 brought a war within a war to Missouri. The war was but a few months old, and the Republic found itself on paths never trod before, never anticipated by founding fathers, and never dreamed of by frightened citizens North or South. The "90-day war" touted by Americans from Congress to the dirt farmer was stretching out already by that first winter, becoming longer, more difficult, more painful, and more costly in human life than anyone could have known. The early bravado and parade mentality that rang from every county courthouse across the continent had diminished somewhat as the early casualty lists were read aloud in town squares. Rioting broke out in previously quiet, prosperous villages above and below the old Missouri Compromise line. And Missouri, an affront to the Union, a slave state, projected herself boldly into Federal territory, fiercely divided, and violently rent asunder.

Lincoln, keenly aware of the delicate political balance within the

Border States, had treated Missouri gingerly, with the care of one touching a hot stove, when he had forced his overeager commander, John Frémont, to rescind a rash and premature order freeing slaves within the state. Lincoln recognized all too well the splinters of the old Democratic Party, the Southern Unionists and Whig secessionists, in Missouri. The governor, Claiborne Fox Jackson, was a Douglas Democrat, and in those early months of war, he had unwisely waited for a state convention to affirm his determination to lead Missouri out of the Union to join the new Confederate nation. The governor, clean shaven, pious, and as verbose as a circuit-riding clergyman, had refused on constitutional grounds Lincoln's first call for ninety-day recruits. Backed by a fractious majority of the state legislature, Governor Jackson had prepared to secure direct communication with Confederate president Jefferson Davis, whose military aid he had requested, and preside over the hastily convened state convention. The early sessions met in Jefferson City and were dominated by pro-Confederate delegates.

After a rousing floor fight, however, the site of the convention was moved in March 1861 to the spacious new assembly chamber of the Mercantile Library Hall in St. Louis. From that time forward, power began to swing to Northern supporters. It was clear that if Missouri held for the Union, St. Louis was the linchpin. Tensions ran high as the convention toiled toward the final outcome, and many of the pro-Union delegates were enraged by the sight of a secessionist flag flying from the rooftop of the old Berthold Mansion at the corner of Fifth and Pine in clear view of the delegates. The convention held for the Union, but Governor Jackson still refused President Lincoln's first call for troops in April, again denouncing it as "illegal, unconstitutional and revolutionary."[25]

At this point, with St. Louis under martial law, McPheeters and other known Southerners were arrested and required by the mayor of the city and by the Federal military authorities to sign an oath of allegiance to the U.S. government. The oath stipulated that the citizen signing would not render any service or support, real or moral, to the Rebel cause. McPheeters could not, therefore, sign such an oath, believing as he did that the South had a right to withdraw from the Union and knowing all too well that his own kinsmen and childhood friends from North Carolina would serve the Confederate cause. As he refused the oath under the avenging eye of the military authorities, McPheeters knew that his own imprisonment would be the ultimate result. It was only a question of time.[26]

He carefully followed events in the city during 1861, and there were several that frightened and outraged him. The first of these came on May 10 and became known to history as the Camp Jackson Affair, though called "The St. Louis Massacre" by McPheeters. So shocking was this violent event that the doctor wrote of its anniversary in his wartime journal two years later.[27] It was this incident, more than any other, that demonstrated to McPheeters that the social-political environment of the city would no longer tolerate his presence as a known Southern sympathizer even if he remained silent on political questions. As polarization in Missouri continued apace, there was no middle ground anymore, no neutrality permitted by enflamed citizens and officials, for the moderate man of reason. After the Camp Jackson Affair, McPheeters knew there was no hiding place.

Camp Jackson, named for the governor and located on the outskirts of St. Louis, was a training ground for the pro-Confederate militia known as the Missouri State Guard. Opposing this organization was another armed band, pro-Union, known as the Home Guards. As both paramilitary groups trained and paraded in the city, rumors of spying, sabotage, concealed identities, and sneak attack ran wild, and on May 10 the Unionists, joined by regular U.S. troops, surrounded the Missouri State Guard and easily captured them. All this was an effort to secure possession of the St. Louis Arsenal for the Federal government rather than allowing it to fall into Rebel hands.

The secessionist captives were ordered to stack arms and then were marched through the streets of the city toward the arsenal, which was to serve as a military prison. Along the streets excited citizens of St. Louis rushed to see the spectacle. Some threw rocks and cursed the Yankee soldiers, while others brought picnic lunches and beer to enjoy on grassy lawns as the captives trooped by. On Olive Street the procession stalled for almost twenty minutes, and tension mounted when an angry mob suddenly ran toward the anxious soldiers. Shots were fired and the people panicked, running away in all directions and leaving behind dead and wounded picnickers. The final death toll was at least twenty-eight. The military procession, disordered and frightened, attempted to dress ranks and march their prisoners away as a brave fifer nervously began to pipe "Yankee Doodle."[28]

The Camp Jackson Affair placed St. Louis squarely in Union hands, and if military authorities had felt some measure of restraint imposed upon them by President Lincoln's cautious policies toward Missouri, the events of May 10 swept all moderation away. The names of forty prominent Confederate sympathizers were posted in public places. Arrests were made on city streets, in offices, or cafes during daylight hours. Protestant ministers were monitored by military officials for signs of secessionist persuasion or simple neutrality, and they were often exiled without benefit of a hearing from the state altogether and forbidden to preach.

In June 1861 there was another outburst of violence in the city, which took place less than a block from the doctor's home and office. McPheeters clipped the article from a daily newspaper and carefully pasted it into a scrapbook among his personal papers:

> The Recorders Court (now known as the Police Court) was at that time held in the second story of the engine-house occupied by the hook and ladder company on Seventh Street between Pine and Olive. One June 17, 1861, McNeil's Regiment the United States Reserve Corps, marched from their quarters in Turner Hall, across Seventh Street. The Recorder's Court was in session, but as the soldiers approached, those free to do so went to the balcony outside the courtroom to look at the parade.
>
> When opposite the engine house a shot or volley, for subsequent testimony was conflicting, rang upon the air, and several people fell dead, several others wounded. A prisoner on trial fell dead, while the Recorder, Major Valentine J. Peers, retained his seat, though shot were about him like hail. The dead all told were seven. . . . During the excitement, a man impelled by curiosity stopped on the corner of Seventh and Olive. . . . [H]e sought safety in a nearby store, into which one of the soldiers followed him, piercing him through the breast with his bayonet. A coroner's inquest was held over the victims of the shooting.[29]

By the end of the year, McPheeters was to see clearly that his hope to remain with his family in "peace and security," was an empty dream. The third alarm sounded when a new directive issued from President

Lincoln's commander of the Department of Missouri, Maj. Gen. Henry W. Halleck. It was a new and deeper crisis for McPheeters after that general order was posted publicly in St. Louis on December 24:

> The suffering families driven by rebels from Southwestern Missouri, which have arrived here, have been supplied by voluntary contributions made by Union men. Others are to arrive in a few days. These must be supplied by the charity of the men known to be hostile to the Union. A list will be prepared of the names of all persons of this class who do not voluntarily furnish their quota, and a contribution will be levied on them of ten thousand dollars, in clothing, provisions, and quarters, or money in lieu thereof. This levy will be made on the following classes of persons in proportion to the guilt and property of each individual: 1st. Those in arms with the enemy who have property in this city. 2nd. Those who have furnished pecuniary or other aid to the enemy . . . 3rd. Those who have verbally, in writing, or in publication given encouragement to insurgents and rebels.[30]

The general order further announced the creation of a board of assessors consisting of three military commanders and a Unionist citizen and charged with the levying of fines on those found guilty.

Two weeks later in the newspaper, McPheeters and twenty-three well-known individuals in St. Louis, obviously those intended as the "class" to be fined, fired back an open letter to General Halleck protesting his harsh new order:

> The Federal authorities are breaking up the government themselves under the guise of preventing its being broken up by others. . . . What remains is revolution in the garb of government and depending for its legitimacy upon bayonets. . . . [W]e do not mean to resist the proceedings against us under the orders complained of, unjust and oppressive as we deem them to be. We are powerless in the premises. You have the armed hand to enforce your orders and decrees. We are defenseless and resistance would be idle. We cannot, however, give to your authority in the premises even such recognition as might be implied from our voluntary payment of the sums required of us. We have, therefore, concluded respectfully to protest and remonstrate against it, and to decline paying the same.[31]

Their restrained and dignified protest did nothing but isolate the like-minded Southerners and make them easier targets. Gov. Claiborne Jackson and other political leaders of the secessionist party had fled the state by the end of 1861.

As the first year of Civil War hardened into place, Missouri, and St. Louis in particular, experienced its own war. Not only was the presence of Federal troops disturbing to the people but the splintering of familiar institutions and community groups, even families, also was of serious concern. St. Louis was a microcosm of the nation in 1861. As the city lost its prized and widely advertised social order, men went about the busy streets armed in broad daylight. Neighbors closed their shutters against roaming gangs of all political persuasions out seeking random violence. Rumors swept through the city, and there were days when merchants kept their doors locked and their produce or retail items safely indoors.

William McPheeters's younger brother, Samuel Brown McPheeters, lived with his family in St. Louis at this time. Samuel, a well-respected and popular Presbyterian minister, was pastor of the Pine Street Church, where William served as elder and Sallie was a leader of activities for women. Curiously, the doctor made no mention of his brother in his diaries or papers, yet it is evident that each complicated the life of the other after the implementation of martial law. Theirs may well have been one of those family bonds rent asunder by the war, for the two brothers chose divergent paths when faced with the final crisis and never joined hands again.

Samuel surely depended upon the saving grace of his close friendship since college days with Col. Frank Blair, who in 1861 commanded the 1st U.S. Volunteers in St. Louis. Also Samuel himself held a commission as chaplain in the U.S. Army, and he had been awarded in 1859 an honorary doctorate of divinity by Westminster College in Missouri.[32] With such distinguished credentials in the community and in his church, Samuel McPheeters was sure that he sealed the safety of his position in St. Louis when he signed the oath of allegiance to the Federal government.

At the same time, a few blocks away at Tenth and Olive, his older brother, William, agonized over the moral question of the oath and decided to "act on principle" no matter what the cost and refused to sign. Samuel's congregation reflected the divisions in the city itself, and a faction of Unionists demanded that Reverend McPheeters denounce the Confederacy from his pulpit and lead them in a prayer for President Lincoln. In the furor that followed these demands, Reverend McPheeters was arrested in December 1862 for "unmistakable evidence of sympathy with the rebellion." Maj. Gen. Samuel R. Curtis, now U.S. commander of the Department of Missouri, ordered Samuel to cease preaching within the borders of Missouri and officially banished him and his family from the state within ten days. At this point a few members of the pastor's congregation traveled to Washington, D.C., to put the case before the president.[33]

Besieged by many vexing problems from Missouri, Lincoln warned Curtis that "the U.S. Government must not undertake to run the churches," and he countermanded the decree of banishment against the minister. The local presbytery, however, after fiery debate removed Rev. Samuel McPheeters from his post at the Pine Street Church. Samuel traveled to Washington and managed to gain an appointment with Lincoln. Following that interview, the president knew that Samuel was, in his heart, a Rebel sympathizer. However, he did not want him punished unless the minister committed an overt act of support for the Confederacy.[34] The president further believed that this closed the case, leaving arrangements needed to carry out these instructions to General Curtis and his staff in St. Louis.

More than a year later Lincoln discovered that, contrary to his direct order, Samuel McPheeters had been forbidden to preach at all in Missouri. This time an angry Lincoln countermanded an order and wrote in exasperation to his military officials, "I have never interfered, nor thought of interfering as to who shall or shall not preach in any church; nor have I knowingly or believingly, tolerated any one else to so interfere by my authority." Although St. Louis newspapers carried the president's admonition, it was too little to salvage Samuel from public humiliation and the loss of his vocation. In failing health, he remained in St. Louis through part of the war and then accepted a call from Mulberry Church in rural Kentucky.[35]

For Dr. William McPheeters, the end began one month after Samuel's arrest. On January 23, 1862, he wrote, "my house was entered in broad daylight by the United States police officers and robbed of over $2000 worth of furniture, and this too at a time when one of my children was lying at the point of death in the house, and did die a few days thereafter." The entire household knew the officers were coming from the clatter in the street, where a crew of four dirty warehouse workers jumped down from their heavy delivery wagon and walked across the lawn toward the McPheeters home. A double team of draft horses tossed their heads in harness and waited in the street, edging the huge wagon forward. Accompanying them, though keeping his distance, was a young red-faced lieutenant who had ridden up on horseback to supervise the removal of the household belongings. Two of the men in filthy caps and jackets pulled the doorbell several times, waiting impatiently and stomping on the floor of the porch. The lieutenant, obviously nervous and uncertain of his role, held official papers rolled up in his fist.

Inside, Sallie McPheeters stood rigidly upright at the foot of the staircase while her husband at the top of the stairs spoke instructions to her in angry, almost whispered tones. His presence was required upstairs at the bedside of their sick child, five-year-old William. One of their household servants held a baby in her arms and raced toward the back of the house, catching her apron on the kitchen door as she went. Two other servants in ankle-length black cotton shirts and shirt waists held George and little Maggie by the hands, urging them to hurry away. Their mother breathed deeply to compose herself and motioned to Henry, a young German servant dressed also in black, to open the front door. The bell clanged crudely again and again.[36] Henry performed his duty at the door with formality and stood back, his hand upon the huge brass knob, his eyes straight ahead, as the workers from the warehouse stormed into the entry hall to face Sallie. The items listed by the provost marshal general removed from McPheeters's home were:

> One buggy and harness—cost $275
> One rosewood piano—cost $350
> 6 rosewood and damask parlour chairs—cost $120
> 2 rosewood and damask sofas—$280
> 1 rosewood marble top table—cost $85[37]

Thirty years later Sallie McPheeters was interviewed by a newspaper reporter concerning events in St. Louis during the war. She gave a vivid account of the invasion of her home on that terrible January day. She remembered in detail the confiscation of her belongings. In describing the atrocity to the journalist, she remembered that the work-men were in a vile humor that morning. "In their wake had followed many a neighborhood boy expressing his opinion of their errand. When they were further hampered by their own ignorance in getting the piano in moving shape, they turned to Mrs. McPheeters for instructions. The lady answered "when thieves come stealing she was not in the habit of helping them." And so they worked by themselves and finally left with the piano, a fine instrument, which had been a gift to Sallie from her father. On February 19 a second levy was made on the McPheeters' household goods. The piano, parlour furniture, horse, and buggy had not sold for enough to pay the assessment, and now the authorities took everything—the cookstove, mattresses and beds, a framed engraving of the U.S. Senate, a marble bust from the entry hall, armchairs, a washstand, a hatrack, and sofas. The house with its bare walls was all that remained. In the interval between the two seizures, the little boy, five-year-old William, had died.[38]

As Sallie and William McPheeters tried desperately to cope with the grief over the loss of their child, the doctor was arrested again and detained by military officials in their effort to force him to sign the oath of allegiance to the Federal government. Later remembering his feelings, he wrote, "I acted from principle," and did not sign. He could not compromise his personal integrity, and the oath was the sticking point. Hounded by police, robbed of his personal possessions, and unprotected by civil law, he knew that his only course was to sign the oath or go to prison. And prison was a very real possibility for him, as the case of a Dr. Rose demonstrated. McPheeters told the story after the war of a Southern physician who had lived in Illinois for thirty years and in 1862 was arrested and thrown into the infamous prison near Alton. No fault could be found with him, and the commandant offered to release him after he had served a long time. Dr. Rose refused, saying that, after residing for thirty years in Illinois, he was in the company of the only gentlemen he had met in all those years. Despite this rather whimsical story, the truth about Alton Military Prison was generally known. A former penitentiary built in 1830, it drew such severe criticism from Dorothea Dix that all inmates were moved prior to the outbreak of the war. In 1860 the abandoned building was opened as a prison for captured Confederates. Starvation and disease as well as neglect and cruelty caused an official count of six to ten deaths per day.[39]

The Alton prison was not the only facility that threatened Confederate sympathizers in St. Louis. At Eighth and Gratiot stood a strange-looking building that had served as McDowell Medical College, Christian Brothers Academy, and the private home of Dr. Joseph Nash McDowell and his family. In the absence of Dr. McDowell, who joined the Confederacy with a few medical students in tow, Federal military authorities seized two of the three connected buildings on the property to use as a prison. Horror stories circulated about treatment of prisoners there, and it was widely known that some people incarcerated at Gratiot Street Prison were never heard from again.

A third prison existed in St. Louis, whispered about, but seen by only a few. That was the underground hold at Myrtle Street known as "Lynch's Slave Pen," where before the war slaves were held prior to auction. It was described as a pair of dungeons under the sidewalk.[40] McPheeters, well aware of such terrifying stories, held the fate of his family uppermost in his mind as they sorrowed together in an empty house.

In the spring of 1862, pressure by Federal military authorities intensified upon McPheeters and his friends. Following the confiscation of their household goods and, in some cases even real estate, many people had sought a safe haven in the South, while others had paid the so-called taxes levied by the military provost. There would be no end to it. By June, McPheeters realized that "the alternative was now forced upon me either to take this oath, which I could not and would not do, go to prison, or else quit my home, family & business, and seek refuge in the South—the only land of civil & religious liberty accessible to me. I unhesitatingly chose the latter alternative."[41]

On June 20 McPheeters made his escape from home at night, traveling with E. C. Wells, a friend who was similarly threatened for his Southern background. He took leave of Sallie and their three children, left a note in the dean's office at the medical school, and resigned as director of the Marine Hospital. The next day, when classes convened at St. Louis University School of Medicine, a student remembered waiting in anatomy class for Professor McPheeters, his favorite instructor, to appear and begin his lecture. Instead, the dean entered the classroom and, standing before the students, he sadly read the letter he had found that morning bidding them all a melancholy farewell.[42]

It took McPheeters two weeks to reach Richmond by horseback, crossing Federal lines somewhere in Tennessee. He arrived on the fourth of July, soon after Rebel forces had defeated Maj. Gen. George B. McClellan's Army of the Potomac in the Seven Days' Battles. He requested to serve under Maj. Gen. Sterling Price, commander of Missouri forces then serving in Mississippi. When McPheeters was commissioned surgeon by the Confederate secretary of war, he was assigned to join Price's staff. The doctor then made his way from the Confederate capital, heading west and south to northern Mississippi, where Price and his Army of the West had been engaged in an unsuccessful attempt to retake the town of Corinth from the Federals. McPheeters caught up with the general in Holly Springs, a small farm town a few miles from Corinth, in late October, and he was given the duty of medical inspector. The number of sick and wounded men overwhelmed Price's medical staff at this point because of recent failed engagements across northern Tishimingo County, so McPheeters rolled up his sleeves and went to work.

In November, Price and his men were ordered to Grenada, Mississippi, one hundred and fifty miles north of the state capital, and three months later they were sent farther south to the vicinity of Vicksburg. The Missourians spent another Christmas far from home, still east of the river, but it was their abiding hope to be ordered closer to Missouri in the new year. When it became Price's unhappy duty to tell his men that they were to remain where they were, he expected desertions en masse, but his men accepted their duty calmly.

Five months later the general was allowed to move west with only the members of his staff. In April, McPheeters accompanied them to Little Rock, where the general was assigned command of two divisions of Arkansas and Missouri infantry.

When McPheeters boarded a ferry to cross the Mississippi River to Arkansas, he entered the Confederate Department of the Trans-Mississippi, a designation by authorities in Richmond for more than 700,000 square miles of territory, reaching as far west as New Mexico and including Texas, Indian Territory, Missouri, Arkansas, and Louisiana. From the outset, the Trans-Mississippi was an administrative nightmare.

For purposes of organization, the Trans-Mississippi had been divided into four military districts (Arkansas, Texas, Western Louisiana, and Indian Territory), but even this move could not compensate for two basic inadequacies in the department as a whole. First, the region was still basically frontier, sparsely settled for the most part by homesteaders who had moved west within that generation to clear and plough smaller plots of ground than Tidewater Virginia or Mississippi Delta plantations. Here and there in this sprawling department there were towns, but they did not rival Charleston, Savannah, or New Orleans. These were farm towns, useful hubs of agricultural commerce connected by farm-to-market roads and the rivers. Second, because the Trans-Mississippi was newer to settlement, developing rapidly but not yet securely wealthy, there were few railroads, and many of these were built east to west. So it was that in military planning, President Davis and his powerful appointees saw the Trans-Mississippi primarily as a gigantic warehouse, a source of supply and men for the armies of the East, for it was there in the valleys of Virginia where they committed Confederate hopes. The war in the West was, for the Rebel military command, of secondary importance. Jefferson Davis, always blindly loyal to his constellation of West Point cronies regardless of their inepitudes or failings, sent so many unsuccessful officers to the West that the Trans-Mississippi has been called by one historian the "junkyard of the Confederate army."[43]

Therefore, it is understandable that as late as 1862 there was still no medical department in the Trans-Mississippi, and only after the battle of Shiloh, when unprecented numbers of wounded and dying men urgently needed medical care, did President Davis issue an order to create a medical department west of the river. One of the surgeons assigned to this task described in his notes his impressions of the department. He found

> not a commissioned officer nor an enlisted soldier west of the Mississippi River, unless it was a few [officers] who were away from the army on furlough. There was not an ounce of medicine, nor an article of hospital furniture or bedding belonging to the government.
>
> The same is true of the Commissary and Quartermaster departments. . . . The Medical Director . . . proceeded as best he could to organize that department; his first step being to organize an Army Medical Board composed of Drs. J. W. Lawrence, Wm.

Lawrence, and Dr. P. O. Hooper, who, upon his recommendation were commissioned Surgeons and, at once proceeded to examine applicants for the rank of Surgeon and Assistant Surgeon.

In order to collect medicines for the army being raised, every druggist in [Arkansas] was appealed to sell to the Medical Purveyor as much of his stock as he could without depriving the people of what they needed. Scouts, agents, or smugglers were employed to bring out medicines from Memphis, St. Louis and Cairo, and all other available points in the Federal lines . . . and very soon a full and ample stock was accumulated at Little Rock. The Examining Board worked earnestly and faithfully and very soon an able Corps of Surgeons and Assistant Surgeons were selected after rigid examinations.

A laboratory for manufacturing medicines was established at Arkadelphia under charge of Dr. Chas. O. Cuitman and large quarters were furnished by him. Large and commodious hospital was constructed at Little Rock and Dr. C. M Taylor was the first medical officer assigned to duty, he being assigned as senior surgeon of post in charge of all hospitals.

In four or five months, an army of 25 or 30,000 men was organized by volunteering and conscription and with the exception of appropriate fire arms, was well equipped. In the fall of 1862, after the organization had been completed, General Theophilus Holmes of the Army of Virginia took charge of the department, relieving General Hindman of the department command and placing him in command of the army.[44]

When McPheeters arrived in Little Rock in April 1863, the medical department was a year into its operation, but the fifth commander of the Trans-Mississippi Department, the elderly, fumbling Theophilus Holmes, had been just recently replaced (though he now held district command in Arkansas). To fill the position of commander number six, President Davis sent a fellow graduate of West Point and veteran of the War with Mexico, a Floridian whose talents were hoped to be administrative since they were clearly not military. Lt. Gen. Edmund Kirby Smith assumed command of the vast area west of the river that constituted his department, and it was more than a year before he could come to grips at all with the problems of the Trans-Mississippi.

Little Rock, the capital of Arkansas, was a prosperous town before the war, occupying the southern and higher bank of the Arkansas River, with a population of slightly over four thousand. It boasted a cluster of churches, two hotels, two daily newspapers, a college, a female academy, study and music clubs for ladies, and a couple of saloons, and while the wide streets of the capital were unpaved, there were numerous brick houses with wide lawns and shade trees, gardens, and stables. The capital building, or State House as it was called, centered the town with Greek Revival dignity, overlooking the nautical traffic on the Arkansas and commanding the business of town traffic on Markham Street.

Stationed in Little Rock, McPheeters was obliged to secure his own quarters, so he rented a room in a civilian household. In addition to his military medical duties, he was expected to care for local civilian patients as well as the families of officers accompanying the army. This policy of allowing military doctors to conduct private practices in towns near their duty stations was used by both armies, North and South, and had been in place since the War of 1812. Nonmilitary patients paid the usual fee for medical care. McPheeters soon became acquainted with a few of the citizens of Little Rock and visited with them when his duties allowed.

On June 1, 1863, in the evening, McPheeters sat at a table in his modest room and, taking up a newly devised pen, wrote a daily entry in his wartime diary. The diary itself is no more than a pocket-sized notebook the doctor made by first folding sheets of pale blue writing paper in half. He had then sewn the pages together, creating a spine. To save paper and to bind a book small enough to be carried in his coat pocket, McPheeters wrote in miniature with his steel pen. It is probable that he had started the diary earlier, perhaps when he reached Richmond on July 4, 1862, because there is no title page to the remaining document, no dedication, or commemorative beginning, as was the style of the day. Perhaps those early pages were lost. Regardless, this stained, faint journal was created to chronicle in intimate detail the wartime ordeals of this steadfast and decent man who became part of the titanic and ultimately unsuccessful effort of the Confederacy west of the Mississippi River.

June 1st 1863. General [Sterling] Price[45] and staff left Little Rock today for Jacksonport on the White River, the division which he commands having preceded him the day before. At the request of

Major [Thomas L.] Snead,[46] I remained behind in Little Rock to attend to his child who was quite sick with scarlet fever; Snead himself remaining also. I also had under my charge Col. [Austin M.] Standish[47] and Ben Chambers. Mrs. Gen. Churchill[48] and Mrs. Johnson and Jordan united in the request for me to remain, which I did cheerfully, still retaining my room and boarding at Mrs. Kates.

June 2nd. Visited Snead's child three times, it being quite sick and Mrs. Snead very uneasy. [I] also visited Col. Standish, who is staying at the Arsenal,[49] and Ben Chambers[50] whose brain is seriously affected. Took tea and spent the evening at Mrs. Mary Johnson's.

June 3rd & 4th. [I] was a good deal occupied with Minnie Snead and Ben Chambers both of whom are quite ill, the former with ulcerated sore throat, the latter with profound stupor and decided brain symptoms. Col. Standish [is] improving. While unoccupied with my patients [I] kept to my room reading Macaulay's *History of England* during the day and spent the evening at Mrs. Johnson's.

June 5th & 6th. Still occupied as on the two previous days. Minnie Snead is improving slowly, while Ben Chambers is worse and will run a narrow chance for his life–coma profound. Blistered him to back of neck.[51]

June 7th. Ben Chambers somewhat better but still very ill. Dined today at old Mrs. Johnson's with Lt. Gen. [Theophilus Hunter] Holmes. We struck up an acquaintance and as he says we went to school together in Raleigh [North Carolina] when boys, he however, being some ten years my senior. He was very polite and talkative.[52]

June 8th. As his child improves Mr. Snead himself was taken sick from watching all night and exposure. [He] had chills and high fever. [I] visited him twice and spent some time in conversing with his wife about people and things in St. Louis. Ben Chambers is improving finely.

June 9th. Spent the day visiting my sick and in reading Macaulay. Snead still has fever. Took tea and spent the evening at Old Mrs. Johnson's.

June 10th. After visiting my patients who are improving, [I] rode down this evening with Maj. Nick Hill[53] in his buggy to Mrs. Mary Johnson's farm 12 miles down on the Arkansas River where she has been for several days and wrote me a pressing note to visit her. [I] got there just at dark, met the young ladies riding to meet us on horseback. Lt. [Theophilus Hunter] Holmes [Jr.][54] and Capt. [Charles W.] Broadfoot[55] arrived soon after. It commenced to rain soon after and rained hard until late in the night.

June 11th. Spent a delightful night. [I] was kindly and hospitably entertained by Mrs. Johnson. Miss Cass Rider and Miss Carroll are staying with her which added to the enjoyment, at least of the young gentlemen. The place is a pretty one just on the bank of the river. Arose early this morning and heard the birds singing cheerfully and the sun shining brightly, the storm having subsided. After a sumptuous breakfast Maj. Hill and I took his buggy and drove back to Little Rock having had a pleasant visit. On going up to the Hotel met Gov. [Thomas Caute] Reynolds who has just arrived from Shreveport.[56]

June 12th. Visited all my patients and found them improving. Also visited Gov. Reynolds. Took dinner with Mr. Worthen [and] several of his friends, male and female.

June 13th. Day hot but passed off as yesterday.

June 14th. Mrs. Johnson came up from the country this morning, her son having had a severe chill. She came to town to be near me. Having been sent for, I called to see him and found him with high fever and very nervous. [I] stayed a good part of the day and all the night at the house, his mother being very uneasy when I left him.

June 15th, 16th, 17th, 18th, & 19th. Walt Johnson continued ill and grew worse during all these days, so much so, that at the earnest request of his mother I spent a good part of the days and all the nights at her house, still however, retaining my room at Mrs. Kates. During the intervals of absence [I] visited the Rev. Mr. Welch, Presbyterian minister, whose family I had become acquainted with and taken several meals with them. Also visited Maj. and Mrs. Snead, both he and his child having recovered. Also Ben Chambers. Walt was very sick and his mother painfully anxious. She would frequently call me up during the night to quiet her apprehensions. Mrs. Churchill and Mrs. Jordan were constantly there and in attendance. In the evening I would sit out on the porch and smoke my pipe. On the 18th and 19th he began decidedly to improve but was still weak and fretful. The time, however, that I spent in Mrs. Johnson's house passed off pleasantly. I have never met with more kindness or hospitality in my life than from this whole family.

June 20th. My little patient having so far improved as not to render it necessary for me to be so constantly with him—even in the opinion of his anxious mother—I returned again to my boarding house at least to sleep, still taking most of my meals at one or the other Mrs. Johnson's. Today [I] visited several acquaintances and friends preparatory to starting for the army on Monday next— Mr. Welch's family, Mr. Worthen, Mrs. Green, and others.

June 21st. Sunday. Went to the Presbyterian Church where I heard Mr. Welch preach one of his plain, practical, [and] good sermons. Took dinner with Mrs. Mary Johnson and tea with old Mrs. Johnson and Mrs. Jordan. After tea took leave of them all.

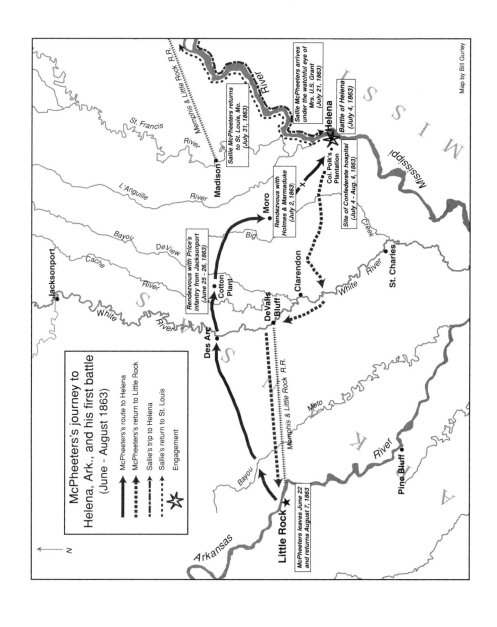

McPheeter's journey to Helena, Ark., and his first battle (June - August 1863)

McPheeters's route to Helena
McPheeters's return to Little Rock
Sallie's trip to Helena
Sallie's return to St. Louis
Engagement

N

MISSISSIPPI

St. Francis River

Memphis & Little Rock R.R.

River

Sallie McPheeters returns to St. Louis, Mo. (July 31, 1863)

Sallie McPheeters arrives under the watchful eye of Mrs. U.S. Grant (July 21, 1863)

Madison

Helena

Battle of Helena (July 4, 1863)

L'Anguille River

Mississippi

Col. Polk's Plantation

Moro

Rendezvous with Holmes & Marmaduke (July 2, 1863)

Site of Confederate hospital (July 4 - Aug. 4, 1863)

Bayou DeView

Big

Creek

Cache River

Rendezvous with Price's Infantry from Jacksonport (June 25 - 26, 1863)

Cotton Plant

Clarendon

White River

St. Charles

Jacksonport

White River

Des Arc

DeVall's Bluff

Memphis & Little Rock R.R.

Meto

River

Bayou

Pine Bluff

Little Rock

McPheeters leaves June 22 and returns August 7, 1863

Arkansas

ARK

Map by Bill Gurley

CHAPTER I

The Helena Campaign, 1863

I waited patiently upon the Lord,
He stooped to me and heard my cry.

Helena, Arkansas, a river town of considerable wealth, was important to both armies because of its location—across the Mississippi River from and about a hundred miles north of Vicksburg and seventy miles south of Memphis. In the days before the war, the landing at Helena had been a regular stop for river traffic bound for Vickburg, Natchez, and New Orleans, and it was the terminus for East Arkansas cotton. The wealth that poured into Helena was both agricultural and commercial, and the tall smokestacks of riverboats tied up at the quay of Helena were as thick on some days as the bristles of a hairbrush. The side- and stern-wheelers brought to town all kinds of goods as well as a wild variety of people working the river for pleasure or profit.

In July 1862, following the battle of Pea Ridge, Federal forces had occupied Helena, developed the town as a supply depot for the Northern siege against Vicksburg, and turned it into a center for their highly remunerative trade in cotton. Union strategists considered the town a perfect base for their inevitable campaign against Little Rock; however, the Rebel high command saw it simply as a military target that, if engaged, might relieve to some degree the pressure against Vicksburg, which was sustaining a prolonged siege of immeasurable anguish.

The Confederate drive toward Helena in June 1863 was just that—a chance to recapture the town and to divert Union forces focused upon Vicksburg. At that time Vicksburg and her counterpart two hundred miles downriver in Louisiana, Port Hudson, protected the only segment of the Mississippi still in Confederate hands. Commanding the high sheer bluffs on the east side of the river, Vicksburg brandished thirty-seven heavy guns, located at various elevations above the flood plain, that delivered a deadly fire to all shipping below. Until these guns were silenced, Union control of the Mississippi was incomplete, and Maj. Gen. Ulysses S. Grant had spent months attempting to achieve that goal.

First using Memphis as his headquarters, Grant had devised military plans to take Vicksburg via an overland route through northern Mississippi, but when Confederate cavalry destroyed his supply base at Holly Springs, he abandoned that approach. His next scheme employed his army as construction crews to dig a canal through the wet bottoms and bayous of Louisiana west of Vicksburg in order to bypass its batteries. When this option faltered the general had Adm. David Dixon Porter's naval flotilla attempt to exploit a circuitous system of rivers, creeks, and bayous as a means of positioning Union troops above the city. This highly criticized effort was also doomed to fail. The bluff city still held. Finally, after weighing his few remaining options, Grant marched his army down the western bank of the river opposite to and beyond range of Vicksburg's heavy guns in the hopes of making a lodgment on the eastern bank somewhere below the city. As the Yankee foot soldiers trudged through the swamps and bayous of eastern Louisiana, Admiral Porter, with eleven ironclad gunboats and transports, ran the gauntlet of Vicksburg's batteries. Aided by Porter's vessels, Grant crossed his army about forty miles below Vicksburg and secured a bridgehead at the little hamlet of Bruinsburg on April 30, 1863. Then, in one of the boldest maneuvers of the war, Grant marched his forty thousand men two hundred miles through the state's interior, defeating the Confederates in five pitched battles and capturing the state capital at Jackson all in a span of eighteen days. By the end of May, Vicksburg was besieged.[1]

From Richmond, Jefferson Davis and the members of his cabinet had pressured the commanders of the Trans-Mississippi for more than a year "to do something" to divert Federal forces away from Vicksburg. At stake was the vital Vicksburg–Port Hudson corridor, the loss of which would slam the door shut on communication with the Trans-Mississippi Department and access to its human and material resources, including much-needed European war goods imported through Mexico. Moreover, Union control of the Mississippi River meant the Confederacy would be cut in two. These entreaties fell upon the ears of three Confederate principal players with whom Dr. William McPheeters was well acquainted—Lt. Gen. Theophilus Hunter Holmes, Lt. Gen. Edmund Kirby Smith, and Maj. Gen. Sterling Price.

Holmes, a West Point crony of President Davis, had been transferred west following a poor performance with the Army of Northern Virginia to command the Confederate Trans-Mississippi Department in October 1862. Holmes's inadequacies stemmed, in part, from deteriorating health that had left him practically deaf, abnormally anxious, and with a proclivity to burst into fits of rage when a courier or telegram brought him bad news. A Missouri surgeon described the general as being "about sixty years old, six feet high, [with] large gray eyes, a long nose, and sallow complexion. He is hunchbacked and makes a very ungraceful appearance either on foot or on a horse. He is in his dotage and is apt to insult his best friend." Understandably, his men often referred to him derisively as "Granny Holmes." When Holmes received strong suggestions from Richmond to assist Vicksburg along the Mississippi, he was paralyzed by fear that he could not advance and leave the valley of the Arkansas River undefended. Confederate defeats at Prairie Grove and Arkansas Post in December 1862 and January 1863 had brought the myopic old general to this panic. At moments in various disjointed and tangential conversations, he intimated that he wished to be relieved of command.[2]

Thus in March 1863 President Davis sent yet another West Point graduate, Lt. Gen. Edmund Kirby Smith, to replace Holmes as departmental commander. During the reorganization, Davis allowed Holmes to retain command of the District of Arkansas, a decision that assured the old general's diffidence toward cooperation would be maintained. Blame for the Trans-Mississippi's unresponsiveness toward the developing crisis east of the river, however, cannot be placed exclusively upon Holmes. Once Smith arrived at his headquarters in Shreveport, he immersed himself in the task of untangling the extensive command-and-control problems plaguing the massive department. Smith explained to Holmes that he would "be too far away" to help direct affairs in Arkansas. Such an arrangement forced Holmes to act as on his own volition, which, in effect, meant no movement toward Helena would be immediately forthcoming.

The other major Confederate personality influencing the Helena campaign was Maj. Gen. Sterling Price of Missouri, a veteran of the

Mexican War, U.S. Congressman, and former governor of the state. Price had played a crucial role in the organization of Missouri's secessionist government, and it was the driving purpose of his military service as commander of Missouri troops to lead them back to Missouri and bring their state into the Confederacy where it belonged. After all, Missouri's star was prominently affixed to the Confederate "Stars and Bars." In June, while Price and his infantry division were at Jacksonport, Arkansas, Smith received a message from Secretary of War James A. Seddon pressing the issue of an attack on Helena. Smith, in turn, passed the message on to Holmes, instructing him "to act as circumstances may justify." When Holmes discussed the feasibility of such an attack with Price, the venerable Missourian conveyed that his troops were in excellent condition and that success was assured provided the attack were "conducted with celerity and secrecy." Holmes, however, remained unconvinced.[3]

On June 14 the district commander received information that caused him to reconsider. Confederate cavalry commander Brig. Gen. John S. Marmaduke reported that recent efforts to reinforce Vicksburg had seriously depleted the garrison at Helena. Concomitant with the news from Marmaduke came another message from Seddon exhorting a movement against Helena. This coupled with Price's enthusiasm prompted the usually doleful Holmes to telegraph Smith with an unusually optimistic request: "I believe we can take Helena. Please let me attack it." Several days later Smith replied, "Most certainly do it."[4]

Thus the Helena campaign was born in the minds of Holmes and Price and authorized by Smith. Designed not for its own purposes but to serve those elsewhere, the logistically ill-coordinated plan called for Price's division of infantry to leave Jacksonport on June 22 and approach Helena from the north. Brig. Gen. James F. Fagan's infantry brigade, accompanied by Holmes, would depart Little Rock and move toward Helena from the west. The cavalry brigades of Lucius M. Walker and John S. Marmaduke operating in eastern Arkansas were to rendevous with the infantry near Helena. Together the three columns would bring to bear almost eight thousand men.[5]

As McPheeters rode along with the gray column on that first day out, carrying fancy "eatables" in a champagne basket provided by a Little Rock matron, the Rebel force defending Vicksburg was already running desperately low on food. Those citizens who had not earlier fled were living in caves nearby and were close to starvation. Confederate Lt. Gen. John C. Pemberton, commanding the garrison at Vicksburg, was compelled to put his ravished men on quarter-rations—two ounces of fat pork and a biscuit per day. Symptoms of scurvy had begun to appear among them, causing men to faint after about twenty minutes of duty manning the heavy guns on the bluff. Pemberton, isolated from his fellow commanders in the field, cut off entirely from Richmond, starving, and at the tragic end of the siege, could not have known that three ragged butternut columns were making their toilsome way across half of Arkansas to throw themselves against his attackers. Had he known this, he would also have known that the effort was too little, too late.

Price had stated that "celerity and secrecy" were crucial to the success of the Helena campaign. By the second day of the march, secrecy was lost as word passed swiftly through the countryside to the Yankee commander at Helena, Maj. Gen. Benjamin M. Prentiss, that the gray host was moving toward him. Prentiss had his personal reputation on the line, for he shouldered the ignominy of having been surprised and captured during the battle of Shiloh fifteen months earlier. As soon as word reached him of the Confederate advance toward Helena, Prentiss vowed not to be unprepared again.

In what could be seen only as an overreaction to his earlier error, Prentiss ordered reveille sounded at 2:30 every morning, rousting out his four thousand Union infantry to battle-ready alert. His fortifications consisted of artillery redoubts that rimmed all landward approaches to Helena and the gunboat *Tyler* riding at anchor near the landing below the town. The Federals positioned their batteries to provide mutual fire support, and these positions were fronted by an abatis of felled trees, thus creating an impenetrable barrier for man and beast. In addition, rifle pits situated so as to take advantage of the unusually steep hills and deep, brush-choked ravines connected the batteries.

All these preparations were under way at Helena as the Confederates took up the line of march from Little Rock and Jacksonport. McPheeters was often on horseback, sometimes riding in an ambulance wagon among the infantrymen, listening to tall tales of home and battles won. Rumors were flying about Gen. Robert E. Lee's foray into Maryland and Pennsylvania; the boys hooted about stringing up "Old Abe" and General Grant from a chinaberry tree.

Their mood began to darken when they were assailed by unantic-
ipated summer storms and their pace was slowed on some days almost to
a standstill. Accordingly, the celerity also deemed essential by Price was
disabled as the men slogged in mud up to their knees, hauled and shoved
wagons and mules through deep sloughs, and forded a host of flooded
creek and river bottoms. Delays in traversing the submerged delta lands
of eastern Arkansas precluded Holmes from properly reconnoitering the
approaches to Helena. Upon their arrival, the Confederates discovered
felled trees blocking all roads leading into town. Furthermore, the pre-
cipitous hillsides protecting the outskirts of Helena thwarted any off-road
conveyance of the artillery and support vehicles. With no time to clear
the obstacles, Holmes ordered the artillery left behind; the assault would
be made by the infantry alone. Awaiting them was the enemy, alert and
hunkered down behind carefully designed fortifications.[6]

McPheeters composed himself as he looked into the faces of the
silent young men, and the fear he felt was for them. His own mind was
calmed by early lessons learned in his parents' home, by the faith they
had lived and taught, and by passages of Scripture that he and his sib-
lings long ago had memorized. His interior universe was orderly and
knowable as he affirmed his call to duty. McPheeters knew that his
Creator had called him, not to triumph or to victory, not to justice or
even to affirmation, but to service, to duty. He had only to perform
that unstintingly, courageously, never shrinking, and without com-
plaint, and the knowledge of this would be his fulfillment, God's grace.
His spirit was laced with these absolute assurances. The boys were silent
as their ordeal drew near. Some were surely praying.

June 22nd. Monday. Left Little Rock today at noon in an ambulance to join the army at Jacksonport accompanied by Maj. Snead,
Capt. [John] Mhoon, and Chas. Perry on horseback.[7] Mrs. Johnson
had put up and sent me a large champagne basket full of choice eatables to supply us on the road. Just as we were about leaving we
ascertained that the army had moved from Jacksonport in the direction of Helena with the view of attacking that place. This caused
us to change our course so as to intercept them on their march. On
crossing the Arkansas River at Little Rock, which we did on a pontoon bridge, a very amusing incident occurred. The river had

swollen so as to render the bridge too short by some 30 yards, which had to be crossed by boat. When nearly across on the boat Capt. Perry proposed for a wager to jump his horse off the bank into the river and swim to us who yet remained on the bridge. Snead took his wager and sure enough, fool like, he plunged in. The day was hot and the water deep. The horse capsized and the rider fell off and went under. For a few moments horse and rider struggled but finally both got safely to land. The scene was very ludicrous and gave rise to much merriment. [We] went 21 miles by night passing Gen. [James F.] Fagan's[8] camp and spent the night at Mr. Adams, a very comfortable place.

June 23rd. Started off after an early breakfast this morning but had not proceeded more than three miles when one of the fore wheels of our wagon gave way and down it came, the hub breaking and all the spokes coming out. Fortunately, we were near a house where we—Snead, Mhoon, and myself—took shelter from the sun. After some delay we succeeded in getting an old carriage a mile or two ahead to which we hitched our mules, left the broken ambulance, and proceeded on our journey. Found Mrs. Johnson's snack vastly convenient and acceptable. Reached Des Arc on White River about 6 P.M. Put up at the Hotel. Snead and I took supper with Capt. [Hamilton B.] Ware,[9] Snead staying all night and I returning to the Hotel.

June 24th. Rained hard all night and to a late hour in the day. Sent our carriage back, or rather left it and hitched our team to a wagon in which we proceeded, the carriage being too weak to stand the horrible roads of the Cache [River] bottom, famous for its almost impassibility. About dark [we] got to Mr. Harrelson's, 4 miles from Cotton Plant, where we spent the night. Rain still continuing.

June 25th. After breakfast [we] crossed the country three miles in our wagon to Mr. Hill's, still 4 miles from Cotton Plant. Here we sent our wagon and team back and waited for the army to come up, this being their road. About 1 P.M. Gen. Price and party arrived, the troops being still behind. When the army left Little

Rock I sent on with it my horse, trunk, and other baggage, returning only a few articles. To my great disappointment I found on joining my mess here that Dr. [Thomas D.] Wooten[10] had left horse and all at Jacksonport, expecting me to go there. Having no horse along, Maj. [Isaac] Brinker[11] furnished me with an open ambulance in which I proceeded. We remained the remainder of the day and night at Mr. Hill's.

June 26th. Remained at Mr. Hill's quietly all day today to allow the troops to come up, who were detained by the bad state of the roads. It continued to rain all day and night. I remained in the house and improved the time by writing to Mrs. Johnson.

June 27th. Saturday. The train having come up, the General and the staff left Mr. Hill's this morning. After going five miles we were stopped by the washing away of bridges during the heavy rains of the three days and nights past. Went into camp at 10 o'clock A.M. and remained until 4 P.M., in the meantime taking dinner and then starting again. Had an awful time in crossing Bayou de View, it being very much swollen.[12] Went a few miles further when we came to Caney Creek which we could not pass as it had increased to the size of a big river. Camped on its banks and slept out in the open air on some pieces of an old house. Slept soundly, however, the rain ceasing.

June 28th. Sunday. Was detained here until late in the evening in constructing a raft to cross the wagons on—Caney Creek presenting a formidable appearance. The soldiers—bodyguards—were engaged all morning in swimming the horses across and had a merry time swimming and playing in the water. During the morning I went to Maj. Brinker's quarters where Rev. Mr. [Enoch M.] Marvin[13] was and he read a chapter in the Bible and we engaged in religious excercises. About 4 P.M., the raft being completed, the wagons commenced crossing on it. The horses having all been taken out and swam across, the men pulled the wagons on the raft. It was an exciting and amusing scene. The creek was 150 yards or more wide. One or two wagons rolled partly off creating a great hurrah. Finally, however, we all, that is, the headquarters train, got safely over and we went a few miles on the other side and encamped for the night. I passed the night on the ground under a tree and slept soundly.

June 29th. Remained in camp until 1 P.M. to allow the brigades to cross Caney Creek. [We] then took the line of march and came 5 miles and encamped on the prairie. Again [I] slept under a tree without a tent.

June 30th. Arose at 3 [A.M.] and got underway at 4 A.M. in the meantime having eaten breakfast. Marched 17 miles today through some deep and bad bottoms and crossing some deep streams. Reached Moro about 11 A.M. and went into camp tired and hot. Slept out without tents again. We have our tents along but would not take the trouble to put them up.

July 1st. Made a short march of two miles today arriving at Spring Creek about 9 o'clock A.M. where we spent the day and night. The whole country around turned out to see and pay their respects to Gen. Price. In the afternoon, Dr. Wooten, Mr. Marvin, myself, and several others went swimmimg in the creek, which we found refreshing after the heat of the day. Our camp today had been recently occupied by the cavalry and we were greatly annoyed at night on finding our blankets and bedding all terribly *"fly-blown."*

July 2nd. Started at ½ past 5 this morning [and] came seven miles when we came up with Gen. Marmaduke's cavalry command.[14] Here we halted and was soon joined by Lt. Gen. Holmes and staff. As the generals were consulting we had nothing to do but amuse ourselves. [I] was invited by Mr. Geo. Smizer, formerly of St. Louis, to dine with him at Mrs. Geo. R. Johnson's, a widow lady residing 2 miles further on from our camp and 16 miles from Helena. She has a large house, lives well, and gave us a nice dinner. As I was more comfortable there than in camp or rather out of doors, I spent the night with her as the army would have to pass in the morning.

July 3rd. Started at ½ past 3 A.M. having first taken a cold breakfast prepared by Mrs. Johnson. Marched 10 miles and reached Col. Allen Polk's who resides six miles from Helena.[15] Here the command halted and went into camp nearby. Both generals and their staff went into Mr. Polk's. [I] found that I knew all his kinfolk and he mine so we struck up an agreeable acquaintance. After an hour or two [I] went to our camp. The evening was spent in making preparations for the fight, which was to come off on tomorrow. Got my instruments, bandages, morphia, chloroform, and etc. all ready and placed them in my haversack to carry with me on the field. As we were to start on the march to Helena a little after midnight, I retired early, but before doing so I went to Mr. Marvin's tent to join him in evening prayer. He prayed most fervently for our preservation and commended us to Him in whom alone there is safety. I felt solemn in view of the conflict of the morrow.

July 4th. 1863. Battle of Helena. About 1 A.M. all hands were on the march for Helena. The night was dark, the soldiers marched in profound silence, and as I rode the lines the scene impressed me very seriously. I never witnessed a more solemn procession and the thoughts would arise in my mind: before the sun sets many of these poor fellows will have bit the earth and their spirits have departed to Him who gave them, and perhaps I may be of the number. It was indeed a melancholy march, silent and dark. We reached the neighborhood of Helena about daybreak when line of battle was formed. The road that we had to approach the town was very bad, steep, rugged, and full of felled timber. The attack commenced a little after daylight. Gen. Price commanding the center, Gen. Fagan the right, and Gen. Marmaduke the left wing.[16] I had determined to accompany Gen. Price on the field remembering that Gen. Albert Sidney Johnston probably lost his life by not having a surgeon with him.[17] But when I had been on the field for some time and seen the shower of grape and cannister pass thick around me, hearing the whiz of the minie ball and crash of the cannonball as it passed, one of which took off a limb just over my head, Maj. Snead rode up to me and stated that a number of wounded had been carried to the rear without a surgeon and requested me to attend to them. I at once went back 50 yards where they were, dismounted and gave my horse to an orderly and commenced dressing the wounds of those brought off the field. After this I saw little of the fight. True, I heard the shout of our brave division as they charged the enemy's battery and heard and saw the cannonball as they passed and felled down the timber, still my business was with the wounded and to them I stuck. I soon found the position I occupied too much exposed to the fire of the enemy for the safety of the wounded or myself, as we were in momentary danger, so I had them removed across the brow of a hill just back and there went to work. Here there was no water and I again moved to a position still farther back which had been selected for the General Hospital. Here I found Drs. [Francis. D.] Cunningham, Wooten, [Caleb Dorsey] Baer, [R. M.] Slaughter, and in fact most of the surgeons of the division.[18] There was enough for us all to do as the wounded were being rapidly brought back. The first limb that I amputated was the left arm of a young man from Little Rock to whom Mr. Marvin called my attention. Mr. Marvin was very busy and efficient in attending [and] administering to the wounded. And thus I was engaged while the battle lasted.[19] This is not an account of the battle, but only a note. The result of the battle is soon told. Gen. Price's Division stormed and took the battery on Graveyard Hill and our soldiers occupied it, but the fighting on our right and left wing was not good, nor successful and we were soon informed that our army was "falling back."[20] The Infirmary Corps first brought these tidings. Our object now was to suspend operations and remove all the wounded off the field to Col. Polk's house which had been selected as a hospital. The fight ceased about 10 [A.M.] and by 2 P.M. we had all the ambulance trains at work and most of the sick off the ground. When they had all gone I mounted my horse and rode back to Col. Polk's coming up in the meantime with Gen. Holmes and Price and our gallant but defeated army. The rest of the day and until 12 o'clock at night was spent in the hospital attending to the wounded and endeavoring to make them as comfortable as possible. [I] retired at this late hour tired and sick at heart.

July 5th. Sunday. Our army started back this morning leaving me behind in charge of the wounded, some 168 in all. Col. Polk's whole house and everything about it being given up for that purpose and many put in his negro cabins. Drs. Baer, [James H.] Swindell, [Andrew N.] Kincannon, and [Jacob F.] Brookhart were left behind with me in charge of the wounded.[21] Worked hard all day in endeavoring to get the wounded in a comfortable situation. Col. Polk was both accommodating and kind exceedingly so, and worked hard himself in nursing the wounded.

July 6th. Our cavalry, which remained in the rear, came this morning and formed in line just beyond the hospital and there remained some time. This drew out the Federals. About 12 M. they placed a battery on a point about 2 miles east of the hospital and commenced firing shot and shell, but our men had gone some hours before. Some 6 or 8 shot struck immediately about the building, one in fact went through a cabin where some of our wounded were. This created so much alarm that I ordered a large white flag to be raised fearing that we might be injured by the shell falling thick around us. In a short time the firing ceased and soon thereafter Col. [Powell] Clayton of the Kansas 5th Federal rode up with a squad of cavalry and asked why the white flag was raised.[22] I told him that this was a hospital, and as he had not respected our yellow flag I had ordered the white one raised to [prevent] our wounded being injured.[23] He stated that he had not observed our yellow flag. A parley ensued and soon Gen. Ross and other Federal officers and soldiers came up.[24] Before they came up, however, I had sent 56 of the more slightly wounded to Trenton and thence on to Little Rock to keep them out of their hands. Gen. Ross behaved very cleverly. [He] offered to take charge of our wounded and etc., which I declined. He then offered to send us out what we needed and also forward a letter to my wife, which he did. He informed me that he would send out and have the wounded paroled, a list of whom were furnished him. After remaining some time in general conversation and taking a drink of our whiskey, which they relished much, they departed much to my satisfaction. Before going, however, they informed me that Vicksburg had surrendered to Gen. Grant on the 4th with 20,000 prisoners. This was sad news to me and although I did not fully credit it—the Federals being such enormous liars—it nevertheless disturbed me no little.

July 7th. Had another visit from the Yankees today. About noon Dr. [Isaac] Castleberry,[25] Gen. Prentiss' Medical Director, came out with a corps of surgeons and train of ambulances bringing with them some medical supplies and offering to take all our wounded in. This I declined stating that we preferred caring for them ourselves. This visit was characterized by courtesy on their part. Indeed, Dr. Castleberry was kind in his deportment to me and stated that he knew me by reputation. He was lavish in his promises, much more so than in his performances.[26]

July 8th. Spent the day in attending to the wounded, in procuring and making mattresses for them, and in dressing their wounds. Several of the worst cases have died. [I] sent a dispatch to Gen. Price.

July 9th. Sent Dr. Swindell into Helena this morning under [a] flag of truce with a communication to Dr. Castleberry and Gen. Prentiss asking to be allowed to purchase supplies for our wounded. He returned in the evening bringing word that the supplies needed would be furnished. Dr. Swindell was not permitted to purchase anything for himself or any one else. The Federals still claim to have taken Vicksburg.

July 10th. The supplies promised by Dr. Castleberry or rather a portion of them came out today including a hogshead of ice, which is very acceptable as the weather is very hot. Received a communication from Dr. [Godfrey N.] Beaumont[27] at Trenton in charge of the wounded sent over there and replied to it. [I] took quinine and blue mass, feeling symptoms of intermittent fever.[28] Seven of our wounded have died up to this date.

July 11th. Still unwell, however, [I] did not relax my exertions to render the wounded comfortable. Dr. Castleberry came out today with a few other supplies, not all that I asked for or that he promised, however, [he] promises to send others tomorrow with some tobacco for my own smoking. One of our wounded died today, poor fellow.

July 12th. Sunday. [Today is] but little like a home Sabbath. No church of course and I am still unwell. Weather very hot. Dr. Castleberry did not send out as he promised, but why should I expect a Yankee to keep his promises? Still I have no reason to complain of him or them.

July 13th. Thanks to a kind Providence I feel better today. A great change in the weather. Today it is cloudy and cool. A fire is quite comfortable. Performed the first secondary operation, amputated the arm of a man injured in the elbow joint.[29] This afternoon several parolled persons from Vicksburg called by on their way home thus confirming the sad news of the fall of that city.

July 14th. The fall of Vicksburg and our repulse here has made me feel very sad, but not [to] despair, we will yet rally and "never give up the ship." No never. The Federals also claim to have defeated Gen. Lee—very improbable.[30] [I] was visited both by leaders from Helena and the surrounding country today. They come to do what they can for our wounded. The ladies in this neighborhood have been very kind and attentive. Our wounded are doing well some others of them not. Weather still cold rendering a fire necessary to comfort.[31]

July 15th. Another secondary operation today. Amputated a man's leg above the knee today, it being his only chance for life and that a slim one.[32] The knee joint was terribly shattered by the screw cap from a shell. One other patient died today. Received a lot of supplies today from Trenton. Weather more seasonable.

July 16th. Went this morning, accompanied by Dr. Swindell, to Dr. Rice's and after paying him and family a visit, we went accompanied by Dr. Rice to visit the other hospital some two miles off where the wounded of Shelby's command were left, some 18 Missourians and fine looking men, most of them doing well. Returned and took dinner at Dr. Rice's. Some 5 or 6 of [Archibald S.] Dobbins' Confederate Cavalry dined there also.[33] After dark sent off a refractory nurse under arrest. A large scouting party of Federals passed up the road today. We are visited alternately by the Yankees and by our men.

July 17th. The poor fellow whose leg I amputated died today. He was conscious of his approaching end and was anxious to see a minister, but as there was none near I read him passages from the Scriptures and tried to point him to the Lamb of God as best I could. Another patient also died. Two young ladies from Helena came out and took dinner with us.

July 18th. Day passed off quietly. [I] wrote a letter to Mrs. Johnson, Gen. Holmes, and Dr. Cunningham of Little Rock.

July 19th. Sunday. No church privileges, [I] went over to Mr. Smizer's to see [a] wounded man this morning. On returning with Dr. Kincannon [I] was overhauled by [a] Federal scout and taken back to Col. [William E.] McLean who on hearing who we were promptly released us and rode over to [the] hospital with us.[34] Federals went out on heavy scout, several hundred, [and] returned in [the] afternoon. Officers visited us going and coming. [I] visited Mrs. Polk. Received supplies, flour, and meal from Col. Dobbins' command.

July 20th. Day passed off quietly. Very warm. [I] was visited by some young ladies in the neighborhood, Miss King, and another from Dr. Rice. Wrote a letter to Gen. Price and Dr. Wooten sent by nurses returning to command.

July 21st. Spent the morning in fixing double inclined plane for Capt. [Walter C.] Robinson over at Mr. Smizer's who has a compound fracture of [the] upper third of [his] femur.[35] Took dinner there. On returning to hospital [I] found Dr. Kyler and other

Federals out with [a] flag of truce to see what we needed. Near sundown Mrs. Dorsey Rice came from town and stated that my wife was in Helena. I offered tidings, [it] being too late for me to go in. God bless her. I hope to see her in the morning. Lost a patient today, a young fellow from St. Louis wounded in the leg. [He] died of pneumonia.

CHAPTER 2

The Womenfolk, 1863

Whither thou goest, I will go.

Sallie McPheeters did indeed make the journey to Helena, intent upon seeing her husband behind enemy lines. For her, the news of Union victories on July 4 at both Vicksburg and Helena and resulting euphoria among Federals in St. Louis had been her signal to apply for permission to travel. As the church bells of St. Louis rang and shots fired in celebration, Sallie McPheeters paid them no mind. She had a serious, perhaps even dangerous, project in mind, and she enlisted the cooperation of a close friend and fellow Confederate, Mrs. Allen Polk.

Early in the war, Union military officials had a policy in place of travel-with-permission for regions occupied by Federal forces. Official passes were issued by military provosts to specific individuals for specific dates of travel, whether by steamboat or by rail, and pro-Southern women made their way south to visit or remain permanently with their husbands in the Confederate army. These women carried with them essential items in their excessive baggage—trunks, parcels, and satchels. Almost every woman traveling this way took the risk of smuggling contraband, such as food, clothing, bolts of fabric, leather goods, and quantities of medicine. And they carried an even more precious item— letters from home to the soldiers in the field. The Confederacy had no formal mail service.

Union authorities began tightening regulations governing this traffic, and soon baggage and persons were carefully searched, often either confiscated or taken into custody, and the travelers might be sent without trial or hearing to a Federal prison. The bold and defiant spirit of pro-Southern women became such a vexation to the military that official reports sent to district headquarters were filled with the antics of Confederate sympathizers.

When the war was in its first year, the newspapers of St. Louis reported the colorful encounters of these ladies and officers in blue on the streets of the city:

> FEMININE SECESSIONISTS IMPRISONED—Yesterday morning as the prisoners from Pittsburg [the battle of Shiloh] were passing under escort from the steamer *Woodford* to the McDowell College prison, a small rebel flag was displayed by a lady at the residence of Wm. Bell, on Eighth street near the prison. Other ladies waved their handkerchiefs, and made other demonstrations of sympathy with the captives.
>
> On being satisfied as to the facts, Provost Marshal Leighton ordered a guard placed at the house, with orders to prohibit all ingress or egress by any persons whatever, making the house a prison for the confinement of its inmates. Should the stock of family supplies fall, these ladies will be served with army rations and treated as other prisoners. The same course will be pursued, we understand, towards certain ladies in this city, unless they exhibit a more decent regard for propriety than they have recently done.
>
> Our citizens need not be surprised to see a guard in front of the houses of any of our leading secessionists elsewhere in the city. They who call themselves ladies, yet persist in disgraceful conduct of the kind referred to, should and will be made to feel that they also are to be held to severe account.[1]

Wives and daughters of Confederate soldiers who were left behind in St. Louis banded together to support one another as they faced the extended period of martial law, and Northern officers stationed in the city also faced the certain knowledge that the war was passing them by. At best theirs was a police action merely to maintain relative order in a civilian population. And for the waiting Southern women, their only relief from boredom was to annoy the Union military with a series of seemingly harmless pranks designed to infuriate them. A crescendo of frustration was building between these two groups, as another journalist reported.

> WORE CONFEDERATE COLORS—During all this time the ladies of St. Louis were much in evidence. They carried to the prisons and to the hospital all in the way of food and clothing allowed. But as the war grew, the feeling grew, and some of the ladies were

quite pronounced in their views and acts, especially the younger ones. Many, many were there in St. Louis who had some one in the Confederate Army. "Red, white and red" were the Southern colors. The ladies delighted to wear just inside their bonnets three large roses, a white one in the center, a red on each side, "red, white and red." No matter how else they might be attired, the bonnet thus adorned must be worn.

It was also the custom to line dark wraps of all kinds with bright red, the wind was so apt to flap the cloak back and forth; or perhaps, the turn of a deft hand might do so "When a woman wills, she will." Miss Augustine Chouteau, who lived then on Eighth street near the McDowel College prison, wore a long black cloak lined with the very brightest red to be found. In the afternoons, the prisoners were allowed to congregate for awhile on the porch of that part of the prison that had been Doctor McDowel's residence. It was a queer-looking place, house and college. In the days when Dr. McDowell was a good Whig, and the Democratic papers wanted to be funny at his expense, they spoke of the octagon-shaped college, with its sloping roof, as McDowel's "Pepper Box."

The home adjoining, on the northwest corner of Eighth and Gratiot, had its porch inclosed in a kind of outside wall with openings, and here it was the prisoners could be seen in the afternoons. That was the time for the ladies to pass by, displaying their colors. " . . . Of course, it would be childish for the authorities to issue orders against any article of dress worn by ladies, but it was conduct that gave 'aid and comfort to the enemy.'"[2]

By the time Sallie McPheeters and Mrs. Allen Polk applied for their passes south on the river, there was another policy in place in all regions held by the Union—banishment. Known Southerners called to the attention of the occupying military would find their names on publicly posted lists.

With only twenty-four hours to prepare, these people were required to leave the city or state from which they were banished and, in some cases, to be taken by steamer or rail to a place near the Confederate army. (In early April 1863 Sallie McPheeters's friend, Mrs. Frost, the wife of Confederate brigadier general Daniel M. Frost, was expelled from St. Louis and sent south.) Some women traded fine horses and buggies for more durable mules and wagons to make the journey alone overland. By this policy, the occupying army hoped to gain some degree of control over the civilian population under their jurisdiction, and it was an effective technique, for every Southerner dreaded banishment. When exiled pro-Southern women, often the wives of officers, found their husbands, they remained thereafter as close to the army encampments as possible in rented quarters, moving when the army moved. Indeed, there was a civilian community that followed the army in Arkansas, almost as an encumberance, though McPheeters delighted in the company of these Southern ladies when nearby.

Sallie McPheeters must have felt certain of the good humor of the military provost in St. Louis on July 16, 1863, when she and Mrs. Polk entered the office to request a pass to travel south on the river. The trio of triumphs, Gettysburg, Vicksburg, and Helena, just twelve days earlier, was still generating joy in the hearts of her captors. She and Mrs. Polk were issued a travel pass; Mrs. Polk allowed to travel with her infant and a female slave.[3]

On the appointed day the two ladies and the slave, carrying the baby in her arms, boarded a steam packet at the St. Louis landing, the first passenger boat to go downriver since Vicksburg. Their courage and boldness were silently intact because before the war no lady ever went out into the city unaccompanied or unescorted even for a few hours, and travel without a gentleman as escort and protector was not to be considered. Casting decorum and their own safety aside, Sallie McPheeters and Mrs. Polk were intent upon their mission, and they stepped aboard the steamer having no idea what lay ahead of them.

The decks and salons were crowded with Northern politicians, their gold watch chains visible, their fine clothing the height of fashion, and their loud talk indicative of their newly garnered importance. They stood along the rails exchanging pleasantries with the Federal officers on board. A coterie of Northern women were also passengers, wives and friends of Federal officers, and their finery was obvious, their conversation loud, and their boasting of patriotism to the Union unceasing.

Soon these women discovered that Sallie McPheeters, standing quietly by herself in the salon of the boat, was a Rebel sympathizer, and the insults, from which Sallie was in no mood to shrink, began to fly. With spirited contempt she announced the purpose of her trip to her fellow passengers. Describing this experience years later, Sallie said,

"Their indignation was aroused to the highest pitch and they became exceedingly disagreeable to me in diverse ways, by word and deed, succeeded in rendering my position on the boat anything but pleasant."[4]

Seizing an opportune situation, the political gentleman denounced this Southern wife as a "rebel mail carrier" and "rebel woman," demanding that her luggage and her person be searched for contraband. Summoning the captain of the vessel, the passengers demanded that Sallie McPheeters "be put ashore at the nearest weighing station." The captain refused this request and was at least polite to McPheeters, but he could not diminish the disparaging remarks from his passengers. At last, Sallie recalled, "to rid myself of their insolence, I found it necessary to absent myself from the cabin and from the public table of the boat and to confine myself to my stateroom."

Also on board was a black woman who witnessed Sallie's mistreatment and her subsequent retirement. She made her way to Sallie's stateroom to ask a favor of her; she needed help "cutting and fitting a dress." Sallie asked why she did not enlist her new friends from the North, and the black woman answered that when she really needed help, she always asked a Southern lady. When the project was finished, a woman from Iowa asked indignantly how such a fine fit had been achieved, and the black woman said that the dress was "cut and fit on my person." The Iowa woman was aghast and said to Sallie, "Why, you didn't touch that horrid creature, did you? I would never do such a thing myself," adding, "But we don't intend that you should have them to wait on you."

Reaching Memphis, the steamer docked at the foot of Beale Street to take on a celebrity and her entourage, Mrs. U. S. Grant, her two boys, and their military escort. She was bound for Vicksburg to join her husband after a long stay at the Gayoso Hotel in Memphis. The general had brought her and the boys from their temporary home in Holly Springs to Memphis when his presence was required to direct the final campaign against Vicksburg. With the Mississippi River under Federal control, Mrs. Grant could now travel in relative safety with a military escort. Quickly surrounded by her fellow passengers, she was told of the "ostracized rebel woman on board."

To the great surprise of her audience, Julia Dent Grant called for the captain of the boat and asked the identity of the absent passenger, and then she asked the captain to present her compliments to this lady. When Sallie appeared, Mrs. Grant asked if she were "the wife of Dr. McPheeters of St. Louis?" When Sallie said that she was, Grant replied that she "had pleasant recollections of him" and invited Sallie to join her. "Mrs. McPheeters," she continued, "do not let these women, nor anyone else on board annoy you. I will see that you are not molested, and when the boat reaches Vicksburg, I will make General Grant take you to your husband in his buggy." Sallie told her that Helena was her destination and that the town was quite a ways north of Vicksburg. Julia Grant replied, "Very well, I will see that you get to your husband in safety."

Shocked, the Northern women on board asked Mrs. Grant how she could associate with a Confederate woman. She answered that she harbored no ill feelings toward Southerners and that, in fact, many of her friends were in the South. She added, "Besides, we do not know how soon the tables may be turned and we may be under the necessity of asking for favors at their hands." When the steamer came to at Helena, Julia Dent Grant and Sallie McPheeters made their warm farewells, and Mrs. Grant sent one of her aides ashore with a message for Maj. Gen. Benjamin Prentiss requesting proper treatment and safe passage for Sallie through the lines.[5]

Sallie McPheeters, not always sharing her husband's disciplined spirit and economy of expression (as his diary reflects), had come to him in person at some risk in order to speak privately rather than to write the description of another tragedy in their life together. Death had claimed their second son, George, during McPheeters's absence from home. Sallie had made this pilgrimage in order that they might share the terrible sorrow together, even in an alien, hostile land controlled by their enemy.

> *July 22nd.* Went into Helena after an early breakfast this morning for the purpose of seeing and bringing out my wife. At the picket station a guard accompanied me in. [I] reported to [the] Provost Marshal then to Dr. Castleberry, Medical Director. Found [my] wife well and hearty at Col. Moore's. Got [a] pass from Gen. Ross and [an] ambulance and started out to [the] hospital about 12 M. Arrived about ½ past 1 P.M., Miss Alexander and Miss Otey accompanied us. Found Federals out parolling our wounded. In the evening took my wife over to Dr. Rice's where she will stay.

Very comfortable. Delighted to see and talk with her, but this can't be expressed.[6]

July 23rd. Came over to hospital after breakfast to look after matters. Returned to dinner. [My] wife [is] well though fatigued by excitement and trip. The account of the death of poor George fills me with irrepressible sadness.[7] After dinner [I] went over to the neighboring hospital and amputated the thigh of one of the wounded—gloomy prospect of recovery, still [his] only chance. Federals came out this afternoon and paroled nurses and infirmary corps, an unusual procedure. Happy in the society of my wife. God be merciful to us.

July 24th. Spent the day with [my] wife and at the hospital. Talked over home affairs and etc.

July 25th. Visited hospital after breakfast and attended to affairs there. Returned and took dinner at Dr. Rice's with [my] wife. [In the] evening visited patient whose leg I amputated. [He is] weak and fading.

July 26th. Sabbath, but no church. [I] went to the hospital. Mrs. Polk and Mrs. Snider called to see [my] wife. [I] wrote to the command [and] spent the afternoon with my wife.

July 27th. Sent off some of the wounded from the hospital. Spent most of the day with [my] wife. Received letters from Snead and others.

July 28th. Went over to Judge Jones to see [a] sick child. Visited Mrs. Polk and Mr. Smizer. Federal surgeons came out from Helena to [the] hospital with supplies. [I] sent off a lot of patients. [My] wife complaining. Wrote to Mrs. Gen. Frost.[8]

July 29th. Came over to the hospital and remained several hours this morning. Made arrangements with Mr. Allen Polk to send in our wives in the morning to take a boat for their respective homes.

[I] then returned and spent the remainder of the day with my wife. Her visit has been a very gratifying one to me indeed. Sorry that it is to be so short, but she ought to return to her children and I to my command. She has fixed me up nicely.

July 30th. My wife accompanied by Mrs. Polk started in to Helena on their return home. Mr. Polk and I accompanied them nearly to the pickets, but thought it best not to go in so we had to bid them good bye and commit them to God and the tender mercies of others. God grant my wife a safe return to her home and that she may find her children well. It is sad to part with her not knowing when we will meet again, still I am grateful for her visit. Mr. Ramsey who went in with my wife returned late in the evening. They got in safe, no boat however, and she will have to lie over until tomorrow.

July 31st. Went over to Dr. Rice's this morning with Mr. Tilden, then over to Mr. Ramsey's. Mr. Cook came out from Helena this afternoon bringing tidings and a note from my wife, she gets off this evening and will send me out some things tomorrow. God bless her. [I] went over to Mr. Smizer's this afternoon to see Capts. Robinson and [Amos F.] Cake[9]—both doing well.

August 1st. Had an accession of 8 patients, wounded and sick from Port Hudson, sent out from Helena today. After dinner [I] went over to the other hospital and amputated the left arm above the elbow of a Mr. [Rufus] McPeters[10] wounded on the 4th— third secondary amputation that I have performed. Received a lot of clothes from Helena this evening purchased and sent out by my wife.

August 2nd. Spent an unprofitable Sabbath today—no church. Spent it in the hospital. In the evening [I] went over to Dr. Rice's.

August 3rd. Expected to have started for the command today but before doing so [I] sent Dr. Brookhart up to Mr. Blunt's to learn about a conveyance. He returned late in the evening reporting that he will have one for me, so God willing I will start in the morning. Several ladies visited us today. Made my arrangements to get off in the morning.

August 4th. Tuesday. Turned over the hospital this morning to Dr. Baer and started for Little Rock to join Gen. Price.[11] Went over to Mr.Blunt's, 6 miles off, where we got a carriage. Mr. Allen Polk accompanied me as far as Mr. Blunt's. Drs. Brookhart and [Thomas G.] Kelly[12] from the hospital go with me. Drs. Baer, Swindell, and Kincannon remain behind. Took dinner at Mr. Blunt's then passed Mrs. Johnson's and came on to Col. Taylor's across Big Creek where we spent the night. [I] had a slight fever.

August 5th. Started and came about 20 miles to Mrs. Brown's where [we] took a good dinner and after resting 2 hours turned off from [the] Clarendon Road and came to Harris' Ferry. [We] couldn't get over so [we] went to Judge Black's—a poor place— and spent the night.

August 6th. Crossed White River this morning at Mr. Harris' Ferry—long ferriage—and went over to the DeVall's Bluff Road some 7 miles and stopped at Mr. Miller's.

August 7th. Left Mr. Miller's at 2 A.M. and rode 14 miles by moonlight to DeVall's Bluff. Arrived at 6 o'clock and awaited cars.[13] Rode at night to avoid prairie flies. At ½ past 12 M. the cars arrived. On board was Maj. and Mrs. Snead and Capt. [George W.] Kerr.[14] The two latter en route for Helena under a flag of truce. Mrs. Snead will go to St. Louis if she can. [At] 2 P.M. cars started back and arrived at Little Rock at 5 P.M. Put up at Anthony House. Met numerous friends and acquaintances. After tea called on Mrs. Mary and old Mrs. Johnson and families. Saw Lt. Gen. [Edmund] Kirby Smith.[15]

CHAPTER 3

The Loss of Little Rock, 1863

He lifted me out of the desolate pit
out of the mire and the clay.

McPheeters's return to Little Rock was like a homecoming as he greeted friends in town. Good manners dictated that the recent failure of the army should not be mentioned on that first evening. The Trans-Mississippi Department was depleted now, without orders, and only in remote contact with Richmond, isolated by the loss of the Mississippi. Whatever the future held, McPheeters knew he was where he belonged—at the side of Maj. Gen. Sterling Price, his good old general and friend, whose health he tended carefully.

The cotton-making days of summer gripped Central Arkansas as McPheeters arrived in Little Rock, and the city, once gracious and shaded, prosperous and clean, had been converted in 1862 to a "hospital city," for the Confederate command had decided to send wounded to the capital city from any battle in the region. Remaining in town were women, children, old men, and a few slaves as long trains of ambulance wagons jolted into town laden with suffering men whose screams could be heard from a considerable distance. Sometimes the ambulances came by steam ferry across the Arkansas River, and after the battle of Pea Ridge in March 1862, a pontoon bridge had been constructed at Little Rock, and the convoy of wounded from that engagement had lurched ashore, ending a trek of two hundred miles across backcountry. Many had died en route and had been hastily buried in shallow shared graves in the woods.

There had been two hospitals organized by the newly established Trans-Mississippi Medical Department as the summer began, one in the buildings of St. John's College, a Masonic college for men that was closed at the outbreak of war, and the second, Rock Hotel Hospital, in the center of town. Following the battle of Shiloh, wounded again arrived in droves, by boat, by train, and overland in "meat wagons," as the men called the ambulances. To meet this crisis, eight more hospital sites were created—both the Presbyterian and Episcopal churches at Eighth and Scott were emptied of pews so wounded could be packed into the sanctuaries on straw strewn thinly on the wooden floors. A row of businesses on Main Street that had been padlocked were forced open and used for the wounded, and these buildings came to be known as the Main Street Hospital.

The women of Little Rock had organized themselves into a sewing, knitting, and weaving enterprise, but they hastily gave up their needlework to begin nursing and cooking. Old men who once had dozed and gossiped in the shade of the State House on Markham Street were now busy around the clock, digging graves, unwinding bandages from the dead to be rinsed and used again, and helping distribute food to patients.

The Sisters of Mercy came out of their cloister at Eighth and Louisiana, with the permission of their bishop, to work among the wounded, and the nuns gave up their quarters to be converted into another hospital site. Across the street there was a coffin factory that turned out forty coffins a day, but the bodies of soldiers could not be sent home as the dying had hoped. The city's people were scarcely able to survive in such a crisis, which seemed to have no end.

The winter of 1862–63 was unusually severe, and the Confederate cavalry in Central Arkansas had not been assigned winter quarters; the men slept on the ground with few blankets and no tents. The incidence of pneumonia increased among them as well as among the sick and wounded quartered in Little Rock. During these months, there were at least 2,500 Confederate wounded in the city at any one time, with an average of eight deaths a day. The city council bought property to enlarge Mount Holly Cemetery, but gravediggers were urgently needed elsewhere.

Some time later the nuns made an official report of the crisis and of their nursing duties. "For a while there was almost a famine . . . , for want of sufficient food and clean clothing was partially the cause of the high death rate."[1] And conditions in mid-nineteenth-century hospitals of both armies actually fostered infection, putrefaction, "hospital gangrene," blood poisoning, and tetanus since the principles of asepsis were yet unknown. Not until 1867 were Joseph Lister's teachings widely published and surgeons began to wash their hands and perhaps their instruments between operations.

McPheeters himself was one of the countless, well-trained, yet barehanded military surgeons who operated wearing a butcher's apron or a bedsheet pinned across his chest, amputating limbs of wounded men held down on the operating table by fellow soldiers. Moving rapidly from one patient to another, the surgeon simply wiped the wide-bladed knife on his apron or a rag before beginning another operation. Even cotton used in previous surgery was rinsed to be used again and again.[2] One person recalled: "There was a nauseous aura overhanging many areas of Little Rock at this time, days were warming and just about everybody had the smell of putrification in his nostrils. Amputated arms, legs, as well as bodies, of the dead were buried as expeditiously as possible. But the odor of festering sores and of death could be detected whenever anyone went near any of the improvised hospitals. Virtually every man, woman and child had suffered the shock of unsightly mangled bodies."[3]

Early in 1863, beginning with the fall of a Confederate bastion at Arkansas Post in January, Arkansans became desperately anxious about the fate of their state, realizing that the army that controlled the Mississippi would inevitably control them. A newspaper editor put it clearly: "Anyone with a thimble full of brains ought to know that the fate of Arkansas rests intimately upon that of Vicksburg." Once the Union controlled the length of the great river, they were free to focus their attention westward. One target of particular interest was the weakly defended Lower Arkansas River Valley, gateway to the upper reaches of the fully isolated Trans-Mississippi Department. The key to the area was Little Rock, the capital and geographic center of Arkansas. Federal strategists eyed the city as an easy mark, for after Vicksburg and Helena, Little Rock was vulnerable to attack either by river or land.[4]

The panic of the civilian population, who understood the situation more clearly than Lt. Gen. Edmund Kirby Smith in Shreveport, pressured the governor of the state to move the seat of government to Washington, a small town in Hempstead County in southwestern Arkansas. A Confederate surgeon stationed at St. John's Hospital in

Little Rock, facing reality, wrote to his wife: "Things look rather gloomy about here. . . . [A]ll government property is being removed from town. . . . I consider it merely a matter of time when Little Rock falls." Lt. Gen. Theophilus Holmes and General Price entreated Smith to send reinforcements, but the department commander replied: "I can give you no assistance. You must make the best disposition you can with troops at your disposal." The two generals continued to stew, and when Smith finally sent an infantry brigade in June, both commanders saw the futility of this small number of men. They still asserted firmly that "the enemy are about to send a force of 60,000 men into this State."[5]

Echoing this alarm was the governor of Arkansas, who bombarded Pres. Jefferson Davis and the Confederate Congress with complaints about Arkansas's exposed position. At last the president wrote the governor: "I cannot suppose that your apprehensions that General Smith proposes to surrender the Valley of the Arkansas can be well founded. It is his duty to defend every portion of the territory embraced by his command." In August, Smith visited Little Rock to reassure both civilian and military personnel of his intention to defend the city and what was left to the Confederacy of the state. He glad-handed officials, even breakfasted with McPheeters, and wrote a stirring letter of reassurance for the *Washington (Ark.) Telegraph* addressed to the people of Arkansas.[6]

All his comfortable words notwithstanding, General Smith privately reconciled himself to the loss of Little Rock. August unfurled the devastating heat of high summer over the weary men in and around the city, and by then all but one of the hospitals in Little Rock had been closed. However, as always, everyone suffered from "southern fevers," malaria, typhoid, and dysentery to such a degree that little more than half the aggregate strength of Confederate forces could be mustered for duty. Even General Holmes took to his bed, relinquishing temporary command of the District of Arkansas to Sterling Price.[7]

The Missourian, for his part, set forth quickly to fortify the northern and eastern approaches to Little Rock "with barely 8,000 men of all arms"; he relied on the rapidly falling Arkansas River and one infantry brigade to cover the southern flank. The thin defensive line consisted of six miles of hastily dug rifle pits along the river opposite Little Rock, and these were manned by soldiers who were remnants of other infantry brigades plus a small contingent recently summoned from Pine Bluff.

Recognizing the difficulties of defending two banks of an easily ford-able river, Price ordered the construction of three pontoon bridges across the Arkansas at Little Rock to facilitate the escape of his infantry if all defenses failed. These rickety bridges were indeed crucial to the survival of Price's army since, as it turned out, when the battle commenced, most of his force was defending the wrong side of the river. And farther east of the city, toward Brownsville, DeVall's Bluff, and Clarendon, Price ordered the two cavalry commands of Brig. Gens. L. M. Walker and J. S. Marmaduke to sweep the countryside to obstruct and delay any Federal advance.[8]

Back in Helena, Maj. Gen. Frederick Steele had replaced Maj. Gen. Benjamin Prentiss, despite the latter officer's gallant defense of the town July 4. Steele, newly arrived from Vicksburg, where his effectiveness at division command had caught the eye of fellow West Point classmate Ulysses S. Grant, was given command of the Arkansas Expedition Army with orders to seize Little Rock and the Central Arkansas River Valley.[9] By August the roads, which June rains had transformed into ribbons of mud during the Confederate approach to Helena, were dry, dusty thor-oughfares that allowed Steele's force of seven thousand infantry, six artillery batteries, and six thousand cavalry to march 150 miles to the out-skirts of Little Rock in less than one month's time.

With the enemy approaching overland from Helena, Confederate military morale closely parallelled that of the capital's people, and deser-tions severely reduced the number of defenders. Many civilian families sent their children in groups out of the city to live with friends or kin-folk in safer areas to the south. A month passed between McPheeters's return to Little Rock and the fall of the city to Union forces, and dur-ing that interval, civilians horded food, usually burying what they could get their hands on, and boarded up their houses, preparing to make a hasty escape. Their lack of faith in their defenders proved correct.

McPheeters went about the city paying social calls and visiting a few patients in an almost dazed state as if he were preparing for a long pleas-ure trip. The undertow of anxiety during this lull produced more con-fusion among both the frightened defenders and would-be deserters.

During the month of August, the Confederate cavalry, outnum-bered and outmatched, skirmished with the Federals on a daily basis, gradually falling back toward Little Rock. Confident that Steele's only viable military option for taking the city was a direct assault on the defenses north of the Arkansas River, Price placed the majority of his infantry and artillery in those earthworks and waited. Steele, however, countered the Missourian by dividing his army in the face of the enemy. He sent his cavalry and artillery southeast of Little Rock to force a crossing of the rapidly falling river while his infantry proceeded up the northern bank to feign an assault on the fortifications.

With covering fire provided by twenty artillery pieces placed at the base of a large horseshoe bend in the river, Steele's engineers safely constructed a pontoon bridge for crossing the cavalry at Terry's Ferry. By midmorning on September 10, the blue riders were across and moving west toward Little Rock. A Confederate cavalry brigade and two artillery batteries tried desperately to impede the advance but were forced to fall back slowly to Fourche Bayou, only four miles from the capital. There the fate of Little Rock was sealed. Confederate troopers made an obstinate stand, inflicting the largest number of casualties upon the Federals during the entire campaign. In the end, though, enfilade fire from Steele's artillery and coordinated Union assaults proved too much for the contentious Southern horsemen. Price, not wishing to "suffer another Vicksburg," evacuated his infantry across the pontoon bridges without them ever firing a shot.

Soldiers and civilians alike streamed south out of Little Rock. Marmaduke's cavalry, acting as rear guard, screened the evacuation. As General Holmes turned his back on the city, he responded to a query posed by Marmaduke: "Steele will not pursue us. His government will not seek to disturb us now. We are an army of prisoners and self-supporting at that." By 5 P.M., the gray exodus was complete.[10]

The blue coats marched into Little Rock with the 3d Minnesota Infantry ceremoniously in the lead down Markham Street past the State House, its bands playing. The town seemed to be deserted. The streets were empty, and there seemed no one present to make the official surrender. But one city councilman, James Henry, whose house faced the river, hoisted a bedsheet at the foot of Ferry Street. He was accosted by an officer of Price's staff who promised to shoot the alderman if the flag were not lowered at once. Henry obeyed the order, but when the officer rode away, he again ran the bedsheet up the flagpole. Threatened soon after by a neighbor who came running armed with a shotgun, he lowered the flag once more.

Across the river on the northern bluff inspecting abandoned gun emplacements was General Steele. Through their field glasses, he and his staff observed the white flag going up and down, and the general decided to accept this somewhat informal surrender. Alderman Henry at last draped the bedsheet lengthwise over a picket fence on the riverfront. He believed he had saved the city from destruction.[11]

August 8th. Saturday. Took breakfast at 8 [o'clock] this morning at Mrs. Johnson's with Gen. Smith. Afterwards [I] called on Gen. Price and others. Spent the day pleasantly. Took tea in the evening at Mrs. Mary Johnson's with Gens. Kirby Smith, Price, Frost, etc.

August 9th. Sunday. Went to church and heard Mr. Welch preach a good sermon. After church [I] went to see Mrs. Johnson's sick child. Took dinner with Mr. Parmer and tea with Mrs. Newton. Gov. Reynolds, Gen. [Daniel M.] Frost,[12] and Col. [John W.] Polk[13] smoked with me late. Weather hot.

August 10th. Visited Mrs. Johnson's child then Mrs. Hanger with Dr. Webb.[14] Gen. Smith left this morning. Took tea at Mrs. Johnson's. Had an opportunity to write to my wife through Col. Dobbins and Mr. Rice, which I availed myself of. Col. Dobbins spent the night with me.

August 11th. Was assigned to duty today as Examiner of Conscripts here by my own consent. Took tea at old Mrs. Johnson's. Weather very hot.

August 12th. Day passed off pleasantly though hot.

August 13th. Arranged to begin duties. Procured an office [this] afternoon. [In the] forenoon [I] rode to [the] Penitentiary with Col. Polk.[15] Changed room at the hotel. Visited Mrs. Johnson at night.

August 14th. Commenced regularly the work of examining conscripts today—an ingracious business. Took tea with Rev. Mr. Welch.

August 15th. Got [a] straw hat at [the] penitentiary. Occupied in office. Mrs. [Harriet] Snead returned last evening unable to get through.[16]

August 16th. Spent a quiet Sabbath. Went to church in the morning [and] heard Mr. Welch preach. Took tea at Mrs. Johnson's. Visited Maj. Snead's child. Weather hot.

August 17th. Finished and sent a letter to [my] sister Lavinia. After tea visited at Gen. [William E.] Ashley's—nice people.[17]

August 18th. Day passed off quietly.

August 19th. Changed offices to a room in [the] Land Office building. Took dinner out at Col. Polk's place with his family and Mrs. Frost—good dinner.

August 20th. Day passed off quietly and warm. After tea accompanied Mrs. Polk and Frost and Col. Polk to Mrs. Mary Johnson's. Passed a pleasant evening.

August 21st. Day set apart by President Davis for fasting, humiliation, and prayer. Went to church in the morning and heard a good discourse in the Presbyterian Church from Mr. Marvin. Church not full—our officers don't attend as they should. [I] went to prayer meeting at night. Dr. Wooten came in [but] we took no dinner. Oh that the Lord would hear and answer the prayers of his people.

August 22nd. Attended to duties [and] visited several sick.

August 23rd. Sunday. Considerable excitement in town on the subject of advance of the Federals. Said to be approaching in large force. Went to church [and] heard Mr. Welch preach a good sermon. Town excited.

August 24th. Excitement great, many persons and families going off, Mrs. Frost and Polk among the number. Feds on their way here. Baggage of army all sent across Arkansas River yesterday. Weather hot and dusty.

August 25th. Weather turned cool rendering thick clothes comfortable. Excitement of citizens moving off in great numbers continued. Army movements brisk. All excitement and turmoil. Took leave of the Johnson's who leave tomorrow. Fighting today by pickets.[18]

August 26th. Sold my broken down horse today at auction for $132, net $120. Stampede of citizens continues. Enemy not advancing much. Prospect of a fight tomorrow.

August 27th. Spent the day pretty much in trying to buy a horse without succeeding. Heavy fighting all day today by our cavalry and the Yankee advance guard. We are holding them in check. Citizens still leaving. Sent all my baggage out to camp today.

August 28th. Went out to camp this morning on a visit with Col. John Polk. While there [I] had a chill. Returned to hotel and kept to bed all day. Col. Polk bought a horse for me, price $375. [It is a] small bay. [I had a] fever and felt bad all day.

August 29th. [I feel] better but [am] still under the weather. [I] took quinine. No news of the Yankees advancing. No fighting along our lines. Weather cool. All quiet in front and in town. Rode my new horse out to camp towards evening—pleased with him.

August 30th. *Sunday.* Delightful and cool day. Instead of going to church as I would have liked I went this morning by order to the convalescent camp 4 ½ miles south of town to inspect and return back to duty all men fit for service. [I was] occupied with others several hours in this duty. Got back about 2 P.M. At night [I] went to church and heard Mr. Marvin preach a good sermon. Some skirmishing along our lines today. Yankees not making any headway as yet.

August 31st. Rode down to the convalescent camp this morning in a buggy with Dr. Swindell. [We] had an upset on the way, but nobody [was] hurt. After returning [I] rode over the river with Col. Polk first to Gen. Frost's headquarters and then to our fortifications. They are very creditable and if the Yankees run against them they will be repulsed. All quiet along our lines today. Called to see Miss Cass Rider and after tea paid a short visit to Mrs. Mary Johnson's. Weather cool and pleasant.

September 1st. Commenced examining conscripts again today—confidence having been somewhat restored. Rode out to camp and after took tea with Mr. Parmer.

September 2nd. Day passed off quietly. No excitement in camp or town, but rumors of a victory in Virginia, recognition, etc. In the evening [I] rode across river to Gen. Frost's headquarters with Maj. Snead and Col. Polk. Attended a citizens meeting after supper for home defense—it is high time.

September 3rd. Spent the morning in camp fixing my cot. No excitement in front today. All quiet.

September 4th. All quiet along our lines. No news of the enemy's advance. All confident.

September 5th. Day passed off quietly. No news of the Yankees in front, they seem to have fallen back. Our troops are ready and anxious for a fight. Citizens over the conscript age have formed themselves into a company for home defense.[19] Visited diverse patients among others, Mr. Palmer. Took dinner and tea with his family.

September 6th. Sunday. The town was thrown into a state of excitement this morning by the announcement that a duel was fought early this morning on the other side of the river between Brig. Generals Marsh Walker[20] and Marmaduke both of the cavalry. Before breakfast Gen. Walker was brought in mortally wounded. A sad and disgraceful affair under the circumstances.[21]

Poor Walker has a devoted wife and two children—how I pity her. Quite a disposition is manifested to get up bad feelings between the Missourians and Arkansians growing out of this duel, which is all wrong. Heard two good sermons today by Rev. Mr. Marvin in the Presbyterian church. Col. John Polk left to join his family this morning. All quiet in front today. No news of the Yankees whatsoever, they seem to have fallen back for the present.

September 7th. Gen. Marsh Walker died this evening of the wound received yesterday in a duel. He acknowledges that he did wrong and fought contrary to his convictions of right, but thought it necessary to preserve his honor. Alas for his poor wife. And this is *"honor"* falsely so called. All excitement today on account of the advance of the Federals. They are reported as trying to cross the Arkansas River at Terry's Ferry 8 miles below, cavalry and also infantry in front. A fight will probably come off tomorrow and if we are flanked we will have to fall back. Dined with Mr. Palmer. Sent a letter to my wife today. Weather warm. Several patients on hand.

September 8th. The Yankees did not make their appearance today as they seemed to threaten yesterday; consequently, there was no fight today as was expected, but all quiet in front. Gen. Walker was buried today with military honors. Took tea tonight with Mr. Palmer.

September 9th. All quiet today with no incidents. Visited several patients, mostly officers.

September 10th. Retreat No.2. The quiet of yesterday was broken in at an early hour this morning by a brisk fire of artillery down the river and a report that the Federals had effected a crossing of the river 8 miles below the town, thus going around our breastworks. This rendered our position critical and a retreat was determined upon—no doubt wisely. Our trains were put in motion and all was bustle and confusion. The gunboat here was burnt, also other boats.[22] Fixed up my affairs and prepared for a march.

About 12 M. troops began to move through the city and kept up a continuous stream. Citizens in great consternation. After a hurried dinner I mounted my horse and joined Gen. Price at his headquarters. Took leave of Mrs. Newton and Palmer. About 4 P.M. started with Gov. [Harris] Flanagin[23] and rode out 16½ miles to our camp where we took a cold snack and went to bed under the wagon.

September 11th. Started at daylight this morning. Gov. Flanagin and I rode to Benton and there remained for some time waiting for Gen. Price. [We] then went 2½ miles to the bottom of Saline River where we camped. [I] went to bed under a tree.

September 12th. Left camp at 10 A.M. today and came 12 miles to Mr. Rayburn's where we went into camp about 5 P.M. After eating a hearty super with a good relish [we] retired in camp it looking like rain.

September 13th. Was aroused about 3 A.M. this morning and started off in advance of [the] train and rode 7 miles to Rock Port, county seat of Hot Springs Co., to look after sick, accompanied by Drs. Wooten and Slaughter. Started without breakfast [and] arrived about 6 o'clock. Started off sick train to Arkadelphia, then came to camp some 2 miles below town. [I] got breakfast about 12 M. [and] ate with keen relish. After smoking, I rode with Dr. Wooten 2½ miles in advance to Gen. Price's camp to pay him a visit. For the first time in my life [I] was at fault today about this being Sunday [and] did not find it out until towards night, such is the confusion of a retreat. Camped out in an open field [with] no shade.

September 14th. [I] was aroused at 2 o'clock this morning and after a hurried cup of tea and a cold snack [we] struck our tents and got on our way at 3 A.M. [I] rode ahead with Dr. Wooten and Maj. [Edward Carrington] Cabell.[24] Marched 12 miles to the Ouachita River on the bank of which we are camped. Got into camp about 10 o'clock having waited for [the] train. Had a fine appetite and enjoyed [my] camp dinner hugely. Towards evening [I] bathed in the river, the weather being warm and dusty—very refreshing. Retired early and slept soundly.

September 15th. Got up again at 2 o'clock and started train but did not leave myself until daybreak. [I] then accompanied Gen. Frost and staff who first saw all the troops underway. After a march of 12 miles arrived at Arkadelphia about 11 A.M.[25] Crossed the Ouachita River just at town and went into camp on [the] south bank. Here I hope we will rest for a while. Made myself comfortable in camp. Enjoyed my dinner. Weather warm with rain towards evening [and] continuing during the night.

September 16th. Had a good night's sleep. [I] was not aroused to make an early start. Rained hard during the night and my tent having no fly the rain poured in upon me so as to wet bed and bedding affording me a taste of soldier's life. After breakfast, [I] rode up town and saw numerous army acquaintances. Called at Gen. Price's quarters then returned and spent the afternoon in camp.

September 17th. Hard rain during the night; wetting me completely in bed. Rather a wet, uncomfortable night. Rained all forenoon. Spent day in camp reading, drying bed clothes, etc.

September 18th. Weather clear but cool. Went into town at 10 A.M., attended to some business and entered upon duties examining conscripts. Dined with Gov. Flanagin and others. A good plain dinner. Spent evening in camp.

September 19th. Went to town then to Gen. Price's headquarters. Returned to office; visited [Edwin A.] Hickman;[26] examined conscripts; returned to camp and ate a hearty dinner. At night [I] sat around [the] campfire, discussed affairs of the nation with friends and retired and read *Flower of the Flock*.

September 20th. Sunday. Did not forget that it was the Sabbath today. In the morning I went to the Methodist Church in the

College—all the church buildings being used as hospitals. [I] heard a tolerable sermon. It is a treat to go to church and to worship God in these times of trouble and wickedness. Spent afternoon and evening in camp. Dr. [Charles B.] Mitchell, Senator in the Confederate Congress, stayed with us all night and gave us many encouraging facts with regard to public affairs.[27]

September 21st. Day passed off quietly. [In the] forenoon [I] went to [my] office and examined several conscripts. Late in the evening I visited Hickman at Gen. Price's headquarters. At night I wrote to my wife to send up by Col. [Joseph O.] Shelby's command who start for Missouri tomorrow.[28]

September 22nd. Spent the day in [my] office examining conscripts and in camp reading, smoking, etc.

September 23rd. Went up to town early after breakfast with Dr. Wooten to see Col. [Henry] Clay Taylor,[29] thence to my office and then to camp. At 4 P.M. [we] removed from our camp on the banks of the Ouachita to the rear of town some 200 yards in the woods—a pleasant place. The change was rendered necessary by the felling of trees to give the artillery command of the two ferries should the Yankees attempt it. Weather pleasant and night bright.

September 24th. Arkadelphia. [I] like our new camp [very] much. It is quiet, shady, and withall near to headquarters. Attended to office duties. Visited a Miss Smith [who is] very sick, in consultation with a resident doctor. Lt. Gen. Holmes returned last evening and will assume command in a day or two. Finished reading *Flowers of the Flock*. [I] read by a pine knot fire [which was] very bright.

September 25th. Gen. Holmes took command of the District and Gen. Price [took command] of our division today. Mr. Marvin spent the day with us. Rumors of recognition and the arrival of Iron Clads. After returning from the office I spent the day quietly in camp. Visited Miss Smith again.

September 26th. Day passed off quietly without notable incident. Passed the day in the office, in camp, and in other diversions.

September 27th. Sunday. Arose early and went through a thorough camp ablution and dressed clean from head to foot. Went to the Methodist Church, or rather their place of preaching—all the churches being occupied as hospitals. Upon the whole, the services were solemn and impressive though the minister, an Arkansas army chaplain, was far too confident of the mind of the almighty and what his designs towards us as a nation are—better not be wise above what is written. Spent the afternoon in camp. Lt. Gen. Kirby Smith arrived this evening.

September 28th. Day passed off quietly in camp and office. Went several times to see Maj. Henry Tracy who is very sick.[30] Spent the evening around the camp fire smoking and discussing the affairs of the nation. Had several visitors during the afternoon, among others, Rev. Mr. Beatie, pastor of the Presbyterian Church.

September 29th. On awakening this morning [I] heard the pattering of the rain on the tent with prospects for a rainy day. Maj. Tracy is no better, rather worse. Wrote a letter tonight to my wife to send by Mr. Smizer to Mrs. Dr. Rice near Helena to be sent across the river. It rained all day. Dry and comfortable in camp.

September 30th. At. Arkadelphia. Rained all night but was dry and comfortable in camp. It was cloudy but did not rain much during the day. Maj. Tracy is somewhat better this morning and more decidedly so this evening. Maj. [Thomas W.] Scott[31] formerly a long time ago of St. Louis called to see me today and took dinner with us in camp. [We] renewed old acquaintances and talked of old times. Dr. Kincannon also took dinner with us. He has just returned from near Helena and brings me tidings of the safe return of my wife home and of the well being of the children. We leave here in the morning at daylight to go some 32 miles southwest near Washington [Ark.]. [I] wrote a short letter tonight to my niece, Sue, to be sent by Maj. Scott who goes to Richmond.

October 1st. Gen. Price's command left Arkadelphia this morning for the Little Missouri River some 30 miles below Arkadelphia and 20 miles from Washington, Ark. Arose this morning early, took breakfast by daylight and immediately thereafter started off with train. Overtook Gen. Price and party a mile or two out of town. Called by Gov. Reynolds and Gen. Smith's headquarters. Remained a few moments and then rode with the Gen. some 16 miles to Parson Hill's who invited us to dine with him, which we did, together with Gen. Frost. A most sumptuous dinner it was, a rare treat. A charming old man and his wife worthy of him. Near Mr. Hill's we encamped for the night.

October 2nd. Took breakfast this morning before daylight with old Parson Hill's and a fine breakfast it was. At daylight [I] started with the General. Rode 11 miles to the camp where we will remain for some time. Arrived at 9 A.M. and the rest of the day was spent fixing up.

October 3rd. Spent a quiet day in camp prescribing for the sick, writing letters, sitting around the campfire, smoking, and chatting with Gen. Price and others. [I] wrote to Dr. Taylor, Col. [Benjamin F.] Danley,[32] and the enrolling officer. Dr. Wooten and Maj. Cabell, who remained behind in Arkadelphia, came up to camp tonight bringing news of a fight between Bragg and Rosecrans in which the latter was defeated.[33]

October 4th. Sunday. No church in camp or neighborhood today. Spent a quiet day in camp. By courier tonight the General received additional intelligence of the fight between Bragg and Rosecrans. According to the accounts we have gained a decided victory over the Yankees. God grant that it may prove to be true to the fullest extent. I expect to start for Washington, Ark. in the morning on a short visit—distance some 26 miles.[34]

October 5th. Started after breakfast this morning for Washington, 27 miles distant, accompanied by Maj. Cabell and a 4 mule wagon. On the road we engaged at the farm houses all the provisions that we could to take back to camp. Took a comfortable dinner 12 miles from Washington. About 5 P.M. [we] stopped at Judge Lowry's one mile from Washington and there spent a comfortable night.

October 6th. Raining this morning. About 9 A.M. [it] held up when Maj. Cabell and I went into Washington. Spent the morning in attending to business and seeing acquaintances. Here [I] met an old friend, Mrs. Eakins, formerly Miss Betty Erwin. [I] spent a couple of hours pleasantly with her talking of old times. Rode out with Maj. Cabell 3 miles to Col. Tom Smith's and took a hospitable dinner. There I met Mrs. John Polk. After dinner [we] got all our commissary stores loaded on our wagon and about dusk went again to Judge Lowry's and spent the night. Rained.

October 7th. Started back for camp after breakfast. On the way purchased 8 turkeys at $3 each, 12 chickens at 50 cents each, 9 bushels of sweet potatoes at $1.50 per bushel, onions and other things all for our own mess. Took dinner at Mr. Warren's and got into camp about dusk having made a prosperous trip.

October 8th. The news of the victory of Gen. Bragg over Rosecrans grows bigger and bigger and even more glorious than at first supposed—seems to be a complete rout. God be praised and grant that it may be decisive in its results. Spent a quiet day in camp. By courier at night we got the gratifying intelligence of the capture of Gen. Burnside, his staff, and most of his army, adding to the glory of the late victory near Chattanooga which grows in magnitude daily.[35] Weather fine.

October 9th. The monotony of camp life was broken in upon today by a visit of some dozen ladies to Gen. Price. Among them Miss Snodgrass of St. Louis, a famous patient of mine who was banished in May last from St. Louis for her Rebel sympathies. [I] had a long talk with her. By courier this evening got Yankee account of our splendid victory near Chattanooga. They admit the whole thing, but try to make the best of it by speaking of their gallant fighting. Thank God for this victory. Dined today on a fine venison killed by one of our mess and enjoyed it much.

October 10th. The morning passed off quietly in camp. Dr. Wooten and others went deer hunting but brought back nothing. I did some writing. Towards evening Lt. Gen. Holmes and staff arrived from Arkadelphia making quite an addition to our camp party. We fed and slept them, however, the best we could. Col. [Franck S.] Armistead[36] and others stayed with our mess. Judge [George C.] Watkins[37] and Gen. Holmes also sleeping with us.

October 11th. Sunday. No religious service in or about camp. Passed the day quietly reading, smoking, and talking. [I had] some visitors. A few newspapers from Shreveport [were] received giving, however, no additional news from the great battle in northwest Georgia between Bragg and Rosecrans. Weather fine and mild. Col. [J. H. R.] Cundiff[38] of Gov. Reynolds staff spends the night with us.

October 12th. Morning passed off quietly reading, darning socks, etc. This evening [we] received the gratifying intelligence that on the 27th ult. Gen. Bragg at Chattanooga took 16,000 prisoners and had the remainder of Rosecrans' army in a critical position. God grant that they may all be captured or annihilated. Gen. [Thomas Fenwick] Drayton[39] arrived about dark confirming the news from Bragg's army. We also have intelligence of another battle in Virginia between Gens. Lee and Meade in which the former has defeated the latter. God grant that it may prove to be true. Threatening rain all day, but only threatening.

October 13th. Went about noon today some 12 miles on the Arkadelphia Road to see Maj. Tracy who has had a relapse on his way to the army. Found him at a country house, but not so bad as I feared. [I] prescribed for and cheered him up. Took a camp dinner and started back for camp about 4 P.M. accompanied by Col. Cundiff. Arrived just at dark [and] found them all at our tent around a bright pine fire. Today the elections in Ohio, Indiana, and Pennsylvania take place. If [Clement L.] Vallandigham and the Democrats carry these states Lincoln will go up.[40] Tomorrow we move our camp some 40 miles southeast of this.

October 14th. Arose before day. Everything in camp in a stir preparatory to a march. Took a hurried breakfast, packed up, and got off a little after sunrise. Rode on quietly behind the rest with Maj. Cabell and Jo[seph L.] Thomas.[41] Went 18 miles and got into camp on the roadside about noon. [We] made ourselves comfortable for the night with a huge pine fire. Slept soundly.

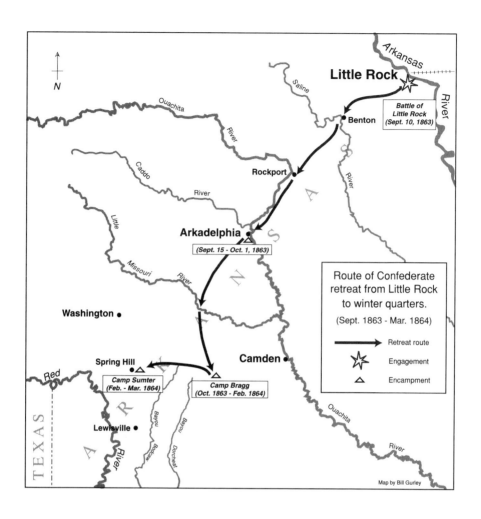

Route of Confederate
retreat from Little Rock
to winter quarters.

(Sept. 1863 - Mar. 1864)

→ Retreat route

☆ Engagement

△ Encampment

Little Rock

Battle of
Little Rock
(Sept. 10, 1863)

Benton

Rockport

Arkadelphia
(Sept. 15 - Oct. 1, 1863)

Washington

Spring Hill

Camp Sumter
(Feb. - Mar. 1864)

Camp Bragg
(Oct. 1863 - Feb. 1864)

Camden

Lewisville

TEXAS

Arkansas

River

Saline

Ouachita

Caddo

River

Little

Missouri

River

Red

River

Bayou

Bodcaw

Bayou

Dorcheat

Ouachita

River

N

Map by Bill Gurley

CHAPTER 4

Winter Quarters, 1863–64

*He preparest a table before me in the presence
of mine enemies.*

The autumn of 1863 ushered in a much-needed respite for the weary foot soldiers serving the Confederate District of Arkansas. Over the past ten months the district had diminished considerably. Failures on the fields of Prairie Grove, Helena, and Little Rock had relegated the Rebels to the state's southwestern corner. With Maj. Gen. Sterling Price's veteran infantry now one hundred miles closer to the Red River, Lt. Gen. Edmund Kirby Smith undoubtedly felt more secure in his prospect of confronting and thwarting any future Federal threats aimed at Shreveport and East Texas. The loss of Little Rock and the Arkansas River Valley, however, was indeed a bitter pill for Smith to swallow, but in his mind a dose of strong medicine was necessary if the Trans-Mississippi Department was to endure the blue contagion.

Furthermore, the threat of Federal encroachment, so virulent during the months of August and September, had seemingly gone into remission by October. Ironically, Maj. Gen. Frederick Steele himself appeared to be the curative, for once Little Rock had been secured, he seemed content to simply rest upon his laurels. The campaign's real tactical objective—the destruction of Price's army—had gone unrealized, thanks, in part, to the Confederates' speedy retreat but more so to Steele's diffidence toward pursuit. The Federal commander's hesitancy effectively transformed his army from one of invasion to one of occupation, thereby squandering a golden chance to crush the disheartened Rebels. This missed opportunity would have grave consequences in the months ahead.

On paper, the Federals controlled almost two-thirds of Arkansas. In reality, the country lying between the occupied cities of Fort Smith, Little Rock, Pine Bluff, and Helena was a virtual no man's land, vulnerable to the sorties of guerrilla bands and Southern cavalry. In fact, the commands of Brig. Gen. John S. Marmaduke and Col. Joseph O. Shelby were free to operate as they pleased, and they did just that. Just two weeks after the retreat from Little Rock, Shelby demonstrated how easily the Federal cordon could be penetrated. The Missourian led a group of more than one thousand Rebel troopers on a successful raid deep into the interior of his home state. Upon his return to Arkansas, Shelby was promoted to brigadier general. Until the close of the war, the Shelby-Marmaduke tandem would wreak havoc on the Yankee infrastructure west of the Mississippi River.[1]

Functionally disassociated from the rest of the Confederacy, the Trans-Mississippi Department would be further isolated during the autumn of 1863 due to events east of the Mississippi River. Reports of the signal Southern victory at Chickamauga, coming just ten days after the fall of Little Rock, cheered the discouraged Trans-Mississippians. Their newfound hope, however, was short lived. Just two months later the Army of Tennessee suffered what was perhaps its most humiliating defeat at Missionary Ridge. All hope of any cooperation between the two western Confederate armies had disappeared by the end of 1863. With his department completely adrift, Smith, at the behest of Pres. Jefferson Davis and the Confederate governors of Arkansas, Louisiana, Missouri, and Texas, assumed military and civil responsibilities that were heretofore unprecedented. Smith effectively became king of the Trans-Mississippi, and his realm became known as "Kirby Smithdom."[2]

In late October the five thousand Arkansas and Missouri foot soldiers constituting the bulk of the district's army settled into winter quarters west of Camden.[3] There, safe from the threat of Federal incursions, they ensconced themselves in a small town of log cabins erected in the wilderness of southwestern Arkansas. During their tenure in the rustic sanctuary of Camp Bragg, the army spent its time recuperating, reorganizing, and refurbishing. Like most of the other inhabitants of Camp Bragg, Dr. William McPheeters would spend his second consecutive Christmas separated from wife and family. In an effort to counter the boredom of camp life and divert his thoughts away from his family's plight, McPheeters immersed himself in his profession. During this time, he was instrumental in organizing the Army Medical Association, a group of regimental, brigade, and divisional surgeons who met monthly to discuss pertinent medical issues. An integral part of their meetings focused on the presentation of interesting cases and the discussion of scientific papers—the equivalent of what is known in academic medicine today as a "journal club" and "grand rounds." Keeping abreast of current issues in battlefield medicine would serve the physicians well, for the upcoming spring would provide plenty of opportunities to test their newfound knowledge.[4]

October 15th. Thursday. Arose before day and got under way about daylight after eating a hearty breakfast. Came 22 miles and got into camp about 1 o'clock P.M. Here we will probably remain awhile, but how long is uncertain. We are in Ouachita Co. about 20 miles southwest of Camden. Busy all afternoon in fixing up camp. Succeeded in making ourselves very comfortable. *Today 22 years ago I first arrived in St. Louis.*

October 16th. Day passed off quietly in camp. Ate, drank, smoked, talked around the campfire, and discussed the affairs of the nation, etc. Threatening rain.

October 17th. No rain today as it threatened last night. The brigades are coming up. Two have already arrived, the others will be on one each day. Prepared smoking tobacco—Arkansas script. After dark Rev. Dr. [Benjamin T.] Kavanaugh preached for us at headquarters a sensible sermon.[5] [I am] glad to hear preaching in camp at all times.

October 18th. A delightful and peaceable Sabbath day for which I desire to thank God. Attended preaching at ½ past 10 in Gen. Fagan's Brigade near by. Dr. Kavanaugh preached a good sermon in the woods surrounded by camps. It was a solemn and impressive occasion—soldiers very attentive. I love to worship God in camp. Would that we had divine service regularly. [The] rest of the day passed off quietly. Dr. [Bennett H.] Clark, formerly of St. Louis, arrived yesterday.[6]

Monday Oct. 19th. At Camp Bragg. A windy, dusty, disagreeable day. Remained in camp enduring the dust from the road kicked up by scores of forage and other wagons passing. Had a large group around our campfire at night. Read Wilberforce's *Practical View*.

October. 20th. Weather warm, windy, and threatening rain. Not so dusty as yesterday. It is probable we will move our quarters tomorrow to a more comfortable place some 3 or 4 miles off. A rumor reached camp this evening that Rosecrans had surrendered to Bragg at Chattanooga with 55,000 men. Too big and too good to be true I fear. Rained about dark some.

October 21st. No rain today. After breakfast [we] packed up and moved headquarters 3 miles. Spent the rest of the day in fixing up our new camp. Succeeded in making ourselves very comfortable. Weather a little colder.

October 22nd. Notwithstanding it was threatening rain all day, and did rain several times, [I] attended a country barbecue at the house of Mr. Christopher given to Col. [Samuel S.] Bell's regiment[7] who are mostly from this neighborhood. Gen. Price and staff were invited and at 11 A.M. we rode over. Quite a number of the natives, male and female, were present. A good dinner and plenty of talk. Returned to camp about 3 P.M. While there heard what seems to be confirmation of the surrender of Rosecrans' army. God grant that it may be true. Weather cold and rainy.

October 23rd. A bright and beautiful day. Clear and cold. [I] went with Dr. Wooten first to Fagan's Brigade then to see Dr. Madden some 3 miles off, with whom we took a family dinner, and after rode back to camp. Read Wilberforce's *Practical View* by [a] campfire of pine knots. No news or even rumors today. A chilly night. Would that I could be with my family tonight. God bless them.

October 24th. [I] was engaged during the morning in making improvements in camp. Built a large log fire place and a terrace in front of our tents, a decided improvement. Met Gen. [Thomas J.] Churchill[8] at Gen. Price's quarters. [I] heard from his good wife, Mrs. Johnson, and Mrs. Jordan and got kind messages from them.

Late in the evening [I] rode over to Gen. Drayton's headquarters to send a letter written during the afternoon to [my] brother, Alexander, by an officer who goes across the Mississippi River. Rode back by moonlight.

October 25th. Sunday. Rode with Drs. Wooten and Slaughter this morning to church, the Synod of the Cumberland Presbyterian being in the neighborhood. Preaching indifferent, congregation large, and a good house of worship, ministers rough, altogether not edified. Gen. Price came over to our camp and paid us a visit during the afternoon. News of Rosecrans surrender seems to be confirmed. God grant that it may prove to be true. We hear also that Gen. Blunt and his staff (Federals) have been killed by Quantrill and his men.[9] A beautiful moonlit night. A group [is] around our campfire. Weather cool but delightful.

October 26th. Day passed off quietly in camp without notable incident. Maj. [Jilson P.] Johnson, inspector from Richmond, dined with us.[10] Intimations of a move soon. Rosecrans probably not captured. Rumors doubtless false.

October 27th. Accompanied Maj. Johnson on his inspection of the sick of Gen. Drayton's Brigade this morning, occupying an hour or two. Dr. Slaughter left for Washington, Ark. for medical supplies. Rained this morning [but] cleared off towards noon. Spent [the] afternoon and evening in camp and at Gen. Price's quarters.

October 28th. Spent the day in camp. [I] had numerous visitors. Several surgeons returned from Memphis where they have been with our wounded from Helena. Revs. Mr. Marvin, Dr. Kavanaugh, and Col. Clay Taylor took dinner with us. The former has a very sore eye—ulceration of the cornea. [I] prescribed for him. Yankee news gives the defeat of Vallandigham for governor of Ohio.

October 29th. Went with Maj. Cabell after breakfast to Mr. Blake's to see Dr. Clark and get provisions. Brought back 2 turkeys, 6 chickens, and 4 lbs butter—turkeys $5 for the two, chickens $5, and butter $4. Rode back in drizzling rain. Dr. Cunningham and Col. Taylor dined with us on a fine turkey. Read and smoked at night.

October 30th. Rained hard last night and this morning. Took breakfast in [my] tent. Rain ceased about 9 A.M. Towards noon Dr. Wooten and I rode to Parson Moore's to see Mr. Marvin. Had a pleasant visit and returned to camp about dusk.

October 31st. Spent the day in camp. In the morning [I] mended pantaloons and fixed up clothes generally. [I] have all these things to do myself. Had many visitors during the day. Dr. Clark dined with us.

November 1st. The Blessed Sabbath. Dr. Wooten left this morning for Texas on a 60 day leave to visit his family. In his absence [I] was assigned to duty by Gen. Price as Chief Surgeon of his division. Received this morning a present of two pair of fine yarn socks from Mrs. Irene Jordan, knitted by her own fair hands and accompanied by a kind note—many thanks to her. Capt. Kerr and myself rode over some 4 miles to a Methodist church where we heard a good sermon from a preacher from Missouri on the resurrection of Christ—house crowded. [I] enjoyed the excercises much. Thank God for the Sabbath and the sanctuary. After church [I] rode over to Mr. Moore's to see Mr. Marvin whose eye is very sore. Took dinner there and spent a pleasant time with an agreeable family. Returned to camp and spent the evening around our own campfire.

November 2nd. Busily engaged all day in attending to medical duties. Wrote to my wife a short letter by an opportunity presenting itself. [I] hope that she will get it—doubtful however. Also wrote to Mrs. Jordan thanking her for her nice present. Rained in the morning; cleared off after and was quite warm. [I] went to Gen. [James Camp] Tappan's Brigade[11] to see Maj. Tracy. Drs. Clark and Swindell took dinner with us.

November 3rd. Another day spent quietly in camp busy in prescribing for the sick and other official duties. From the *Chicago Times* and other Yankee papers received today, we learn of a series of battles running through 8 days between Gens. Lee and Meade, in which the latter Yankee Gen. and army were driven all the time from position to position behind the entrenchments at Washington City—good for Gen. Lee.[12] Met Col. [Sidney D.] Jackman at Gen. Price's quarters this evening who is just from his guerrilla operations in Missouri where he has stirred up the Yankees considerably.[13] Weather warm.

November 4th. Rode over with Maj. Cabell this morning to visit Gen. Churchill and pay our respects to him. Found him absent on a visit to his family. [I] then visited a sick soldier 2 miles further on and then visited Gen. [Mosby Monroe] Parsons[14] and Lt. Gen. Holmes, each at their headquarters. [I] also visited Dr. Cunningham and others of Gen. Holmes' staff. Found the Gen. very complaisant. Returned home and partook of a good dinner— a fine turkey. Judge Watkins dined with us. Late in the evening [I] received a note from Mr. Marvin asking me to come and see his eye which he thought [was] worse. Rode 5 miles and got to Mr. Marvin's about dark. [I] cauterized and otherwise attended to the ulcer on his cornea. Spent the night [with this] plain but pleasant and intelligent Christian family. Young ladies played and sang. [We] had family worship, etc. Threatening rain.

November 5th. Raining slowly this morning. After breakfast and attending to Mr. Marvin's eye, [I] started for camp in the rain. Rode two miles out of the way to call by Mr. Blakes to see Dr. Clark. Arrived at camp wet having ridden 7 miles in the rain. Dried up and spent the day in camp quietly if not pleasantly. After dark, [I] wrote a long letter to [my] sister Lavinia by John P. Ingram[15] who goes over to Grenada [Mississippi] to establish a tri-weekly line of couriers between that place and our army.

November 6th. The chief incident of today was the receipt of a letter from my beloved wife of date of Oct. 4th and 6th, brought by a messenger just returned from St. Louis. Thank God she and my children were well at that time. This is the first tidings from them since parting with my wife at Helena in July last, and a great comfort to me. Visited a sick soldier 4 miles off. Weather delightful.

November 7th. A dull day in camp. Felt a little under the weather. Sun quite hot. After tea, [I] wrote a long letter to my wife in reply to hers of yesterday. [I] hope that she will get it. Nothing of interest in camp today.

November 8th. A lovely Sabbath day. Arose early, bathed, and put on Sunday clothes. After breakfast [I] rode to Mr. Moore's to see Mr. Marvin's ulcerated eye. Found him about [the] same. [I] took dinner and returned to camp. Had not the privilege of going to church. After tea, [I] read Arthur's *Tongues of Fire* (a good book) by firelight.

November 9th. Morning spent in trying to get in reports of surgeons from brigades and in writing a long letter to Dr. Wooten. Maj. Johnson, inspector from Richmond, visited and inspected our quarters. Weather rather colder than of late.

November 10th. After breakfast and smoking [my] pipe, [I] rode over to see Mr. Marvin's eye accompanied by Capt. Kerr. Orders to be in readiness to move at a moments warning indicate some move. Weather cool but pleasant.

November 11th. Spent the day in camp attending to official duties, reading, etc. Read *The Dairyman's Daughter,* I think for the first time. An admirable and simple story of humble piety. No news in camp today. Lt. Crittenden spent the day and night with us.

November 12th. Spent the day pretty much in the saddle. After breakfast [I] rode 5 miles to see Mr. Marvin. On returning [I] found a message for me to visit Col. [Charles S.] Mitchell[16] and also a young Missourian two miles beyond Gen. Holmes' headquarters and 5 miles from camp. Found him quite sick, threatened with phthisis.[17] On returning from the latter place while riding through the woods [I] had [an] occasion to dismount. My foot [got] caught in the stirrup and in attempting to disengage it my horse took fright, threw me down, and dragged me some distance. [I] lost the reins and was in a most perilous position when providentially my foot got loose and I was left unhurt in the road though badly frightened. Thank God for this deliverance. My horse returned to the house half a mile where I walked to get him. It was near dark when I got back to camp and got dinner.

November 13th. Spent the day in camp superintending the building of a log and mud chimney to [our] tent. Had all the negroes at work and after a day of steady labor succeeded in constructing a very fine one if it will only draw well. It is built some 8 feet from and in front of the tent, the space between to be boarded up and roofed which will give me a comfortable house in case of bad weather. Threatening rain tonight. Maj. Snead, who has been absent on a 60 day furlough, returned this evening.

November 14th. Day passed in camp without notable incident. Visited sick in quarters and prescribed for others at my own camp. Col. [Ignatius] Szymanski and Capt. [Andrew] Sigourney took dinner with us.[18] Dr. Bond arrived before dark and spends the night with us.

November 15th. Sunday. Arose this morning by times and after indulging in the luxury of a bath and of clean clothes took a hearty camp breakfast. After which [I] went 4 miles to a country Methodist church, where I heard the circuit rider preach to a good congregation of soldiers and citizens. After church [I] went on a mile further to visit Mr. Marvin; his eyes [are] somewhat better. Cauterized them and after spending a couple of hours with him and taking dinner, [I] returned to camp. Late in the evening Maj. Cabell and I rode over to pay our respects to Mrs. Gen. Tappan. Paid her an agreeable visit and returned to camp by moonlight. Spent a pleasant evening around a large bright campfire, Snead, MacLean and [Duncan C.] Cage[19] being of the party. Weather pleasant.

November 16th. Engaged pretty much all day in building a shed, connecting tent, and chimney. Now in case of a rain we will be comfortable. No news or other incidents of interest in camp. An animated discussion at night around campfire on the merit and demerits of West Pointers between Snead and [William M.] Seay.[20]

November 17th. [I] was called up at 2 o'clock this morning to see Maj. [James H.] Reynolds[21] who had a convulsion from drink. Spent the morning in working on house and other fixtures around. Weather mild and delightful. No news from the enemy or anywhere else. Slaughter returned from Lewisville this evening. Dined on venison today.

November 18th. Spent the morning in examining applicants for furlough from the Texas Cavalry Brigade and in working on our house, etc. Col. Armistead and Capt. [John W.] Hinsdale[22] of Gen. Holmes' Staff took dinner with us. [I] went this evening to visit Mrs. Gen. Tappan who is sick. Finished Arthur's *Tongues of Fire,* a most excellent work. No news in camp.

November 19th. Today was set apart by Gov. Flanagin of this state as a day of fasting and prayer for the blessing of God on our cause in this state and throughout the Confederacy. After a late breakfast [I] went over to the church 5 miles off and attended an interesting meeting of prayer. Quite a number of army chaplains, officers, soldiers, and others were present. Would that God would hear the prayers offered up today and grant us peace and independence. After church, [I] rode over to Parson Moore's to see Mr. Marvin; his eye is improving I am happy to say. On returning to camp [I] called to see Mrs. Tappan who is also better. After dark [it] commenced raining—our cabin is vastly comfortable. Paid Gen. Price a visit tonight and sat an hour.

November 20th. A damp day. Found our log house and chimney with its bright fire very comfortable. Spent the day in camp [and] had diverse visitors. After dark [I] visited the General and had an interesting conversation on the early history of the war and the political events immediately preceding it. Tonight we have rumors of another victory by Bragg and Lee in Tennessee and Va.—hope they are true but the rumor needs confirmation.

November 21st. Examined cases for furlough and discharge sent up from the Texas brigade of cavalry; made out morning report of sick of [the] division consolidated from brigade surgeons reports; wrote a letter to my wife and one to Dr. W. M. Lawrence[23] of Washington, Ark.; and had several visitors. Thus the day—a beautiful one—passed off.

November 22nd. Went over to the Methodist Church this morning accompanied by Dr. Slaughter. Heard a very good sermon from Chaplain [C. F.] Dryden.[24] Afterwards, [we] went over to Parson Moore's to dinner. Mr. Marvin's eye greatly improved; he was out today. Returned to camp about 4 P.M. and after tea read Alexander's *Evidences of Christianity*. Maj. Cabell started for Shreveport today.

November 23rd. A rainy day. Our cabin and mud chimney [are] vastly comfortable. Spent the day in examining Texas cavalry for furlough and in reading Alexander's *Evidences of Christianity*. After dark, Dick Morrison[25] came to my tent and read poetry—a break.

November 24th. A bright but windy and cold day. Made other improvements in our cabin to obviate the smoking of the chimney if possible. Several officers—Lt. [John Edward] Drayton, Capt. Jones, [Benjamin H.] Hart, and Dr. Brookhart—took dinner with us.[26] After tea, [I] wrote a long letter to Hon. George Davis[27] in behalf of Col. Dobbins. Late at night Snead and MacLean came into my cabin and talked until after 12 by the bright "light wood" fire blazing in the fire place.

November 25th. Spent the morning in ironing handkerchiefs, sewing on buttons, etc.—womanly work that I don't like but have to do—and reading Alexander's *Evidences of Christianity*. Dr. [John McC.] Lacy[28] of Fagan's Brigade dined and spent the night with me. After dark [I] read. Late at night [I] was sent for by Snead to go to his tent. Found him and others in a gay mood and having a good time. Did not remain long and got off unharmed.

November 26th. The day passed off quietly in camp and without noteworthy incident. About dark Col. Jo Shelby, who has recently returned from his raid into Mo. paid us a visit. His presence drew others and we had quite a gay time around our council fire. The band serenaded him also. Some of them kept it up to a late hour, but I retired about 11 o'clock.

November 27th. A rainy stormy day—thunder and lightning though not violent. A dull day of course. Had several visitors, spent time in cabin and tent and found it very comfortable. Read Alexander's *Evidences of Christianity* and attended to ordinary duties.

November 28th. Rained hard all night, became cold towards morning and had a slight fall of *snow*. A cold but clear and windy day. Had a good deal of writing to do in transmitting orders to brigades and other official business. After dark read the *Chicago Times* and Alexander's *Evidences of Christianity*. Had numerous visitors. Our snug cabin and cheerful fire attracts outsiders. Capt. [Edward B.] Stonehill[29] spent the evening with me. All quiet in camp.

November 29th. Sunday. A very cold night for the southern part of Arkansas. This morning ice a half inch was on all the water. I, however, slept warm and comfortable. Ate breakfast out of doors —a cold business. After breakfast and a smoke [I] rode over to Gen. Drayton's Brigade and was accompanied by him to church 5 miles off. Heard Mr. Marvin whose eye has almost recovered. After church we went to Parson Moore's and partook of a good dinner and met clever Christian people. As we were about to leave, Col. Taylor drove up having with him his wife, Mrs. Schaumburg, and Mrs. Dr. Scott, just arrived from St. Louis via Camden and Little Rock.[30] It was a great pleasure to meet them as they had seen my beloved wife and children just before starting. They represent her as well and "looking younger and prettier than ever." Thank God for their well being—would that I could see and be with them. Remained until near dark when Gen. Drayton and I rode briskly to camp.

November 30th. Weather still cold but somewhat moderated. After breakfast [I] rode over with Gen. Price to Parson Moore's to visit Mrs. Schaumburg, Scott, and Taylor. After paying them a pleasant visit and making arrangements for their comfort, [we] came back to camp by Lt. Gen. Holmes' headquarters. Found him gone to Camden. Transacted some business with Dr. Cunningham, saw Judge Watkins, and then returned. Found Mrs. Scott already at Gen. Price's quarters, having previously sent my ambulance for her. After a serenade by the band and seeing numerous acquaintances, she started for Washington to meet her husband accompanied by Gen. [William L.] Cabell[31] and Lt. Morrison.

December 1st. Rode with Gen. Price this morning to Gen. Churchill's headquarters to see Mrs. Churchill. Found her well and as usual very agreeable. Paid her a pleasant visit after which, accompanied by Gen. Churchill, we visited his brigade and then returned to camp. After a late dinner (4 P.M.), Maj. Snead and I rode over to Parson Moore's 6 miles to visit Mrs. Shaumburg and Taylor. Arrived just before dark and remained until 9 P.M. Took tea and talked over St. Louis people and affairs. Mrs. Schaumburg and Taylor brought me a pair of spectacles and a beautiful woolen helmet cap worked and sent by my beloved wife. God bless her. [It is] valued most of all for being her handy work. Dark ride home but not unpleasant.

December 2nd. Morning spent in camp in official duties. About 3 P.M. Maj. [Lauchlan A.] MacLean[32] and myself went over to Parson Moore's accompanied by the band to serenade the ladies from St. Louis—Mrs. Schaumburg and Taylor. They played numerous airs much to the delight of the ladies and family. Remained with them until near dark and got back to camp a while after dark and took a hearty dinner. Snead stayed with me last night and this. I neglected to mention that a day or two since I received $30 and two fine linen handkerchiefs from Mr. Worthen of Little Rock whose child I attended while there.

December 3rd. This is my birthday, but I prefer not recollecting exactly how old I am for fear that I might be compelled to admit that I am growing old. Received a visit this morning from Gen. Churchill and Dr. [Charles H.] Smith,[33] also from Dr. Clark, Col. [James D.] White,[34] and others. Mrs. Schaumburg and Mrs. Clay Taylor came to headquarters, having sent my ambulance for them, and dined at MacLean's and Snead's mess. Gen. Price and I dined with them—a most excellent dinner too it was for camp. The ladies afterwards returned to Parson Moore's. Maj. Cabell, my camp mate, returned from Shreveport this evening.

December 4th. A soldier in Gen. Tappan's Brigade was to have been shot today for desertion, but was pardoned by Lt. Gen. Holmes. Wrote several letters—one to sisters Kate and Jane, [one] to Dr. Lawrence, and to Francis Valle of the cavalry,[35] the latter on business. Rainy tonight.

December 5th. Cleared off and became a beautiful day. Spent the forenoon in camp. Had a visit at our quarters from Gen. Price. By invitation I dined with Gen. and Mrs. Churchill at his head-quarters where they are very comfortably fixed. Gen. Tappan also dined there. Had a most excellent dinner and enjoyed the good company. At night [I] read Daniel's *Life of Stonewall Jackson* just out and published in New York—good.

December 6th. Sunday. A bright and delightful Sabbath day. No church in the neighborhood and my horse being sick, [I] spent the day in camp. Sent out orders to the brigades and attended to other official duties. Paid the General a visit after dark and read Stonewall Jackson's life. Thus passed the day rather unprofitably for the holy Sabbath.

December 7th. A rainy, disagreeable day. Wrote a letter to Dr. [John M.] Haden,[36] Medical Director of Department at Shreveport enclosing receipts of monies expended in hospital near Helena under my charge and asking that my accounts be settled and closed. $2000 was placed in my hands for benefit of the wounded, all of which is accounted for.

December 8th. Lt. Crittenden who has been with us for several days started this morning for Richmond. By him wrote a long letter to sisters Kate and Jane. Commenced building a stable. Had numerous visitors.

December 9th. Drew up and forwarded monthly return of medical officers of this division for November, after which [I] worked on [our] stable until 3 o'clock P.M. when Maj. Cabell and I rode 3 miles and dined with Capt. [A. C.] Dickinson of the Engineer Corps.[37] At night [I] wrote a long letter to my wife to send by Capt. [J. M.] Wills[38] who starts to St. Louis in a day or two.

December 10th. A raw and cloudy day. Visited Col. Mitchell of Drayton's Brigade who is laboring under orchitis, the result of injury.[39] The remainder of the day [I] worked hard in completing the stable. Maj. [W. Watkins] Dunlap[40] and Capt. Stonehill spent the day with us. Unfavorable news from Bragg's army today—hope that it is not true as it comes through Yankee sources.

December 11th. Finished Stonewall Jackson's life. A cloudy day with slight rain towards night. Day spent in camp. Had a visit from Gen. Churchill. By evening mail received a letter from Dr. Wooten dated Oct. 23 at Bonham, Texas—the first since he left. The news from Bragg's army today via Shreveport is more favorable—hope that it may turn out true.

December 12th. Weather mild and cloudy. Spent the day quietly in camp. Read Alexander's *Evidences of Christianity* and a stray copy of the *St. Louis Republican* without getting much news, however. I have felt down in the mouth tonight over the news from Bragg's army. We have contradictory reports, but fear that he has met with a reverse, but still hope for the best—God grant us success.

December 13th. Sunday. A cold, windy, disagreeable day. After breakfast, Gen. Drayton and I rode over to church 5 miles off. Parson Woods, a chaplain in Parson's Brigade preached a good sermon from [the] text "Redeeming the time because the days are evil." After church, went to Mr. Moore's where we took dinner and saw Mrs. Clay Taylor and others. On returning, stopped at Gen. Tappan's headquarters to pay our respects to Mrs. Tappan. After dark, sat some time with Gen. Price and others in the General's quarters. Maj. Tracy just up from Shreveport spent the night wth us. He is hopeful of Bragg's success.

December 14th. Was aroused at a late hour last night by a roaring in our chimney, having piled on a huge fire before going to bed, the night being cold. Found our chimney in a light blaze and soon our cabin and tent would have been consumed. Awoke Majors Cabell and Tracy and then the negroes. By their aid and an abundance of water, the flames were soon extinguished and we went to bed in security. Had, however, to pull down part of our chimney. Wrote to Dr. [John B.] Bond,[41] Medical Purveyor, at Lewisville, Ark. on business. Weather clear but cold and calm. Day passed in camp in ordinary routine of duties. Had a visit from Gen. Churchill and Lt. [Ambrose H.] Sevier.[42] News encouraging this evening from Bragg and Longstreet.

December 15th. Occupied most of the day in making new mud jambs and back to cabin chimney. Received several official communications requiring transmission to brigades. Day cloudy with rain towards night.

December 16th. Rained hard all night and to a late hour this morning. Gen. Price went to Camden this morning to meet Lt. Gen. Kirby Smith and Holmes in consultation as to army operations. At 4 P.M. went over to Gen. Tappan's by invitation to dine. Major Cabell and MacLean also dined there. Mrs. Tappan was present and we had a good camp dinner. A blustery cold evening and night. In [the] cabin with our large fire it is very comfortable.

December 17th. 1863. A cold but clear day. Engaged all morning in transmitting orders and official papers to the brigades. Very cold and disagreeable eating out of doors. Gen. Price not yet returned from Camden. Passed a quiet and pleasant evening reading Alexander's *Evidences of Christianity* by light wood firelight. No news today.

December 18th. Gen. Price returned from Camden this evening where he has been for several days, but brings no news. The General and his staff were invited to dine at Gen. [Thomas P.] Dockery's today some 15 miles off on the Lewisville Road,[43] but owing to the General's absence the rest of us declined going. Wrote a professional letter to Dr. Bond and attended to other official duties. A clear, cold day.

December 19th. Weather still clear and cold especially for the southern part of Arkansas. Spent the day quietly in camp rather busy in attending to official duties and in receiving calls and answering inquiries of brigade surgeons.

December 20th. Sunday. There being no preaching in the neighborhood today, after the morning hour Maj. Cabell and I rode down to Gen. Churchill's headquarters to visit Mrs. Churchill, but finding her gone to Lewisville—the General having been transferred to the cavalry—we went to Dr. Madden's where we took dinner. From the Dr. got 2 vol. of Carlyle's *Miscellanies*—a treat. On returning to camp found an order for me to go to Camden as a witness before the Examining Board in session there, so "Deo volente" I will start early in the morning for that place.[44]

December 21st. Started this morning after an early breakfast (½ past 7) for Camden in a four mule ambulance accompanied by Capt. Perry. Arrived in Camden ½ past 12. Went to courthouse where Lt. Gen. Holmes has the office of his headquarters. Saw Dr. Cunningham and others of his staff and diverse other acquaintances. At 3 P.M. dined with Judge Watkins and Gen. Holmes and spent a pleasant hour in conversation with them. The General offered me the Chief Surgeon of Marmaduke's Division of Cavalry, which, however, I declined. After dinner, [I] gave my testimony in the case of Maj. [Benjamin D.] Chenowith[45] arraigned on charges, etc. Also visited Mrs. Gen. Churchill staying at Dr. Seay's. At night visited Mrs. Col. Clay Taylor at Mr. Buchanan's, Capt. [Benjamin] von Phuls[46] accompanying me. At 10 o'clock, [I] returned and spent the night with Mr. Davidson.

December 22nd. Took breakfast at Dr. Cunningham's mess with him and Dr. Haden, Medical Director of the Department. Had an agreeable chat and understanding with him about my position in Gen. Price's Division and on other army medical affairs, all of which was perfectly satisfactory. After breakfast and a smoke [I] saw several persons, attended to some business, and about 11 o'clock started back to camp where I arrived about 5 P.M. after a trip without incident. Took dinner and after dark visited the General and brought up my business to date. Weather pleasant but rather cloudy.

December 23rd. Was engaged all morning in sending out instructions to all the brigades to be prepared in the event of a move of which there is a probability. Ordered infirmary corps to be organized, bandages, ligatures, etc. to be got in readiness and begin providing for the sick who will have to be left. Also wrote on business to Dr. Bond, Medical Purveyor, and Dr. Cunningham. Afternoon and night read Carlyle's essay on Voltaire. Weather mild but not very clear.

December 24th. Major Cabell and I took an *egg nog* this morning, the first of the season. At 10 o'clock Gen. Price accompanied by his staff reviewed Gen. Parsons' Brigade and a fine appearance they made, double-quicked particularly well. Received an invitation through Gen. Drayton to take Christmas dinner tomorrow at Parson Moore's. Dr. Haden, Med. Director of the Department arrived this evening and will spend the night with me. Christmas Eve—would God that I were at home with my family tonight.

The return of this anniversary brings sad reflections—Death has entered the home circle since last Christmas and my first born is no more; God bless his mother and the remaining children.[47] May they be happy though we are separated and I a wanderer and a refugee living in a tent, but I repine not—our cause is just and I have no regrets for my course though it may cost me the loss of all my earthly possessions.

December 25th. Christmas. Dr. Haden spent the night with us. Maj. Cabell and I bundled together in my bed and Dr. Haden in the major's, all on the floor. Commenced the morning by making a big big bucket of *egg nog* of which the General and most of his staff and others partook and seemed to enjoy hugely for it was good and good cheer prevailed. At eleven o'clock Gen. Drayton and myself started off on horseback. First we went to Mr. Blake's to call on his family, here we took egg nog also then rode 2 miles across to Mr. Moore's where partook of a good Christmas dinner. Col. and Mrs. [Richard H.] Musser, Col. [John B.] Clark [Jr.], and some 4 or 5 other officers and others were also there.[48] Remained an hour after dinner and then returned to camp. After dark quite a fuss was heard in Gen. Drayton's Brigade with the fire of one piece of artillery in which the General ordered out his staff and body guard and we all rode over to quell any disturbance that might be brewing, which fortunately did not occur and with a reprimand for the unauthorized shot we all returned. There is a party at Gen. Tappan's quarters tonight to which, however, I did not go, preferring to remain at home. A merry Christmas to my dear wife and children—God bless them. How my heart yearns towards them tonight and how I long to be with them, but [I] know not when that happy day will arrive—not until this cruel war is over. God speed its end and grant us an honorable peace [and] our independence with all the blessings of home and peace.

December 26th. A rainy, gloomy day. Kept close to quarters. Wrote letters to Dr. Cunningham and Lt. Franke Valle on business and to Rev. Mr. Marvin at Shreveport. It is now at night raining hard. How my thoughts turn towards home and the dear ones there and if I were disposed to be sad I could easily become so, but will not. The Lord in compassion bless my beloved wife and children and grant us a speedy reunion.

December 27th. A raw disagreeable day. Had no opportunity of attending divine service. About 12 M. the staff were ordered out to cavalry drill in preparation for the review to be given to Lt. Gen. Smith tomorrow. Spent an hour in the various evolutions to be gone through with in accompanying the General on the field under command of Maj. MacLean. After dinner I was called to Gen. Drayton's Brigade to see a case of strangulated hernia. [I] gave [the] man chloroform and used taxis for a long time without effect.[49] Intended to operate before tonight but fortunately reduction took place. After dark spent an hour or so at the General's quarters. Maj. Snead reading Carlyle.

December 28th. According to previous notice Lt. Gen. Holmes reviewed Gen. Price's whole division at 1 P.M. today. The review passed off well and was witnessed by hundreds of persons from the neighborhood. In riding around with the Generals we went at full speed and was quite and animated scene. Gen. Holmes paid us a visit in our cabin and took a smoke with us after dinner then goes on to Washington.

December 29th. A bright, beautiful day. Spent the forenoon indoors mending stockings, etc. Visited Gen. Tappan, who is sick, twice. Spent the evening writing and in reading Carlyle. But little of interest going on in camp.

December 30th. The surgeons of this division (Price's) have recently formed themselves into an Army Medical Association for purposes of mutual improvement while we are in permanent encampment to which they have done me the honor of electing me President. Today the Association held its second meeting at Dr. Herndon's headquarters. So rainy and disagreeable as it was I rode 3 miles to Gen. Parsons' Brigade in order to attend. Some 12 or 15 surgeons were present. On taking the chair I made a short speech returning thanks, etc. We had quite an interesting meeting. Three papers on the peculiarities of intermittent fever in the army were read and discussed. There was a general interchange of ideas. These meetings will I doubt not be profitable. The subject for the next meeting is pneumonia in the army. Evening and night spent in quarters reading Carlyle, etc.

December 31st. The last day of 1863 and a cold, blustery, snowy day it is. About breakfast time the wind shifted, it became cold and the rain was converted into snow, which continued pretty much all day. Rode over to the Body Guard to see a sick soldier. Returned and kept pretty close to quarters the remainder of the day. Stewed some molasses candy by way of amusement and our cook being disabled [I] gave Frank[50] a practical lesson in making beef brisket. Succeeded pretty well. Dr. Wooten who has been absent for two months on a visit to his family in Texas returned this evening. Weather cleared off toward night—very cold. This is the last of '63. Many sad and solemn reflections crowd on me to which I cannot here give expression.

January 1st, 1864. A bright but very cold day this New Years day is, the ground covered with snow. My thoughts recur to home and family—God bless and protect them. Well do I remember New Years in days of yore, and the recollection brings back sad reflections in which I will not stop [to] indulge now. God grant me wisdom and direction during its days and months and may it be a year of prosperity to our beloved country and may it bring to us blessed peace. Arose at the usual time. Breakfasted late and afterwards had an egg nog in our quarters of which Gen. Drayton and others participated. At 11 A.M. today the mercury stood at 10° above zero—cold weather for southern Arkansas. After dark [I] spent an hour or two with Gen. Price and others in his quarters.

January 2nd. Weather somewhat moderated but still cold and cloudy. Spent the day pretty much in quarters. Maj. Cabell reading aloud "Corrine."

January 3rd. Sunday. The first Sabbath of the year. Sleeting all day and forbidding out. Spent the time in my cabin reading and thinking of the "loved ones at home"—God bless them. No preaching in the neighborhood that I know of. At all events weather too inclement to turn out.

January 4th. Weather still gloomy and sleety—trees all covered with ice. Somewhat unwell all night and this morning, but thanks to a kind Providence [I] feel better this evening. Spent the day quietly indoors reading, etc. No news or anything of interest in camp.

January 5th. Weather again very cold and inclined to snow and sleet. Read President Davis' message to Confederate Congress—a noble state paper which with a masterly hand depicts Yankee perfidy and English unfriendliness, worthy of the man and of our young Confederacy. Shelby's Cavalry passed today and we were visited by numerous of his officers. Rumors today of another grand victory in Virginia.

January 6th. Weather clear but still very cold—resembling Missouri weather. Spent the morning in improving stable for the comfort of my horse. Tried my hand on fritters today (in showing the cook how to make them), succeeded admirably. Gen. Rust visited us this afternoon. Read physiology at night. Gen. [Albert] Rust though a Virginian by birth and a brigadier in the service is far from being sound on the "Goose question."[51]

January 7th. Day passed off quietly and without incident in camp. Weather still very cold.

January 8th. Weather still clear and cold. Spent the morning in tinkering in various ways at little comeforts. Dined at 4 P.M. Had a visit from Gen. Price this afternoon. After dark [I] wrote a long letter to Gov. Reynolds in matters and things in general. Tonight we have still further news of a glorious victory by Gen. Lee in Virginia over Meade and the Yankee army—God grant that it may prove to be true and more than true.

January 9th. Another cold day spent in camp reading, principally, and in attending other matters of minor importance.

January 10th. Sunday. A bright day somewhat more moderate than for the past week. Did not go to church as there was none in the neighborhood. Maj. [John] Tyler [Jr.][52] and Capt. Celsus Price[53] returned this evening, both of whom had been in Texas for some time. The rumors that we have heard about battles and victories in Va. and Tenn. probably all false.

January 11th. Weather mild and delightful. Dr. Cunningham paid us a visit this morning on his way to Camden having been off on a short leave. As our army has gone into winter quarters and will probably be stationary here for several months, Gen. Price started today on a 60 day leave to visit his wife in Washington, Texas. In his absence, Gen. Drayton, senior brigadier will command the division. Spent the day quietly reading and attending to diverse small matters. Major Tyler took dinner with us.

January 12th. Spent a busy day hard at work rebuilding and redaubing our chimney and making other improvements in our cabin.[54] The chimney now does finely and gives me great satisfaction. Weather mild and pleasant. No news from any quarter and no incidents in camp. Major Tyler came into our tent, after the above was written, with Maj. Snead and others and discoursed us largely on the subject of Texas and his exploits there much to the satisfaction and amusement of all present.

January 13th. Rode down to Gen. Parsons' Brigade this morning with Dr. Wooten to attend the Army Medical Association which met in Dr. [Robert J.] Bell's quarters.[55] Had quite an interesting meeting. Several papers were heard on pneumonia in the army and an intelligent discussion took place on the subject. About 1 P.M. [we] adjourned for dinner. [I] dined with Dr. Herndon, smoked, and then resumed our meeting. Dr. [Robert J.] Christie gave an interesting demonstration of the heart using an ox heart for the purpose.[56] Had a spirited ride home. After dark [I] ate

broiled venison and ho cake [in my] tent. Spent the evening reading and smoking.

January 14th. A bright and beautiful day spent in camp quietly
and ingloriously. Paid Gen. Drayton a visit and had a visit from
Gen. Churchill. After dark, stewed some molasses and we had a
regular candy pulling by way of vanity; after which, Maj. Cabell
and I talked over former times until midnight.

January 15th. Received a letter from [my] sister Lavinia from
Raleigh, N.C. of date Dec. 7th, a long and interesting letter
informing me of the well being of all at the home of my childhood. Also received a letter from Dr. Bond. After tea [I] wrote
several letters on business and paid Maj. Tyler a visit.

January 16th. Another beautiful spring-like day. Spent it in camp
reading physiology and tinkering around. At night [I] wrote a long
letter to my wife to send by Col. [Louis A.] Welton[57] who
promises to put it through for me. It is a pleasure to write to her
and would be more so if I could only write unashamedly.

January 17th. Sunday. A rainy day. Spent mostly in camp close
in quarters reading, smoking, talking, and sleeping. Capt. Carville
Wood[58] with his bride arrived this afternoon and occupied Gen.
Price's quarters tonight. She expects to go to St. Louis shortly. [I]
called to see her and spent half an hour agreeably with her and
sent messages to friends in St. Louis. She is quite a nice woman.
From Camden this evening we learn that a flag of truce from Little
Rock states that Lincoln, the Yankee President, is *dead*. This may
or may not be so. If it is I shall rejoice in hopes that it may have
an important bearing on the war, but in such matters, and in all
matters, God knows what is best.

January 18th. A clear and cold day. Was occupied all morning in
superintending the erection of buildings for our negroes. Paid
Snead a visit after dark and had a long talk with him and Maj.

Cabell on affairs in general. Read physiology after returning to cabin. Hearing that Mrs. McCluer of St. Louis is on the other side of the river and in want. We raised funds from the Missourians for her benefit. I cheerfully contributed $50. Several thousand dollars have been raised.

January 19th. Another bright pleasant day. The moon shines beautifully tonight creating in me a strong desire to be at home with my family. Oh, that this war was over and our independence achieved! Yet I have no desire to withdraw until that is accomplished, *nor do I repent* the course I have taken, not for one moment. Spent the day about quarters without accomplishing much. Received a letter from Gov. Reynolds at Marshall, Texas in reply to one written to him some two weeks ago. No news or other matters of interest in camp.

January 20th. Dr. Jo Scott[59] and wife arrived at our camp today from Washington on route for Camden where she expects to meet Mrs. Schaumburg and with her proceed to Little Rock and St. Louis under a flag of truce. [I] was glad to see her as she will see my wife. Mrs. Newton, just out from Little Rock, arrived this afternoon at Gen. Churchill's headquarters on her way to Lewisville, Ark. Wishing to see her, Majors Cabell, Snead, and I rode down to visit her after a late dinner (5 P.M.). Spent an hour or two very pleasantly; heard such news as she had from Yankeedom; took tea and then rode home by moonlight. After getting to camp and taking a smoke [I] called to see Mrs. Scott at Maj. MacLean's tent whose guest she is. Found diverse officers there. Col. J. B. Clark and Maj. Snead, and Cabell came to our tent afterwards where for a long time we consulted as to army and public affairs which need not be mentioned here. 12 o'clock at night, time for retiring. God bless our young Confederacy.

January 21st. Another beautiful spring-like day and a magnificent moonlit night. Spent the day quietly in camp. Maj. Tyler dined with us. After dark [I] paid Mrs. Scott a visit. She was serenaded by the band from two of the brigades.

January 22nd. Gen. Drayton had a review of the division today which went off well. Wrote a long letter to [my] sister Lavinia this afternoon to send across the river by a gentleman going over in a day or two. Hearing that Mrs. Schaumburg was at Parson Moore's this evening on her way to Camden and thence to St. Louis, Maj. Cabell and I rode over towards night and paid her a visit and by her sent messages to my wife. Took supper and rode home by moonlight 5 miles—very pleasant. I have some idea of going to Camden tomorrow to see yet more of her.

January 23rd. Started for Camden at 11 A.M. this morning on a 4 days leave on horseback accompanied by Maj. Cabell. Weather delightful and roads good. Went ten miles and stopped for dinner— plain country fare. Resumed our journey after a rest of an hour. Some five miles from Camden [we] fell in with several officers, Capts. Broadfoot and [Lionel] Levy[60] and Mr. Davidson acquaintances who had been out netting partridges, and rode in with them. Arrived about sunset. Stopped with Dr. Cunningham. After brushing-up, [I] went with Maj. Cabell to call on Mrs. Bruce at Mrs. Thompkin's. Found her a beautiful and accomplished lady. Took supper with her, after which we went to see Mrs. Schaumburg and Mrs. Scott. Found Mrs. Clay Taylor there also besides several St. Louis gentlemen. Spent an hour agreeably and then returned and spent the night with Dr. Cunningham.

January 24th. Sunday. Took breakfast with Dr. Cunningham at his mess and after smoking called up to take leave of the ladies about to start for St. Louis under a flag of truce, and to send last messages to my wife by them. Was detained in consequence of them not getting off until it was too late to go to church. At Gen. Holmes' headquarters saw diverse [members] of his staff and others and heard of the arrival of Gen. Bragg on this side of the river as Assistant Sec. of War—glad of it. Dined with Mrs. Bruce by invitation. Saw her sisters, Mrs. Thompkins and Miss Lowry, and Mr. Lowry her father all refugees from Louisiana and *nice* people. Had a good dinner, a fine cup of coffee and most of all enjoyed the society of the family. In [the] course of [the] afternoon [I] visited

Gen. Holmes and Mrs. Capt. Jo Chaytor, an old patient of mine and a banished refugee from St. Louis.[61] After dark [I] visited Judge Watkins and Maj. Snead, the Judge accompanying me on the last visit. On the way we were stopped by the sentinels and as I had forgotten the countersign [I] had to go several squares with them to get it. A magnificent moonlit night.

January 25th. Spent last night and took breakfast this morning with Dr. Cunningham. After breakfast met Mr. Bass of Nashville [Arkansas] and spent an hour or two with him and other gentlemen. Saw also [several] other acquaintances and attended to some business. At 1 P.M. [I] took leave of Dr. C. and called by Mr. Thompkin's and took dinner with him, immediately after which Maj. Cabell and I mounted our horses and started back for camp a little after 2 P.M. Rode along quietly and arrived at Gen. Churchill's headquarters about dark. Here we halted and took tea with the Gen. and Mrs. C. and met also Mrs. Newton there—all agreeable people. After supper and the rising of the moon [we] rode on to camp where we arrived about 9 o'clock P.M. after a most delightful trip of three days.

January 26th. Weather still continues delightful. Maj. Tyler who has been a guest of ours started for Richmond, Va. today. Wrote to Lt. Fergus MacRae by him.[62] Paid Gen. Drayton a visit. No news or other excitement in camp. Spent the day quietly.

January 27th. The Army Medical Association met this morning at our quarters—a good attendance. Two lengthy and good papers were read. One on masturbation and the other on typhoid fever were read and the discussion of these subjects occupied the time of the meeting for several hours pleasantly and profitably. Late in the evening [I] accompanied Maj. Cabell in a walk.

William McPheeters at age forty-five, 1860, one year before the war broke out. *(Missouri Historical Archives, William McPheeters Papers)*

Sallie McPheeters. *(Photo courtesy of General Sterling Price Museum)*

VIEW OF THE CITY OF ST. LOUIS, MISSOURI.

St. Louis as it appeared from the Illinois side of the Mississippi River in 1854. (*Missouri Historical Archives, William McPheeters Papers*)

Julia Dent Grant, wife of Gen. Ulysses S. Grant, was a long-time friend of
Dr. McPheeters. This friendship proved invaluable to Sallie McPheeters
during her harrowing trip to Helena, Arkansas, in July 1863.
(Photo courtesy of the Library of Congress)

Lieut. Gen. Theophilus H. Holmes served as the controversial commander of the
District of Arkansas from 1862 until his removal in March 1864. "For Gen. Holmes
personally I have none but the kindest feelings, said McPheeters, "but his incompetency for the position he has occupied is patent to the whole army and country."
(Photo courtesy of the Library of Congress)

Gen. E. Kirby Smith commanded the Trans-Mississippi Department from 1863 until its surrender in May 1865. *(Photo courtesy of the Library of Congress)*

As his medical inspector and later chief surgeon, McPheeters was a great admirer
of fellow Missourian and District of Arkansas commander, Maj. Gen. Sterling Price.
(Photo courtesy of the Texas State Library and Archives Commission)

April 28th Thursday. An order was received late last night to have two days rations cooked – to leave the wagons, artillery & all sick & barefooted who are not able to stand hard marching & to start at 6 oclock. Am. Artillery & train come on as soon as the pontoon bridge is complete. Arose by daylight & after taking a refreshing cup of coffee started off to look after the sick of the Division – Left a surgeon to see that all those left are properly housed & cared for, & then went to the river where the army was crossing, the Yankees took their pontoon & of course left the Wahchetaw river between them & us, without the means of crossing. During the night a foot way was constructed by means of which the soldier went over in single file – of course it was a slow process & there was a great jam – Major & Brigadier Generals, Col's & other officers in large numbers. It was 9 oclock before the troops crossed – our horses were crossed on a flat boat – about 10 a. m. we fairly got under way in pursuit of the fleeing yankees. The whole road was which we travelled offorded unequivocal signs of great perturbation on the part of the yankees – The whole road was strewn with old boots, shoes, overcoats, blankets, pantaloons & every other article of dress, & various other things – besides tents, wagons & other camp equipage were left half burned, shewing that they were anxious to get rid of all unnecessary baggage in their flight – It was a gratifying sight for an enemy who advanced with so much confidence & boasting that they would march unopposed through the country & take possession of the Trans. Miss. department – Genl Govt has been gracious to us. Gen. Kirby Smith passed us on the way – Gen. Price being in advance. We came 14 miles on the Princeton road & then went into camp. at 4 P.m. Took a cup of coffee & a cold lunch – will bless under a tree tonight & go on in pursuit of yankees the day left.

April 29th We were ordered to march this morning at 3 Am. consequently had to get up at 2 oclock after a nap under a tree. But in consequence of having to go in the rear of Gen. Walkers division who were slow in moving we did not get off until after three oclock & were all day delayed by the horses in advance – Passed through Princeton about 3 P.m. in a hard rain & came out 8 miles beyond in the neighbourhood of Tulip, but on a different road. It was near night when we went into camp, without tents, in the rain & with but scant rations. Orders to march again at 12 oclock m. I slept the short time all others to that occupation on the seat of an ambulance covered by an oil cloth to keep the rain off – This business of forced marches in pursuit of an enemy & without a train is rather a rough business, but all bear it cheerfully.

April 30th Saturday Battle of the Saline River. Took up the line of march promptly at mid night dark rain, & very muddy. all together a horrible march & truly do I pity & admire the poor privates who foot it through the much & mire & water uncomplainingly – Gen. Kirby Smith passed us on the road & we came up with Gen. Price soon & all pushed on to Jenkins Ferry on the Saline where the enemy were supposed to be engaged in crossing the river. Arrived within 3 miles of the ferry about 7 Am. Supposing that only a small part of the enemys force was on this side of the river Gen. Churchills division was at once sent forward to attack them – the cavalry having been skirmishing all morning & at 8 oclock the battle

A page of McPheeters's diary. The battle on Saturday, April 30, 1864, which he calls Battle of the Saline River is known as the Battle of Jenkins' Ferry. *(Missouri Historical Archives, William McPheeters Papers)*

CHAPTER 5

"No Abiding Camp," Winter 1864

No place to lay his head.

January 28th. A move of camp has been determined upon for convenience of forage. This morning [I] rode with Dr. Wooten over to the brigades of Gens. Drayton and Tappan to select the quarters of one of them as a hospital to leave the sick of the division. We selected Tappan's. At my own suggestion I will remain behind in charge of the hospital. Day spent in making other preparations for the move.

January. 29th. 1864. Friday. Our army commenced moving this morning for the new camp near Spring Hill [Arkansas] in the neighborhood of Red River. The brigades of Generals Drayton and Tappan went today. The other two will follow tomorrow. After breakfast [I] rode over to the quarters evacuated by Gen. Tappan where all the sick will be concentrated and left under my charge. Saw to matters over there, Selected the cabin occupied by the general for my quarters. Saw to procuring rations and medicines for 188 sick who will be left. On returning got a note from Gen. Churchill asking me to call down to his brigade and see his wife who is sick. Got there about dinner time. Prescribed for Mrs. C. and took dinner with the Gen. and Mrs. Newton on a fine turkey. Afterwards, [I] rode back with Gen. C. who came up to see the commanding general (Drayton). Col. Clay Taylor just from Camden dined with us at a late hour. Saw Gen. Drayton about the conduct of the hospital, etc. Weather not so fine as of late. Rained a little during the day.

January 30th. Rained hard last night. Threatening rain all day. Gen. Drayton and most of his staff left this morning for the new camp near Spring Hill some 35 miles off. Our mess did not get off until 1 P.M. Wooten, Slaughter, and Jo Thomas with all the wagons except mine went on in the direction of camp, whilst I moved over to Gen. Tappan's cabin to take charge of the Division Hospital. Thus remaining behind. Maj. Cabell who intends visiting his plantation on the Mississippi River came over with me and will spend the night. Spent most of the morning looking after the wants of the sick. Fixed up very comfortable in my new quarters. Assistant Surgeons [Jesse E.] Thompson and [Thomas H.] Kavanaugh remain behind with me.[1] Hearing of a sick soldier in distress some 8 or 10 miles off [I] sent them late this evening [to] look after him. After tea [I] read [the] *St. Louis Republican* of [the] 12th. Wrote a letter for medical supplies, etc. Raining hard, prospect of a rainy night.

January 31st. 1864. Sunday. Spent the morning in visiting and prescribing for the sick in [the] cabin hospital and in attending to their other wants. Rained occasionally during the day with hard wind. Maj. Cabell did not go to Camden but spent the day with me. There was no preaching in the neighborhood during the day. Tonight a Hardshell Baptist preached a short distance off, but I *declined* to hear him. Wrote to Dr. Slaughter tonight for medicines.

February 1st. Maj. Cabell left me after an early breakfast this morning for Camden. Spent all the forenoon in visiting, prescribing for, and getting a list of the patients in hospital. After dinner rode a mile and a half to see a young Missourian who is quite sick. After tea [I] was engaged in drawing off a list of patients. Drs. Thompson and Kavanaugh assisted me. Received a note from Gen. Churchill and sent some medicine to his children. He leaves in the morning to join his command. His family leaves for Lewisville [Arkansas]. Day bright and beautiful.

February 2nd. Spent the day quietly in hospital duties and in reading. I am very snugly and pleasantly situated. At night read *Home Influences*.

February 3rd. Another day quietly spent in hospital duties and in reading. Maj. [Thomas] Monroe[2] returned from Camden this evening en route for camp. He brings no news. By him [I] wrote a letter to Dr. Wooten tonight.

February 4th. Spent the morning in visiting the sick under my care and what remained of it and the afternoon in reading *Home Influences*. Dined with Capt. [William B.] Langford[3] in his quarters —a good camp dinner. Late in the evening rode a mile and a half to see a sick soldier. Read until 1 o'clock.

February 5th. Dr. Slaughter arrived this evening from camp via Lewisville bringing medicine for our sick—all getting on well in camp. He spends the night with me. It has been a delightful day spent quietly and peacefully in reading and in hospital duties.

February 6th. Slaughter left after breakfast for Camp Sumter[4] where the army now is and the day was passed peaceably, pleasantly, and alone. Read and was interested in *The Mother's Reward* the sequel to *Home Influences*—interesting volumes. The quiet of my present position is exceedingly grateful to my feelings and I shall not be in a hurry to quit this place. I have time and inclination to think often of the "loved ones at home," my dear wife particularly. God bless them.

February 7th. Sunday. A quiet and peaceful day spent in visiting the sick in hospital and in reading. There was preaching some three miles off but I did not feel like going though the day was delightful so [I] remained at home in quiet. Sent 5 patients back to their commands recovered.

February 8th. As the number of patients in the hospital is not enough to require the attendance of three medical officers, I relieved Dr. Kavanaugh this morning and he returned to the command. About noon [I] was pleased by a visit from Major Snead en route from Camden to camp. He has just returned from a visit to Little Rock with a flag of truce. He took dinner and spent several hours with me and then went on not spending the night as I wished as he was anxious to get on. He brings no news of interest seems cheerful and hopeful and even thinks that this year will see the close of our struggle. God grant that it may be so. Oh how I long for peace that I may return to the bosom of my beloved family. [I] was pleasantly employed during the day and evening when not professionally engaged in reading the *Mother's Recompense.*

February 9th. The only incident of the day was the making and drinking of an egg nog. Capt. Langford and Dr. Thompson came in about noon with a basket of eggs which was soon served up as above stated. Day mostly spent in reading after visiting all my patients. Weather delightful. No news from any quarter—"all quiet on the Potomac."

February 10th. Visited all the patients in the hospital this morning, Dr. Thompson being unwell. After getting through these duties [I] attended to sundry duties of a private and domestic kind and spent the remainder of the day quietly reading. I have before expressed how delightful the quiet and calm of my present position is. I have no desire to return to the turmoil of camp speedily.

February 11th. Finished reading *Mother's Reward,* a most pleasing tale. Wrote to Col. Clay Taylor and at night a letter to Gov. Reynolds; otherwise, the day passed as yesterday and the day before.

February 12th. Sent off twelve patients today to their commands, the others are so rapidly recovering that we will soon be able to break up this establishment. Wrote to Dr. Wooten a short letter this forenoon. Took a solitary ride on horseback this evening. After supper wrote a long letter to my brother, Alexander.[5] Thus has passed the day and thus far the night.

February 13th. Capt. [R. A.] Kidd[6] arrived from camp today bringing me some news of army proceedings on the other side of the river. About 11 A.M. an ambulance train, 15 in number, arrived from the command to convey our convalescents thither. They brought me a letter from Dr. Wooten. With as little delay as possible they were loaded with men and their baggage and started back. Sent off some fifty-one or two, which with those previously discharged leaves me only some 10 or 15 remaining. Wrote to Dr. Wooten by the train.

February 14th. Sunday. For the past two weeks the weather has been balmy and beautiful. Last night it clouded up and rained a little and today it has rained slowly all day increasing after night. [I] was prevented from going to church on account of the weather. After visiting the few patients I have, [I] spent the day indoors reading. About nine o'clock tonight Dr. Thompson and Capt. Langford came in and we made an egg nog and enjoyed it much. 11 P.M. raining hard with every prospect of its continuing.

February 15th, 1864. Monday. At Hospital, Camp Bragg. The rain of yesterday and last night ceased this morning and the weather became clear and we had a clear and delightful day. Visited and prescribed for my patients, mended some clothes, darned stockings, then read Sir Edward Seawell's *Narrative,* a very pleasing book. This I did before and after dinner and after tea. I have a quiet, nice time and my thoughts often, very often, recur to my dear wife and children. Oh how I long to be with them. Persons from Camden bring reports of the taking of Memphis by Gen. Forrest and others. [This] was news of interest, but these reports are wholly unreliable and, therefore, I do not place confidence in them. Oh that this war would end, but it can only cease by the independence of the South being recognized, which is not likely soon to be done, and until it is done the war must go on. God grant us a speedy peace and independence.

February 16th. Weather changed during last night becoming cold and windy. After visiting patients in hospital, spent remainder of day in my cabin writing up my papers and arranging matters. Maj. Monroe arrived this evening from camp giving me all the news from our headquarters, which however, is not much. They are to have a big ball there on Monday night next, the 22nd. I will try and not get there until it is over and thus miss the "noise and confusion" incident thereto.

February 17th. Weather quite cold. Thin ice on the water this morning. Visited my sick and prescribed for them all. Maj. Monroe and Capt. Langford paid me a visit this morning talking over the affairs of the army and country. The remainder of the day and evening was spent in writing and reading Sir Edward Seawell's *Narrative,* an interesting and to all appearances truthful narrative. A gentleman who arrived this evening from Camden states as the news from that place that Gen. Forrest has attacked Memphis.

February 18th. Weather clear but still cold. After visiting my patients and attending to their wants returned to my comfortable cabin and spent the time in reading Sir Edward Seawell's *Narrative,* in which I am much interested. Spent a half-hour after tea in conversation with Maj. Monroe then returned to my quarters where by a bright fire read until 11 [P.M.] then, as my custom is, read the Bible. I cannot but thank God for the quiet and comfort of this quiet and delightful "sick camp" and for all his many mercies to me. The present is truly delightful, calm, soothing, and profitable alike. I trust to my feelings and heart. God bless my dear absent wife and children.

February 19th. Two men, Arkansians belonging to Tappan's Brigade, were to be shot today in our division for desertion. This seems to be a harsh remedy, but many of these trifling Arkansians are constantly deserting and it is absolutely necessary to preserve discipline in our army. One of them had gone over to the Federals and I hope that this execution, which I presume came off, will have a salutory effect. Spent the day in hospital duties and in reading. Weather still quite cold.

February 20th. Persons up from the command today state that the two deserters who were to have been shot today escaped from the guard night before last, no doubt with the connivance of the guard as they were in irons. They state also that the guards have been arrested and put in irons. I hope most heartily that they will shoot every one of them. Such scoundrels are a disgrace to the service. Another day spent peaceably and quietly in hospital duties and reading. The weather has moderated considerably.

February 21st. Sunday. Dr. Thompson with nine discharged convalescents started for the command this morning, his wagon having arrived yesterday evening. I have now only some 6 or 8 patients remaining awaiting the arrival of ambulances when all will be sent to the command. After visiting my patients this morning and reading several chapters in the *Acts of the Apostles* and attending to usual morning devotions, I ordered my horse and rode four miles to a Methodist church, but finding that there was no preaching went on a mile further to Parson Moore's where I paid a pleasant visit, took dinner, and sat an hour after. Then returned to my cabin again where I arrived about 4 P.M. Since Dr. Thompson's departure, Dick, my servant and wagon driver, and myself are all that is left about the premises so that it looks lonely enough, though I cannot say that I feel lonely. Spent the evening and night reading. Weather mild and pleasant again.

February 22nd. This is not only Washington's birthday but also the anniversary of the inauguration of President Davis, President of the Confederate States. The event is to be celebrated at our camp, Camp Sumter, by a grand ball which comes off tonight and at Camden by a sham fight. As before stated I am right glad that I am absent from the command so as to avoid the "noise and confusion" of the ball.[7] Four of Gen. Holmes' body guard came here this morning stating that they were ordered to come and remain here until Gen. Holmes arrived from Camden en route for some place they knew not where, but after remaining for some hours and the General not making his appearance they returned to Camden. A woman living in the neighborhood came over this afternoon and stated that two soldiers came to her house and took all the money and other valuables she had and notified her to leave the country in two days. It seems that her husband has lately deserted from our army and that she and he are suspected of Union sentiments. There is no doubt [of] some disloyalty among the people in this neighborhood and the soldiers are determined to make the country too hot for such, still I do not approve of a war on women and children, it is too much like the Federals. Late this evening [I] went a half-mile off to visit a sick woman. Weather mild and delightful.

February 23rd. My patients are so far recovered that they are able to be sent to their commands and I only await the arrival of an ambulance train to send them off and join the army myself. Expecting dispatches and letters from our headquarters I sent the steward this afternoon over to Baird's to the courier station to get them if there were any, but he returned without anything for me— quite a disappointment as I know that I have letters and probably orders at the command awaiting my arrival. Gen. Holmes passed on the other road this morning going to our camp, but I did not see him. Received $5 for the visit I paid yesterday in the neighborhood. Finished reading Sir Edward Seawell's *Narrative* in which I have been *much* interested. In it I find the origin of the expression, "All in the eye Betty Martin." It had its origin in a Romish prayer to St. Martin in which this Latin expression occurs, "O Mihi! Beate Martini," literally, "Oh to me blessed Martin" from which the phrase originated.

February 24th. Sent over to Baird's today again expecting dispatches from the command, but was again disappointed, so I will quietly await the arrival of the ambulances, which will probably be here tomorrow. Spent the day in prescribing for the sick and in reading in perfect quiet with [my] mind quiet and serene.

February 25th. As I anticipated, the ambulances made their appearance about noon today. All the patients will be sent off tomorrow and "Deo volente," I will proceed myself to the command now at Spring Hill, some thirty-five miles off. Spent most of the day in reading. This afternoon I went about two miles to see a negro woman sick as women not unfrequently are, bled her, did what was necessary to be done, received $10 for my visit and returned home having been absent about an hour.

February 26th. Friday. Packed my trunk and other effects last night. Arose early this morning, took a thorough ablution as my custom is and took an early breakfast. Immediately after breakfast started off the ambulances with all the sick for their respective commands and soon thereafter loaded my own wagon, sent it off and then started myself on horseback taking leave of Camp Bragg where I had remained some four months, the last four weeks of which time was very quiet and to me delightful on account of the quiet having been left in charge of the sick of the division. Half a mile from the camp I stopped to visit the woman I went to see two days ago, received $5 for the visit, and then went on my way to Camp Sumter where our army now is. My object was to go within three miles of Centerville on the Washington road then take to the left and come to Spring Hill, but owing to the stupidity of those who directed me I turned off at the wrong place and so missed the road and travelled on some twelve miles in hog paths and by-paths through the woods. [I] finally succeeded onto the main road but now owing to my own stupidity I took the wrong end of the road and went about four miles in the opposite direction from that in which I wished to go. When inquiring at a house I found that I was 6 miles from Falcon and 10 from Spring Hill. It was now late in the evening, but nothing daunted but a good deal put out by the mistake I had made. [I] wheeled around and doubled my tracks determined to reach Spring Hill, our headquarters, tonight. When five or six miles off it began to grow dark and the last two miles it was very dark; however, I made the trip having ridden at least 47 miles since 9 A.M. Arrived an hour after dark and was warmly received by Dr. Wooten and others. Took a cup of tea at our mess, smoked, and for an hour or two talked over the affairs of the country and of camp with the various staff officers and then retired for the night. My wagon and baggage did not come the whole way. Our headquarters is at Spring Hill near Red River and mid-way between Lewisville and Washington. The staff officers occupy a large female seminary building admirably adapted for accommodating the staff officers with comfortable rooms for officers and sleeping apartments.

February 27th. Camp Sumter. Took a comfortable breakfast at our new mess, after which [I] was appointed on a Board of Survey to examine and report on a lot of quartermaster's goods. This occupied me a couple of hours. Paid my respects and reported to Gen. Drayton [who is] in command during Gen. Price's absence. About noon my wagon arrived whereupon I fitted myself up very comfortably in a large room in the seminary building selected for Maj. Cabell and myself in our absence. Dined about 3 P.M. and soon after learning that Mrs. Snead had just arrived from St. Louis and was at Maj. [Richard] Pryor's about a mile distant,[8] I at once went over to see her and spent a couple of hours hearing and asking questions about my family and friends in St. Louis. She saw my beloved wife and children just before leaving and gives me the gratifying intelligence that they were well. My wife is very anxious to come south and only awaits an invitation from me. I wish that she had come with Mrs. Snead. Oh how I long to see her. Mrs. S. could bring no letters but she gave me many messages and some flannel and other things including likenesses of my dear wife and children, which I have not yet received. It is a great pleasure to hear from those we love and to see their dear faces on paper. In a number of the *Republicans*[9] that she brings I am sorry to see announced the death of Judge H. R. Gamble who for two years past has been acting as governor of Missouri.[10] While I differ from Judge G. and regret deeply his course in the present revolution, I respect him and regret his death. He was I doubt not a good man.

February 28th. Sunday. Took a cold bath and dressed in clean clothes from head to foot this morning in honor of the day. Soon after breakfast it commenced raining and rained hard all day; consequently, I could not go to church as I had hoped as there is a Presbyterian church here. Spent the day indoors read several chapters of Paul's Epistle to the Corinthians and having no other suitable for Sunday [I] wrote a letter to Dr. Haden. About 4 P.M. Dr. Taylor arrived from Camden and took dinner and spent the night with us. MacLean came in after dark and sat an hour in my room. 11 P.M., still raining hard.

February 29th. This being leap year February has twenty nine days. The rain of yesterday turned into snow and sleet during the night and on awakening this morning was surprised to find the ground white with snow. During the entire day it has been sleeting and snowing and with all quite cold. A marked contrast from the delightful spring weather that we have had of late. Owing to the state of the weather the review that was to have come off today was postponed. Gen. Holmes arrived about noon and soon went on to Lewisville. After dinner, notwithstanding the horrible state of the weather, I rode out to Maj. Pryor's to see Mrs. Snead and paid her a visit of over an hour. She has so recently seen my dear wife that it is a pleasure for me to see and converse with her on that account, as well as her own. After tea [I] read Yankee papers and wrote a letter to Col. Clay Taylor at Camden.

March 1st. Tuesday. The sun arose clear this morning, the wind shifted to the south, and the snow of yesterday began to disappear rapidly and before night was well nigh gone. Wrote a letter to my beloved wife to be enclosed in one sent by Mrs. Snead which I hope that she will get, but think it very doubtful. In it I left it to her own choice to come south or not as she thinks best. She seems so anxious to join me that I cannot oppose her coming any longer for God knows I desire above all things to have her with me now and ever and my advising her to remain where she is has all along been from the fact that I knew that she was more comfortable than I could make her here, but if she comes I will be but too glad to see her. Read Yankee papers during the afternoon. After dark Gen. Drayton called up to see me and sat an hour in conversation.

March 2nd. The Army Medical and Surgical Association held its meeting in Gen. Churchill's Brigade today and as I have the honor of being President I rode with Drs. Thompson, [Robert] Duncan, and [Paul Christian] Yates this morning.[11] The meeting was pretty well attended and was interesting. Several well-written papers were read and discussed. The subject was gunshot wounds of the abdomen. About 3 P.M. returned to my quarters just in time for dinner. The remainder of the day passed off without incident. After dark, read sketches of travels on the coast of western Africa. Capt. Celsus Price spends the night with me.

March 3rd. Had a visit this morning from the Rev. Mr. Boyd, Pastor of the Presbyterian church here. He resides a mile and a half off, is a Virginian, and for some time after the commencement of the war was a Capt. in the Virginia army, but meeting with an accident by which his spine was injured had to resign and is now quite an invalid from that cause. After dinner (4 P.M.) rode out with Maj. Snead and Maj. Pryor to see Mrs. Snead. Her trunks having arrived she gave me the photographic likenesses of my two children, dear Maggie and Sally, and the ambrotype of my beloved wife—all good. What a pleasure it is to look upon their beloved faces. As I gaze on them, memory brings back my once happy home and all the endearments I have left behind to engage in the glorious cause of Southern independence. It is a pleasure to see their faces on paper and steel as I am denied the greater pleasure of being with them, but trusting in the goodness and mercy of God I hope ere long to be again reunited to them. Remained until dark and then returned to my quarters. This morning received a long letter from Gov. Reynolds in public affairs and one from Dr. Bond on business. Weather pleasant.

March 4th. The morning passed off quietly and without incident in reading, smoking, etc. Wrote a letter to Dr. Bond at Lewisville on business. Dined at 4 P.M. after which Drs. Wooten, Slaughter, and myself rode out to the Rev. Mr. Boyd's where we paid a very pleasant visit, took a hospitable and good supper, and remained smoking and talking until nine o'clock when we returned by starlight to our quarters. So passed the day.

March 5th. Received a letter from Dr. Bond this morning stating that his wife expected to go to Little Rock and would take a letter for me. I therefore wrote a long letter to my wife and sent to

him by the return courier. In it I discuss the propriety of her coming south and after telling her the difficulties and inconveniences
leave it to her own judgement whether or not to come. Should
she determine to come I will be glad to see her and will welcome
her with all my heart though for her sake I rather hope that she
will remain where she is now comfortable. A pleasant day passed
in quarters and after finishing and sending off my letters read travels
on the western coast of Africa. A great dearth of news.

March 6th. Sunday. 1864. Took a cold bath and put on clean
clothes in honor of the day. At 11 o'clock walked over to the village church where I heard the Rev. Mr. Boyd, Presbyterian pastor of the church, preach a good sermon from these words, "How
long halt ye between two opinions" and read several chapters in
the new testament and this evening several Psalms. While standing out on the upper porch late this evening [I] saw two of the
body guard taking a tall middle-aged man over to one of the
brigades to be kept under guard, all on horseback. On inquiry I
learned that he was a Baptist preacher who had been arrested in
one of the adjoining counties for preaching disloyalty and distributing Lincoln proclamations and otherwise attempting to
excite the people to disloyalty. When the party got a few miles
off and within half a mile of the brigade they were going, the
Reverend Scoundrel attempted to make his escape by running his
horse. He was twice fired at by the guard, both shots taking effect
and the last killed him instantly. He was no doubt guilty and richly
deverved his fate. I have thought much of my home and family
today and long to be with them. May God in infinite mercy bless
and preserve them and me and bring us together again soon in
peace and safety. Oh blessed peace, when will we be blessed with
thy presence? Peace and independence is what we desire. Weather
mild and delightful.

I wish here to put on record a conclusion to which I have
recently come after much reflection. It is this, that the result of
this war will be the adoption of some system of *gradual emancipation* in the South. There is no denying the fact that the sentiment
of the world is against us on account of slavery, which nothing

but a tremendous convulsion such as we are now experiencing could accomplish. This may do it. The future will tell. We are fighting not for slavery, but for the right of self government. God's will be done.

March 7th. Monday. At Camp Sumter. Wrote a long letter this morning to Dr. Cunningham, Medical Director of the Department, on personal and army matters. About noon, Gen. Price arrived after an absence of nearly two months. We are, all officers and men, delighted to see him and have him return to duty again. He looks well and has had a pleasant trip and was everywhere received by the people with marks of distinction. Spent the day quietly feeling somewhat under the weather—took quinine. About dark Major Cabell also returned and occupied the same room with me. Received a note from Mrs. Jordan this evening requesting me to come down to her place near Lewisville to see her mother, Mrs. Johnson, who is quite unwell. Providence permitting I will go down in the morning. After dark the whole of Parsons' Brigade came in person to pay their respects to Gen. Price on his return. It was a gratifying sight. The General made them a speech and the band made music.

March 8th. Left camp at Spring Hill 10 o'clock this morning for Lewisville, Ark. to visit Mrs. Jordan and her mother, Mrs. Johnson, near which they temporarily reside being refugees like the rest of us. Rode the distance, 18 miles, alone and on horseback. Mrs. Jordan lives one and a half miles this side of Lewisville in a nice comfortable place. Arrived 1 P.M. [and] was warmly received and hospitably entertained for they are whole-souled nice people. Soon after arriving partook of a sumptuous dinner. Mrs. Churchill, Mrs. Newton, and Mrs. Dick Johnson came out after dinner and paid a visit. Maj. John Adams[12] arrived from Washington and also spent the night occupying the same room with me. About 4 P.M. rode into Lewisville in the carriage and paid Dr. Bond, Medical Purveyor, a visit and after remaining an hour returned to Mrs. Jordan's where I found Col. Dick Johnson, her brother, who took tea and remained until bedtime. Passed a pleasant evening and retired about 11 o'clock. Found old Mrs. Johnson very feeble but cheerful and as ever intelligent. Prescribed a tonic for her.

March 9th. Was aroused before day by a thunderstorm accompanied by wind and hard rain which continued until about 9 A.M. when it cleared off and was clear the rest of the day. Took a nice breakfast about 9 o'clock and about 10 A.M. rode into town in the carriage with Miss Sally Johnson. Paid Dr. Bond a visit and examined the Purveyor's Office and then went to see Mrs. Bond and afterwards rode down to see Mrs. Churchill and Mrs. Dick Johnson. Sat an hour with them in pleasant and animated conversation and about 1 P.M. returned with Miss Sally to the country. After dinner rode down in the carriage with Mrs. Jordan and Miss Sally Johnson to see Mrs. Wright who lives a mile below town on the Shreveport Road. She has a fine place, lives in good style, and is a fine woman, hospitable and wealthy. Spent an hour with her very agreeably. Reached Mrs. Jordan's on our return about dusk. Passed a pleasant evening. Rained again tonight and turned quite cold.

March 10th. Concluded this morning as the weather was favorable to return to camp. About 11 A.M. [I] started having paid a most charming visit and being urged to repeat it, which I promised to do and will certainly do if the army remains long here. On the ride up fell in with Lt. Wm. Von Phul[13] on his way from Shreveport to Spring Hill. He came as far as Gen. Drayton's Brigade. Rode leisurely and arrived at our headquarters about 2 P.M. Found things in status quo though there are some indications of a move of the army soon. We have news also of a victory of Gen's. Polk and Breckenridge over Sherman (Federal) in Mississippi, as well as of Forrest over Grierson's Cavalry after a three days fight.[14] Hope that they may both prove to be true and that they will be followed by yet other victories which may God grant.

March 11th. Spent the morning in writing official communications to the brigades, in assisting Maj. Cabell in counting his pay funds, etc. We counted eighty thousand dollars. Late in the evening rode out to Maj. Pryor's with Maj. Cabell and Snead to visit Mrs. Snead and the family of Maj. Pryor. Spent a pleasant evening and partook of a sumptuous supper, one which reminded me of the delightful peace times. About 10 P.M. we rode home by moonlight and smoked several pipes of some good tobacco which I have just procured—Arkansas scrip as it is called. Several of the staff officers called, some of whom sat until a late hour, inconveniently late.

March 12th. By the courier this morning from Camden received a letter from Dr. Cunningham in reply to one I wrote him several days ago and also a letter from Lt. Col. Clay Taylor. Both letters state that they have received news by telegraph of the defeat of Sherman by Polk and of the arrival of Sherman in New Orleans on the 1st instant, and also of the defeat of Grierson by Gen. Forrest. If this news proves to be true as it seems to be confirmed it is a glorious achievement and will tell on the events of the coming campaign. If Gen. Sherman and staff are in New Orleans it is evident that his army must have been scattered. God grant that it may prove to be true and more than true.

March 13th Sunday. Arose early and as my custom is underwent a thorough ablution. Breakfasted alone, all the other members of the mess being absent except Dr. Wooten who is unwell. After breakfast read several chapters in the Bible. A dispatch from Shreveport by courier this morning brings the gratifying intelligence that Gen. Holmes has been relieved from the command of the District of Arkansas and ordered to Richmond. I am glad of this as every one else is, as it will remove an incubus on our army and cause in this quarter. For Gen. Holmes personally I have none but the kindest feelings, but his incompetency for the position he has occupied is patent to the whole army and country.[15] At 11 o'clock went to church where I heard a good sermon, a Presbyterian minister from a distance, and again in the afternoon when the Rev. Mr. Boyd preached. After church rode out home with Mr. Boyd where I took tea and spent a pleasant evening. Reached home about 11 P.M., found Capt. Jo Thomas just arrived from Marshall, Texas.

March 14th. Monday. The removal of Gen. Holmes places General Price in command of the District of Arkansas. Last night he got orders to that effect and this morning started for Camden to assume command. Whether this is to be a permanent or only a temporary arrangement does not yet appear, I hope, however, that it is the latter. Gen. Price is an instance of "the right man in the right place," and I would be sorry to see him permanently removed from this division. Gen. Drayton will command the division in the meantime. Wrote a note to Mr. Jordan and one to Dr. Bond both of Lewisville by the courier. Commenced reading *The Dutch Republic.* Spent the day quietly indoors. Weather windy and a little cold. All quiet in and about camp. The time is approaching, however, for us to begin the move. Maj. Snead left today for Shreveport.

March 15th. Tuesday. Received a letter this morning from R. H. Johnson of Lewisville desiring to know if in case he sent up for me, I would go down and attend on his wife in case of her expected confinement, his family physician being absent. To which I returned an affirmative answer. Also got a note from Gen. Tappan asking me to ride out to Col. Hervey's and visit his wife who is sick which I did—a distance of two miles. Found her complaining a good deal; cheered and prescribed for her. A letter was received today from Maj. Cabell at Camden giving us the news from the east of the Miss. River; defeats of the Federal army in Florida by Gen. Finnegan,[16] also the failure of Banks' attack on Mobile at Pascagoula Bay—our forces repulsed and drove him back. Also told of the cavalry under Gen. Forrest routing the Federal Generals Smith and Grierson's cavalry force, which defeat caused Sherman's army to fall back from beyond Meridian to Vicksburg—all of which is cheering. During the time not otherwise occupied read *The Dutch Republic,* an interesting and well-written history. Jo Thomas returned this evening from Washington Ark. as drunk as a fool, wet to the skin, and muddied from head to foot, his horse having fallen down with him in a muddy creek. After tea Gen. Drayton paid me a visit and sat an hour conversing on the condition of affairs, the news, etc, etc.

March 16th. Wednesday. Rode to Gen Parsons' Brigade this morning with Dr. Wooten to attend a meeting of the Army Medical Association. It met in Dr. Herndon's quarters and was upon the whole interesting. As President it was my place to preside. Gunshot wounds of the joints was the subject for consideration. One or two papers were read, and a number of cases related. After the meeting took dinner with Dr. Herndon—a good camp meal. After smoking the pipe, returned to our headquarters about four o'clock. A letter was again received from Maj. Cabell today giving us an account of another attempted raid by the Yankees on Richmond. They got within five miles of that envied city, but they were driven back and defeated, the Yankees admitting a loss of 240.[17] This doubtless far greater if they admit so much, as they were never known to tell the truth. Spent the evening and night in reading *The Dutch Republic;* the style of which is fine.

March 17th. Thursday. Received a letter from Dr. Cunningham this morning offering me the position of Field Inspector of the District if I would accept it. I replied that I would. In case the assignment is made it will involve my removal to Camden and place me on the District staff. Wrote a letter to Maj. Cabell. Gen. Price ordered his personal staff, bodyguard, and band to Camden today. This looks as though he expected not to return to this division soon. Received a note from Mrs. Jordan this afternoon accompanying a set of buttons for a coat, just what I am in want of. I have spent most of the day in reading *The Dutch Republic* in which I am quite interested.

March 18th. Friday. Had a visit from Generals Churchill and Tappan this morning, the latter came to consult me about his wife. It is emphatically true in the army that we have no abiding camp, much less can we tell what a day will bring forth. About two o'clock today a special courier arrived from Camden ordering the entire division to move down to Camden at once. The order is from General Price. The news rapidly spread and in a few moments all was excitement and bustle. Orders were issued from all the departments and the notes of preparation were heard all around.

We will not be able to get off however until day after tomorrow. As to the cause of this sudden and unexpected move we are left to conjecture. It looks as though it were intended to meet an advance of the enemy. At all events it is something urgent. Finished reading the first volume of the *Dutch Republic* this evening.

March 19th Saturday. I mentioned above that an order came yesterday directing this division to go at once to Camden. This morning another order came from Lt. Gen. Smith (Kirby) ordering us to proceed with all dispatch to Shreveport and as he is the ranking officer his orders will have to be obeyed, so we proceed to Shreveport in the morning. The enemy it seems have landed at Alexandria La. and are threatening Shreveport, hence the latter order. We are to join Gen. [Richard] Taylor's[18] command and give battle to the Yankee invaders. God grant that we may be successful in driving them back. Everything and everybody have been busy today getting ready for the move. A letter was also received from Maj. Cabell at Camden giving us good news from the other side of the river. The Yankees have been defeated at all points. Spent the morning in getting ready for the move of tomorrow and in reading. This afternoon rode out to Maj. Pryor's to see Mrs. Snead. She has just received a letter from St. Louis and gives me the gratifying intelligence that my wife and family are well. While there Gen. and Mrs. Churchill and Mrs. Newton arrived from Lewisville to see the command off. After remaining a short time, rode over to the Rev. Mr. Boyd's to take leave of him and his family and then returned again to Maj. Pryor's and took tea. Gen. Parsons also came in and we had a pleasant evening and a delightful supper. Remained until 10 o'clock and then returned to headquarters. Tomorrow, Sunday as it is, we will be on the move. "Deo volente." I have yet some preparations to make before starting.

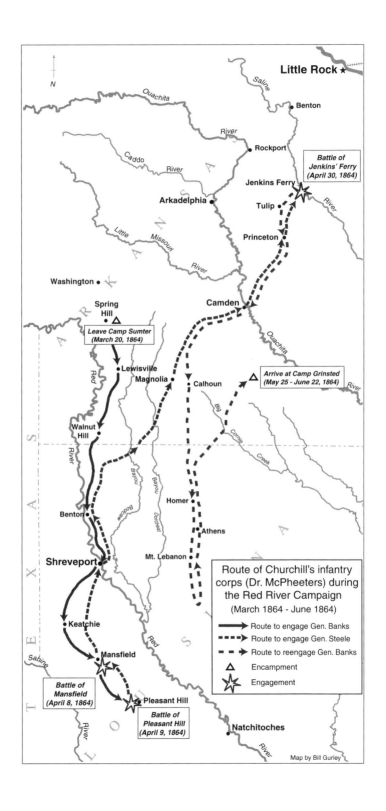

Little Rock ★

N

Ouachita

Saline

Benton

River

Rockport

Caddo

River

*Battle of
Jenkins' Ferry
(April 30, 1864)*

Jenkins Ferry

A R K A N S A S

Arkadelphia

Tulip

River

Princeton

Little

Missouri

River

Washington

Camden

Spring
Hill △

*Leave Camp Sumter
(March 20, 1864)*

Ouachita

River

Lewisville
Magnolia

Calhoun

△ *Arrive at Camp Grinsted
(May 25 - June 22, 1864)*

Red

Big

Cornie

Walnut
Hill

River

Creek

Bayou

A R K A N S A S

Benton

Bayou

Bodcaw

Bayou

Dorcheat

Homer

L O U I S I A N A

Shreveport

Athens

Mt. Lebanon

**Route of Churchill's infantry
corps (Dr. McPheeters) during
the Red River Campaign**
(March 1864 - June 1864)

T E X A S

Keatchie

Red

→ Route to engage Gen. Banks
┅► Route to engage Gen. Steele
╌► Route to reengage Gen. Banks
△   Encampment
✶   Engagement

Sabine

Mansfield

*Battle of
Mansfield
(April 8, 1864)*

Pleasant Hill

*Battle of
Pleasant Hill
(April 9, 1864)*

Natchitoches

River

River

Map by Bill Gurley

CHAPTER 6

Red River and Jenkins' Ferry, 1864

Be Thou our guard while troubles last.

Spring 1864, the third seed time for the fractured republic, arrived. Rains washed the wounded soil, swelling rivers and gullies and mud-dying the run-offs and valleys where once kitchen gardens had flourished. Early jonquils came up, edging little farm pathways in bright yellow—to the smokehouse, to the shed and privy, or beside ruined porches. And there, on the darkened, raw horizon were standing chimneys, "Sherman's tombstones," remembering plantations and home places laid low by the war. Wild violets and rangy dandelions came up in clumps in empty pastures, but there was no one to see except columns of weary, ragged soldiers walking past or deserters skulking by, all starving, all angry, and all wishing for home in the greening air.

Along the corridor of land between the South Arkansas bayous and the Red River, there were no farmers toiling behind their homemade mule-drawn ploughs to set the furrows for seed, no calving to increase domestic herds, and no clotheslines filled with spring bedding or bright quilts, flapping in the brisk early winds. For long stretches, the country was bare; people were gone. In the despair of war, their own army had confiscated their animals, emptied their smokehouses and root cellars, and burned their cotton to keep it out of enemy hands. The entire Trans-Mississippi, once the supply pantry of the Southern nation, the frontier of farmers, mule skinners, preachers, and plain folk, lay now wasted and spoiled, swept aside as worthless by Richmond, targeted for easy pickings by the Union—all except Texas.[1]

In Sam Houston's old republic lay cotton fields under cultivation, a few foundries, shoe factories, and a degree of prosperity not shared by the remainder of the Trans-Mississippi. Stored in the cotton sheds of East Texas and piled at railheads were thousands of cotton bales beyond the reach of Yankee scalpers and Rebel blockade runners alike. With Northern textile mills standing idle, cotton alone made Texas the obvious Union target. Then too there was a foreign policy matter that vexed Pres. Abraham Lincoln and his secretary of state—Napoleon III had taken it upon his empire to install a Hapsburg, Maximillian, the younger brother of Austrian emperor Franz Josef, upon the throne of Mexico. Backed by the presence of a French army on Mexican soil, Maximilian was a potential ally for the Confederacy. With this in mind, Lincoln was the driving force behind talk of a Texas invasion, and Union commanders had long discussed what the nature of such a campaign should be. For two years an offensive to secure portions of Texas had been on the Yankee drawing board. It first called for an expeditionary force commanded by Maj. Gen. Nathaniel P. Banks, which had sailed from New York in late 1862. This army was initially ordered to join Maj. Gen. Ulysses S. Grant in his difficult campaign to secure the entire length of the Mississippi for the Union, and after the fall of Vicksburg and Port Hudson in July 1863, the approval for Banks's Red River campaign was given.[2]

It was Maj. Gen. Henry Halleck who saw West Louisiana, South Arkansas, and the Red River as the natural portal into East Texas, and he urged this route upon the man of the hour, Banks. The resulting plan called for an amphibious force commanded by Rear Adm. David Porter to move, in conjunction with a massive infantry column, up the Red River toward Shreveport. A second Union column under Maj. Gen. Frederick Steele would move south from Little Rock to Shreveport, creating a massive converging attack upon Confederate troops there defending what was left of the Trans-Mississippi Department.[3]

Banks brought into action a host of thirty thousand men, most of whom were seasoned veterans, and a flotilla of sixty vessels, including thirteen ironclad gunboats. But the obvious weakness of any plan for a combined military operation is timing—the possibility of delay, low water, skirmishers, sharpshooters, thunderstorms, fevers, breakdowns, wagon jams, or mixed signals. In the case of the Union's Red River campaign, so perfect on paper, so beautiful on the outstretched military maps, things began to go wrong with the first step of the first infantryman on the road and the first head of steam of the first gunboat on the river.

Nevertheless, the U.S. Navy flotilla moving up Red River man-

aged to seize all the stored and hidden cotton bales onshore within range
of its 240 guns. Dividing the profits among officers and crew amounted
to a rich and widely envied take when sold to New England cotton
agents waiting at New Orleans for supplies of the South's money crop.
The resale value of cotton to the silent textile mills of the North gen-
erated a vigorous commercial enterprise. On March 15, 1864, the Ides,
Admiral Porter's fleet had anchored at Alexandria, Louisiana, because
their voyage to Shreveport was halted by a series of shallow cascades.
Porter was becoming aware of the capriciousness of the Red River.

Maj. Gen. Richard Taylor and his 8,800 Confederates defending
the District of Western Louisiana drew the seemingly impossible assignment of impeding the blue horde. To improve Taylor's odds of success,
Lt. Gen. Edmund Kirby Smith had ordered Maj. Gen. Sterling Price to
send Brig. Gen. Thomas Churchill's and Brig. Gen. Mosby M. Parsons's
infantry divisions, about 4,400 men, to Shreveport. After four months
in winter quarters at two different encampments, the Arkansas and
Missouri veterans faced a springtime resumption of the war having not
been newly provisioned or equipped. There were no eager fresh recruits
parading up to join them. At best the Confederates could hope to field
13,000 bayonets to confront Banks's juggernaut.[4]

The blue army came into the spring campaigns well fed, well clad,
newly equipped, and intensely purposeful, while the butternut boys
picked up their old weapons, patched their worn uniforms, and prepared to face their strengthened foe. President Lincoln, keenly aware
of the political necessities of this presidential-election year, made a significant change in his high command, appointing Ulysses S. Grant, now
a lieutenant general, as general in chief of the Union armies. With this
change Lincoln hoped for a season of stunning victories to silence the
nagging press and those scattered peace-at-any-price movements.

With the fall elections only seven months in the offing, Banks, a
former Speaker of the House, also realized success on the battlefield
spelled success at the ballot box. As commander of a mighty Federal
army, the ambitious politician envisioned not only the conquest of
Louisiana and Texas but the presidency as well. The Red River, therefore, would be the course to his own political victory, the presidency.
Time, Nature, and the Rebels, however, posed a threat to Banks's well-
laid plans.[5]

General Grant had never been keen to the idea of invading north-ern Louisiana, yet he reluctantly agreed to lend Banks three of Maj. Gen. William T. Sherman's crack divisions, about eleven thousand men, led by Brig. Gen. A. J. Smith. Repayment of this loan, however, was due on April 15. After that date, Smith's troops were to be transported east for participation in Sherman's campaign for Atlanta.[6]

Nature compounded interest on the loan. Instead of the usual springtime rise in the Red River's navigable pool, the stream continued to drop, and Admiral Porter's fleet was faced with the threat of being grounded. Thus Banks's grand designs, both military and political, hinged on a swift seizure of Shreveport. With only two weeks before the expected return of A. J. Smith's divisions, the combined expedi-tion had reached Grand Ecore, just seventy miles from their objective. Confidence abounded. Any idea that the Confederates might disrupt the Federal timetable with a vigorous defense seemed almost an afterthought. This was especially so given the token resistance encoun-tered during the first weeks of the campaign.[7]

Even Edmund Kirby Smith seemed willing to accommodate the Federals. Faced with the decision of which invasion force to attack first, the Southern commander vacillated on his choice of targets: Steele's smaller, more distant column; or Banks's behemoth, currently looming at Shreveport's door. Smith's equivocation played into Banks's hand. "Dick" Taylor, though, incensed by his superior's indecision, argued vehemently for an immediate strike, preferably at Banks. Due to a lack of reinforcements, Taylor, a Louisiana planter and politician, had grudg-ingly retreated almost two hundred miles in the face of Banks's army; now with his back to the wall, he had no intention of abandoning his state without a fight.[8]

Anxious to settle the issue and close the operation, Banks made a decision that sealed the campaign's fate. Instead of marching up the river-bank supported by the heavy guns of Porter's flotilla, Banks turned his massive infantry column westward, away from the river. By advancing over the single road that led through the hamlets of Pleasant Hill and Mansfield south of Shreveport, the blue column expected to rendezvous with the gunboats in a couple of days. Based on the available maps, the move appeared militarily prudent. In reality, the road amounted to a nar-row tunnel meandering through thick pine forests. Compounding the

problem was the order of march. The wagon train of the cavalry advance
was placed between it and the following infantry column. This pattern
was repeated for each of the infantry divisions, resulting in the Union
army being strung out over twenty miles of road. Any numerical advantage the blue horde enjoyed generally was effectively neutralized by the
combination of confined road space and unit dispersion. Furthermore,
the situation portended disaster if a rapid and orderly reversal of the
column became necessary. The thought of a setback, however, never
entered the minds of the Federal officers.[9]

If Banks was oblivious to the predicament confronting his army,
Taylor was fully cognizant of his opponent's tactical vulnerability. If he
could strike the head of Banks's column as it marched along the confined roadway, an almost three-to-one numerical advantage would be
his reward. Taylor also realized that if Banks's column reached the crossroads town of Mansfield, three routes led directly to Shreveport and a
reunion with Porter's fleet. The time to strike was imminent, Kirby
Smith be damned. At Sabine Crossroads just south of Mansfield, Taylor,
now reinforced with units from Texas, halted and blocked the road
with over eight thousand vengeful Confederates.[10]

Within supporting distance of Taylor at Keatchie, Louisiana, was
Brig. Gen. Thomas Churchill's division of Arkansas and Missouri
infantry. Eighteen days earlier they had begun the over one-hundred-
mile trek from Arkansas. In the column rode their newly appointed
division surgeon. The Red River campaign began for Dr. William
McPheeters on another uncommemorated Sabbath day.

March 20th Sunday. Farewell to Camp Sumter. All the Brigades
commenced moving this morning in the direction of Shreveport.
Arose early, took a thorough ablution, the last that I will probably
get for some days to come, as a march is not favorable to personal
cleanliness or personal comfort. Took a hurried breakfast, had my
wagon loaded and soon we were all mounted and on our way.
Gen. Drayton and staff got off about 8 A.M. Weather cloudy, cold,
and threatening rain. The command all camped in the neighborhood of Lewisville 18 miles off. I stopped at Mrs. Jordan's 2 miles
from Lewisville, and as it was cold, raining, and our train not
arrived and the kind family was urgent in their invitation, I

remained, took dinner and spent the night instead of going to camp, and a great improvement it was over camp—such a night. Gen. Parsons also stayed all night and we occupied the same room. About 10 P.M. there was a heavy hail storm, the ground was covered in a few moments and our poor soldiers were all out in it. Old Mrs. Johnson, Mrs. Jordan, Miss Sally and the others made themselves very agreeable and the evening passed off pleasantly; but not much like a Sabbath has this been.

March 21st. Monday. After breakfast took leave of the family and rode into Lewisville. [I] saw Dr. Bond, and also called to see Col. R. H. Johnson[11] and family. By these delays I fell behind the rest of the staff and got mixed up with the troops and the wagons. Left Lewisville about 11 A.M. and traveled 14 miles through bad roads and amid troops and wagons innumerable. Got to camp about 2 P.M. took a camp dinner, smoked our pipes and sat around a log fire. The weather is dreary and cold and spitting snow this evening. This is written in camp on a board. We have commenced the Spring campaign in earnest.

March 22nd. Tuesday. On the march. Retired early last night and arose at 3 o'clock this morning. Took breakfast and commenced the march about 5 [A.M.] just as the day was beginning to dawn. Rode twelve miles to Walnut Hills, through which we passed and came nine miles south of it in the edge of Louisiana where we pitched our tents for the night having made a march of 21 miles.[12] Part of the road was tolerably good while the others parts were horrid. A pretty good days journey for our infantry. On getting into camp sent the servants off foraging. They brought back 10 doz. eggs for which we paid $2 a dozen and $5 a peck for black-eyed peas. These are war prices. We are getting on finely and our troops are in fine spirits. All feel as though we were going to whip the Yankees—God grant that we may.

March 23rd. Wednesday. Encamped last night in Louisiana. Retired early and arose this morning at 4 o'clock and by half past 5 was on the march in advance of all the brigades. Passed through Collinsville a one horse town, and a number of handsome residences doubtless the abode of gentlemen. A marked contrast in this respect from Arkansas. On the way [I] met Col. John Polk's servant who informed me that Mrs. Polk was near by at the beautiful residence of Dr. Newman, whereupon Maj. MacLean and I rode back a short distance and paid her a visit, and was glad to see her cheerful face. Came on to Benton where we went into camp. Benton is a small place on Red River 14 miles from Shreveport. We have made a march of 22 miles today and got into camp about 1 P.M. our train coming in about an hour afterwards. Took dinner about 3 P.M. with a good appetite. Weather pleasant with cold nights and mornings. Tomorrow, Providence permitting, we will go into Shreveport as it is probable that boats may be sent up tonight to take our infantry and artillery down. The enemy that we hope to meet and whip are said to be at Alexandria La. 14,000 strong, waiting for a reinforcement of 10,000 coming from some other quarters to join them. We expect to reinforce Gen.'s Taylor and [John G.] Walker[13] and then offer them fight. They have gunboats at Alexandria which as yet have not been able to get beyond that point.

March 24th. Thursday. Arose before day and took breakfast by candle light this morning and started on the march before sunrise. Weather cloudy, very windy and cold. Had 14 miles to make to Shreveport. Our march was on the banks of the Red River—the country is beautiful and the farms magnificent. I have never seen so beautiful and fertile a valley for farming purposes as that of the Red River. The country is levied all the way and the trees hung with moss. The last two miles of the way was in a cold beating rain which rendered it unpleasant. Arrived opposite Shreveport about half past 9 A.M. took shelter from the rain under an old cotton shed while Gen. Drayton reported to Lt. Gen. Kirby Smith for orders. In the mean time we quit the shed and took refuge in a house just opposite the town—here we took dinner for which we paid each $2 and a very plain dinner it was. The pontoon bridge during the morning was partially removed to allow boats to pass. Quite a number of which [did pass], including two or three gunboats. About 4 P.M. it was put down and our train and the General and his staff rode over it into and through Shreveport to a mile the other side where we went into camp, the rain in the mean time having ceased, but the roads [were] very muddy. In camp, and tolerably comfortable. I hear tonight that Gen. Smith has made a new arrangement of our division. Gen. Drayton relieved. The two Missouri brigades constituted into a division under command of Gen. Parsons, and the two Ark. brigades into another to be commanded by Gen. Churchill. This arrangement which is probably only temporary may give rise to other changes. What effect it may have upon my position I cannot say as yet. The enemy are said to be within 40 miles of this place and advancing, so we will probably have a fight in a few days.

March 25th. Friday. Rigged out in clean clothes this morning and after breakfast rode into town with Maj. Dunlap. Called on Dr. Haden, Medical Director of the Department, and Dr. [Solomon. A.] Smith, Director of Hospitals.[14] At the office of the former met Dr. David Yandell, formerly of Louisville Ky.[15] After spending some time with Dr. Haden called at the Hospital to see Dr. [George W.] Riggins[16] and with him took dinner—a plain affair. Also met Col. William Broadwell,[17] besides met several other acquaintances. Shreveport is not as large a place as I expected, apparently not containing over 2,000 inhabitants, with not many elegant residences that I have seen yet. The steamboats at the levee look very natural to me reminding me of St. Louis on a small scale. Recieved a letter by courier from Col. John Polk and one from Dr. Bond. Remained in town until two o'clock. In the mean time our camp was moved from where we halted last night to a mile southeast of town. Here we have a comfortable location but will probably not be permitted to occupy it many days.

March 26th. Saturday. Went into town this morning. Called first at the Medical Purveyor's on business, then visited the Gunboat *Missouri* lying at the wharf—a very formidable craft, carrying 8 guns.[18] Then called on Wm. Broadwell and at his office wrote two letters to my wife which he promised to send by different routes through his brother Moses in N. York. At ½ past 3 P.M.

dined in company with Dr. Wooten and Slaughter with Dr. [George C.] Catlett formerly of St. Joseph Mo. now post surgeon.[19] He gave us a good dinner which we enjoyed very much. Capt. Charley Green, Gen. [Benjamin] Huger and others dined with us.[20] After dinner saw Dr. Haden who promised to arrange things to suit me and asked me to call tomorrow. Five o'clock returned to camp after spending a pleasant day.

March 27th. Sunday. Took a thorough bathing in camp this morning and fixed up for the day. Had many visitors and much caucasing in regard to an order reducing our transportation. All [are] trying to keep their baggage and plunder together. At 11 A.M. rode in with Dr. Wooten to church at the court house in which the Presbyterians worship. Heard a sound, logical, good sermon from the Rev. Mr. Mosley, pastor. The room is a good one and the services were orderly and reminded me of the pleasant Sabbaths at home when I was surrounded by my wife and children and in my own seat in the sanctuary—Oh for a return of those happy days. After church spoke to the minister, then called at the Medical Purveyors and Medical Directors office. At 2 P.M. [I] dined at Dr. Haden's mess with him, Dr. Yandell, Maj. [Thomas G.] Rhett,[21] and others—they live well. At 4 o'clock returned to camp. Towards evening called in the neighborhood to see Rev. Mr. Mosely and wife. He is a Missourian and his wife an old acquaintance of my brother's wife, Eliza. Maj. Cabell returned and joined us this evening—glad to welcome him back. The weather windy and disagreeable and the night dark.

March 28th. Monday. There was a review of our troops this morning by Gen. Kirby Smith which I did not attend however not wishing the trouble. Had a visit from the Rev. Mr. Marvin. [I] was glad to see him and to find that his eye is better than when I last saw him. About 11 o'clock rode into town (Shreveport) to attend diverse matters of business. While there I had my hair cut for which I paid $2, bought a bridle without bit for $11.50, halter $10, curry comb $2. I mention these as war prices. These articles were purchased from the government at cost price. Maj. Cabell who was with me bought privately a pair of spurs for which he paid $50. Returned to camp about 2 P.M. [This has been] a disagreeable day— very dusty, and tonight cloudy.

March 29th Tuesday. An excessively disagreeable day. Windy, blustery, and cold, such a day as renders camp life very unpleasant. Remained in camp all day read *The Dutch Republic.* It was too windy however to stay out of doors by our camp fire and too cold to be comfortable in tent without fire. We expected to have moved today towards the enemy and made all our arrangements accordingly, but the order did not come and of course here we remained. This evening had a visit from the Rev. Mr. Mosely. At night had quite a gathering around our camp fire discussing matters personal and public.

March 30th. Wednesday. The wind has lulled and we had the only pleasant day that we have had since arriving at Shreveport. Remained in camp all day having no business in town. Wrote a letter to my wife hearing of an opportunity of sending it by a man going to St. Louis. The remainder of the day was occupied in reading, smoking, and entertaining those who called. As I mentioned several days ago, Gen. Drayton has been relieved and ordered to Texas and two divisions formed out of one. Today, by an arrangement between Gens. Churchill and Parsons, the staff was divided by these two generals commanding divisions. This will divide our staff. I go with Gen. Churchill by choice. Drs. Wooten and Slaughter and Maj. Cabell [go] with Gen. Parsons. This arrangement will probably only be temporary.

March 31st. Thursday. Wind, wind, wind. The wind has blown a hurricane all day with clouds of dust. A much uncomfortable day in camp. This morning received an order assigning me as Chief Surgeon of Gen. Churchill's Division. Reported to the General and made arrangements while in town to get all necessary supplies for the campaign on which we are about to enter. From the Med. Purveyor got a case of amputating instruments and receipted for hospital and other supplies. At 10 A.M. a large party of officers went on board and examined the gunboat *Missouri* lying at the wharf—a formidable craft. Capt. [Jonathan H.] Carter in command exhibited to us the working of the guns, all of which was very satisfactory. Would that we had more such with which to clean out the Yankees from our rivers and harbors. Attended to diverse matters in town and returned to camp about 2 P.M. and the rest of the day endured the wind and dust as best I could. After night the wind still keeps up. Called to see Gen. Drayton. In a day or two our staff and headquarters will be broken up and the members of the staff scattered among the two new divisions.

April 1st. Friday. After breakfast rode down to Gen. Churchill's headquarters to issue orders to the brigade surgeons in reference to their monthly reports. Remained an hour with the General, while there he had a present from a lady in the neighborhood of a nice looking cake in the shape of a large heart all done up nicely in flowers. He invited me to eat it with him, but when we cut into it behold the center was filled with cotton, when we remembered that it was the first of April. On returning divided all the medical stores with Dr. Wooten. I have a large six mule wagon for transporting mine. I only need a tent to complete my outfit which I hope to get in [a] few days. Spent the evening and night at my own quarters but had quite a number of vistors. Weather more pleasant, less wind.

April 2nd. Saturday. Rode into town after breakfast in ambulance with Dr. Wooten and Maj. Tracy. [I] went first to Maj. [William H.] Haynes, Quart. Master, to get an order to have a suit of clothes cut out.[22] Got the order and went to government shop with cloth and after some little palavering had my measure taken and by 12 M. the suit was cut out for which I paid the moderate price of $3. Then took my bundles to the Hospital where by the aid of Dr. Riggins I expect to get them made by one of the inmates of that establishment and consider myself fortunate in so doing. This done called at the Med. Purveyor's where I met several acquaintances. [At] half past one [I] returned to camp. After dinner rode rode down to Gen. Churchill's Hd. Qts. where I

found several papers for me to act on and other business to transact. After dark Maj. Cabell and myself rode into town to pay Lt.
Gen. and Mrs. Kirby Smith a visit. We found them at home and
just taking coffee in the parlour. Spent an hour or more very pleasantly. Gen. Smith I have frequently met before and his wife once.
Here we met Judge Jones formerly of N.C. now on the bench in
La. and an ex-member of Congress. On leaving Gen. S's he took
us to his house where we sat with him for a couple of hours smoking and talking, with a drink of La. rum. [I] returned to camp about
11 o'clock.

April 3rd. Sunday. All is bustle and confusion in our camp this
morning in consequence of a move of our headquarters, or rather
a breaking up of the old and going to our respective new Hd.
Quarters. Packed up and loaded our wagons after breakfast and
parted company with the mess mates with which I have been so
long. Maj. Cabell and Dr. Wooten and Slaughter go to Gen.
Parsons, while I go to Gen. Churchill as Chief Surgeon of his
division. Gen. Drayton goes to Texas. His son left him last night
and intends crossing the Miss. River. About 9 A.M. having sent
my wagons, Med. stores, and servants I rode down to Gen.
Churchill's quarters and after fixing things in tent and looking
around awhile rode up with the Gen. and Lt. Sevier in ambulance
to church. As the Presbyterian minister did not preach I went to
the Episcopal Church where I heard a very moderate sermon and
for the first time in my life I communed with that church. The
invitation was broad and as we have so few opportunities in the
army of partaking in the sacrament I was anxious on this occasion
to acknowledge Christ before the world. May he give me grace
so to live that I shall not bring a reproach upon him in the profession I have made. Soon after church returned to camp. Gens.
Smith and Churchill and other officers partook of the sacrament.
I will now mess with Gen. Churchill. Weather still very windy
and horribly dusty and disagreeable. After tea [I] accompanied
Gen. Churchill and Lt. Sevier to see the ladies at Cal Watson's
who lives in the neighborhood.[23] [I] found them very agreeable
and intelligent young ladies.

April 4th. Monday. In the high wind of last night my tents blew down enveloping me in canvas. I went out in my night clothes but seeing no chance of putting it up in the high wind I concluded to grin and endure it until morning; it was just after midnight. This morning rode into town in ambulance with Dr. Duncan, but before getting back it broke down three times. The tires of three wheels came off causing us no little annoyance and delay. While in town by skillful arranging I succeeded in getting a fine new tent for myself and also 50 tin cups for hospital purposes. Attended also to diverse other matters of business and saw numerous acquaintances. Returned to camp 2 P.M. and while engaged in taking a snack, an order came to move at once which cut short my dinner. Packed up and loaded at once and started about 5 P.M. to meet the enemy, or in that direction. The brigades started about the same time and we rode at the head of the column. Marched 8 miles being about 10 miles from Shreveport and went into camp after dark just beyond where Gen. Parsons' command was camped, and after taking supper spread our beds and retired surrounded by troops.

April 5th. Tuesday. Was awoke at 3 A.M. this morning by reveille and at once got up and dressed. Took breakfast at 4 and at ½ past 4 before the break of day mounted my horse and moved with the Gen. at the head of the column. The morning was calm and pleasant though cool. Rode 15 miles over good road to Keachi, La. where we arrived before 9 A.M. Here we halted and when our wagons came up which was a couple of hours later pitched our tents just in the edge of town. One of the divisions encamping on either side of the town. Having received my new tent I stretched it for the first time. It is a very large elegant tent and is vastly comfortable. I consider myself very fortunate in getting it. Maj. Cabell, Dr. Slaughter, and Capt. Thomas came by and paid me a visit. Soon after getting into camp was called on by Dr. Polk a refugee from Miss., now residing here but a native of N.C. who invited Gen. Churchill and myself to dine with him at 2 o'clock. Accordingly at that hour we went accompanied by Maj. Cabell and Capt. Thomas, and enjoyed his hospitality in the shape of a good dinner preceded by a mint julip. On arriving here Gen. C[hurchill] reported by letter to Gen. [Richard] Taylor 20 miles off at Mansfield and we now await his orders. The evening and night passed off quietly.

April 6th. Wednesday. Still at Keachi. Gen. Churchill started at an early hour this morning to Mansfield 20 miles off to see Gen. Taylor and returned this afternoon. Spent the day in my magnificent pavilion, reading, smoking, and sleeping. Was visited by several of the surgeons of the division on business. Took advantage of our stay here to get an office desk made, and was fortunate enough to meet with a carpenter shop with a negro for a workman, who after diverse explanations made me such a desk as I wanted. I am now well fixed up. After supper went over to Dr. Polk's to visit his family and also Mrs. Gen. Tappan who arrived this evening to join her husband. The day has been pleasant.

April 7th. Thursday. At 10 o'clock this morning rode out with Gen. Churchill to Gen. Tappan's camp to review the troops of the latter. The review went off well. We rode around rapidly. The troops marched and appeared well, and quite a number of ladies and citizens were present. On returning from the review found Maj. Cabell and Col. [Aaron H.] Conrow M[ember of] C[ongress] from Mo. at our camp,[24] they remained and dined with us on a fine turkey and after dinner Gen. Tappan, Dr. [Thomas G.] Polk,[25] Col. [Lucien C.] Gause,[26] and others also called when we sent 3 miles in the country and got some ice and mint and had an iced mint julip. After dark it commenced raining. Nine o'clock tonight a courier arrived from Gen. Taylor ordering us to hold ourselves in readiness to move at early dawn. So we may be off in the morning.

April 8th. Friday. Today has been set apart by Pres. Davis as a day of fasting, humiliation, and prayer throughout the Confederacy, and our people are praying for the success of our cause—may God in mercy answer them. I have endeavored to observe the day as best I could under the circumstances. Another courier arrived at one o'clock last night ordering our army to start at daylight for Mansfield, La. 20 miles off. Arose before day took no breakfast save a cup of coffee and at sunrise started with Gen. Churchill on our march, the troops having previously started. By 10 o'clock we marched ten miles and rested temporarily in a magnolia grove. Here a courier met us from Gen. Taylor urging us to push on as rapidly as possible. In less than half an hour another and still another met us saying that a fight was progressing and we were needed. After a short rest the whole column started and arrived at Mansfield about 2 P.M. making the days march from Keachi to Mansfield 20 miles. On arriving General C[hurchill] reported at Gen. Taylor's Hd. Qts. Gen. T[appan], however, was on the field.

The Battle of Mansfield. At Gen. Taylor's quarters we received orders to proceed one mile out on the Stony Point Road and there await orders. Here we rested and hard bread was distributed among our troops who were tired and hungry. While here the roar of artillery and musketry was heard on the Pleasant Hill Road at a distance of some 5 or 6 miles and from the perpetual peal it was evident that a desperate conflict was going on between our forces under Gen. Taylor and the Yankees under Gen. [Nathaniel P] Banks.[27] I could but feel that it was a good day for us to fight when our people throughout the Confederacy were praying for our success, and so it turned out the news soon came in that we were driving the Yankees capturing many prisoners, wagons, ambulances, etc, etc. Our division was not needed and we were not ordered into the fight but 3 miles further on the same road to camp. On going back into town late in the evening to get my medical supplies in readiness for the morrow I witnessed the gratifying sight of seeing some 1200 federal prisoners in one group, just brought in from the field. It was a glorious victory, the Yankees were completely routed and fled in great confusion. The Battle of Mansfield will in all time be regarded as one of the most brilliant victories of the war.[28] We whipped them with a number one third less and captured 2000 prisoners and 200 wagons loaded with stores and other things innumerable. We lost, however, many valuable lives among others Gen. [Alfred] Mouton of La.[29] Thank God for the victory of this good day. I returned to camp after dark and took a cold snack and then laid down under a tree and slept a few hours, our train being all in the rear.

April 9th. Saturday. Ride over the Battlefield of Mansfield—The Battle of Pleasant Hill. An order came at 1 o'clock for us to start at 3 A.M. so promptly to the hour we were on the march having just taken a bite only of cold food. By the aid of a guide we crossed over from the Rocky Point to the Pleasant Hill Road five miles. On coming into the latter road we got on the battlefield of the evening before and in the woods and along the roads were evidence enough of the terribleness of the conflict, dead Yankees and horses, guns, cartridge boxes, sabres, etc., etc., were seen in all directions. Went a mile or two further on the Pleasant Hill Road and drew up in line of battle, but hardly had the line been formed when Gen. Taylor rode up rapidly and ordered us to advance, [saying] that he "had heard news" the Yankees were in full retreat. So after allowing several thousand Texas Cavalry to pass in hot pursuit of the fleeing Yankees, our infantry also pushed on. During the march for the next 12 miles such a sight I never beheld, such gratifying evidence of the utter rout and precipitate retreat. I cannot now do justice to the subject. The bodies of dead Yankees were numerous for the first 3 or 4 miles and all the way dead horses, broken wagons, ambulances, thousands of muskets and rifles, sabres, bayonets, and all manners of implements of war were scattered in every direction. Trunks, wearing apparel, knapsacks, cooking utensils, and something of almost everything else were scattered along the road and in the woods, showing that the Yankees fled in a panic throwing away all their supplies. Our captures were very great and our soldiers supplied themselves with many things that they needed. It was a glorious sight. The Yankees were retreating all night and went into Pleasant Hill 20 miles from Mansfield. We pushed on to within 3 miles of that place where we arrived about 12 M. Here we rested several hours. The Yankees our scouts reported were making a stand at Pleasant Hill. We ate nothing today. About 3 P.M. Gen Churchill in command of his own and Gen. Parsons' Division started and marched across

to the Fort Jessup Road to take position on our extreme right, it
being our intention to attack the enemy. Gens. Walker, [Camille
Armand] Polignac,[30] [Tom] Green,[31] and others occupying the
center and left wing. It was 5 o'clock before we got into position.
In the rear of the line of battle I selected my site for a field infirmary, and made every necessary arrangement for attending to the
wounded, gave directions to surgeons and asst. surgeons, etc., etc.
A few moments after 5 P.M. the attack commenced and soon
became terrific. The wounded began to be brought in and I
became busy in looking after them. As the firing became more
continuous and more terrible, Confederate and Federal wounded
were brought to the rear. The news from the field of battle was
that we were driving the enemy and soon some 200 or 300
Yankee prisoners passed by. I was in high spirits and dressed
wounds with alacrity, but soon another and different report came
and I was startled by the announcement that our lines were broken and our army falling back at all points. This took me by surprise and filled me with distress. The fact is that our army after
the most gallant fighting were outnumbered and outflanked by
the enemy and had to fall back which they did in great confusion.
It is said that the Missourians broke first and soon the whole line
gave way. I shall not attempt to describe the scene. A complete
panic and stampede defies description.[32] I soon saw that I would
have to abandon the hospital or fall into the hands of the Yankees
as I thought—so the wounded were put into ambulances and
every other available vehicle and sent back. I remained until all
our wounded save 2 or 3 Federals were sent off and then detailed
a surgeon to look after them.[33] It was near night when Maj. [James
Knox] Campbell[34] rode up and told me that if I longer delayed I
would be a prisoner so I determined to go. In going to my horse
I found that my orderly had run off taking my overcoat and blanket but leaving my horse, which I mounted with my amputating
case under my arm. On riding along the road minie balls were
whistling all around me and one or two near were struck. Maj.
Campbell now suggested that safety required us to take to the
woods, which we did and such a ride I never had; such a scene I
never witnessed and hope never to see again. [We] rode through

the woods and bushes for 5 miles and in the dark, then came into
a road that we did not know, but rode on until 10 P.M. when we
were about 10 miles from the battlefield. Tired, my horse jaded,
hungry, and thirsty, Maj. Campbell and myself holed up in a barn
lot by the road side. Here we got feed for our horses, built a fire,
and laid down in the lot with nothing to cover us but our saddle
blankets (and the night was chilly). Here we slept until daylight
with groups of soldiers all around us and having passed hundreds
on the road. Thus ended the day ingloriously to us as it seemed
to me then, but there is a sequel not so inglorious as will appear
from what follows.

April 10th. Sunday. This is the Sabbath but I scarcely knew it.
Arose by daylight, saddled my horse, and started to get to our
command. In going across the country several miles from where
I started came up with Gen. Parsons, Col. [Joseph H.] Kelly,[35]
and others at the house of Gen. ———— whose wife gave us a fine
breakfast—the first meal for me in 30 hours. After breakfast rode
6 miles with Gen. P[olignac] over to the "Mill" on the Mansfield
Road where Gen. Taylor had his Hd. Qts. On arriving was gratified to learn the Yankees, not knowing the advantage they gained
over us the evening before, had retreated during the night leaving their dead and wounded on the field and a part of our army
holding possession of the battlefield so that instead of being badly
routed we have all the advantages of a substantial victory, and our
cavalry are pushing on in pursuit of the fleeing foe. On joining
Gen. Churchill I found him just on the eve of going to the front
and visiting the battleground 8 miles off. I accompanied him. On
the way we constantly met groups of Yankee prisoners being
brought in by our cavalry amounting to several hundred. I rode
all over the battlefield. It was sad to see the dead on both sides
lying all cold and ghastly on the ground; the Yankees however,
greatly outnumbering our dead. But I will not attempt a description of this scene. I went also to the field infirmary. It did not fall
into the hands of the enemy as I thought it would. I also went
into the hospital in Pleasant Hill to look after our wounded. Here
I found most of our surgeons at work, and the wounded being

brought in from the field. Remained in discharge of medical duties until late in the evening and then rode back with Dr. Wooten to camp, 8 miles. [I] found them all at the "Mill." Took a snack and spread my blanket on the ground without tent and slept soundly.

April 11th. Monday. Of the startling events and horrid sights of the past few days I can not pretend even to give a synopsis. Slept last night at the "Mill" 8 miles from Pleasant Hill in the open air. After an early breakfast rode down to Pleasant Hill with Dr. Wooten to see our wounded. Remained there until 4 P.M. busy all the time in amputating limbs, adjusting fractures, elevating depressed skulls, and etc., etc.[36] All the slightly wounded were sent off to Mansfield. After making our own wounded as comfortable as the nature of the cases would admit, I visit[ed] the two hospitals where the Federal wounded are. [I] found a large number, some 200, with only one Yankee surgeon to attend to them. Our surgeons, however, are rendering him all the assistance in their power. Most of them are severely wounded and many of them will never return home again. They came here to butcher our people and got butchered themselves. On the outside of the hospital I counted 17 dead bodies of Yankees unburied lying in the sun. At 4 P.M. started for camp on the way met Dr. Yandell, Drs. [Joseph T.] Scott, [P. O.] Hooper, and Lawrence,[37] on their way down to assist in attending to the wounded, but Dr. Wooten and myself assisted by the surgeons of our respective divisions had already done most of the work. Instead of having 8 miles to ride back we had 20 as since we left camp the command has moved back near Mansfield near the camp that we left on the 9th. Arrived about 8 P.M. found my tent up and occupied. Maj. [Henry M.] Clark spent the night with me.[38]

April 12th. Tuesday. After breakfast rode into Mansfield with Gen. Churchill. [I] first called at Gen. Taylor's Hd. Qts. where we remained a while and saw several acquaintances. Afterwards [I] rode a mile on the other side of town to see Capt. Ben Johnson, Gen. Churchill's Adjutant General, a gallant young officer who was wounded in the left arm in the late battle. Found him comfortable.

Visited the general hospital and other smaller hospitals. [I] found them all crowded with the wounded from the two late battles. There are hundreds of these poor fellows. It makes me sad to behold them, but everything is being done that can be done to make them comfortable. Returned to camp (4 miles from town) just in time for dinner. Maj. [D. Herndon] Lindsay dined with us.[39] This evening received a new suit of clothes that I left in Shreveport to be made. [They were] sent by Dr. Riggins [and] they fit very well. I am now well off in clothes. All quiet, but expecting to move soon.

April 13th. Wednesday. Was engaged all day until late this evening in the various hospitals in Mansfield in attending to and making our wounded comfortable. After hard work I succeeded in getting everyone of the wounded belonging to our division placed on a matress and pillow. Besides this I attended to the wants of other wounded. The ladies of the town and country are very kind and very attentive. The hospitals present a sad picture. This afternoon met with a relative of mine Dr. W. A. McPheeters of the famous Cresent Regiment of La.[40] Also met with a Federal surgeon from Iowa who attended lectures in our college in St. Louis and knew me. He is not strongly imbued with Lincolnism and among other things told me that we had come nearer *conquering* those of them who had fallen into our hands by the kindness we had shown them than we could in any other way!! Our cavalry have been fighting the enemy on Red River yesterday and today, attacking their gunboats and transports. The news this evening is that they are playing wild with the Yankees and butchering them terribly. The only one reported killed on our side is Brig. Gen. Green of the Texas Cavalry—a sad loss. Having whipped the Yankees in La. and driven back and defeated Banks' grand expedition we will now turn our attention to Gen. Steele in Ark. and to that end start in the morning at daylight for Shreveport en route for Arkansas. God grant that we may be as successful there as we have been here and that the department may be rid of Yankees.

April 14th. Thursday. Left our camp 4 miles out from Mansfield La. a little after daylight this morning on the Kinston Road for

Shreveport. Gen. Churchill's Division in advance, Gen. Parsons' following on the same road and Gen. Walker's taking the middle road. My labors of yesterday and the day before have rendered all our wounded comfortable so that in going off I leave nothing unattended to. The road on the march was very dusty, but keeping at the head of the column we were enabled to avoid most of it. [Our army] passed through Kinston, a one horse village, and came on some 14 miles, making our march 17 miles and camped near a large bayou, making our Hd. Qts. in a church hard by—a Baptist church I think from the indications—a very good building, the use of which supercedes the necessity of putting up tents. Arrived about 10 A.M. our train coming up about 2 P.M. In the meantime indulged in a nap stretched out on the benches with the Bible for a pillow. Weather cloudy and pleasant, not hot. On our march we passed Gen. Polignac's command some 6 miles from Mansfield. He is a Frenchman, a prince, connected with Louis Napoleon, who has come over to help us in our struggle and has just been promoted to a Maj. Gen. He fought gallantly in the battle on the 8th.

April 15th. Friday. Arose at 3 A.M. this morning, took breakfast before day and started off by daylight. Gen. Parsons went forward today and we were somewhat delayed in consequence both in starting and on the march. Came up also during the day with Gen. Walker's Division and long train, which also delayed us. Marched 24 miles to Shreveport and encamped on the same spot that I left some 10 days ago. Went into town to see the Medical Purveyor's on business but found him (Dr. [Henry C.] Rogers) too much in liquor to do business.[41] Returned to camp late and ate a hearty dinner having taken nothing since before day. Weather cool and clean. Tired and sleepy—will retire.

April 16th. Saturday. Arose about 3 this morning and got under way a little after daylight. Came into Shreveport and was detained there for a short time in seeing to getting supplies and etc., etc. Crossed over the pontoon bridge and took the road for Camden to intercept Gen. [Frederick] Steele in his retreat on that place.[42] Our campaign in La. has been eminently successful and now we turn our attention to Arkansas. On the way met Col. John Polk who informed me that his wife was staying some few miles ahead, whereupon I called by and paid her a short visit. Gen. Walker's and Gen. Parsons' Divisions are also on the march for Camden making in all some 10,000 infantry with which I trust we will be able to drive the Yankees before us. At Benton, 14 miles from Shreveport, where we stopped for the troops to get up, Lt. Gen. E. Kirby Smith passed us on his way to Ark. also. Came 4 miles from Benton and camped near Mr. Dixon at which place Mrs. Snead is staying. After tea [I] called over to see her with Gen. Churchill and spent an hour with her very pleasantly. Mrs. Tappan was also there. The band came over too and serenaded the ladies.

April 17th. Sunday. A Sabbath on a march is but a compensation for the quiet and delight of a Sabbath at home and in time of peace. As usual arose at 3 A.M. this morning and got underway at early dawn. Got off our Hd. Qts. train in advance of the troops. This has been the warmest day that we have had yet and quite dusty, though riding ahead of the column avoided much of this. Passed through Collinsburg [La.] and came on 17 miles where we went into camp near Dr. [J. M.] Standish's.[43] Three miles from where we started passed the house where Mrs. Col. Clay Taylor is staying and having a letter to her from her husband I called by for a moment to see her. She was not up but I talked to her through the crack of the door. Just as we were going into camp Dr. Standish came over and invited Gen. Churchill, Lt. Sevier, and myself to his house to dinner and as it was near by we went. He lives in elegant style [and] gave us a good dinner. [He] has 3 handsome, intelligent, and sprightly daughters who made themselves very agreeable. All together it was a pleasant visit and one of those delightful episodes in a soldier's life. Returned to camp at 4 P.M. Read several chapters in the Bible and tried to remember that it was the Sabbath.

April 18th. Monday. Got off as usual at daylight this morning. After coming 10 miles had to cross the Bodcaw [Creek] in a flat boat which detained us some time. We, however, got into camp in good time. Got out my desk and commenced making out my report of the late battles, which I completed and have it now ready to send forward. In our division we had 24 killed and 113 wounded. Maj. Snead called by this afternoon on his way to Shreveport and gave us the news from Gen. Price. The Yankees are in Camden. I hope that we will be able to dislodge them. The day has been very pleasant. I am glad to get my report off my hands.

April 19th. Tuesday. Camped last night on the edge of Arkansas, having marched out of Louisiana after a most successful campaign. Got off just as day was breaking this morning and marched 22 miles to Magnolia, half a mile beyond which we camped. Here we receive the gratifying intelligence that on yesterday Gen. Price attacked a foraging party of the Yankees some 18 miles from Camden with a heavy guard, capturing some 200 wagons and killing a large number of the enemy.[44] The day has been pleasant [and] we are getting on finely in our march. [We are] ahead of the other columns, and will probably join Gen. Price tomorrow or the day following. Sent my report of the Battle of Pleasant Hill off today accompanied by a letter to Dr. Yandell. Having to get up at 3 o'clock in the morning and nothing to keep us up at night we retire early and sleep soundly.

April 20th. Wednesday. Arose at the usual hour while on march and after breakfast and sending our head quarters train forward, Gen. Churchill and his staff rode back into Magnolia to see the columns pass through, which they did in good style. After which we took up the line of march and passed the troops again and rode 12 miles where we came up with Gen. Kirby Smith and his staff on the roadside. Here we remained two hours and then came on 6 miles further where we went into camp and where I hope that we will be permitted to rest the troops at least for one day. Gen. Parsons' and Walker's Divisions have not yet come up. After getting dinner wrote a letter to my beloved wife and sent it to Shreveport to be sent to Moses Broadwell in N.Y. and thence to St. Louis—may she receive it. I propose tonight to luxuriate in a thorough spring bath and wash off the dust of the last two weeks march. We camp tonight in 19 miles of Camden and of course to the Yankees.

April 21st. Thursday. Remained quietly in camp all morning and until 1 o'clock when just about to sit down to dinner an order came from Gen. Price to whom we now report ordering us to move forward within 10 miles of Camden. So in half an hour we were packed up and ready for the march and soon were underway. Came 6 miles to the Seminary and went 2 miles beyond where [we] camped. On the way had a shower of rain. Nothing of interest today.

April 22nd. Friday. Took up the line of march at an early hour this morning and came some ten miles and took a position within nine miles of Camden on the Woodlawn Road. The command is some half mile in advance of our headquarters in a good position for battle should the enemy come out. We have all the roads picketed and other commands are posted on the roads so that we are gradually investing Gen. Steele. Got into camp early. Was visited by several of the brigade surgeons and made preliminary arrangements for an engagement. We will probably have hot work in a few days. God grant us success.

April 23rd. Saturday. This day two weeks ago the Battle of Pleasant Hill took place, the scenes of which I shall never forget. Today we remained quietly in camp until about one o'clock when an order came directing us to move immediately forward to within two and a half miles of Camden. Immediately all was activity and in half an hour the whole division was in motion and after a march of 7 miles in two hours we reached the point indicated. Here we met Gen. Price and staff, and simultaneously with our own arrival Gen. Parsons' Division came up on another road and both moved forward one mile to a bridge where the enemy's pickets were in force. About this time Gen. Kirby Smith rode up and in a short time a brisk artillery fire was opened on the enemy's pickets. For a while everything looked like a battle, but it was a demonstration to cover a movement of our cavalry in another quarter. After some 30 or 40 shots and the enemy not replying but skedadling, our troops withdrew and the skirmish ended. It was now late in the evening and we started back to camp. Simultaneously with the march of the troops our baggage train had been across to Buena Vista on the Seminary road and to that place we returned. It was after dark before we arrived. Took up our quarters for the night in a vacant house. Gen. Churchill bunked with me on my mattress. The afternoon and night was quite cold and inclined to rain.

April 24th. Sunday. An alarm was given this morning by a report coming in that our pickets were warmly engaged just in front. Immediately the troops were under arms and in line of battle and baggage was packed and Gen. Churchill rode to the front. It proved, however, to be a mistake and all arose from the regiment of Choctaw Indians shooting hogs turned over to them for rations.[45] About 9 A.M. rode over with Gen. C. four miles to Gen. Price's Hd. Qts. Here [I] saw him and all my former associates, and Dr. Haden, and Yandell just from Shreveport. Dr. Wooten who has just been announced as Med. Director of the District of Ark. instead of Dr. Cunningham, who at his request has gone to Va. I saw and congratulated him. Maj. Snead informed me that his wife had heard from St. Louis as late as April 1st. and that my beloved wife and children were well. Thank God for this. I have great and constant cause for profound gratitude! Lord give me a greatful heart for all thy blessings. No preaching today. The enemy just in front. All is watchfulness.

April 25th. Monday. Today and yesterday are the only days that our army have rested since we left Mansfield, La. On the march down and up we went 250 miles averaging daily 20 miles and fighting a battle in the meantime. This is good marching for infantry. Spent the day in official duties, in looking after the wants of the division, getting in and forwarding requisitions, and reading the *History of the Dutch Republic.* This afternoon news came in from the cavalry that our pickets had been driven in by the enemy on several roads and the troops were ordered to be in a state of readiness. Later it was stated that a big smoke was seen in the direction of Camden. Perhaps the Yankees may be on the eve of leaving that place and taking the back track—we shall see. Drs. Taylor and Smith from Gen's Price and Marmaduke's Head Qts. came over and took tea with us. After dark Gen. Tappan's band gave us a serenade.

April 26th. Tuesday. Passed the day quietly in camp. No picket fighting or other excitement, but all quiet in front. Made arrangements for establishing a division hospital to provide for our sick. Day quite warm. Finished the second volume of the *Dutch Republic.* A dispatch was received this evening giving an account of another victory of our cavalry in La. over Bank's army 30 miles below Nachitoches. That army is thoroughly demoralized. Gen. Steele has made no demonstrations today, nor have we.

April 27th. Wednesday. Soon after breakfast this morning we received the gratifying intelligence through Gen. [Samuel Bell] Maxey of the Cavalry,[46] that Camden had been evacuated by the Yankees during yesterday evening, last night, and this morning. Soon after we received the additional tidings of another victory of ours arms—Gen. Fagan with his cavalry on the other side of the Ouachita River has defeated the enemy, taken 300 wagons, 1000 prisoners, 7 pieces of artillery, and killed and wounded 500.[47] This is glorious and no doubt led to Gen. Steele's retreat. Anticipating an order to push forward, I arranged for all the sick of the division and made all necessary provisions for their comfort. Soon the order to move came and at one o'clock the whole command started for Camden, 11 miles. Weather very hot. Arrived in Camden about ½ past 4 [P.M.]. [The] citizens [were] delighted to see us. Yankees all gone with a big scare on them. Camped in edge of the town. As we passed through ladies waved their handkerchiefs and all came out to see and welcome us. Took a late supper. This is written in [my] tent after all have retired.

April 28th. Thursday. An order was received late last night to have two days rations cooked, to leave the wagons, artillery, and all sick and sore-footed who are not able to stand hard marching, and to start at 6 o'clock A.M. Artillery and train to come on as soon as the pontoon bridge is brought up. Arose by daylight and after taking a refreshing cup of coffee started off to look after the sick of the division. Left a surgeon to see that all those left are properly housed and cared for, and then went to the river where the army was crossing. The Yankees took their pontoon and of course left the Ouachita River between them and us, without the means of crossing. During the night a footway was constructed by means of which the soldiers went over in single file. Of course it was a slow process and there was a great jam—Majors, Brigadier Generals, Colonels, and other officers in large numbers. It was 9 o'clock before the troops crossed. Our horses were crossed in a flat boat. About 10 A.M. we fairly got underway in pursuit of the fleeing Yankees. The whole road over which we traveled afforded unequivocal signs of perturbation on the part of the Yankees. The whole road was strewn with old boots, shoes, overcoats, blankets, pantaloons, and every other article of dress, and various other things, besides tents, wagons, and other camp equipage were left half-burned showing that they were anxious to get rid of all unnecessary baggage in their flight. It was a gratifying sight for an enemy who advanced with so much confidence and boasting that they would march unopposed through the country and take possession of the Trans-Miss Department. Truly God has been gracious to us. Gen. Kirby Smith passed us on the way, Gen. Price being in advance. We came 14 miles on the Princeton Road and went into camp at 4 P.M. Took a cup of coffee and a cold lunch. [I] will sleep under a tree tonight and go on in pursuit of Yankees at daylight.

April 29th. Friday. We were ordered to march this morning at 3 A.M.; consequently, had to get up at 2 o'clock after a nap under a tree. But in consequence of having to go in the rear of Gen. Walker's Division who were slow in moving, we did not get off until after three o'clock and were all day detained by the troops in advance. Passed through Princeton about 3 P.M. in a hard rain and came out 8 miles beyond in the neighborhood of Tulip but on a different road. It was near night when we went into camp without tents, in the rain, and with scant rations, having come 26 miles. Orders to march again at 12 o'clock M. I slept the short time allotted to that occupation on the seat of an ambulance covered by an oilcloth to keep the rain off. This business of forced marches in pursuit of an enemy and without a train is rather rough business, but all bear it cheerfully.

***April 30th. Saturday. Battle of the Saline River* [Jenkins' Ferry].**[48] Took up the line of march promptly at midnight—dark, rainy, and very muddy, altogether a horrible march and truly do I pity and admire the poor private who foots it through the mud and mire and water uncomplainingly. Gen. Kirby Smith passed us on the road and we came up with Gen. Price and all pushed on to Jenkins' Ferry over the Saline where the enemy was supposed to be engaged in crossing the river. Arrived within 3 miles of the ferry about 7 A.M. Supposing that only a small part of the enemy's force was on this side of the river, Gen. Churchill's Division was at once sent forward to attack them. The cavalry having been skirmishing all morning and at 8 o'clock the battle began [with] only Churchill's Division and the cavalry being engaged. It was soon discovered, however, that instead of a small portion of his army, Gen. Steele had his whole force on this side for the fight opened hotly and increased in fury. Gallantly did Churchill and his men charge and drive the enemy, and for 2 hours and a half they bore the brunt of the battle at which time Parsons' Division was ordered in double quick, and finally Walker's Division was also sent in and the engagement became general. The fighting was very, very heavy and such volleys of musketry and so continuous for hours I never heard. Reports came back that we were not only holding our own but slowly driving the enemy, still I felt extreme anxiety until the battle was decided. This, however, did not prevent me from exerting myself to the utmost to make provisions for our wounded. Selected a house in the rear for a hospital then rode to the front to send ambulances and infirmary corps on the field and to see that they went forward. Our wounded now came in large numbers and with the other surgeons I went to work at the hospital taking off legs and arms and directing things generally. About 12 M. the enemy drew off and crossed the river having been fairly whipped after an obstinate fight on their part—leaving their dead and wounded in our hands, their pontoon bridge, and destroying large numbers of wagons. The Yankees had no artillery in the fight and the ground was such that ours could not act with efficiency, so that the battle was fought and won with small arms. Our victory cost us the lives of many valuable and patriotic officers—Gen. [William R.] Scurry of Texas mortally wounded,[49] Col. [Hiram L.] Grinstead[50] and [Col. John B.] Cocke[51] of our division killed on the field and many, many others. As soon as I could be spared from the hospital I rode over the battlefield with Dr. Swindell and visited the Federal hospital. The battlefield was the valley of the Saline and it had been raining and it was a perfect quagmire for miles. It is almost incredible how men could wade through such mud and water and fight as they did. The battlefield presented a sad picture, dead officers and men lying in all directions, horses scattered here and there, and further on dead and wounded Yankees.[52] It was a dreadful sight, officers and men that a few hours before I had seen and talked with now lying cold and ghastly on the ground—War is a dreadful thing.[53] At the Federal hospital I saw over 100 wounded, the rest they took off.[54] After going over the field and seeing that our wounded were removed, I returned to the hospital and there worked hard until night when exhausted and with the worst headache I ever had, having ate nothing all day. I went to camp hard by and then after some mutton broiled on the coals without bread I went to bed on the ground and tried to sleep, but could not for a long time so violently did my head ache; however, I got through the night though very uncomfortably after an eventful and never to be forgotten day.[55]

May 1st. Sunday. Returned to the hospital after getting a snack of cornbread and sheep and then went to work again. [I] will not attempt to describe the scene there—200 horribly wounded at least in the house and out of doors. It was a sight that beggars description. Let those who prate about the glories of war witness such a scene and then talk of glory—this is the sad part of the picture. At 10 A.M. the command moved up to Tulip, I remained

behind of course. All day long until late in the evening I was operating, taking off arms and legs and whatever else was needed to
be done. I never took off so many in one day before. [I'm] sorry
that it was necessary to remove so many.[56] Late in the evening
after all the operating necessary to be preformed had been completed, I started for Tulip to make preparations for removing our
wounded to that place. On the way up (8 miles) found the roads
very bad and all along encountered the cavalry. Arrived at camp
about dark, too late to go into Tulip tonight so took a snack and
went to ground and blanket after a day of disagreeable labor.

May 2nd. Monday. Went into Tulip after an early breakfast. At
Gen. Price's Hd. Qts. saw Dr. Wooten and Taylor about making
arrangements for our wounded. Saw the General, Maj. Cabell and
many others, all have much to say about the recent fight. Selected
a church for our hospital and had bunks made, etc., etc. After dinner went again to Tulip and completed arrangements for our
wounded with which I am well pleased—left all necessary hospital
stores. Saw many officers and friends. Our army moves at daylight
for Camden there to get up supplies and out at the Yankees again.
Having left Surgeons to attend to our wounded I will go on with
the command. Have worked hard and faithfully for the past few
days to get our wounded fixed up and have the satisfaction to know
that I have succeeded. Today by special act of the Confederate
Congress we hold an election for members of Congress from
Missouri. The election was held in all the Mo. Brigades and all soldiers from Mo. and citizens expelled have a right to vote. I voted
in Gen. Parsons' camp, voting for Thos. L. Snead as the representative from St. Louis—he will no doubt be elected.[57]

May 3rd. Tuesday. Agreeable to orders we started on our march at
daylight on our return to Camden. On the way stopped at Gen.
Price's Hd. Qts. in Tulip [and] saw the General, Snead, Dr.
Wooten, and others. Then called with Gen. Churchill at our two
hospitals to see after our wounded. Found them as comfortable as
could be expected. I have left Dr. Parsons in charge of our
wounded.[58] After visiting the hospitals started on to overtake the

command. Gen. Price came on today also. Rode 8 miles to Princeton and passing through came on six miles beyond where we went into camp in a comfortable place. Reached camp at ½ past 10 o'clock and the train came up two hours afterwards. Marching and counter marching has been the order of each day since the opening of the spring campaign. We have marched 300 miles and fought two pitched battles in both of which we whipped the enemy after a hard fight, but both were decided victories. I have stood the fatigue and hardships of the campaign as well as anyone in the army. Slept out of doors, gone without food, rode through rain, for all of which I thank God for giving me health and strength.

May 4th. Wednesday. The events of today are soon recorded. Broke up camp and commenced the march at sunrise—a delightful morning—came 14 miles and went into camp 13 miles from Camden—Tomorrow, "Deo Volente," we go in. We are taking it by slow marches, our men having been on forced marches so long that they are wearied and tired and need rest. For the last month we have averaged from 19 to 26 miles a day and fought two pitched battles 200 miles apart. This evening Drs. Wooten and Slaughter came by and stayed a short time, just from the hospital at Tulip. They report our wounded comfortable and doing well. After getting into camp read the Bible and then the *Dutch Republic.*

May 5th. Thursday. In Camden. Arose at daylight and started on the march at sunrise. Rode 13 miles and came into Camden by 8 A.M. Came on what is known as the Lone Pine Ferry Road and crossed on the pontoon bridge. All the way the vandalism of the Yankees may be seen in the ruins of dwellings burned to the ground and a general destruction of property. Indeed this has been the case everywhere when we have followed in the path taken by this so-called "Union Army." These fiends in human shape have literally carried fire and sword wherever they have been. Standing crops have been destroyed, houses burned down, cattle killed, and a defenseless people, women and children, turned out of doors, robbed of their substance, and literally beggard; and yet, these are the hypothetical scoundrels who pretend to be fighting for the restoration of a once honored, and now dispersed and abhorred union, as though the people of the South with such evidence of Yankee barbarity everywhere before them could ever consent to live with such a set of vandals. On coming into town called at Gen. Price's head quarters and after remaining awhile and seeing him and numerous acquaintances came out one mile from town to what is known as the Whitfield House which Gen. Churchill took for his Hd. Quarters. Here we are comfortable in a good house. I took a room and soon made it habitable by placing in it my cot, desk, and etc. Here we will probably remain awhile. Spent the day quietly and agreeably, reading and etc., and tonight sleep in a house—the first for a long while.

May 6th. Friday—Camden Ark. Rode into town this morning after breakfast with Gen. Churchill. Called first at Gen. Kirby Smith's headquarters and then at Gen. Price's. At the former place saw Dr. Yandell and others. Called also to see Maj. Dunlap who was wounded in the late fight. Took a toddy with Maj. Hill [and] met Dr. Haden, Col. Bass,[59] and others. On my way out paid Mrs. Clay Taylor a visit. During the afternoon [I] was engaged in writing orders to the brigades for reports and in making out my report of the killed and wounded in the late engagement of the division. Day pleasant and passed off quietly.

May 7th. Saturday. Spent the day in quarters. Was very busy all morning in making out my report of the killed and wounded of the late battle at Jenkins' Ferry just one week ago today. It follows: Churchill's Division; killed 65, severely wounded 143, slightly wounded 116, total 324. Was also engaged in preparing other official documents. Had a visit from Mr. Garrett of St. Louis, of the firm of Tealman, Robinson, and Co. He was known in St. Louis as a southern man and was twice imprisoned by the Yankees for his "secesh" proclivities, but he is now here a prisoner on parole in our hands. He came with Steele's army to speculate in cotton and was taken by our cavalry while returning with a train of 300 wagons to Little Rock, which was captured. Thus the hope of gain demoralizes and seduces our friends from their principles—

a dirty business this trading in cotton with the enemy. Spent a portion of the afternoon in reading. Would that I could see my dear wife and children tonight. God bless and watch over them. Oh for a reunion with them.

May 8th. Sunday. After breakfast rode over to church and as there was no service in the Presbyterian Church went to the Episcopal where I heard a very appropriate sermon. After service called with Gen. Churchill to see Mrs. Bruce and Mrs. Col. Polk, also called to see Drs. Wooten and Slaughter. At 3 o'clock dined with Maj. Hill where I met Gov. [Trusten] Polk for the first time since his release from his imprisonment by the Yankees.[60] After returning home wrote a long letter to my brother, Alexander. After tea rode into town to see Mrs. Clay Taylor and Mrs. Gen. Tappan. From indications today I think it almost certain that we will be ordered again to Louisiana and that very soon.

May 9th. Monday. Was engaged all the morning in writing official letters, making out reports, and in preparing for our expected march to Louisiana. Gen. Smith left for Shreveport today, but prior to going he promoted Gen. Churchill to the rank of Maj. General to date from the Battle of Jenkins' Ferry. This is a well-deserved tribute and I am glad of it. He also promoted to the same ranks Gens. Parsons, Fagan, and Marmaduke. To Maj., Capt. Ben Johnson, and to Capt., Lt. Sevier both of Gen. Churchill's staff and both gallant young men. A cloudy, rainy day. This afternoon rode into town transacted some business, called to see several gentlemen, and then visited Mrs. Snead. After tea wrote a letter to my beloved wife to send by Mr. Garrett when he is exchanged—would that I could write freely and unreservedly. Also wrote to Dr. Yandell and others. A dark and rainy night. We do not, however, move tomorrow.

CHAPTER 7

A Summer's Respite, 1864

He makes me to lie down in green pastures.

It was clear to McPheeters and the other Trans-Mississippi Confederates that they had accomplished an astonishing feat in April 1864. In Louisiana, Maj. Gen. Nathaniel Banks and his thirty thousand Federals had been repulsed. In Arkansas, Maj. Gen. Frederick Steele and his battered blue column skedaddled back to Little Rock. Luck, gumption, and the miscues of their opponents had allowed the rag-tag columns of Lt. Gen. Edmund Kirby Smith, Maj. Gen. Richard Taylor, and Maj. Gen. Sterling Price to accomplish the seemingly impossible task. The integrity of the Trans-Mississippi Department, or what remained of it in 1864, had been maintained. It was, however, to be the final flare of success for Confederate forces in the region. They had kept the enemy out of Texas, but theirs was, and always had been, a position of diminishing strength, and while the modest glory of the Red River campaign brightened their spirits, they had to know, obliquely, dimly, that they were outmanned and outgunned.

The frighteningly obvious difference between the two armies was that the Union could sustain losses like those along the Red River and regroup, rebuild, repair their military, and fight another day in another place. The Confederacy could not. At least Confederate forces in the East could not, and it was there that Lt. Gen. U. S. Grant, general in chief of all Federal forces, chose to concentrate his efforts. By the summer of 1864, Grant's strategy for bringing a close to the war hinged on simultaneous thrusts at three principal targets in the eastern Confederacy: Gen. Robert E. Lee's Army of Northern Virginia near Richmond; Gen. Joseph E. Johnston's Army of Tennessee in northern Georgia; and the port city of Mobile, Alabama. At this juncture in the conflict, the Trans-Mississippi West did not figure heavily into the Union equation for winning the war. Having already detached that region from the rest of the Confederacy, Federal military authorities could easily sustain their grand strategic objectives simply by maintaining the status quo west of the Mississippi River. For all practical purposes, Smith's Trans-Mississippians, though flushed with victory, posed no serious threat to Grant's overall strategy for victory for the union.

General Smith also realized that his April successes would have little bearing on events east of the river. Though isolated and adrift, the western commander could count on the facts that his department was self-sustaining and that his men could rest, recuperate, and replenish their arms and accoutrements. For the time being, this could be accomplished with the assurance that another threat of aggression would be months in the offing.

Furthermore, Smith recognized that, in terms of men and matériel, his department could do nothing to assist the Confederate war effort in the East. The taste of victory in April had whetted the appetite of many Arkansans and Missourians for mounting a Confederate offensive, one disruptive to Federal war plans back east. For Sterling Price, such a project could have only one objective—Missouri. But realization of such plans, should they materialize at all, lingered months away on the horizon.[1]

> **May 10th. Tuesday.** This is the anniversary of the famous "Camp Jackson" affair and St. Louis massacre—a day ever memorable to all Missourians. It suggests many reflections in which I cannot now indulge. Gen. Churchill started for Lewisville, Ark. to see his wife—he will join us on the march. In his absence Gen. Tappan will command the division. We start on the march for Louisiana at daylight in the morning. My boy Frank was struck on the head by one of the negro boys and severely hurt. [He] has been insensible all day. I fear that I will have to leave him behind. Spent the morning in quarters preparing for our journey. Had a heavy rain last night. After dinner went in town on business. Procured some medical stores then called to see Mr. Garrett who will go to St. Louis soon. [I] gave him a letter to my wife and had a long talk with him and sent many messages to friends in St. Louis. While in town heard of a gratifying success of our armies

in North Carolina—the taking of Plymouth, 2500 prisoners, 3 gunboats, 31 pieces of artillery, 100,000 lbs. bacon, 1000 barrels flour, and much other garrison stores.[2] Verily God has been with us of late and has granted us many signal victories for which I desire to thank him. Saw Maj. Cabell just returned with flag of truce from near Little Rock. He brings evidence of the demoralization of Steele's army. Saw also a group of 10 Federal prisoners just brought in. The weather is quite cold tonight. Had a long visit from Col. [G. W.] Sappington this morning.[3] He has just returned from near the Mississippi River.

May 11th. Wednesday. Left Camden this morning at sunrise for Louisiana. Gen. Tappan [is] commanding the division in the absence of Gen. Churchill. Called by and rode out with him at the head of the column. Came on the Wire Road to Shreveport to a point 14 miles out where we went into camp early. Took coffee and eggs with Gen. T. then a nap and read the *Dutch Republic* for the rest of the day. Received by courier two letters from my sister in N.C. containing much of interest. At 5 P.M. partook of a good camp dinner—Mrs. Tappan, who accompanies the expedition, dining with us. Retired early as we start at daylight in the morning.

May 12th. Thursday. Started at daylight this morning and marched 16 miles and went into camp 3 miles from Calhoun and six miles from Magnolia east, near the residence of Mr. Dixon. On the way bought five spring chickens cheap at one dollar each. Got into camp early, took a snack, and at 5 o'clock had a good dinner at which Mrs. Tappan was present. Soon after getting into camp a train from Shreveport with a lot of whiskey and other hospital stores [arrived destined] for Camden. Having an incline to that effect I stopped the train and took out two barrels as a reserve supply in case of a battle. It has been a delightful day. We camp tonight 30 miles from Camden.

May 13th. Friday. Arose at ½ past three this morning, took breakfast before daylight and the train got off by early dawn. Gen. Tappan and I remained behind at Mr. Dixon's with Mrs. Tappan for an hour and a half until the command and all the train had passed, then rode through and had the annoyance of passing the whole train which we finally accomplished and got into camp 17 miles from where we started by 11 A.M. Encamped in the woods where the ticks are as thick as blackberries. Took a snack and a toddy and my cot being spread took a long nap. At 5 P.M. had a good camp dinner graced by Mrs. Tappan's presence. Read some and retired early. The day pleasant but warmer than yesterday.

May 14th. Saturday. The same old story. Started at daylight having arisen about ½ past 3 A.M. and taking coffee and eggs for breakfast. Came 14 miles and went into camp early. A few miles after starting came into Louisiana in which state we camp tonight and will remain for some time. Pitched tent, spread my cot, and after eating a snack and smoking a pipe took a nap and then read until dinner. At 5 P.M. ate a hearty meal enjoying the luxury of green peas and lettuce with spring chicken—a sumptuous repast for rebel soldiers on a march. Now I will read my Bible and retire. Weather delightful and roads good. Thank God for his many blessings.

May 15th. Sunday. Another Sabbath on a march and of course no Sabbath at all—Oh! When will this cruel war cease and we be allowed to return to our homes, our families, our altars, and our sanctuaries? Arose as usual at 3 A.M. took breakfast before day and got off at the head of the column by daylight. By these early starts we avoid the annoyance of passing through the troops and train and set early to camp. Came 13 miles to Homer, a nice little town in Claiborne Parish, La. where there is a Methodist College and fine court house and other evidence of thrift besides several churches. Passed through by ½ past 8 A.M. and came out 4 miles near the residence of Mr. Dixon who has a fine establishment. The old gentleman invited us to dine with him which we did between 12 and 1 P.M. which did not, however, destroy my appetite for a good camp dinner of spring chicken, lettuce, and green peas between 5 and 6. About sundown Mr. Dixon's family and some young ladies from the neighborhood came to camp when Gen. Tappan's band came up and played several pieces;

among others, "Home Sweet Home," "Old Hundred," and other sacred music appropriate to the day.

May 16th. Monday. Started as usual at early dawn this morning and made a long march, 22 miles, passing through first the one horse little town of Athens, and then some twelve miles distant, Mount Lebanon, a snug and thrifty village some two miles beyond which we camped. Got into camp later than usual. The troops came along looking weary and tired an hour or two later. Passed the day as usual—a snack and a nap, then dinner, reading and etc. after Lt. [William C.] Gibson from St. Louis now in the La. Cavalry called to see me in the afternoon and spent an hour.[4] Heard today of a victory of Gen. Lee in Va. in which he captured 7000 prisoners and defeated one wing of the Yankee army.[5] Thank God for this victory. A lovely moonlit night, weather growing warm.

May 17th. Tuesday. Got off at the usual hour—daylight this morning—Mrs. Tappan remaining behind, and came 15 miles camping 3 miles in advance of the troops in Bienville Parish. Soon after getting up tent, taking a snack, and lying down for a nap, a courier arrived from Shreveport stating that the enemy had evacuated Alexandria and ordering us to return to Camden and recruit our army preparatory to a move in the direction of Missouri. This was joyful news to us all. Tomorrow the command rests and then take the backtrack. The troops are delighted at this. The Lt. Governor of La. who resides in the vicinity of our camp, Gov. Pierce, came over, paid us a visit, and took camp dinner with us.

May 18th Wednesday. On the march from La. The command rest today before entering upon the march back to Camden, but as our headquarters were some three miles in advance of the column, after a late breakfast we moved back, which is now forward some 7 miles, putting us 4 miles in advance of the troops. Encamped at a mill dam where we have fine water and plenty of it which the couriers and servants enjoyed by bathing. After getting our tents up we had a fine refreshing rain which will lay the dust render our march tomorrow comfortable. No incidents today.

May 19th. Thursday. Being some distance in advance of the command started about 6 o'clock this morning and rode on leisurely to Mount Lebanon and encamped in a beautiful grove in the town. Gen. Churchill and Capt. Sevier joined us about noon having come up with his family. The General of course takes command and Gen. Tappan returns to his command. Near where we are encamped resides Dr. [Beletha] Powell in charge of the hospital at this place.[6] His mother-in-law is Mrs. Harvey, whom I have met at Mr. J. J. Holliday's in St. Louis. On learning that I was here, she sent over for me to go see her and I found her a charming lady. Took tea and enjoyed a fine cup of coffee and a delightful supper with her—spring chicken and afterwards a mint julip. During the afternoon visited Mrs. Churchill. While there the Miss Doiters came in—beautiful young ladies—one of them remarkably pretty, beautiful to behold. Spent a pleasant evening at the Doiters. Saw in the papers Gen. Lee's dispatches to the Sec. of War giving an account of two days fighting in Va. in which he had defeated the Yankees with great slaughter. There are rumors of a third days fighting with a complete rout of the Yankees— God grant that it may be so.

May 20th. Friday. Got off in good time this morning and came 14 miles, encamping 8 miles from Homer. Got into camp early, before 9 A.M., and had a long day. Mrs. Churchill and family accompany us and took dinner and breakfast with us.

May 21st. Saturday. Came 15 miles today passing through Homer and coming four miles on the other side and went into camp on the roadside in the shade. Got comfortably fixed, tent up, cot and mattress spread by eleven o'clock and spent the rest of the day quietly and agreeably. The weather is getting quite warm. I am very pleasantly situated at present. Mrs. Churchill being along messes with us, or rather, we take our meals with her thus affording us the pleasure of the society of a very charming lady which is a rare treat in camp life—would that my own beloved wife were along also.

May 22nd. Sunday. This has been a Sabbath indeed. As our command is weary and there is no necessity now for our hurrying on we rested today much to my gratification, as I like to observe the Sabbath whenever it can be done, even in time of war. Being 4 miles from Homer and the weather being hot and the roads dusty I did not go in town to church, but spent the day quietly in camp. Since the arrival of Gen. Churchill's family our mess has been rather large with an excess of servants, so today we divided, Maj. Ben Johnson,[7] Capt. Sevier, and myself forming a new mess leaving the Gen. and his family together. This afternoon commenced a letter to my beloved wife to be sent by Mrs. Maj. Clark who expects so to go to St. Louis. She will, I hope, see my wife— would that I could have that pleasure. My thoughts have frequently and fondly recurred to the dear ones at home today—God bless and protect them from all danger and harm. Gen. and Mrs. Tappan came over this afternoon to see Mrs. Churchill. An order came from Gen. Price this evening directing us to proceed 25 miles from Camden and there remain until further orders. We go in the morning, God willing.

May 23rd. Monday. Took up the line of march this morning at the usual early hour and came 16 miles, getting into camp on the Big Cornie Creek about 10 A.M. Weather quite hot and roads dusty but once in camp with tent up and cot spread it was comfortable with a stiff breeze blowing. We left La. today and came into Arkansas (Union Co.). Gen. Parsons, who has also been ordered back, I understand camps within a few miles of us—his drums can be heard.

May 24th. Tuesday. Took breakfast before daylight and got under way by early dawn. Came 22 miles by 10 o'clock [and] went into camp. Here we are ordered to remain until further orders. This is doubtless to rest the troops and for convenience of forage. After dinner got my desk out and wrote a letter to Dr. Wooten then finished the letter commenced several days ago to my wife to send by Mrs. Clark, and after tea wrote Maj. Cabell a long letter.

May 25th. Wednesday. As our headquarters are not very comfortable, we moved this morning after a late breakfast several miles on the Camden Road where we soon pitched our tents and are now comfortably fixed. Gen. Churchill and family occupying a room in a house. Wrote a letter this afternoon to Col. Clay Taylor, also to Malcolm Graham[8] of Parsons' Division and one to Maj. Monroe on business. Here I hope that they will have an opportunity of resting and recruiting for several weeks. Since breaking up our winter quarters at Camp Sumter about two months ago we have marched 650 miles and fought two pitched battles, so that our troops require rest. Had visits from several surgeons of the division today on business. Our camp is known as *"Camp Grinstead"* in honor of the gallant Col. Grinstead who was killed at the Battle of Jenkins' Ferry on the Saline River, Ark. April 30th, 1864, when we whipped the Yankees under Gen. Steele after a hard fight.

May 26th. Thursday. A delightful day spent quietly in camp. Had various visits from surgeons and others on business. Received a letter from Dr. Wooten giving me the Yankee account of the great battle recently in Va. from which it is obvious that Gen. Grant was badly whipped by Gen. Lee. They the Yankees admit a loss of from 27 to 43000 in killed, wounded, and prisoners, and that Grant has fallen back. This is a big admission although Grant with usual Yankee impudence denies a defeat. I look with interest for the accounts from our side of the house. Doubtless it was a great and telling victory but as usual obtained with the loss of many valuable lives on our side. Thank God for this victory.[9] Wrote a long letter to Dr. W. in reply, also wrote to Maj. Snead. Read among other books, *The Last Days of Jesus* by Dr. Moore of Richmond.

May 27th. Friday. Another day spent quietly in camp in the ordinary routine of official duties. Received and wrote several business communications, etc., etc. By courier this evening from Camden we received news respecting recent great victories in Va. and elsewhere. Lee's victory over Grant seems to have been very complete and must tell on the northern people, the Yankee finances, and on the final result. Providence is evidently smiling on our cause for which I desire to be thankful. After tea, commenced a long letter to [my] sister Lavinia in Raleigh. Several of the young members of the staff came over and paid me a visit and have just left.

May 28th. Saturday. Spent the morning in sending out instructions to the brigade respecting certain reports that I wish them to furnish me and in making out forms for the same. Had a long visit at my tent from Mrs. Churchill. By courier this evening received a note from Mrs. Snead stating that she expected to start for St. Louis in a few days, and if I wished to write to my wife she would carry the letters. Of course I will avail myself of her kindness and go to Camden also to see her that my wife may have the pleasure of seeing one who has recently saw me. Retired early tonight with a severe headache.

May 29th. Sunday. No preaching today anywhere near that I know of, so spent the day quietly in camp, read the scriptures and *The Last Days of Jesus* by Dr. Moore. Finished a long letter begun several days ago to [my] sister Lavinia. Wrote also to Dr. Yandell. The courier from Camden brought me several official communications also a letter from Dr. Wooten. This afternoon had visits from several surgeons and others. Capt. T. T. Taylor[10] took tea with us. After tea called up to see Mrs. Churchill. Tomorrow, Providence permitting, I propose going to Camden to see Mrs. Snead before she leaves for St. Louis.

May 30th. Monday. Took breakfast at an early hour this morning and at 7 o'clock started for Camden accompanied by Maj. Ben Johnson and Capt. Taylor in a tricoach and two mules. After a ride of 23 miles through dust and sand reached Camden at 1 P.M. Went to Dr. Wooten's quarters just in time for dinner. Talked over army and other matters. Late in the evening called to see Mrs. Snead and had a long talk with her and sent many messages to my wife who I hope she will shortly see. Called to see other acquaintances. Spent the night with Dr. Wooten.

May 31st. Tuesday. After breakfast and a smoke, called to see Dr. Bond, Med. Purveyor, on business then called on Gen. Price at his Hd. Qts. Found the old gentleman well, and hearty, and in good spirits. Spent some time with him and after attending to other matters, the object of my visit having been accomplished, at 11 A.M. started with Maj. Johnson on our return to camp. Had a hot and dusty ride and reached camp about 6 P.M.—found things in status quo. After tea wrote several business letters and disposed of diverse official documents.

June 1st. Wednesday. Was very busy this morning in making out my monthly return of medical officers, requisitions for battle supplies, and other reports preparatory to a move. Malcolm Graham from Parsons' Division called to see me and spent an hour or so. I gave him $50 in greenbacks sent him by his mother, and as he was very destitute of clothing gave him two pair of new socks and a shirt. Had visits from Drs. [Benjamin A.] Jandon, [David S.] Williams, and Swindell.[11] At 6 o'clock this evening Gen. Churchill had a review of the division in a rough field about a mile off. There was quite a turn out of citizens. In riding around, which we did in a sweeping gallop, my horse fell and came near throwing me but fortunately I escaped without being unsaddled. At the close of the review it commenced blowing and threatening rain, and rained some during the evening—a good rain is very much needed. Capt. [L. M.] Nutt[12] took tea and spent the night with us.

June 2nd. Thursday. It did not rain much last night as was expected, nor during the day, but tonight we are having a fine season which is very much needed by the crops. Was busy during the morning sending up other reports respecting medical transportation and etc. This afternoon wrote another letter to my sister in N. Carolina to send across the Mississippi River by Capt. Nutt who spent the day with us and leaves in the morning. Capt. T. T. Taylor arrived from Camden this evening, took tea and will spend the night. He brings news of various fights on the river and in Virginia, all of a cheerful character. Gen. Marmaduke has taken and scuttled two gunboats and burned two Yankee transports.[13] Sat in my tent after tea while it rained out, smoked and thought of home and family while others were chatting gaily around. 10 P.M. raining hard.

June 3rd. Friday. Had little in official business to transact today, but in lieu thereof wrote several letters. First and foremost one to my beloved wife to be sent by Mrs. Snead, also a letter to Mrs. Snead asking her to say some things to my wife that I did not wish to put in my letter to her. Also wrote to Col. John Polk and Dr. Wooten, all of which were sent to Camden. By courier this evening received a batch of circulars from Richmond and Shreveport (Surgeon General and Med. Direct. of Department) containing instructions to med. officers all of which have to be transmitted to the brigades. Had a fine rain last night but none today. Lt. Fulton Wright[14] arrived this evening, took tea, and will spend the night with us.

June 4th. Saturday. Another day passed quietly in camp without any incident of note. Was engaged for a while during the morning in sending out instructions to the brigade surgeons. Then read and slept, ate dinner, smoked, read, and then slept again. Arose after sleep was no longer refreshing, washed and fixed up, then read a while. Walked around the encampment, went to see Maj. Johnson, etc., etc. After tea, called to see Mrs. Churchill who presented me with a magnificent magnolia blossom, which is now by me giving forth its delightful fragrance. How I wish that I could give it to my dear wife who would appreciate it highly—God bless her.

June 5th. Sunday. After enjoying the luxury of a bath and a thorough change of underclothes, took breakfast, read the Bible, and attended to other duties. At 10 o'clock I rode one and a half miles to a Methodist church where I heard a good and sensible sermon by Dr. Kavanaugh. The church was crowded by soldiers but I regret to say that I saw but few officers present. Our officers are sadly deficient in their duty in this respect and set but a poor example to the men. After sermon, went to the house of Maj. [John C.] Wright who lives in the neighborhood.[15] He lives in comfortable style and is an intelligent gentleman and his wife an agreeable lady. He is an elder in the Presbyterian church. Gen. and Mrs. Tappan are staying with him. All parties insisted on my staying to dinner, which I did and got a good meal—plenty of good vegetables and raspberries and cream, the first I have enjoyed this season. After dinner a heavy rain came up which detained me until after 5 P.M. Taking advantage of a lull in the storm returned to camp. By courier from Camden received a letter from my

niece, Sue, in Raleigh, N.C. and dated April 12th. She writes a
good letter and gave me much interesting news. After dark rain
still continues. Confined to my tent which is dry and comfortable, but camp is dull in wet weather, so I have to retire early in
self-defense.

June 6th. Monday. A dull, disagreeable day in camp. Rained all
morning. Ate, smoked, slept, and read, finishing the *Last Days of
Jesus* and commenced Cummings' *Great Preparation*. The necessity
for other messes existing at our headquarters Maj. Ben Johnson left
our mess and formed another with [Charles E.] Royston and
[Charles E.] Mitchell.[16] Read President Davis' message, a short sensible document.[17] After tea, paid Mrs. Churchill a visit and spent
an hour with her.

June 7th. Tuesday. Still laying over quietly in camp awaiting orders
and preparations that are being made for a grand move. Read,
smoked, slept, and ate. This afternoon had a visit from Capt.
Reynolds[18] from Parsons' Division on his way to Camden. Wrote
several letters. By courier received a batch of circulars containing
instructions to surgeons to be sent down to the brigades. A heavy
rain came up about 5 P.M. which continued until dark and which
prevented our cook from getting us supper. We, however, procured some cold ham and bread and made out finely. After supper,
or rather snack, read Cummings' *Great Preparation,* an interesting
religious work. Thus has passed another day in camp. Oh that these
days may soon be over and we permitted to return to our homes
and our families!

June 8th. Wednesday. Still raining. It has rained off and on all day,
sometimes very hard, and tonight is dark and rainy and forbidding. Tent life is disagreeable in wet weather but it is better than
being out of doors as many of our poor soldiers are, and as I have
a fine large tent I ought to be contented. Had a batch of orders
to issue this morning and numerous discharges and furloughs to
act on with other official duties to perform—all, however, not
occupying me very long. Read Cummings' *Great Preparation* and

found comfort from it in my present condition, especially from the fact elaborated that there is no chance, no accident but God ruling and governing in all things even the most minute events. This I know full well and I do rejoice that he does reign and will over rule all things for his own glory. May he speedily speak peace to our beloved country and give us with it *independence*. Gen. Churchill and Capt. [Charles E.] Kidder[19] went up to Camden today. We have received no news for several days past. May the news be cheering when it does come.

June 9th. Thursday. Another day of showers and sunshine. Towards evening it rained very hard for an hour after which the sun set clear and the new moon came out bright giving promise of a clear day tomorrow. Read Dr. Cummings pretty much all day. Was greatly interested in his views and in the beauty of his style and his enlarged Catholic spirit. He believes in the second advent of our savior and in his personal reign—so mote it be. Gen. Churchill returned from Camden this evening but brings us no definite news. It is rumored that Johnston has defeated Sherman, capturing large numbers of prisoners, but rumors are unreliable.

June 10th. Friday. As predicted last night the rain has passed off and today it has been clear and tonight the moon shines brightly and all nature seems fresh and washed—too beautiful for the pall of war that hangs over the land. Would God that this war was at an end and that peace once more smiled on the land. Had but little of official duty to perform and read most of the day. Finished *The Great Preparation* and for want of something better commenced *Moss Side*, a romance. This evening took tea with Gen. and Mrs. Churchill. Had a good supper with canned oysters. Was visited by Drs. Swindell and [Edwin E.] Harris.[20] This lovely night fills me with desire to be with my beloved wife and family—Oh for a reunion with them.

June 11th. Saturday. The rain not over yet as I had hoped. Had several hard showers today interspersed with bright sunshine. Had little to do and when not entertaining visitors spent the time in

reading *Moss Side*. By courier this evening from Camden received
a long letter from Maj. Cabell, partly on business but giving me the
news from the other side of the Miss. River and from the Yankee
papers. The report of Sherman's defeat by Jo Johnston is still
received and may be true but still needs confirmation. If so it is a
most important victory. Col. Colton Greene[21] has attacked a party
of Federals on the Miss. River, killing 200 of them and driving them
to their boats. After supper went over to see Mrs. Churchill.

June 12th. Sunday. Weather still cloudy and threatening rain, too
much so to venture out 6 miles to church. So I remained in camp
and spent the morning and afternoon in camp reading and sleeping. Late this evening Maj. [Charles B.] Moore[22] and I rode over
to Maj. Wright's and took tea and spent a pleasant evening. Had
a fine supper, good clabber and raspberries, etc., which to a soldier living in camp on beef and bread is a great treat. Returned to
camp about 10 P.M. Weather cool but cloudy. Received by courier
a note from Maj. Maclean giving me some Yankee intelligence
of not much general interest but interesting to me. All quiet in
camp. Will read my Bible and retire.

June 13th. Monday. This has been a lovely day, cool and pleasant, and the weather settled once more. Wrote a long letter to
Maj. Cabell and a short one to Maj. Maclean, also read a good
deal. Young Fulton Wright arrived this evening and will enter
upon duty as one of Gen. Churchill's staff. He will mess with us.

June 14th. Tuesday. Still resting in Camp Grinsted with no
prospect of an immediate move that I can see. Spent the morning quietly reading—finished *Moss Side*. Not a very pleasant story
though there is some fine delineations of character in it. This afternoon rode down to Gause's Brigade and [William D.] Blocher's[23]
Battalion of Artillery to visit the surgeons and see how they are
getting on. Had a pleasant ride and an agreeable visit. By courier
this evening received dispatches from Camden and orders to send
all ambulances of the division needing repairs there without delay.
The news of Sherman's rout by Johnston still comes in and I hope

that it is true. The Yankee papers claim that Grant is within seven miles of Richmond, but this is very doubtful. But McClellan got even nearer than that two years ago and was driven back and so I trust it will be with Grant. A lovely moonlit night—cool, and pleasant. After tea went up to see Mrs. Churchill and the General and spent an hour pleasantly. P.S. ½ past 10 P.M. I have just been out enjoying this lovely moonlit night and thinking of my beloved wife and children and wishing Oh how ardently that I were with them and could see them. God bless them!

June 15th. Wednesday. The middle of June—the month is rolling rapidly. Important events are transpiring on the other side of the Mississippi but as yet we are ignorant of them. Had but little to do and nothing on hand to read. For lack of something else read a stray volume of *The Hstory of the French Revolution*. The courier from Camden this evening brought me orders but no news of recent events in Va. or elsewhere which most of all interests us at present. Dr. Smith, Maj. [Thomas W.] Newton, and Capt. [Alex K.] MacLean arrived this evening from Gen. Marmaduke's headquarters on the Miss. River—all members of his staff—but add nothing to our stock of news.[24] Spent the day in camp. Another beautiful moonlit night.

June 16th. Thursday. Spent the day quietly in camp. Copied some circulars from Shreveport and sent them to the brigades—they contain instructions to surgeons. Having nothing of special interest to read, took up *The French Revolution* and read it. Had another hard rain for two hours about the middle of the day. Gen. Marmaduke and Gen. John B. Clark Jr.[25] called by, the former on his way to Camden and the latter from Parsons' Division and spent several hours taking dinner. Our visitors of yesterday left this morning for Lewisville, Ark. taking with them Lt. Wright. Capt. Sevier also went this evening to attend a party so I am quite alone tonight. Took my tea by myself tonight out in the open air in front of my tent with the frogs singing around me. Enjoyed the plain quiet repast but my thoughts would recur to my home and once happy family group two of whom are now in heaven as I trust. God grant

a speedy reunion of those of us that are left. The courier from
Camden this evening brought us no news.

June 17th. Friday. Read, smoked, and slept during the morning.
Had a visit from Gen. Tappan and Col. [Robert G.] Shaver,[26] and
in the afternoon from Dr. [Edward L.] Hamilton.[27] At 5 o'clock
this evening rode over to Maj. Wright's in the carriage with Gen.
and Mrs. Churchill where we spent the evening very pleasantly
and partook of a good supper. Rode back to camp by moonlight
where we arrived about 10 o'clock. The courier from Camden
brings us news of another battle between Gens. Lee and Grant
near Richmond. Not a general engagement but a considerable
affair in which 2 or 3 corps of Grant's army was defeated. Lee capturing some 1500 prisoners besides killing and wounding many
and driving back the invaders. The reported defeat of Sherman
by Johnston in Georgia turns out to be all a mistake—one of the
many false rumors to which we are so subject. A large transport
was captured a few days ago by our cavalry on the Arkansas River
loaded with cotton and other valuables. The boat and cotton was
burned and the other things including 40 prisoners taken off.

June 18th. Saturday. This has been the hottest day of the season
and having nothing to take me out I have kept quietly in camp
and in the shade. Had several visitors among the surgeons of the
brigade. While remaining quietly here with but little to do, my
thoughts naturally recur to my wife and children and home.
Today I have thought of them much and longed so ardently to
be with them. It is now within a day of two of two years since I
left St. Louis and all that I hold most dear! Oh when will this cruel
war end and we be allowed to return to each other? It has been
a long time since I even heard from my beloved wife. If I could
only hear from her regularly it would be such a comfort. But all
that I can do is to commit her and them in faith to a covenant
keeping God, which is indeed a great comfort. Gen. Churchill
had a drill of the whole division this afternoon which attracted all
the females in the neighborhood but as it was very hot I did not
turn out, not having much military ardor. By the courier from

Camden this evening I received a long and interesting letter from Maj. Cabell giving me all the news as culled from the Yankee papers. Lincoln and Andy Johnson have been nominated by the Republicans as their candidates for president and vice president on an extremely radical platform, breathing death and destruction to the "Rebs" and ultra on the negro question, which is perhaps the best for us. Fremont and Cochran have been nominated by the ultra-radicals or abolitionists.[28] The democrats have yet to make their nomination and lay down their platform and then will comence the triangular fight for the Yankee presidency, which I hope will result in a revolution at the north. The news from the two great armies confronting each other in Virginia and Georgia is favorable to us. The issue at stake is immense but trusting in God, in the justice of our cause, and in our gallant armies and their heroic leaders, I hope and believe that we will be successful. There is no doubt but that events at the north are culminating and if with the blessing of Providence Lee and Johnston both defeat the Federal armies opposite them, I should not be surprised to see a revolution in the north resulting in peace to us. I cannot but say God grant and speed it.

June 19th. Sunday. There is a brightness and beauty and sacred stillness about the Sabbath, which does not belong to any other day. So it has seemed to me today as I have looked out from my tent on the beautiful park in which we are located. I had hoped to have gone to Mount Holly to attend Presbyterian Church there, but my horse which has been loose for two days could not be caught so I had to forgo the privilege and remain at home. Read the Bible which, by the bye, I do daily and not merely on Sunday, then the *Sunny Side,* a very good Sabbath school book. Late this evening rode over to Maj. Wright and there spent the evening and took tea with Gen. and Mrs. Tappan and Maj. and Mrs. Wright very pleasantly and at 10 o'clock rode home by moonlight alone.

June 20th. Monday. Today two years ago I left home, wife, and family, and business, and all that is most dear to me in this life to

take part in this war for Southern independence. Since then I have
been constantly with the army in the field and have gone through
many exciting and trying scenes, but thanks to a kind Providence
I have enjoyed excellent health and have been enabled to endure
the fatigue and exposure of a soldier's life well. Had I known when
I first left that I would be absent two long years from my family,
I would have hesitated long, but the fact there was no alternative
left me but to go to prison, take an oath which I *could not* in good
conscience take, or to leave and join the southern army. When
the choice between these alternatives became inevitable, I could
not and did not hesitate, and though the separation from my
family has been exceedingly bitter to me and the life that I have
been compelled to lead is foreign to my taste and habits, yet I have
never regretted the step, but only the necessity of having to take
it. And now after two years absence the future is all dark before
me and I can form no idea when I will be able to rejoin my family,
but I hope for the best. God grant that the day may not be very
distant. Today my thoughts recur to home and family. The morning was very hot. About noon we had a fine rain which cooled off
the weather finely. Soon after the rain Dr. [Charles M.] Taylor,[29]
Medical Inspector, arrived from Camden and will spend the night
with us. He brings news that Forrest and Polk on the other side
of the Mississippi have routed Grierson and Sturgis who with a
force of 8000 were marching to destroy the Mobile and Ohio
R. R. The rout is said to be complete. The fight occurring in Miss.
and the commands were both mixed cavalry and infantry.[30] He
also gives other rumors of victories but as they are only rumors I
will not mention them lest they not be confirmed. Gen. Churchill
and various members of the staff spent a good part of the evening
with us. By the courier from Camden received a batch of orders,
circulars, etc., from district headquarters. Dr. Taylor spends the
night with us. By invitation from Gen. Churchill he and I took
tea with him and Mrs. Churchill and spent a pleasant evening.

June 21st. Tuesday. After breakfast Dr. Taylor and myself visited
all the brigades and each regiment belonging to each and made a
thorough inspection of them. This occupied us nearly all morning. After getting through with Gen. Tappan's Brigade about

1 P.M. we went to Maj. Wright's and took dinner with him and Mrs. Tappan. Here we also met the Rev. Mr. Patterson and Squire McRae from Mt. Holly who gave me pressing invitations to visit them. Returned to camp about 3 P.M. shortly after which Dr. Taylor left for Gen. Parsons' Division. Dr. Swindell came over and sat a long time with me. By courier from Camden an order came directing our command to proceed to Camden without delay. So we start in the morning and will bid adieu to the quiet and delightful retirement of Camp Grinstead after a stay here of just four weeks. The object of the move I do not know, time will develop. I am sorry to leave but if there is any necessity for it a soldier must always yield his own comfort to the good of the service. By return ambulance from Lewisville tonight Lt. Wright sent us a large jar of butter, a big basket of chickens, several cakes, and etc., but did not come himself on account of an indisposition. This is a most acceptable addition to our mess supplies.

June 22nd. Wednesday. Took an early breakfast and commenced making preparations to move at an early hour this morning. Packing and loading occupied an hour. Bid adieu to Camp Grinstead about 7 A.M. The troops got off at daylight en route for Camden. Accompanied by Maj. Moore [I] rode by and took leave of Maj. and Mrs. Wright whose liberal hospitality I had enjoyed while in the neighborhood. The weather was cloudy and there were several showers during the morning. Rode on with Maj. Moore, other members of the staff and the General being either before or in the rear. Passed through train and troops. The command encamped within 2 miles of Camden, I however, rode on and came in town arriving at Dr. Wooten's quarters just at dinner time. In the evening went with Maj. Cabell around town. Called on Dr. Bond, Col. Taylor, and Maj. Brinker, and intended to wind up by a visit to Gen. Price but was prevented by a rain. After tea Capt. Seay called to see me and sat sometime. Spent the night with Dr. Wooten and Maj. Cabell.

June 23rd. Thursday. In Camden. Spent the day in Camden. After a restless night, rendered so by the fleas, which invaded my bed and preyed upon me at a merciless rate, arose at an early hour this morning. Breakfast over, the reading of a chapter in the Bible and a long smoke, went down town. Called first at Gen. Price's headquarters and had a long conversation with him and a shake of the hand with diverse members of his staff. Then read a recent Yankee paper from which I got no news of interest and spent an hour or two in talking with acquaintances. About 1 o'clock returned with Maj. Cabell to his and Dr. Wooten's quarters and took dinner with them and several other surgeons. During the afternoon we discussed army medical matters at length. Late in the evening walked down town again and remained in conversation with such acquaintances as I met until near dark when I returned to my temporary quarters and spent the evening in smoking and conversation. Gen. Price reviewed Dockery's Brigade this afternoon, but the weather was hot and I had no particular fancy for such pageants so I did not turn out.

June 24th. Friday. Still in Camden. After breakfast called with Dr. Wooten to see Maj. Brinker. From him I got a good pair of shoes for which I paid $10—at ordinary times they would have been worth one dollar and a quarter. Then called on Gen. Price and by him was shown dispatches from Richmond to the 14th instant giving an account of army operations in Va. to the 13th, all encouraging—a defeat of the enemy cavalry with a capture of 500 prisoners. About 1 P.M. Dr. Wooten, Maj. Cabell, and myself received a message from Gen. Price asking us to come up to his quarters to see a St. Louis paper of very late date containing important news. On riding over we read the *St. Louis Republican* of the 18th only 6 days old. The telegraphs from Washington and other points state that Grant with his army had crossed to the south side of James River and attacked Petersburg which place they claim to have taken, but from an analysis of the dispatches and the well known proclivity of the Yankees for lying there is very considerable doubt about this. Still the news is of such a character as to cause very great anxiety, but we must wait and hope for the best. My trust is that under God General Lee will yet defeat him as he has heretofore done and drive him from the soil of Va. It also announces the return of Vallandigham to Ohio and contains a bold and defiant speech from him against the Lincoln despotism.[31] While at the General's he received a dispatch from Shreveport announcing the death of Lt. Gen. (Bishop) Polk of the army in Georgia.[32] Thus the workmen die, but I trust that the work will go on. At 3 o'clock Maj. C., Dr. W., and myself dined by invitation with Maj. Maclean in company with Cols. Gause, Shaver, and White. He gave us a good dinner for war times. Of course the conversation turned on the recent news from Virginia. All were excited on the subject, but the majority hopeful doubting the Yankee statements. God grant that it may prove unfounded. About 5 P.M. called to see Gen. and Mrs. Churchill (who are now staying in town), Governor Polk, and Judge Watkins. Spent a half hour very pleasantly with them, all occupying the same house in pleasant quarters. Late in the evening rode out to camp with Col. Gause where I arrived about dark. Tonight I occupy a schoolhouse hard by, my tent not having been put up.

June 25th. Saturday. Was engaged several hours this morning in pitching my tent and making myself comfortable, in which I succeeded very well indeed. Have a nice camp with my large tent all to myself, which of itself is luxury. The weather was very warm and by the time I got fixed up it was necessary to cool off and wash up. Spent the rest of the day quietly with no incidents worthy of note. Gen. Tappan paid me a visit during the morning and sat for some time. No news from Camden or elsewhere today and tonight there is nothing for me to do but to read and sleep, would that I could have pleasant dreams of the "dear ones at home." If thinking of them in my waking hours would secure this, I would dream of them nightly.

June 26th. Sunday. The day was so hot that I did not think [it] prudent to ride to Camden to attend church so [I] spent the day quietly in camp reading the Bible and Bunyan's Life written by himself, or as he calls it *Grace Abounding*—giving an account of his remarkable trials and inward struggles against the corruption of his nature and the temptations of the Evil One. An interesting and instructing narrative introductory to his *Pilgrim's Progress,* which I propose next to read and which candor compels me to say I never yet read systematically through. During the morning Gen. Tappan and Col. Gause paid me a visit and sat awhile. About 2 P.M. a heavy rain came up which lasted several hours cooling the air and remaining cloudy and damp for the rest of the day. Lt. Wright returned to our mess in the evening, having been on a visit home. No news from Camden or elsewhere. After tea continued to read and reflect until drowsiness came on and disposed me to retire early, which I did and slept soundly and sweetly but without dreams.

June 27th. Monday. Col. [Charles J.] Turnbull,[33] Department Inspector, reviewed and inspected the division this morning at 8 o'clock. I did not, however, turn out. Mrs. Clay Taylor and two young ladies of Camden came out to the review and after it was over called by and stayed a short time at our camp. Maj. Hill and Lt. Frank Von Phul[34] accompanied them. Maj. Dunlap came out and spent the day with us. He and Col. Turnbull dined with us, the latter also took tea with us. By a flag of truce, which goes up to Little Rock in the morning, I wrote a short letter to my wife and sent it in by Maj. Dunlap. Hope that she will get it, but have but little hope that she will do so, still I write by every opportunity. No additional news from Virginia as yet. It is rumored this evening that Gen. Lee has defeated Grant, but rumors are so unreliable that they can never be depended on. The day has been hot but clear. Where not otherwise engaged I read Bunyan's *Pilgrim's Progress*.

June 28th. Tuesday. After breakfast this morning rode down to Dr. Williams quarters, Tappan's Brigade to meet and arrange the Medical Examining Board for this division before which all cases applying for furlough and discharge are to come. Four or five cases came before us, all of which were disposed of and sent forward. After getting through with the Board rode over to see Gen. Tappan at his quarters and stayed a short time then returned to camp by one o'clock. Had various matters of official duty to attend to on getting back. By the courier from Camden received a letter from Mrs. Churchill enclosing one from Mrs. Wooten directing and asking my opinion and advice about Mrs. Dick Johnson's case. This letter I answered at some length giving such advice as I deemed advisable. Col. Turnbull took tea with us after which he made inspection of my office, papers, etc. We had a good deal of talk on army matters and movements respecting many of which we differed widely in our opinions, especially with regard to men (officers). In conversation with [one] who occupies the position that he does at Gen. Smith's Hd. Qts. some insight is obtained as to the views entertained at Shreveport though I would hold no one else responsible for his opinions.

June 29th. Wednesday. Rather a dull day—hot and spent quietly in camp without incident and with but little to do. Read Bunyan's *Pilgrim's Progress,* smoked, and slept as much as the fleas would allow me to. No reliable news from any quarter today.

June 30th. Thursday. The last day of June. The summer is advancing and still this huge war progresses, still Richmond is not taken by the Yankees, at least so far as we know or have cause to believe, thanks to a preserving Providence. Two years ago this time I was on my way to Richmond and desperate fighting was going on around that devoted city and McClellan and his hosts were driven back after seven days of hard fighting. Still the Yankees are yet infesting it and Grant with his tens of thousands are still there contending with our gallant army for the possession of our capital. God grant that Gen. Lee may be again able to drive him back. One year ago I was on the march with our army to Helena where on the 4th of July we met with a repulse. Such are the mighty incidents of this war that almost every day is an anniversary. Spent the day quietly in camp reading and trying to keep cool. Late this evening Gen. Tappan called by on his way out from Camden and gave us encouraging news from Va. and elsewhere just received by northern papers. Petersburg was not taken at latest accounts as the Yankees boasted was the case. Thank God for this and for all his mercies to us. We also have news that Shelby has captured a boat on White River and one on the Arkansas River taking 400 prisoners.[35] These small successes are also encouraging.

July 1st. Friday. Today the new currency law goes into effect on this side of the river. The old issue of Confederate money ceases to be circulated except at a discount of 33⅓ percent, and we are to have a new issue, but as yet I have seen none of it.[36] After breakfast rode to Gause's Brigade and there sat on the Medical Examining Board. Had five or six cases before us for furlough, transfer, etc., all of which we disposed of, if not to the satisfaction of the parties applying, at least as we thought just and right. After dinner drew up my monthly return of medical officers of the division, prepared other documents for being forwarded, and attended to other duties. By the courier from Camden this afternoon I received a short letter from my beloved wife dated April 8th sent by flag of truce. Though of old date it is a great comfort to me— at that time she and the dear children were well. She hears from me very seldom though I write quite often by every opportunity that presents itself. Her last letter from me was March 6th and before that she had not heard for three months. This letter has put me to thinking about home and my family and fills me with desire to be with them. I have read and reread it over and over again though coming as it does by flag of truce, and having to be inspected, it is of course general in its character. All that I can do is to commit my wife and children to God and ask his protection of them and hope and pray for a termination of this "cruel war" that we may be reunited again.

July 2nd. Saturday. Another warm day spent quietly in camp reading, sleeping, and attending to such official duties as came before me. Capt. Sevier and Lt. Wright went into Camden this morning leaving me to take dinner and supper alone. Hearing that a flag of truce would leave Camden in the morning for Little Rock, I wrote a short letter this afternoon to my wife to send by it. I will enclose it to Col. [John L.] Chandler[37] at Little Rock and request him to send it to my wife under care of Mr. Wickham. In this way I trust that she will receive it knowing what a comfort it is to her to hear from me as it [is] to me to hear from her. By persons coming out of town this evening, we hear that news has reached there that Grant has been driven across the James

River with great loss. I hope that this is true and if it is a glorious
result and one that calls for profound gratitude to almighty God.

July 3rd. Sunday. Arose early this morning and after enjoying the
luxury of a cold bath dressed out in clean clothes. After an early
breakfast, which I took alone, rode into Camden where I arrived
about ½ past 7. First hunted up the Flag of Truce that was going to
Little Rock and gave to the Lt. in charge a letter for my wife, also
$10 in federal greenbacks to purchase me a hat, comb, brush, etc.
provided he can get them. [I] then called at Mr. Lowry's to see Mrs.
Thompkins, his daughter, who goes with the Flag on her way to
Louisville, Ky. and obtained from her the promise to write to my
wife on her arrival there informing her of my health and well being.
In this way I hope that she will hear from me as I have but little
confidence that she will get my letter by the Flag of Truce. Then
[I] went to Maj. Cabell's and Dr. Wooten's quarters, put up my
horse and at 10 o'clock went to the Methodist Church where I
heard a very sensible and good sermon from the pastor. After
church [I] had a talk with Gov. Polk. Both of us then called to see
Dr. Taylor where we met with Gen. Churchill and others and
heard the contents of a Yankee paper of the 27th ult. just received
to the effect that the Yankees had been thwarted in all their attempts
to take Petersburg, Va., having been repulsed in various assaults
with great loss. Evidently from the showing of the Yankees themselves affairs around Richmond look encouraging for us. Took dinner with Dr. Wooten and Maj. Cabell and intended to return to
camp in the evening but a heavy rain came up which kept me in
town all night. After the rain was over, Maj. Cabell and myself
called to see Dr. and Mrs. Hardin and then Gen. and Mrs. Churchill
and after remaining until nearly dark [we] returned to his quarters.

July 4th. Monday. This is rather a sad anniversary to us. This day
one year ago Vicksburg was surrendered to the enemy with its garrison and our army was repulsed at Helena, at which I was present.
Doubtless if Grant and his army are yet in the neighborhood of
Richmond. There is heavy fighting going on there as the Yankees
will no doubt try to avail themselves of the enthusiasm which the

day naturally inspires and attempt to take the Confederate capitol, and then add this proud city to the list of their 4th of July victories. God grant that they may be thwarted in their designs and driven away, routed and in confusion. Two years ago today I arrived in Richmond just at the close of the Seven Days fighting before that famed city in which McClellan was defeated by the peerless Gen. Lee. Still the Yankees persist in their attempts to get possession of Richmond, having failed many times since. After breakfast this morning, [I] called to see Gen. Price and after a long conversation with him, rode out to camp where I arrived about noon and spent the remainder of the day in usual camp occupations.

July 5th. Tuesday. This brings the day for our Examining Board to meet. After breakfast, I rode down to Gen. Tappan's Brigade to meet the other members: Dr. [John H.] Gaines,[38] acting Surgeon of the Brigade, and Dr. Jandon. Some five or six cases came up before us, all of which were disposed of. Returned to camp about 12 M. In due time [I] took dinner, a smoke, and a nap, though between the heat and the flies my nap was anything but refreshing. Dr. Swindell paid me a long visit during the afternoon. Capt. Sevier went to Mt. Holly this afternoon to attend a party tonight at Mr. Snead's. The young people are disposed to enjoy themselves in spite of the war, which covers the land as with a dark pall. This has been a day without news and even without rumors—would that when it does come it may be of a cheering character. Heavy cannon firing was heard yesterday in the direction of the Arkansas River or maybe Pine Bluff.

July 6th. Wednesday. I have been busy all day today in making out my semi-annual return of medical and hospital stores required by regulations. It is a long and troublesome report, a full yard and a half long, including all the medications and reserved hospital supplies that I have received and issued out to the surgeons of the division and left at the various hospitals where our wounded have been left. Have nearly completed it. Had a visit this morning from Col. Shaver now commanding the post of Camden. From him I learn that a paper has been received of the 28th ult.—Yankee—

confirming Grant's discomfiture at Petersburg and Richmond, Va. The weather has been hot but I have not suffered.

July 7th. Thursday. Have been occupied today in completing my semi-annual return and in arranging and assorting my medical stores. This occupied me for several hours, which together with reading, smoking, and other necessary occupations beguiled the day tolerably well. By the courier from Camden [I] received several official documents and a note from Maj. Cabell on business which I answered. No news of interest today, but several rumors which are of too unreliable and doubtful a character to be recorded or believed. Took dinner alone—my mess mates having gone into town. Finished reading *Pilgrim's Progress* in which I have been interested and edified. The day has been hot, but the night is cool.

July 8th. Friday. In camp near Camden. Our Examining Board met this morning in Gause's Brigade. At nine o'clock I rode down and passed upon four or five cases of furloughs and transfers. On my way home [I] called by Blocher's Artillery Battalion on business and returned to camp by noon. The remainder of the day was occupied in fixing up official documents for being forwarded &c., &c. No news of interest or other excitement. A quiet, hot day. The command remaining inactive awaiting the troubling of the waters in official circles. In the mean time, the summer is passing off and the destinies of the nation are being settled by the action of our armies on the other side of the Mississippi River and by lapse of time and the logic of events that are transpiring, as well as for their not transpiring. Gold in New York is at a premium of 138 percent. This clearly shows that the Yankee cause is on the wane and is the surest thermometer of the Yankee pulse.

July 9th. Saturday. Passed the day quietly and undisturbed in camp. Having sent off all my reports for the past month and quarter, [I] had but little official duty to discharge so [I] spent most of the time reading *St. Valentine's Day, or the Fair Maid of Perth,* one of Scott's novels. No news of any kind. Altogether a day without incident of any note. Weather hot but showery towards evening.

July 10th. Sunday. After breakfast this morning, [I] rode into Camden with Maj. Moore and Lt. Wright to attend church. On arriving, called at Gen. Price's headquarters where I saw the General, Gov. Polk, Maj. Cabell, and other friends and there remained until time to go to church. While there, a dispatch was received from Shreveport stating that Johnston had defeated Sherman with heavy loss, killing the Federal Generals Hooker and McCook.[39] This needs confirmation. Gov. Polk and myself then went to the Methodist church; subsequently, Gen. Price and Col. Clay Taylor came in. [We] heard a good sermon from Chaplin [Horace] Jewell.[40] From church [I] went home and took dinner with Maj. Graham, formerly from North Carolina, all of whose friends I know as well as those of his wife who was a Miss Washington. Col. and Mrs. Taylor also stay at his house. Had a good supper and was hospitably entertained. After dinner and a smoke, rode over to Dr. Wooten's quarters where I remained until near dark. Gen. Churchill called in late and I remained talking with him until after sunset, then [I] rode out to camp by moonlight alone. The ride was solitary but cool and delightful. [I] arrived too late for supper but that is of but small moment to one who has had a good dinner.

July 11th. Monday. Spent the day in camp and having but few professional or official duties to perform, read as much as the heat of the weather and the annoyance of the flies would allow me. As for sleep that was quite out of the question with the thousand and one flies humming around and crawling over me. Both my mess mates went off on short leaves today leaving me to eat my meals alone. Dr. Swindell called by this evening on his way out from Camden and informs me that a *St. Louis Democrat* of the 2nd inst. has been received there which announces or rather admits the defeat of Sherman by Johnston, that gold is $290 in New York, that Chase, Lincoln's Secretary of the Treasury, has resigned and that the seige of Richmond is suspended for the present and Grant [is] falling back. All this is good and glorious news and for which I desire to render thanks to the Gens. of [the] victories. God grant that the ill success with which they have met during the present year may so discourage the Yankees as to incline them to peace.

July 12th. Tuesday. Our Medical Board met at Tappan's Brigade this morning and at 9 o'clock I rode down there where we had diverse cases to act on which were duly attended to. Remained in session a couple of hours and then returned to camp by noon. The rest of the day was spent in reading *St. Valentine's Day, or the Fair Maid of Perth.* No news of any importance today. There is a rumor that Grant has been defeated again by Gen. Lee and driven from Bermuda Hundred—a complete rout. Hope that it is true. Gold in St. Louis is said to be $325. This is reducing Federal green backs to a very low figure and if true shows a bad state of Yankee affairs. We shall see.

July 13th. Wednesday. Another hot day spent quietly in camp reading principally. When the army is stationary the life of a staff officer is one of comparative indolence. As Chief Surgeon of the division my duties are light except at the beginning of the month, and after an engagement when they are arduous and responsible. Had numerous visitors from surgeons and others which occupied a portion of my time. No recent news today from any quarter but all that we do get is most cheering even that obtained from Yankee papers, on which we have mainly to rely on at present.

July 14th. Thursday. Today was spent as yesterday—in camp with but little to do. Finished reading the *Fair Maid of Perth,* and for want of something better commenced one of James' *The Convict* —certainly not an attractive title. We have news today of the destruction of the Confederate war steamer, *Alabama,* in the Mediterranean Sea by Yankee cruisers.[41] If this be so while it is to be regretted it is not to be wondered at. She has had a long run and has destroyed many Yankee crafts and an immense amount of property. It is also said that Seward, Blair, and Bates of Lincoln's cabinet have resigned as well as Chase.[42] This looks like a breaking up of the corrupt Black Republican cabal which has ruled at Washington with such desperate and despotic sway. May it prove beneficial to the cause of southern independence.

July 15th. Friday. The Medical Examining Board met as usual this morning in Gause's Brigade and thither at 9 o'clock I repaired. We had diverse cases before us requiring the exercise of judgment and professional skill, all of which were disposed of. On my way back to camp about the middle of the day passed Blocher's Battalion near to which was a large arbor of brush erected and a large congregation of soldiers and others were assembled engaged in religious exercises, conducted by the chaplains of the army of the Methodist denomination. They are holding a protracted meeting, and as is usual under such circumstances with this class, a good deal of excitement and wild confusion was exhibited. Still I hope that good will be accomplished, though there is not as much order and discretion as the solemnity and importance of religion demands. Quite a revival I understand is in progress. In Gen. Parsons' Division similar meetings have been held with better results. Far be it from me to discourage such meetings though for the honor of religion and the permanent good that is likely to result I could desire more prudence in their management. Would to God that our entire army—officers and men—were persuaded by a strong religious feeling and that the Holy Spirit were poured in our entire people in copious effusion for there is a great need of it. And we ought in all humility to humble ourselves before God for the many and great victories with which he has crowned our armies during the present campaign. Oh that our people felt this as they should. Spent the remainder of the day in reading. Late in the evening amused myself for an hour in pitching quoits with the young gentlemen of the staff.[43] No news today. The weather warm, the night bright and beautiful.

July 16th. Saturday. Still another hot day passing quietly and inactively in camp reading, smoking, and eating, though the latter operation forms but a small part of my existence as the scanty fare of camp is anything but tempting to the appetite. One advantage in a retired camp [in] this hot weather is that I can adopt my dress or undress to the weather and bathe as often as I like which is a great luxury. Capt. Royston, just out from Camden, states that the *Memphis Bulletin* of the 10th has been received which represents Johnston in full retreat before Sherman and [that] Grant is demanding the surrender of Petersburg. But this is such a lively sheet that there is no reliance to be placed in it.

July 17th. Sunday. After breakfast this morning [I] rode into Camden with Lt. Wright. Called at Gen. Price's headquarters for a short time to hear the news, but there was none. Then went to the Episcopal Church. In addition to the ordinary service a child was baptised. If language can convey anything, clearly it is obvious that the Episcopal service, as read today, teaches the doctrine of baptismal regeneration and all the Romish tendencies of the Pupils are to be found in the prayer book which must be reformed if ever that erring church itself is reformed. Instead of giving us a regular sermon, the preacher, Mr. Curtis, delivered an extemporaneous lecture on the propriety of infant baptism of which I never had a doubt, but the whole system of sponsors as well as the Romish doctrine of Baptismal regeneration I for one utterly reject and condemn. After church, [I] went to Gen. Churchill's and Gov. Polk's quarters with whom I took a late dinner, Mrs. Churchill presiding. Spent the long interval between church and dinner (dined at 4 P.M.) in conversation on the war and other matters. Between 5 and 6 o'clock [I] rode up to Dr. Wooten's quarters and there remained an hour, by which time the sun was nearly down and Lt. Wright and myself had a cool ride out to camp, the latter part of the way by moonlight. Heard no news of any kind in town though the tone of feeling is not as confident and satisfactory as it was a week ago. Most of the reports that we have heard of late are evidently false. It is amazing that we can never get the truth second handed. Learning of an opportunity to write across the Mississippi River by a gentleman going over. I will avail myself of it and write to my niece Sue McPheeters.

July 18th. Monday. A clear hot day spent quietly in camp. Finished reading *The Convict,* a very readable book. Finished a long letter commenced last night to my niece in North Carolina and sent it this morning to be conveyed across the Mississippi River and mailed it on the other side by Capt. [Henry W.] Pflager.[44] Commenced reading Dickens' *Little Dorrit.* Manfactured enevelopes, and late in the evening pitched quoits for an hour by way of amusement and thus passed the day. No news of any interest from any quarter.

July 19th. Tuesday. Rode down to Gen. Tappan's Brigade this morning where an Examining Board met. We had as many as a dozen cases for examination mostly for furloughs. As regards short furloughs for men who have been or are sick, I am disposed to be lenient, but when it comes to discharges I am designedly rigid. After getting through our business [I] had a long conversation with Capt. [H. W.] McMillan[45] of Fagan's Cavalry Division who is just from the Arkansas River and from him learned of their operations against Yankee boats etc. Got back to camp just before dinner. By Lt. Wright just from town, I learned that a flag of truce would start for Little Rock in the morning, and by which I wrote a letter to my beloved wife and sent it in by Capt. Royston. My letter I enclosed to Col. Chandler, a Federal at Little Rock, and requested him to forward it to my wife—I trust that she will get it. In my letter I intimated to her that if in the fall she desired to come south that I would not oppose it but would be heartily glad of it. I hope that she will come. Late Yankee papers have been received but they contain little or no news of importance. Affairs in Virginia and Georgia remain unchanged. God protect our armies and grant them victory over their enemies.

July 20th. Wednesday. We have exciting and cheering news today to the effect that our army is within 8 or 10 miles of Baltimore, cutting off and threatening Washington City and that Grant is on the retreat from Petersburg and Richmond in the direction of Washington.[46] Late Yankee papers seem to foreshadow something of the sort and those who profess to have seen and read the *Chicago Times* of the 14th say that such is contained in that paper. But we have been too often deceived by such reports to place implicit confidence in them. Still it may be so and I hope that it is. There has undoubtedly been great excitement in Baltimore—the ringing of bells and forcing the citizens to arms and etc. If Grant has been forced to withdraw from the neighborhood of Richmond it is glory enough for one day. Spent the day in camp reading *Little Dorrit*. Late this evening we had a refreshing shower, which has cooled the air very much and tonight it is very pleasant.

July 21st. Thursday. A letter from Camden this morning informs us that a dispatch has been received from Col. Cad Polk[47] at Monticello stating that he has seen and read in a Yankee paper of the 14th inst. that our forces have taken Baltimore and Arlington Heights, that Grant is retreating from Petersburg with Beauregard in pursuit and etc. It may be true that we have taken Baltimore, but there is probably no truth in the story about Arlington Heights. The whole statement, however, needs confirmation as the Yankees, when they are scared, sometimes publish sensational reports which may prove to be all false, or they may do it to get the Northern people to enlist in their army. I hope, however, that it is true. God grant that it may be true and that it will tell in final result. Spent the day in camp reading and doing such official duty as devolved on me. My mess mates being all absent in town, [I] took dinner and supper alone and poor meals they were. Beef, miserable corn-bread and an ear of green corn for dinner, and for tonight biscuits, salt bacon and a cup of cold water for supper—camp fare. I do not complain, however, as my health is good and my appetite fine, thanks to a kind Providence. There is a wedding in town tonight. Col. White of Missouri weds Miss Frazer. Some of our staff are in attendance, but not having curiosity enough I did not go in. We had another fine shower this evening. General Tappan sent me a fine watermelon today which we enjoyed the eating of this evening. Had several visitors during the day.

July 22nd. Friday. A great change in the weather since the rain of yesterday. It is cool and pleasant this morning. After breakfast and smoking my pipe [I] went down to Gause's Brigade to attend the meeting of the Medical Examining Board. We had 8 or 10 cases before us some of whom required careful examination so our meeting was rather protracted. When it was over [I] sat by some time conversing with Drs. Swindell and Jandon on polemic theology until Dr. Swindell's dinner was announced, whereupon I took dinner with him. Returned to camp between 2 and 3 P.M. On arriving [I] found a note from Mrs. Churchill saying that the General was quite sick and asking me to ride into Camden and see him. So after finding my horse and fixing up, I went in. On arriving [I] found him quite unwell—very nauseous. Despairing of my coming he had sent for Dr. Wooten who I found there when I arrived. We prescribed for him and cheered him up and promising to return and spend the night with him, I called up at Gen. Price's quarters and spent an hour in conversation with him and others there. He had a *Cincinnati Commercial* of the 13th inst., a rabid abolition journal, which was filled with accounts of the great excitement and consternation at the north occasioned by the movement on Washington and Baltimore. They seem to anticipate the most severe results. Two officers who have just arrived from the river state that they have seen Yankee papers as late as the 16th that our army under Ewell entered Washington on the morning of the 14th at 4 A.M. and also that Johnston has defeated Sherman in Georgia. If all this be true—and God grant that it is—it is glorious, most glorious. After remaining for a long time with Gen. Price [I] rode over to Dr. Wooten's quarters and remained to tea, [after] which [I] mounted my horse and rode out a half a mile to the place where I had agreed to meet Capt. Royston to say to him that I would not return to camp with him as agreed upon. Then [I] went up to Gen. Churchill's quarters and after seeing him again and giving directions for the night, prior to going to bed, [I] had a long talk with Governor Polk and Judge Watkins, who occupy the same house, on the state of the country and the exciting news which we have been receiving for a day or two past. These exciting subjects too occupied my thoughts after I retired.

July 23rd. Saturday. Spent last night in Camden and as was natural from the nature of my thoughts before going to sleep dreams of our success and imagination went into St. Louis with our victorious army. But it was only a dream. Took breakfast with Mrs. Churchill, Gov. Polk, and Judge Watkins who mess together. The General is better this morning, put him on treatment for the day. Dr. Wooten called up and we rode down to Gen. Price's headquarters where I read a letter to Col. [John Q.] Burbridge[48] from his adjutant on the Arkansas River giving him a synopsis of papers up to the 16th inst. which state that Gen. Breckenridge with 15,000 men stormed and took Baltimore on the 14th. Confirmed the defeat of Sherman by Johnston and etc. If we have really taken Washington and Baltimore as there seems to be every reason to believe it is certainly one of the greatest military exploits of the age, and stamps Gen. Lee as the great General of the age. But I forebear comment until the papers confirming the facts are received. After remaining in town until about 11 A.M., [I] returned to camp where I arrived about noon. Both of my mess mates are away. Capt. Sevier went yesterday to Little Rock with a flag of truce and Lt. Wright went home to Lewisville on a visit, so I am alone. A wagon sent several days ago to Mrs. Wright's at Lewisville for provisions arrived last night bringing butter, chickens, flour and a number of very acceptable delicacies which are highly appreciated in camp, and which are particularly acceptable to me just at present not feeling very well and not relishing the coarse fare of camp. Spent the after-noon and evening in official duties and in reading. Gen. Tappan paid me a long visit this evening and took tea with me. The weather tonight is cool and pleasant.

July 24th. Sunday. Took breakfast this morning with Capt. Royston after which [I] rode into Camden with Gen. Tappan. Weather pleasant. On arriving at Gen. Price's headquarters, [I] learned that a Cairo paper of the 15th inst. had been received which contradicts the cheering news that we have been receiving for several days past. [It] denies that Washington or Baltimore have been taken by our forces and says that no battle has taken place between Sherman and Johnston. The source from which this information comes is not very reliable and may be incompatible with what is said to be con-tained in the papers of the 16th. Still it creates very great doubts on the whole subject and we must await further news to resolve these doubts. From Gen. Price's headquarters I went up to see Gen. Churchill. [I] found him not quite so well as yesterday but still mending. After paying this visit [I] went to the Methodist church where I heard a very good sermon on the duty, importance and reasonableness of prayer by the Pastor Rev. Mr. Radcliff. Hearing that Mrs. Thomas Smith had recently arrived from St. Louis, I called to see her hoping that possibly I might hear from my wife by her.

She had not seen her but heard through a friend that she was well. [I am] glad even of this doubtful information. After paying a short visit, [I] went to Dr. Wooten's quarters where I had the pleasure of seeing his wife and children just arrived from Texas. [I] took dinner with them. Gen. Tappan came over with Maj. Cabell also for dinner. Remained talking, smoking and napping until 5 o'clock when I again rode out to camp alone, where I arrived just after sunset. [I] took a light supper alone and here I am in my tent prepared for a quiet night.

July 25th. Monday. Feeling rather unwell today—bowels somewhat out of order—so [I] did not go in to visit Gen. Churchill as I would otherwise have done. Spent the day quietly reading, lounging and taking medicine. Captains Royston and Kidder took dinner with me. No good or cheering news today. Yankee papers still deny all about the taking of Washington or Baltimore and there is doubtless no truth in the stories that we have heard. It is amazing the false reports that we get. They even say our army is leaving Maryland and that Johnston is falling back. There is certainly nothing cheering in the aspect of affairs at present, but trusting in God I will hope for the best.

July 26th. Tuesday. The weather for several days past has been cool and pleasant. [I am] still a little unwell. [I] went, however, to Tappan's Brigade this morning to attend the meeting of the Medical Examining Board. [We] had quite a number of cases before us, all of which were disposed of. Finished reading *Little Dorrit;* [I] can't say that I am much pleased with it. Dickens is a bad man and by making his characters who profess piety hideous, seeks to prejudice the public against religion—a mean mode of attack. His characters are mostly overdrawn and not true to life. Still there are some good take-offs in the book. No news today. By the courier this afternoon, [I] received official dispatches rendering it necessary for me to issue orders to the brigade surgeons.

July 27th. Wednesday. Thanks to a kind Providence I feel better today. After breakfast, [I] went into town. Called on Gen. Churchill

[and] found him improving. [I] then called for a moment at Gen. Price's headquarters but learned no news, in fact, there was none in town. Wishing to return a book and get another to read, I called on Dr. and Mrs. Harding for that purpose and got Dicken's late book, *Great Expectations,* which I brought out to camp. Took dinner with Maj. Cabell on a fine piece of tenderloin beef. Remained until 5 P.M. then called again to see Gen. Churchill. On returning late in the evening to camp, [I] got a letter from Mrs. Newton who is sick at Lewisville entreating me to visit her and prescribe for her. [I] don't know yet whether I can go or not.

July 28th. Thursday. Spent the morning in answering letters. Wrote to the Rev. Mr. Boyd of Spring Hill from whom I received a letter a day or two ago since, in which he stated that he had sent me some watermelons, which by the bye have not yet come to hand. Also wrote to Mr. John H. Simpson[49] of Parson's Division in answer to a letter from him. [With] this over [I] read *Great Expectations.* Rather a novel incident occurred, at least to me today. Ned, Capt. Sevier's servant, disobeyed me and was impudent, whereupon I attempted to correct him when he ran off and defied me. I sent two couriers and had him caught and brought to me where I administered a sound thrashing to him much to my satisfaction and that of the rest of the staff. Maj. Ben Johnson, who has been absent on leave some 20 days, returned this evening. Capt. Kidder took breakfast with me, Capt. Royston dinner, and Maj. Johnson tea with me. We had a fine rain this evening. No news today though recent Yankee papers have been received. Had a visit from Gen. Tappan this morning.

July 29th. Friday. Attended the meeting of the Examining Board at Gause's Brigade this morning, and after getting through with all the cases on hand [I] learned that Dr. Swindell, senior surgeon of the brigade, was under arrest for some misunderstanding with the Col. of the regiment. Returned to camp and spent the rest of the day as usual in reading, doing some official duty, and etc. No news today. It is raining hard tonight while I am snug in my camp house—would that our soldiers were all as comfortable.

July 30th. Saturday. Spent the day in camp reading and in transmitting official communications to the brigade. This afternoon [I]
received a note from Dr. Wooten requesting me to come in town
tomorrow prepared to go to Shreveport. Gen. Price expects to start
there early the next morning and wishes him or myself to accompany him as he has been sick and may need medical attendance on
the way, and as Dr. Wooten dislikes to leave on account of his
wife's being here, he asks me to go. Although I had rather not take
the trip, yet to accommodate Dr. Wooten and Gen. Price, I will
do it provided the arrangements are such as suit me when I go in
tomorrow. So I will go in prepared for the trip. We have news
today that a battle has been fought near Atlanta, Georgia. The
Yankees claim to have defeated our army and to have taken Atlanta,
while our accounts are to the effect that Sherman was defeated with
great loss.[50] We will have to wait and see which account is true.
The Yankees are enormous liars and if our account is official from
Richmond as it purports to be there is no question as to which is
entitled to belief.

July 31st. Sunday. The last day of July '64. Agreeable to the letter
that I received last evening I arranged my affairs this morning
preparatory to a visit to Shreveport, La. About twelve o'clock I
rode into town with Maj. Dunlap. Just before starting, Capt. Sevier
arrived in camp having returned from a trip to Little Rock with a
flag of truce. He did not get into the town and did not bring me a
letter from my wife as I had hoped, thus deeming me to another
disappointment. It is hard to be separated from one's family without the means of hearing from them. This is one of the saddest features of this sad war with thousands of those whose families and
friends are within the enemy's lines. Arrived in Camden about 1
P.M. and at Dr. Wooten's quarters just in time for dinner. When
over and after a smoke, Dr. Wooten, Maj. Cabell and myself rode
over to Gen. Price's quarters. Found him better and sitting up. It
was arranged that we should start in the morning at sunrise in a four
mule ambulance. After seeing him, [I] called around to visit Gen.
and Mrs. Churchill. Found him improving but still in the bed.
Returned again to Dr. Wooten's quarters where I spent the evening

and night. My boy, Frank, came in from camp with my carpetsack and took out my horse, as I have no need for him on the trip. We have no news today from any quarter. I did not get in town in time for church; consequently, this has been an unprofitable Sabbath to me. Oh, that this war was over and peace habits once inaugurated.

August 1st. Monday. Rained during the night. Arose at daylight this morning and repaired to Gen. Price's quarters and took an early breakfast with him, but owing to a heavy shower of rain did not get off as soon as we expected. It was 7 o'clock when we embarked in a four mule ambulance. Rode 21 miles on the Wire Road by 1 P.M. when we stopped and took a plain meal at a plain house on the roadside. [The] husband of the woman [has] gone to the war and she widowed for the time. This is the case with thousands, in fact, with almost every house. The woman though poor would receive no pay for our dinner and feed for our horses, saying that she "never charged soldiers." This is true patriotism. After resting a couple of hours we started again and came on 15 miles further to Magnolia, making a trip of 36 miles. The first part of the day was pleasant on account of the rain, the latter part hot. On the way [I] read a long and interesting letter from Maj. Snead to Gen. Price from Mississippi on army and public affairs. At Magnolia [we] put up at the hotel kept by Mr. Parker who exerted himself to make us and especially Gen. Price comfortable. Retired early.

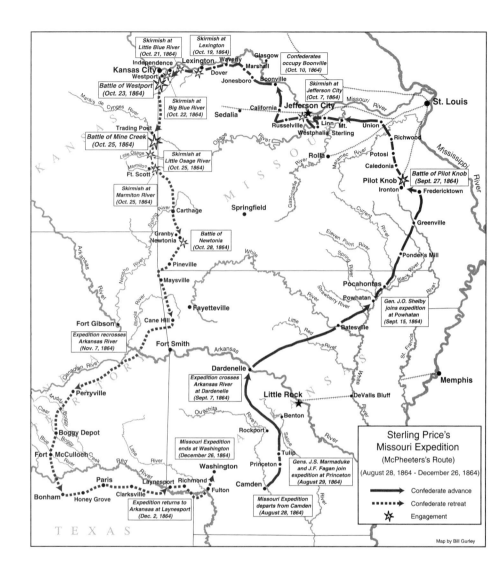

Skirmish at
Little Blue River
(Oct. 21, 1864)

Skirmish at
Lexington
(Oct. 19, 1864)

Independence • Lexington • Waverly • Glasgow
Kansas City • • • Marshall
Westport • Dover
• Jonesboro • Boonville

Confederates
occupy Boonville
(Oct. 10, 1864)

Battle of Westport
(Oct. 23, 1864)

Skirmish at
Big Blue River
(Oct. 22, 1864)

• California • Sedalia • Jefferson City

Skirmish at
Jefferson City
(Oct. 7, 1864)

Missouri   River   • St. Louis

• Trading Post

Battle of Mine Creek
(Oct. 25, 1864)

• Russelville • Linn • Mt.
• Westphalia Sterling • Union
Osage   River   • Richwood

Skirmish at
Little Osage River
(Oct. 25, 1864)

Little Osage
• Marmiton
• Ft. Scott

Skirmish at
Marmiton River
(Oct. 25, 1864)

• Rolla   • Potosi
• Caledonia

Battle of Pilot Knob
(Sept. 27, 1864)

• Pilot Knob
• Ironton   • Fredericktown

• Carthage
• Springfield

• Greenville

• Granby
• Newtonia

Battle of
Newtonia
(Oct. 28, 1864)

White

Eleven Point River

Spring River

• Ponder's Mill

• Pineville

• Maysville

• Pocahontas
• Powhatan

Gen. J.O. Shelby
joins expedition
at Powhatan
(Sept. 15, 1864)

• Fort Gibson

Expedition recrosses
Arkansas River
(Nov. 7, 1864)

• Cane Hill • Fayetteville

Little

Red

• Batesville

• Memphis

• Fort Smith

Arkansas

• Dardenelle

Expedition crosses
Arkansas River
at Dardenelle
(Sept. 7, 1864)

• Little Rock   • DeValls Bluff

White

• Benton

• Perryville

Ouachita

• Rockport

• Boggy Depot

Fort • McCulloch

Missouri Expedition
ends at Washington
(December 26, 1864)

• Washington

• Tulip

• Princeton

• Paris • Laynesport • Richmond
Bonham • • Honey Grove   • Fulton
• Clarksville

Gens. J.S. Marmaduke
and J.F. Fagan join
expedition at Princeton
(August 29, 1864)

• Camden

Expedition returns to
Arkansas at Laynesport
(Dec. 2, 1864)

Missouri Expedition
departs from Camden
(August 28, 1864)

T E X A S

Sterling Price's
Missouri Expedition
(McPheeters's Route)
(August 28, 1864 - December 26, 1864)

→ Confederate advance
▪▪▪▶ Confederate retreat
★ Engagement

Map by Bill Gurley

CHAPTER 8

The Grand Expedition, 1864

Send us forth into the world to do Thy will.

William McPheeters's friendship with Maj. Gen. Sterling Price had deepened during their months of campaigning together. Their long evenings in the general's quarters, smoking and talking, had provided them time to share their private thoughts as well as their goals for the army. One hope, which remained fixed in the mind of the aging general, was to return to Missouri with an army strong enough to conquer his home state for the Confederate nation. Price and McPheeters agreed that Missouri had been illegally pirated for the Union during the early days of secession. After all, there was in the Confederate flag a star for Missouri, a slave state. McPheeters had seen people of "quality" supporting the Southern dream of independence, and if Price could return with his gray army, these people would flock to his banner. This was their firm belief. This would redeem the Trans-Mississippi, restore the waning Confederacy, and validate their months of heroism in the field of battle so far from home.

The grand plan distilling in the minds of the general and his staff was an invasion force that would make its way due north up the full length of Arkansas, crossing into Missouri at its southeastern corner. They believed that countless recruits would join their expedition and that they would march into St. Louis triumphantly, capture the arsenal, and equip their army and the new recruits with the latest Yankee weapons stored there. So confident was the general of this outcome that, in his preparations for this fifteen-hundred-mile trek, he included a wagonload of newly polished brass band instruments and an ensemble of terrified musicians. He imagined himself in full regalia leading his triumphant host down Front Street to the accompaniment of martial music.

With a deep sense of purpose, McPheeters rode with Price toward

Shreveport and the headquarters of Lt. Gen. Edmund Kirby Smith to receive final orders and funding for the invasion force. As physician and friend, McPheeters was concerned for the fifty-four-year-old Missourian who had achieved substantial bulk during his military ordeal and now weighed well over three hundred pounds. On this trip he and McPheeters rode in a double mule-team ambulance, but as part of the preparation for the expedition to Missouri, his men fashioned for him a sturdy wagon that they padded with quilts. Indeed, when it was necessary for Price to ride a horse, his aides brought forward a carefully groomed draft horse equal to the task. McPheeters was increasingly attentive to the general's state of health.

To wrench Missouri from the Federals' grasp, the key was speed, and speed meant cavalry. Realizing this, General Smith preferred another officer to lead the expedition besides Price. To Smith, the Missourian's military accumen was questionable; other officers were more suited to the task. What Price brought to the table, however, was rank and political influence, especially with the people of Missouri. After considerable deliberation, Smith reluctantly handed the expedition reins over to the weary old infantry officer.

For the department commander, the objectives of the operation were strictly military—capture St. Louis, divert Federal troops away from the eastern theater, and accrue as many recruits, arms, and livestock as possible. But Price the politician had additional motives— reestablish Missouri's elected government and rally Confederate Missourians to the flag and the cause. Simply put, the goals for the expedition were lofty, and its realization was bold.

The blueprint for success required cooperation among the cavalry divisions of Brig. Gens. J. O. Shelby, John S. Marmaduke, and James F. Fagan, all officers with solid reputations whose core commands had proven themselves on numerous fields. Like many of their previous raids into Missouri, the columns were expected to move quickly and be mutually supportive. This campaign, however, would necessitate a force much larger than any these officers had managed heretofore. To assure success, veteran cavalry units were liberally supplemented with mounted infantrymen, guerrillas, bushwhackers, and almost four thousand unarmed recruits. The result was a force of twelve thousand men poised to strike into Missouri. A drawback to the arrangement was the threat of plunder and desertion among the novice, undisciplined horsemen. Furthermore, such a sizeable force required a wagon train of equal proportions, and this was an even greater problem. Hundreds of wagons would impair the column's quickness and maneuverability—elements crucial to the mission's success and the survival of its participants.[1]

August 2nd. Tuesday. Arose early this morning [and] took breakfast and got off by sunrise. The landlord of the hotel charged us $35 for our supper, breakfast and nights lodging, that is, for Gen. Price, myself, the driver and 4 mules. This is war prices. On the way [we] bought a watermelon for $2 which was very refreshing, the weather being very hot. We came 42 miles today, part of the road being very bad. After going 25 miles, [we] stopped for dinner at the plain house of a poor woman who had a sick child. I was glad to have it in my power to prescribe for it and give her medicine—one of her children recently died. She would charge us nothing for our dinner—another instance of disinterested patriotism. Started again about 3 P.M. and came 17 miles crossing the ferry of the Bodcaw [Creek] and arrived at Dr. Standishes' just about dark. Here we were received and entertained most hospitably. The young ladies (3 accomplished and charming girls) were very anxious to see Gen. Price and were greatly obliged to me for bringing him to their house. Mrs. Standish informed me that one of the young ladies had promised that if an officer would bring Gen. Price to see them that she would make him a fine Palmetto hat. Of course I claimed the hat and she promised to make it. Spent a pleasant evening and retired about 11 P.M. enjoying a fine nights rest.

August 3rd. Wednesday. Breakfasted at 6 A.M. and after remaining an hour talking with the ladies resumed our journey. Dr. Standishes' is a delightful place, intelligent and refined, and they insisted on our stopping on our return, which we promised to do. It is a great treat to get with such people. The road today was good. About 1 o'clock we stopped at Dr. Vance's, 10 miles from Shreveport, and took dinner and rested two hours. At 3 P.M. we resumed our journey and drove along Red River in the bottom and arrived at Shreveport between 5 and 6 [P.M.]. [We] put up at the Verandah Hotel but soon after Gen. Smith called and took Gen. Price up to his quarters. I was out at the time, [having gone] to the barber's to have my hair cut, for which I paid $3. Took tea at the hotel, saw Col. Mitchell, and talked with him. After tea, Dr. Yandell called and insisted on my going also to Gen. Smith's, saying that the General had directed him to bring me up, so I went. There I found Governor Reynolds and others and spent a pleasant evening. [I] smoked a good cigar, got a toddy of fine brandy, and passed the time agreeably. Retired after 11 o'clock.

August 4th. Thursday. Took breakfast, a fine meal, good coffee, etc., with Gens. Smith, Price, Gov. Reynolds, Drs. Yandell and Smith, and others. After breakfast, [I] went down into town on business for Gen. Price. Received a letter from Maj. Cabell of Camden giving me several commissions to do for him, all of which I executed, and [then] returned to Gen. Smith's quarters about 1 o'clock. Here [I] met Generals [Simon Bolivar] Buckner[2] and [John H.] Forney,[3] was introduced to them, and had some conversation with them. While down [the] street [I] met Col. [Matthew R.] Cullen,[4] formerly of St. Louis, but more recently of Richmond, who has come over to this department as Military Judge. He returned with me to pay his respects to Gen. Price. At 11 o'clock, General Smith started on a steamer on a short visit to Alexandria, leaving us at his quarters in charge of several of his staff. At the request of the Chief Quartermaster, Gen. [William R.] Boggs,[5] I took charge of and gave my receipt for $100,000 in new issue to be delivered to Maj. Brinker in Camden. Took a toddy of fine old brandy with several of the military dignitaries, and before Gen. Smith left he presented us with a bundle (25) of fine cigars for our smoking on the way, which is a great treat, both the cigars and brandy [during] these times of war and blockade. On settling my bill at the hotel for the poor supper I got last night, I paid $5. [I] also paid $1.50 a paper for small papers of matches— worth five cents at ordinary times. Such are the enormous prices charged for everything now! At 1 P.M. we took a snack and at 2 P.M. started again on our return to Camden, having remained in Shreveport less than one day during which time Gen. Price had an interview with General Smith and arranged for the former going into Missouri. The visit though short was, therefore, satisfactory. I had no desire to prolong my stay in Shreveport as it was very warm and very sickly there. Got across Red River in the ferry boat by ½ past 2. [We] rode ten miles through the bottom to Dr. Vance's where we delighted and partook of a fine watermelon then resumed our journey. The farms of Red River bottom I have spoken of as most magnificent and exceedingly fertile, all teeming with corn now ripe. With the blessing of Providence there is no prospect of our army in the department starving at least for a year to come. At dusk, having traveled 21 miles, we stopped for the night at the fine residence of Mr. Adges, a wealthy planter formerly from South Carolina, where we were kindly welcomed and most hospitably and luxuriantly entertained.

August 5th. Friday. After a fine night's rest and a sumptuous breakfast, [we] resumed our journey this morning. During the night there was a storm of wind and some rain which laid the dust and rendered it much more pleasant travelling today. [We] came 12 or 14 miles to Dr. Sandidge's, arriving about 11 A.M. and remained to dinner. I have before, on more than one occasion, spoken of this family as one of the most agreeable and charming that I ever met. Here we met Gen. Marmaduke and Maj. [Manning M.] Kimmel[6] also on their way from Shreveport. With the young ladies and other members of the family we had quite a dinner party and one that would not have disgraced the most luxurious board in peace times. It is pleasant to get among such people and would be agreeable to remain longer but we have no time to enjoy ourselves now, so at 3 P.M. we again resumed our journey and by sundown came 14 miles to Walnut Hill, 7 miles beyond the Louisiana line in Arkansas. [We] stopped for the night at Dr. Peterson's, also a wealthy Red River planter formerly from Georgia. Here also we were most hospitably and elegantly entertained. Mrs. Peterson is a very pretty, young, intelligent, pious, and interesting lady. Having been greatly annoyed and pained all day by a boil on my seat, I got the doctor to lance it for me, which gave me great relief after the pain of the operation was over.

August 6th. Saturday. [I] was not in a hurry to start this morning
as we were in pleasant quarters, had not far to travel, and as a rain
during the night had cooled the atmosphere. Got off, however,
after a delightful breakfast and rode 18 miles to Lewisville and
arrived at Mrs. Wright's, one mile west of the town. Arrived
between 2 and 3 P.M. Mrs. Wright lives in an elegant house, is very
wealthy, and has about her all that wealth and a cultivated taste can
suggest for her own comfort and that of her friends. She is
unboundedly hospitable. Here again we came up with Gen.
Marmaduke and Maj. Kimmel who left soon after dinner. We also
found her son, Lt. Wright of Gen. Churchill's staff and one of my
mess mates; Capts. Taylor and Watkins; also Miss Rayburn, a beautiful young lady and belle of Little Rock; Mrs. D. Payton and her
sister, Miss Sophy Crease, a perfect nondescript character of
a woman, all here as visitors, who together with Mrs. Wright's
daughters formed a gay, happy, interesting family group. After fixing up and resting awhile, I rode into Lewisville to Col. Dick
Johnson's to see my friend Mrs. Newton, who had written beg-
ging me to call and see her professionally. [I] found her and her son
laboring under dysentery. [I] advised with and prescribed for them
and Mrs. Johnson, who is also sick, and then returned to Mrs.
Wright's in time for a sumptuous supper such as would do credit
to any board in prosperous times of peace. After supper, the young
ladies played on the piano and sang. Then the young folk danced
awhile, promenaded, conversed, and finally played several old fashioned games. In the meantime, the General retired, but I was so
charmed with the rarity of the entertainment that I remained up
until long after eleven and almost felt that I was young again, and
if my beloved wife had been there [I] would have enjoyed it hugely.
I wonder where she is and what she is doing tonight, and my children too, where are they? I will not tell all that I said to the girls
and particularly to Miss Rayburn. As I had made an engagement to
breakfast with Col. Johnson in the morning, I reluctantly took leave
of the ladies before retiring and then went to the gentleman's quarters and took a smoke before going to bed.

August 7th. Sunday. Before I was up this morning, Col. Johnson
sent a horse out for me to ride to his house for breakfast. So after

making my toilet, I rode in leaving Gen. Price behind, who is to call for me after breakfast at Col. Johnson's. [I] met Dr. [Isaac] Folsom,[7] a hospital surgeon stationed here and who is in attendance on Mrs. Newton, her son, and Mrs. Johnson, and after consulting with him on their cases, partook of a good breakfast. About 9 A.M. Gen. Price called by for me and after paying a short visit, we started on our journey, Sunday though it be. I do not like it, but I am under orders. We came only 18 miles to Lamartine to the residence of Mrs. Dockery, the mother of Brig. Gen. Dockery, where we arrived about 2 P.M. and spent the remainder of the day and night. She too has a fine house and lives in great comfort. Here we found the General, her son, and his pretty and agreeable wife and spent a pleasant time, being warmly welcomed. I must here remark that the private residences at which we have stopped on the trip cannot be beat for elegance and refinement and hospitality. In so many days march in any county, I care not where, and but for the fact being constantly the subject of conversation, one would hardly know that we are engaged in a gigantic war, and that our ports are blockaded.

August 8th. Monday. Left Mrs. Dockery's at 7 o'clock this morning after a good night's sleep and a comfortable breakfast. After a ride of 32 miles over a hilly road and passing some six or seven long trains of government wagons, [we] arrived in Camden about half past 3 P.M. We did not stop on the way for dinner. The fact is neither Gen. Price nor myself desired any dinner, having fared so sumptuously of late we both felt replete and it was a comfort to give our stomachs rest. Took the General to his quarters, and then drove around to Dr. Wooten's and Maj. Cabell's quarters and there took out my baggage. After resting awhile and fixing up, [I] mounted my horse, which had been brought to me from camp, and rode to Maj. Brinker's to deliver up the one hundred thousand dollars brought from Shreveport for here—public funds. After that [I] called to see Gen. and Mrs. Churchill, but not finding them at home [I] went up to Gen. Price's quarters where I met numerous officers and friends. About dusk, [I] returned, took tea and spent the evening and night with Dr. Wooten and Maj. Cabell.

August 9th. Tuesday. Called down at Gen. Price's headquarters
this morning where I met Gen. Churchill and Fagan and many
other officers. The weather being extremely hot I soon returned
and cooled off. [I] had a long conversation with Dr. Wooten and
Maj. Cabell concerning Gen. Price's contemplated trip up into
Missouri from which I ascertained that Dr. Wooten does not wish
to accompany the expedition on account of his wife and family
being here. At his request, Maj. Cabell and I waited on Gen. Price
and stated the case and asked that Dr. Wooten be excused from
the trip. The General readily and kindly consented and then
requested me to go with him as his Medical Director, stating that
he preferred me to any one else, that is, I presume next to Dr.
Wooten who has been with [him] since the commencement of
the war. I readily assented to his proposition. He stated that he
would relieve me from my present position and order me to
report to him. He then told me to make all my arrangements for
the trip. At 3 o'clock [I] dined with Gen. and Mrs. Churchill by
invitation. Gen. Marmaduke, Gov. Polk, Judge Watkins, and
Capt. Sevier also dined with them. After dinner, [I] had a long
talk over our contemplated move and army affairs generally.
Having some business with the Medical Purveyor, [I] went to see
him about 5 P.M. then returned to where I am staying and spent
the evening with Dr. and Mrs. Wooten and Maj. Cabell. Hearing
of an opportunity of sending a letter to my beloved wife, after tea
I wrote to her telling her all that I dared to communicate but in
general terms. Would that I could write to her freely and fully.

August 10th. Wednesday. Had diverse business arrangements to
make this morning preliminary to the contemplated move. So after
breakfast [I] rode down to Maj. Brinker's quarters and made
arrangements to join his mess on the march and on our campaign
into Missouri. I prefer being with him and it seemed to be agreeable to him also. Attended also to processing of transportation and
next saw Dr. Bond, the Medical Purveyor, and with him settled
the matter of medical supplies for the expedition. [I] then went to
District Headquarters and there saw a number of officers and others.
Having finished my business, [I] returned about 12 M. to Dr.

Wooten's quarters to cool off. Dr. Slaughter, who has been on the
Mississippi River for some time past, returned about noon but without succeeding in getting what we went for—medical supplies.
Gen. Cabell came in before dinner on his way to his command,
and with him we all took a mint julip. Late in the evening [I] rode
out to camp with Maj. Dunlap intending to spend the night and in
the morning removing my effects into town where it is necessary
for me to be in order to complete my arrangements for getting off
in the early part of next week. Arrived at camp before sunset and
was warmly welcomed by Gen. Churchill's staff whom I was glad
to see and who I regret to part company with, but such is the fate
of war.

August 11th. Thursday. After breakfast this morning, [I] commenced packing up my effects preparatory to moving into town.
In due time, [I] struck my tent and loaded up my wagon and
started off, after which I took leave of Camp Yell and relinquished
my position as Chief Surgeon of Churchill's Division to become
Medical Director of General Price's Corps. Before leaving camp,
[I] traded horses with Lt. Wright, he having a fine chestnut sor-
rel named Grease and having fears that my horse would not stand
the long trip before me. I was anxious to get his. I gave him my
horse, $75 in gold, and $10 in greenback for his. I hope that he
will prove a servicable animal. About 11 o'clock, [I] rode into
town (Camden) with Capt. Kidder, Majs. Dunlap and Johnson,
and Lt. Wright. On arriving I stored my things at the Medical
Purveyor's and went to Dr. Wooten's quarters in time for dinner. During the afternoon it rained hard. Late in the afternoon [I]
rode up to visit Mrs. Maj. Graham, who is sick and prescribed for
her. After tea, [I] conversed for a long time with General and Maj.
Cabell and others on our personal experience of men and things
as we have found them during the war. My experience has been
altogether favorable to the hospitality and liberality of the people
that I have met.

August 12th. Friday. Gen. Cabell left for his command this morning. Soon after breakfast I went to the Medical Purveyor's to make

arrangements for my medical supplies for our expedition, all of
which were satisfactory. [I] got all that I wanted. Saw Maj. Brinker
and secured additional transportation; I want two wagons instead
of one. This done, I went to Gen. Price's headquarters on business
then visited Mrs. Graham and Mrs. Churchill. At noon, hearing
that Mrs. John Polk had just arrived from St. Louis where she
had been imprisoned and otherwise maltreated, I went to Maj.
Monroe's quarters to see her hoping to hear from my wife by her,
which I did. She saw my wife just before leaving St. Louis and
informs me that she and my children were well, which is of course
gratifying. While there a heavy rain came up and detained me
some time. At 3 o'clock [I] dined with Gen. and Mrs. Churchill.
Gen. Price, Maj. Cabell, Gov. Polk, and Judge Watkins were of
the party. Late in the day [I] returned to my quarters. Capt. Jo
Thomas returned from the river bringing with him Mr. Parkman
of Memphis, [who] came out on business with Gen. Smith at
Shreveport. After tea, Gen. Parsons came in and spent the night
with us. We will probably be delayed in Camden several days yet
before starting for Missouri. Yankee papers of the 6th inform us
of another repulse of the Federals at Petersburg; I judge a disastrous one to them.

August 13th. Saturday. I was relieved from duty this morning
with Churchill's Division by order of Gen. Price and ordered to
report to him preparatory to entering upon the duties of Medical
Director of the Army Corps about to advance. After which [I]
was engaged for some time at the Medical Purveyor's office in
transferring to Dr. Jandon the Division Medical Store, and in having my supplies for the expedition put up. After dinner [I] enjoyed
a nap of sleep and late in the evening rode up to see Mrs. Graham,
whom I found some better. I also saw Mrs. Clay Taylor. After
supper, [I] had a long discussion with Gen. Parsons, Mr. Parkman,
and others on the general subject of oath taking to the Federal
government. I taking strong grounds against the whole system and
condemning it in toto. The conversation grew out of an oath produced by Mr. Parkman, which he had taken in Jackson, Tenn. in
common with other citizens.

August 14th. Sunday. Rained hard during the night, rendering it necessary for me to move my cot to avoid a leak in the roof. A dull rainy morning. After breakfast [I] went to the Medical Purveyor's and from thence to the Methodist Church where I heard Parson Moore, whom I had known at Camp Bragg, preach. It was communion Sabbath and for the first time in my life I communed with that denomination. There are so few opportunities of this kind presented in the army that I do not like to allow an occasion to pass without availing myself of it, besides I have been pleased with the spirit of these Methodist ministers that have been thrown in with the army and can fraternize with them heartily. Then too I like on all suitable occasions to acknowledge my allegiance to the Lord Jesus. It may be a long time before I shall be permitted to enjoy another communion season. Spent the afternoon at home. Late in the evening [I] called to see Gen. and Mrs. Churchill and spent some time with them. Gov. Reynolds who has just arrived from Marshall, Texas to accompany us into Missouri, took tea with us after which we had a long and interesting conversation on public affairs.

August 15th. Monday. Rain, rain, rain. It rained last night and to a late hour this morning. After it held up so that I could go out, [I] visited Major Brinker and Morgan to arrange about transportation and my ambulance train. Four new ambulances arrived today from Washington, but without covers. This I had to see to with the aid of Dr. Wooten. After dinner, [I] snoozed and later in the evening called to see Mrs. Graham and Mrs. Jordan who arrived today and is staying at Gen. Churchill's. [I] found her the same bright intelligent agreeable woman that she has always been. Today we received news of the Surrender of Fort Gaines before Mobile and of the capture of several of our ironclads.[8] The saddest part of it is that the fort was surrendered in all probability by the treachery of Col. [Charles D.] Anderson of an Alabama regiment—base miscreant.[9] These disasters will probably lead to the loss of Mobile. Gov. Polk took tea with us tonight.

August 16th. Tuesday. Clear this morning. Rained hard about noon. Attended to diverse matters in the forenoon in preparation for our expedition. The probabilities are that we will not get off yet for several days awaiting the arrival of the ammunition train. After dinner, [I] slept and afterwards mounted my horse and visited Mr. John Polk and Mrs. Churchill and Jordan. After tea, Maj. Cabell and I called to see Gen. Price and Gov. Reynolds and afterwards Maj. MacLean.

August 17th. Wednesday. Still rainy and damp. Our expedition is still delayed on account of the rain and other causes. [I] was occupied during the forenoon in completing my arrangements. I am now well nigh ready to start at short notice. Visited Gen. Price at his headquarters this forenoon. Spent the afternoon and evening at home on account of the rain. No news, good or bad, today.

August 18th. Thursday. Rained all the morning keeping me in doors. Slept and wrote a letter to [my] sister Lavinia to send across the Mississippi River by courier informing her and my friends in North Carolina of my contemplated trip to Missouri. After dinner, [I] went into town and attended to diverse matters of business. Saw Gen. Churchill and from him obtained his pay account for $301, money that I advanced him some time since. After tea, [I] wrote a letter to Miss Sandidge to be sent by Maj. Cabell who goes to Shreveport in the morning. No news today. Our expedition [is] not yet ready to start [and] will probably be delayed several days.

August 19th. Friday. No rain but cloudy and cool today. Spent the forenoon down the street in fixing up diverse of my personal effects and in completing my arrangements for our contemplated trip into Missouri, but owing to the non-arrival of the ammunition train we are still detained and will be for some days. All parties are becoming anxious to get off, and it is very important that we should do so as soon as possible. Maj. Cabell started this morning for Shreveport. Spent the afternoon at home fixing up a matress to take along with me. Had visits from several surgeons on business connected with the expedition. No news from any quarter today and no Yankee papers.

August 20th. Saturday. Visited Gen. Price at his headquarters this morning, then Maj. [George A.] Gallagher[10] who is sick, and afterwards the Medical Purveyor. Arranged my mattress and blankets for the trip and attended to other matters of detail. After dinner, as there is no need of my being here for some days to come, I concluded to accompany Maj. [A. S.] Morgan[11] on a visit to Maj. Wright to spend the Sabbath with him. So about ½ past 3 P.M. we set off on horseback and after a ride of four hours arrived at Maj. Wright's about dusk, a distance of twenty-one miles from Camden. Was kindly and hospitably received by the Major, his wife being somewhat sick. Enjoyed a hearty country supper with good clabber and cream in abundance. After tea, [I] prescribed for Mrs. Wright and had a long talk with the Major on the affairs of the country and at a reasonable hour retired to a comfortable bed and enjoyed a quiet sleep without mosquitoes.

August 21st. Sunday. A quiet Sabbath in the country. Arose at a reasonable hour and after the rare privilege of uniting with Maj. Wright in family worship, enjoyed a country breakfast. After smoking my pipe, [I] rode with the Major to Mount Holly Church five miles distant, a neat Presbyterian Church of which the Rev. Mr. Patterson is pastor. Quite a genteel and good congregation assembled. The Rev. Dr. Kavanaugh, Chaplain at Large, preached a sensible discourse from the text *Lovest thou me?* On the way home, [we] called by Maj. Morgan's, saw his lady-like wife, and ate part of a very large watermelon which must have weighed 50 lbs. Returned to Maj. Wright's to dinner and spent the afternoon and evening in social discourse, and the night in comfortable sleep.

August 22nd. Monday. After an early breakfast, Maj. Morgan called by for me and I took leave of Maj. Wright's hospitable home and about 7 o'clock we started for Camden. The morning being pleasant we had an agreeable ride. Called by Gen. Churchill's headquarters and paid my associates on his staff a short visit and arrived in Camden a little after 11 o'clock. Found things in status quo, nothing of a stirring nature having occurred since I left and no news of interest having been received. Spent the afternoon partly at home and partly down the street looking after the affairs of the expedition. Saw numerous acquaintances.

August 23rd. Tuesday. Attended to various matters this morning, such as arranging my ambulance train and etc. Called to see Gen. Price at his headquarters and visited others on business. Thus passed the morning. At 2 P.M. [I] accompanied Col. Clay Taylor to Mrs. Graham's and took dinner with her—a comfortable family meal—and after dinner called to see Gov. Reynolds at the Generals quarters. Spent the afternoon at home, several surgeons calling on business. After tea, [I] attended and joined a *secret order,* having reference to military and political affairs, and took two degrees in the order. Enough said of that subject. Received a letter from Mrs. Jordan asking the loan of her books that I have and which I will cheerfully loan her. By the 2 o'clock courier to Shreveport, [I] wrote a short letter to Maj. Cabell. Received news from the other side of the river today, though not of a very stirring character. Affairs at Richmond and Atlanta remain about as at last dates.

August 24th. Wednesday. Wrote a letter to Mrs. Jordan this morning before breakfast and sent her *The History of the Dutch Republic* and *Sir Edward Sewall's Narrative.* After breakfast [I] took them to Dr. Taylor to be sent to her. [I] was occupied with various matters of business during the morning and saw diverse persons. Gen. Price and his two sons, [as well as] Gov. Reynolds, and Majors MacLean and Tracy dined with us today. We had a pleasant social time and gave them a good dinner for the times preceded by a tolerably good mint julip. Received a letter from Mrs. Newton at Lewisville thanking me for attending on her and asking advice in the case of her son laboring under dysentery. Later in the day [I] got a letter from Maj. Cabell at Shreveport stating that he had sent me up a palmetto hat made and kindly sent to me by Miss Fanny Lu Sandidge of Louisiana, for which I feel duly thankful to her.[12]

About dusk [I] was called to see a man just on the edge of the town who had been thrown from his horse and seriously injured—the doings of whiskey. We received an account of a most gallant feat of two young scouts on the Arkansas River. They captured and burned a steamer heavily laden with Federal stores and guarded by 15 Federal soldiers. [They] took all on board prisoners and burned some 8 or 10 of the soldiers with the boat who refused to surrender, but took refuge in the hold of the boat. They also captured a fine race horse of Gen. Steele's on board besides other valuables. Such acts of heroism deserve to be recorded.

August 25th. Thursday. Our grand expedition into Missouri still hangs fire, detained by the non-arrival of our ordnance train. Spent the morning in arranging my tent and other personal effects, and in seeing to the getting together and outfitting ambulances, etc. By the 2 o'clock courier, [I] wrote a letter to Maj. Cabell at Shreveport. Spent the afternoon and evening indoors, the weather being hot.

August 26th. Friday. As the time for the departure of our expedition approaches, business accumulates. We will probably get off day after tomorrow. This morning I was busy visiting the quartermasters getting my ambulance train filled up with mules, drivers, etc., and this afternoon in filling up medicines, assigning surgeons, and other necessary things. I am now nearly ready. Col. Cullen arrived about noon from Shreveport and took up his lodgings with us. I received today a beautiful palmetto hat made and sent to me by Miss Sandidge of Louisiana, which I prize very highly for its own value and for the sake of the fair donor.

August 27th. Saturday. An intensely hot day. Had my two wagons loaded this morning with medical stores in readiness for starting the train early in the morning. Next saw that all the ambulances were in readiness. By dinner time had all my arrangements all completed. Effected an exchange of saddles with Col. Clay Taylor by which I now have a first rate outfit—horse saddle and bridle. Saw numerous surgeons and others on business. Spent the afternoon at home the weather being too hot to venture out unnecessarily. Late in the evening rode down street on business. Spent the evening in quarters conversing and smoking with Col. Cullen, Dr. Wooten, and others. Tomorrow, Sunday though it be, we expect to start on one of the grandest expeditions of the war—a march of 600 miles into the enemy's country is certainly a considerable undertaking. God grant that it may prove a success and may his blessings attend us and preserve us from danger. I desire especially to implore the divine blessing to myself personally that I may have wisdom to guide me and strength to endure the fatigues of the trip.

August 28th. Sunday. Arose early this morning finished packing and put my personal effects in my wagon. Several of the ambulances reported and one was sent to Maj. Gallagher who is sick and wishes to go along and another to Kavanaugh who was kicked by a horse. Having all things in readiness took breakfast after which I took leave of Mrs. Wooten and other friends then mounted my horse to join Gen. Price and his staff and set out on our grand expedition. Dr. Wooten accompanied me. On going down the street I found that the General had passed on and was at the ferry. We repaired and came up with him just on the opposite bank from the town. It was ½ past 8 A.M. when we bid adieu to Camden. We were now fairly on our march, the day exceptionally hot and the roads dusty. Rode 12 miles when we found it necessary to rest our horses. While at the house where we halted a violent storm of rain, hail, and wind came up which cooled the atmosphere much. All the staff did not come up until late in the day. On another occasion I will give the names. After the rain, came 4 miles further and went into camp at Dr. Drake's, 16 miles from Camden. On this trip I enter into new mess arrangements going in with Maj. Brinker and Gov. Polk. Put up our tent in due time and enjoyed my first meal on the march and with my new mess mates. Weather showery during the evening. My mess arrangement promises to be very agreeable. Retired early, sleeping on the ground in Maj. Brinker's tent with others.

August 29th. Monday. Arose, dressed, and took breakfast before daylight and by sunrise was on our way, weather and travelling more pleasant than yesterday. We have quite a cavalcade along. The staff of the General, the attachés, hangers-on, and body guard form a large company. By 11 A.M. arrived at Princeton 16 miles from our place of encampment. Here we met General Fagan, Marmaduke, Cabell, and Clark with their commands. Here I also met with Mrs. Bruce just out by a flag of truce from Louisville Ky. via Little Rock. She brought me a letter from my beloved wife dated July 29th, one month old. It is a rare treat to hear from home and I am greatly delighted to know that wife and children were well at the date of my letter. Mrs. Bruce gave me a good deal of news about persons and things in Mo. and Ky. My wife's letter, however, delights me more than all. Had an interview with the Chief Surgeons of both the divisions and arranged all matters necessary to be determined upon. Saw many officers and citizens and spent the afternoon and evening agreeably. Slept under a fly and retired early. Today the Yankee Democratic Convention meets at Chicago to nominate a candidate for President. If they nominate a peace candidate and can elect him all will be well. The night clear and warm.

August 30th. Tuesday. In my notes on this trip I shall be brief. Was aroused before day this morning by a threatened storm. It did not, however, rain until we had finished breakfast. Having a short march today we were not particular in starting soon. Got off; therefore, about 6 A.M. after the General and most of his train had gone on. Rode with Gov. Polk, soon after we started it commenced raining and continued to do so all morning. I was, however, well protected by overcoat and india rubber cloth. Came 8 miles to Tulip where we stopped for the day to allow trains all to get up and get everything in order. Here went into a vacant house as it was raining hard. Turned over to Dr. [Joseph L.] Moore[13] one of my 4 mule ambulances and attended to other official duties. The rain ceased towards afternoon. Had a good deal of running about in the rain. Wrote a letter to Dr. Wooten by courier giving him an account of our journey thus far. I am well pleased with my mess—we live well and they are quiet sober gentlemen. Visited Maj. Gallagher several times and prescribed for him. Retired early sleeping on the floor of the house we occupied.

August 31st. Wednesday. The last day of August and of summer. Started at sunrise this morning—Marmaduke and his command in front. Gen. Price, staff, and train next, and Gen. Fagan in the rear. Made a long march today coming 27 miles and at Mr. Claridy's where we went into camp at 3 P.M. The early part of the morning was cloudy and pleasant but it became very warm. We will soon be in the neighborhood of the Yankees and must keep a sharp lookout. Encamped on the roadside and made ourselves comfortable.

Sept. 1st. Thursday. Arose and took breakfast at the usual hour, but owing to a bridge out of order and the consequent detention of the train we did not get off until near 7 o'clock. Gen. Fagan goes in advance today and Marmaduke in the rear, headquarters in between. After coming 3 or 4 miles left the main Little Rock road and came a way through the woods between Benton and Rock Port, a beautiful shady road interspersed with numerous fine rocky streams. Marched 18 miles and encamped about 1 P.M. on a branch of the Saline. We are now in the region of the Jayhawkers, Greybacks, and Yankees. The weather is very hot and the march today was fatiguing but we have a fine camp, plenty of water and fine bathing.

Sept. 2nd. Friday. Got up at 3 A.M. this morning and after an early breakfast got underway before sunrise. Last evening luxuriated in a bath in a fine rocky creek hard by. Came 17 or 18 miles over a rocky and mountainous road with numerous cold streams. The day was excessively hot and the march a tedious one. Arrived in camp about 2 P.M. having been frequently detained by the command in front. Had a bad headache which was made worse by the sting of a yellow jacket, a nest of which we encountered near our camp. Tired and sleepy I retired early after eating a hearty dinner and paying the General and Maj. Gallagher a visit. Slept under a fly.

Sept. 3rd. Saturday. Started at daylight having arisen at 3 A.M. and breakfasted before daylight. The road today was exceedingly rough and mountainous, often the scenery was sublime. The weather yesterday was excessively warm, today it was more pleasant but still warm. Came 16 or 17 miles to the La Fourche [River] where we went into camp at 1 P.M. Our mess wagon broke down today detaining us somewhat in our dinner after getting into camp. Maj. Gallagher is somewhat better today but still very sick and his dysentery not checked. He came along without my advice and I fear he will not stand the trip. Poor fellow, I pity him very much—to be so sick on such a march and under such circumstances is truly pitiable. Have a poor campground today, nothing but warm creek water to drink and but half rations for our horses, yet thus far we have got along well and quietly and should be thankful. God grant us a safe and prosperous journey.

Sept 4th. Sunday. This has not been a Sabbath to me in any respect. As usual we got under way this morning at daylight, Gen. Marmaduke in advance and Fagan in the rear—they alternate daily. The road was exceedingly rough and stony with one mountain, several high hills, and numerous streams, all covered thickly with huge boulders. By the tardiness of the command in front we were frequently detained and for a long time so that it was 3 P.M. before we got into camp 16 miles from where we started in Perry County. As usual all hands were tired and glad to rest and wash off the dust of travel although it has not been so excessively hot today as for several days past. No incidents save the usual to camp. No Federals as yet, though some talk of Jayhawkers. Had a good many sick to prescribe for and visit after getting into camp. The exposure to the hot sun having developed fevers of various kinds. Relieved about 9 P.M.

Sept. 5th. Monday. Started at the usual hour and came 20 miles over a better and much less mountainous and rocky road than yesterday and the day before. The weather was warm though not as oppressive as it has been. The ride was somewhat disagreeable and dusty. Got into camp in Yell County, 14 miles from the Arkansas River about 2 P.M. After washing off the dust and resting a while, visited diverse of the sick of the train and prescribed for them. On the march had a long conversation with Gov.

Reynolds about matters and things in general. Late in the day we had dinner which I enjoyed much, having ate nothing since before daylight this morning. After the fatigues of the march and the early rising it is my custom to retire early. Thus far we have got along well for which I desire to be thankful.

Sept. 6th. Tuesday. After all hands had gone to bed last night a gust of wind and threatening storm came up blowing down our fly and leaving us enveloped with canvas. The mishap, however, was soon remedied and we got through the night comfortably. Started at daylight this morning and came 14 miles to Dardenelle on the Ark. River. The crossing the Arkansas has been regarded as the most difficult part of our task. We find no Federals here but hear of trains and other bodies not far off on the other side, for whom scouts have been sent out. The probabilities are that we will cross the river unmolested and get along without interruption from the Yankees. Late in the evening a part of the ordnance train fording the river. In the morning, Providence permitting, the whole train will cross. Was very busy during the afternoon and evening in prescribing and seeing to the sick. There are at least 300 men and officers attached to these headquarters and of course a good many are sick. Found it necessary to leave some of the worst cases behind but found no difficulty in getting ladies among the citizens to take charge of them. As a courier returns to Camden in the morning wrote a letter to Dr. Wooten.

Sept. 7th. Wednesday. Crossing the Arkansas River at Dardenelle. At an early hour this morning the train commenced fording the Arkansas, the water coming up to the bed of the wagon. Having breakfasted, seen to the sick, and having my things so arranged in my wagon as not to get wet, I mounted my horse soon after sunrise and rode down to the riverbank already crowded by wagons, some 250—artillery and cavalry by the thousands. Soon I waded in and passing wagons and horsemen crossed over, the water coming up to the middle of my horses sides but by keeping my feet up kept them dry. On reaching the opposite side I had a full view of the crossing. It was really grand and picturesque and is well worthy of being sketched and perpetuated. I cannot now pretend to describe it but I shall never forget it. We all succeeded in getting across without difficulty by doubling teams and with but one small accident— Maj. Tracy's wagon in coming down the steep bank capsized and upset all in it. This, however, was soon righted and by 9 A.M. we were on the road again and by ½ past 1 P.M. had marched 15 miles to Dover, Pope Co. Ark. where we went into camp and went through the usual routine. It rained slightly in the morning but cleared off toward the middle of the day and was altogether the most pleasant day's march that we have yet had. After dinner (5 P.M.) paid Gov. Reynolds a visit at his camp accompanied by Gov. Polk. Was invited to a party given to the Gen. and staff tonight but it was too much trouble to fix up, so I decline, preferring to sleep.

Sept. 8th. Thursday. Got up and ready to march at the usual time just after daylight, but owing to some delay in Fagan's Division in advance we were delayed until 9 o'clock—the latest start that we have made yet and I may add the slowest and most tedious though we came but 14 miles. Our camp is not a very pleasant one though it will do for one night. It was 3 P.M. before we got in and of course late in the day before we got fixed up and ate dinner.

Sept. 9th. Friday. Got a good night's sleep having taken an early start. Got off on the march this morning at an early hour, between daylight and sunrise. Came 18 miles on the road to Batesville or in that direction and went into camp in the woods, I think in Van Buren Co. After getting into camp had a good many sick to prescribe for and provide for. Visited a case of supposed varioloid[14] with Dr. Smith, Chief Surgeon of Marmaduke's Division. Owing to the breaking down of our mess wagon on the road it was late in getting and consequently late when we got dinner. Weather clear and hot, nights cool.

Sept. 10th. Saturday. Started just after daylight. Marched 21 or 22 miles and went into camp on Little Red River still in Van

Buren Co. I think. On the road we have heard reports of Federals in the neighborhood. One of our forage masters came in and reported over 200 some 2 miles off having captured the horse of one of the foraging party, whereupon, a detachment was sent out to take them in if possible. They have not yet returned, but I fear the Yankees will take to their heels and escape. Young Arthur Brinker[15] captured two Feds while out with the foragers. We got into camp at 2 P.M.

Sept. 11th. Sunday. Took a good bath and swam in the Little Red River yesterday evening and this morning put on clean underclothes in honor of the day. Started at early dawn this morning, Sunday though it is, but came only 15 miles and went into camp at 11 A.M. at Kinderhook, [the] house of [a] Mr. Murphy. [We are] still in Van Buren Co. Our advance guard this morning encountered a band of Jayhawkers or Greybacks killing one and probably wounding others. Col. [Robert C.] Wood[16] yesterday surprised and took from them 30 horses and saddles. The report of 200 Yankees being in a few miles of us on yesterday proved on investigation to be untrue. Came over spurs of mountains today, one of which was steep, rocky, and bad. Today we have been just two weeks on the march and Providence has favored us thus far with a peaceful and safe journey. Personally, I have just cause for gratitude. In these mountain regions of barren lands the poor ignorant and debased are Union but where we meet with persons of any intelligence they are uniformly loyal to the South.

Sept. 12th. Monday. Started at daylight and marched 30 miles over unparalleled bad roads crossing a range of mountains some 12 or 15 miles in extent. Rocky, steep, rough, and exceedingly rough, and the whole way without water for stock or man. The day too was hot. This was all together the roughest and worst day's march that I have ever made. I have seen and read of bad mountain roads but this far exceeded anything that I had imagined and is all together impracticable for loaded wagons—huge rocks, steep cliffs, and deep cuts for miles down the mountain and yet our trains had to come over it and did come. Some 3 or 4 wagons were smashed up others were upset. My medical wagon was capsized, broke many of my bottles, and turned out everything on the mountain but fortunately the damage was not very serious. Our mess wagon was broken down and did not get into camp until after one o'clock at night. Other wagons fared the same fate. We on horseback traveled from early dawn to near dark and went into camp on a stream in the valley two miles from White River. Owing to the accident to our wagon we got no supper so I parched an ear of hard corn and supped on it. Though I had ate nothing since before day and had come 30 miles over such roads I suffered but little from hunger, thirst, or fatigue. Slept under my wagon on an empty stomach.

Sept. 13th. Tuesday. Owing to the disasters to our train on yesterday and the lateness of the hour at which many of them arrived in camp, we did not get off this morning until late. The ordnance and other trains were left behind to fix up and Gen. Marmaduke's command left with them while Gen. Price and his staff started about ½ past 10 o'clock for Batesville some 18 miles distant. Gen. Marmaduke will [take] another road and rejoin us in a few days. The road today was rocky and rough and very bad but not to be compared with that of yesterday. We reached Batesville—rather a nice town—just about sundown and went into camp on a stream in the edge of the town. I enjoyed my breakfast this morning after a fast of 24 hours hugely. My horse today is lame from a sore foot cut by a rock.

Sept. 14th. Wednesday. Our 18th day's march. Started at the usual hour, daylight. Marched 30 miles in a northeasterly direction toward Powhatan over tolerably good roads and went into camp on Strawberry River about ½ past 4 o'clock. Always on reaching camp and in the morning before starting I have a good many sick to look after and prescribe for. The weather today was pleasant and tonight feels fall-like. We are tonight 13 miles south of Powhatan in Independence Co.

Sept. 15th. Thursday. Got off at the usual hour and came 14 miles to Powhatan on Black River by half past 9 A.M. where we found Gen. Shelby awaiting our arrival and his troops nearby. Here we went into camp and spent the rest of the day. At Gen. Shelby's Hd. Qts. under a tree we spent some time overseeing and conversing with him and his officers and after smoking a good cigar and taking a drink of good whiskey with him went to our camp. I had various matters to attend to and when in camp am generally busy. Shelby has a large force which united with ours will constitute Gen. Price's command for going into Missouri. Here we learn that McClellan has been nominated by the Cincinnati convention and read their platform.[17] McClellan is small potatoes and the platform unsatisfactory.

Sept. 16th. Friday. Left Powhatan before sunrise this morning and came 18 miles to Pocahontas Ark. in Randolph Co. on the Black River. Got into camp before 1 P.M. Here we will probably lie over tomorrow to organize the command generally, and my charge will be to organize the Medical Department. I have daily official duties to perform and all the time sick to look after and prescribe for which with other duties on the march keeps me busy after getting into camp. This is our 20th day's continuous march. For several days past we have seen it stated in the Yankee papers that Atlanta has fallen, but from their own account there is some doubt about it.[18]

Sept. 17th. Saturday. Today we rested at Pocahontas, a deserted village. The first rest since we started for the purpose of fixing up the command. I have been busy all day in organizing the Medical Department, issuing medical supplies, sending out orders, prescribing for the sick, and in attending to my lame horse. Discovered this morning that by some accident my carpet sack has got wet and all my shirt collars and other clothes are nearly spoiled by mildew— a sad account this but I must bear it as best I can. Late in the evening went over to Dr. Paine's, spent the evening, and took tea. He resides near the town and is a clever intelligent old gentleman. It is probable that we will rest again tomorrow as our train has not yet come up but it will not be much of a Sabbath. I have had a quite many visitors on business today.

Sept. 18th. Sunday. Rested again today at Pocahontas, although I am sorry to say that it was not because it was the Sabbath but because the command was not fully organized. Got up early this morning and went over to Dr. Paine's accompanied by Gov. Polk and took breakfast with him. Was occupied during the day with the details of official duties. Tomorrow we start for Missouri moving in three columns. Would that I could spend the day as it should be.

Sept. 19th. Monday. After two days of very acceptable rest started on our march this morning leaving Pocahontas but not crossing Black River. Traveled 24 miles, crossed the Arkansas line and *entered the State of Missouri* after going 20 miles and encamped 4 miles on this side of the line about ½ past 3 P.M. In honor of our entrance into Missouri, Maj. Brinker opened a bottle of native wine at dinner which we enjoyed both in the occasion and in itself. Twenty-seven months ago tomorrow I left the state of Mo. an exile and a refugee. Today I enter it with an army which God grant may be a victorious one and relieve this down trodden state.

Sept. 20th. Tuesday. Marched 20 miles into Mo. and went into camp [at] 3 P.M. at Ponder's Mill on the Little Black River in Ripley Co. On the way passed three houses, or rather the smoldering ruins of three residences, burned on yesterday by a company of Yankee cavalry. It was pitiable to see women and children standing out without the vestige of shelter, furniture, or clothing to protect them. Hearing of their depredations a scout was sent out after them and this morning they had a fight in which 3 or 4 were killed, 7 or 8 wounded, and 8 prisoners. The march today and yesterday has been fatiguing owing to the cavalry in advance moving so slow. Weather pleasant but roads very dusty.

Sept. 21st. Wednesday. Twenty-fourth day's march, 26th day out. Left the Little Black River on which we camped and made a short march of 13 or 14 miles on the road to River Station on the Big Black River and about 8 miles distant therefrom. Before the rest of the command started this morning I rode over a mile and a quarter on another road to see the wounded in the skirmish of yesterday. Found 4 of our men and one Yankee lieutenant—two of our men died during the night. Had those that could be transported brought on in ambulances and left the worst cases. On the way we passed a house in which there was a Federal shot through the chest. He made his way in last night having been wounded on yesterday. Got into camp early and had full time to fix up and attend to all matters. I have a huge appetite and thanks to a kind Providence have enough to satisfy it. I enjoy good health and stand the fatigues of the march well.

Sept 22nd. Thursday. One of the wounded men that I brought along on yesterday was so bad that I had to leave him behind at a house this morning, indeed he will hardly live through the day I think. Left at the usual hour and made a march of 22 miles crossing the Big Black River—a very pretty stream—8 miles from where we started. Went into camp about ½ past 2 P.M. at Greenville, the county seat of Wayne County on the St. Francis River. Our camp is just on the riverbank and it is an interesting sight to see the cavalry and trains pass. Gen. Shelby is on our left and Gen. Marmaduke on our right from 10 to 20 miles distant.

Sept. 23rd. Friday. 25th day's march—4th day in Mo. Came 18 miles today over a rough, hilly, rocky road leaving Greenville at the usual hour just after daylight and went into camp about 1 o'clock P.M. near a fine spring in Wayne Co. I think. Gen. Shelby on our left attacked Patterson on yesterday where there was a small garrison of Federals. The greater part of the troops left on hearing of his approach. He took the town and in the fight he killed fourteen Yankees and wounded others, how many I do not know. Tomorrow we concentrate at Fredricktown.

Sept. 24th. Saturday. It rained hard last night and consequently we had no dust today. Came 20 miles to Fredricktown, Monroe Co.,

Mo. by 1 P.M. and went into camp. Gen. Shelby had preceded and taken possession of the town, the Federal troops having fled before him. Here we found a good many stores much needed by our army. On arriving I went up to see if I could procure anything in the way of medical supplies that I need. Found a Dr. Goff who knew me and who had some articles that I needed, which I got. The officers and troops were as thick as blackberries and as busy as bees about town in securing whatever was for sale. Spent the afternoon and evening in procuring supplies. Ate a hearty dinner late and spent a quiet night.

Sept 25th. Sunday. Another Sunday which is no Sabbath to me. We rest here today. Had many things to do and see to. Got all my medicines and personal effects secured then spent the day as quietly in quarters as I could. Many things crowd on me to say but I must be brief. This is the town in which Jeff Thompson[19] had a fight with the Feds. three years ago and damaged them so badly—in coming in yesterday I passed over and examined the battleground. It is not yet determined which direction we will go from here, but we are getting far in the enemy's country and must expect soon to meet opposition. Late this evening I received a message from Mrs. Dr. Fleming—formerly Mary Lee whom I know well and formerly knew intimately as a young man—to come out to see her. She and the Dr. live at Mine Lamotte 4 miles from this place so Maj. Kimmel and I rode out, took tea, and spent a very pleasant evening with them talking over old times, war times, and St. Louis affairs. Mrs. F. saw my wife last spring in St. Louis and before leaving the house wrote a short letter to my wife and left it to be forwarded by Mrs. Fleming. On returning to camp about 10 P.M. we encountered 5 or 6 picket stands and were stopped by them all and closely questioned and although we had a pass to go and return it was with difficulty that we got in, so faithfully did the pickets discharge their duties.

Sept. 26th. Monday. Left Farmington early this morning, Gen. Marmaduke having come up during the night and came 12 miles on the Ironton Road and went into camp about 12 M. Gen. Fagan has gone forward to invest Ironton and Gen. Shelby has gone around to destroy the Iron Mountain R.R. We are 8 miles distant from Ironton. While at dinner about 4 P.M. cannon were heard in the direction of Ironton—so the ball has opened. It ceased in half an hour, however, but will doubtless be renewed again as we will attack and I hope take the place tonight or in the morning. There are about 1500 Yankees there it is supposed. God grant us success.

Sept. 27th. Tuesday. [Battle of Pilot Knob.] Started at an early hour for Ironton and rode 8 miles over a rough road and in the rain. Our march was hurried by an occasional peal of artillery which, however, ceased before we arrived. The news reached us that the enemy had evacuated and gone to Pilot Knob, 2 miles off, so we went in and found Gen. Fagan already in possession of the town. Here we found many stores which were taken possession by the chiefs of the various departments. Gen. Price made his Hd. Qts. at an abandoned fort which commanded a fine view. The troops were all brought in and arrangements made to invest and attack Pilot Knob where the Yankees have a strong fort and some 1000 or 1500 men.[20] It took a long time to arrange the artillery on the hills and get all our men in line of battle, but during the whole time this was being done the Yankee batteries were occasionally firing upon us. At 3 P.M. the attack commenced and for an hour and a half the musketry and artillery were very rapid. I will not attempt a description. The Yankees had a strong position and after driving them and fighting desperately our men were repulsed, but not badly. It was determined to renew the attack and take the place but it was thought best to defer it until morning as it was now late. I was very busy with the wounded at the various hospitals and performed the first amputation. Our wounded were quite numerous and some of them very severe. It was after dark when I left things in charge of the division surgeons. Our train remained 8 miles off and did not come up so I spent the night at a store with Maj. Brinker and others where we fared well and had plenty to eat and drink. I had a fatiguing day and one which will long be remembered though I pour over it so hurriedly.

Sept. 28th. Wednesday. Before day this morning a tremendous explosion was heard, shaking the whole earth. The Yankees had blown up their magazine and at daylight had evacuated Pilot Knob so our troops took possession and pressed on in pursuit.[21] After an early breakfast went to the hospital to look after the wounded. Found the number a good deal increased. Saw that they were all attended to. Rode up and down and then to the Knob where I met the Yankee Medical Director, Dr. [Seymour D.] Carpenter,[22] and exchanged civilities with him. They left their wounded, some 60 or 80. A large drug store was turned over to me but there were but five things in it that I needed so I left it unmolested. About 10 o'clock the General started in the direction of the enemy and in an hour after I followed on too and overtook him on the way. We came 12 miles and went into camp near Caledonia, Washington Co. where we spent the night.

Sept. 29th. Thursday. Took up the line of march again this morning. It rained a little during the night and bid fair to be a rainy day, but fortunately it rained but little and we had a pleasant travel. Came 22 miles passing first through Caledonia and then Potosi, county seat of Washington Co. and went 8 miles west and encamped about 4 P.M. in an orchard. Gen. Shelby had a fight and took the town with some 200 prisoners day before yesterday. Near town I saw two of his wounded and attended to them. Gens. Marmaduke and Shelby have gone in pursuit of the fleeing Yankees and I hope we shall hear a good account of them. Gen. Jeff Thompson and Capt. Pflager joined us about night and stayed with us.

Sept. 30th. Friday. Came only 12 miles to the Richwoods and went into camp early to allow the train and rear guard to come up. At this writing we have received no official account from Gens. Shelby and Marmaduke but unofficially we hear that they have captured 500 Yankee infantry. We are now 80 miles from St. Louis and must expect fierce opposition. Would that I could communicate with my family—God bless them. This is the last day of September. Received a long letter from Dr. Wooten at Camden.

October 1st. Saturday. Left at the usual hour in the rain, went 12 miles from Richwoods, crossed the Merrimac by ford and proceeded 8 miles further to St. Francis Station on the S.W. branch of the Pacific R.R. It had previously been entered by our troops, a few Federal soldiers driven out, the depot burned, and the railroad torn up. Gen. Cabell was sent 15 miles below to Franklin to destroy the main stem of the Pacific R.R. which he did killing a few Yankees and burning the depot and stores there. At St. Francis Station we met Gens. Marmaduke and Shelby who had returned from the pursuit of the Yankees. After remaining in town an hour went a mile out to camp having marched 21 miles. We camp tonight 55 miles from St. Louis and 10 miles from the Missouri River. So near and yet I fear I will not be able to see or even communicate with my beloved wife and children—God bless and watch over them. I fear that the Yankees will persecute them on my account. Many of the citizens come to see and welcome us. All are anxious to get a look at Gen. Price. We get many recruits also.

Oct. 2nd. Sunday. At an early hour this morning the General and staff rode into Union the county seat of Franklin Co.—a pretty little town 8 miles from where we camped. Shelby had entered it the evening before killing some Federal militia, taking about 60 of them prisoner, driving the rest out, and taking possession of the town. We found the town free from Dutch all of whom had fled on our approach, but crowded with soldiers and good southern people who came in to see and welcome Gen. Price and his army. It is cheering to see the bright faces of the ladies at the prospect of being rid of Dutch and Yankee domination and the alacrity with which the young men join our army. Here I attended to several of our wounded brought from Franklin. With Gov. Polk, Maclean, and others I remained in town several hours after the General left and talked with the people, sent messages to my wife, and attended to such duties as devolved on me. Late in the evening rode out to our camp 7 miles out with Gen. Shelby and staff and Gov. Reynolds. On the way passed a dead Yankee lying by the roadside killed in the fight of yesterday. I also witnessed a brutal act of one of our soldiers to another. Camped in a meadow.

Gov. Reynolds and Gen. Jeff Thompson took dinner with us near sundown. This is another Sunday which was no Sunday to me.

Oct. 3rd. Monday. Rained again this morning, consequently, we had a rough, muddy, and disagreeably wet march of 15 miles on the road to Jefferson City and went into camp in the woods about 2 P.M. Gen. Clark was sent forward on yesterday and took Washington on the Missouri River and Pacific R.R., the Yankees crossing the river and fleeing. Thus far we have met no serious opposition but this cannot last always.

Oct. 4th. Tuesday. Started in the rain this morning and came 17 miles then crossed the Gasconade River and went one mile further and went into camp. The last two miles of the road was horribly rough and muddy. Forded the Gasconade at Mt. Sterling, Osage Co. Two miles from camp I was called to see a wounded soldier laboring under tetanus. I fear the poor fellow will die. He was wounded in the foot at Pilot Knob. This has been by all odds the roughest days march that we have yet had. This is written almost in the dark.

October 5th. Wednesday. No rain today but any quantity of mud. Came 14 miles over bad roads to Sterling, county seat of Osage Co. and went into camp in the bushes. Weather raw and inclined to rain. We are now within 20 miles of Jefferson City. Marmaduke yesterday took Herman with some 250 stand of arms.

October 6th. Thursday. Left Linn and came 18 miles to Princes Ford over the Osage River 8 miles from Jefferson City. Before arriving and while moving we heard heavy firing in the direction of the ford. It turned out to be Shelby attacking some 400 or 500 Federals guarding the ford. He soon dispersed them killing some 8 or 10 Yankees and perhaps more. The only casualty on our side was the severe perhaps mortal wounding of Col. [David] Shanks,[23] one of Shelby's Cols. On hearing the firing the Gen. and his staff rode up rapidly. We crossed the Osage fording it easily and rode some mile and a half in advance in pursuit of the fleeing Yankees.

After seeing how things were going we recrossed and encamped on the Osage County side of the river—just opposite us is Cole Co. Altogether it has been an exciting day. We may expect hot work from this time on. God be with us and give us success. Some 7 or 8 miles from camp this morning we passed through the Dutch town of Westphalia. Dr. [John F.] McGregor and Col. [Isaac N.] Hedgepeth[24] took tea and spent the night with us. The Dr. is an old pupil of mine and wished to make me a present of a horse, but could not get anything to ride home on so I had to forgo the horse.

October 7th. Friday. Recrossed the Osage River early this morning and proceeded towards Jefferson City. At Moro Creek 4 miles from Jefferson we encountered the Federals. They made a stand there so as to oppose our progress. Here we had a sharp skirmish. Gen. Fagan in the advance fought them. We gradually drove them before us and finally ran them into their entrenchments in the city. By this time it was late, the day too far advanced for storming the fortifications. They probably have a strong force at Jefferson City and it may be prudent for us to give it the go by. In the skirmishing today we had some wounded and I established a hospital 3 miles from town at Mr. Berry's house. Here we had some 10 or 12 of our own wounded and 2 Federals. I took off the right arm of one man and one was killed, shot through the head. It was late when I got through at the hospital and the firing which was brisk during the day had ceased so I started off with Dr. Slaughter and Capt. Thomas to hunt up Gen. Price. Went 4 miles across to Riggin's Mill to Gen. Fagan's camp where I expected to meet him but not finding him and it being now night I determined to bivouac in the edge of a meadow. Made my supper of a piece of chicken cooked by myself on a stick and a piece of cold bread and slept on some hay covered with my saddle blanket and overcoat—the night was cold but we had a big fire.

Oct. 8th. Saturday. Got through the night comfortably though in the open air. Took a piece of bread and a cup of coffee for breakfast and started off with Gen. Fagan in search of Gen. Price. After riding across the country 4 miles finally came upon him and Gen.

Marmaduke. It was determined not to attack the Yankee fortifications at Jefferson so we resolved to move on. The Yankees commenced advancing on us and during the day as we moved slowly
forward in the direction of Versailles there was constant fighting
with our rear and their advance. All day we heard firing. We came
out 17 miles to a little town and went into camp (Russelville).
Arrived just about sundown—hungry—got a good dinner and
set a man's broken arm. Today and yesterday have been exciting
days. Thus we go and we are experiencing the hardships of a soldier's life.

October 9th. Sunday. Started at daylight and marched some 8 or10
miles on Versailles Road passing through a beautiful prairie country then turned to the right near High Point and took the road to
California, which town we passed through about 1 P.M. and came
some 9 miles on the Boonville Road and went into camp in
Wonder County on the Wonder Creek, 19 miles from Boonville.
Gen. Marmaduke in our rear was fighting all day with the enemy's
cavalry some 2500 strong. Late in the evening after we got into
camp the artillery firing was quite brisk but it finally ceased, the
enemy having in all probability been driven back. Gens. Shelby
and Thompson have been sent forward to take Boonville which
town we expect to reach tomorrow night. We have marched 26
miles today—Missouri impresses me as a beautiful country and
one that is worth contending for. This has been another Sabbath
poorly spent. Oh, how I long for the return of quiet Sabbaths and
home comforts—God grant their speedy return.

October 10th. Monday. Started with the advance guard at daylight this morning accompanied by Majors Brinker, Tracy, and
others to go into Boonville in advance of the army, Gen. Shelby
having taken the town last night with 300 Yankee prisoners. After
a spirited ride of about 19 miles and passing through a brigade of
cavalry we arrived in Boonville about 9 o'clock. Found the town
in possession of Shelby and the citizens in great excitement and
all the southern portion of them overjoyed at our arrival. Many
friends long separated met and tears of joy were shed. Oh how I

wish that my own beloved wife and children were here. I cannot describe the scene that I witnessed. They were varied and interesting. I met some acquaintances and many that knew me. Took breakfast at the City Hall with Col. [James R.] Shaler.[25] About 11 o'clock Gen. Price arrived. The citizens flocked to see him and for the rest of the day the scene baffles description. Took dinner at the hotel. Watered my horse in the Missouri River. Our camp is at the fairground.

October 11th. Tuesday. Boonville, Mo. Had a quiet night in camp. Arose early, washed, put on a white clean shirt and my best suit, and after breakfast went into town. Repaired to the City Hotel, [which is] the General's Hd. Quarters and the resort of a hundred ladies and sympathizing friends. Attended to diverse matters of official business. Called on Rev. Mr. Morton (Presbyterian minister) and Mrs. Dr. Lutt. Left with Mrs. Dr. Lutt a letter to my wife which she promises to send to her. Towards noon firing on our rear was heard and the report came in that our pickets had been driven in and that the enemy were pressing our men. Soon there was a stir—troops were ordered out [and] the General went to the front. I fixed up my affairs, mounted my horse and made hospital and other arrangements—took the Thespian Hall for a hospital. Soon the wounded in few numbers began to come in and the firing increased. Six or eight wounded and one dead man was brought in. [I] assisted in two amputations. Took dinner and tea at the hotel, [and] saw and conversed with hundreds. Firing and the fight brisk, skirmishing continued until dark. Our train moved from the Fair Grounds to 2½ miles out on the Georgetown Road. After dark, but by moon light, [I] with others of the staff rode out to camp and there spent the night expecting all the while to be ordered off at a moments warning. The above gives but a poor idea of the day's doings, but it will be suggestive.

October 12th. Wednesday. Went into Boonville after breakfast— fighting still going on in front. Went to the hospital [where] some 25 or 30 wounded [were] brought in. Spent all the morning in the hospital directing the operations—amputations and resections.

Hundreds of kind ladies came and gave every assistance in their power—a busy scene and to them no doubt painful. Some 3 or 4 [of the wounded] have already died and the rest doing well—all were well cared for. Dined with Rev. Mr. Morton. Made all necessary arrangements for the wounded. Towards evening the enemy were driven back and quiet prevailed in town. I had a busy day, but I think [I] attended to everything devolving on me. Late in the evening [I] came out to camp expecting to start tonight in pursuit of the enemy. I write this just on the eve, as I expect, of a night march.

October 13th. Thursday. As I anticipated we had a night march last night. The command commenced moving soon after dark. About 10 P.M. the General left Boonville and we all fell into line soon after, taking up the line of march in the direction of Georgetown and Lexington. The night was cool and pleasant [with] bright moonlight. We came 9 or 10 miles to Cheauto Sulphur Springs in Cooper Co. and halted. It was 1 o'clock in the morning when we arrived but our wagons did not arrive until ½ past 3. [It was] 4 A.M. before I got to bed. Had a few hours sleep. The sun was up when I arose and we made a late start marching 12 or 15 miles only and going into camp near the Black Water [River], I think in Saline Co. We have heard nothing of the Federals today and all has been quiet.

October 14th. Friday. Made a short march of only 7 miles and got into camp by 10 o'clock at Jonesborough, Saline Co. Several expeditions have been sent off—one to Glasgow and one to Sedalia—we will await their operations. Recruits in large numbers are all the time joining us. The people of Missouri are thoroughly aroused and it is evident that the great heart of the people are thoroughly with us if they will only act in accordance with their principles—Now is the time for their deliverance. We hear nothing of the Federals today.

October 15th. Saturday. Twenty three years ago today I arrived in St. Louis, though now an exile in the cause of liberty. In looking back over the past I have great cause to thank God for his goodness and many mercies and I do from my heart thank Him. But I cannot now dwell on the past, the present is too exciting and important. Started at the usual hour, passed through Marshall, the county seat of Saline Co., and came on to the Saline [River] making in all 17 miles march. The country through which we passed is a beautiful and rich agricultural country—verily Missouri is a fair land. At Marshall I halted for an hour and procured a few valuable medical stores—got into camp early. Recruits are coming in by the hundreds, as many as 700 reported yesterday and last night. Our success thus far exceeds my expectations—God grant us complete success. Today we hear of another splendid victory of Gen. Lee's on the Potomac.[26]

October 16th. Sunday. Our army rested in camp today but with this exception it was not much like a Sabbath. No preaching in camp or in the neighborhood, in fact the minds of all are too much excited and there are too many comings and goings and etc. for any calm religious excercises. All had an opportunity of washing and fixing up, which is certainly a luxury. A great many ladies and others—friends and relatives of officers and men—called to see their friends and the General. The wife of the General's son, Edwin Price, a brother and niece of Maj. Brinker and two other ladies took dinner with [us] and spent the night at our tent. We managed to make them all comfortable and gave them a first rate dinner. In the afternoon [I] sat the thigh of a Capt. who was so unfortunate as to get it broke by a fall from his horse. Had other official and professional duties to perform. Glasgow surrendered on yesterday evening to Gen. Clark and Sedalia to Gen. Jeff Thompson. Some 1000 prisoners and arms, and large quantities of quartermaster stores, etc. fell into our hands by these captures. The report is that the Yankees are following us with infantry and cavalry.[27] This has been an interesting and exciting day.

October 17th. Monday. Took a good breakfast of which the ladies partook and at a reasonable hour. Soon after, the order was to be read to move at a moments warning so everything was packed and loaded up. Our visitors left for their homes, but Gen. Clark's command not having arrived, Gen. Price was unwilling to leave before his arrival. He did not come up until night so we spent the day where we were—passed quietly. New recruits and visitors constantly coming in. The Yankees are evidently moving on us, but our army is constantly increasing and soon we will be able to meet them.

October 18th. Tuesday. Started our march this morning at a late hour and came 12 miles to Waverly in Lafayette Co. on the Missouri River, 20 miles [from] Lexington. We learn that Carrollton was captured yesterday with 800 horses. Thus far we have swept everything before us but this cannot last. We must have hard fighting—God defend us.

October 19th. Wednesday. An exciting day. Pursuing, fighting, and driving the Yankees all day. Started at daylight, came 10 miles to Dover, a nice little town, still in Lafayette Co., then marched 12 miles to the neighborhood of Lexington. The Federal pickets were driven in by our advance early in the morning, and believing that they were in considerable force and would probably give us a fight Shelby was sent on to engage them. Skirmishing began some 6 or 8 miles from Lexington and we gradually drove them to some 5 or 6 miles beyond the town. As the firing became brisk Gen. Price went to the front. I accompanied him and it was a beautiful and exciting scene to see the Yankees fleeing before the fire and charge of our men. We followed them until night put a stop to our pursuit. [James G.] Blunt, [Jim] Lane, and [Doc] Jennison, a beautiful trio of scoundrels,[28] with about 2500 cavalry were in Lexington but we drove them out and our men occupied the town. We, however, encamped some 2 miles out at Gen. [James] Shield's[29] place, a beautiful place, but terribly gutted and mutilated by the cowardly Kansas Yankees on yesterday. It was night when we went into camp—dark, cold, and inclined to rain. It was late when we got supper and I had a first rate appetite.

October 20th. Thursday. Accompanied by Gov. Polk I rode into Lexington soon after daylight to procure medical stores, etc.

Found the town guarded by our soldiers and but few troops there. Stores all closed. Called on Dr. Ruffin and from him got the status of those with whom I wanted to deal. Found good stocks of goods in the drug store—secured some valuable drugs, also a pair of common boots. [I] was very busy until the order for all the troops to leave the town rendered it necessary to send my wagon out. Saw several acquaintances and was very busy. About 11 A.M. started to join the command accompanied by Gov. Polk. We rode through several brigades and had a most dusty and disagreeable ride. It was late when we reached camp on a creek bottom having marched 16 miles on the Independence Road. Weather inclined to snow a little and rain.

October 21st. Friday. Another exciting day. Fighting the Yankees most of the day. Started at an early hour for Independence but after marching some 8 or 9 miles to the Little Blue River we found the Yankees occupying the hills across the river having burned the bridge—a strong position. Gen. Shelby being in advance attacked them about noon. The firing of musketry and artillery was very heavy and for a while it seemed that the Yankees were going to give us a hard fight. Shelby, however, drove them from the strong position with considerable loss to them and some loss to his own forces. Having routed them (Lane, Jennison, and [Maj. Gen. David] Hunter)[30] he followed them into and beyond Independence. Dead Yankees were strewn all along the road. It was night when we went into Independence and late before we got our supper and retired. On coming into town I secured Jones' Hotel as a hospital and made arrangements for bringing in our wounded. I also found a Yankee hospital with 10 wounded under the care of Dr. [James P.] Ericson,[31] a Yankee Missourian. I extended to him every courtesy and facility for his wounded. The Yankees also took away with them quite a number of their wounded with them, the citizens say about 100. At all events we drove them and punished them severely. But I cannot do justice to the events of the day so full of interest and crowded with incidents.

October 22nd. Saturday. At Independence. After an early breakfast rode up into town to superintend to preparations of the hospital and making our wounded comfortable—we have here about 30. [I] also visited the Yankee hospital. At 9 o'clock the army moved out on the Westport Road following the fleeing Yankees. I remained until 12 M. when having completed my arrangements I started towards the army. I left Dr. [John H.] McMurry[32] in charge of our wounded. In the mean time another column of the Yankees probably lead by [Maj. Gen. William S.] Rosecrans[33] came up on our rear and attacked Gen. Marmaduke in our rear. In front we fought all afternoon the force in our front and that in our rear. In front Shelby drove those in the advance capturing one 24 lb. how-itzer and some 60 prisoners and several wagons. While in the rear Marmaduke and Fagan held in check the heavy force behind, not, however, without some loss of men and two pieces of artillery from Gen. Cabell. Progressed only some 12 miles today fighting in front and rear all the way.[34] Established a hospital at the house of a widow lady adjoining the field of battle in which some 27 of our own and 7 Yankee wounded were brought. [I] was occupied until long after dark in getting them attended to. Slept out in the open air and tak-ing only a snack. It has been a busy day and full of excitement not without apprehension. For several days past [we have been] travel-ling through the border counties of Mo.—Jackson, Bates, and Cass —every house has been burned and the whole country devastated by the Yankees.

October 23rd. Sunday. It is now evident that the Yankees have a heavy force in our front and rear and are trying to get us in a tight place and with some prospect of succeeding. I hardly knew that this was Sunday so busy and excited have I been all day. Early in the morning completed my hospital arrangements and left Dr. [Caleb] Winfrey[35] in charge of our wounded. The army com-menced moving at daylight. Shelby attacked the force in front and drove them into and beyond Westport. The fighting was very severe but he whipped and drove them. In the meantime, how-ever, the strong force from Independence advanced on and struck our rear and came near using up Shelby as he returned from pursuit of Blunt and company, but he cut through and escaped with some loss.[36] It was now evident that the Yankees had doubled teams on us to such an extent to be too strong for us and that to save our large train we must retreat in a southerly direction. About noon, therefore, we commenced retreating and came 25 miles, fighting all the way, and encamped on a stream in the southern part of Cass County, getting into camp after dark. The day was one of excitement as we marched along the broad and beautiful prairies. Bodies of Yankees could be see attempting to flank us on the right and left and frequently our men were drawn up in line of battle, but we had no severe fighting save in the morning. Once we threw shells and stampeded a few of the Yankees near our right flank. It was a beautiful sight. [Having] started off without breakfast [I] had nothing to eat all day until night. Got into camp about 9 P.M. after an eventful day.

October 24th. Monday. Started at daylight and continued our retreat in the direction of Fort Gibson. Came 35 miles and went into camp in Kansas at Marais de Cygnes River near [a] trading post. Had no fighting today; the enemy appeared in our rear but did not offer battle, so we kept on. The country through which we passed today is most beautiful. Found several stores at [the] trading post from which a good many goods were obtained. Had a hard march.

October 25th. Tuesday. This has been a disastrous day! Slept under the wagon—the night dark and rainy—[and] was aroused at 2 A.M. [I] took a hurried breakfast in the rain and prepared for a start before day, but did not get off until about daylight. Traveled on quietly for some 15 or 16 miles to the Little Osage [River] which we crossed. Here we halted for a while. Gen. Marmaduke in the rear sent word that he was pressed hard by the enemy and immediately Gen. Price ordered Gen. Fagan to his aid. Gov. Polk and myself rode on a mile in advance on the prairie and there awaited the arrival of the General. Soon, however, the wagon train commenced passing rapidly and we were informed of a fight in the rear. One part of Shelby's Division in front was left to guard the train and the other was ordered to the aid of Marmaduke and Fagan. In a short time before I thought that the fight was begun, news came that we were routed and retreating in confusion. This was surprising. The scene that followed beggars description and I shall not attempt it. Marmaduke's command was charged by the Yankees with sabres and revolvers. This charge he undertook to receive on horseback when his men gave way and a rout followed. Gens. Marmaduke and Cabell were either captured or killed. Other officers and probably a good many privates fell into the hands of the enemy. Shelby, however, checked and kept back the enemy but the whole army was in retreat.[37] We traveled some 10 or 12 miles on the prairie, having come into Missouri again, until about 3 o'clock P.M. When the enemy appeared in our rear a line of battle was formed on the prairie, both armies being in full view of each other. It was a beautiful sight. Fighting commenced about 4 P.M. and for a while we held our own and even drove the enemy, but our troops were demoralized by the transactions of the morning and gradually our whole army commenced falling back. I saw the whole fight and cannon balls and shells frequently burst around and near me. About sundown we left the field and marched some 8 or 10 miles to our train [and] took supper. We were now in full retreat with our army demoralized and some 500 or 600 unarmed troops. It was ordered to destroy part of our train. [I] rearranged and consolidated my baggage and medicines and gave up one wagon. We were to start at 2 A.M. and it was 1 A.M. before I completed my arrangements. [I] destroyed a great many valuables and personal effects. We had a bon fire of wagons and other things. The command moved at 2 [A.M.] but we did not get off until ½ past 3 [A.M.] so I got no sleep.

October 26th. Wednesday. An unparalleled long march. It was very dark and inclined to rain. We wandered through the prairie and got out of the road. Our train became scattered and my wagon ran into a ravine and in the hurry and stampede—the enemy pressing us in the rear—it was abandoned by which I lost all my medicines and instruments, most of my clothes, and all my papers and personal effects, which I regret very much, but there is no use in grieving over [them] as these losses are incident to the life of a soldier. We continued the march until 9 o'clock when we reached Carthage in Jasper Co. or rather where it once was, for it had been destroyed by the Yankees—a march of over 60 miles. I was in the saddle some 17 hours. I was tired and hungry when we got into camp having had no breakfast and nothing to eat during the day still I got along well and adjusted a broken limb after getting into camp. It was after 11 P.M. before we got supper and 1 A.M. before I got to bed, but slept soundly when I got at it.

October 27th. Thursday. Started late, 11o'clock [A.M.], and came 16 miles to Shoal Creek in Jasper Co. not far from Neosho and Granby. No enemy heard of today—got into camp at dark. I write this out of doors and at night. We are on the retreat as rapidly as possible.

October. 28th. Friday. Just two months today we left Camden on this expedition. Started at the usual hour and came 12 miles and went into camp passing through Granby or what was once that town (the vile Yankees have burned almost every house in it) and Newtonia, the county seat of Newton Co. Went into camp 3 or 4 miles from that town. Having heard nothing of the enemy in the rear I had hoped that we were out of reach of them, but soon it was stated that Gen. Shelby was skirmishing and just as I had sat down to dinner between 3 and 4 P.M. the roar of cannon and crack of small arms was heard very near at hand, and it was obvious that a fight was going on a short distance off. After a hasty meal I proceeded to the field, Gen. Price having preceded me. Our train was hurried off 5 or 6 miles to the rear. The battle was on the south side of Newtonia about one mile. The musketry was quite heavy and the cannonading brisk. As I rode over the field to look after and direct the transportation of the wounded to the hospital established in the rear, the cannon balls and shells fell uncomfortably thick around me. It was evident, however, that we were getting the best of the fight and that Shelby was driving them. The action lasted until sundown, the Yankees falling back all the time until they withdrew altogether. It was a decided victory for which we are indebted to Gen. Shelby who is by all odds the first cavalry officer on this side of the Mississippi River.[38] In the hospital we had some 24 or 25 wounded men and officers. These occupied my attention until 9 or 10 o'clock at night. As in all such cases it was a sad scene. Having got them all dressed and as comfortable as possible and detailed a surgeon to remain in charge of them, I rode to camp some 8 miles calling by Gen. Fagan's Hd. Qts. and accompanying him and his staff to our Hd. Qts. It was 11 P.M. when I arrived. [I] slept out in an open field.

October 29th. Saturday. Marched about 30 miles today. Passed through Pineville, county seat of McDonald Co., a complete mess of ruin, and going into camp near Rutledge on Cow Skin River— a beautiful stream. The whole country through which we have passed for days has been desolated by the Yankees—a commentary on Yankee civilization.

October 30th. Sunday. Another Sabbath without rest. Started at the usual hour and marched 18 miles to Maysville, Ark. We passed out of Missouri about 7 or 8 miles from our starting point. Farewell Missouri for the present. The heart of thy people is right but the tyrant's heel is heavy on thy neck. The day of deliverance I hope will come. Got into camp in good time just on the border of the Indian Nation where Ark., Mo., and the Indian Nation come together. Country all desolated. No news of the Yankees today or yesterday. No forage for our horses tonight.

October 31st. Monday. Our camp last night was in the Cherokee Nation instead of in Ark. as I supposed. Started at a very early hour this morning. Marched 17 or 18 miles and got into camp on Illinois Creek in good time. The country through which we passed today and yesterday has been desolated and almost depopulated by the Yankees and Pin Indians; consequently, we got no forage for the horses last night and got none tonight. We are now in N.W. Ark., Benton Co.

November 1st. Tuesday. Was aroused before day by the water coming into our tent and under our bedding. [I] hurriedly bundled them up and put them in the wagon and prepared to march. Started in the rain and traveled all day in a cold rain—the beauty of army life—roads rough and mountainous withall. Came 20 miles to Cane Hill, Washington Co., Ark., 16 miles from Fayetteville and near the Boston Mountains—went into [it] in the rain. There has been so much thieving of late that in order to keep our horses our mess have established a private watch. I take my turn of two hours tonight.

November 2nd. Wednesday. Weather horrible, cold and rainy. [The] army rested today and luxuriated in the mud and rain. [I] was occupied in establishing a hospital to leave such of the wounded as cannot be carried along. Issued orders to Chief Surgeon of [the] division but had to see to it myself. A most disagreeable day and a gloomy prospect ahead in the way of roads, forage, and subsistence. We have the Boston Mountains to cross [which] are far-famed for roughness—The Lord protect and preserve us.

November 3rd. Thursday. The rain of yesterday turned into snow last night. The army remained stationary again today. Indeed in the state of the command, stock, and weather it would have been almost impossible to have moved. A miserable, cold, snowy, muddy disagreeable day it has been. [I] was occupied in getting the sick and wounded housed and cared for. [I] find it difficult to get surgeons to attend to their duties. [I] had numerous calls on business and went around to visit all the wounded in all the buildings and hospitals. Altogether spent a most unpleasant day. At night [I] took my turn on the watch from 12 to 2 A.M.

November 4th. Friday. Cleared off during the night and clear weather today. Started on our march this morning at 10 o'clock [A.M.] after a rest of two days at Cane Hill from which point we take a westwardly course through the Cherokee Nation. [We] came into the Indian Territory in about 6 miles after leaving camp. Our route will be through the Nation thus avoiding the Boston Mountains. Forage is very scarce and our horses fare badly, as yet I have had no cause to complain of my own fare. Came 15 miles and went into camp on a fine stream. Every house that we passed was either burned or rendered desolate. Not a sign of life was visible— the work of the Federals.

November 5th. Saturday. Second days march in the Indian Nation. [Our army] came about 20 miles over roads first rough and rocky then rough prairie though very good land and went into camp on a large stream (creek), the name of which I do not remember. Today and yesterday we have passed through the region of the Pin Indians, that portion of the Cherokees who went with [John] Ross to the Federals and they are, consequently, hostile.[39] One of our men was shot by one of them on the road today. Every house that we passed during the march was empty and desolate. Had a comfortable camp, good water and plenty of wood. [I] enjoyed my supper hugely. Col. [Wedig] Von Snelling[40] took dinner and spent the night with us. I have been greatly blessed on this trip with good health and a good appetite and with something to gratify it, while many others no doubt suffer of hunger.

November 6th. Sunday. Another Sabbath unnecessarily desecrated. Marched about 18 or 20 miles and went into camp on the Arkansas River about mid way between Forts Smith and Gibson. A part of the country through which we passed was very picturesque indeed, some beautiful landscapes and views. The march, however, was a tedious and dull one. Took my turn on the watch last night between 4 and 6 A.M. giving me a good opportunity to watch and clean up by a large fire, which I availed myself of. Arrived in camp late and have no forage for our horses and have to rely solely on grazing, which however, is very good in the bottom—grass and cane. How I would like to be with my wife and family tonight. God bless and protect them and bring us together soon.

November 7th. Monday. Recrossing of the Arkansas River. Two months ago today we crossed the Arkansas River at Dardenelle on our way up. Today we recross it on our way back under very different circumstances and much further west, midway between Forts Smith and Gibson in the Indian Nation. [We] had to cut a road two miles along the banks of the river from where we camped to the ford through a thicket of cane and brush which occupied some time. We reached the ford about 12 [P.M.] and got across by one [o'clock]. The train of course [arrived] much later. [We] then came some 3 miles across the bottom to the high ground and went into camp, so we did little less than cross the river today but that is a good deal. Our supply of commissaries is very limited. Our men are all eating meat (beef) without bread or salt. We get no forage for our horses and many of them are giving out and in all probability we will see much harder times yet before we get to an inhabited land. We are now in the Choctaw Nation and the country through which we will have to pass for the next 10 days has nothing for man or beast except grass on which our stock subsist. In our own mess we have to limit ourselves in our rations of food, but we fare well compared with others and have great cause for thankfulness.

November 8th. Tuesday. Owing to the state of our teams feeding on grass we made only a short march of 10 miles today and got into camp early. Sent our horses out to graze which today is very indifferent. A rainy disagreeable day. [We are] still in the Indian Nation. Our sick are on the increase and the scarcity of provisions and hardships of the trip will make yet more. I have multitudes of applications daily for transportation and other attention to broken down and disabled men.[41] The night promises to be disagreeable. Gov. Reynolds dined with us today. We have numerous applications daily for food. Today [is] the election for President in the U.S. Lincoln will no doubt be elected.

November 9th. Wednesday. It rained hard all night last and became cold. It was a very inclement night. About dark we received intelligence that it was designed by the command—a portion of them—to charge our headquarters train and take possession of our eatables. They seem to think that we have large quantities of flour and etc., all of which I regret to say is a mistake. However, we had a strong guard put out and made all necessary preparations for their reception, but they did not come. At breakfast some twenty or more charged our breakfast table and ate all our breakfast. They were almost famished and we cheerfully *divided* our meal with them. We came 12 miles today over a prairie road. It was exceedingly uncomfortable, cold, and muddy on the march and I suffered from cold and hunger, but we came along cheerfully. [We] went into camp early, built a big fire, and sent our horses out to graze and rather poor grazing at that. We have passed no inhabited house today or for 3 or 4 days past. We are en route for Perryville and Boggy Depot.

November 10th. Thursday. We camped last night on the Canadian [River] and are still in the wilderness, an uninhabited region without forage or subsistence for man or beast. Provisions are very scarce, nothing but wild beef without bread or salt. Hundreds of horses are daily giving out and being abandoned. Horses, saddles, bridles, etc., are left on the road side. We are probably from 80 to 100 miles from food and forage, but I trust that we will get through. My watch last night was from 2 to 4 A.M. Today the weather has been fine. [We] came 12 miles and encamped in a skirt of woods with tolerable grazing. We are now enduring the hardships of a soldier's life—Let us bear this like men.

November 11th. Friday. Another day's march of 15 miles in the wilderness with half-starved, wearied, [and] jaded horses. Our men [are] feeding on hickory nuts, acorns, and dead horse flesh. As yet I have succeeded in getting about half rations and therefore ought to be satisfied, nay more gratified. Govenor Polk, Dr. Johnson,[42] and myself hunted up a hickory nut tree and ate heartily off the nuts. The weather is pleasant. Wolves were howling around us tonight.

November 12th. Saturday. My watch last night was between 11 P.M. and 1 A.M. and the night being bright, mild, and beautiful, and having the camp fire all to myself, I improved the occasion to take a thorough washing and a change of clean undergarments. Had a comfortable breakfast under the circumstances and started at the usual hour and came 3 miles to Gaines' Creek where we found Gen. Fagan encamped and an abundance of beef and fine grazing of cane and grass. It was determined to remain here the rest of the day, which was very grateful to man and beast especially as we have discovered a good many beef in the bottoms so all hands will luxuriate in meat tonight. Our march today was therefore a short one, only 3 miles. On yesterday several left our mess to go forward to Boggy Depot to gather up and send to us stock and provisions. I trust we will all get safely through. A part of the command has also gone forward.

November 13th. Sunday. Started at daylight and made a march of 17 miles passing through Perryville that was formerly a trading post for the Indians with only two or three houses now a heap of ruins and encamped about a mile beyond on a creek where there is tolerable grazing. This being the Sabbath and having plenty of beef and good grazing I suggested to the General that we had best rest today, but he thought it best to continue the march so we violated the Sabbath again. My horse was sluggish and wearied today. My boy Frank, contrary to my orders rode him all over the country yesterday afternoon in search for an Indian pony without getting one. I, however, chastised him for disobedience. During my watch last night from 11 to 1 A.M. the wolves could be heard howling all around.

November 14th. Monday. The army rested today on the creek near Perryville. Last night a supply train of 7 or 8 wagons with flour meal and salt arrived from Boggy Depot greatly to the joy of men and officers, all of whom have been eating beef without salt or bread for the past two weeks. All enjoyed the luxury of bread and salt and are consequently in better spirits today. I was occupied all this morning in sending forward all the sick and wounded of the whole command, including some 6 or 8 cases of small pox recently developed in the command, to Boggy Depot some 40 or 50 miles distant. Placed them all under charge of Dr. [Homer Lee] Parsons.[43] It is a great relief to get them off under such comfortable circumstances. Grazed my horse and kept Frank pulling grass for the night and tomorrow. Had diverse visits and calls on business.

November 15th. Tuesday. By the lone camp fire during my watch last night when all in camp was still and quiet, I thought of my home, wife, children, and friends and wished: Oh! How heartily that "this cruel war was over" that I may return and be with them. As it was I could only think and pray for their safety—Dear God please watch over and protect them. After a days most welcome rest, left our camp near Perryville and came 17 miles on the road towards Boggy Depot and went into camp about 1 P.M. when the daily routine had to be gone through; grazing horses and preparing for the night. Weather cloudy and rather cold. Roads good.

November 16th. Wednesday. Started at daylight and made a short march of 7 miles and went into camp at 9 o'clock A.M. on a creek where there was fine grazing a mile from the road. Here we rested all day giving our horses and mules an opportunity to fill their stomachs with grass. Also spent an hour or two in pulling grass for the night and kept Frank at the same. Had venison for dinner. We are now living well having plenty of flour, meat, and coffee. We are still in the Choctaw Nation about 25 miles from Boggy Depot. Heard from Dr. Parsons in charge of the sick train in advance—getting on well.

November 17th. Thursday. Another days march in the wilderness of the Choctaw Nation under difficulties. Came 15 miles through prairie and plain in a cold disagreeable rain, occasionally very hard, but with gum cloth and overcoat I managed to keep dry and tolerably comfortable. Crossed Muddy Boggy Creek near which was Gen. Stand Watie's[44] headquarters—commanding Choctaws. Here we stopped for an hour during the hardest of the rain and the General, Gov. Polk, and MacLean took dinner with him. [I] went on to camp afterwards, 2 miles off, and spent the afternoon in looking after the sick and in efforts to make myself and horse comfortable. The night was rainy and disagreeable and my watch a dreary one.

November 18th. Friday. Another disagreeable march of 10 miles in raw drizzly weather to Boggy Depot, the place to which we have looked with so much anxiety for so long a time. [We] camped near the town where the grazing was good. The place is a trading post of some importance with the Choctaws and rather a nice town with some good houses. Gen. [Douglas H.] Cooper[45] is in command; a fine looking officer-like man. On his staff is Dr. [W. J.] MacCain,[46] formerly a pupil and graduate of ours in the St. Louis Medical College. With him and the Post Surgeon I made arrangements to get our sick in the hospital here where I hope they will be comfortable until they can be sent forward. Another rainy day. Here we hear of big and glorious Confederate victories in Virginia and Georgia—hope that it will prove true.

November 19th. Saturday. The night was dark, rainy, and very disagreeable and the morning likewise. [I] was busy after the departure of the army in arranging with Dr. [William E.] Dailey,[47] Post Surgeon, for the accommodation of our sick which I did satisfactorily; he taking charge of them all and doing the best he can for them; I [am] leaving a surgeon from the command to assist him. This accomplished, about 9 o'clock Gov. Polk and I rode on in the direction that the army had gone, towards Bonham [Texas]. On the road we met a wagon with corn for Gen. Cooper from which we begged two ears and gave it to our horses on the roadside, which is the first they have had for two weeks. Came 9 miles and went into camp near Mrs. Lafore's where we had an agreeable surprise by finding forage for our horses—corn, hay, and oats. Truly this is a godsend to our half-starved and weakened horses. The weather cleared off and the latter part of the day was clear and pleasant. [We] have a good camp and enjoyed a hearty meal before night.

November 20th. Sunday. Made an early start and marched 10 miles and went into camp at an early hour. In our march [we] crossed the Blue River and Ft. McCulloch just beyond the Blue where there is a large earthwork erected by Gen. [Albert] Pike[48] while in command here. We are still in the Choctaw Nation and for the past two days we have passed several inhabited houses, before that all was desolation or dreary solitude. No Sabbath again today. Would for God [we had] a return of Sabbath and sanctuary privileges.

November 21st. Monday. Soon after getting into camp last night a strong norther sprang up which blew a perfect hurricane all night and was excessively unpleasant, especially as our tent and fire were placed wrong for the wind. Our march today of 15 miles was cold and disagreeable. Camped on a branch of Allen's Bayou, 4 miles from Carriage Point, where I stopped and warmed at an Indian house—very clean people. Weather cold.

November 22nd. Tuesday. Having passed through the Cherokee, Choctaw, and Chickasaw Nation today after a march of 17 miles, about 1 P.M. we emerged from the wilderness, crossed Red River, came into Fannin Co., Texas, and encamped on the south bank of the river. [When] crossing [we] forded at Kemps Ferry on the road to Bonham. Day very cold and the march, therefore, an unpleasant one.

November 23rd. Wednesday. First days march in Texas. Left the bank of Red River this morning and after a march of 15 miles came to Bonham, county seat of Fannin Co. The ride across the prairie was a very disagreeable one. Cold cutting wind blew the whole way and Gov. Polk and myself, who always ride together, suffered considerably in hands, feet, and face. On approaching Bonham, Maj. [Andrew J.] Dorne[49] rode out to meet the General to invite him and his staff to go to his house. [I] called on Dr. [Albert B.] Hoy,[50] Hospital Surgeon, to make arrangements for our sick and wounded who may come this way, in which I succeeded. While at his office I was so unfortunate as to encounter Maj. Tracy in liquor, with whom I had a passage at arms in words. A good many of the staff officers drank too much and got into a disgraceful fight which resulted in Maj. Tracy, Maj. Morrison, Lt. Seldon,[51] and

Lt. Von Phul's being placed under arrest by the General. Took dinner with Dr. Hoy and [William Carson] Boon.[52] In the afternoon [I] called to see Maj. Dorne and family and declined an invitation to dinner having some matters of business to attend to. Bonham is a small town of some 300 or 400 inhabitants and not very prepossessing in appearance.

November 24th. Thursday. After breakfast at daylight and getting ready for the march, I rode uptown to see some acquaintances and complete some business. Called at Major Dorne, [William] Quesenberry,[53] and Col. and Mrs. Jackson's, all pleasant visits and agreeable people, then on the Medical Purveyor, Dr. [John W.] Madden,[54] and Dr. Hoy. About 9 o'clock Gov. Polk and I rode out behind the army but with the General. Came 14 miles on the road to Paris where we found our train camped. The day [was] mild but cloudy. We are now on what is called the "Blacklands" of Texas, which in wet weather is very muddy, stiff, and bad.

November 25th. Friday. Marched 12 miles today and went into camp early in Lamar Co., Texas, 14 miles from Paris. We find forage and provisions abundant in this part of Texas. The day has been cloudy and disposed to rain though the prairie roads over which we haved passed have not been bad, black wax land though it be. Passed through Honey Grove, a small town connected with Davy Crockett in the early days of Texas.

November 26th. Saturday. Marched 14 miles and encamped near Paris, county seat of Lamar Co. After selecting camp, Gov. Polk and I rode up to see the town. Rather a good looking place of 500 or 600 inhabitants, the people of which I judge are not remarkable for their loyalty if the enormous prices at which they sell everything and the low value they set on Confederate money [are an indication]. Our march today was through a prairie country tolerably well peopled. Day pleasant. Learning that the quarterly meeting was in progress, after supper which was also dinner, Maj. Brinker, Gov. Polk, and myself walked up to the Methodist church where we heard a very good sermon. Here on the frontier of Texas was the first sound of the gospel that I have heard since starting on the expedition, just 3 months ago lacking one day.

November 27th. Sunday. Another Sabbath desecrated as I think unnecessarily by marching when we might have rested. Would that Gen. Price was a stricter observer of the Sabbath. Came 13 miles on the Clarksville Road and went into camp in the edge of Lamar Co. on a lake or pond of poor water. Col. [Thomas Coke] Bass[55] called to see us.

November 28th. Monday. Just three months ago today we left Camden. Marched 17 miles today to Clarksville, county seat of Red River Co., a right sharp town. Here we rest for several days. Gov. Polk, Maj. Brinker, and myself rode on in advance of the General and arrived in town an hour or two in advance of him and the command. I occupied this time in visiting the Post Surgeon and in inquiring into the facilities for taking care of our sick. We camp just in the edge of town while the General remains at the Hotel.

November 29th. Tuesday. A day of acceptable rest to man and beast. After breakfast [I] walked up town where I was engaged all the forenoon in starting and furnishing a hospital for the accommodation of all our sick. Saw numerous persons and officials, wrote orders, and transacted other business. Called to see the General and had an interesting talk of half an hour. He read me a letter from Gen. Parsons in which I was interested. Returned to camp after mid-day and spent the time in the ordinary routine of camp life.

November 30th. Wednesday. Another days rest. After a late breakfast and smoke [I] went uptown and was occupied most of the morning in completing hospital arrangements and providing for and provisioning them. [I] saw numerous officers. Met with an opportunity of writing to Mrs. Dr. Rice of Phillips Co., Ark. near Helena and requested her to write to my wife and inform her of my whereabouts and well being. In this way I hope that she will hear from me. Would that I could hear from her.

December 1st. Thursday. Struck tents this morning after a rest of two days and left Clarksville. Came 18 miles on the Laynesport Road camping near Mr. Pope's in Bowie, Co., Texas. Thus far we have skirted the border counties only of Texas. The march today was a pleasant one. Weather pleasant though cloudy.

December 2nd Friday. Started at daylight and came 18 miles to Red River which we forded at Laynesport and went into camp near the banks of the river in Sevier Co., Ark. Thus we have bid adieu to Texas for the present. Gen. [Richard] Gano[56] is encamped in the neighborhood and we will in all probability go into winter quarters in this region near here. Just before getting into camp a heavy rain came up which, however, lasted but a short time though long enough to render camp disagreeable.

December 3rd. Saturday. This is my birthday. I am bordering hard on 50 years old and yet I can scarcely realize it and certainly do not feel that old. My mother used always to write me a letter on this day, but she has gone to heaven. My wife no doubt recurs to the fact. Would God I could spend the day with her and my children rather than here in the frontiers of Ark., Texas, and the Indian Territory. We rested today and I spent the most of the day in mending my old clothes—beautiful employment for ones birthday. Last night we had another Norther. The wind blew furiously and came near wrecking our tent. I weighed a few days ago at Paris, 135 lbs.

In 1864 Maj. Gen. Thomas J. Churchill appointed McPheeters chief surgeon for his Arkansas infantry division. *(Photo courtesy of Arkansas History Commission)*

Commander of an Arkansas infantry brigade in Churchill's division, Brig. Gen. James C. Tappan became a close friend of Dr. McPheeters. *(Photo courtesy of UALR Archives and Special Collections)*

As commander of the Confederate Missouri infantry division serving in the Trans-Mississippi, Maj. Gen. Mosby M. Parsons befriended McPheeters and often accompanied the doctor to church services while in camp. *(Photo courtesy of General Sweeny's Museum)*

The McDowell Medical College at Eighth and Gratiot in St. Louis was taken over by Federal authorities after Dr. McDowell joined the Confederate Army. It became an infamous Yankee prison and Sallie McPheeters was briefly incarcerated there before her banishment from St. Louis.

Following the war, when this picture was taken, a group of physicians rented the building from Dr. McDowell in order to establish a medical school. William McPheeters joined this faculty. *(Missouri Historical Archives, William McPheeters Papers)*

Dr. William M. McPheeters, circa 1875.
(Photo courtesy of State Historical Society of Missouri)

A newspaper photograph of Sallie McPheeters taken
at the celebration of the McPheeters' fiftieth wedding
anniversary, May 10, 1899. *(Missouri Historical Archives,
William McPheeters Papers)*

Planter's (House) Hotel where McPheeters lived when he arrived in St. Louis, October, 1840. It was in the refurbished Planter's Hotel that a banquet was hosted by the Medical Society in 1903, honoring McPheeters and three of his elderly colleagues. *(Missouri Historical Archives, William McPheeters Papers)*

CHAPTER 9

Arkansas Again, 1864–65

Thy will be done on earth.

By December 1864, the war had changed, had mutated from its early form to become now a static war rather than one of movement. The Union had redefined its own nature in the very effort to preserve itself intact, and by the end of this difficult year, the Northern people had come to accept the prolonged anguish necessary to achieve it. Pres. Abraham Lincoln had been reelected after a period of social and political outcries for peace from his weary electorate. His steady purpose for the war itself, his focus upon the nature of the federal union, articulated in so few words at Gettysburg, together with his own toughness and singleness of mind, brought the conflict by winter 1864 to a new echelon.[1]

It was now a war of exhaustion. Gen. Robert E. Lee, the master tactician, had been able in the early days of the war to snare brilliant, dashing victories from the Yankee Goliath, but as that giant lumbered toward organization, tested military leaders, found them wanting, and chose others, the massive potential for men and matériel became focused.[2]

As William McPheeters and the scrawny remnant of the Confederate's Missouri Expedition waited, shivering in makeshift tents on the banks of the Red River in southwestern Arkansas, three Yankee armies were massed, poised to strike what everyone knew could be the final blow. Maj. Gen. William T. Sherman was in Savannah; Lt. Gen. Ulysses S. Grant was at Petersburg, and Maj. Gen. George H. Thomas was in Tennessee.

Americans were experiencing total war for the first time. McPheeters, like General Lee and his commanders, were gentlemen at arms, citizen-soldiers of grace and polish, and they were horrified by acts of war committed against civilians. Even the Yankee press criticized Sherman for tearing up railroad tracks, blasting bridges, burning farm houses, and killing chickens. His soldiers had become vandals, they said, criminals of the rudest stripe, rapists, and thieves. But if the enemy came over this ground again, the general reasoned, if he fought here another day, there would be nothing left to sustain him.[3] In the end the war destroyed in the Confederate states two-thirds of the assessed wealth and property of 1860, including the value of slaves.

In the Trans-Mississippi, however, the vast majority of the region's interior had yet to feel the hard hand of war. Those small farms and plantations that had been ravaged by the Union war machine lay primarily on the department's eastern periphery, along the Red, Arkansas, and Mississippi Rivers. Yet by 1865 the threat of Yankee despoliation was far less pressing to the region's inhabitants than the daily economic strain gripping the department. The dilemma was rooted in the Trans-Mississippi's saving grace—cotton.

Cotton, the army's medium of exchange for everything from domestic goods to foreign commodities coming through the blockade and Mexico, so plentiful in 1863 and 1864, was no longer abundant. Numerous factors—the destruction caused by enemy invaders, the activities of speculators, the demands of legitimate trade, the competition between Confederate and state supply agencies, the voluntary reduction of acreage devoted to the cultivation of commercial staples, a drought in Texas, and the scarcity of transportation—had all conspired to reduce severely the stocks of cotton available to pay the Trans-Mississippi Department's debts. Without it, the financial underpinnings of the region were in peril.[4]

To compound the problem, negotiable currency was in short supply, and what was in circulation had so depreciated that it was hardly worth the paper it was printed on. Many regiments whose service pay had been in arrears for more than a year threatened to mutiny. Inflation was such that farmers, merchants, and plantation owners refused to accept either Confederate notes or vouchers toward the army's purchases. Lt. Gen. Edmund Kirby Smith had implemented a number of "Bureaus" —Quartermaster, Ordnance, Subsistence, Conscription, Medical, and Cotton—to contend with departmental demands, but without supplementary procurements from the local citizenry, the army faced starvation and collapse. Out of desperation he authorized a policy implementing the seizure of provisions without issuance of vouchers, and when necessary, armed force was sanctioned to wrest property from its owners.

Adding to the chaos, roving bands of deserters and absentees preyed upon local inhabitants. Accordingly, many farmers and merchants in the region wondered just who the real enemy was. Faced with few remaining options, families in southern Arkansas and northern Louisiana departed for Texas simply to be rid of the army. A planter in Alexandria, Louisiana, voiced the sentiments of many of his neighbors: "almost everyone is going [to Texas.] . . . [W]e cannot live here for our own men, they will not let us live, but destroy everything we can make." Texas, many would find, offered little solace. Thus, in 1865 the civilian populace of the Trans-Mississippi found the Confederate army to be a greater menace than the Yankees.[5]

The last year of the war also ushered in a shortage of provisions. Until that time the availability of food and forage had rarely been an urgent problem for the department, especially for the District of Arkansas. The campaigns of 1864 and the added pressure of billeting ten thousand Confederate soldiers for two consecutive winters, however, had taken their toll on southern Arkansas' agricultural resources. As testimony to the region's predicament, a Union cavalry officer described the results of a minor raid through southern Arkansas and northern Louisiana in January 1865: "No squad of men much less an army can live anywhere we have been. The people have neither seed, corn, nor bread, or the mills to grind corn in if they had it. . . . [I] cannot imagine that one company of cavalry can obtain subsistence . . . in the whole country." It is little wonder that when McPheeters went hunting with a few of the men near the Red River to augment their meager rations, they never even saw a squirrel.[6]

Maj. Gen. Sterling Price took leave of his men once his Army of Missouri made it to a secure and supplied campsite, and he traveled on to seek council with fellow officers of the Trans-Mississippi at Washington, Arkansas. He desperately needed to find safe winter quarters for his command. Winter was well on its way and would have a devastating effect upon his men, who slept in the open near Richmond, Arkansas.

> **December 4th. Sunday.** Rested in camp today but there was no preaching near and I therefore remained quietly in camp. Read the Bible, paid the General a visit, wrote a letter to Dr. Wooten, and received numerous calls on business.

December 5th. Monday. Left Laynesport on the banks of Red River and marched 20 miles to Richmond, Sevier Co., Ark. in the neighborhood of which we will probably remain for some time. Maj. Gallagher joined us today.

December 6th. Tuesday. In camp at Richmond, Ark. near Red River. Gen. Price started this morning for Washington, Ark. to have an interview with Gen. [John B.] Magruder[7] commanding the district. We will remain here until he returns when we will learn where our winter quarters will be. Made ourselves as comfortable as possible in camp. Gen. [William Elliott] Ashley who has a farm near this called to see us and invited Gov. Polk and myself to dine with him, so at 2 o'clock we rode out to the plantation 3 miles from camp and took a comfortable family meal with him and several other gentlemen. His wife is not with him. Returned to camp in good time.

December 7th. Wednesday. Spent the day in camp writing official communications and etc. Received a letter from my niece Sue at Raleigh N.C. dated Sept. 20th. Though of old date it is gratifying to read it and to know that my friends in N.C. are all well and in good spirits. Our mess were engaged in constructing a hominy mortar and in beating hominy. It succeeded well and we will now have that palatable article. Weather cold and windy. Went squirrel hunting.

December 8th. Thursday. Another day spent in camp in the ordinary routine of duties, mending old clothes and the like. Wrote several official letters of instruction. Day windy, cold, and disagreeable.

December 9th. Friday. Spent the day in fixing up my tattered and depleted wardrobe and in such official duties as presented themselves. Weather pleasant.

December 10th. Saturday. Gen. Price not yet returned; consequently, we still remain here not knowing whether it will be our permanent winter quarters. Still engaged in repairing my wardrobe.

Purchased some tolerable smoking tobacco at $3.50 per lb. in leaf, very moderate for this country. The wind changed and we had a regular norther and it became very cold.

December 11th. Sunday. Weather very cold and windy, a sudden change. Ice forms in a short time. In the absence of preaching today we had a pleasant service in our tent. Gov. Polk read us a good sermon prefaced by prayer and reading of the scriptures. It was a delightful truce from the ordinary duties of camp life. [I] had diverse visits from the brigades and some on business. At night we had another sermon read and wound up the day with prayer. Thus passed the most rational and agreeable Sabbath of the campaign.

December 12th. Monday. Gen. Price returned from Washington, Ark. today having had a satisfactory interview with Gen. Magruder. [I] rode out several miles in the country with Gov. Polk to get some cotton to stuff his mattress. By courier today received four letters from my beloved wife which have accumulated during my absence, however, none of them later than September. Oh, it was a great treat and real pleasure to read lines traced by her dear hand and learn that she and my children are well. Thank God for his goodness to them and to me. The reading of these letters turned my thoughts homeward. Oh, how I long to be with the loved ones at home—My noble wife, God bless her. I also received a letter from my brother Alex and niece Sue in Raleigh N.C. which were exceedingly gratifying. Also received other letters, some on business and some friendly. The reading of these numerous letters occupied all my spare time.

December 13th. Tuesday. Rode 5½ miles in the country this morning to see a soldier's wife who is quite sick. On returning answered numerous letters. Wrote to Maj. Clark, Malcolm Graham, Dr. [Thomas A.] Lonergan,[8] and others. Also endorsed papers and attended to other official business. It is probable that we will remain here (Richmond, Ark.) for 5 or 6 days longer. Had a visit from Gen. Price. Maj. [Washington L.] Crawford[9] dined with us and spent the night. Weather cloudy, warm, and inclined to rain.

December 14th. Wednesday. At Richmond, Ark. in camp. Occupied all morning in writing official and unofficial letters and in attending to other matters in and about camp. At 4 P.M. dined by invitation with Dr. [Alexander] Lovett[10] of this place in company with Gen. Price and son, Gov. Polk, and several ladies of the town. Had a good dinner and enjoyed the company. Weather mild and pleasant.

December 15th. Thursday. Morning occupied in sending order blanks to the division, also wrote several business letters and a long official letter to Gen. Churchill giving him an account of our expedition. Late in the evening dined with Dr. Hamilton of Tappan's Brigade who lives here and is now at home on leave. Gen. Price, his two sons, Dr. Slaughter, and several ladies of the town constituted the party. Mrs. Hamilton is a nice lady. The dinner went off well.

December 16th. Friday. This is a day of prayer and religious worship set apart by Gen. Smith to be observed in this department in lieu of this day a month ago set apart by the President—Davis— as his proclamation did not reach us in time. May the day be properly observed and may the hearer and answerer of prayers speedily answer by granting peace and independence to our beloved and bleeding land. Finished and sent my letter to Gen. Churchill. The rest of the day spent quietly in camp, there being no preaching in the neighborhood. Weather warm, cloudy and inclined to rain. Towards evening Gov. Polk read us a good sermon from the text, "All things work together for good to them that love God," and at night learning that there was preaching went to church where I heard rather an indifferent discourse. There was a ball in town tonight which I did not attend. It was very inappropriate I think.

December 17th. Saturday. Spent the morning in camp attending to the ordinary round of official duties. At 4 P.M. dined by invitation with Mrs. Williamson in company with the General, several of his staff, Gov. Polk, Judge [Freeman W.] Compton,[11] and several ladies. A nice dinner party and good dinner.

December 18th. Sunday. Rainy and disagreeable. No church. Rode out to see a wounded officer then called on Dr. and Mrs. Hamilton and paid a pleasant visit. On returning to camp wrote to my niece, Sue, in N.C. to send across the Mississippi River by Col. [William I.] Preston[12] who leaves in the morning. This is our last day at Richmond, Ark. We (Gen. Price and staff) start early in the morning en route to Washington [Arkansas].

December 19th. Monday. A very rainy inclement morning. We had breakfast at an early hour and commenced making preparations to move to Washington. I was making arrangements to get Capt. Pflager into a private house as he is too sick to travel when an unfortunate affair occurred which will prevent our starting and probably detain us here several days longer. Colonels Wood and MacLean had some difficulty about a pass in the adjutants office. Meeting soon after in MacLean's quarters they got into a fight which resulted in Wood's stabbing MacLean twice in the back part of the chest. I was summoned to see him and found him seriously wounded and suffering; [he] supposing himself mortally wounded, but I hope not.[13] To get out of the ruinous mess [we] moved to a house which we found much more comfortable than in camp this wretched day and night. I am glad that we are not on the road, but I regret the cause that detains us. MacLean [is] seriously but I hope not mortally wounded.

December 20th. Tuesday. Weather still cold, rainy, and forbidding. Our indoor quarters [are] far more comfortable than our outdoor ones. MacLean doing tolerably well. [I] commenced a long letter to Maj. Cabell now at Camden. After dark, as the nights are long, we amused ourselves by listening to the reading of Shakespeare. Mr. [Samuel] Fowler[14] read last night *The Merchant of Venice* and tonight *Othelo,* a rational way of spending an evening when one is deprived of the comforts of home and the pleasure of the society of his wife and children.

December 21st. Wednesday. Weather clear and cold. Furnished my letter to Maj. Cabell and sent it by courier. Having but little

to do in the way of official duties occupied myself in the interesting business of darning stockings and mending up old clothes.
If my beloved wife could see me at it I know that she would be
amused, but I am becoming quite adept with the needle.

December 22nd. Thursday. I was called up this morning at
2 o'clock to see Col. MacLean who was suffering very much. [I]
remained with him an hour and left comparatively easy. On visiting him after breakfast [I] found that symptoms of pleurisy[15] with
effusion had developed themselves and he soon began to sink. Saw
him frequently during the day [and] it became evident early in the
day that he was dying. About sundown this evening he breathed
his last. Alas, poor L. A. MacLean. His death and the cause which
lead to it is deeply regretted by us all. We have news today that
Nashville [Tennessee] has been taken by our troops. I have said but
little of [the] news of late because of the unreliable nature of the
reports that we hear.[16]

December 23rd. Friday. Made a post mortem examination of
Col. MacLean this morning. Found as I had anticipated that the
lung had been penetrated about half an inch. Violent pleuro-
pneumonia with effusion had set in of which he died. This afternoon we buried him in a church yard a mile from town. In the
absence of a minister, Gov. Polk read a part of the Episcopal service. We left him alone in solitude. This is the last of poor MacLean.
After dark paid a visit to Dr. and Mrs. Lovett and spent an hour
very pleasantly. Tomorrow, God willing, we leave Richmond for
Washington.

December 24th. Saturday. After a stay of near three weeks we left
Richmond, Ark. after early breakfast this morning for Washington.
The weather cloudy, damp, and chilly and the roads muddy. Came
18 miles and went into camp about 2 P.M. near Dr. Jones' plantation, now occupied by Maj. [Lemuel] Sheppard,[17] two miles from
Red River. After getting into camp we made an egg nog in honor
of Christmas Eve. It was very palatable. We drank to our absent
wives and families. God bless them. How I would like to be with
them at this time.

December 25th. Sunday and Christmas. Though Sunday and a time-honored holiday, we spent it on the road. Before starting, however, and after getting into camp in the evening we of our mess took an excellent egg nog. Came 5 miles and crossed Red River on a ferry boat at Williams' farm. It took a long time to get all our wagons over the river. After crossing [we] marched 7 miles, making 12 in all, and went into camp near Dr. Pope's farm in Lafayette Co. on the bank of Red River just below the mouth of Little River.

December 26th. Monday. Marched 2 miles starting at daylight and crossed the Red River at Fulton [Arkansas]. By thus crossing and recrossing the river we avoided most of the bad roads which we would otherwise have encountered. From Fulton to Washington is 14 miles the first 6 of which was very bad. Arrived at Washington about 12 M. Before arriving [we] met Maj. Ben Johnson and other acquaintances. At Col. [John R.] Eakin's[18] printing office read Gov. Reynold's outrageous attack on Gen. Price with unmixed regret.[19] Late in the day our wagons arrived and we went out about ½ a mile north of the town and went into camp. It took us until dark to get fixed up.

December 27th. Tuesday at Washington, Ark. Assisted this morning before leaving camp in making out an inventory of the late Col. MacLean's effects. Capt. Sevier called out to see me and Judges Watkins and Walker to see Gov. Polk. We all rode into town. [I] first called to see Capt. Royston then rode out to visit Mrs. Johnson and Jordan—paid a pleasant visit. At 3 P.M. dined by invitation with Col. Eakin in company with Gen. Price, Gov. Polk, Judge Watkins and Walker, and several other gentlemen and ladies. Mrs. Eakin is an old and valued friend of mine, Betty Erwin that [she] was. She gave us an excellent dinner; turkey, mince pie, and egg nog. After dinner rode out to camp. By this time it was fully dark.

December 28th. Wednesday. At noon today Gen. Price and staff called on Gen. Magruder in a body for the purpose of paying our respects to him. We were of course courteously received. Saw also Malcolm Graham, a clerk in his office, and loaned him $40 dollars. Afterwards I called on Rev. Mr. and Mrs. Boyd of Spring Hill now here. Still later Gov. Polk and I rode out 4 miles to call on Mrs. Hill recently Mrs. Jim Johnson with whom I was so intimate at Little Rock. She was absent and we did not see her. We saw, however, Miss Carroll. Called at the hospital on the way in and got some medicines to answer my present wants. After dark called to see Dr. Wilson and family in the neighborhood of our camp—paid a pleasant visit to a very nice family. Saw his daughter, Mrs. Fleming Bates, who used to be a neighbor of mine in St. Louis; found her very agreeable and we talked over home affairs. After remaining until 10 o'clock [I] returned to camp and enjoyed sound sleep.

December 29th. Thursday. Went into Washington after breakfast. Called on and saw several acquaintances among others Rev. Mrs. Boyd and Mrs. Eakin. The latter in reference to having some shirts made, which she kindly and cheerfully consented to have made for me and as I am bad off in that respect it will be a great accommodation to me. Returned to camp and spent the evening and night around the campfire.

December 30th. Wednesday. The year is rapidly coming to a close. [I] rode into town and spent an hour or two very pleasantly in seeing and conversing with gentlemen acquaintances. Took the material for making 4 shirts to Mrs. Eakin and had an agreeable talk with her about our early friends and acquaintances and old times generally. Returned to camp about 3 P.M. and as usual spent the evening and night around the campfire and in [my] tent. Weather clear and cold.

December 31st. Saturday. This is the last of 1864. The close of the year brings sad reflections. I am separated from my beloved wife and children and at this season my thoughts and affections naturally recur to them. The war still goes on and no one can tell when it will end and then the rapid flight of time reminds me that I am growing old, but I will not indulge in these reflections. The year that has past has been an eventful one, but thanks to a kind

Providence our cause has generally prospered and today our prospects are much brighter than they were this time last year. So far as I am individually concerned I have great cause to be thankful and I trust I am thankful for all the unnumbered mercies and blessings of the year. Oh, for grace to live and act more than heretofore as I ought. During the past year I have been on very active duty; have been on three long campaigns, two into Louisiana and one to Missouri in which I have marched near 2500 miles, but I cannot now review the deeds of the past. Rode into town after breakfast; saw several acquaintances; called on Mr. Boyd and Mrs. Ashley, and late in the day returned to camp. Judge Watkins rode out and dined with us. Farewell to 1864.

January 1st. 1865. Sunday at Washington, Ark. All hail to the New Year this bright Sabbath day. May the blessing of God be with me through the year that is to come and on which we have just entered. At eleven o'clock went into town to church. Attended the Presbyterian church and heard a sensible and solemn sermon from the pastor, Rev. Dr. Williamson, appropriate to the season. After church called at Capt. [Thomas] Rector's[20] and saw his family and took a lunch. There [I] met Generals [Henry Hopkins] Sibley[21] and Jeff Thompson then returned to camp. Col. [Michael W.] Buster[22] dined with us. I was also surprised and gratified by the arrival of Dr. Wooten from Spring Hill. He will spend the night with us. We called to see Gen. Price and spent much time in talking on army affairs.

January 2nd. Monday. Having got through with the expedition to Missouri and the large cavalry command which Gen. Price has had undergoing reorganization and a portion of them being dismounted, a new arrangement of troops will be made in the spring and Gen. Price no doubt put in command of infantry. To effect these changes will require time and as all active military operations will be suspended during the winter. Gen. Price will leave in the morning on a 60 day leave to visit his family in Texas, and all his staff who desire it have been offered a like leave, but as I do not desire it I have declined to leave. As most of them go off there was a general breaking up of our headquarters and our mess today. Maj. Brinker with whom I messed lately started to go into winter quarters, but as Gov. Polk and myself who remain have not yet completed our arrangements for quarters we concluded to remain at our campfire tonight. After going into town to see about some matters there, I rode out to Mr. Thomas Smith's, 3 miles from town, to see if I could procure board and lodging while I remain here; fortunately, I succeeded. He lives in a good house and has everything very comfortable about him and I shall no doubt be pleasantly situated. Late in the day [I] took a family dinner with Dr. Wilson and then returned to our campfire and by the light of pine knots read until 10 o'clock.

January 3rd. Tuesday. Before breakfast went over to Dr. Wilson's to take leave of Gen. Price who started early on his visit to Texas. After seeing him off [I] went over and took a good camp breakfast with Maj. Gallagher. After breakfast Gov. Polk and I broke up our camp and sent our baggage to our new quarters, he to Dr. Wilson's and I to Mr. Smith's. My things having been sent off to the country [I] went into town having been summonsed to give evidence before the court martial in the case of Col. Wood, on trial for the killing of Col. MacLean. It was late before I was called to the stand. I was examined as to the nature of the wound, the cause of death, etc. [I] got through about 2 P.M. and rode out to Mr. Smith's and here I am now quietly and snuggly in a room to myself and almost as comfortably as in peace time.

January 4th. Wednesday. At Capt. Tom Smith's.[23] With the exception of a visit to Dr. Wilson's plantation a mile and a half off to see a sick soldier, Mr. Venable,[24] I spent the entire day in my room writing letters, etc. [I] first wrote to my wife and enclosed it in a long letter to Col. John W. Polk, near the Mississippi River, to be forwarded for me. Also wrote to Maj. Cabell at Camden and Dr. Wooten at Spring Hill. The quiet and retirement of my present retreat is delightful to me. Here I have a comfortable room all to myself and I enjoy it much.

January 5th. Thursday. Intended going to town today but it rained slowly all day so I contented myself to remain quietly in my room: reading, doing little jobs of sewing, and etc. After tea Capt. Smith and his sons sat with me for an hour. They bring out the report from town (Washington) that Sherman has captured Savannah [Georgia] with 35,000 bales of cotton. It is a Yankee account and I hope is not true.[25]

January 6th. Friday. The rain having ceased and the weather cleared off after breakfast, I rode over to Dr. Wilson's farm to see Mr. Venable. [I] found him doing very well. This visit over, I rode into town and meeting with Gov. Polk we both called to see Mrs. Eakin and paid her a pleasant visit. In town [I] saw numerous acquaintances but heard no good news. Savannah has probably fallen into the hands of the Yankees, which I regret very much, but we must not be discouraged by these disasters. Returned at 2 P.M. in time for dinner. Spent the afternoon in reading and after tea had a long chat with Capt. Smith about mutual acquaintances in Virginia and elsewhere.

January 7th. Saturday. Spent the day in my room having no disposition to go out or go to town. Occupied myself in reading, mending clothes, and in writing letters.

January 8th. Sunday. Intended going to town to church today but it rained in the morning and thus prevented me. Spent the day in doors reading and writing. Finished a long letter to Hon. Thos. L. Snead, Richmond, Va., giving him an account of our trip to Missouri.

January 9th. Monday. A rainy boisterous day. [I] did not venture out but spent the whole day in doors reading, sewing, and writing. Made a calico pillow slip. How I wish my dear good wife could see me engaged at this kind of work, it would amuse her much. As the evening shades gather around me, Oh how I long to be with my family, but I will not and do not repine, yet from the bottom of my heart I wish that this cruel war was over.

January 10th. Tuesday. The ground was thinly covered with snow this morning but in due time the sun arose and it soon vanished away. Rode over this morning to Dr. Wilson's farm to see Mr. Venable and thence to town. Called at the post commander's, deposited some letters, saw and talked with diverse acquaintances, got some mending done on my bridle and breast strap, and then returned to the country. Received a letter from Dr. Wooten saying that he had procured me board at Hervey's near Spring Hill where I expect to go in 4 or 5 days.

January 11th. Wednesday. Rode to town this morning. On the way in [I] called at Dr. Wilson's residence to visit the family and Mr. Bates [who had] just arrived from Texas. After remaining in town a short time [I] went 3 miles beyond to pay Mrs. Jordan and Mrs. Newton a visit [where I] remained an hour or more. On the way back [I] stopped again in town where I met several acquaintances and on the way out called to see Gov. Polk staying in Dr. Wilson's office. Returned [at] 4 P.M.

January 12th. Thursday. Rode into town again this morning and attended to some business. Collected $125 interest on my interest bearing notes. Called with Gov. Polk to see Mrs. Hempstead, formerly Miss Gratiot of St. Louis, a very agreeable lady residing here. [I] then called alone at Gen. [Grandison D.] Royston's[26] to see his son and family. Saw diverse acquaintances in town and heard of a chance of sending a letter to my wife. On returning to the country [I] wrote her another letter, which I enclosed to Capt. A. McCoy[27] on the Mississippi River, and which I fondly hope she will receive. God bless her. After tea, Mr. Smith's two little girls came in to see me. They remind me of my own dear children about their ages and set me to thinking of my once happy home now broken up. The Lord in mercy restore it again.

January 13th. Friday. Went down to Capt. Smith's plantation to see a sick negro this morning then to Dr. Wilson's to visit Mr. Venable and from there rode into town. Called on Mrs. Eakin to see about some shirts that she is having made for me. [I] paid $50 for making 4 shirts, I furnishing all the material. Attended to other matters in town and then returned to the country. Gov. Polk rode out with me and spent the night.

January 14th. Saturday. After breakfast Gov. Polk and myself rode into town and called to see Miss Harriet Snodgrass who is about to go into the Yankee lines and to St. Louis, and by her I sent messages to my wife. Through her I hope that my wife will hear from me as Miss Snodgrass has promised to see her. Saw numerous acquaintances, among others Col. Clay Taylor. Tried to make arrangements to get my baggage taken to Spring Hill where I wish to go early next week. Loaned Malcolm Graham $40 making in all $100 [that I have] loaned him. About 2 P.M. returned to the country and spent the afternoon in writing to my brother, Alex, in N.C., and [in] other matters.

January 15th. Sunday. It was my desire and intention to go to church today, but soon after breakfast I received a message from Mrs. Jordan urging me to come and see her son who was quite sick. Of course I went and as it was 5 miles off I was denied the privilege and pleasure of attending divine worship. I found the boy suffering a good deal and remained with him several hours and took dinner. Maj. and Mrs. Hill also dined there. It was near dark when I got back.

January 16th. Monday. Started to town this morning. On the way [I] met a messenger from Mrs. Jordan asking me to come out again and see her son. So after remaining in town a short time and attending to some business, [I] rode out. Remained there an hour or two and then went over to Col. [Charles S.] Mitchell's[28] Brigade several miles across the country. Saw the Col. and several other officers. On the way home [I] called at Dr. Wilson's to see Col. Polk and it being about dinner time, 4 P.M., dined with him and returned to my quarters about dark. Spent the evening reading.

January 17th. Tuesday. On going in town this morning received a long letter from Maj. Cabell at Camden which I read with interest. After spending a short time in town, went out to Mrs. Jordan's to see her son who I found better and after remaining some time returned to my lodgings in the country and spent the evening and night in reading Prescot's *Phillip the Second*. Gen. Magruder gave a large party at his quarters last night which I did not attend, being in the country and not caring to ride out 3 miles afterwards.

January 18th. Wednesday. Remained at home during the morning reading *Phillip the Second* and writing letters, one to Capt. [Richard S.] Harper[29] at Minden [Louisiana] and another to Maj. Brinker on business. About 2 P.M. had my horse saddled and called by Dr. Wilson's for Gov. Polk when we rode out to Mrs. Jordan's where we took dinner by invitation. Maj. Hill dined there also. Had a fine dinner and of course agreeable company. It was nearly night when we started back and quite dark before I reached home.

January 19th. Thursday. Went into town this morning to make preparations to go to Spring Hill tomorrow. Received a letter from Gen. Churchill and also from Dr. Wooten, the latter urging me to bring him some commissary supplies when I come to Spring Hill, which I will endeavor to do. Saw diverse friends but got no news. Called to see Col. Wood now under confinement for the killing of Col. MacLean. Returned to the country about 2 P.M. and read *Phillip the Second*. After dark Gen. Price's band now here with Gen. Magruder came out and gave the family a serenade and took supper. They gave us some fine music.

January 20th. Friday. Mrs. Jordan kindly offered me a wagon to carry my baggage to Spring Hill, which offer I accepted. [After] breakfast I packed up my duds and in a short time the boy with a two mule team arrived when I took leave of Capt. Smith and family where I have remained and been hospitably entertained since the 3rd. instant and took my departure. He would receive no pay for my staying with him. Frank, my servant, and my baggage [rode] in the wagon and I on horseback. Rode through Washington and attended to some business then rode by Mrs. Jordan's to bid her and Mrs. Johnson good bye, the wagon in the mean time going on. It was 12 M. when I left her house. [I] overtook and passed the wagon on the road and after a ride of three hours over horrible roads reached Col. [Calvin Monroe] Hervey's,[30] 2 miles from Spring Hill, where I had previously engaged board. Arrived in time for diner at 4 P.M., the wagon arrived soon after. Here I find myself comfortably housed. Col. Hervey [was] not at home but his wife [is] very kind. Maj. [John S. H.] Rainey[31] of Camden, brother-in-law to Mrs. Hervey, also spent the night at Col. Hervey's. Here I expect to spend a month or six weeks should something occur to prevent it. Rode 17 miles today.

January 21st. Saturday. At Col. Hervey's near Spring Hill. After a comfortable night's rest and a fine breakfast rode into Spring Hill to see Dr. Wooten and family staying in the seminary building. Soon Dr. Slaughter came [and] we spent the morning smoking and conversing. It was near 4 P.M. when I returned to my lodging in time, however, for a late dinner. Mr. Hervey returned this evening. [I] spent an hour or two conversing in the parlor then retired to my room and read the life of Mary, Queen of Scots.

January 22nd. Sunday. Notwithstanding it was threatening rain, went to Spring Hill to church at 11 o'clock where I heard a very sensible sermon by a Methodist minister by the name of Davies on the sin of profane swearing and Sabbath-breaking, two great evils of our army and country. After church [I] returned home. In the evening, having turned cold, it began to snow and bids fair to be a deep snow. How thankful I am that I am in such comfortable quarters.

January 23rd. Monday. The ground was covered but slightly with snow this morning, it having cleared off cold during the night. After breakfast, rode over to Dr. Wooten's quarters and there remained an hour or two. By courier received a letter from Dr. Bond. After returning to my lodgings, spent the rest of the day reading the life of Mary, Queen of Scots.

January 24th. Tuesday. Weather clear but cold. Spent the day indoors. First [I] wrote a long letter to Gen. Price after which [I] read the sad story of Mary, Queen of Scots. Thus quietly passed the day.

January 25th. Wednesday. Weather unchanged; clear and cold. Rode over to Dr. Wooten's quarters after breakfast. There [I] met several gentlemen and learned that the Yankee papers team with recognition of the Confederacy by England and France which they anticipate will soon take place. God grant that it may be so, for with recognition the dawn of blessed peace would soon appear. Returned to my quarters about 2 P.M. Finished the sad and tragical story of Mary, Queen of Scots and having nothing more substantial to read commenced *Rob Roy* by Scott.

January 26th. Thursday. Spent the day indoors. Wrote a long letter to Dr. Bond [in] Gilmer, Texas in reply to his and giving an account of our Missouri expedition and then read *Rob Roy*. The quiet of the country is delightful.

January 27th. Friday. Spent the entire day indoors reading. I have now been at Col. Hervey's one week where I am quietly and delightfully situated. Col. Hervey is a wealthy planter having a plantation on Red River [and] lives in good style. I occupy a large room on the first floor. We eat two meals a day, the last about 4 P.M.

January 28th. Saturday. Rode over to see Dr. Wooten after breakfast. Called also to see Mrs. Thompson and her daughter, Mrs. Lucas, who live in the same house and are connected with my brother's wife. Returned about 2 P.M. and read *Rob Roy*. Dr. King,[32] a surgeon recently from Texas, an agreeable gentleman, arrived at Col. Hervey's and spent the night in my room. After tea, he and the ladies gave us some good music.

January 29th. Sunday. No church in the neighborhood. Spent the day at home. Dr. King left for Washington after dinner. Later in the day Gen. Jeff Thompson arrived and still later Maj. Kimmell and Lt. Smith of Gen. Magruder's staff came, and all spent the night with Col. Hervey. Gen. Thompson occupied my room with me. He amused us by relating incidents in his experience in prison life among the Yankees and other incidents in the war. We sat up late talking over the affairs of the war and the country.

January 30th. Monday. Weather rainy and sleety. Maj. Kimmell and Lt. Smith left this morning en route for Shreveport, but Gen. Thompson remained all day. Spending the whole day indoors we had much talk together, which with some reading occupied my time. No news from any quarter.

January 31st. Tuesday. Gen. Thompson left this morning for Washington. Gen. Magruder passed down on yesterday en route for Shreveport, but on hearing of a Yankee raid near Camden he stopped at Lewisville until its extent and magnitude could be ascertained. While sitting in my room reading Macaulay about 12 today, Maj. Hill called by in his buggy and proposed to take me home with him near Washington, stating as a reason that his wife wished to see and consult me. So without a moments notice I jumped in and went with him. After a ride of three hours we arrived in time for 4 o'clock dinner. There I found in addition to his wife, Miss Amy Rayburn, two Miss Carrolls, and Col. [Edward P.] Turner,[33] Gen. Magruder's Adjutant General. All were agreeable persons. We spent the night until 12 A.M. in conversation and in various amusements such as "consequences" and the like, childish sports which, however, were innocent and amusing.

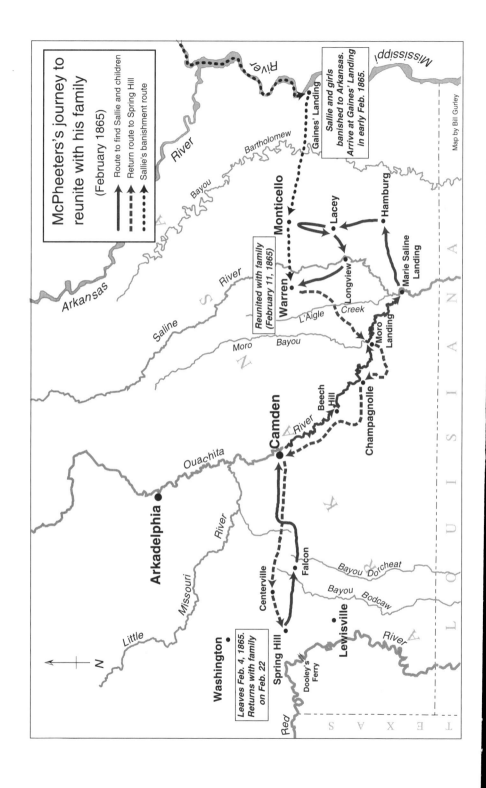

McPheeters's journey to reunite with his family
(February 1865)

→ Route to find Sallie and children
--→ Return route to Spring Hill
•••→ Sallie's banishment route

Sallie and girls banished to Arkansas. Arrive at Gaines' Landing in early Feb. 1865.

Reunited with family (February 11, 1865)

Leaves Feb. 4, 1865. Returns with family on Feb. 22

Map by Bill Gurley

Mississippi River
Bartholomew Bayou
Arkansas River
Saline River
Moro Bayou
Ouachita River
Missouri River
Little River
Red River
Bayou Dorcheat
Bayou Bodcaw
River

Gaines' Landing
Monticello
Lacey
Hamburg
Warren
Longview
Marie Saline Landing
L'Aigle Creek
Moro Landing
Beech Hill
Champagnolle
Camden
Arkadelphia
Falcon
Centerville
Spring Hill
Washington
Lewisville
Dooley's Ferry

ARKANSAS
LOUISIANA
TEXAS

N

CHAPTER 10

Banishment and Reunion, 1865

*The Lord will help them and rescue them . . .
from the wicked.*

Federal military authorities in St. Louis, enforcing martial law, had grown frustrated and annoyed at a single defiant, vainglorious segment of the civilian population—pro-Confederate women. For three years Union officers had placed many of these women under surveillance, candidates for banishment or military prison, only to see them released by their friends in high places. Approaching their wits' ends over subtle displays of Southern defiance, the officers forbade women to wear the color red as ribbons on their bonnets or other clothing, silk linings in their capes, or petticoats. The pro-Confederate ladies taunted the soldiers under whose control they had lived for so long, and officials responded by issuing ever more punitive regulations. Military reports by the provost of St. Louis vented his fury to his district superiors, describing the antics of these "active, intelligent, wealthy women."[1]

For a long while, military clerks had been kept busy opening the mail delivered under a flag of truce addressed to the women under surveillance. The clerks were searching for any phrase or sentence that might qualify as offensive or treasonous communications. Sallie McPheeters had been closely watched, and her mail had been opened for a long while. Finally, in December 1864, she composed a cover note to accompany a letter to her husband. Addressed to Maj. Gen. J. J. Reynolds, newly appointed commander of the Federal Department of Arkansas, it was not just defiant, it was sassy:

St. Louis, December 21st, 1864

General Reynolds

Dear Sir:
I take the liberty of writing to you to beg that you will do me

a favor by sending the enclosed letter to my husband Dr. Wm. M. McPheeters, formerly of St. Louis now on Gen. Price's staff. I have often heard my husband speak of you in the highest regard when you resided here a few years ago and hoping the war has not changed you as it has many others from gentleman to fiends. I presume to seek this favor of you. Should the Dr. send a letter by return flag of Truce *please forward* and you will have the *thanks* of a Rebel "though she be."

Respectfully yours,
Sallie McPheeters

"A Rebel though she be"—these were the words the Office of the Provost Marshal had long sought, an admission of disloyalty. Moreover, her insinuation that war had transformed his colleagues from "gentlemen to fiends" proved especially irksome to Reynolds.[2] The missive was incriminating, and regardless of her innocent intentions, Sallie would have to pay.

On January 17, 1865, Sallie was arrested and incarcerated in the Gratiot Street Prison, which, coincidentally, was the old McDowell Medical School built by Dr. Joseph Nash McDowell in the 1840s, where her husband had attended lectures as a young physician. Here, in the dark, crowded, stinking interior of the octagon-shaped former medical school, Sallie spent two days and nights. Disease was rampant among the tattered soldiers packed into rooms on every floor. Sallie was in one room on the third floor used to imprison women, and she could look through the bars of the window to see her little girls on the street corner below as a friend brought them there at a designated hour. Had William McPheeters seen the newspaper two days later, he would have read: "BANISHED—By order of General Dodge, the following female sympathizers have been banished beyond the lines of the Federal forces via Gaines' Landing: Miss Georgia T. Reed, Mrs. Sallie McPheeters, Miss Jane Ward, Miss Mattie Anderson, Miss Mollie Anderson."[3]

With only a few hours to prepare, Sallie and her two daughters were put on a freight train bound for Cairo, Illinois. They had no money, one trunk, and a few satchels containing their belongings. At Cairo they were herded onto a riverboat along with five other banished women from St. Louis.

Their destination lay 437 miles down the Mississippi, a wilderness of swamps and bayous in the southernmost corner of Arkansas. By the time Sallie McPheeters and the tiny band of lost souls from St. Louis were rudely put ashore by their captors, the plantations along the big river had been stripped of horses, mules, and cotton. Her ordeal had taken nearly three weeks, in a variety of riverboats that tied up at night and pulled ashore often to take on wood or to seek safe haven from the raging Mississippi. The rain never stopped; it seemed to be the end of the world by flood.

February 1st. Wednesday. Rained all night and misted all day. [I] did not return to Col. Hervey's, but after [a] late breakfast rode into Washington (4 miles) with Maj. Hill. Here I met numerous acquaintances and received the painful intelligence from the *St. Louis Republican* of the 18th instant that my beloved wife had been arrested and confined in the female department of Gratiot Street prison, St. Louis, on the charge of general disloyalty.[4] This news filled me with sorrow and regret, the more painful because [I could] do nothing to aid her in this hour of severe trial. Oh my dear darling wife, how my heart bleeds to think of your trials and persecutions! Would God I were able to serve you or even to be with you now. I pray God that he will give you strength and fortitude and grace to bear up under these trials and that they may result in nothing worse than your being banished from among the detested Yankees. After remaining in town several hours [I] returned to Maj. Hill's by late dinner time. The evening and night passed off cheerfully to others but my thoughts were with my poor persecuted wife and I could think of nothing else and was poor company for anyone.

February 2nd. Thursday. It rained hard all night. My earliest thoughts this morning as well as my latest were of my beloved incarcerated wife. What can I ever do to repay her for all that she has so heroically endured for me and in our noble cause? I should be unworthy of her if it is not the study of my life to make her happy. May the arms of omnipotence be around her and my dear children in this dark hour. After breakfast, though the day was unpromising, I started back to Col. Hervey's, 12 miles, on horse-back with a servant to bring the horse back. The recent rains had so swelled all the streams that I met with great difficulty. [I] took the wrong road and had to swim my horse over four creeks, a thing which I very much dislike, and of course got thoroughly wet in all the lower part of my body. The bottom of the Bois d'Arc was all a lake up to my horse's flank, but by dint of perseverance and deter-mination arrived at Col. Hervey's hospitable residence about 2 P.M. I exchanged my wet clothes for dry ones and was kindly welcomed by Mrs. Hervey and Miss Derrick, a very intelligent and agreeable young lady. During the afternoon [I] wrote to Maj. Cabell and Dr. J. N. McDowell,[5] both in Washington [Arkansas].

February 3rd. Friday. Felt unusually depressed all day. The thoughts of my dear wife being imprisoned oppresses me. After breakfast [I] rode over to see Dr. Wooten but was ill at ease. [I] returned and tried to divert my mind by reading Macaulay. Old Mrs. Johnson on her way to Lewisville called by Col. Hervey's and stayed all night. [I] was glad to see her. After dark Col. Hervey came from Washington bringing me a note from Col. Shaler stat-ing that he had received a note from Capt. McCoy at Monticello [on] Jan. 29th, in which he said he had that day met my wife and two children travelling in a wagon between Gaines' Landing and Monticello and [she] would be in Monticello the next day. This intelligence took me by surprise. She has undoubtedly been ban-ished and is now exposed to all the trials and hardships of a severe journey. I shall start for Camden in the morning hoping to meet her. God bless and protect her.

February 4th. Saturday. Soon after breakfast [I] arranged my affairs and started on horseback for Camden leaving my servant and bag-gage at Col. Hervey's. Slept but little last night. Called by Spring Hill to see Dr. Wooten. It was ½ past 10 before I left there. Went via Falcon. Passed through Falcon, 18 miles from Spring Hill, [at] 3 P.M., which before reaching I had to pass over the two Bodcaws [Creeks], which nearly swam my horse for a long distance. From Falcon [I] went on to Parson Moore's near Camp Bragg 15 miles further. The [Bayou] Dorcheat was very high and almost swam my horse in the bottom after crossing the bridge. [It] commenced raining towards evening. [I] arrived at Parson Moore's after dark in the rain having traveled 33 miles through mud, high water, and rain.

February 5th. Sunday. Rained hard all night. Although it is the Sabbath and raining hard I felt obliged to go on to Camden in search of my wife and children. The rain of last night added to those of several days ago, causing all the streams to become very much swollen. [I] found great difficulty in getting on. On reaching Mr. Baird's, at his suggestion, [I] went across some 7 miles to the Old Washington Road and went past Poison Springs to avoid swimming creeks. As it was, it was just as much as I could do to get over the water courses, every branch being a river. After a long ride of 35 miles through rain, mud, and high water, [I] arrived at Camden after dark and stopped at Dr. Taylor's quarters where I spent the night. My first inquiry was for my wife, but could hear nothing of her. It is now impossible to get from Monticello for the high water. The Lord protect my family. On the way today [I] stopped at Dr. Madden's to inquire the way just at dinner time but had no appetite to eat.

February 6th. Monday. Spent a restless night. The thoughts of my wife being out in the mud and rain and the uncertainty as to where she is troubled me. After breakfast went to the Adjutants Office to inquire about the courses to Monticello. Wrote to my wife there and to two gentlemen to look after her and aid her getting in. Saw Col. and Mrs. John Polk and others and made all necessary inquiries about the roads to Monticello. Learning that a boat, the *Gen. Fletcher,* would go down the Ouachita River this evening, I determined to go down on her as far as she goes and then cut across to Magnolia if I do not hear of my wife in the mean time. So I made my arrangements accordingly; got passports from Gen. Magruder; and embarked myself and horse on the boat which got off about 4 P.M. Col. John W. Polk goes down with me. The boat goes down on government business in charge of Maj. [John B.] Burton[6] and has a good many officers on board.

By dark we arrived at Beech Hill, some 30 miles, where we laid up for the night. The thoughts of my wife, and anxiety about her, has kept me uneasy all day.

February 7th. Tuesday. Spent a restless night on the boat. [I] could not sleep from anxiety about my dear family. The boat started at daylight and by 12 o'clock P.M. ran down to Moro Landing. Hearing no news of my family as I had hoped, [I] left my horse here in charge of Capt. Mhoon and continued on the boat down to Careyville Landing where we arrived ½ past 2 P.M. Owing to the fear of encountering the Yankees below, the boat was afraid to go down further so Col. Polk, Mr. Sharp of Memphis, and myself embarked on board the yawl or lifeboat to go down to Marie Saline Landing, some 40 miles below on the Ouachita River, my objective being to get to Monticello by the most practical route. It was 3 P.M. when we started in the yawl with two stout negro men to row us and a white man to steer. The river was high and the current strong so we ran well and made good time. About dark and 20 miles below where we started we suddenly came upon a steamer—*The Nelson*—stopped at a wood yard. Our first impression was that it was a Yankee boat and that we had all gone up. We soon found, however, that it was one of our own boats loaded with corn going up to Camden. So after going aboard, taking supper, and inquiring [of] the news below we reembarked on our frail craft and after a cold but safe run by moonlight until 11 P.M. we arrived at Marie Saline having rowed 40 miles since three o'clock. Here we went on shore by walking over some 1000 yards of crazy trestle work and spent the night in the house of a poor old woman with a blind son, sleeping on a dirty bed with no covers save our overcoats and saddle blankets. [I] could get no news here from Monticello or of my family, but learned that the Yankees, some 4000 strong, on a raid were at Hamburg on our route 22 miles ahead and that the whole country was in alarm.

February 8th. Wednesday. Took breakfast with the old woman at the landing, sent the yawl back to Moro Landing, and Col. Polk and myself went out to Mrs. Buffington's—a very clean woman— 3 miles off. Here we got horses and Col. Polk and I started for

Hamburg. Called by at Mr. Bate's, 2 miles off, and took dinner and hearing that the Yankees had left Hamburg went on to that place where we arrived about sundown and put up with Dr. Dickenson's —a very clean gentleman. On the way we were stopped and came near having a difficulty with 3 cavalrymen. Here again I am disappointed in not hearing of my family. [The] Yankees have gone on towards Gaines' Landing.

February 9th. Thursday. Owing to the difficulty of getting horses and the fear of encountering the Yankees at Monticello, I found it impossible to get off today, so [I] spent an anxious day at Hamburg at the house of Dr. Dickenson. Providence permitting I will renew my journey in the morning and hope to reach Monticello in the morning where I hope to meet my beloved wife.

February 10th. Friday. Having procured a mule to ride, [I] started off from Hamburg after breakfast with Col. Polk for Monticello, distant 33 miles. Passed through Lacey and when 7 miles from Monticello met a courier with a dispatch saying that my wife, when last heard from, was at Warren. Thus doomed again to disappointment I determined to go on to Monticello and thence to Warren. Late in the evening when two miles from Monticello we were met by a man just from town who warned us not to go into Monticello, as the Yankees were momentarily expected there on a raid from Pine Bluff, and who told us that most of the men had left the town. On receiving this news we deemed it safest not to venture in, so we turned back and spent the night at a house 4 miles from town in some apprehension all night of the Yankees.

February 11th. Saturday. Fearing to go through Monticello the nearest way, I parted with Col. Polk at daylight and went back to Lacey, thence to Longview where I crossed the Saline River in a ferry boat and went to Warren where I arrived late in the evening having traveled 40 miles. Here I was fortunate enough to meet my wife and two children at the hotel and who were anxiously looking for me. It was a joyous meeting after so long a separation. My dear wife was well and looking well though she has had a dreadfully rough trip. The children, Maggy and Sally, were very much grown in 3 years and would not have known me, nor I them. The reunion was a happy one.

February 12th. Sunday. Accompanying my wife were 5 ladies: two old ones, Mrs. Groners, one 62 and the other 84 years old, [and] three young ones, two Miss Andersons and a Miss Ward. Before my arrival they had made arrangements to hire two wagons to take the whole party to Camden. So as we were still in dread of the Federals, we started off from Warren this morning, Sunday as it was. Soon after breakfast the two two-horse wagons were loaded up with baggage and the 8 females and we started; I on mule back. After going about 12 miles we had to cross the L'Aigles, three noted creeks with a desperate bottom. Here we met with difficulty. One of the bridges was gone and the water covered the bottom for ¾ of a mile. In going out of the road to avoid the destroyed bridge our teams stalled in the mud and deep water. The drivers had to get down in the water waste deep, get the ladies out, and double the teams to get out. After a delay of a couple of hours and much hard work and other difficulties, we finally got through these dreadful L'Aigles and went two miles beyond to a plain country house where we spent the night, most of us sleeping on the floor.

February 13th. Monday. After an early breakfast [we] started for Moro Landing 16 miles off. Here we arrived about 1 P.M. and were kindly met by Capt. Mhoon and Lt. Walker. [We] went into their quarters, warmed, took a snack, and then were ferried over the Moro and Ouachita by Capt. Mhoon's men and also over a deep slough on the other side when Capt. Mhoon took leave of us. The Ouachita had risen so much that we had to encounter another deep and wide slough two miles further. The crossing here was difficult and dangerous, but by elevating the things in the wagons and doubling teams we got over safely and spent the night in a common house just on the other side.

February 14th. Tuesday. Came on today through desperate roads and high creeks to Champagnolle. Here I hoped to get a boat but was disappointed. Had to turn out of the direct road onto the Lisbon Road to avoid swimming creeks. About 7 miles from

Champagnolle and when near Mr. Medlock's the axle of one of
our wagons broke and we had to stop all night at Mr. Medlock's,
a plain but comfortable place. Here little Sally who was unwell
all day became quite sick. I was up with her frequently during the
night and was very much alarmed about her towards morning,
but thanks to a kind Providence she got better.

February 15th. Wednesday. By the time the wagon was mended
Sally was able to go on, but it was 10 o'clock before we got off and
after plodding through the mud until night [we] got within 20 miles
of Camden. [We] put up at a Parson Mullin's, a most miserable
filthy place with coarse vulgar people. Our food all along has been
coarse. This was dreadful. My wife was very much annoyed and
spent an uncomfortable night on the floor as did the rest of us.

February 16th. Thursday. Got up at 3 A.M., built [a] fire, and got
ready to start by daylight. [I was] glad to get out of so filthy a place.
After encountering more mud [we] arrived in Camden about 3 P.M.
and put up at Mrs. Ritchie's boarding house. The trip from Warren
of 5 days was a very hard one through mud, water, and all sorts of
difficulties, but thanks to the good Lord it was a safe one. The other
ladies of the party put up at Mrs. Richmond's.

February 17th. Friday. Spent the day quietly in Camden. Some
few Missourians called to see my wife. I saw Gen. Parsons and
secured his ambulance to bring my family to Spring Hill and also
got the promise of a wagon for the baggage. We are comfortable
at Mrs. Ritchie's.

February 18th. Saturday. Expected to start for Spring Hill this
morning but the wagon not being ready [we] remained quietly
in Camden.

February 19th. Sunday. This being the Sabbath I preferred not
travelling and so remained. Maggy, Sally, and I went first to the
Methodist church, but could not get in so we went to the
Episcopal church where we heard Dr. McGill, a lay reader, read
the service—a poor sermon. Yesterday evening we went out to

Col. [Levin M.] Lewis'[7] quarters and witnessed dress parade—the first Confederate soldiers that my family has seen.

February 20th. Monday. Ambulance and wagon reporting [we] left Camden this morning between 9 and 10 A.M. [We] came 20 miles before sundown and spent the night at Mr. Christopher's very comfortably. [The] roads were bad but not impossible.

February 21st. Tuesday. Came 24 miles to Centerville on the Washington and Camden Road. Encountered a heavy shower and arrived at Centerville in the rain about 3 P.M. Here I found it very difficult to get lodging for the night but finally succeeded in getting in at Mr. Dickinson's, a very poor place, where we spent a tolerable night. It rained hard until some time in the night.

February 22nd. Wednesday. Started in good time this morning having 12 miles to come. Turned off the Washington Road and came towards Spring Hill. [The] roads were rough but not deep. Arrived at Col. Hervey's hospitable residence about 1 P.M. where we were kindly and cordially welcomed and where we expect to make our home for a short time. We are all glad to be at rest. My wife has had a horrid trip from Gaines' Landing. [It] commenced raining soon after we got to Col. Hervey's and rained hard all night. Our teamsters returned after leaving us here.

February 23rd. Thursday. At Col. Hervey's with my family. Rained hard all last night and was cloudy and disagreeable all today. Stayed indoors with my family thankful that we are in such pleasant quarters and not in the mud and water on the road. Col. Hervey who has been at his plantation returned after breakfast. A quiet and peaceful day.

February 24th. Friday. Remained at home again today. Dr. Wooten called this morning to see my wife and sit an hour or two. After he left [I] engaged myself in mending and fixing up Maggy's trunk and in other jobs rendered necessary by the jolting of the long hard trip. My wife having bought me a razor today I cut off my mustache after wearing it ever since leaving home, now near three

years. It is less trouble to shave my upper lip than to be troubled
with a mustache. Raining again tonight. After dark [I] wrote a letter to Capt. Pflager on business and in reply to one from him.

February 25th. Saturday. Weather still cloudy, windy, and
unsettled. After breakfast [I] rode over to Spring Hill and paid Dr.
Wooten a visit at the Seminary. While there [I] wrote a letter to
Mack Graham and one to Dr. Haden reporting my whereabouts.
Returned and spent the rest of the day with my family. Towards
evening Mrs. Musser and Fleming Bates en route from Washington
to Lewisville called by and staid all night. After supper [I] wrote a
letter to Maj. Cabell and one to Gov. Polk giving them information brought by my wife in reference to their families and inviting
them to pay us a visit. These gentlemen are now at Lewisville.

February 26th. Sunday. A bright beautiful day. No preaching in
the neighborhood. Mrs. Musser and Mr. Bates left after breakfast
for Lewisville. Mr. [and] Mrs. Murphy came over to pay Mrs.
Hervey a visit. He is the Episcopal minister here and in Washington
but this is not his day for holding forth. Spent the day quietly. Read
and prayed with my family as in the days of old when at our happy
home in St. Louis without two boys [who] now I trust [are] in
heaven. During the morning Dr. Slaughter and Mr. Thompson
came over to visit my wife and spent an hour. Col. Hervey returned
from his plantation and reports Red River rising with the prospect
of an overflow. After dark Col. Mitchell and Maj. Tracy came and
spent the night with Col. Hervey.

February 27th. Monday. Spent the day at home with my family
reading Macaulay, writing letters, etc. After dinner took a ride on
horseback with Maggy, Molly Hervey,[8] and Sally, the latter riding in front of me. We went several miles and had a pleasant
ride—all for the benefit of the girls.

February 28th. Tuesday. Went over with Col. Hervey and the chil-
dren after breakfast this morning to a sale in the neighborhood. The
Rev. Mr. Murphy, Episcopal preacher, was selling out to go to
Texas. I bought a few small articles, but there was not much of

value offered, though what was sold brought war prices. After returning wrote a letter to Surg. Haden, Chief of Medical Bureau, Marshall, Texas, asking to be relieved from field duty and assigned to some post or hospital where I can be with my family. Capt. and Mrs. Lindsay and Capt. [S. M.] Frost[9] spent the night at Col. Hervey's. Weather pleasant.

March 1st. Wednesday. Rode over to Spring Hill this morning but did not find Dr. Wooten at home so paid but a short visit. Read Macaulay and spent the rest of the day pleasantly with my family. Capt. and Mrs. Lindsay stayed all day.

March 2nd. Thursday. Rained pretty much all day and very hard as night advanced. Kept indoors all day. Towards evening Col. [William A.] Alston,[10] Gen. Magruder's Adjutant, on his way from Lewisville to Washington called by and spent the night with Col. Hervey. Malcolm Graham also accompanied him coming on a visit to my wife and to get the things she brought from his mother.

March 3rd. Friday. Rained hard all night and continued rainy most of the day. There seems to be no end to the rain this spring. Remained at home reading and otherwise amusing myself with family and friends.

March 4th. Saturday. The sun came out bright and beautiful this morning. Capt. and Mrs. Lindsay and Mac. Graham left for Lewisville. After breakfast rode over to Spring Hill to see Dr. Wooten. Remained an hour or two and received several letters among others one from Gov. Polk. This is the day on which Lincoln is to be inaugurated for his second term [as] president of Yankeedom and on which it is said foreign powers will recognize the South and raise the blockade. God grant that it may be so.

March 5th. Sunday. Again no preaching in the neighborhood. Day bright and spent quietly indoors reading and otherwise endeavoring to improve the time. Took a long walk with wife and children late in the evening. Capt. [Edward F.] Pearson[11] called by and spent the night.

March 6th. Monday. Another bright beautiful day spent quietly in the country with my family. Read and otherwise amused myself. Late in the evening took a long walk with wife and children.

March 7th. Tuesday. Went over to Spring Hill this morning to pay Dr. Wooten a visit but got no news whatever. Day passed off quietly. Maggy and Molly Hervey took a horseback ride in the evening. My wife cut me out a full suit of summer clothes out of a large shawl brought out by her.

March 8th. Wednesday. A lovely day passed quietly at home. Gen. Jeff Thompson and Charles Perry called by en route for Lewisville to Washington and took dinner, but gave us no news. Toward night the weather changed and became much colder and for awhile hailed hard.

March 9th. Thursday. Weather cold, cloudy, and forbidding during the morning. Remained at home. Col. Alston and Capt. Rector en route for Lewisville called and paid my wife a short visit. By special courier from Lewisville this afternoon I received a note from Capt. [John W.] Lewis,[12] Gen. Price's adjutant, stating that the General wishes me to report for duty before Monday next, at which time he expects to move with his command. This renders it necessary for me to go to Lewisville tomorrow. Col. [Thomas H.] Murray[13] and two other officers from Parsons' Division spent the night.

March 10th. Friday. After breakfast this morning [I] started for Lewisville on horseback. After several hours ride [I] arrived, a distance of 20 miles, between 1 and 2 P.M. [I] met Gov. Polk soon after arriving and called on Mrs. Churchill where I was invited to stay. [I] then called to see Gen. Price with whom I had a long talk. [I] got a leave of 20 days from Monday next to return and provide for my family. Then returned, took dinner with, and spent the evening with Mrs. Churchill [where I] was kindly received and hospitably entertained. On the way to Lewisville [I] met Mrs. Johnson who promised to call by and pay my wife a visit.

March 11th. Saturday. After a comfortable breakfast and taking leave of Mrs. Churchill [I] went to Gen. Magruder's office to get my leave approved. Saw Col. Turner, Malcolm Graham, and others. Col. Turner cheerfully approved my leave. Did not see Gen. Magruder as he had not come to his office, which I regret. Having finished my business [I] started on my return to Spring Hill accompanied by Gov. Polk who came up to visit my wife. We arrived about 3 P.M., having taken it leisurely, [and] found all well. Weather delightful. During the evening talked over St. Louis affairs with Gov. Polk and my wife.

March 12th. Sunday. No church in the neighborhood again today. Gov. Polk spent the day with us. Dr. Wooten came over and paid a long visit. Day passed off quietly but not to my satisfaction in a moral point of view.

March 13th. Monday. Gov. Polk returned to Lewisville this morning [and I] rode with him as far as Spring Hill to see Dr. Wooten. Got no news. [The] rest of the day [was] spent quietly at home. In the evening Maggy and Molly Hervey went to a little party at Maj. Finley's[14] accompanied by Mrs. Hervey to matronize them.

March 14th. Tuesday. Col. Turner, Gen. Magruder's adjutant, called by today bringing me some letters and giving us the sad news that Charleston had been evacuated by our forces and burned to the ground before leaving it. This is greatly to be regretted, but I rejoice that it has been destroyed rather than it should be polluted by Yankee occupation. Malcolm Graham came up this evening to visit my wife.

March 15th. Wednesday. A rainy disagreeable day spent indoors reading Macaulay's History. Dr. Wooten called by en route for Washington but had no news.

March 16th. Thursday. Wrote several letters during the morning and [read] Macaulay. Late in the evening [I] took a walk with the girls. No news and no incidents.

March 17th. Friday. Arose before day and accompanied Col. Hervey hunting. We rode several miles but saw neither deer nor turkey though they are said to be abundant in the woods. The weather is delightful. General Magruder, Col. Alston, and Capt. [Stephen D.] Yancey[15] en route from Washington to Lewisville called by and took dinner at Col. Hervey's and spent several hours in conversation with my wife. [They] then went over to Spring Hill and spent the night with Dr. Wooten. The General has been ordered to Texas and will, therefore, leave this district much to the regret of everyone. Late in the evening [I] took a ride on horseback with the girls—Maggy, Molly, and Sally.

March 18th. Saturday. After breakfast rode over to see Dr. Wooten [and] found Gen. Magruder there. He offered to ask for me to be assigned to duty at Galveston if it would be agreeable to me. In my assuring him that it would he promised to do so and took a note to that effect. After the General left, Dr. Wooten, Dr. [Thomas] Brandon,[16] Mr. Thompson,[17] and myself went deer hunting. I took a stand. We started several deer and one of the party got a shot, but none came near me. Mr. Thompson, however, killed a fine large wild turkey-gobler. Late in the evening I took the gun and went in the neighborhood to a favorite resort of deer—for they are numerous here—but did not see any.

March 19th. Sunday. Again without preaching [I] spent the day indoors reading, catechizing the children, and reading to them. Oh, for the return of regular Sabbath privileges.

March 20th. Monday. A rainy blustery day, uninviting out of doors, and as I had nothing to take me out [I] remained in the house reading and attending to domestic duties of various kinds. We have rumors today of a battle in North or South Carolina in which Beauregard and Sherman, the commanders of both sides, are said to have been killed and the Yankees defeated.[18] But as rumors are so conveniently unreliable, the report is entitled to but little credit. I sincerely hope that Beauregard has not been killed; we cannot spare such a man.

March 21st. Tuesday. Rode over to the seminary this morning to hear the news and see Dr. Wooten, but heard nothing but additional reports of a battle between Lee and Grant in which the latter was defeated as usual. God grant that it may be true, but there is no reliance whatever on lame rumor.

March 22nd. Wednesday. Mrs. Jordan, on her way to Lewisville, called by today and paid my wife a visit and gave us a kind and pressing invitation to visit her at her residence near Washington. Weather delightful. Remained at home. No news and but little to interrupt the monotony of country life.

March 23rd. Thursday. Went deer hunting this morning with Dr. Wooten, Mr. Thompson, young Finley, and Brandon. One of the party killed a doe. I saw but did not get a shot at another. Brought home a ham. Received a letter from Gov. Reynolds at Marshall, Texas congratulating me on the safe arrival of my wife and family in the Confederacy. Mrs. Hervey, my wife, and the girls went visiting to see Mrs. Wooten and Thompson.

March 24th. Friday. Paid a visit today to Col. Hervey at his plantation on the other side of Red River, 13 miles distant. Started after breakfast and called at the seminary to see Dr. Wooten who would have accompanied me but for the indisposition of his wife. Crossed Red River at Dooley's Ferry on a government pontoon bridge and rode four miles before reaching his farm. Found him spaying hogs. His farm is a beautiful one, the land very fertile and lies finely. After dinner [I] vaccinated a lot of young negroes. Walked about the farm. Bought from a country woman 6 yds. of jeans and a coarse shirt for Frank for which I paid $50 and considered it a bargain, as indeed it is.

March 25th. Saturday. Arose early and took a good farm breakfast. Soon after which, accompanied by Col. Hervey, started back for Spring Hill where we arrived about 12 M. having paid a pleasant visit. On the way up we met Capt. Mhoon at Dooley's Ferry where he is now stationed. Found [my] wife and children well.

March 26th. Sunday. Attended church this morning at Spring Hill. Heard a plain good gospel sermon from a Methodist brother. Rev. Mr. Boyd and Dr. King came home with us and stayed to dinner. We have rumors today of battles on the other side of the Mississippi River and of recognition by foreign powers, all of which must be received with many grains of doubt. Spent the evening and night in reading.

March 27th. Monday. Went out deer hunting after breakfast. Dr. Slaughter killed a buck. Took another drive after dinner. Col. Clay Taylor and several others joining in the hunt, but we did not get a shot. Saw several officers from Washington but got no reliable news. Wrote to Gov. Reynolds in reply to his late letter of congratulation and other official letters. Weather cloudy and disposed to rain. Mrs. Dr. Scott and Miss Eliza Dean, en route for Louisiana, called by and paid my wife a short visit this morning.

March 28th. Tuesday. Rode over to Spring Hill and visited Dr. Wooten and Dr. King this morning but heard no news. Spent the rest of the day reading and otherwise amusing myself. Maj. [Samuel] Gibson[19] of Churchill's Division spent the night.

March 29th. Wednesday. A rainy disagreeable day. Maj. Cabell called on his way to Washington to see my wife and self and spent an hour; glad to see him. The rest of the day was spent quietly indoors. Finished reading the *Heart of Midlothian*. Still no orders.

March 30th. Thursday. Went over to Spring Hill about noon today. While there, Gen. Price arrived from Lewisville on his way to Washington where the court of inquiry into the conduct of the Missouri Campaign is to meet.[20] He took dinner with Dr. Wooten and in the evening came over to Col. Hervey's and spent the night to pay my wife and the family a visit. They were glad of an opportunity to see him. He looks very well and is in very good spirits. My wife and he talked over Missouri affairs in which he takes great interest.

March 31st. Friday. Gen. Price left a while after breakfast for Washington. As I am at present on his staff and as he is not now on duty, owing to the investigations of the court, which he has requested and which is about to meet, I will probably not be on duty for sometime, except [that] I should be ordered to duty at some post as I have requested to be. Rode over to Spring Hill during the morning to hear the news. Called to see Dr. King and Wooten. Spent the rest of the day reading and otherwise amusing myself.

April 1st. Saturday. For the amusement of the children, we all went on a fishing party today in which several families in the neighborhood joined: Maj. Finley, Dr. Brandon, Dr. Wooten, and Mr. Thompson. After breakfast we went to the Bois d'Arc Creek some 3 miles off. My wife and children, Col. and Mrs. Hervey, his daughters, and Miss Derrick went from this house in a wagon. The Col. and I on horseback. At the creek we met the rest of the party and commenced fishing which we kept up for an hour with poor success, owing no doubt to the high water in the creek. We caught a few small fish, but all parties soon became discouraged and repaired to the rendezvous where in due time we enjoyed a fine lunch brought by the ladies; Molly and Maggy having cotton cakes to April Fool the party. We returned home about 4 P.M. after which we joined in a deer hunt in the neighborhood and killed a fine deer; shot by Col. Hervey. I have not yet succeeded in getting a shot. The day was pleasant though the sun was hot.

April 2nd. Sunday. Spent the day at home as there was no preaching in the neighborhood. Mr. Fowler called by to see me on his way to Washington and spent the night.

April 3rd. Monday. Took a deer drive this morning but was not fortunate enough to start a deer and so [I] got no venison. Maj. Cabell called by again on his way from Washington to Lewisville and paid a short visit. After dinner [I] went fishing with Maggy and Molly, but had poor success. Dr. King and Lt. [Frank S.]

Reed[21] came over after tea, spent the evening, and gave us some good music.

April 4th. Tuesday. Maj. Brinker called by to see me this morning. He is just from Washington but brings no news. Spent the most of the day in writing letters. Wrote a long one to my brother Alex in North Carolina, a still longer [one] to Maj. Snead in Richmond, Va., and entrusted them to Capt. Chas. Greene at Shreveport to be forwarded by him by the first opportunity across the river. Capt. Sogran[22] and Mr. Hannah stayed all night with us at Col. Hervey's.

April 5th. Wednesday. It rained very hard during the night and continued to rain most of the day so as to raise all the water courses very much. Spent the day indoors reading Kenilworth for lack of something more substantial.

April 6th. Thursday. Went to Spring Hill where I received a letter from Dr. [Lewis T.] Pim[23] in reply to one written to him. Returned and read until late in the evening when I took a walk with my wife. Thus quietly passed the day.

April 7th. Friday. Went on a deer drive this morning with Dr. Brandon and others, but did not succeed in getting a deer. One of the party, however, killed a fine wild turkey-gobbler, young and fat. While I impatiently wait here daily expecting orders, I have leisure in which to engage in hunting, but I had rather be at something more useful. Took a long walk with my wife in the evening.

April 8th. Saturday. This day a year ago the Battle of Mansfield was fought in which we whipped Banks and the Yankees under him so badly and near which I was. A cold and cloudy disagreeable day. Finished Kenilworth. After dinner [I] took Maggy and Molly and went out on a deer drive, or rather a deer stand—Bob Brandon[24] acting as driver—but owing to the rain which came up did not do much. [I] saw no deer and of course did not get a shot.

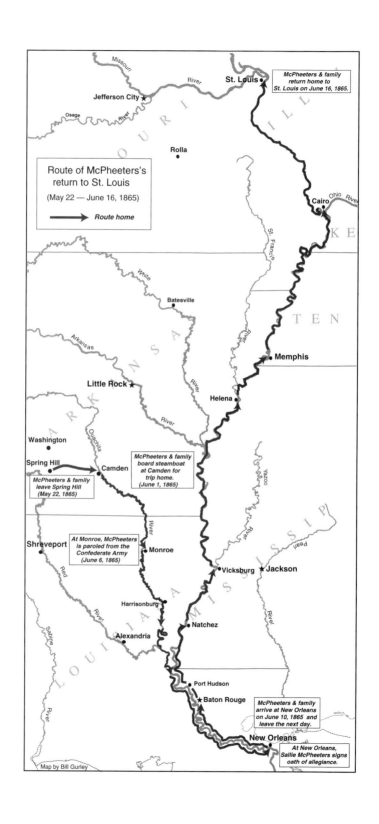

Missouri River

St. Louis •

Jefferson City ★

McPheeters & family
return home to
St. Louis on June 16, 1865.

Osage River

• Rolla

Route of McPheeters's
return to St. Louis
(May 22 — June 16, 1865)

→ *Route home*

Ohio River

Cairo ★

St. Francis River

White River

• Batesville

TEN

Arkansas River

Memphis •

Little Rock ★

River

Helena •

Washington •

Ouachita River

Spring Hill •

Camden •

McPheeters & family
board steamboat
at Camden for
trip home.
(June 1, 1865)

McPheeters & family
leave Spring Hill
(May 22, 1865)

Yazoo River

Pearl River

River

Shreveport •

At Monroe, McPheeters
is paroled from the
Confederate Army
(June 6, 1865)

Monroe •

Vicksburg ★ Jackson

Red River

Harrisonburg •

River

• Natchez

Sabine River

Alexandria •

River

LOUISIANA   MISSISSIPPI

• Port Hudson

★ Baton Rouge

McPheeters & family
arrive at New Orleans
on June 10, 1865 and
leave the next day.

River

New Orleans •

At New Orleans,
Sallie McPheeters signs
oath of allegiance.

Map by Bill Gurley

CHAPTER 11

Surrender, 1865

Not my will, but thine be done.

April 1865 marked the one-year anniversary of William McPheeters's participation in the Red River and Camden campaigns. Those halcyon days had done much to bolster the spirits of soldiers and citizens alike. Misfortunes in the department during the twelve months that followed, however, quickly tempered Confederate morale west of the Mississippi.

Self-sustaining for more than three years but now burdened with a tenuous economic infrastructure and shouldering a war-weary populace, the Trans-Mississippi Department stood like a house of cards. As always, events to the east dictated the region's future. And on April 9, 1865, when Gen. Robert E. Lee surrendered the Army of Northern Virginia, the cards began to tumble. News of Lee's surrender struck the department like a thunderbolt, and morale, already shaky, plummeted. Men and officers alike began leaving their units en masse. Whole regiments and even brigades disbanded. Lt. Gen. Edmund Kirby Smith, Maj. Gen. Sterling Price, and a host of other officers, realizing they would soon be generals without armies, appealed to the rank and file to persevere and continue resistance. Their words, however, rang hollow. Several units, most notably Brig. Gen. J. O. Shelby's Missouri cavalry division, vowed never to surrender, preferring "exile to submission, death to dishonor," but most realized the futility of further resistance and simply walked away.

The tempest of panic reached full crescendo with news of the capitulation of Gen. Joseph Johnston's Army of Tennessee on April 26 and Lt. Gen. Richard Taylor's Department of Alabama, Mississippi, and East Louisiana on May 4. At that point there was no longer any regular Confederate force under arms east of the Mississippi; only Smith's Trans-Mississippians remained.[1]

On May 8 terms for surrender of the department were delivered to Shreveport by a Federal envoy. Smith refused them: "Your proposition for the surrender of the troops under my command are not such that my sense of duty and honor permit me to accept." He then summoned the governors of Arkansas, Louisiana, and Missouri to a conference at Marshall, Texas, where a set of terms more liberal than those accepted by General Lee was proposed. The Federals promptly rejected the amended terms, but instead of gathering an overwhelming force to crush the defiant Rebels, they merely bided their time; they too realized that whether Smith surrendered or not, his army was rapidly disintegrating.[2]

Between May 18 and May 26, virtually all of the organized units in Texas disbanded of their own accord, leaving only what remained of the Missourians and Arkansans encamped near Shreveport and a few regiments in the Indian Territory as organized fighting units. Smith, in a quixotic effort to bring some order to the chaos, moved his headquarters to Houston on May 18. Upon his arrival nine days later, the general discovered that the army he claimed to command no longer existed. The previous day, May 26, his chief of staff, Lt. Gen. Simon Buckner, and Sterling Price formally surrendered the surviving fragments of the Trans-Mississippi army at New Orleans. The war in the West was over.[3]

Surrender of the department did not mean capitulation of all affected parties. Some like Shelby and his Missourians refused to surrender and hastily struck out for Mexico, where they envisioned a continuance of their struggle beyond the Rio Grande. Others despondently signed their paroles but then, fearing governmental reprisals if they returned home, exiled themselves to Mexico, Cuba, or England. Among the more notable of Dr. McPheeters's colleagues who chose Mexico over Missouri were Sterling Price, Brig. Gen. Mosby M. Parsons, Gov. Thomas C. Reynolds, and Col. Trusten Polk. For McPheeters, however, the end of his three-year ordeal, principled though it was, had arrived, and the notion of seeking asylum in a foreign country was simply unacceptable. Home would be his destination, home to St. Louis.[4]

April 9th. Sunday. Anniversary of the Battle of Pleasant Hill, a memorable fight already recorded in these pages. A rainy forbidding day. No church in the neighborhood so remained at home reading the Bible and such few religious books as I have and instructing my children. General Price called and paid us a short visit on passing today. His court has been ordered to convene at Shreveport whither he is going.[5]

April 10th. Monday. Went over to a sale at Spring Hill where I spent most of the morning without, however, buying anything. A man by the name of Reynolds is selling out. Things were very high. Wheat, $18 per bushel; sugar, $4.50 per lb., and other things in proportion. Such are the fabulous prices now ruling all over the Confederacy. Spent the rest of the day reading, etc.

April 11th. Tuesday. Went out on a deer drive this morning. One of the party killed a fine buck, but I was not fortunate enough to get a shot or even see a deer. I am a poor sportsman and were it not that I am here awaiting orders and having nothing else to do I would give up hunting as a poor business. Lt. [David C.] Knox[6] stayed all night at Col. Hervey's. Weather rainy and disagreeable.

April 12th. Wednesday. Rained slowly all day, and having nothing particularly to take me out, I spent the day indoors reading, smoking, etc. Maj. [John D.] Trimble[7] and Dr. Baxter spent the night at Col. Hervey's.

April 13th. Thursday. Went to Spring Hill after breakfast and spent an hour or two. Received a letter from Capt. Chas. Green at Shreveport. In the evening Col. Hervey and I went deer hunting and took the girls with us—Molly and Sally—but we were not fortunate enough to start a deer. It was nearly dark when we returned.

April 14th. Friday. Rain, rain. This has been a remarkably wet spring. Rained again all day. Spent the time indoors reading and otherwise amusing myself.

April 15th. Saturday. Weather clear today. Dr. Brandon, his son, and young Finley came over after breakfast and was joined by Col. Hervey and myself in a deer hunt. We killed a fine buck, shot by

Bob Brandon. After this we went to a sale at Mrs. Gelson's. Here I learned through a letter just received of the evacuation of Richmond by our forces.[8] This event, though not unexpected, created a damper on my feelings. No doubt this was rendered necessary by the movements and recent successes of the enemy and we have been looking to it for some time as not improbable. Still it is greatly regretted as it shows that our army is greatly pressed on the other side of the river. This seems to be our darkest and most gloomy hour and God only knows what is to become of our beloved country. Still trusting in Him, I hope for the best and will not despair of success; no, never. After dinner took another deer hunt. In this we were joined by Maggy, Molly, and Miss Sally Brandon. I also took little Sally with me on my horse. The girls seemed to enjoy the sport much. Started two deer and shot at them four times without getting them.

April 16th. Sunday. Went to Spring Hill to church this morning. Rev. Mr. Boyd preached. All the family went. My wife received a letter from Mrs. MacRae today dated St. Louis Feb. 20th, which was gratifying to her as it gave her tidings of our dear friends at home. They express great sympathy for her.

April 17th. Monday. Took a short deer drive this morning with the girls as it was Easter Monday and they were relieved from their school duties. The latter part of the day it rained hard and was spent indoors.

April 18th. Tuesday. Rode over to Spring Hill and spent the morning with Dr. Wooten, but learned no news of interest. Rest of the day spent in reading. Visited our turkey pen and found one hen turkey in it, which I secured and brought home.

April 19th. Wednesday. Intended going today with my family to Washington to pay Mrs. Jordan a visit of a few days but was prevented by the rain, which it seems will never cease. Wrote a letter to Col. W. A. Alston of Gen. Magruder's staff warning him of a certain man, Clifford, who my wife thinks is a Federal spy. Rained very hard during the evening and night.

April 20th. Thursday. This has been a day of sadness and gloom. Early this morning Mr. Dickson called by on his way from Washington bringing distressing tidings that on the 9th of this month Gen. Lee with his army of 43,000 men surrendered to Gen. Grant. This is a sad and I fear almost fatal blow to the prospects of our cause. It was no doubt necessary in the situation in which Gen. Lee was placed, but it is nonetheless deplorable. For the first time the appalling fact stares me in the face that we are in great danger of being subjugated by the Yankees. May God in mercy forbid it, but should it be His will while I bow with reverence and submission to His decrees I am yet as firmly convinced as ever *that we are right,* nor do I regret the course that I have taken in giving my poor aid to the South in her struggle for independence. Rained hard most of the day; nevertheless, [I] went over to the village this morning to console with friends.

April 21st. Friday. Spent the day at home not feeling very well in body and of course gloomy in mind. With the loss of the Virginia army I see not how we are to maintain ourselves without aid from abroad, which it is not at all probable that we will receive. I will not dwell on this gloomy subject, nor depict the ten thousand horrors attending subjugation by such a race as the Yankees, but hope for the best.

April 23rd. Sunday. The Rev. Mr. Davies, Methodist preacher, spent last night with us. This morning feeling better [I] went to Spring Hill to hear him preach. He gave us a moderate sermon. He is not an educated man. Spent the rest of the day in home duties.

(The 22nd was overlooked; did nothing)

April 24th. Monday. Col. Hervey and myself rode up to Washington this morning to hear the news. Called by to pay Mrs. Jordan a visit who lives 3 miles from Washington. Found her and Mrs. Johnson well and as ever agreeable but in low spirits owing to the sad news respecting our cause on the east side of the Mississippi River. On going into Washington saw various persons, all gloomy. Learned nothing cheering but on the contrary all reports going to show the desperateness of our cause. There are reports that Johnston's army has surrendered which needs confirmation. I hope that it is not true. Took dinner at 3 P.M. with Col. Eakin but did not see his good wife who is "in the straw." Just before leaving town on the return home saw a letter from Dr. Taylor at Shreveport giving an account of the assassination of President Lincoln and Secretary Seward on the night of the 13th inst. in Washington City. The report is circumstantial and no doubt true. Lincoln was shot in the theater, Seward in his room. I do not sorrow at the death of these two guilty authors of this war with all its untold horrors, but [I] cannot approve of the manner in which they came to their end. Assassination is a horrid thing. We have indeed fallen on degenerate times. God only knows what is to become of this once happy, now divided, and almost ruined country. Reached home about dark having rode 26 miles.

April 25th. Tuesday. Rode over to Spring Hill after breakfast [and] there got two letters. One from John W. Polk about a mule that I rode when going after my wife and the other from Capt. Chas. Greene [at] Shreveport confirming the death of Lincoln and Seward. After dinner went on a deer drive for the amusement of the girls, Maggy and Molly, who accompanied us. Not that I feel at all like engaging in such sports. Went over to Dr. Brandon's where we were joined by Miss Sally and others. Made two drives but got no deer. Dr. Wooten gave me a letter on the drive from Gov. Polk containing a short bulletin giving some account of the Washington City tragedy. Booth, the actor, it seems was the assassin of Lincoln. The murderer of Seward has not yet been ascertained. I forbear speculation as to the effect that this will have on the war or on the northern people. While this act has been perpetrated by men no doubt claiming to be Southern and doubtless sympathizing with us, the South is in no way responsible for the deed.

April 26th. Wednesday. Was unwell this morning. Threatened with dysentery so [I] remained quietly at home and took medicine. Col. [Caleb] Perkins[9] called by and spent the night. He brings rather more cheering accounts of our recent disasters on the other side of the "river." They are not so bad as we have had represented by the Yankee papers. Gen. Lee probably surrendered only about 8000 or 10000 and Johnston's army is intact.[10]

April 27th. Thursday. Went to Spring Hill. Received a letter from Dr. Pim, Assistant Chief of [the] Medical Bureau stating that if I would indicate a point to which I wished to go in Texas that I should be gratified. I am at a loss in the present state of affairs to decide where I ought to go. I wish to get out of reach of Yankee invasion and at present all is doubt and uncertainty. Col. Mitchell and two Missouri Lts. stayed all night. Col. Mitchell has recently been married to Miss Reeler of this state.

April 28th. Friday. Death of Lincoln and Seward confirmed beyond a doubt.[11] Andy Johnson, the renegade, is now President of the U.S. I fear that we will have a worse man than Lincoln to deal with. Went a deer driving both morning and evening. Killed a doe in the morning's hunt, Capt. [R. M.] Littlejohn[12] being the fortunate shot. I got a shot but was too far off to do any execution. In the evening the girls accompanied us but we did not start a deer.

April 29th. Saturday. Wrote two letters this morning, one to Dr. Pim at Marshall [Texas] and the other to John W. Polk, both in reply to letters from them on business, and took them over to Spring Hill to be forwarded by courier. Rest of the day spent in reading. Dr. King spent the night with us.

April 30th. Sunday. No preaching today. Remained quietly at home. Dr. King remained with us.

May 1st. Monday. Still at Col. Hervey's near Spring Hill awaiting orders. No military movements on foot at present in this department. This quiet cannot long continue. Wrote to Dr. Pim applying to be sent to San Antonio, Texas if compatible with the good of the service. I am not at all sanguine that the request will be granted, but as I have been called on to make a choice I have fixed on this as upon the whole the best. Wrote also to Capt. Mhoon.

May 2nd. Tuesday. Went deer hunting this morning with Dr. Brandon and quite a party. Spent the whole morning and killed no game. I got a shot and ought to have killed a deer but missed him, my gun going off too soon before I got aim. The fact is I take no interest in hunting and only go because I have nothing else to do. The condition of our cause gives me great concern. I have serious apprehensions that we will come short of our independence. God forbid.

May 3rd. Wednesday. Maj. Cabell and Drs. [R. A.] Burton[13] and Wooten came over and took breakfast with us this morning on their way to Washington. Mrs. Hervey started for Camden on a visit. Wishing to go to Fulton to get some articles of clothing from the quartermaster, I rode over this morning with Dr. Brandon, distance 12 miles, over horrible muddy roads. Got there about 11 A.M. [and] saw Cols. Buster, [Robert C.] Newton, and Drs. Duncan and [Randolph] Brunson.[14] [I] took dinner with the doctors. Could get only a pair of shoes and two undershirts. Remained two or three hours and then returned home again where I arrived between 4 and 5 P.M. Dr. King spent the night with us.

May 4th. Thursday. Spent the day at home reading and otherwise diverting myself as best I could, but found it difficult to interest myself in anything.

May 5th. Friday. Went deer hunting this morning with Dr. Brandon, Col. Hervey, and others. We were to have been joined by a party from Washington, but they did not come down, so we went it alone, but killed no deer. I, however, saw one but too far off to shoot at. Maggy and Molly accompanied us and went on the stand with me. They had a sight of the deer as he passed. Weather getting warm.

May 6th. Saturday. Having nothing better to do I joined a fishing party today with Maggy, Molly, Dr. Wooten and family, the Brandons, Finleys, Col. Thompson,[15] and others. We went to Red Lake near Dooley's Ferry on Red River some 7 miles off. Some of the party went in wagon and ambulance. I [went] with the girls on horseback. We started after an early breakfast. Before reaching the Lake it commenced raining and continued to rain most of the day. Still we fished with good success, the fish biting rapidly. We caught near two hundred perch [both] small and good size. Towards noon we adjourned to a church near by, cleaned and fried our fish, and had a good meal which I enjoyed much. The ladies had amply provided other things. Our repast being over we concluded not to fish [any]more on account of the rain, but started for home about 2 P.M. Had a disagreeable ride home where we arrived between 4 and 5 P.M. On reaching home, found Gov. Polk at Col. Hervey's having come up from Lewisville on a visit to us of a few days. [I] was glad to see him and talk with him on the state of our affairs.

May 7th. Sunday. No preaching in the neighborhood. Spent the morning in conversation with Gov. Polk on the desperate condition of our cause. Col. Hervey returned from Washington bringing information that Gen. Joe Johnston and Sherman had agreed on terms for capitulating our army and arranging for peace, but their agreement was disapproved of by Andy Johnson, the Yankee President, and his cabinet and the arrangement has probably failed. So we must await further developments. Booth the murderer of Lincoln has been killed and captured by the Federals. He refused to be taken alive, preferring death by a bullet to a halter. During the afternoon Gen. Price and his son Capt. Celsus Price called by on their way to Washington from Shreveport where his court of inquiry has been ordered.[16] The old hero looks well and is in better spirits than many others. He spent the night with us. Several other officers also spent the night. Weather intended to rain.

May 8th. Monday. Gen. Price left after breakfast for Washington, Ark. Gov. Polk spent the day with us. We rode over to Spring Hill where I received by courier two letters, one from Mrs. Hervey in Camden giving no news except the reported surrender of Johnston's army, which is probably not true, and one from Malcolm Graham from Alexandria. La. of the 3rd. inst. speaking of the arrangements between Johnston and Sherman before alluded to. Spent the remainder of the day in conversation, etc.

May 9th. Tuesday. Gov. Polk returned to Lewisville this morning. I went with him as far as Spring Hill. There [I] saw a bulletin of yesterday from Washington confirming what we have previously heard and, showing a disagreement and probable difficulty between Sherman and his government about his recent agreement with Johnston, what I hope will result in good. Johnston, at last accounts, holds out. What the result will be God only knows. May He overrule all things for our good. Maj. Cabell stayed all night with us.

May 10th. Wednesday. This is the anniversary of my wedding and of the Camp Jackson Massacre in St. Louis. Sixteen years ago today I was married to my beloved wife. Since then busy time has made many changes. We are engaged in a war with the U.S. for independence and I regret to say with but little hope of success and I am an alien and refugee from my home. God only knows what lies before me, but trusting in His mercy I will go forward. Rode over to Spring Hill with Maj. Cabell on his way to Lewisville. There I learned that Gen. Joe Johnston has surrendered his army and the war east of the Mississippi River is probably virtually at an end. What the result on this side will be cannot yet be divined.

May 11th. Thursday. Wrote a letter to Malcolm Graham and enclosed him $50 in green backs sent to him by Miss Eliza Dean at his request. I may as well here mention that I paid Maj. Cabell a day or two ago $350 in Confederate money by Col. Hervey for the hire of boy Frank up to last of May inst. Learned of no news. A meeting of the Governors of this Department is now being held at Marshall, Texas at which Federal commissioners are present. I hope that they will agree on honorable terms of capitulation; otherwise, there is no alternative but to fight on to the bitter end. God grant us a happy issue out of our troubles. Mrs. Hervey returned from Camden this afternoon bringing with her sister, Mrs. Rainey, and child and Miss Eliza Armstrong. They bring us no news.

May 12th. Friday. Went over to Spring Hill this morning to see Dr. Wooten, hear what news is afloat, and consult on what is best to be done under exisitng circumstances. Heard no news however. Nothing from the conference of governors now in session in Marshall.[17] Spent the evening at home.

May 13th. Saturday. We hear today that the Federals are at Arkadelphia on their way down in this direction. Under the impulse of this report, for it may be only an unfounded report, we commenced getting ready to move across Red River so as to have that stream between us and the Yankees should they advance in this direction. After dark Col. Hervey and I rode over to Spring HIll to see if we could get any news, but got none. The reported advance of the Yankees is no doubt untrue.

May 14th. Sunday. Col. Musser and Capt. Celsus Price called by this morning and the General (Price) went down the road en route for Shreveport, his court not having met in Washington. I rode over to Spring Hill where I saw him for half an hour. The old hero bears our misfortunes with philosophic composure. The Rev. Mr. Boyd preached in the village church and I got there late in the excercises. Spent the remainder of the day quietly at home. Received a note from Lt. Col. Clay Taylor enclosing a scrip containing intelligence from St. Louis and among other items it was mentioned that my brother had gone to Kentucky to live—no doubt driven off by the persecution of the Federals.[18]

May 15th. Monday. Went over to Spring Hill and awaited the arrival of the courier but got no news. General Fagan and two of his staff, Maj. [William F.] Rapley[19] and Capt. Mhoon, came by and stayed all night. Gen. Fagan has been ordered to Shreveport and is on his way thither, probably for consultation with the military authorities. There is no longer any doubt of Gen. Joe Johnston's surrender.

May 16th. Tuesday. Rode over to Spring Hill as usual this morning hoping to hear news. It is rumored that this department has been surrendered. If so, it is submitting to inevitable and dire necessity. We are a conquered, subjugated people. God help us. I will not dwell on the horrors of such a fate, but I desire to submit with resignation to the desires of an all wise Providence as hard as it may be knowing that "the judge of all the earth will do right" though it may involve our destruction as a people. Still I have always believed and I still firmly believe that the South was right in this contest. We were fighting for the right of self government and with the downfall of the Southern Confederacy perishes the last hope of free governments. The Yankees themselves will one day find to their cost that they have been fighting against their own interest and the fundamental principles on which their government was founded. Their liberties are gone as well as ours and they will find out when it is too late.

May 17th. Wednesday. Spent the morning at Spring Hill with Dr. Wooten who leaves in the morning with his family for Bonham, Texas on a leave of 30 days. Long before his leave expires in all probability our armies in this department will be disbanded and the war brought to a close on terms most disastrous to the South. Dr. Wooten's family has resided in Bonham since the war. I parted with him with regret as we have been associated together more or less ever since I have been in the army, now near three years, and for a long time messed together. In the afternoon [I] wrote a letter to Maj. Rainey at Camden and Capt. Charles Green [at] Shreveport inquiring about the probability of getting a boat at those points preparatory to a return homeward so soon as the fate of this department is determined and it will be safe for me to take my family back.

May 18th. Thursday. Rode over to Spring Hill about the time for the courier to arrive but got no news. Spent the remainder of the day at home awaiting the result of affairs and ruminating on the prospects ahead.

May 19th. Friday. Spent the morning in supine inaction. In the afternoon [I] rode over to Spring Hill but got no news. Maggy

and Molly went with Col. Hervey this afternoon to his plantation on horseback across Red River some 12 or 14 miles. Mr.
Knox from Washington spent the night.

May 20th. Saturday. Spent the day in supine inaction. Remained
at home and tried to read but found it a dull business, my mind
being so much occupied with other matters. Maggy and Molly
returned this evening.

May 21st. Sunday. No church in the neighborhood today so [I]
spent the day at home except [for] a ride to Spring Hill late in the
evening. The couriers have stopped between this and Shreveport
so we are cut off from getting news. Mrs. Rainey's wagon arrived
this evening from Camden and I have agreed to return with her.

May 22nd. Monday. Made arrangements to start for Camden
tomorrow morning en route for Memphis making my way back
to Yankeedom. The war is over and I have nothing to do but
return. Was busy all day in packing and getting ready for my trip
and so was my wife. I have been at Col. Hervey's now three
months where I have been most kindly and hospitably entertained.
I feel everlasting obligations to them. Wrote letters this morning to
Mrs. Jordan, Gen. Price, Governor Polk, and Maj. Cabell. Saw persons from Shreveport who represent things in a horribly demoralized condition, the army disbanding and the people thoroughly
whipped. There is no alternative left us but to submit to Yankee
domination.

May 23rd. Tuesday. Left Spring Hill early this morning having
spent three months very pleasantly there at the hospitable residence of Col. Calvin M. Hervey. Mrs. Rainey of Camden and
her child, Miss Eliza Armstrong, my wife and two children, and
Waddy Finley,[20] together with myself constituted our travelling
party. I disliked to leave very much, but the desire to get to
Camden and there take a boat endeavored me to leave earlier than
I would otherwise have done. The day was cloudy and pleasant
for travelling. [We] came through Centerville and thence on the

Washington and Camden Road. By night [we] made 35 miles and stopped at Mr. Hadley's, 33 miles from Camden, [with] half of our party remaining two miles behind at Mr. Simpson's.

May 24th. Wednesday. Got an early start and reached Camden about 4 P.M. Stopped at Maj. Rainey's. The day has been hot but we met with no difficulty on the way. We get no news here as all mails and couriers have stopped. After tea [I] wrote to Col. Hervey to send back by Waddy Finley who returns in the morning.

May 25th. Thursday. At Camden, Ark. As I will probably have no further use for my riding horse, Grease, I sent him back this morning by Waddy Finley [as] a present to Col. Hervey—a small return for his kindness to myself and family while under his roof. He is a fine horse and has carried me thousands of miles and I feel attached to him, but as the war is over I will probably not need a riding horse again. I prefer the Col.'s having him to selling him. I am disappointed in not finding a boat here but hope to get one in a few days. [I] went down [the] street this morning and saw several acquaintances but heard no news. As the weather is hot [I] returned early and spent the rest of the day until evening quietly at home.

May 26th. Friday. No boat, no news. The telegraph wires between this and Shreveport are down and I see no way of getting away from this place. No mails and no way of communicating with anybody or any place. Everything throughout the country [is] in a state of confusion. It is not yet known whether this department has yet surrendered.[21] I am at a loss [for] what to do, in fact, there is nothing left for me to do but to wait quietly here until something turns up. I and my family are, however, very comfortable at Maj. Rainey's. The weather for several days past has been very hot; today it is quite pleasant.

May 27th. Saturday. Another day of anxiety—no boat, no telegraph, no news, and no way of getting on my journey homeward. This morning [I] saw Gen. Dockery en route for Little Rock to make arrangements for surrendering the Reserve Corps of the state. Weather cool and pleasant. Late in the evening [I] paid Mrs. Maj. Graham a visit. She lives in the neighborhood.

May 28th. Sunday. Went with [my] family to the Methodist church this afternoon, it being the only church open. Heard Rev. Mr. Radcliff preach a pretty good sermon. In the afternoon [I] met with and conversed with Capt. Lewis just from the east of the Mississippi River. He has nothing, however, particularly new. The telegraph wires [are] not yet up to Shreveport.

May 29th. Monday. Spent the morning at Maj. Rainey's office in conversation with diverse gentlemen, but elicited no news. We have no intelligence as to the surrender of this department as all our means of communication is cut off. As there is but little prospect of getting a boat here, I am now desirous of getting a conveyance to Pine Bluff on the Arkansas River [and] there to embark for Memphis, but before doing this I wish to hear of the surrender of the army on this side and procure a parole.

May 30th. Tuesday. Made partial arrangements today for getting a wagon to take myself and family to Pine Bluff on the Arkansas River day after tomorrow. I hope to complete the arrangements and with the blessing of Providence to get off on Thursday. At Pine Bluff I hope to get a boat for Memphis. Persons arrived today from Shreveport and Little Rock, but did not add much to our stock of information. Weather hot.

May 31st. Wednesday. I have been at Camden just a week today waiting the arrival of a boat, but had just despaired of one coming and had made arrangements to go to Pine Bluff by land when about noon today the *Twilight* made her appearance. She is an old boat [and] a good deal torn to pieces. Still, as I am anxious to get to Monroe [Louisiana] and the mouth of the river, I embarked on her with my family about 6 P.M., a few moments after which we started down the river and ran some fifteen or twenty miles and laid up for the night. While at Camden we have been hospitably entertained by Maj. Rainey and his family.

June 1st. Thursday. On the Ouachita River. The boat started off by daylight this morning. I slept indifferently, the accommodations are poor, and the fare coarse, but it is preferable to an overland trip in a wagon. Trusting to a kind Providence, I hope that we will get on our journey safely and well. The boat stops frequently for cotton, wood, etc. Mr. Gallagher, telegraph operator for a long time at Camden but formerly from Liberty, Mo., accompanied us on the trip. About dark [we] reached Careyville, a wood yard, where we laid up for the night. The children went ashore and amused themselves by moonlight.

June 2nd. Friday. Slept comfortably last night—no mosquitoes or bed bugs. Got off by daylight and made a good run. Took on 40 bales of cotton and about mid-day came into the state of Louisiana. Providence permitting we will reach Monroe this evening. There I hope to meet with a boat going to the Mississippi River, but may be detained for some time. [At] 8 P.M. [we] arrived at Monroe, La. Soon after arriving the boat was taken possession [of] by a squad of Marmaduke's cavalry—Greene's Regiment. Guards were put aboard and no one allowed to come on or go off. They had an idea that there were large amounts of goods on board purchased by government cotton, which they wished to get possession of. For a while we had quite an excitement. Some on board were very much frightened, but Col., now Gen. Colton Greene soon arrived and assured me that the ladies need not fear, etc. It was, however, thought to be most prudent to run the boat up to Trenton several miles above and there spend the night, a guard remaining on all night. As there were a good many loose and desperate soldiers about and some excitement, I sat up until a late hour to see that all was secure. Had a long talk with Gen. Greene in which he acquainted me with what had been going on among military men for the past few weeks. Sometime after midnight I retired and slept safely.

June 3rd. Saturday. At Monroe, La. Gen. Greene came aboard after breakfast and to satisfy the soldiers instituted a search of the boat, which was conducted very orderly. Some shoes, hats, and other articles of clothing were distributed among the soldiers which seemed to satisfy them and they retired without any disturbance. Some few trunks and other baggage were robbed during the night. After the search, the boat dropped down again to Monroe and there laid up. There is no other boat here and I fear that we will have to remain here for several days before getting to the mouth of Red River to get up the Mississippi. Capt. George Kerr came on board to see my wife and later in the day Dr. Harding called to see me. [I] went on shore to look for quarters in case we have to remain here long and late in the evening removed family and baggage to the Ouachita House kept by Mr. Sheffield. An indifferent hotel where we are only tolerably comfortable, but will make out.

June 4th. Sunday. On awakening this morning [I] learned that two Federal gunboats had arrived during the night and late in the day the steamer, *White Cloud,* came up with a regiment of negro troops, a part of whom landed here with their officers to establish a post, while the remainder went on to Camden. Their arrival created some excitement, the negro troops being somewhat of a curiosity and not to the taste of the people, but the sooner we get used to the Yankee rule the better. [We must] realize the fact that we are a conquered people and have to submit to whatever indignities our conquerors choose to inflict on us. There was no service in any church but the Catholic, so I did not go out. Late in the evening [I] went with my wife and children to Mrs. Delaries and paid a visit. She gave us a good cup of coffee. The weather [is] hot and dry. The steamer, *Twilight,* on which we came down, was taken possession of by the gunboats, so it is fortunate that we left her.

June 5th. Monday. No prospect of a boat as yet to go down the river. Yankee negro troops [are] garrisoning the town. Called this morning to see the Col. commanding the post to inquire about parole and learned that he has no power to grant them. Spent the day indoors as it was very hot. Late in the evening the steamer, *Emma,* came up with a lot of paroled Confederate prisoners and paroling officers who will commence giving paroles as soon as the

Confederate commissioner arrives. This also affords a chance of getting down the river in a day or two.

June 6th. Tuesday. The commissioners of parole commenced operations today and I took my parole as a prisoner of war of the U.S. pledging myself not to take up arms against the U.S. until regularly exchanged. On their part they guaranteed that I shall not be molested by the Federal authorities so long as I observe my parole and obey the laws in force where I reside. I never had any disposition to fight against the U.S. All I sought was southern independence and the right of the South to make their own government. Having failed in this I propose to live in peace the rest of my life if I am permitted to do so, but where my future home will be, God only knows, but trusting in his mercy I hope to find some safe asylum. The weather is intensely hot. Still expecting a boat. Called to see Dr. and Mrs. Harding who called to see us on yesterday. Monroe is a pretty though very dusty place.

June 7th. Wednesday. The *White Cloud* came down early this morning and will go down to the mouth of Red River this evening. [I] was very busy all morning in getting ready to go down on her. Having made all my arrangements and paid my bill at the hotel, [I] embarked on board of the *White Cloud* with my family about 4 P.M. and about 6 P.M. she started, bound for Baton Rouge, where my objective is to get a boat going up the Mississippi. The boat is not in good condition though we are passably comfortable. The weather [is] intensely hot, but when we commenced running it was comfortable. The night [was] bright and beautiful. Several other families [are] on board, one of whom is under my care.

June 8th. Thursday. Passed a comfortable night. The boat made a good run during the night. Early this morning [we] passed Harrisonburg and Trinity. The former nearly burnt down by the Yankees, and the latter a good deal injured by shot and shell and both now under water; in fact, all the country in this region is submerged. With the blessing of Providence we will reach the

Mississippi River this evening where I hope to meet a boat going up. About sundown [we] got to Port Hudson. Here [we] stopped for an hour and then proceeded to Baton Rouge where we arrived about 10 P.M. Could not get in at the hotel, Hainey House, so [we] had to remain on the *White Cloud* all night. Retired very late. [The] night [was] bright and beautiful.

June 9th. Friday. Went ashore at Baton Rouge early this morning. It is a beautiful and business-like place; much larger than I expected. Soon found a boat, the *Mattie Stephens,* going to New Orleans so [I] concluded to go down there in order to secure a good boat and suitable accommodations. Embarked about 9 A.M. and was soon on the way down river. [I] hope to reach New Orleans tonight. [We] did so, but very late after 12 M. [I] sat up until we got into port.

June 10th. Saturday. Awoke finding myself in New Orleans this morning. A Federal officer was on board requiring all on board not paroled to take the oath of allegiance to the U.S. before going ashore. My wife had to take it much to her regret. My parole let me off though I will doubtless have it to do before or after reaching St. Louis. Went ashore early and took lodging at the City Hotel. Spent the morning in walking over the city and in purchasing some things; my wife shopping. New Orleans is a fine city and impressed me favorably. My object in coming to the city was to get a good boat and as the *Arthur* was to leave at 5 P.M. [I] took passage on her, the Capt. giving me a fine elegant room. She is a large splendid boat. Got off at the time specified. Several acquaintances [were] aboard [including] Col. [Charles] McClaren of St. Louis, Col. S. Chambry of C.S.A., and others.[22] Had a fine run [but] the boat [was] very much crowded.

June 11th. Sunday. En route for St. Louis on steamer *Arthur.* Day spent pleasantly enough but not profitably. Passed Baton Rouge about noon and Port Hudson later. Our boat runs well and we live finely. Numerous soldiers of both armies on board.

June 12th & 13th. Monday & Tuesday. Still on the Mississippi River. Time passes off as usual on [the] steamboat. We are crowded but comfortable. Passed Natchez and Vicksburg and [are] getting on well. Today, Tuesday, [we] also passed [the] mouths of the Arkansas and White [Rivers]. Weather warm.

June 14th. Wednesday. Arrive at Memphis about 9 A.M. this morning and as the boat remained there several hours I went ashore and walked over the town. [I] was surprised at the improvement since my last visit many years ago. It is now a fine, large city. Got under way about 12 M.

June 15th. Thursday. Arrived at Cairo [Illinois] about 5 P.M. when we were fortunately relieved of most of our passengers rendering the boat vastly more comfortable.

June 16th. Friday. Arrived at St. Louis about 5 P.M. this evening after an absence of three years lacking 4 days. I will not attempt to record my feelings on this occasion. I did not anticipate returning under such sad circumstances, but God's will be done. I have the proud consciousness that I have done my duty, and the failure of the South to achieve her independence is owing to no fault of mine. Took lodging at the Lindell Hotel. [I] saw many of my friends and was warmly received by all. Here these notes of my movements close properly. One or two incidents I will note down and then close the record.

June 17th. Saturday. Saw numerous friends and acquaintances all of whom welcome me back warmly. My wife and children went to Mrs. Graham's this evening to spend the Sabbath. I, however, remained in town [and] reported to Maj. Gen. John Pope.[23] He received me *very kindly indeed*. After seeing him [I] went to the Provost Marshal's and took the oath of allegiance to the U.S. Under other circumstances I would regard this as dishonorable and would suffer martyrdom before doing it. Now I look back upon it in a different light and hesitated not to do it.

June 18th. Sunday. Went to Dr. Anderson's church and in the afternoon went out to Mrs. Graham's to join my family and see the friends in the country.

June 19th. Monday. Returned to the city. Mr. Wickham and family dined with us at the Lindell.

June 20th. Tuesday. Moved into Mr. Wickham's home at 17th and Lucas Place, his family being absent in the country.

Finis

The Homing, 1865–1905

Be there at our homing and give us, we pray,
Your peace in our hearts, Lord at the end of the day.

McPheeters closed his wartime diary shortly after he and his
family returned to St. Louis. The discipline of his diary, so
faithfully kept during the war, may have been an instrument
of his survival. At home once more, he took care to preserve his small,
hand-sewn book, stowing it away unchanged, perhaps even unread, as
a relic of his wartime experience. The record of his life from that point
became his private papers and his scrapbook, housed in the William M.
McPheeters Collection at the Missouri Historical Society Archives in
St. Louis.

In private McPheeters wrote: "And now after the disastrous termination of the war—which God knows I most deeply deplore, and
upon a review of the past I find nothing to regret in the course which
I have pursued. I acted from principle, as I trust in the fear of God, &
from a high sense of duty, and were the whole thing to do over with
the lights that were before me, I do not see that I could act otherwise
than I did. That the South failed of achieving her independence is
lamentably true, but I have the proud consciousness of knowing that I
did my duty, and that no part of her failure is justly chargeable to me."[1]

He promptly addressed himself first to the question of his own
amnesty or pardon. "On the 17th of June 1865 I returned to this city
a paroled prisoner, after an absence of three years lacking three days,
and as was required took the oath of allegiance to the U.S. Government.
This oath under the circumstances I regarded as involving no point of
honor to say the least, as it is the duty of every one to bear allegiance
to the government under which he lives, and the necessities of the case
require that I shall live under the Yankee government." The words—

amnesty, pardon, parole—had ever-changing definitions. He had been paroled, had signed pledges of loyalty to the U.S. government, and as soon as he had his family ensconced in the Lindell Hotel had walked to the office of the provost marshal to begin the process of his own recovery. This involved a letter to Pres. Andrew Johnson: "Having returned to St. Louis where I have long resided, I desire to remain in peace and quietness having taken the prescribed oath of allegiance, and now I ask that a special amnesty be granted me."[2]

At this point, the long wait for an official reply began. A few months later, he wrote again, substituting the word "pardon" for "amnesty," and this time he wrote on the letterhead of the insurance company with which he had once again found part-time employment. One year later the president's affirming letter arrived. In the meanwhile, however, McPheeters had taken steps to repair his career.

When John Wickham and his family returned from their summer home, the McPheeters family left the Wickham city residence and moved into their former home at Olive and Tenth Streets. McPheeters left nothing in writing concerning his method of maintaining this property. So perhaps, like other banished Confederates, he had left money with a trusted friend, money to pay taxes and to maintain the property. Certainly, John Wickham would have performed this duty since he remained in St. Louis throughout the war, although his name had appeared on the list of forty Southern sympathizers posted in 1862. Perhaps he had paid the tax assessed by Federal military authories, pehaps he had bribed them, but in any case, he and his family had remained in St. Louis, unmolested throughout the war. As the first friend whom McPheeters contacted upon his return, Wickham might well have been the one entrusted with the McPheeters home.[3]

St. Louis in this period took on almost a dual character. The streets of downtown teemed with men returning from both armies, and unemployment was widespread. Riverboats converted to military use jammed the docks, confused in returning to civilian commercial use. Veterans and freedmen hung around the shipping offices seeking work. Plying the river were boats overloaded with soldiers from both armies going home. The other aspect of St. Louis was the old city, showing the ragged edges of former grace, and professional and social groups eager to reestablish importance in the postbellum city, laying aside in gentlemanly style the vicious divisions of North and South. For this group, however, the general leaning was and always had been toward the Southern cause. McPheeters returned to this echelon.

Within a year of their return, Sallie and William McPheeters stepped back into their former social position in St. Louis. Preserved in his scrap-book, the record of their activity survives. Two decades later, when the Civil War was romanticized by a younger generation, an enterprising reporter interviewed Dr. McPheeters, who told him his story:

> Immediately after the late civil war the ladies of this city got up a grand event known as the Southern Relief Fair. By the united and enthusiastic efforts of the ladies, aided by the liberality of a generous public, this fair proved to be a most brilliant success. The handsome sum of $140,000 was realized. Before this money was turned over to the committee of gentlemen who so faithfully and judiciously distributed it to all parts of the then stricken and impoverished South, thus affording timely relief to thousands of desolate homes, I went to the lady managers and requested of them to turn over to me $5,000 of the amount realized, and ask no ques-tions. No intimation was given as to the disposition I proposed to make of the money; but the ladies had sufficient confidence that it would not be misapplied, as at once, and without hesitation they granted my request. At that time Mr. Davis was confined at Fortress Monroe, a State prisoner. Through my brother then resid-ing in New York, I sent him $3,000 of the amount received, stat-ing that it was an offering from the ladies of St. Louis. I still have in my possession a letter from Mrs. Davis acknowledging on the part of her husband, the receipt of the draft, and in the most appro-priate terms expressing gratitude for the spirit which prompted the gift as well as the gift itself.[4]
>
> After Mr. Davis was released from prison, on his way to his Southern home, he came by St. Louis, and before I knew he was in the city, he drove to my residence for the purpose, as he stated, of paying his respects. It is hardly necessary to say that this visit was most highly appreciated both by myself and my family.
>
> At this same juncture, Missouri's brave and gallant chieftain, Major-General Sterling Price, had just returned from Cordova [sic] Mexico, where he had gone after the surrender broken down in health and well nigh bankrupt in fortune, though not by any means in reputation. The remaining $2,000 I personally handed

over to him, rejoicing that I was thus enabled to minister to his necessities, and I have the best reason to know that the gift was as timely as it was gratifying to him.[5]

The war had been over for three years when a group of St. Louis physicians began to reorganize the Missouri Medical College, originally founded by Joseph N. McDowell. On March 16 they met in the strange old building at 8th and Gratiot Streets, the former Federal military prison, which was now vacant. The holes in the walls, chiseled by escapees, were still there. The part of the building used by the McDowell family as their home was littered with trash, and the roof leaked.

Dr. McDowell was present that evening in March. Those attending hoped to rent the building, repair it, and reopen the medical school. This was both a professional and a financial enterprise for these physicians, for in accordance with the proprietary or for-profit principle (under which they organized), the faculty of the medical school also became its owners; many schools were established this way throughout the nation at this time. McPheeters was appointed professor of Materia Medica, General, and Special Therapeutics—in the first published catalog of the school, his address was given as 10th and Olive Streets, with his office at the rear of the property. It was the intention of the group to use the McDowell Building as a temporary location for their medical school, planning to build a new facility, which they accomplished two years later.[6]

The catalog for the 1870–71 academic year described the medical school as "located at 6th and Elm, under the same roof with St. Luke's Hospital." Students purchased lecture tickets from each professor, and graduation required that they attend every lecture offered, a complete course in two years. In 1872 the catalog boasted of St. Louis as a city of "nearly 400,000" and the school with teaching facilities at City Hospital, Marine Hospital, Quarantine Hospital, and the Small Pox Hospital as well as St. Louis County Insane Asylum and St. Louis Western Dispensary.[7]

McPheeters resigned his professorship at Missouri Medical College four years later to become the full-time medical examiner for the St. Louis Mutual Insurance Company, the enterprise with which he had become affiliated on a part-time basis in 1865.[8]

Always astute in medical politics, he became active once again in

the American Medical Association and was elected a national vice president in 1873, and his position with the insurance company enhanced
the family's financial situation. They moved from Olive Street to a
newer, more fashionable area of the city with a home at 3452 Pine
Street. It was a tall two-and-a-half story stone house with a columned
porch across the facade. In the latest style, it had a rather narrow ter-
raced lawn to the sidewalk.[9]

In 1894, when McPheeters was seventy-nine years old, he was
invited by the medical society to give a retrospective address on medical progress during the past century. In his address McPheeters made it
manifestly clear that he was a man who lived purposefully in the present, and as a medical educator, he was focused upon the future of his
profession.[10]

At the University of Pennsylvania as a young medical student,
McPheeters had been solidly trained in the rational medical therapeutics of the early nineteenth century. He was taught to identify fevers,
to treat each one differently, and to try to prevent one fever from evolv-
ing into another by heroic therapies as Benjamin Rush had taught at
the University of Pennsylvania. New, young doctors traveled far and
wide from this and every other medical school in the country, bleeding, purging, and blistering their patients. McPheeters treated his own
malaria in 1863 by purging himself drastically, and one of his fellow surgeons dosed himself with large amounts of gunpowder for the same disease. Because McPheeters finished his medical training in 1840, he was
on the cusp of a new trend, empiricism, taught in French medical
schools at the time. His statistical analysis of the St. Louis cholera epidemic of 1849 reflected this approach, and in the literature of American
epidemiology, it is a first.

The Civil War caught American medicine on a plateau in terms
of progress, in the preanesthesia, preasepis days when infected wounds
were thought to be healing and raging fevers in postsurgery patients
were considered merely part of a normal healing process. Wartime
surgery, performed in the most primitive situations, sent thousands of
veterans home mutilated and permanently disabled, and the public, in
despair, began to demand better medicine. These veterans brought
home with them horror stories about field hospitals, and the image of
the perpetually drunk post surgeon carelessly slashing and cutting on

improvised, filthy operating tables became fixed in the public mind. The rationalism of the early decades of the nineteenth century had given way to empiricism by midcentury, and McPheeters was so eager to keep abreast of changes that he organized the medical journal club in the wilds of Arkansas to bring together surgeons in order to discuss their major problems in dealing with the sick and wounded.

His address to the medical society in 1894 described each of these developments in medical therapeutics. He found them exciting rather than threatening, a challenge rather than an obstruction because, in his stoic fashion, McPheeters moved with change, never clinging to the past. In the waning years of the nineteenth century, his profession underwent another fundamental change, wedding science and medicine to produce yet another rationalism, this time to bring the scientific practice of medicine to the bedside. And so, in his seventy-ninth year, the elderly doctor stood firmly in the center of the stream of medical progress, manifesting his lifelong credo that change is the essence of life.

The twentieth century approached, brimming with American promise, and for St. Louis it meant new bridges proposed across the Mississippi River, new sewer systems, taller buildings than ever imagined thanks to new structural steel, and electric trolley cars lurching at terrifying speeds into the suburbs of the city. St. Louis in the midst of the Gilded Age was leading the nation as its major shoemaker, producing a hundred thousand pairs a year, and Anheuser-Busch, competing successfully with the brewers of Milwaukee, was thirty years old.

Accompanying this new spirit of material progress was a sentimental fascination with the Civil War. McPheeters, always the archrealist, always seeking to find "a happy issue out of affliction," declared in another public address, "It is high time all the asperities of the conflict—everything calculated to engender strife and alienation—should be forgotten, buried, in the oblivion of the past." This was also part of his credo, although the political life of the nation, and certainly of Missouri, still endured in mended places the phantom pain of the Lost Cause.

The McPheeters family, prominent once more in St. Louis, was frequently the target of social attention, as on the occasion of their golden wedding anniversary on May 10, 1899. A social editor of the *St. Louis Republican* described the gathering as a "celebrated affair. Their Pine Street home was festooned with American Beauty roses on mantles, in vases, on marble tables, in baskets and over doorways. . . .

[A] great many friends came to call. The celebration was held in a social yet thoroughly informal manner."[11]

McPheeters was eighty-eight years old in 1903 when he and three other elderly doctors were honored at a banquet held at the new Planters House Hotel under the auspices of the St. Louis Medical Society of Missouri. One of McPheeters's final projects was to serve on a committee whose mission was to provide funding for new quarters for the medical society, and even at his advanced age, he was apparently tireless in his work on this project. Largely through his efforts a building was purchased that housed the society and library.[12] At the Planters House Hotel, McPheeters and four contemporaries were feted with an elaborate eight-course dinner. Toasts were offered and McPheeters rose, third on the program, to give his cordial, decorous response.[13]

McPheeters was the most elderly physician in St. Louis. His career began in the horse-and-buggy days when doctors routinely bled patients, blistered them, and searched for the causes of disease in the ambient air before Joseph Lister's principles of asepsis. His career ended with the advent of the automobile and telephone, of which he was one of the earliest subscribers in St. Louis. He was active when Robert Koch discovered the tuberculosis bacillus, he quickly adapted the use of the X-ray machine, and he witnessed the control of cholera, diphtheria, smallpox, and malaria.

During the blustery days of March 1905, McPheeters became ill and took to his bed. His younger colleagues diagnosed pneumonia, and after a week of illness, William McPheeters died in his home on March 15. His funeral was held at the Grand Avenue Presbyterian Church, formerly the Pine Street Church, renamed and moved west since the days of Samuel McPheeters's ministry.

Ten days after his death, the St. Louis Medical Society devoted an evening to the commemoration of William McPheeters's career. The committee remembered him in their addresses as a superbly trained physician, an innovative editor, a medical educator, and a tireless public servant. They recalled his deep religious faith as well as his discipline, his value as both colleague and friend. His service in the Confederate cause was mentioned with great tact. McPheeters was honored and, by implication, absolved by the young speaker as having been, in all the seasons of his life, a man of principle.[14]

APPENDIX

Extant Reports

Apart from his personal diary, very few of William McPheeters's official reports and personal correspondence survived the war. The items included in this appendix represent unpublished inspection reports and orders, official reports regarding care of the wounded after the battle of Helena, and private reminiscences prepared immediately after the war.

ITEM 1

Dr. McPheeters and Dr. Thomas D. Wooten conducted an inspection of infantry camps near Little Rock in the spring of 1863. At this time McPheeters was medical inspector for Maj. Gen. Sterling Price's infantry division. Very few medical inspector's reports from the Trans-Mississippi Department have survived, and these two provide an excellent insight about the importance medical officers placed in maintaining camp hygiene with regard to disease prevention. McPheeters was an early proponent of public health, and this is evident in the reports below.

Report regarding present and proposed cantonment of Price's Division

Head Quarters, Little Rock Ark.
April 4th 1863

General,

At your suggestion we have visited and carefully inspected the camp grounds on which the troops under your command are now located, as well as the position to which it is proposed to remove them, and beg leave respectfully to submit the following report.

The grounds on which the various Brigades are now encamped are well selected with reference to the healthiness of the site, being high and rolling, so that in case of rain any impurities which may have collected on the surface is thoroughly washed off. The ground in and about the camp has been completely cleared leaving no trace of vegetable matter, the decay of which might generate disease. Each Brigade has erected at a considerable expense of time and labor, large and well-arranged hospitals for the accommodation of its own sick. These will be floored and properly ventilated, which render them desirable receptacles for the comfortable treatment of the sick without the delay and expense incident to their removal to a general hospital.

Such of the men as are furnished with tents have them floored with plank, thus avoiding the dampness of the ground in wet weather; while those who are without tents—comprising the major part—have erected for themselves comfortable and commodious log cabins with floors and large open fire places, rendering them at once convenient and healthful abodes, such as are rarely to be met with in the army. Besides there are stables, work shops, and drill grounds which have been prepared with care, and with reference to the wants of the command—in fact we have rarely met with camps as well furnished with all the appliances necessary for the health and comfort of the troops, and which must have required months of labor to bring them to their present state of completeness.

With regard to the location adjoining and in the vicinity of Cunningham's or Clear Lake, we do not regard it as either healthy or desirable site for a large camp. There are in the neighborhood small parcels of ground where a regiment or two might be eligibly located, but the great body of the ground is low, flat, damp and interspersed with small wet weather streams. The ground is also covered to some extent with dead and decaying vegetable matter, which is well calculated to generate disease when acted on by the heat of the sun.

Without going into further details we are satisfied that not only the comfort, but also the health of the troops would be seriously jeopardized by the removal from the present to the proposed location.

> Respectfully,
> T. D. Wooten, Chief Surg.
> W. M. McPheeters, Med Insp.

Maj. Gen. S. Price

"Report of Inspection of Division Commanded by Maj. Gen. Price, May 18, 1863."

Division Head Quarters
Little Rock, May 18th 1863

General,

On the 15th Inst. we visited and carefully inspected each regiment belonging to the Brigades commanded by Brig. General Parsons and McRae, now encamped three miles distant on the north side of the Arkansas River.

The ground occupied by them as encampments is well selected, high, sufficiently shaded, and to all appearance healthy. In Gen. McRae's Brigade the tents are regularly and systematically arranged, and sufficiently remote from each other as to admit of being properly policed, and in point of fact are kept with a commendable degree of neatness. Sinks are prepared and regularly used both for the reception of the offal accumulating in cooking, and other purposes. Each company is divided into messes of ten, and to each mess one man is detailed to cook, who is exempt from ordinary military duty while in camp. This salutary arrangement is common to the entire Division, while Gen. McRae's Brigade alone the cooking is all done adjacent to but outside of the encampment, thus avoiding the smoke as well as the unpleasant accumulations which are apt to occur when cooking is done between the rows of tents. The health of this Brigade is at present good, the average number of sick for each regiment reported on Surgeon's call the morning of our visit being twenty-seven, and most of these cases of slight indisposition.

There are, however, in this Brigade no Hospital tents, nor other arrangements for isolating the sick; consequently, they have to be crowded into their small tents along with the well to the material injury of both parties. There is also a scarcity of water, the scanty supply thus far obtained is derived from wet weather branches which are gradually drying up. Attempts have been made to supply this defect by the sinking of wells in various localities, but thus far with little or no success owing to the strata of slate rock some five or six feet below the surface which cannot be penetrated by the implements on hand. It is obvious to remark that a sufficient supply of water, not only for drinking and cooking purposes, but also for washing the clothes and keeping the persons of the soldiers clean is essential to the health of an army.

In Gen. Parsons' Brigade the police arrangements are not as complete as they should be; there is not that evidence of cleanliness and order in and around the tents that is desirable, and the camps are rather too much crowded together for a permanent encampment where economy of space is not rendered necessary. These remarks are particularly applicable to Col.'s Hunter and Pickett's regiments but may be due to temporary causes and to the fact of their recent removal to their present location. This Brigade has recently been furnished with one Hospital tent for each regiment, so that the necessity of crowding together the sick and well will no longer exist in this case. The health of the Brigade is comparatively good, the average number of sick to a regiment being thirty-eight most of whom are only slightly indisposed.

The solitary case of Small Pox which occurred in Col. White's regiment a few weeks ago was promptly isolated by the Surgeons in charge, his mess mates quarantined, and a system of vaccination instituted. No other case has as yet made its appearance, and consequently all fear as to the spread of the loathsome disease may be dismissed.

On the 16th Inst. we visited and in a like manner inspected the Brigades under command of Brig. Generals Tappan and Fagan located on this side of the river four miles distant. The site occupied by these Brigades is in most respects eligible, having the advantage of shade and a good supply of water. The only objection to it is that immediately in the rear there is a swamp of considerable magnitude. This may not prove injurious in the present state of the weather, but during the hot months of July, Aug. and Sept. it would undoubtedly give rise to disease of a malarious character.

The police and sanitary regulations of both these Brigades are as complete as could be expected, and the hygienic condition of the troops good. The great majority of the cases of sickness reported are of a very mild character; we, however, witnessed two cases (one in each Brigade) of sudden and very violent disease which have doubtless proved fatal before this—one being violent congestion of the lungs, and the other inflammation of the brain.

The average number of sick per regiment in Gen. Tappan's Brigade is fifty-eight, while that in Gen. Fagan's is forty-seven.

In both these Brigades there is a deficiency of proper hospital tents, while in the entire Division there is a very great want of ambulances both for the removal of the sick to the General Hospital, or for conveying the wounded from the battlefield in case [of] action. It is respectfully recommended that these ambulances when furnished be placed in charge of the Surgeons of the regiments, who shall be responsible for their preservation, so that they may be kept for their legitimate use, and not subject to the order of other parties who may wish to employ them for foraging and other purposes.

There seems to be some hesitation on the part of regimental surgeons in sending their seriously sick to the General Hospital. It is obvious that in the present unsettled state of the command, the severe and protracted cases of disease can be better cared for and their dietetic and other wants more speedily met in the General Hospital than can be in camp. It is therefore respectfully suggested that an order covering these cases might have a salutory effect.

Very Respectfully,
T. D. Wooten
Chief Surg., Price's Div.
W. M. McPheeters
Surgeon & Med. Insp.

Maj. Gen. Price

ITEM 2

While in charge of the wounded at Mr. Allen Polk's near Helena, McPheeters submitted three reports to Maj. Gen. Sterling Price. Although much of the information contained in the reports mirrors that found in the diary, McPheeters tended to be somewhat more specific when reporting on the status of the wounded and the activity of the Federals at Helena in his official correspondence.

HOSPITAL AT MR. ALLEN POLK'S
July 6, 1863.

SIR: A squad of Federal cavalry, under command of Colonel Clayton, took possession of this hospital about 1 P.M. today. General Ross, whose brigade was stationed nearby, soon came up, when all the wounded remaining on hand were paroled, amounting to 72 in all. I had previously sent off on yesterday and today 63 of the more slightly wounded, including 5 nurses. Prior to the arrival of the troops, some five or six shot and shell were fired at the hospital, some of which came within a few feet of the main building, and one struck and fell inside of one of the cabins in which the wounded were lying. This induced me to address a communication to the Federal commander, informing him that this building was occupied as a hospital, and asking him to respect our wounded, but before it was sent Colonel Clayton came up, to whom it was delivered. He stated that he had not observed our yellow flag, but that as soon as he saw it he had sent back and ordered the artillery to cease firing. They remained about an hour. We had nothing to complain of in their treatment. Indeed, General Ross stated that, if we desired it, our wounded here might be sent into Helena, where they could have ice and other comforts; but as they are comfortable here, and as we will probably have an opportunity to send most of them forward to Trenton, where the others have gone, I think I shall not avail myself of his offer. Our wounded are almost all doing remarkably well. Only one death has yet occurred—Private [E.] Strickland, Company I, Gause's regiment, McRae's brigade. As yet I have had no means of ascertaining, with any certainty, the number of our killed and wounded remaining in possession of the enemy. The officers and men varied very much in their statements, some estimating the number at 400, others at 800, showing evidently that it was all guesswork with them. One officer stated to me that they had sent off 570 prisoners on one boat, on the evening of the 4th, including Colonel [Levin. M.] Lewis. Captain [J. R.] Morris, of Company H, Gause's regiment, who was reported killed, they say was taken prisoner. In the confusion of their occupation of the hospital, I was unable to learn as to the fate of others of our command. [Federal] officers and men seemed to be in the finest possible spirits over the surrender of Vicksburg, which they assert took place on the 4th, unconditionally, and without a fight, with 22,700 prisoners. General Grant, they say, first sent up a boat with the news of the surrender, and subsequently another giving the number of prisoners. He massed his forces, they say, and marched in unopposed. As marvelous as this is, the officers and men evidently believe it, and when Port Hudson is taken, they say they will have complete possession of the Mississippi River. I could get no definite information as to General Lee's army. One officer remarked that the news from Pennsylvania was "very much mixed." As soon as the wounded here are sent off, or in a condition to be left, I shall start to join your headquarters. Dr. Cunningham left yesterday evening for Trenton, thence for Little Rock, thinking that he could do more good in the latter place. Drs. [C. D.] Baer, [J. H.] Swindells, [A. N.] Kincannon, and Burckhart [*sic*, Brookhart] are still here. Mr. Polk is exceedingly kind, giving not only his house and everything in it, but his personal services to our wounded.

I have the honor to be, very respectfully, your obedient servant,

W. M. McPheeters

Maj. Gen. Sterling Price.

P.S.—Since writing the above, Private John W. Haynes, Company A, Glenn's regiment, has died. Dr. McNair, of Bell's regiment, has also arrived from Helena, having been released, with his infirmary corps of 13 men, all of whom are en route for General Fagan's brigade. He states that all our wounded have been sent up to Memphis. Colonel [S. S.] Bell wounded, and a prisoner. The enemy estimate their loss at 200 killed and wounded. He heard the report of the capture of Vicksburg, but seems not to credit it himself. He was not permitted to bring out or to see a paper.

Item 3

In a follow-up to his July 6 report, McPheeters provided further details of the Federal visit to the Polk Hospital.

Hospital at Mr. Allen Polk's
July 7, 1863.

General: I had the honor of writing you on yesterday, giving report of the condition of our wounded here, of a visit from the Federals, and the current news, as far as I could get it, which letter I hope you will receive. This morning the medical director, a corps of surgeons, and an ambulance train came out to take possession of our wounded, and, if desired by me, to take them into Helena. They brought out such medical and hospital stores as they supposed we needed—sugar, tea, coffee, potatoes, bandages, &c., and were, I must say, very polite and kind, indeed. I declined sending the wounded in, preferring to keep them here, where we will be able to make them comfortable; whereupon the medical director promised to send us out ice and such other articles as we stand in need of, a list of which I furnished him. I must repeat it again that they were exceedingly kind, and I wish to give them full credit for it. One of their ambulances, horses, and driver, sent out, as they say, to bring in our wounded, was captured, I understand, by General Fagan's command. This they complain of very much. I promised to report the fact to you, assuring them that if the facts were as stated you would certainly have it returned. All the surgeons who were left in Helena, and have since returned, speak in high terms of their attention to our wounded, and, as they claim that it was sent out for the benefit of our men, I am satisfied that we would consult our interest by having it promptly returned.

Colonel [R. A.] Hart was wounded in the left leg, not dangerously; has gone to Memphis. Adjutant [Edward] Warburg lost his leg. Lieutenant [W. F.] Rector was killed, or rather died; lived six hours. These are the only additional particulars that I have received since my last. Our wounded here are doing as well as could be expected. I am doing all that I possibly can to make them comfortable. Up to this time three deaths only have occurred. I write in great haste, as the messenger is anxious to get off. I will report from time to time.

Very respectfully, your obedient servant,
W. M. McPHEETERS.

Maj. Gen. STERLING PRICE.

P.S.—No additional news from Vicksburg.

ITEM 4

McPheeters's last official report from Helena, written on July 14, discusses details of the Federal capture of Vicksburg.

HOSPITAL AT MR. ALLEN POLK'S
July 14, 1863.

Maj. Gen. STERLING PRICE:

DEAR SIR: I wrote you on the 12th by one of our scouts. This morning another opportunity presents itself, of which I will avail myself. Yesterday evening five of our infirmary corps who were detained in Helena came out, and will go on to the army this morning. They were allowed to come out without being paroled. Accompanying them is a paroled officer from Vicksburg, who fully confirms the sad news of the surrender of that gallant city on the 4th instant. I had hoped until seeing and conversing with him, that there might still be some mistake in the Federal reports on that sub-ject, but unfortunately they turn out to be true. The reason that he assigns for the surrender was want of provisions. The army, he states, had for some weeks been on quarter rations, and the day prior to the capitulation mule meat was issued to the men. This, with the inability of General Johnston to relieve them, was stated to the men as the reason for the surrender. On the 3d, General Pemberton sent a flag of truce to General Grant proposing terms, which was replied to by General G. on the 4th, when the Federals came in and took possession; a sad Fourth of July to us this has proved. From what I can learn, the terms of surrender were about these: Officers and men all to be paroled on the spot, and to be marched out in a body, the officers retaining their side arms and the men their personal effects. Everything else the Federals took possession of. He knows very little about individuals, but says that a great many of our men were sick; he thinks that there were not more than 10,000 men fit for duty, and as they were kept daily on duty on quarter rations, they were very much exhausted. He thinks that, on the evening of the 4th, a large part of Grant's army started toward Jackson, in pursuit of General Johnston, and he heard it reported in Helena yesterday that they had cut Johnston up very badly and taken a large number of prisoners. This same report I heard from Federal surgeons, who were out a day or two since. This, however, may all be Yankee gasconade.

The men brought out no papers from Helena, and I am, there-fore, unable to give you any definite information from General Lee's army. They say, however, that the Yankees still claim a vic-tory over him in Pennsylvania, but that our friends in Helena do not credit it. One man who read the papers states that the tele-grams were so confused and contradictory that he could make nothing out of them. You may have received more recent and reliable news on all these points than I have, still I give you such information as I have received. Citizens here are not allowed to go into Helena, nor to receive papers therefrom, so that we are very much cut off from all sources of news, and have to depend on papers occasionally smuggled out and on chance passers-by. Our pickets (some 50 or 60) went by this yesterday, within a mile or so of town. The Federals (I mean their cavalry) have not been out for several days, but may do so at any time. I have made inquiry, but cannot ascertain that any gunboats have gone up

White River. I have not heard to write on any other subject. Our wounded are getting on very well. I would be glad to learn your whereabouts, and to know whether I will have to join you in Texas or elsewhere.

I have the honor to be, most respectfully, your obedient servant,

W. M. McPHEETERS

ITEM 5

The following item was obtained from the "Service Records of Confederate General and Staff Officers" for Maj. Gen. Sterling Price.

> On the retreat from Missouri when transportation for the sick began to be scarce owing to the great numbers who were giving out, and the limited supply of wagons, I wrote the following order, but before issuing it submitted it to Gen. Price. He directed me to take it to the adjutant and have it approved and issued to the Chief Surgeons of Divisions with instructions that it should be strictly enforced.

Hd. Qts. Army of Missouri, in the field
November 7th, 1864

> Medical officers of the army are authorized and required—in addition to ambulances and other medical wagons—to use all other wagons and other vehicles for the transportation of the sick, wounded, and disabled as far as it is possible to do so. Whenever one or two can be accommodated in wagons used for other purposes, they will see to it that they are thus accommodated. Should any difficulty arise in carrying out this order they will call on the nearest military commander for a guard sufficient to enforce it.

By order of Maj. Gen. Price
W. M. McPheeters

ITEMS 6 AND 7

Immediately upon his return to St. Louis, McPheeters composed an account of the two signal events that most affected him during the war: the circumstances behind his joining the Confederate army, and the arrest and banishment of his wife, Sallie.

"Reasons for Quitting Home and Joining the Southern Army"

When in 1860 Messrs. Lincoln and Hamlin were elected President and Vice President of the United States, by the people of the Northern States exclusively—Elected as sectional candidates, and because they were sectional candidates, and opposed to the domestic institutions of the South, I believed that every consideration of honor, self protection, and patriotism demanded of the South a withdrawal from the Union, and the formation of a separate and distinct Confederacy. Hence I became an avowed secessionist, a disunionist! I believed then, and still believe, that they had the right to separate without involving them in a war with the remaining states of the Union. Again, when in the spring of 1861 Mr. Lincoln and his Cabinet by a course of policy evidently designed to bring on an attack on Fort Sumter, and which finally succeeded in inducing said attack, and thus inaugurated the war between the two sections, and then called out 75,000 men to crush the South, my sympathies were all with the South, and my daily prayer to God was that He would strengthen the South effectually to resist this army of invasion.

During the whole of 1861 and the early part of 1862 while I remained in St. Louis, inside the Federal lines, I witnessed with amazement the deep animosity, & diabolical hatred of the people of the North against the South. The press, the pulpit and all classes of society breathed out threatenings of the fiercest and most malignant character, and with savage ferocity, & fiendish malignity seemed to thirst for their blood, and for their utter annihilation. Not by any means participating in these feelings, I was known as a "Southern Sympathizer"—as from the bottom of my heart I was. Yet under the rigor of Martial Law, I learned to keep my opinions to myself, and to put a guard on my tongue. I had certainly violated no law, civil or military, but was quietly practicing my profession, when by order of Maj. Gen. Halleck U.S. Commander at St. Louis with the knowledge and approval of the President of the U.S., my house was entered in broad daylight by the United States police officers and robbed of over $2,000 worth of furniture, and this too at a time when one of my children was lying at the point of death in the house, and did die a few days thereafter.

But notwithstanding such were my views, & feelings, and such the treatment which I had received, I should have felt it to be my duty to remain at home, and take care of my family, & attend to my business, had I been allowed to do so in peace and security. Such however was not the case. An arbitrary military order was issued requiring all persons to take an oath which honor, and conscience alike forbid my taking, and police officers were put on my track to enforce this odious oath on me. The alternative was now forced upon me either to take this oath, which I could not & would not do, go to prison, or else quit my home, family & business and seek refuge in the South—the only land of civil & religious liberty accessible to me. I unhestitatingly chose the latter alternative. The sacrifice of leaving my family and all accumulated interests of over twenty years hard labor was great—how great I will not now undertake to say. On the 20th of June 1862 accompanied by Dr. Wm. Webb I left St. Louis hurriedly, made my way through the Federal lines in Tennessee and repaired to Richmond Va, where I arrived on the 4th of July just at the close of the memorable battles before that city in which Gen. McClellan was so badly defeated by the Confederate forces. On the 8th of July I was commissioned by the Secretary of War as Surgeon in the Confederate Army, and at my own request was ordered to report to Gen. Bragg, for assignment to duty with Gen. Price then commanding the army at Tupelo Miss. From this time until the close of the war in the spring of 1865, I continued with the army in the field, first on the east, & then on the west side of the Miss. River, doing the duties of Surgeon to the best of my ability, in the various positions assigned me.

And now after [this] disastrous termination of the war—which God knows I most deeply deplore, and upon a review of the past I find nothing to regret in the course which I have pursued. I acted from principle, as I trust in the fear of God, & from a high sense of duty, and were the whole thing to do over, with the lights that were before me, I do not see that I could act otherwise than I did. That the South failed of achieving her independence is lamentably true, but I have the proud consciousness of knowing that I did my duty, and that no part of her failure is justly chargeable to me.

On the 17th of June 1865 I returned to this city a paroled prisoner, after an absence of three years lacking three days, and as was required took the oath of allegiance to the U.S. Government. This oath under the circumstances I regarded as involving no point of honor to say the least, as it is the duty of everyone to bear allegiance to the government under which he lives, and the necessities of the case require that I shall live under the Yankee government.

William M. McPheeters

St. Louis Mo. July 24th 1865

"Arrest, Imprisonment, and Banishment of My Wife"

I wish to put on record the facts connected with the arrest, imprisonment and banishment of my wife and children beyond the military lines of the United States in the winter of 1865, as an evidence of the manner in which "the best government in the world" waged war on women & children, and as setting forth one of the many reasons which I have for entertaining a deep & ardent attachment to the aforesaid government of the United States.

On leaving St. Louis in 1862 to join the Southern army, as a matter of necessity I left my family behind me. During the time that Gen. Steele was in command at Little Rock my wife was in the habit of enclosing to him open letters to me, with the request he kindly complied. Subsequently Gen. Reynolds—whom I had formerly known in this city while one of the Professors in Washington University—superceded Steele. To him also my wife enclosed an open letter to me, and in her note to him she alluded to the fact of my having known him &c. and concluded by expressing the hope that he "like some others had not changed from a gentleman to a fiend." To this language, intended as a complimentary piece of pleasantry he took exception, considering it as an indignity through him to his government. Whereupon he returns the letter to Gen. Dodge, Yankee commander at St. Louis, with this endorsement "send Mrs. Sally McPheeters down & I will put her through the lines at once." Upon the receipt of this communication, by order of Gen. Dodge, my wife was arrested & thrown into Gratiot Street Prison, and two days thereafter was banished with her children— in mid winter—January 17th 1865, with only a few hours notice in which to make her preparations for leaving home.

The mistake which my wife made in this manner—and into which I no doubt led her—was in supposing that this fellow Reynolds ever was a gentleman.

The greatest sympathy was manifested by the community for my family at being thus suddenly & ruthlessly torn from their home, & the utmost indignation was expressed at the brutal conduct on the part of the Federal authorities.

They were sent by rail to Cairo, with some four or five other banished females, under charge of U.S. detective police officers, and from Cairo, by boat, and were landed on the west side of the Mississippi River at Gaines Landing in Arkansas, at a time when the whole country was flooded & when by reason of the horrible roads they had the utmost difficulty in getting to the interior of the country. From Gaines Landing they went in a wagon to Monticello through mud & water where they remained a week for want of transportation, during all of which time they were threatened by a Yankee raid then going through that country robbing, burning & murdering as was the custom of these savage emissaries of the "best government in the world," but fortunately they escaped them & thus were not robbed of their baggage, as they undoubtedly would have been had they encountered them.

At the time they were sent out I was not on duty & having just returned from the Missouri Expedition—and was staying at the hospitable residence of Col. C. M. Hervey, Spring Hill, Hempstead Co. Ark.—While on a visit to Washington, Ark., I saw at Gen. Magruder's Head Quarters a *St. Louis Republican* which mentioned the fact of my wife's arrest, and the next day heard intelligence by courier that she was near Monticello. Whereupon I started in search of her & the children—travelling under great difficulties on account of high water & almost impassible roads & finally joined them at Warren, Ark. some four weeks after they left St. Louis. From that place we went in a wagon to Camden—Here I procured comfortable transportation on to Col. Hervey's, where we were most comfortably & agreeably situated, and where we remained for three months & until the surrender of the Trans. Miss. Dept.

The war having terminated so disastrously to the South, and all my interests being in St. Louis, there was nothing left for me but to return again to this city. So in the latter part of May, I left Col. Hervey's with my family, came to Camden & after the delay of a week took a miserable boat for Monroe La. from thence went to Baton Rouge & to New Orleans & on to St. Louis where I recommenced the practice of medicine.

Such are briefly the facts connected with the banishment of my wife.

W. M. McPheeters

St.Louis Mo. July 27th 1865

NOTES

ABBREVIATIONS

AHC   Arkansas History Commission, Little Rock.

CSR-Ark. *Compiled Service Records of Confederate Soldiers Who Served in Organizations from the State of Arkansas,* M317, National Archives (microfilm).

CSR-Mo. *Compiled Service Records of Confederate Soldiers Who Served in Organizations from the State of Missouri,* M322, National Archives (microfilm).

MHS   Missouri Historical Society, St. Louis.

MLWU Bernard Becker Medical Library, Washington University School of Medicine, St. Louis.

O.R.   *The War of the Rebellion: A Compilation of the Official Records of the Union and Confederate Armies.* 130 vols. Washington, DC: Government Printing Office, 1880–1902. [All references to series 1 unless otherwise indicated.]

PREFACE

1. Major L. Wilson, "The Country Versus the Court: A Republican Consensus and Party Debate in the Bank War," *Journal of the Early Republic* 15, no. 4 (winter 1995): 619-47.

PROLOGUE

1. W. M. McPheeters, "Situation as Resident Physician and Surgeon in the Philadelphia Hospital at Blockley" (diary), May 25, 1840–Jan. 1856, MLWU. [Hereafter cited as McPheeters, Blockley diary.] This earlier diary by McPheeters includes descriptions of his year of postgraduate professional training and, in less detail, his move to St. Louis.

2. A physical description of McPheeters was included on the document he signed in St. Louis on June 17, 1865, swearing loyalty to the U.S. government. Oath of allegiance, W. M. McPheeters Collection, MHS.

3. J. Thomas Scharf, *History of Saint Louis City and County, from the Earliest Periods to the Present Day,* 2 vols. (Philadelphia, 1883), 2:1521; "Records of the Medical Society of Missouri," Dec. 25, 1835, St. Louis Medical Society Library. Scharf writes, "Regular meeting of St. Louis doctors was held at City Hall Nov. 23, 1829, to establish fees." William Beaumont, M.D., post surgeon at Jefferson Barracks near St. Louis and a widely recognized physiologist, had been involved in a dramatic murder trial in September 1840, the year before McPheeters's arrival. Reginald Horsman, *Frontier Doctor: America's First Great Medical Scientist* (Columbia: University of Missouri Press, 1996), 246–53; Cynthia DeHaven Pitcock, "The Involvement of

William Beaumont, M.D., in a Medical-Legal Controversy: The Darnes-Davis Case, 1840," *Missouri Historical Review* 59 (1964): 31–45.

4. McPheeters, Blockley diary, Nov. 3, 1841.

5. W. M. McPheeters, "Matters and Things in General—A Brief Retrospect of a Half a Century" (paper presented before the St. Louis Medical Society, Dec. 15, 1894), MHS; R. O. Muether, M.D., "The Evolution of the St. Louis Medical Society," in Joseph A. Hardy Jr. et al., *St. Louis Medical Society Centennial Volume* (St. Louis: n.p., 1939), 15–19; R. E. Schlueter, "Joseph Nash McDowell," in ibid., 77.

6. McPheeters, Blockley diary, June 11, 1846.

7. W. M. McPheeters, "War Reminiscences: Mrs. Grant's Kindness to a Lady in Distress. Interesting Paper Read by Dr. W. M. McPheeters before the Southern Historical and Benevolent Society," in scrapbook, William McPheeters Collection, MHS. McPheeters's address was delivered at Lucas Place, probably the residence of his close friend and fellow Southerner John Wickham, on December 14, 1894. Lloyd Lewis, *Captain Sam Grant* (Boston: Little, Brown, 1950), 100–102. Ulysses Grant was a second lieutenant when he reported to Jefferson Barracks in 1843. His roommate at West Point, Frederick Dent, was Julia's brother. Grant visited the Dent's country home, White Haven, a large, two-story farmhouse on 925 acres. Mr. Frederick Dent, Julia's father and St. Louis attorney and businessman, also maintained a home in the city for his wife and eight children. This house was at Fourth and Cerre Streets and was where Julia and Ulysses were married in August 1848. William C. Winter, *The Civil War in St. Louis* (St. Louis: Missouri Historical Society Press, 1995), 8–9.

8. McPheeters, "Matters and Things."

9. McPheeters, Blockley diary, Nov. 3, 1841.

10. Ibid., Oct. 15, 1842.

11. Ibid., June 11, 1846.

12. McPheeters, "Matters and Things."

13. "Society Proceedings, St. Louis Medical Society, Meeting of March 25, 1905: In Memoriam—Dr. William McPheeters," *Journal of the Missouri State Medical Association* 1, no. 11 (May 1905): 619–31.

14. Victor Fourgeaud, M.D., "Mortality among Children in St. Louis," *St. Louis Medical and Surgical Journal* 1 (Mar. 1844): 12, 181–95. The editors studied mortality rates among children for a three-year period, 1841–43, and compiled the number of deaths in five disease categories: cholera, convulsions, consumption, brain fevers, and "unknown."

15. Marion Hunt, "St. Louis Children's Hospital," *Overlook Magazine* 16, no. 2 (summer 1979): 1–7. Incorporated in 1879, St. Louis Children's Hospital operated in a rented house at 2845 Franklin Avenue in the center of the city until 1884, when the "new" hospital building opened its doors on the corner of Adams Street and Jefferson Avenue. The medical and surgical staff were homeopathic physicians from the opening of the hospital until 1910. For a discussion of the development of children's hospitals in the United States, see Charles E. Rosenberg, *The Care of Strangers: The Rise of America's Hospital System* (New York: Basic Books, 1987), 104, 114, 268–70.

16. McPheeters, "Matters and Things."

17. *The (St. Louis) Daily Union,* May 2, 1850. McPheeters wrote that the cholera epidemic lasted for a year but struck with particular severity from May to August. During the months of June and July, there were 5,108 deaths from cholera, and the

total number of fatalities at the end of the year was 8,108. McPheeters kept careful records, charting the progress of the epidemic in a scientific way.

18. McPheeters, Blockley diary, May 10, 1849. McPheeters's groomsmen were J. S. Smith; John Wickham; and a Lieutenant Wilcox, U.S. Army; E. C. Wells, with whom McPheeters would later flee the city (in June 1862) to join the Confederate service. The bride's attendants were two daughters of the Graham family, Fanny and Lilly; Almira Russell; and Charlotte McRay.

19. Unidentified newspaper clipping, May 11, 1899, in scrapbook, McPheeters Collection, MHS.

20. McPheeters, "Matters and Things."

21. *St. Louis City Directory, 1856,* 165. McPheeters's office and residence were listed on the "north side of Olive between Fifth and Sixth." *Kennedy's St. Louis Directory, 1860* (335) lists McPheeters's office and residence at 150 Olive Street. This location continued as the family residence until 1878.

22. James M. McPherson, *Battle Cry of Freedom* (New York: Oxford University Press, 1988), 170–81; Walter Ehrlich, *They Have No Rights: Dred Scott's Struggle for Freedom* (Westport, Conn.: Greenwood, 1979), 37–38; *Missouri Democrat,* May 21–22, 1863; John Richard Anderson Vertical File, MHS.

23. McPheeters, Blockley diary, Nov. 4, 1844.

24. The last public auction of slaves in St. Louis was held on the steps of the Old Court House on January 1, 1861. An abolitionist crowd of two thousand gathered for this event and disrupted the attempts of the auctioneer to enlist bids. Winter, *Civil War in St. Louis,* 27.

25. James O. Broadhead, "St. Louis during the War," James O. Broadhead Papers, MHS, 23–24.

26. Both the mayor of St. Louis, Daniel Taylor, and the Federal military authorities required all persons holding public positions to sign the following oath: "I do solemnly swear that I will support the Constitution of the United States and of the State of Missouri; that I will not take up arms against the Government of the United States; nor the Provisional Government of the State of Missouri; nor give aid nor comfort to the enemies of either during the present civil war." Winter, *Civil War in St. Louis,* 29–30. The signed oath of Herman Kahte, justice of the peace for the city of St. Louis (1861), is on permanent display at the Missouri History Museum, St. Louis.

27. W. M. McPheeters diary, May 10, 1863, McPheeters Collection, MHS.

28. William H. Lyon, "Claiborne Fox Jackson and the Secession Crisis in Missouri," *Missouri Historical Review* 58 (July 1964): 434; James W. Covington, "The Camp Jackson Affair, 1861," *Missouri Historical Review* 55 (Apr. 1961): 197–212; William Bull, "Memoir," William Bull Collection, MHS.

29. Scrapbook, McPheeters Collection, MHS; *Leslie's Illustrated Newspaper,* June 29, 1861; *Missouri Democrat,* June 18, 1861; Scharf, *History of St. Louis,* 2:523; Winter, *Civil War in St. Louis,* 69–70.

30. Office of the Provost Marshal Department of the Missouri, St. Louis, Special Order 95, Jan. 21, 1862, in scrapbook, McPheeters Collection, MHS.

31. Ibid.; Protest to Major General Halleck, St. Louis, Dec. 26, 1861, McPheeters Collection, MHS.

32. Walter B. Stevens, *St. Louis: The Fourth City, 1764–1909* (St. Louis: S. J. Clarke, 1909), 1002–3.

33. David Herbert Donald, *Lincoln* (New York: Simon and Schuster, 1995), 451–52.

34. Ibid.

35. William Hyde and Howard L. Conrad, eds., *Encyclopedia of the History of St. Louis*, 4 vols. (New York: Southern History, 1899), 3:1407–10; unidentified newspaper clipping, 1863, in scrapbook, McPheeters Collection, MHS.

36. The U.S. Census of 1860 lists the McPheeters household as follows: William M., age forty-three; Sarah, thirty; George B., ten; Margaret, one; and William, five. Servants living on the property were: Mary Germer, age forty-three, born in Ireland; Mary Meyer, nineteen, born in Germany; Mini Meyer, sixteen, born in Germany; and Henry Volker, fourteen, born in Germany.

37. W. M. McPheeters, "The Following Articles," *Missouri Republican,* Jan. 23, 29, 1862, in scrapbook, McPheeters Collection, MHS.

38. Newspaper clipping, interview of Sallie, in scrapbook, McPheeters Collection, MHS; W. M. McPheeters, "Private Paper No. 1. Reasons for Quitting Home and Joining the Southern Army," McPheeters Collection, MHS.

39. Newspaper clipping, Scrapbook, McPheeters Collection, MHS; Alton Military Prison commemorative plaque, undated, placed by the Alton (Ill.) Historical Society.

40. Abasalom Grimes, a river pilot, friend of Samuel Clemens, and Confederate mail carrier who served time in several Federal prisons, described the facility at Myrtle Street as "an excavation in the ground which had been lined with boiler iron and this in turn with boards. There were two apartments or cells in the box, each about eight feet square and seven feet high." There was no light, heat, or ventilation, and Grimes was imprisoned there in abject darkness during winter. Milo M. Quaife, ed., *Absolom Grimes, Confederate Mail Runner* (Shawnee Mission, Kans.: Two Trails, 1997), 158–59.

41. McPheeters, "Private Paper No. 1."

42. "Society Proceedings, St. Louis Medical Society, Meeting of March 25, 1905: In Memoriam—Dr. William McPheeters," 629.

43. Albert Castel, *General Sterling Price and the Civil War in the West* (Baton Rouge: Louisiana State University Press, 1968), 141.

44. James M. Kellar, "Organization of the Medical Department in the Trans-Mississippi," 1893, Joseph Jones Collection, Howard Tilton Memorial Library, Tulane University, New Orleans.

45. Sterling Price had been a successful planter, U.S. congressman, Mexican War general, and governor of Missouri, qualifications that at the war's outset garnered him command of the Missouri State Guard and soon after a commission as major general in the Confederate army. Known affectionately as "Old Pap," he led his Missouri and Arkansas troops in many significant actions on both sides of the Mississippi River. His popularity, however, far exceeded his success on the battle-field. As one of the ranking officers in Trans-Mississippi Department, Price would command the District of Arkansas for more than a year and greatly influence military operations in that theater. Castel, *Sterling Price;* Robert E. Shalope, *Sterling Price: Portrait of a Southerner* (Columbia: University of Missouri Press, 1971).

46. Thirty-six-year-old Maj. Thomas Lowndes Snead served as chief of staff and assistant adjutant general to Sterling Price. Snead participated in all the major battles

in which Price was involved and was a loyal follower and staunch defender of the general. In May 1864 Snead was elected to the second session of the Confederate Congress, representing the First Missouri District. Robert E. Miller, "Proud Confederate: Thomas Lowndes Snead of Missouri," *Missouri Historical Review* 79 (Jan. 1985), 167–91.

47. In June 1863 Ireland native Austin M. Standish served as assistant adjutant general on the staff of his brother-in-law, Brig. Gen. Mosby M. Parsons. *Service Records for Confederate General and Staff Officers,* series M331, roll 235, National Archives (microfilm).

48. Daughter of a U.S. senator and wife of Brig. Gen. Thomas J. Churchill, Anne Maria Sevier Churchill was "a petite brunette of beauty, sparkling intellect, vivacious[ness], and admired by a large circle of friends." Anne McMath, *First Ladies of Arkansas* (Little Rock: August House, 1989), 91–96.

49. The Federal Arsenal at Little Rock was the scene of the first confrontation in Arkansas between state forces and U.S. troops in January 1861. Bobby Roberts and Carl Moneyhon, *Portraits of Conflict: A Photographic History of Arkansas in the Civil War* (Fayetteville: University of Arkansas Press, 1987), 20–21.

50. Ben Chambers was a planter from Craighead County, Arkansas. U.S. Census, 1860, Population, Craighead County, Arkansas.

51. Blistering entailed the administration of a chemical counterirritant or vesicant (often a preparation of Cantharis beetles) to the skin, which produced a large blister at the affected site. It was believed that the watery fluid that collected under the skin would reduce inflammation and "relieve torpor" by diverting "the impetus of the blood from the part affected to the part of application." J. Worth Estes, *Dictionary of Protopharmacology* (Canton, Mass.: Watson International, 1990), 36–37.

52. Lt. Gen. Theophilus Hunter Holmes was, like McPheeters, a native of North Carolina. The school referred to by the general is probably Raleigh Academy, which McPheeters attended prior to entering the University of North Carolina. From July 1862 until February 1863, Holmes commanded the Trans-Mississippi Department. His reluctance to assist Confederate forces east of the Mississippi during this period resulted in his being replaced by Lt. Gen. Edmund Kirby Smith. Holmes, however, was allowed to retain command of the District of Arkansas, a position he held until March 1864. William M. McPheeters File, Alumni Records, University of Pennsylvania, Philadelphia; Anne Bailey, "Theophilus Hunter Holmes," in *The Confederate General,* 6 vols., ed. William C. Davis (National Historical Society, 1991), 3:116–17; *Service Records of Confederate General and Staff Officers,* series M331, roll 130.

53. Maj. Nicholas S. Hill was the purchasing commissary for the District of Arkansas. Two months later he was appointed chief of commissary and subsistence for the district. Hill held this position until January 1865. *Service Records of Confederate General and Staff Officers,* series M331, roll 127.

54. Nineteen-year-old 1st Lt. Theophilus Hunter Holmes Jr. served as his father's aide-de-camp while in the Trans-Mississippi and continued in that capacity until the general and his staff were ordered to North Carolina in April 1864. On June 3, 1864, as a member of the 5th North Carolina Cavalry, Holmes Jr. was killed "while leading a line of skirmishers" in battle near Ashland, Virginia. *Service Records of Confederate General and Staff Officers,* series M331, roll 130.

55. Charles W. Broadfoot also served as an aide-de-camp to Lt. Gen. Theophilus

Holmes. Returning with the general to North Carolina in 1864, Broadfoot became lieutenant colonel of the 1st North Carolina Junior Reserves. Joseph H. Crute Jr., *Confederate Staff Officers, 1861–1865* (Powahatan, Va.: Derwent, 1982), 89; *O.R.,* 47(1):1062.

56. Thomas Caute Reynolds became Missouri's second Confederate governor after the death of Claiborne Fox Jackson. Robert E. Miller, "One of the Ruling Class, Thomas Caute Reynolds: Second Confederate Governor of Missouri," *Missouri Historical Review* 80 (July 1986): 422–48.

1. THE HELENA CAMPAIGN

1. Warren E. Grabau, *Ninety-eight Days: A Geographer's View of the Vicksburg Campaign* (Knoxville: University of Tennessee Press, 2000).

2. Steven E. Woodworth, "Dismembering the Confederacy: Jefferson Davis and the Trans-Mississippi West," *Military History of Texas and the Southwest* 20 (1990): 1–22; Robert L. Kerby, *Kirby Smith's Confederacy: The Trans-Mississippi South, 1863–1865* (New York: Columbia University Press, 1972), 112–15; William R. Geise, "The Department Faces Total Isolation: Part IX, February–July, 1863," *Military History of Texas and the Southwest* 15 (1979): 35–48; Geise, "Isolation: Part X, July–December, 1863," *Military History of Texas and the Southwest* 15 (1979): 31–42; Anne Bailey, "Theophilus Hunter Holmes," in *The Confederate General,* 6 vols., ed. William C. Davis (National Historical Society, 1991), 3:116–17; Steven E. Woodworth, *Jefferson Davis and His Generals: The Failure of Confederate Command in the West* (Lawrence: University Press of Kansas, 1990), 179–80; Dr. R. J. Bell diary, Aug. 12, 1863, Mosby M. Parsons Papers, MHS.

3. Woodworth, "Dismembering the Confederacy," 17–22; Kerby, *Kirby Smith's Confederacy,*106; Albert Castel, *General Sterling Price and the Civil War in the West* (Baton Rouge: Louisiana State University Press, 1968), 142–44; Edwin C. Bearss, "The Battle of Helena, July 4, 1863," *Arkansas Historical Quarterly* 20 (autumn 1961): 256–57.

4. John M. Harrell, *Arkansas,* vol. 10 of *Confederate Military History,* ed. Clement A. Evans (1899; reprint, Secaucus, N.J.: Blue and Grey, n.d.), 179; Bearss, "Battle of Helena," 258–59.

5. Castel, *Sterling Price,* 144.

6. Bearss, "Battle of Helena," 261–69; Bell diary, June 24–27, MHS; Castel, *Sterling Price,* 145–47; Thomas A. DeBlack, "1863: 'We Must Stand or Fall Alone,'" in *Rugged and Sublime: The Civil War in Arkansas,* ed. Mark K. Christ (Fayetteville: University of Arkansas Press, 1994), 79–81; Harrell, *Arkansas,* 181–83.

7. John Mhoon at this time held the rank of lieutenant in the 4th Confederate Engineer Troops and served as engineer on Sterling Price's staff. Charles T. Perrie was a volunteer aide-de-camp on Price's staff. Joseph H. Crute Jr., *Confederate Staff Officers, 1861–1865* (Powahatan, Va.: Derwent, 1982), 158–59; "Trans-Mississippi Order Book," Apr. 1, 1863, MHS; *Service Records for Confederate General and Staff Officers,* series M331, roll 196, National Archives (microfilm).

8. James Fleming Fagan led a brigade of Arkansas infantry in the District of Arkansas until September 1863, when he was assigned command of a cavalry brigade. Promoted to major general in April 1864, Fagan eventually assumed control

of all cavalry in the District of Arkansas and for a brief period in 1865 was placed in charge of the entire district. *Service Records of Confederate General and Staff Officers,* series M331, roll 90; Anne Bailey, "James Fleming Fagan," in *Confederate General,* 2:115–16.

9. This was probably Capt. Hamilton B. Wear, commanding Company I, 36th Arkansas Infantry. *CSR-Ark.,* 36th Infantry, roll 222.

10. In April 1863 Thomas Dudley Wooten was appointed chief surgeon for the District of Arkansas and one year later named medical director for the district. Wooten served on Sterling Price's staff for the duration of the war. *Service Records for Confederate General and Staff Officers,* series M331, roll 273; R. French Stone, *Biography of Eminent American Physicians and Surgeons* (Indianapolis: Carlon and Hollenbeck, 1894), 570–71.

11. A member of Price's staff since January 1862, Maj. Isaac Brinker was chief quartermaster for the District of Arkansas. *Service Records for Confederate General and Staff Officers,* series M331, roll 33; "Trans-Mississippi Order Book," Apr. 1, 1863, MHS.

12. Dr. Robert Joe Bell, surgeon in the 10th Missouri Infantry, gives a more detailed account of the arduous crossing of Bayou DeView:

> June 28th. We marched two miles and managed in this distance to cross Bayou de View and the swamp contiguous. This bayou and most of the swamp were bridged. In the road along which we marched the water was from two to five feet deep. In the course of our march, the men stripped off all their clothes with the exception of their shirts and boldly waded through the mud and water carrying their guns and knapsacks. While in this condition several of the planter's daughters appeared on the road. Seeing the soldiers partial state of nudity they quietly retired. As we marched along this side of the bayou, the drummers and fifers on board a flat[boat] floated along down the stream and regaled the brave suffering soldiers with some excellent national airs. This swamp is heavily timbered. Emerging from the soil are numerous cypress knees adding to the dismalness of the surrounding scenery. I hope that I shall never again witness such dreadful times.

Bell diary, June 28, 1863, MHS.

13. Enoch M. Marvin, a Methodist minister from St. Louis, was staff and division chaplain for Sterling Price. Marvin was instrumental in establishing the very popular "Army Church," an interdenominational institution organized in the District of Arkansas by Methodist and Presbyterian ministers. Crute, *Confederate Staff Officers,* 158; Charles F. Pitts, *Chaplains in Gray* (Nashville: Broadman's, 1957), 59–60, 129–30.

14. Brig. Gen. John Sappington Marmaduke played a pivotal role in all the major campaigns in the Trans-Mississippi's District of Arkansas, gaining a reputation as one of the Confederacy's finest cavalry officers. Captured during the battle of Mine Creek, Kansas, Marmaduke was confirmed as the Confederacy's last major general while still a prisoner of war. Edwin C. Bearss, "John Sappington Marmaduke," in *Confederate General,* 4:154–57.

15. A former lawyer from Tennessee, Allen J. Polk moved to Phillips County, Arkansas, in 1849 and became a successful planter. His plantation served as a Confederate field hospital following the battle of Helena. *The Goodspeed Biographical and Historical Memoirs of Eastern Arkansas,* (Chicago: Goodspeed, 1890), 792.

16. In the Confederate plan of battle, Fagan and his Arkansas infantry were to assault the Federal left, anchored by Battery D atop Hindman Hill. Employing Parsons's Missourians and Dandridge McRae's Arkansans, General Price had the ominous duty of ascending Graveyard Hill against Battery C, which constituted the Federal center. The extreme Federal right, secured by Battery A on Rightor Hill, was to be seized by the dismounted cavalry brigades of Marmaduke and Brig. Gen. Lucius M. Walker.

17. McPheeters is referring to the death of Confederate general Albert Sidney Johnston on April 6, 1862, during the battle of Shiloh. Johnston, after ordering his personal physician, Dr. David W. Yandell, to attend to wounded soldiers, was himself severely wounded in the leg a short time later. For want of prompt medical attention, Johnston bled to death, making him the highest-ranking officer on either side to be killed during the Civil War. According to McPheeters, Price's response to his request was, "Doctor, I would be very glad if you would do so." Wiley Sword, *Shiloh, Bloody April* (New York: William Morrow, 1974), 271; W. M. McPheeters, "War Reminiscences," *The St.Louis Republican,* Dec. 17, 1893.

18. Since October 1862, Dr. Francis. D. Cunningham had been medical inspector for the Trans-Mississippi Department; however, on March 19, 1863, Theophilus Holmes appointed him medical director for the District of Arkansas. Cunningham held this position until May 2, 1864, when he was ordered to Virginia. Dr. Caleb Dorsey Baer was chief surgeon for Mosby M. Parsons's Missouri infantry brigade. In July 1863 Surgeon R. M. Slaughter was the medical field purveyor for Sterling Price's infantry division. Seven months later Slaughter would be named medical purveyor for the District of Arkansas. *Service Records for Confederate General and Staff Officers,* series M331, rolls 68, 162, 226; Crute, *Confederate Staff Officers,* 145.

19. In his official report on the attack against Helena, Sterling Price made special mention of the efforts of Dr. McPheeters and Mr. Marvin: "To my chief surgeon, Thomas D. Wooten, to Surg. William M. McPheeters, and to Assistant Field Purveyor R. M. Slaughter, my constant thanks and commendation are due for the sedulous manner in which they have at all times devoted themselves to the sick and wounded, but never more humanely or more conspicuously than upon this occasion. These gentlemen tell me that they owe their grateful acknowledgments to the Rev. Mr. Marvin for the very important services which he rendered at their hospitals, not only offering the consolations of his holy office to the dying, but ministering assiduously to the wants of the wounded." *O.R.,* 22(1):416–17.

20. Just after 4:00 A.M., Brig. Gen. James Fagan opened the battle south of town. Because he advanced an hour ahead of Price, Fagan drew the attention of gunners on both Hindman and Graveyard Hills, and the resulting crossfire stalled his attack in front of Battery D. In the Confederate center, Price's well-coordinated charge saw his Arkansas and Missouri troops race up and over Battery C, capturing its two field pieces and several prisoners. As the gray infantry milled atop Graveyard Hill, heavy shells from Fort Curtis and the gunboat *Tyler* rained down, wreaking havoc among the Southerners. Seeking refuge from the maelstrom, many made their way into Helena, only to be captured. To the north, Marmaduke and Walker's assault degenerated into a desultory affair that never seriously challenged the Federal right flank anchored on Rightor Hill. By 10:30 A.M., after almost seven hours of vicious combat, Holmes acknowledged the futility of the situation and ordered a withdrawal. In the

aftermath he would report suffering 1,636 casualties out of roughly 8,000 men engaged. The Union defenders lost only 239 men in killed, wounded, and missing. Bearss, "Battle of Helena," 271–93; Castel, *Sterling Price,* 148–51; J. H. McNamara, "Paper by McNamara," *(St. Louis) Missouri Republican,* Dec. 5, 1885.

21. Dr. James H. Swindell was the surgeon for Lucien C. Gause's 32d Arkansas Infantry. Dr. Andrew N. Kincannon was surgeon for Col. Lebbeus A. Pindall's 9th Battalion of Missouri Sharpshooters. Dr. Jacob F. Brookhart was assistant surgeon for Col. John E. Glenn's 36th Arkansas Infantry. *Service Records of Confederate General and Staff Officers,* rolls 35, 149, 239.

22. Col. Powell Clayton was commander of the Union cavalry during the battle of Helena. Later in the war he commanded the Federal garrison at Pine Bluff. In 1868 Clayton was elected governor of Arkansas. Bearss, "Battle of Helena," 294; Bobby Roberts and Carl Moneyhon, *Portraits of Conflict: A Photographic History of Arkansas in the Civil War* (Fayetteville: University of Arkansas Press, 1987), 192.

23. Yellow was the color adopted by the Confederate medical corps. Yellow flags were typically flown over hospitals to denote their noncombat status.

24. Since no Union officer named Ross holding the rank of colonel or higher was present at the battle of Helena, McPheeters is most likely referring to Col. Samuel A. Rice. Rice commanded the Second Brigade of Brig. Gen. Frederick Salomon's infantry division, which defended the Federal right flank during the battle. Bearss, "Battle of Helena," 278.

25. Dr. Isaac Casselberry was surgeon of the 1st Indiana Cavalry. James W. Wheaton and Ed Gleeson, *Surgeon on Horseback: The Missouri and Arkansas Journal and Letters of Dr. Charles Brackett of Rochester, Indiana, 1861–1863* (Carmel: Guild Press of Indiana, 1998), 227.

26. McPheeters, in a follow up to his July 6 report, provided further details of the Federal visit to the Polk Hospital. See appendix, item 1.

27. Dr. Godfrey N. Beaumont was surgeon of the 11th Missouri Infantry. Wayne H. Schnetzer, *Men of the Eleventh: A Roster of the Eleventh Missouri Infantry, Confederate States of America* (Shawnee Mission, Kans.: Two Trails, n.d.), 6.

28. Quinine, a drug isolated from the bark of the cinchona tree, was used to treat malaria and its accompanying fevers. Blue mass, a dark, slate-colored preparation containing 33 percent elemental mercury, could be shaped into pills and administered as treatment for a variety of ailments. "Intermittent fever" was a general term for fevers that recurred periodically, such as those associated with malaria.

29. Confederate surgeons classified amputations as either "primary" or "secondary" depending on how soon after the injury the procedure was performed. Primary amputations took place within forty-eight hours of the initial injury, while secondary procedures were conducted later. In general, the success rate of primary amputations was better than that for secondary procedures. H. H. Cunningham, *Doctors in Gray: The Confederate Medical Service* (Baton Rouge: Louisiana State University Press, 1993), 222–24.

30. The Federals were referring to the defeat of Robert E. Lee at the battle of Gettysburg, fought July 1–3, 1863.

31. McPheeters's last official report from Helena, written on July 14, discusses details of the Federal capture of Vicksburg. See appendix, item 4.

32. The success rate for secondary amputations above the knee was less than

50 percent. G. A. Otis and D. L Huntington, eds., *Medical and Surgical History of the Rebellion*, 2d ed. (Washington, D.C.: Government Printing Office, 1883), 2(3):407-10.

33. Col. Archibald S. Dobbins commanded the 1st Arkansas (Dobbins's) Cavalry in Brig. Gen. L. Marsh Walker's brigade. Two months later, after Walker's death, Dobbins assumed command of the brigade and led it for the remainder of the war. Bearss, "Battle of Helena," 297.

34. Col. William E. McLean commanded the First Brigade of Salomon's division, which defended the Federal left flank during the battle of Helena. Bearss, "Battle of Helena," 278.

35. While leading Company C, 36th Arkansas Infantry in the assault up Graveyard Hill, thirty-three-year-old Capt. Walter C. Robinson was shot in the thigh, resulting in the fracture McPheeters describes. Robinson later became a lieutenant colonel. *O.R.*, 22(1):419; *CSR-Ark.,* 36th Infantry, roll 228.

2. THE WOMENFOLK

1. *Missouri Democrat,* Apr. 16, 1862.

2. Unidentified newspaper article, n.d., in scrapbook, William McPheeters Collection, MHS.

3. "Office of Provost Marshal, St. Louis, July 16, 1863," McPheeters Collection, MHS; W. M. McPheeters, "War Reminiscences," McPheeters Collection, MHS.

4. Scrapbook, McPheeters Collection, MHS.

5. Ibid. This encounter, in which Julia Dent Grant displayed the social attitudes considered so correct by McPheeters and his Southern friends, was a favorite story that the McPheeters repeated over the years.

6. As a gentleman of the mid-nineteenth century, McPheeters was prevented by rules of decorum from writing, or even articulating, his private feelings at this reunion with his wife.

7. George was the eldest of two sons born to Sallie and William. Unfortunately, both sons (George and William Jr.) died in childhood. Alumni Records, William M. McPheeters File, University of Pennsylvania Archives, Philadelphia.

8. Eliza "Lily" Frost was the wife of Brig. Gen. Daniel Marsh Frost. She had been banished from St. Louis along with eleven other women on April 23, 1863. They were charged with being Southern sympathizers involved in "the business of collecting and distributing rebel letters." Robert E. Miller, "Daniel Marsh Frost, CSA," *Missouri Historical Review* 85 (July 1991): 394.

9. Twenty-five year-old Amos F. Cake, captain of Company C, Pindall's Battalion of Missouri Sharpshooters, was severely wounded during the fighting at Helena. He recovered and was later elected major of Searcy's Missouri Battalion of Sharpshooters. *CSR-Mo.,* 9th Battalion Sharpshooters, roll 149.

10. Rufus McPeters, a private in Company G, 6th Missouri Cavalry, was one of nineteen casualties suffered by his unit at Helena. *CSR-Mo.,* 6th Cavalry, roll 43.

11. Three weeks later Dr. Caleb Dorsey Baer died of an apparent heart attack while attending his charges at the Polk hospital. Brig. Gen. Mosby M. Parsons was so affected by the loss of Baer that he distributed to his men in the field General Order No. 109, which eulogized their former brigade surgeon. Capt. J. H. McNamara, "Parsons' Missouri Brigade in the Red River Campaign," *The Missouri Republican,* Nov. 6, 1886.

12. This was probably Thomas G. Kelly. It is unclear to whose unit Kelly was attached at Helena, but in October 1863 he was assistant surgeon in Robert Wood's 14th Missouri Cavalry. *CSR-Mo.*, 14th Cavalry, roll 78.

13. DeVall's Bluff, situated along the White River, was the terminus of the western stretch of the Memphis and Little Rock Railroad, which originated in Little Rock. The eastern section picked up fifty miles farther east at Madison and continued to Hopefield, opposite Memphis, on the Arkansas side of the Mississippi River. Leo E. Huff, "The Memphis and Little Rock Railroad during the Civil War," *Arkansas Historical Quarterly* 23 (autumn 1964): 260–70.

14. George W. Kerr of Missouri was a captain and ordnance officer in Sterling Price's infantry division. *Service Records for Confederate General and Staff Officers,* series M331, roll 148, National Archives (microfilm).

15. Lt. Gen. Edmund Kirby Smith took command of the Trans-Mississippi Department in February 1863. When that vast department was isolated from the rest of the Confederacy after the fall of Vicksburg, Pres. Jefferson Davis promoted Smith to the permanent rank of general and empowered him with authority to govern the region independently of the administration at Richmond. Smith transformed his command into an independent dominion known to many as "Kirby Smithdom." Joseph Howard Parks, *General Edmund Kirby Smith, CSA* (Baton Rouge: Louisiana State University Press, 1954); Robert L. Kerby, *Kirby Smith's Confederacy: The Trans-Mississippi South, 1863–1865* (New York: Columbia University Press, 1972).

3. THE LOSS OF LITTLE ROCK

1. William W. O'Donnell, *The Civil War Quadrennium* (Little Rock: Civil War Round Table, 1985), 27.

2. Frederick J. Elsas, "The Journal of Henry L. Dye, Confederate Surgeon," *Surgery* 63 (Feb. 1968): 352–62.

3. O'Donnell, *Civil War Quadrennium*, 33.

4. "Who Is to Blame," *Arkansas Patriot,* Jan. 8, 1863; DeBlack, "1863: 'We Must Stand or Fall Alone,'" in *Rugged and Sublime: The Civil War in Arkansas,* ed. Mark K. Christ (Fayetteville: University of Arkansas Press, 1994), 89; *O.R.,* 22(2):945–47.

5. Junius N. Bragg to Josephine, Aug. 25, 1863, in *Letters of a Confederate Surgeon, 1861–1865,* ed. T. J. Gaughan (Camden, Ark.: Hurley, 1960); Robert L. Kerby, *Kirby Smith's Confederacy: The Trans-Mississippi South, 1863–1865* (New York: Columbia University Press, 1972), 226–27; Albert Castel, *General Sterling Price and the Civil War in the West* (Baton Rouge: Louisiana State University Press, 1968), 153–54; *O.R.,* 22(2):941–42.

6. *Washington Telegraph,* Aug. 19, 1863; Joseph Howard Parks, *General Edmund Kirby Smith, CSA* (Baton Rouge: Louisiana State University Press, 1954), 307–10; Kerby, *Kirby Smith's Confederacy,* 134, 226.

7. Paul E. Steiner, *Disease in the Civil War: Natural Biological Warfare in 1861–1865* (Springfield, Ill.: Charles C. Thomas, 1968), 214–28.

8. Leo E. Huff, "The Union Expedition against Little Rock, August–September, 1863," *Arkansas Historical Quarterly* 22 (autumn 1963): 226–27.

9. Ibid., 227–28.

10. John M. Harrell, *Arkansas,* vol. 10 of *Confederate Military History,* ed.

Clement A. Evans (1899; reprint, Secaucus, N.J.: Blue and Grey, n.d.), 216–18; DeBlack, "1863," 90–96; Huff, "Union Expedition against Little Rock," 234–35; John N. Edwards, *Shelby and His Men* (Cincinnati: Miami Printing, 1867), 348.

11. O'Donnell, *Civil War Quadrennium,* 48–49.

12. Brig. Gen. Daniel Marsh Frost was celebrating his fortieth birthday when McPheeters penned this diary entry (perhaps the smoking session was in celebration). That month Frost and his infantry brigade were summoned to Little Rock, where he assumed command of the earthen defenses north of the city. Robert E. Miller, "Daniel Marsh Frost, C.S.A." *Missouri Historical Review* 85 (July 1991), 381–401.

13. What capacity Col. John Widener Polk served in Price's army on August 9, 1863, is unknown. However, in 1864 he served as volunteer aide-de-camp to Brig. Gen. Thomas J. Churchill and later was in charge of the cotton bureau post at Monticello, Arkansas. His wife, Anna Eliza Polk, was arrested on a southbound steamer leaving St. Louis in June 1864 and charged as a probable smuggler and spy. On her person was a considerable amount of correspondence addressed to Confederates in Arkansas; among the letters was one from Sallie McPheeters to her husband. *Service Records for Confederate General and Staff Officers,* series M331, roll 199, National Archives (microfilm); *Union Provost Marshal's Files,* series M345, roll 219, National Archives (microfilm).

14. "Dr. Webb" is probably William C. Webb, surgeon for the 12th Missouri Cavalry, or Frederick F. Webb, assistant surgeon for the 10th Missouri Cavalry. *CSR-Mo.,* 12th Cavalry, roll 61; *CSR-Mo.,* 10th Cavalry, roll 58.

15. Erected in 1842, the Arkansas State Penitentiary was utilized by Confederate authorities during the Civil War to hold prisoners of war. On September 10, 1863, Union troops occupied Little Rock and began imprisoning Confederate captives in the facility, which consisted of five brick buildings enclosed by a stone wall twenty-two feet high. The structure was razed in 1899 to provide a site for the current Arkansas State Capitol. Lewis Barnard, "Old Arkansas State Penitentiary," *Arkansas Historical Quarterly* 13 (autumn 1964), 321–23; *O.R.,* series 2, 7:957–59.

16. McPheeters is referring to Harriet V. Snead, wife of Maj. Thomas L. Snead, as being unable to get through Federal lines in order to return to St. Louis. In June 1864, though, she did manage to get through but was arrested "for crossing Federal lines without proper authorization" and imprisoned. On June 24 she was "paroled under bond of $5,000 to remain at the residence of Walker R. Carter upon the condition that she will receive no visitors except by written permission" of the provost marshal. *Union Provost Marshal's Files,* series M345, roll 219.

17. Son of a U.S. senator, "Gen." William Elliott Ashley had been an Arkansas militia officer, planter, and state representative, and he had most recently been the wartime mayor of Little Rock until the city's capture by Federal troops in September 1863. *Goodspeed's Biographical and Historical Memoirs of Central Arkansas* (Chicago: Goodspeed, 1890), 377, 385.

18. The fighting to which McPheeters refers was the battle of Reed's Bridge on Bayou Meto, twelve miles northeast of Little Rock. The engagement involved the Union cavalry of Brig. Gen. John W. Davidson's command and Marmaduke's Confederate horsemen.

19. On September 4 General Price demanded the services of "every citizen capable of bearing arms or ministering to the wants of the wounded." For the full proclamation issued to the people of Pulaski County, see *O.R.,* 22(2):991–92.

20. In March 1863 Lucius Marshall Walker, the nephew of Pres. James K. Polk, received command of a cavalry brigade in the District of Arkansas. Following the battle of Helena, tensions developed between Walker and Brig. Gen. John Sappington Marmaduke. On September 6, 1863, the strain culminated in a duel between the cavalry officers, which resulted in Walker's mortal wounding. Ezra J. Warner, *Generals in Gray: Lives of the Confederate Commanders* (Baton Rouge: Louisiana State University Press, 1959), 321–22.

21. The confrontation between John S. Marmaduke and Lucius M. Walker was one of the most incredible and tragic vignettes of the Civil War in the Trans-Mississippi. For a detailed account of the Marmaduke-Walker affair, see Leo E. Huff, "The Last Duel in Arkansas: The Marmaduke-Walker Duel," *Arkansas Historical Quarterly* 23 (spring 1964): 36–44.

22. The gunboat was the CSS *Pontchartrain*.

23. Harris Flanagin was colonel of the 2d Arkansas Mounted Rifles, stationed near Chattanooga, Tennessee, when he learned of his election as governor of Arkansas. Returning to Little Rock in November 1862, Flanagin worked diligently for the defense of the capital city and the Arkansas River Valley. Farrah Newberry, "Harris Flanagin," *Arkansas Historical Quarterly* 17 (1958): 3–20.

24. Edward Carrington Cabell was Price's paymaster. In August 1864 Cabell was appointed chief paymaster for the District of Arkansas. Howard L. Conrad, *Encyclopedia of the History of Missouri*, 6 vols. (St. Louis: Southern History, 1901), 1:459–60; *Service Records of Confederate General and Staff Officers*, series M331, roll 44.

25. Located fifty miles southwest of Little Rock along the Ouachita River, Arkadelphia was a primary ordnance center for the Trans-Mississippi Department. The city was the site of a large powder mill, arsenal, tannery, medical laboratory, and salt works until the autumn of 1863, when most of the operations were moved to Marshall and Tyler, Texas. H. B. MacKenzie, "Confederate Manufactures in Southwest Arkansas," *Arkansas Historical Association Publications* 2 (1908): 207–16; William A. Albaugh, *Tyler, Texas, C.S.A.* (Harrisburg, Pa.: Stackpole, 1958), 30–42.

26. This is probably Edwin A. Hickman, former first lieutenant of Company B, 6th Missouri Infantry. A severe leg wound received during the siege of Vicksburg led to Hickman's transfer to the Trans-Mississippi Department in September 1863, where he was eventually assigned to duty as assistant quartermaster at Bonham, Texas. *Service Records for Confederate General and Staff Officers*, series M331, roll 126.

27. Charles Burton Mitchel, a former U.S. senator from Arkansas, represented the state in the Confederate Congress from 1861 until his death on September 20, 1864. James M. Woods, "Devotees and Dissenters: Arkansans in the Confederate Congress 1861–1865," *Arkansas Historical Quarterly* 38 (1979): 237–38; Michael B. Dougan, *Confederate Arkansas* (Tuscaloosa: University of Alabama Press, 1976), 37–38, 83, 124.

28. Joseph Orville Shelby's famous Iron Brigade participated in all of the significant cavalry actions that took place in Arkansas and Missouri during the war. His stellar performance on the battlefield earned him a reputation of being one of the finest cavalry officers in the Civil War. McPheeters mentions Shelby on the eve of the cavalryman's first independent raid into Missouri. Daniel O'Flaherty, *General Jo Shelby: Undefeated Rebel* (Chapel Hill: University of North Carolina Press, 1954); W. L. Webb, *Battles and Biographies of Missourians* (Kansas City: Hudson-Kimberly, 1900).

29. Lt. Col. Henry Clay Taylor, a volunteer aide-de-camp to Sterling Price in 1862, was named chief of artillery for Price's infantry division in June 1863. From November 1863 until January 1865, Taylor served as chief of ordnance for the District of Arkansas. *Service Records for Confederate General and Staff Officers,* series M331, roll 242.

30. Maj. Henry W. Tracy served as a volunteer aide-de-camp to Brig. Gen. Daniel Frost for the first two years of the war. He then served on the staffs of Price and Brig. Gen. Mosby M. Parsons as chief of subsistence. In August 1864 he was appointed chief of commissary and subsistence for the District of Arkansas. *Service Records for Confederate General and Staff Officers,* series M331, roll 250.

31. This is probably Maj. Thomas W. Scott, chief of subsistence for Brig. Gen. Louis Hébert's brigade in the Department of Mississippi and East Louisiana. *Service Records of Confederate General and Staff Officers,* series M331, roll 220.

32. In 1862 Maj. Gen. Thomas C. Hindman appointed Benjamin Franklin Danley as provost marshal general for the District of Arkansas, a position he held until the war's end. It is possible that McPheeters was writing to Benjamin's older brother, Christopher Columbus Danley. C. C. Danley was wartime editor of the *Arkansas Gazette,* and he too was often referred to as "colonel." Stewart Sifakis, *Compendium of the Confederate Armies: Arkansas* (New York: Facts on File, 1992), 56; *Arkansas Gazette,* June 1, 1877; Fred. W. Alsop, "History of the Arkansas Gazette," Small Manuscript Collection, AHC.

33. McPheeters is referring to the battle of Chickamauga, fought September 19–20, 1863.

34. Following the fall of Little Rock, Governor Flanagin and the Confederate civil government relocated to Washington, a small town in Hempstead County in extreme southwestern Arkansas.

35. Much of the "intelligence" that filtered into the Trans-Mississippi from the East was often greatly exaggerated or simply in error. In this instance, neither Maj. Gen. Ambrose Burnside nor his staff or army was present at Chickamauga or Chattanooga; they occupied Knoxville, over one hundred miles to the northeast.

36. Lt. Col. Franck S. Armistead was assistant inspector general for the District of Arkansas from May 1863 until April 1864. *Service Records of Confederate General and Staff Officers,* series M331, roll 9.

37. Formerly chief justice of the Arkansas Supreme Court, George C. Watkins served as judge advocate for Lt. Gen. Theophilus Holmes. After Holmes's resignation from the District of Arkansas in 1864, Watkins continued to serve on military courts in the region. Joseph H. Crute Jr., *Confederate Staff Officers, 1861–1865* (Powahatan, Va.: Derwent, 1982), 90; Clio Harper, "Prominent Members of the Early Arkansas Bar, Biographies 1791–1884," AHC.

38. J. H. R. Cundiff was appointed aide-de-camp to Missouri governor Thomas Caute Reynolds with the rank and pay of colonel of cavalry in the Missouri State Guard. He was later appointed assistant auditor for the Trans-Mississippi Department. *Service Records of Confederate General and Staff Officers,* series M331, roll 68.

39. Thomas Fenwick Drayton commanded a brigade of Missourians during the winter of 1863–64 before Lt. Gen. Edmund Kirby Smith transferred him to the Western Subdistrict of Texas in March 1864. William C. Davis, "Thomas Fenwick Drayton," in *The Confederate General,* 6 vols., ed. William C. Davis (National Historical Society, 1991), 2:76–77.

40. U.S. Congressman Clement Laird Vallandigham was a renowned "Copperhead" and Peace Democrat from Ohio. Frank M. Klement, *The Copperheads in the Middle West* (Chicago: University of Chicago Press, 1960).

41. Capt. Joseph L. Thomas served as assistant quartermaster on the staff of Sterling Price. During the Missouri Expedition in 1864, Thomas was in charge of transportation for the Army of Missouri and later assigned as chief paymaster. *Service Records of Confederate General and Staff Officers,* series M331, roll 245.

4. WINTER QUARTERS

1. Robert L. Kerby, *Kirby Smith's Confederacy: The Trans-Mississippi South, 1863–1865* (New York: Columbia University Press, 1972), 232–37; John N. Edwards, *Shelby and His Men* (Cincinnati: Miami Printing, 1867), 193–240.

2. William R. Geise, "Kirby Smithdom, 1864," *Military History of Texas and the Southwest* 15 (1979): 17–36; Kerby, *Kirby Smith's Confederacy,* 253–81.

3. Kerby, *Kirby Smith's Confederacy,* 237.

4. Cynthia Pitcock and Bill Gurley, "'I Acted from Principle': William Marcellus McPheeters, Confederate Surgeon," *Missouri Historical Review* 89 (July 1995): 394.

5. Benjamin Taylor Kavanaugh, a Kentuckian by birth, was a true Renaissance man. At various times during his life, he could rightfully be called physician, scientist, editor, author, and member of the clergy, which is why McPheeters refers to him as "Rev. Dr." Kavanaugh. During the war, he served as both chaplain and surgeon, being attached to Maj. Gen. Sterling Price's forces. *The South in the Building of the Nation,* vol. 12 (Richmond: Southern Historical Publication Society, 1909), 28–29; Howard L. Conrad, *Encyclopedia of the History of Missouri,* 6 vols. (St. Louis: Southern History, 1901), 5:509–10.

6. Dr. Bennett H. Clark was assistant surgeon to the 32d Arkansas Infantry. *Service Records of Confederate General and Staff Officers,* series M331, roll 56, National Archives (microfilm).

7. "Col. Bell's regiment" was the 37th Arkansas Infantry, commanded by Col. Samuel S. Bell. Stewart Sifakis, *Compendium of the Confederate Armies: Arkansas* (New York: Facts on File, 1992), 119.

8. Thomas James Churchill was given command of the Post of Arkansas on the lower Arkansas River. Outnumbered almost eight to one, Churchill and his entire command were captured on January 11, 1863. Imprisoned for three months at Camp Chase, Ohio, Churchill was exchanged and assumed command of a division of Arkansas infantry. Anne Bailey, "Thomas J. Churchill," in *The Confederate General,* 6 vols., ed. William C. Davis (National Historical Society, 1991), 1:186–87.

9. McPheeters is referring to the battle of Baxter Springs, Kansas, where on October 6 William Quantrill and his band of guerillas attacked and massacred the escort of Union brigadier general James Blunt. Blunt narrowly escaped with his life.

10. In August 1863 Maj. Jilson P. Johnson, a member of Maj. Gen. John C. Breckenridge's staff, was assigned to the Office of the Adjutant and Inspector General in Richmond, Virginia, for "special inspection duties." One of his first assignments was to inspect Lt. Gen. Theophilus Holmes's army in the District of Arkansas. *Service Records of Confederate General and Staff Officers,* series M331, roll 141.

11. James Camp Tappan, a Yale graduate and practicing attorney from Helena, led the 19th and 24th (Consolidated), 27th, 33d, and 38th Arkansas Infantry Regiments as part of Thomas Churchill's division at the battles of Pleasant Hill and Jenkins' Ferry in 1864. Terry L. Jones, "James Camp Tappan," in *Confederate General*, 6:26–27; *O.R.*, 34(1):784.

12. McPheeters is refering to Gen. Robert E. Lee's attempt to turn Maj. Gen. George G. Meade's right flank and move toward Washington, D.C. Beginning on October 9, 1863, a series of small engagements took place between the Rapidan River and Bull Run Creek in Virginia. The most serious of these engagements occurred at Bristoe Station on October 14. The campaign ended on October 22 with Lee falling back behind the Rappahannock River.

13. In the fall of 1863, Col. Sidney D. Jackman carried out several independent excursions throughout Missouri and Arkansas. In the spring of 1864, Jackman's guerrilla band reached regimental strength and was designated Jackman's Missouri Cavalry. He would command a brigade of Missouri cavalry during Price's Missouri Raid in the fall of 1864. Joseph H. Crute Jr., *Units of the Confederate States Army*, (Gaithersburg, Md.: Olde Soldier Books, 1987), 208.

14. Mosby Monroe Parsons was one of the best brigade and division commanders in the Trans-Mississippi Department. Parsons developed a reputation as a determined and respected fighter, leading his Missourians (8th, 9th, 10th, 11th, 12th, and 16th Missouri Infantry, Pindall's 9th Battalion of Missouri Sharpshooters, and Ruffner's and Lesueur's Batteries) in the battles of Cane Hill, Prairie Grove, Helena, Pleasant Hill, and Jenkins' Ferry. Recognizing his leadership capabilities, Lt. Gen. Kirby Smith assigned Parsons to duty as major general in May 1864. From February to April 1865, Parsons commanded the District of Arkansas. Robert E. Miller, "General Mosby M. Parsons: Missouri Secessionist," *Missouri Historical Review* 80 (1985): 35–57; Edwin C. Bearss, "Mosby Monroe Parsons," in *Confederate General*, 4:210–11.

15. John Ingram served in Company E, Elliot's Missouri Cavalry Battalion. *CSR-Mo.*, Elliot's (9th) Cavalry Battalion, roll 54.

16. Charles S. Mitchell was colonel of the 8th Missouri Infantry. "Register of Officers, Parsons Division Missouri Volunteers," MHS.

17. "Phthisis" was a term used to describe tuberculosis.

18. In September 1863 Maj. Ignatius Szymanski arrived in the Trans-Mississippi Department as assistant agent for exchange, establishing his headquarters at Alexandria, Louisiana, the following month. His charge was to provide corrected lists of paroles of Union prisoners, obtain information on both Union prisoners and Confederates captured by the Federals, and to instruct commanders in the proper procedure for prisoner exchange and in the establishment of parole camps. Capt. Andrew Sigourney was chief paymaster for the District of Arkansas. Henry P. Beers, *Guide to the Archives of the Confederate States of America* (Washington: National Archives, 1968), 234; *O.R.*, 34(1):783; *Service Records of Confederate General and Staff Officers*, series M331, roll 225.

19. Duncan C. Cage served as volunteer aide-de-camp and later assistant engineer for Sterling Price. By March 1864, Cage was promoted to captain while retaining the position of assistant engineer. *Service Records of Confederate General and Staff Officers*, series M331, roll 44.

20. In July 1863 Capt. William M. Seay was acting assistant adjutant general to

Daniel M. Frost. But by the following November, he was serving in the same capacity on the staff of Mosby M. Parsons. *Service Records of Confederate General and Staff Officers,* series M331, roll 221; *O.R.,* 33(1):983.

21. On April 14, 1863, Capt. James H. Reynolds was appointed assistant quartermaster on the staff of Mosby M. Parsons. By February of the next year, Reynolds was division quartermaster for Parson's two infantry brigades. *Service Records of Confederate General and Staff Officers,* series M331, roll 209.

22. Capt. John W. Hinsdale had been acting as assistant adjutant general to Theophilus Holmes since December 1862, but in August 1863 he was designated assistant inspector general for the District of Arkansas. He was returned to Holmes's staff in March 1864. *Service Records of Confederate General and Staff Officers,* series M331, roll 128.

23. Dr. W. M. Lawrence served the Trans-Mississippi Department's Army Medical Board, which was responsible for examining surgeons throughout the command. *Service Records of Confederate General and Staff Officers,* series M331, roll 153.

24. C. F. Dryden was chaplain for the 12th Missouri Infantry. "Register of Officers, Parsons Division Missouri Volunteers," MHS.

25. Richard "Dick" T. Morrison was appointed aide-de-camp to Sterling Price in May 1861 and continued in that capacity for the duration of the war. *Service Records of Confederate General and Staff Officers,* series M331, roll 183.

26. Lt. John Edward Drayton was aide-de-camp to Gen. Thomas F. Drayton. "Capt. Jones" could be either A. J. Jones, Company K, Dawson's Arkansas Infantry; B. M. Jones, Company E, 36th Arkansas Infantry; Edward T. Jones, Company C, 37th Arkansas Infantry; J. M. G. Jones, Company G, 39th Arkansas Infantry; or W. J. F. Jones, Company E, 39th Arkansas Infantry. Benjamin H. Hart was captain of Company B, 8th Missouri Infantry. Joseph H. Crute Jr., *Confederate Staff Officers, 1861–1865* (Powahatan, Va.: Derwent, 1982), 51; Janet B. Hewett, ed., *The Roster of Confederate Soldiers,* 16 vols. (Wilmington, N.C.: Broadfoot, 1995–), vols. 8–9; "Register of Officers, Parsons Division Missouri Volunteers," MHS.

27. George Davis was attorney general for the Confederate States of America.

28. John McC. Lacy was assistant surgeon for Col. William H. Brooks's 34th Arkansas Infantry. *Service Records of Confederate General and Staff Officers,* series M331, roll 151; John M. Harrell, *Arkansas,* vol. 10 of *Confederate Military History,* ed. Clement A. Evans (1899; reprint, Secaucus, N.J.: Blue and Grey, n.d.), 382.

29. Capt. Edward B. Stonehill was assistant aide-de-camp to Sterling Price. *Service Records of Confederate General and Staff Officers,* series M331, roll 235.

30. Mrs. H. Clay Taylor, Mrs. Wright C. Schaumburg, and Mrs. Joseph T. Scott were wives of officers serving under Sterling Price and Edmund Kirby Smith. Wives of Confederate officers from St. Louis frequently gained passes to visit their husbands, much like Sallie McPheeters did when she visited her husband after the battle of Helena. Several women had no other choice but to remain with their husbands because they had been banished from Missouri as Rebel sympathizers, smugglers, or spies. Lt. Col. Wright C. Schaumburg was assistant inspector general to E. Kirby Smith, and Dr. Joseph T. Scott was chief surgeon for D. M. Frost's infantry division until his appointment to the Army Medical Board in February 1864. *Service Records of Confederate General and Staff Officers,* series M331, roll 220.

31. William Lewis Cabell, known affectionately as "Old Tige" to his men, commanded a brigade in James F. Fagan's cavalry division. In October 1864 he was captured during the battle of Mine Creek and imprisoned in Boston Harbor until July 1865. Paul Harvey, *Old Tige: General William L. Cabell, CSA,* Hillsboro Junior College Monographs, no. 4 (Hillsboro, Tex.: Hillsboro Junior College, 1970).

32. Maj. Lauchlan A. MacLean served as assistant adjutant general to Sterling Price from July 1862 until March 8, 1864. On August 29, 1864, Price announced MacLean as his senior assistant adjutant general. *Service Records of Confederate General and Staff Officers,* series M331, roll 161.

33. Serving initially as surgeon to the 25th Arkansas Infantry, Dr. Charles H. Smith was assigned as chief surgeon to Brig. Gen. John S. Marmaduke's cavalry division in early 1863. *Service Records of Confederate General and Staff Officers,* series M331, roll 228.

34. James D. White served as colonel of the 9th (White's) Missouri Infantry until April 1863 at which time he was placed on detached duty as scout and informant for Federal troop movements on the Mississippi and lower Arkansas Rivers. Stewart Sifakis, *Compendium of the Confederate Armies: Missouri* (New York: Facts on File, 1992), 127; *O.R.,* 41(3):988–89.

35. Francis Valle was captain of Company G, 8th Missouri Cavalry. *CSR-Mo.,* 8th Cavalry, roll 53.

36. Dr. John M. Haden was medical director of the Trans-Mississippi Department from June 12, 1862, until March 25, 1864. Haden then became chief of the Medical Bureau, which was in effect surgeon general of the Trans-Mississippi Department. J. Woodfin Wilson, "Some Aspects of Medical Services in the Trans-Mississippi Department of the Confederate States of America, 1863–1865," *Journal of the North Louisiana Historical Association* 12 (1981): 123–46; William R. Geise, "Kirby Smith's War Department," *Military History of Texas and the Southwest* 15 (1979): 17–35.

37. Capt. A. C. Dickinson was attached to the Confederate 1st Engineers Battalion in the Trans-Mississippi Department, but he resigned in January 1864. Stewart Sifakis, *Compendium of the Confederate Armies: The Confederate Units* (New York: Facts on File, 1992), 178–79; *Service Records of Confederate General and Staff Officers,* series M331, roll 161.

38. J. M. Wills was captain of Company A, 11th Missouri Cavalry. *CSR-Mo.,* 11th Cavalry, roll 44.

39. Colonel Mitchell of the 8th Missouri Infantry was suffering from orchitis, an inflammation of the testes.

40. Transferred from the Army of Tennessee to the Trans-Mississippi Department in February 1863, W. Watkins Dunlap served at various times as chief of artillery for John S. Marmaduke, Sterling Price, and Thomas Churchill. In August 1864 he was named chief of artillery for the District of Arkansas. *Service Records of Confederate General and Staff Officers,* series M331, roll 81.

41. Dr. John B. Bond was the medical purveyor for the District of Arkansas, with headquarters at Lewisville and later at Camden. Medical purveyors had the difficult and at times almost impossible task of procuring, storing, and distributing medical supplies. Wilson, "Medical Services in the Trans-Mississippi Department," 123–46; *Service Records of Confederate General and Staff Officers,* series M331, roll 27.

42. Ambrose H. Sevier served as assistant inspector general for Thomas Churchill.

Promoted to the rank of captain in May 1864, he served as Churchill's assistant adjutant general until the department's surrender in June 1865. *Service Records of Confederate General and Staff Officers,* series M331, roll 223.

43. Thomas Pleasant Dockery, a planter from southern Arkansas, received his commission as brigadier in August 1863 and soon was commanding a brigade of mounted infantry in James Fagan's cavalry division. In November 1864 the Reserve Corps in the District of Arkansas was placed under his control. Anne Bailey, "Thomas Pleasant Dockery," in *Confederate General,* 2:70–71.

44. *"Deo volente"* is Latin for "if God is willing."

45. Benjamin D. Chenoweth was major of the 21st Texas Cavalry, which served in Arkansas at various times under the commands of William H. Parsons, Lucius M. Walker, and John S. Marmaduke. In the fall of 1863, Chenoweth led a brigade of Texas cavalry composed of the 21st Texas, B. D. McKie's and C. L. Morgan's squadrons, and Pratt's Texas Battery. Anne J. Bailey, *Between the Enemy and Texas: Parsons's Texas Cavalry in the Civil War* (Fort Worth: Texas Christian University Press, 1989), 29, 155.

46. This is likely Capt. Benjamin von Phul, commander of a temporary artillery battery attached to Brig. Gen. Thomas Drayton's infantry brigade. His brother, Lt. Francis von Phul, was an aide-de-camp on the staff of Brig. Gen. John B. Clark Jr. at this time. *O.R.,* 22(2):1086.

47. McPheeters is referring to the death of his first-born son, George. Having lost both sons due to illness since the war's outbreak, only the two young daughters, Sally and Maggie, remained to share the love of their mother and father.

48. Richard H. Musser was lieutenant colonel of the 9th Missouri Infantry, and Col. John B. Clark Jr. commanded the regiment. Both officers had served with the Missouri Confederates in the Trans-Mississippi since receiving their commissions in the Missouri State Guard in 1861. "Register of Officers, Parsons Division Missouri Volunteers," MHS; Anne Bailey, "John Bullock Clark Jr.," in *Confederate General,* 1:194–95.

49. Chloroform (trichloromethane) is a volatile liquid that was used for anesthetic purposes during the Civil War. It was administered by dripping the fluid onto a sponge or cloth held over the patient's nose and mouth. "Taxis" refers to the manual replacement or reduction of a hernia. H. H. Cunningham, *Doctors in Gray: The Confederate Medical Service* (Baton Rouge: Louisiana State University Press, 1993), 225–27.

50. Frank was a negro servant whose services were loaned to McPheeters by Maj. Edward Carrington Cabell.

51. A Virginian by birth, Albert Rust settled in Arkansas in 1837 and became a prominent planter, lawyer, and politician. Though a brigadier general since March 1862, his questionable loyalty to the Southern cause resulted in his being stripped of all military duties in early 1863; the term "Goose question" is a covert reference to the issue of slavery. Rust's criticism of the Confederate government grew as the war's end became inevitable, and he often expressed his sentiment for the Union. Terry L. Jones, "Albert Rust," in *Confederate General,* 5:120–21; Webb Garrison, *The Encyclopedia of Civil War Usage* (Nashville: Cumberland House, 2001), 96.

52. Maj. John Tyler Jr., son of the tenth president of the United States, was a confidant to Sterling Price and volunteer aide-de-camp on his staff during the

Helena campaign. He afterward returned to Virginia and frequently corresponded with Sterling Price, often chastising "the ineptitude of the West Pointers" in charge of local departments at Richmond. John Tyler Jr. to Sterling Price, June 7, 11, 1864, in *Service Records of Confederate General and Staff Officers,* series M331, roll 253.

53. Lt. Celsus Price, son of Sterling Price, served as volunteer aide-de-camp to his father from March 1862 until March 1865. His father nominated him for promotion to captain, but the War Department never confirmed the appointment. *Service Records of Confederate General and Staff Officers,* series M331, roll 202.

54. In the camp of the 8th Missouri Infantry, not far from McPheeters, Capt. Ethan A. Pinnell provided a description of the interior of his own rough-hewn cabin, which was probably typical of the structures constituting Camp Bragg:

> Our house, we call it a house, is twelve by fourteen feet square, built of round logs, daubed with red clay, a wooden chimney in the south, and door in the east. In the back end from the fire are two bunks, beadstead fashion, in which six of us sleep. In the corner between the door and the fire, stands a rough board table, above it a broad board on pegs in the wall on which rest our table furniture consisting of two whole plates, four tin ones, four or five knives and forks, one tea cup and two tin ones. Under the table sitting on the ground our cooking vessels consisting of a small pot, a small skillet with a broken lid and a broken tea kettle. In the opposite corner from the table, a pine box set against the wall on wooden pins which answers the double purpose of a writing desk and trunk. Around the walls hang suspended on pins our scanty supply of clothing and our old sabers. A half dozen wooden stools complete the description.

E. A. Pinnell diary, Mosby M. Parsons Papers, MHS.

55. Dr. Robert J. Bell was surgeon for the 10th Missouri Infantry. In 1864 Mosby Parsons appointed Bell as chief surgeon of his infantry division. "Register of Officers, Parsons Division Missouri Volunteers," MHC.

56. Dr. Robert J. Christie served as surgeon in Col. William Moore's 10th Missouri Infantry. While at Camp Bragg, he and several other surgeons participated in another anatomy lesson, this one involving "a negro killed by another a few miles from the camp." Christie's narrative continued: "We made arrangements to get the body, and got it. . . . We used the subject for careful dissecting and operation. We did our dissecting in a log hut: the cracks were not chinked nor daubed, and to us, on the inside, it was an amusing sight to see a row of eyes peering through the cracks, trying to get a glimpse of the structure of the human form divine. Seeing us dissecting part from part, and perceiving that we seemed to understand their mechanisms, our importance was no doubt magnified in their estimation." "The Memoirs of Dr. Robert J. Christie," <http://www.bcl.net/~flanagan/genealo/memoirs.htm#chvi> (accessed Sept. 29, 2000).

57. Col. Louis A. Welton was involved in a variety of activities, including the impressment of negroes and the shipping of cotton and mules. In 1864 he was captured and court-martialed by the U.S. War Department on charges of spying. Found guilty, he spent the remainder of the war imprisoned in Fort Delaware. *Service Records of Confederate General and Staff Officers,* series M331, roll 263.

58. Capt. Carville H. Wood was an aide-de-camp to Joseph O. Shelby. Crute, *Confederate Staff Officers*, 174.

59. Dr. Joseph T. Scott was appointed to the Army Medical Board and continued in that capacity until paroled in June 1865. *Service Records of Confederate General and Staff Officers*, series M331, roll 220.

60. Capt. Lionel Levy served as judge advocate of the military court in the Trans-Mississippi Department. *Service Records of Confederate General and Staff Officers*, series M331, roll 156.

61. McPheeters's patient was the wife of forty-seven-year-old Capt. Joseph Chaytor, assistant quartermaster for the 4th Missouri Cavalry. *Service Records for Confederate General and Staff Officers*, series M331, roll 53.

62. Lt. Fergus McRae was an artilleryman from St. Louis who served in Cockrell's Missouri Brigade, Army of Tennessee. R. S. Bevier, *History of the First and Second Missouri Confederate Brigades* (St. Louis: Bryan Brand, 1879), appendix, 5.

5. "NO ABIDING CAMP"

1. Dr. Jesse E. Thompson was assistant surgeon for the 38th Arkansas Infantry and later served in the same capacity for the 1st Arkansas (Monroe's) Cavalry. Thomas H. Kavanaugh was assistant surgeon for the 3d Missouri (Leseuer's) Field Artillery. *Service Records of Confederate General and Staff Officers*, series M331, rolls 247, 145, National Archives (microfilm).

2. Maj. Thomas Monroe, a forty-four-year-old Missourian, was chief quartermaster of Sterling Price's infantry division. *Service Records of Confederate General and Staff Officers*, series M331, roll 180.

3. This is probably William B. Lankford, captain of Company K, 33d Arkansas Infantry. *CSR-Ark.*, 33d Infantry, roll 213.

4. Camp Sumter was the name given to the army's new winter quarters in the vicinity of Spring Hill, Hempstead County, Arkansas.

5. McPheeters's brother, Alexander, then resided in New York State. Miscellaneous File, William McPheeter Collection, MHS.

6. R. A. Kidd was captain of Company D in William L Anderson's Arkansas Cavalry Battalion. *CSR-Ark.*, Anderson's Cavalry, roll 31.

7. The military ball held on February 22 in Spring Hill was only open to civilians, members of the headquarters staff, and field officers. Although Dr. McPheeters did not attend, most of the officers did, including Dr. Robert J. Bell and his new wife. In her diary Mrs. Bell provides a description of the festivities:

> Feb. 22d. Dr. Bell left early this morning, but not until he had my consent to attend the ball. I went over with Mrs. Hervey this morning to help set the table and returned at two o'clock. We then left for the party at nine o'clock. I went with Mrs. Hervey but found Dr. Bell waiting for me. I then entered the dancing room and there found a very, very nice assembly. I must say that I never saw more busts displayed with the ladies. The first families of the country were there. I noticed Mrs. Gen. Churchill, Misses Pike, daughters of Albert Pike, Mrs. Newton of Little Rock, Mrs. Gen. Tappan. and many other ladies of rank. I had the pleasure of going to the table with Gen. Drayton,

who is commanding in the absence of Gen. Price. The table was very nicely arranged and everything went off pleasantly. Altogether, I think it was as nice a party as I ever attended.

Mrs. R. J. Bell diary, Mosby M. Parsons Papers, MHS.

8. This is probably Richard Pryor, a planter living near Spring Hill in Hempstead County, Arkansas. Pryor was sixty-six years old at the time; therefore, the title "major" likely refers to a previous militia appointment. U.S. Census, 1860, Population, Hempstead County, Arkansas.

9. McPheeters is referring to issues of the *St. Louis Republican.*

10. Hamilton Rowan Gamble had been chief justice of the Missouri Supreme Court in 1851, when he delivered a dissenting opinion in the court's proslavery decision in the Dred Scott case. In July 1861, after Missouri's Southern-sympathizing governor, lieutenant governor, and secretary of state "abdicated" their positions, the Missouri legislature elected Gamble governor. In December 1863 Gamble slipped on the steps of the state capitol, severely fracturing his arm. Complications from the injury led to his death in St. Louis on January 31, 1864. William C. Winter, *The Civil War in St. Louis* (St. Louis: Missouri Historical Society Press, 1995), 120–21.

11. Although both were Missouri natives, Dr. Robert Duncan was surgeon for the 27th Arkansas Infantry, while Paul Christian Yates served as surgeon for the 38th Arkansas Infantry. John M. Harrell, *Arkansas,* vol. 10 of *Confederate Military History,* ed. Clement A. Evans (1899; reprint, Secaucus, N.J.: Blue and Grey, n.d.), 382, 384.

12. Maj. John Adams was a volunteer aide-de-camp to Brig. Gen. James F. Fagan. Crute, *Confederate Staff Officers,* 58.

13. Lt. William Von Phul was the ordnance officer for Gen. William L. Cabell's cavalry brigade. *Service Records of Confederate General and Staff Officers,* series M331, roll 255.

14. McPheeters is referring to Maj. Gen. William T. Sherman's Meridian campaign. Sherman captured Meridian, Mississippi, on February 14, 1864, being opposed by forces under Lt. Gen. Leonidas Polk. The linchpin of the campaign, though, was a proposed juncture at Meridian with Brig. Gen. William Sooy Smith's cavalry force from Memphis. On February 22 Smith was stopped well short of his objective by Maj. Gen. Nathan B. Forrest's command and soundly defeated at the battle of Okolona.

15. In February 1864 Holmes learned that the governors of Arkansas and Missouri, the Arkansas representatives in both houses of Congress, and even Lt. Gen. Edmund Kirby Smith had been petitioning Richmond to replace the elderly general with "an active, energetic successor, who can win the confidence of the people and excite the enthusiasm of his troops." An angered and insulted Holmes tendered his resignation to Smith, who promptly accepted it. Sterling Price then assumed command of the District of Arkansas. Robert L. Kerby, *Kirby Smith's Confederacy: The Trans-Mississippi South, 1863–1865* (New York: Columbia University Press, 1972), 289; *O.R.,* 34:935; Albert Castel, *General Sterling Price and the Civil War in the West* (Baton Rouge: Louisiana State University Press, 1968), 171.

16. In the largest Civil War battle to take place in Florida, Federal forces under Brig. Gen. Truman Seymour were defeated on February 20, 1864, by the Confederate troops of Brig. Gen. Joseph Finnegan at the battle of Olustee.

17. On March 1, 1864, a dramatic raid on the Confederate capital by two

columns of Federal cavalry under Brig. Gen. Judson Kilpatrick and Col. Ulrich Dahlgren was thwarted, resulting in the death of Dahlgren. Some evidence suggests this raid was an assassination attempt on Jefferson Davis.

18. Maj. Gen. Richard Taylor, the only son of Pres. Zachary Taylor, was commander of the District of Western Louisiana of the Trans-Mississippi Department. During Maj. Gen. Nathaniel Banks's assent up the Red River in spring 1864, Taylor's Confederates fell back 150 miles to the outskirts of Shreveport. Refusing to abandon his adopted state without a fight, Taylor turned on the Federals, and his Louisiana and Texas troops dealt Banks a stunning defeat at Mansfield on April 8. Failing to duplicate his success the following day at Pleasant Hill, Taylor nevertheless forced Banks into a humiliating retreat. T. Michael Parrish, *Richard Taylor: Soldier Prince of Dixie* (Chapel Hill: University of North Carolina Press, 1992).

6. RED RIVER AND JENKINS' FERRY

1. Frank Vandiver, *The Southwest: South or West?* (College Station: Texas A&M Press, 1975), 22–31.

2. Ludwell H. Johnson, *Red River Campaign: Politics and Cotton in the Civil War* (Baltimore: Johns Hopkins University Press, 1958), 3–45; Robert L. Kerby, *Kirby Smith's Confederacy: The Trans-Mississippi South, 1863–1865* (New York: Columbia University Press, 1972), 151–86; William C. Davis, *Jefferson Davis: The Man and His Hour* (New York: Harper Collins, 1991), 574; Joseph Howard Parks, *General Edmund Kirby Smith, CSA* (Baton Rouge: Louisiana State University Press, 1954), 283–84.

3. Johnson, *Red River Campaign,* 40–42, 170–71; Kerby, *Kirby Smith's Confederacy,* 290–92.

4. Albert Castel, *General Sterling Price and the Civil War in the West* (Baton Rouge: Louisiana State University Press, 1968), 173; Kerby, *Kirby Smith's Confederacy,* 290–99; Johnson, *Red River Campaign,* 119.

5. Johnson, *Red River Campaign,* 19–20, 46–47.

6. Kerby, *Kirby Smith's Confederacy,* 292–93; Johnson, *Red River Campaign,* 42–45.

7. Kerby, *Kirby Smith's Confederacy,* 294–97, 301; Johnson, *Red River Campaign,* 89–100; *O.R.,* 34(1):179–80.

8. T. Michael Parrish, *Richard Taylor: Soldier Prince of Dixie* (Chapel Hill: University of North Carolina Press, 1992), 317–38; Kerby, *Kirby Smith's Confederacy* 298–99.

9. Richard Taylor, *Destruction and Reconstruction: Personal Experiences of the Civil War* (New York: D. Appleton, 1879), 159–62; Johnson, *Red River Campaign,* 113–19.

10. Taylor, *Destruction and Reconstruction,* 162; Parrish, *Richard Taylor,* 339–41.

11. "Colonel" Richard H. Johnson was editor of the *Arkansas True Democrat* and brother of Robert W. Johnson, Confederate senator from Arkansas. After the Federal occupation of Little Rock, the *True Democrat* did not resume publication. James M. Woods, *Rebellion and Realignment: Arkansas's Road to Secession* (Fayetteville: University of Arkansas Press, 1987), 74.

12. When Brig. Gen. Mosby Parsons's Missourians crossed the Louisiana state line, one of their bands struck up the tune "Arkansas Traveler." "Parsons's Missouri Brigade in the Red River Campaign," *The Missouri Republican,* Nov. 6, 1886.

13. Maj. Gen. John George Walker's division of Texas infantry gained a reputation for long forced marches in good order from one threatened point to another in

Arkansas and Louisiana, earning them the sobriquet "Walker's Greyhounds." His
Texans fought at Milliken's Bend, Mansfield, Pleasant Hill, and Jenkins' Ferry. In
June 1864 Walker assumed command of the District of Western Louisiana after Lt.
Gen. Richard Taylor asked to be relieved. Norman Brown, "John George Walker,"
in *The Confederate General,* 6 vols., ed. William C. Davis (National Historical Society,
1991), 6:88–89; J. P. Blessington, *The Campaigns of Walker's Texas Division* (1875;
reprint, Austin: State House Press, 1994).

14. Dr. Solomon A. Smith of Alexandria, Louisiana, was a close personal friend of
Lt. Gen. Edmund Kirby Smith and served on the general's staff for most of the war.
In October 1864 Dr. Smith replaced Dr. David W. Yandell as medical director of
the Trans-Mississippi Department. J. Woodfin Wilson, "Some Aspects of Medical
Services in the Trans-Mississippi Department of the Confederate States of America,
1863–1865," *North Louisiana Historical Association Journal* 12 (1981): 123–46; Parks,
Kirby Smith, 202, 419.

15. Prominent Kentucky physician David Wendell Yandell was appointed medical director of the Trans-Mississippi Department in November 1863. In September
1864 a minor dispute over rank with another surgeon resulted in his being replaced
by Solomon A. Smith. Nancy Disher Baird, *David Wendell Yandell: Physician of Old
Louisville* (Lexington: University Press of Kentucky, 1978).

16. Dr. George W. Riggins of Missouri served as one of the principal surgeons at
the general hospital in Shreveport. *Service Records of Confederate General and Staff
Officers,* series M331, roll 212.

17. Col. William A. Broadwell was chief of the Cotton Bureau, instituted by
General Smith to regulate the sale of cotton both abroad and to the United States in
order to pay for foodstuffs, armaments, and matériel. Kerby, *Kirby Smith's
Confederacy,* 155–207; *Service Records of Confederate General and Staff Officers,* series
M331, roll 34.

18. The CSS *Missouri,* commissioned on September 12, 1863, was commanded by
Capt. Jonathan H. Carter. She was built in Shreveport for service on the Red River.
The vessel was 183 feet in length; 53 feet, 8 inches in width; and armed with four
heavy guns (one 11-inch, one 9-inch, and two 32-pounders). Her armor consisted of
railroad iron. The *Missouri* never fired a shot in anger against the enemy, but she did
have the distinction of being the last Confederate ironclad to surrender. William N.
Still, "The Confederate Ironclad *Missouri,*" *Louisiana Studies* (summer 1965): 101–10.

19. George C. Catlett was surgeon in charge of the military hospital at Shreveport.
Service Records of Confederate General and Staff Officers, series M331, roll 51.

20. Charles C. Greene was captain of ordnance and assistant to the chief of ordnance in the Trans-Mississippi Department. Maj. Gen. Benjamin Huger was chief
of the ordnance bureau for the department. *Service Records of Confederate General
and Staff Officers,* series M331, roll 111; William R. Geise, "Kirby Smith's War
Department, 1864," *Military History of Texas and the Southwest* 15 (1979): 45–62.

21. Maj. Thomas G. Rhett was chief of ordnance and artillery for the department.
Rhett was directly subordinate to General Smith rather than to Huger, and the district chiefs, who were primarily responsible to their individual district commanders,
reported to Major Rhett. *Service Records of Confederate General and Staff Officers,* series
M331, roll 210; Geise, "Kirby Smith's War Department," 51.

22. Maj. William H. Haynes was quartermaster and chief of the Clothing Bureau

for the Trans-Mississippi Department. Haynes's able and efficient management of the various textile mills and shoe factories throughout the department resulted in Smith's soldiers being some of the best-dressed troops in the Confederate army. *Service Records of Confederate General and Staff Officers,* series M331, roll 122; Kerby, *Kirby Smith's Confederacy,* 380–81.

23. Cal M. Watson was a forty-nine-year-old planter residing in Caddo Parish, Louisiana. U.S. Census, 1860, Population, Caddo Parrish, Louisiana.

24. Aaron H. Conrow was a representative to the Confederate Congress from the state of Missouri. At war's end, Conrow, Brig. Gen. Mosby M. Parsons, and Col. Austin Standish fled to Mexico, where a few weeks later they were captured and killed by Mexican bandits. Robert E. Miller, "General Mosby M. Parsons: Missouri Secessionist," *Missouri Historical Review* 80 (1985): 35–57; "The Death of General M. M. Parsons," *Daily Tribune,* Feb. 2, 1868.

25. Dr. Thomas G. Polk served as a volunteer aide-de-camp to Brig. Gen. James C. Tappan during the Red River campaign. *O.R.,* 34(1):606.

26. Lucien C. Gause was colonel of the 32d Arkansas Infantry. Against Steele's Camden Expedition, Gause commanded a brigade consisting of the 26th, 32d, and 36th Arkansas Infantry Regiments. Stewart Sifakis, *Compendium of the Confederate Armies: Arkansas* (New York: Facts on File, 1992), 115; *O.R.,* 34(1):786.

27. Maj. Gen. Nathaniel Prentiss Banks was commander of the Department of the Gulf and leader of the Federal thrust up the Red River in the spring of 1864. A former member of the U.S. House of Representatives from Massachusetts and governor of that state, Banks was the consummate politician-general. Ezra Warner, *Generals in Blue* (Baton Rouge: Louisiana State University Press, 1964), 17–18; Johnson, *Red River Campaign,* 19–20.

28. At Sabine Crossroads, three miles south of Mansfield, Maj. Gen. Richard Taylor's combined force of almost 9,000 Texas and Louisiana troops attacked the head of Nathaniel Banks's massive column. In less than three hours, the vanguard of the Federal army was routed. The congested arrangement of Union infantry, artillery, and wagon trains created a massive roadblock that led to the capture of twenty cannon, 156 wagons, and over 1,000 prisoners by the Confederates. Total Union losses amounted to 2,235 men out of almost 12,000 engaged. Confederate losses in killed and wounded totaled close to 1,000. For the Southerners, the battle was one of the most decisive in the Trans-Mississippi theater, and it marked the beginning of the end for the Red River campaign.

29. Brig. Gen. Alfred Mouton, son of a former governor of Louisiana, graduated from West Point in the class of 1850. He commanded a brigade of infantry in the Bayou Lafourche and Bayou Teche regions of Louisiana during 1863. Richard Taylor considered Mouton one of his best officers. On April 8, 1864, Mouton was killed while leading his infantry division in the opening stages of the battle of Mansfield. William Arceneaux, *Acadian General: Alfred Mouton and the Civil War* (Lafayette: University of Southwestern Louisiana Press, 1981).

30. Brig. Gen. Camille Armand Jules Marie de Polignac epitomized the scholar-soldier. An excellent mathematician, Polignac served in the French army during the Crimean War. He befriended P. G. T. Beauregard during a visit to America and offered his services to the Confederacy. Polignac assumed command of Mouton's division when that officer was killed at the battle of Mansfield. Promoted to major

general in June 1864, he continued his service in Louisiana until early 1865, when he returned to France. Jeff Kinard, *Lafayette of the South: Prince Camille de Polignac and the American Civil War* (College Station: Texas A&M University Press, 2001); Alwyn Barr, *Polignac's Texas Brigade* (Houston: Texas Gulf Coast Historical Association, 1964).

31. Brig. Gen. Thomas "Tom" Green was Richard Taylor's most competent and respected cavalry officer. Commanding a division of horse during the Red River campaign, he was decapitated by a projectile fired from a Federal gunboat at the battle of Blair's Landing. Jack D. Welsh, *Medical Histories of Confederate Generals* (Kent, Ohio: Kent State University Press, 1995), 87.

32. The arrival of Brig. Gen. Thomas Churchill's infantry division convinced General Taylor his success at Mansfield could be replicated. Throughout the day of April 9, he pushed his victorious Trans-Mississippians until they caught up with Banks's demoralized refugees late in the afternoon at Pleasant Hill. Taylor planned to strike the Federal center with Walker's Texans, while Churchill's Arkansas and Missouri infantry turned the Union left. The tactic met with some initial success, and a repeat of the previous day's results seemed imminent until a Federal counter-attack caught Parsons's Missourians with their flank "in the air," resulting in a pre-cipitous retreat. It was this retrograde movement that caught McPheeters by surprise. The repulse of Taylor's attack did little to bolster Banks's resolve; the next morning he gave up all designs on Shreveport and continued his retreat south.

33. In his official report on the engagement at Pleasant Hill, Thomas Churchill made special mention of McPheeters's commitment to the wounded: "To my chief surgeon, Dr. W. M. McPheeters, I am especially indebted for the energy displayed upon the battlefield in attending and caring for the wounded of the command. He was ever to be found at his post, and with his usual kindness of heart relieving the wants of our gallant wounded." *O.R.,* 43(1):478.

34. Texan James Knox Campbell was chief purchasing commissary for the Northern Subdistrict of Texas. *General Service Records of Confederate General and Staff Officers,* series M331, roll 55.

35. Joseph H. Kelly, a former colonel in the Missouri State Guard, was at various times assistant adjutant general and assistant inspector general on Mosby Parsons's staff. *General Service Records of Confederate General and Staff Officers,* series M331, roll 146.

36. Cpl. Joseph P. Blessington of the 16th Texas Infantry was slightly wounded in the groin during the battle of Pleasant Hill. Making his way to the field hospital, he was shocked by the grisly scene that befell him: "It resembles a butcher's shamble, with maimed and bloody men lying on all sides—some with their arms off; some with their legs off; some awaiting their time, while the doctors, with upturned cuffs and bloody hands, are flourishing their knives and saws, and piles of bloody-looking limbs are strewn around them, while some who have died on the dissecting table, add to the ghastly picture." Blessington, *Campaigns of Walker's Texas Division,* 201.

37. Drs. Joseph T. Scott, Philo O. Hooper, W. M. Lawrence, and G. W. Lawrence constituted the Army Medical Board for the Trans-Mississippi Department, which was responsible "for examination of [medical] officers in the Trans-Mississippi department, and applicants for appointment in the medical depart-ment invited by the secretary of war." Dr. Hooper, president of the board, later became the first dean of the College of Medicine at the University of Arkansas and vice president of the American Medical Association. John M. Harrell, *Arkansas,* vol.

10 of *Confederate Military History,* ed. Clement A. Evans (1899; reprint, Secaucus, N.J.: Blue and Grey, n.d.), 377; R. French Stone, *Biography of Eminent American Physicians and Surgeons* (Indianapolis: Carlon and Hollenbeck, 1894), 221; Wilson, "Medical Services in the Trans-Mississippi Department," 123–46.

38. Henry M. Clark had been division inspector for Sterling Price since 1862. In April 1863 he was promoted to major and appointed assistant inspector general for the District of Arkansas. *Service Records of Confederate General and Staff Officers,* series M331, roll 56.

39. D. Herndon Lindsay was captain of Company H, 9th Missouri Infantry. *CSR-Mo.,* 9th Infantry, roll 147.

40. Dr. W. A. McPheeters was surgeon of the Consolidated Crescent Regiment of Louisiana. On April 17, 1864 he was appointed chief surgeon of Brig. Gen. Henry Gray's brigade of Louisiana infantry. Maj. Silas Grisamore, assistant quartermaster of the brigade, described McPheeters as "a huge mountain of flesh and jollity, familiarly known as "Big Medicine." Arthur W. Bergeron, ed. *The Civil War Reminiscences of Major Silas T. Grisamore, CSA.* (Baton Rouge: Louisiana State University Press, 1993), 152, 167.

41. Assistant Surgeon Henry C. Rogers was the medical purveyor at Shreveport. *Service Records of Confederate General and Staff Officers,* series M331, roll 215.

42. Following a series of defeats in his ill-fated Camden Expedition, Maj. Gen. Frederick Steele retreated toward Little Rock on April 26. Four days later, while crossing his army over the flooded Saline River, Steele fought a brutal delaying action with the pursuing Confederates at Jenkins' Ferry. Successfully extricating his army from the Rebel trap on Saline River, Steele burned most of his wagons and equipment and marched pell-mell for Little Rock. Warner, *Generals in Blue,* 474–75.

43. Dr. J. M. Sandridge resided in Bossier Parish, Louisiana. Throughout the diary, McPheeters spells Dr. Sandridge's surname as either "Standish" or "Sandidge." U.S. Census, 1860, Population, Bossier Parrish, Louisiana.

44. McPheeters is referring to the battle of Poison Spring, one of Steele's defeats during the Camden Expedition. Three Confederate cavalry divisions (about 3,000 troopers with twelve cannon) under the command of Brig. Gens. Samuel B. Maxey and John S. Marmaduke attacked an enemy foraging party. The Federal force was routed, with a loss of 301 men, 170 wagons, and their four cannon. The preponderance of Union casualties occurred in the 1st Kansas Colored Infantry (117 killed, 65 wounded), for many of its black soldiers were shown no quarter. Edwin C. Bearss, *Steele's Retreat from Camden and the Battle of Jenkins' Ferry* (Little Rock: Pioneer, 1966), 15–41; Gregory J. W. Urwin, "'We Cannot Treat Negroes . . . as Prisoners of War': Racial Atrocities and Reprisals in Civil War Arkansas," in *Civil War Arkansas: Beyond Battles and Leaders,* ed. Anne J. Bailey and Daniel E. Sutherland (Fayetteville: University of Arkansas Press, 2000), 213–29.

45. General Smith had summoned Brig. Gen. Samuel Bell Maxey and two brigades of cavalry from the Indian Territory to assist Price in delaying Steele's advance. The 2d Indian Brigade, led by Col. Tandy Walker, consisted of the 1st and 2d Choctaw Regiments. Bearss, *Steele's Retreat,* 40.

46. A West Point graduate (class of 1846), Brig. Gen. Samuel Bell Maxey commanded all Confederate forces in the Indian Territory. Anne Bailey, "Samuel Bell Maxey," in *Confederate General,* 4:170–73.

47. McPheeters is referring to the battle of Marks' Mill, another Union defeat during the Camden Expedition. On April 25 two Confederate cavalry divisions under Brig. Gens. James F. Fagan and Joseph O. Shelby attacked a Union wagon train near Marks' Mill, thirty miles northeast of Camden. The running battle, which lasted five hours, was a stunning defeat for the Federals, who incurred losses approaching 1,300 men—most of whom were captured. Bearss, *Steele's Retreat,* 42–84.

48. Early on the morning of April 30, in the flooded bottoms of the Saline River, one mile south of Jenkins' Ferry, Confederate pursuit of Steele's column ended. Here, as his wagon train struggled to cross the river over a hastily erected pontoon bridge, Steele deployed Frederick Salomon's Union infantry division as a rear guard. Sensing an opportunity to bag the Federal force, Smith and Price fed the foot-weary Confederate infantry divisions into the battle as they came onto the field. In a series of piecemeal assaults, Churchill's Arkansans followed by Parsons's Missourians and finally Walker's Texans hammered the compact Federal line ensconced in a belt of flooded timber. Slogging through mud and water, at times up to their knees, the Confederate attackers were checked in an open field fronting the Federal position. The submerged battlefield precluded deployment of artillery, which forced the contest to be decided by small-arms fire. After four hours of vicious combat, the Federals withdrew, destroyed their pontoon bridge, and effected an escape. A mix-up in orders had directed the Confederate pontoon train toward Shreveport; thus no Confederate pursuit was attempted. Confederate losses were heavy, especially within the officer corps. Among the killed and wounded were Brig. Gens. William R. Scurry, Horace Randal, and Thomas N. Waul. Bearss, *Steele's Retreat from Camden and the Battle of Jenkins' Ferry,* 114–62.

49. Brig. Gen. William Read Scurry led a brigade of Texans in John G. Walker's infantry division at the battles of Mansfield, Pleasant Hill, and Jenkins' Ferry. He was mortally wounded at Jenkins' Ferry while leading his men into action. Lawrence L. Hewitt, "William Read Scurry," in *Confederate General,* 5:132–35; "General William Read Scurry," Confederate Research Center, Hillsboro, Tex.

50. Hiram L. Grinstead was colonel of the 33d Arkansas Infantry in James Tappan's brigade. Sifakis, *Compendium of the Confederate Armies: Arkansas,* 116.

51. John B. Cocke was colonel of the 39th Arkansas (Hawthorn's) Infantry in Brig. Gen. Alexander Hawthorn's brigade. Sifakis, *Compendium of the Confederate Armies: Arkansas,* 124.

52. J. W. "Watt" Gibson, a member of Company A, 9th Missouri Infantry, assisted in removing the dead from the battlefield at Jenkins' Ferry and left this description of the gruesome task: "I was detailed to help bury the dead. Several large wagons were provided with six mules and a driver to each wagon. Four men to each wagon loaded the bodies in. The end gate was taken out of the bed. Two men stood on each side of a body. One on each side held an arm and one on each side a leg. The second swing the body went in head foremost. When the wagon was full it was driven off to where another squad had prepared a long trench into which the bodies were thrown and covered up. It required most of the day to complete our work." J. W. Gibson, *Recollections of a Pioneer* (St. Joseph, Mo.: Nelson-Hanne, 1912), 155.

53. The casualty rate for both sides exceeded 15 percent, a grim testament to the ferocity of the engagement, particularly if one considers the number of men engaged (approximately 6,000 Confederates and 4,000 Federals), the relatively short duration of the battle (approximately four hours), and the virtual absence of artillery. *O.R.,*

34(1):557; Bearss, *Steele's Retreat*, 161.

54. Dr. William L. Nicholson, surgeon for the 29th Iowa Infantry, remained behind to care for the wounded Federals. He described the encounter with his colleagues in gray: "The rebel surgeons and officers who came along assured us that just as soon as their supply trains came up we would be cared for, but for the condition of the roads and the rapid advance of their army in pursuit of ours, the train was a long way behind. . . . When the Confederate surgeons had completed their own work they came and gave us every assistance in their power, and furnished instruments, medicine, dressings and chloroform." William L. Nicholson, "The Engagement at Jenkin's Ferry," *Annals of Iowa* 9 (1914): 505–19.

55. McPheeters's tireless efforts upon the field of Jenkins' Ferry did not go unnoticed. In his official report of the battle, Thomas J. Churchill wrote: "To my chief surgeon, Dr. W. M. McPheeters, I am especially indebted for the prompt and faithful discharge of his duties in the field, as through his untiring zeal and unceasing attention to the wounded none were left uncared for." *O.R., 34*(1):799.

56. On May 1 Pvt. J. W. Gibson was ordered to assist the surgeons at Jenkins' Ferry in their operations. Gibson recalled his eye-opening experience:

> Next day was the doctor's day. I was ordered to go along and assist. Three doctors went together, and over each wounded man they held a consultation. If two of them said amputate, it was done at once. When they came to a man with a wound on his head they would smile and say, "We had better not amputate in this case." It seemed to me they made many useless amputations.
>
> One doctor carried a knife with a long thin blade. He would draw this around the limb and cut the flesh to the bone. The second had a saw with which he sawed the bone. The third had a pair of forceps with which he clasped the blood vessels, and a needle with which he sewed the skin over the wound.
>
> The first man I saw them work upon was a Union soldier. All three said his leg must come off. They began administering chloroform, but he was a very hard subject and fought it bitterly. They asked me to hold his head and I did so. As soon as he was quiet they went to work on him. When I saw how they cut and slashed I let his head loose. I thought if he wanted to wake up and fight he should have a fair chance. I told the doctors that I did not go to war to hold men while they butchered them . . . but the doctors laughed at me and said they would soon teach me to be a surgeon.

Gibson, *Recollections of a Pioneer*, 155–56.

57. In April 1863 the Confederate Congress passed a bill for the election of representatives in Missouri and other occupied Confederate states. As a means of generating more public interest, particularly among troops in the field, Gov. Thomas C. Reynolds delayed Missouri's November 1863 election until May 1864. Thomas L. Snead handily won election as representative from Missouri's first congressional district. Robert E. Miller, "Proud Confederate: Thomas Lowndes Snead of Missouri," *Missouri Historical Review* 79 (Jan. 1985): 167–91; Robert E. Miller, "One of the Ruling Class, Thomas Caute Reynolds: Second Confederate Governor of Missouri,"

Missouri Historical Review 80 (July 1986): 428–41; Kerby, *Kirby Smith's Confederacy,* 150–52.

58. The "Dr. Parsons" McPheeters mentions could be either Homer Lee Parsons, brigade surgeon for Col. William. F. Slemons's Arkansas cavalry brigade, or Dr. John Durant Parsons, assistant surgeon for the 20th Texas (Bass's) Cavalry. Some evidence suggests that members of the 20th Texas Cavalry were in the area. *Service Records of Confederate General and Staff Officers,* series M331, roll 193.

59. "Col. Bass" may have been either Thomas Coke Bass, colonel of the 20th Texas Cavalry, who apparently accompanied Brig. Gen. Samuel B. Maxey to Arkansas in April and remained in the area after Maxey returned with his two cavalry brigades to the Indian Territory, or John J. Bass, a wealthy planter residing in Ouachita County. *Service Records of Confederate General and Staff Officers,* series M331, roll 18; U.S. Census, 1860, Population, Ouachita County, Arkansas.

60. Trusten Polk was elected governor of Missouri in 1856, and soon after his inauguration the state legislature elected him to the U.S. Senate. He was expelled from the Senate in 1862 for his Confederate sympathies, after which he served as a Confederate military judge in the Department of Mississippi. In September 1863 Polk was captured in Mississippi and confined on Johnson's Island, Ohio, in Lake Erie. Exchanged three months later, he was assigned to the Trans-Mississippi Department and assumed his role as presiding judge of the military court. Howard L. Conrad, *Encyclopedia of the History of Missouri,* 6 vols. (St. Louis: Southern History, 1901), 5:182–83; *Service Records of Confederate General and Staff Officers,* series M331, roll 199.

7. A SUMMER'S RESPITE

1. Robert L. Kerby, *Kirby Smith's Confederacy: The Trans-Mississippi South, 1863–1865* (New York: Columbia University Press, 1972), 331–37; Albert Castel, *General Sterling Price and the Civil War in the West* (Baton Rouge: Louisiana State University Press, 1968), 196–203; Joseph Howard Parks, *General Edmund Kirby Smith, CSA* (Baton Rouge: Louisiana State University Press, 1954), 420–33.

2. With the assistance of the ironclad gunboat CSS *Albemarle,* Confederate forces under Brig. Gen. Robert F. Hoke captured Plymouth, North Carolina, on April 20, 1864. The Federal losses noted by McPheeters were correct.

3. Col. G. W. Sappington was a purchasing agent for Confederate forces in the Trans-Mississippi Department. *O.R.,* 22(2):1144.

4. This is probably Lt. William C. Gibson of the 15th Louisiana Cavalry Battalion. Janet B. Hewett, ed., *The Roster of Confederate Soldiers,* 16 vols. (Wilmington, N.C.: Broadfoot, 1995), vol. 6.

5. McPheeters is likely referring to the battle of the Wilderness, May 5–6, 1864.

6. Dr. Beletha Powell, who began the war as surgeon of the 4th Louisiana Infantry Battalion, directed the hospital at Mount Lebanon, Louisiana. *Service Records for Confederate General and Staff Officers,* series M331, roll 201, National Archives (microfilm).

7. Twenty-two-year-old Capt. Benjamin S. Johnson served as assistant adjutant general on the staff of Maj. Gen. Thomas J. Churchill. *Service Records for Confederate General and Staff Officers,* series M331, roll 141.

8. Malcolm Graham was a private in Company G, 9th Missouri Infantry. *CSR-Mo.,* 9th Infantry, roll 147.

9. McPheeters is probably referring to the battle of Spotsylvania Courthouse, May 8–21, 1864.

10. Capt. Theodore T. Taylor served as assistant inspector general to Maj. Gen. Sterling Price during the Missouri Expedition. *Service Records for Confederate General and Staff Officers,* series M331, roll 243; *O.R.,* 41(2):1090.

11. Dr. Benjamin A. Jandon, surgeon for the 26th Arkansas Infantry, replaced McPheeters as chief surgeon of Thomas Churchill's division when McPheeters was selected as chief surgeon for Sterling Price's raid into Missouri. Dr. David S. Williams was regimental surgeon for the 33d Arkansas Infantry and later appointed chief surgeon for Brig. Gen. James C. Tappan's Arkansas infantry brigade. *O.R.,* 41(3):924, 1065; *Service Records for Confederate General and Staff Officers,* series M331, roll 268.

12. This is probably Capt. L. M. Nutt, a former associate of Thomas Churchill, who commanded a company of Louisiana cavalry in Brig. Gen. Hiram Granbury's brigade in the Army of Tennessee. *O.R.,* 39(2):852.

13. From May 23 to June 2, 1864, Col. Colton Greene of Brig. Gen. John S. Marmaduke's cavalry division operated along the Mississippi River in southeastern Arkansas. During this time, his artillery engaged twenty-one Federal vessels of various descriptions, capturing the steamers *Lebanon* and *Clara Eames,* burning two other vessels, and badly damaging eleven others. *O.R.,* 34(1):950–54.

14. A Virginia Military Institute graduate, Lt. William Fulton Wright served as aide-de-camp to Thomas Churchill. *Service Records for Confederate General and Staff Officers,* series M331, roll 274.

15. This is probably John C. Wright, colonel of the 12th Arkansas Cavalry. Colonel Wright's home was located in Union County, Arkansas, not far from Camp Grinsted. *CSR-Ark.,* 12th Cavalry, roll 37; U.S. Census, 1860, Population, Union County, Arkansas.

16. Capt. Charles E. Royston was an aide-de-camp to Thomas Churchill, while Capt. Charles E. Mitchell served in the same capacity on James Tappan's staff. *Service Records for Confederate General and Staff Officers,* series M331, roll 216, 179.

17. The message was an address by Pres. Jefferson Davis published on February 10, 1864, as General Orders No. 19. The order was "a general acknowledgement" to the "Soldiers of the Army of the Confederate States" recognizing their "patriotism . . . devotion and self-sacrifice . . . of the last two years" and assuring them that in 1864 "success awaits us in our holy struggle for liberty and independence, and for the preservation of all that renders life desirable to honorable men." *O.R.,* 32(2):711–13.

18. "Capt. Reynolds" may be either James H. Reynolds, division quartermaster for Mosby Parson's two infantry brigades, or D. W. Reynolds, captain of Company G, 12th Missouri Infantry. *Service Records of Confederate General and Staff Officers,* series M331, roll 209; Register of Officers, Parsons Division Missouri Volunteers, MHS.

19. Capt. Charles E. Kidder was ordnance officer for Thomas Churchill's division. Later that year he was appointed divisional assistant adjutant general. *Service Records for Confederate General and Staff Officers,* series M331, roll 149.

20. Dr. Edwin E. Harris, surgeon for the 9th Missouri Infantry, died of liver failure just a few months later on September 10. "Henry Dye Case Book," Special Collection, University of Arkansas for Medical Sciences, Little Rock.

21. Col. Colton Greene commanded a brigade in John S. Marmaduke's division. After Marmaduke's capture at the battle of Mine Creek, Greene assumed command of John B. Clark's brigade. In 1865 Lt. Gen. E. Kirby Smith promoted Greene to brigadier general. John C. Moore, *Missouri,* vol 12 of *Confederate Military History,* ed. Clement A. Evans (1899; reprint, Secaucus, N.J.: Blue and Grey, n.d.), 302–3.

22. Maj. Charles B. Moore was chief quartermaster for Thomas Churchill's division. On October 14, 1864, he was appointed chief quartermaster for the District of Arkansas. *Service Records for Confederate General and Staff Officers,* series M331, roll 181.

23. Capt. William D. Blocher commanded the 5th Light Artillery Battalion attached to Thomas Churchill's division. The battalion consisted of Lesueur's and Ruffner's Missouri Batteries as well as McNally's, Marshall's, and West's Arkansas Batteries. Stewart Sifakis, *Compendium of the Confederate Armies: Arkansas* (New York: Facts on File, 1992), 37; *O.R.,* 41(3):968.

24. Maj. Thomas W. Newton was assistant inspector general of Marmaduke's division. Capt. Alex K. McLean was assistant quartermaster and field transportation inspector for Marmaduke. *Service Records for Confederate General and Staff Officers,* series M331, rolls 173, 186.

25. Son of a U.S. congressman and later Confederate representative, John Bullock Clark Jr. began the war in the 6th Missouri Infantry. From January 1863 until August 1864, he commanded an infantry brigade in the District of Arkansas. He would lead a cavalry brigade on Price's Missouri Raid, and upon Marmaduke's capture at the battle of Mine Creek, he assumed command of the cavalry division. Anne Bailey, "John Bullock Clark Jr.," in *The Confederate General,* 6 vols., ed. William C. Davis (National Historical Society, 1991), 1:194–95; Stewart Sifakis, *Compendium of the Confederate Armies: Missouri* (New York: Facts on File, 1992), 125–26.

26. Col. Robert G. Shaver commanded the 38th Arkansas Infantry and led that unit at the battles of Pleasant Hill and Jenkins' Ferry. Sifakis, *Compendium of the Confederate Armies: Arkansas,* 83, 119–20.

27. Dr. Edward L. Hamilton was assistant surgeon for Col. Charles L. Dawson's 19th Arkansas (Consolidated) Infantry. *Service Records for Confederate General and Staff Officers,* series M331, roll 115.

28. Retired major general John C. Frémont was nominated for the presidency in 1864 by a coalition of Radicals, Missouri Germans, and War Democrats. John Cochrane, also a retired brigadier general of the Union army, was Frémont's running mate. The ticket, however, was withdrawn in September 1864, and their support thrown to Abraham Lincoln. Ezra Warner, *Generals in Blue* (Baton Rouge: Louisiana State University Press, 1964), 86–87, 160–61.

29. Former medical inspector for the District of Arkansas, Dr. Charles M. Taylor was designated medical director of general hospitals for the Trans-Mississippi Department in 1864. *Service Records of Confederate General and Staff Officers,* series M331, roll 242.

30. McPheeters is referring to the battle of Brice's Crossroads, fought on June 10, 1864. Maj. Gen. Nathan Bedford Forrest and 3,500 Rebel cavalrymen attacked and routed a Union force of almost 8,000 under Brig. Gen. Samuel Sturgis. Forrest's troopers captured eighteen pieces of artillery and 250 wagons and inflicted 2,200 casualties while incurring losses of less than 500.

31. This speech resulted in Clement Vallandigham's arrest, imprisonment, and eventual banishment to the South.

32. On June 14, 1864, Lt. Gen. Leonidas Polk was struck by an artillery shell and killed instantly at Pine Mountain, Georgia.

33. Charles J. Turnbull, colonel of the 25th Arkansas Infantry, was transferred to the Trans-Mississippi Department and served in the inspector general's department; Col. Benjamin Alston was inspector general of the Trans-Mississippi Department. *O.R.*, 34(2):849.

34. Lt. Francis von Phul served as an aide-de-camp John S. Marmaduke. Crute, *Confederate Staff Officers*, 38, 132.

35. McPheeters is referring to Brig. Gen. Joseph O. Shelby's attack and destruction of the USS *Queen City* on June 24, 1864, at Clarendon, Arkansas, on the White River.

36. By the end of 1863, Confederate currency was severely depreciated. On February 17, 1864, the Confederate Congress, in an effort to reduce the amount of currency in circulation, passed a so-called Currency Act. The law stated "that the holders of all Treasury notes above the denomination of five dollars, not bearing interest, shall be allowed until the first day of April 1864, east of the Mississippi River, and until the first day of July 1864, west of the Mississippi River . . . to fund the same in registered bonds payable twenty years after their date, bearing interest at the rate of four percent." All notes of one hundred dollars not funded by the specified dates would "cease to be receivable in the payment of public dues," be subject to a tax of 33⅓ percent plus 10 percent per month, and "shall not be exchangeable for the new issue of Treasury notes provided for in this act." Notes of lesser denomination were made fundable at the rate of 66⅔ cents on the dollar or exchangeable for new notes at that rate until January 1, 1865. After that date, old notes not funded or exchanged were taxable at the rate of 100 percent. The newly issued Treasury notes, however, did not reach the Trans-Mississippi until October 1864. Claud E. Fuller, *Confederate Currency and Stamps* (Nashville: Parthenon, 1949), 114–15; Kerby, *Kirby Smith's Confederacy*, 386–91.

37. John L. Chandler was lieutenant colonel of the 7th Missouri Volunteer Cavalry and the Federal provost marshal general at Little Rock, Ark. *O.R.*, 41(4):465.

38. Dr. John H. Gaines was surgeon for the 24th Arkansas Infantry, which by July 1864 was a part of Dawson's Consolidated Infantry. John M. Harrell, *Arkansas*, vol. 10 of *Confederate Military History*, ed. Clement A. Evans (1899; reprint, Secaucus, N.J.: Blue and Grey, n.d.), 380.

39. McPheeters is referring to the battle of Kennesaw Mountain, which took place on June 27, 1864. A frontal assault on the entrenched Rebel positions resulted in over two thousand Yankee casualities. Among the mortally wounded was Col. Daniel McCook, who received his brigadier's commission the day before his death on July 17. Maj. Gen. Joseph Hooker was not killed.

40. Horace Jewell was Chaplain for the 33rd Arkansas (Grinstead's) Infantry regiment. *Service Records of Confederate General and Staff Officers*, series M331, roll 140.

41. The USS *Kearsarge* sank the Confederate raider CSS *Alabama* on June 19, 1864, off Cherbourg, France.

42. William Henry Seward was Lincoln's secretary of state, Montgomery Blair was postmaster general, Edward Bates was U.S. attorney general, and Salmon P. Chase was secretary of the treasury.

43. "Pitching quoits" refers to a game in which players toss a rope or ring of flattened metal at a peg in the ground, the object being to encircle it or come as close to it at possible.

44. Capt. Henry W. Pflager was chief of transportation and acting assistant quartermaster for Sterling Price's Army of Missouri. *Service Records of Confederate General and Staff Officers,* series, M331, roll 197.

45. H. W. McMillan was captain of Company H, 1st Arkansas (Crawford's) Cavalry. *CSR-Ark.,* 1st Cavalry, roll 2.

46. McPheeters is referring to Lt. Gen. Jubal Early's raid into Maryland, which threatened Baltimore and Washington, D.C., in July 1864.

47. Lt. Col. Cadwallader Polk commanded the 6th Trans-Mississippi Infantry as part of Alexander Hawthorn's Arkansas brigade. *O.R.,* 41(4):1164; Sifakis, *Compendium of the Confederate Armies: Arkansas,* 124.

48. Col. John Q. Burbridge commanded the 4th Missouri Cavalry in Marmaduke's division. Sifakis, *Compendium of the Confederate Armies: Missouri,* 95.

49. This is probably John L. Simpson, a corporal in Company A, Pindall's 9th Battalion of Missouri Sharpshooters. *CSR-Mo.,* 9th Battalion Sharpshooters, roll 149.

50. McPheeters is referring either to the battle of Peachtree Creek, fought on July 20, or the battle of Atlanta, fought on July 22, 1864.

8. THE GRAND EXPEDITION

1. Jerry Ponder, *General Sterling Price's 1864 Invasion of Missouri* (Mason, Tex.: Ponder Books, 1999), 1–13; Robert L. Kerby, *Kirby Smith's Confederacy: The Trans-Mississippi South, 1863–1865* (New York: Columbia University Press, 1972), 331–41; Albert Castel, *General Sterling Price and the Civil War in the West* (Baton Rouge: Louisiana State University Press, 1968), 196–203.

2. A native of Kentucky, Maj. Gen. Simon Bolivar Buckner figured prominently in both the Confederate Army of Tennessee and the Trans-Mississippi Department. In May 1864 he was transferred to the Trans-Mississippi Department to replace Lt. Gen. Richard Taylor as commander of the District of West Louisiana. Promoted to lieutenant general in September 1864, he commanded the District of Arkansas in April 1865 and surrendered the Trans-Mississippi Department in New Orleans on May 26, 1865. Arndt M. Stickles, *Simon Bolivar Buckner: Borderland Knight* (Chapel Hill: University of North Carolina Press, 1940.)

3. Alabama native John Horace Forney, a major general, commanded Maj. Gen. John G. Walker's old Texas division. Arthur W. Bergeron, "John Horace Forney," in *The Confederate General,* 6 vols., ed. William C. Davis (National Historical Society, 1991), 2:134–35.

4. A practicing attorney in St. Louis prior to the war, Matthew R. Cullen held the rank of colonel of cavalry; however, he served strictly as a member of the military court for the Trans-Mississipi Department. *Service Records of Confederate General and Staff Officers,* series M331, roll 67, National Archives (microfilm).

5. Brig. Gen. William Robertson Boggs, a Georgian by birth, served as Lt. Gen. E. Kirby Smith's chief of staff for several months until a dispute led to his resignation in the summer of 1864. Archie McDonald, "William Roberston Boggs," in *Confederate General,* 1:106–7.

6. At various times during the war, Maj. Manning M. Kimmel served as assistant adjutant general on the staffs of Brig. Gen. Ben McCulloch, Maj. Gen. Earl Van Dorn, Maj. Gen. Sterling Price, and Maj. Gen. John B. Magruder. *Service Records of Confederate General and Staff Officers,* series M331, roll 149.

7. While placing his private practice in Wittsburg, Arkansas, on hold, Dr. Isaac Folsom served as an assistant surgeon at St. John's Military Hospital in Little Rock and later at the general hospital in Lewisville, Arkansas. *Service Records of Confederate General and Staff Officers,* series M331, roll 95.

8. On August 5, 1864, Adm. David G. Farragut, with a fleet of fourteen ships and four monitors, steamed past Forts Gaines and Morgan, forced the ironclad CSS *Tennessee* to surrender, and generally defeated Confederate naval forces at the battle of Mobile Bay.

9. Col. Charles D. Anderson surrendered Fort Gaines, one of two installations guarding the entrance to Mobile Bay, and its six-hundred-man garrison on August 8, 1864, but Fort Morgan remained in Confederate hands. He was censured by his superiors for surrendering the fort without putting up a more valiant effort.

10. Maj. George A. Gallagher served as acting adjutant general on the staffs of Lt. Gen. Theophilus Holmes, Sterling Price, and E. Kirby Smith, respectively, between 1862 and 1865. *Service Records of Confederate General and Staff Officers,* series M331, roll 101.

11. Maj. A. S. Morgan was quartermaster of field transportation for the District of Arkansas with headquarters at Camden. *Service Records of Confederate General and Staff Officers,* series M331, roll 182.

12. Fanny Sandridge was the fourteen-year-old daughter of J. M. Sandridge of Collinsburg, Louisiana. U.S. Census, 1860, Population, Bossier Parish, Louisiana.

13. Dr. Joseph L. Moore, originally surgeon for the 4th Missouri Cavalry, served as brigade surgeon for Brig. Gen. John B. Clark Jr. during the raid. *Service Records for Confederate General and Staff Officers,* series M331, roll 181.

14. Varioloid is a mild but contagious type of smallpox found in those who have had smallpox or have been vaccinated for the disease.

15. Arthur W. Brinker was a member of Company C, 14th (Wood's) Missouri Cavalry Battalion in Col. Colton Greene's brigade. During the raid, Brinker was serving as assistant quartermaster for Brig. Gen. John S. Marmaduke's division. *CSR-Mo.,* Wood's Cavalry Regiment, series M332, roll 78.

16. Lt. Col. Robert C. Wood commanded the 14th (Wood's) Missouri Cavalry Battalion, also known as Wood's Partisan Rangers Battalion. At the end of Price's Missouri Raid, Wood was involved in an altercation with Lt. Col. Lauchlan A. MacLean and stabbed him to death. Stewart Sifakis, *Compendium of the Confederate Armies: Missouri* (New York: Facts on File, 1992), 102; *Service Records of Confederate General and Staff Officers,* series M331, roll 161.

17. In Chicago the Democratic Party nominated George B. McClellan for president on August 31, 1864.

18. Gen. John Bell Hood evacuated Atlanta on September 1, 1864. Maj. Gen. William T. Sherman's army occupied the city the following day.

19. By the time of Price's raid, M. Jeff Thompson, known as the "Swamp Fox," had achieved celebrity status for his martial exploits. He assumed command of one of Brig. Gen. J. O. Shelby's brigades and performed admirably in this capacity. In

1865 Thompson was named commander of the Northern Subdistrict of Arkansas. M. Jeff Thompson, *The Civil War Reminiscences of General M. Jeff Thompson*, ed. Donal J. Stanton, Goodwin F. Berquist, and Paul C. Bowers (Dayton, Ohio: Morningside, 1988).

20. At Pilot Knob, Price refused to bypass the nine hundred occupants of Fort Davidson and its sixteen artillery pieces. Instead, he ordered a direct assault by Marmaduke's and Maj. Gen. James Fagan's cavalry divisions. The ill-advised attack resulted in over five hundred Confederate casualties, while losses to the Federals were less than one hundred. Following this setback, Price realized the futility of capturing St. Louis; Jefferson City became his new objective. Albert Castel, *General Sterling Price and the Civil War in the West* (Baton Rouge: Louisiana State University Press, 1968), 210–21.

21. The Union commander at Fort Davidson, Brig. Gen. Thomas Ewing Jr., stealthily evacuated the fort at 3:00 A.M. Shortly after their departure, a slow-burning fuse detonated the powder magazine. Amazingly, the Rebels believed the tremendous explosion to be accidental and fully expected the garrison's surrender at daylight. Ibid., 216–18.

22. Dr. Seymour D. Carpenter served on the staff of Brig. Gen. Thomas Ewing Jr. as Medical Director of the District of St. Louis. *O.R.*, 41(3): 553.

23. David Shanks was colonel of the 12th Missouri Cavalry, but during Price's Missouri Raid he commanded Shelby's Iron Brigade. On October 6, while forcing a crossing at Prince's Ford on the Osage River, Shanks received a mortal wound. *O.R.*, 41(1):663.

24. This may be Dr. John F. McGregor, former surgeon for the 16th Texas Infantry. Later that year he was designated post surgeon at Tyler, Texas. Isaac N. Hedgpeth was former colonel of the 6th Missouri Infantry, but his exact function in October 1864 remains unclear. *Service Records of Confederate General and Staff Officers*, series M331, roll 171; *CSR-Mo.*, 6th Infantry, roll 135.

25. James R. Shaler, formerly colonel of the 27th Arkansas Infantry and assistant adjutant general to E. Kirby Smith, was inspector general for the District of Arkansas. *Service Records of Confederate General and Staff Officers*, series M331, roll 223.

26. McPheeters is probably referring to the battles of Peeble's Farm and Fort Harrison (September 29–October 2, 1864), which took place along the Petersburg and Richmond fronts respectively.

27. Price's march along the Missouri River was slow, providing the Yankees a chance to concentrate. Maj. Gen. William S. Rosecrans, commanding the Department of the Missouri at St. Louis, sent a force of 2,000 men under the command of Maj. Gen. James G. Blunt in pursuit from Lexington while 4,500 cavalry under Maj. Gen. Alfred Pleasonton and 9,000 infantry led by Maj. Gen. A. J. Smith followed from St. Louis. Howard Monnett, *Action before Westport: 1864* (Boulder: University Press of Colorado, 1995).

28. Maj. Gen. James G. Blunt had garnered a reputation in Arkansas, Missouri, and the Indian Territory as a brash and fearless fighter. James H. "Jim" Lane, U.S. senator and jayhawker from Kansas, served as an aide to Blunt. Commanding the first brigade of Blunt's cavalry division was another Kansas raider, Col. Charles R. "Doc" Jennison. McPheeters's reference to "scoundrels" stems from the harsh depredations exacted upon the pro-Southern populace of western Missouri by these men and their com-

mands. Richard J. Hinton, *Rebel Invasion of Missouri and Kansas* (1865; reprint, Ottawa: Kansas Heritage Press, 1994), 84–91; Albert Castel, *A Frontier State at War: Kansas, 1861–1865* (Ithaca, N.Y.: Cornell University Press, 1958), 37–64.

29. Former U. S. Senator from Illinois and Minnesota, Brig. Gen. James Shields met defeat at the hands of "Stonewall" Jackson in the Shenandoah Valley during 1862. Shields resigned from the army in March 1863 and took up residence near Carrollton, Mo. Ezra J. Warner, *Generals in Blue* (Baton Rouge: Louisiana State University Press, 1964), 444–45.

30. McPheeters mistakenly identified Maj. Gen. David Hunter as one of the opposing Union officers. Although Hunter had been commander of the Department of Kansas until April 1862, in October 1864 he was in charge of the Department of West Virginia. *O.R.,* 8(1):1, 37(1):1.

31. Following the engagement at the Little Blue River, James P. Erickson, surgeon for the 16th Kansas Volunteer Cavalry, was left in charge of the Federal wounded at Independence, Missouri. *O.R.,* 41(1):551.

32. During Price's Missouri Raid, Dr. John H. McMurry was surgeon for the 7th Missouri Cavalry. *Service Records of Confederate General and Staff Officers,* series M331, roll 174.

33. Following his defeat at Chickamauga, Maj. Gen. William Starke Rosecrans was removed from command of the Department of the Cumberland in October 1863 and appointed commander of the Department of Missouri the following January. Failure to destroy Sterling Price's column during the Missouri Expedition led to his second termination as a departmental commander in December 1864. Ezra J. Warner, *Generals in Blue* (Baton Rouge: Louisiana State University Press, 1964), 410–11.

34. Between Independence and Westport, Shelby's division took the van, followed by Marmaduke, with Fagan bringing up the rear. Confronted by Blunt's cavalry division, Shelby skillfully forced a crossing of the Big Blue River at Byram's Ford and cleared the way for safe passage of Price's large wagon train. While Shelby's men met success at Byram's Ford, the other two divisions did not fare as well. Maj. Gen. Alfred Pleasonton's Union cavalry force crossed the Little Blue River, bloodied one of Fagan's brigades (Brig. Gen. William L. Cabell's), and occupied Independence. A few miles west of that town, Marmaduke's division temporarily checked the Federal pursuit. Feeling the noose tighten, Price abandoned his designs on Kansas City and ordered his wagon train south. Monnett, *Action before Westport.*

35. Dr. Caleb Winfrey was the surgeon for Col. David Shanks's 12th Missouri Cavalry. *Service Records of Confederate General and Staff Officers,* series M331, roll 271.

36. In order to buy time for the wagon train's escape, Price ordered Shelby to attack Maj. Gen. Samuel R. Curtis's Army of the Border along Brush Creek south of Westport. The day's fighting consisted of a series of charges and countercharges with neither side gaining a decided advantage. Simultaneously, Marmaduke attempted to hold Pleasonton in check at Byram's Ford on the Big Blue River. The Federal pressure proved too much, and after three hours of desperate fighting, Pleasonton scattered Marmaduke's troopers and gained Shelby's rear. Trapped between two armies, each outnumbering his own by more than two to one, Shelby was forced to cut his way out and "make a run for it." The battle of Westport was the largest engagement in the Civil War west of the Mississippi River and turned Price's raid into an ignominious retreat. Monnett, *Action before Westport.*

37. At Mine Creek, Kansas, two brigades of Union cavalry overtook the rear of the Confederate column. Marmaduke's and Fagan's divisions, stalled by their wagons crossing the ford, formed a line of battle along the creek's northern bank. In what has been described as the largest cavalry charge of the war, the Confederates were overrun, and almost six hundred men, including Generals Marmaduke and Cabell, were captured. Shelby's division arrived in time to fight a delaying action as the remnants of Marmaduke's and Fagan's divisions streamed southward. The scenario was repeated at Little Osage River and again at the crossing of the Marmiton. Price's day-long effort to save the ponderous wagon train covered more than twenty miles and practically destroyed his army. That evening, after realizing the futility of further safeguarding the wagons, Price ordered most of them burned. Lumir F. Buresh, *October 25th and the Battle of Mine Creek* (Kansas City, Mo.: Lowell Press, 1977), 112–80.

38. Following the battle of Newtonia, Federal pursuit of Price's force ceased.

39. John Ross was principal chief of the Cherokee Nation. Steve Cottrell, *Civil War in the Indian Territory* (Gretna, La.: Pelican, 1995), 15–16, 47.

40. Captured in Missouri in May 1863, Col. Wedig von Schmelling spent nearly four months in military prisons before being exchanged and appointed as an aide de camp to Price. *Service Records of Confederate General and Staff Officers,* series M331, roll 255.

41. A shortage of ambulances prompted McPheeters to petition General Price for an order authorizing medical officers to comandeer all wagons necessary for the transportation of the wounded. See Appendix, "Extant Reports," Item 5.

42. "Dr. Johnson" may have been either Jesse W. Johnson, surgeon for Col James C. Monroe's 1st Arkansas Cavalry, but who served with Colton Greene's 3d Missouri Cavalry during the expedition, or Benjamin F. Johnson, surgeon of the 10th Missouri Cavalry. *Service Records of Confederate General and Staff Officers,* series M331, roll 141.

43. Dr. Homer Lee Parsons was chief surgeon for Col. William. F. Slemons's Arkansas cavalry brigade. *Service Records of Confederate General and Staff Officers,* series M331, roll 193.

44. Leader of the pro-Confederate faction of the Cherokee tribe, Stand Watie was elected colonel of the 1st Cherokee Mounted Rifles in 1861. In 1864 he was promoted to brigadier general, the only American Indian to hold this rank in the Confederate army. Frank Cunningham, *General Stand Watie's Confederate Indians* (San Antonio: Naylor, 1959).

45. At the outbreak of the Civil War, Douglas Hancock Cooper was U.S. agent to the Choctaw Nation in the Indian Territory. Cooper persuaded members of the "Five Civilized Tribes" to join the Confederate army, which resulted in his commission as colonel of the 1st Choctaw and Chickasaw Mounted Rifles, rising later to the rank of brigadier general. His wartime tenure was spent entirely in the Indian Territory. Anne Bailey, "Douglas Hancock Cooper," in *Confederate General,* 2:26–27.

46. Dr. W. J. McCain was an assistant surgeon on the staff of Brig. Gen. Douglas H. Cooper. *Service Records of Confederate General and Staff Officers,* series M331, roll 168.

47. Dr. William E. Dailey was post surgeon for the Confederate garrison at Boggy Depot. *Service Records of Confederate General and Staff Officers,* series M331, roll 70.

48. Brig. Gen. Albert Pike, a brilliant lawyer, newspaperman, teacher, public speaker, poet, and exponent of Freemasonry, negotiated treaties with the five tribes

of the Indian Territory and allied them with the Confederacy. He had commanded the District of Indian Territory until his resignation in November 1862. Walter Lee Brown, *A Life of Albert Pike* (Fayetteville: University of Arkansas Press, 1997), 353–419.

49. "Maj." Andrew J. Dorne was a merchant residing in Bonham, Texas. U.S. Census, 1870, Population, Fanin County, Texas.

50. At various times, Dr. Albert B. Hoy served as surgeon in the general hospitals at Fort Smith, Little Rock, and Camden. In 1864 he was assigned to Marmaduke's division before transferring to the military hospital at Bonham, Texas. *Service Records of Confederate General and Staff Officers,* series M331, roll 133.

51. This is probably 1st Lt. A. Shelton, Company H, Coleman's Missouri Cavalry, which was also known as the 46th Arkansas Mounted Infantry. *CSR-Mo.,* Coleman's Cavalry Regiment, roll 66.

52. Dr. William Carson Boon had been surgeon of the 9th Missouri Infantry, but in July 1864 he was named medical purveyor of the Northern Subdistrict of Texas with headquarters at Bonham. *Service Records of Confederate General and Staff Officers,* series M331, roll 27.

53. Before the war, William Quesenbury was editor of the newspaper *Southwest Independent* in Fayetteville, Arkansas. He gained national notoriety for his witty editorials and satirical political cartoons often published under the pseudonym "Bill Cush." During the war, Quesenbury, a major, served as personal secretary and departmental quartermaster under Albert Pike. After Pike's resignation, he continued his quartermaster duties in the Northern Subdistrict of Texas. *Service Records of Confederate General and Staff Officers,* series M331, roll 204; William S. Campbell, *One Hundred Years of Fayetteville* (Fayetteville, 1928), 107–8.

54. Dr. John W. Madden was assistant surgeon for Col. Edward Gurley's 30th Texas Cavalry. Anne Bailey, *Between the Enemy and Texas: Parsons's Texas Cavalry in the Civil War* (Fort Worth: Texas Christian University Press, 1989), 234.

55. Thomas Coke Bass was colonel of the 20th Texas Cavalry and later commandant of the Confederate garrison at Boggy Depot, Indian Territory. *O.R.,* 22(1):1051.

56. Brig. Gen. Richard Montgomery Gano originally led a battalion of Texas cavalrymen under Brig. Gen. John Hunt Morgan before commanding a cavalry brigade in the Indian Territory. Anne Bailey, "Richard Montgomery Gano," in *Confederate General,* 3:154–55.

9. ARKANSAS AGAIN

1. Garry Wills, *Lincoln at Gettysburg: The Words that Remade America* (New York: Simon and Schuster, 1992).

2. James M. McPherson, *Battle Cry of Freedom* (New York: Oxford University Press, 1988), 664.

3. James M. McPherson, "From Limited to Total War: Missouri and the Nation, 1861–1865," *Gateway Heritage* 12, no. 4 (spring 1992): 14–16.

4. Robert L. Kerby, *Kirby Smith's Confederacy: The Trans-Mississippi South, 1863–1865* (New York: Columbia University Press, 1972), 385–86; William R. Geise, "Kirby Smithdom, 1864," *Military History of Texas and the Southwest* 15 (1979): 18–35.

5. Kerby, *Kirby Smith's Confederacy,* 386–91; William R. Geise, "Kirby Smith's

War Department," *Military History of Texas and the Southwest* 15 (1979): 45–62; J. Hynson to T. O. Moore, Jan. 3, 1865, Thomas O. Moore Papers, Louisiana State University Archives, Baton Rouge.

6. Kerby, *Kirby Smith's Confederacy,* 381–85; Carl H. Moneyhon, *The Impact of the Civil War and Reconstruction on Arkansas* (Baton Rouge: Louisiana State University Press, 1994), 117–21; Carl Moneyhon, "1865: 'A Perfect State of Anarchy,'" in *Rugged and Sublime: The Civil War in Arkansas,* ed. Mark Christ (Fayetteville: University of Arkansas Press, 1994), 145–61; *O.R.,* 48(1):805–6.

7. Maj. Gen. John Bankhead Magruder's flair for ostentatious uniforms and his eccentric manner earned him the nickname "Prince John." After service in Virginia and Texas, he commanded the District of Arkansas from August 1864 to March 1865. Paul D. Casdorph, *Prince John Magruder: His Life and Campaigns* (New York: John Wiley and Sons, 1996).

8. Dr. Thomas A. Lonergan served as surgeon for the 16th Missouri Infantry. *CSR-Mo.,* 16th Infantry, roll 169.

9. Washington L. Crawford was a volunteer aide-de-camp to Sterling Price. *Service Records of Confederate General and Staff Officers,* series M331, roll 65, National Archives (microfilm).

10. Dr. Alexander Lovett was a forty-seven-year-old physician who hailed from Sevier County. U.S. Census, 1860, Population, Sevier County, Arkansas.

11. Freeman W. Compton was a justice of the Arkansas State Supreme Court from 1859 to 1864. John Hallum, *Biographical and Pictorial History of Arkansas* (Albany: Weed and Parsons, 1887), 319–23.

12. William I. Preston was lieutenant colonel of the 4th Missouri Cavalry. Stewart Sifakis, *Compendium of the Confederate Armies: Missouri* (New York: Facts on File, 1992), 95.

13. On December 19, 1864, Maj. Lauchlan A. MacLean was stabbed during an altercation with Maj. Robert C. Wood, commander of a cavalry battalion in Shelby's Iron Brigade. The fight stemmed from MacLean's refusal to sign a furlough for Wood due to orders forbidding furlough applications. Three days later MacLean died of complications related to his wounds. Wood was arrested, tried, and condemned to death, but he was later reprieved by Lt. Gen. E. Kirby Smith. M. Jeff Thompson, *The Civil War Reminiscences of General M. Jeff Thompson,* eds. Donal J. Stanton, Goodwin F. Berquist, and Paul C. Bowers (Dayton, Ohio: Morningside, 1988), 272.

14. This may be Samuel Fowler, a thirty-two-year-old farmer and father of two who resided in Sevier County. U.S. Census, 1860, Population, Sevier County, Arkansas.

15. Pleurisy is inflammation of the pleura, a membrane that enfolds both lungs and the diaphragm.

16. McPheeters was correct with regard to the unreliability of the capture of Nashville, Tennessee. John Bell Hood's Army of Tennessee had attempted to invest the city December 2–14, 1864. However, on December 15 and 16, Maj. Gen. George H. Thomas's Army of the Cumberland moved from its camps around Nashville, attacked, and drove the Confederates from the field. The battle of Nashville was a decisive Federal victory that left the Army of Tennessee in shambles.

17. Maj. Lemuel Shepperd served as a volunteer aide-de-camp to Brig. Gen.

William L. Cabell. Joseph H. Crute Jr., *Confederate Staff Officers, 1861–1865* (Powahatan, Va.: Derwent, 1982), 30.

18. McPheeters is referring to John R. Eakin, editor of the *Washington Telegraph*. This newspaper was an ardent voice for Confederate Arkansans throughout the war. Michael B. Dougan, *Confederate Arkansas: The People and Policies of a Frontier State in Wartime* (Tuscaloosa: University of Alabama Press, 1976), 52.

19. Embittered over his missed opportunity at being reinstated in Jefferson City as Missouri's Confederate governor, Thomas C. Reynolds wrote a lengthy and vicious article in the December 23 issue of the *(Marshall) Texas Republican* denouncing Maj. Gen. Sterling Price's conduct during the Missouri Expedition. After an exchange of letters between the two antagonists in the *Shreveport News,* Price demanded and was granted a court of inquiry to clear his name. Albert Castel, *General Sterling Price and the Civil War in the West* (Baton Rouge: Louisiana State University Press, 1968), 256–67.

20. Capt. Thomas Rector, assistant chief of subsistence, had his headquarters at Paraclifta, a town approximately twenty miles west of Washington along Little River. *Service Records of Confederate General and Staff Officers*, series M331, roll 208.

21. Brig. Gen. Henry Hopkins Sibley is perhaps best known for inventing the Sibley tent. In early 1862 the failure of his New Mexico campaign and his surly demeanor relegated Sibley to a series of relatively insignificant posts in Texas and Louisiana for the remainder of the war. Ezra J. Warner, *Generals in Gray: Lives of the Confederate Commanders* (Baton Rouge: Louisiana State University Press, 1959), 276–77.

22. Lt. Col. Michael W. Buster had commanded Clarkson's-Buster's Missouri Cavalry Battalion (also known as the Indian Battalion) and the 9th Missouri Infantry. In September 1863 he assumed command of the 15th Arkansas Cavalry Battalion and was assigned to duty in the Indian Territory. Sifakis, *Compendium of the Confederate Armies: Missouri,* 125, 129; Stewart Sifakis, *Compendium of the Confederate Armies: Arkansas* (New York: Facts on File, 1992), 61.

23. Thomas C. Smith was a forty-five-year-old planter and father of five living in Hempstead County, Arkansas. U.S. Census, 1860, Population, Ouachita County, Arkansas.

24. Mr. Venable is probably Thomas Venable, a former member of Company H, 9th Missouri Infantry and later a lieutenant of Company C, Searcy's Missouri Sharpshooter Battalion. *CSR-Mo.,* 9th Infantry, roll 177; "Register of Officers, Parsons' Division Missouri Volunteers," MHS.

25. The report of Savannah's capture was true. Maj. Gen. William T. Sherman's Federal forces occupied the city on December 21, 1864.

26. Grandison D. Royston was an Arkansas lawyer and politician. His title of "general" stemmed from appointment as adjutant general of the Arkansas militia in 1845. He also represented Arkansas in the Confederate House of Representatives from February 1862 to February 1864. Dougan, *Confederate Arkansas,* 122; "Biographical Sketch of 'General' Grandison D. Royston," Small Manuscript Collection, AHC.

27. Arthur C. McCoy was lieutenant of Company A, 5th Missouri Cavalry until 1864, when he took charge of a band of scouts and spies organized by Brig. Gen. J. O. Shelby. McCoy's command patrolled the Mississippi River and occasionally

attacked Federal vessels, though their primary duty was to report on Yankee movements along the river. *CSR-Mo.,* 5th Cavalry, roll 38; John N. Edwards, *Shelby and His Men* (Cincinnati: Miami Printing, 1867) 493–95.

28. Col. Charles S. Mitchell was in command of the 1st Missouri Brigade encamped near Washington, Arkansas. *O.R.,* 41(3):968.

29. Capt. Richard S. Harper was assistant chief of subsistence stationed at Minden, La. *Service Records of Confederate General and Staff Officers,* series M331, roll 118.

30. Calvin Monroe Hervey was a prominent Red River planter in southwestern Arkansas who contributed liberally to the Confederate cause. After the war Hervey's many accomplishments included operating a line of steamboats on the upper Red River, gaining authorization to practice medicine, patenting an improved riding plow known as the Hervey Sulky Plow, and naming the town of Texarkana. Barbara O. Chandler and J. Ed Howe, *History of Texarkana and Bowie and Miller Counties, Texas-Arkansas* (Texarkana, 1939), 290, 320.

31. Until January 1863 John S. H. Rainey served as assistant chief of subsistence at Camden with the rank of captain. At that time the Camden lawyer tendered his resignation "because my business as executor and administrator of several large estates requires most of my time and attention." *Service Records of Confederate General and Staff Officers,* series M331, roll 149; U.S. Census, 1860, Population, Ouachita County, Arkansas.

32. This could be either Dr. Claudius E. R. King, surgeon for the 33d Texas Cavalry, or Dr. A. W. King, assistant surgeon for Waul's Texas Legion. *Service Records of Confederate General and Staff Officers,* series M331, roll 149.

33. Recently promoted to lieutenant colonel, Edward P. Turner was the senior assistant adjutant general to John B. Magruder in 1865. He had been attached to Magruder's staff since the war's inception, first as a private. *Service Records of Confederate General and Staff Officers,* series M331, roll 252.

10. BANISHMENT AND REUNION

1. *O.R.,* series 2, 5(2):319–21.

2. W. M. McPheeters, "Arrest, Imprisonment, and Banishment of My Wife," n.d., William McPheeters Collection, MHS. (Transcribed in appendix as item 7.)

3. *The Missouri Republican,* Jan. 20, 1865.

4. McPheeters read the following notice in *The Missouri Republican* concerning his wife: "MILITARY ARREST ON OLIVE STREET—Mrs. Sarah McPheeters was yesterday arrested at her residence on Olive Street by order of the Provost Marshal General and committed to the female department of Gratiot Prison on a general charge of disloyalty. The specifications of charges against her are not made known. The husband of Mrs. McPheeters is now a surgeon in the Confederate army." *The Missouri Republican,* Jan. 18, 1865.

5. Dr. Joseph Nash McDowell, founder of the McDowell Medical College, had been a colleague of McPheeters since his early days in St. Louis. Like McPheeters, McDowell fled St. Louis and joined the Confederate army. While in Confederate service he inspected hospitals in the Departments of Mississippi and the Trans-Mississippi. It is very likely that McPheeters was writing to inform McDowell that Sallie was being imprisoned in the old medical school, now Gratiot Street Prison.

Service Records of Confederate General and Staff Officers, series M331, roll 171, National Archives (microfilm).

6. Maj. John B. Burton was chief of the clothing bureau at Little Rock in 1862, but by March 1863 he had been promoted to chief quartermaster for the District of Arkansas. Burton held this appointment until the war's end. *Service Records of Confederate General and Staff Officers,* series M331, roll 42; James L. Nichols, *The Confederate Quartermaster in the Trans-Mississippi* (Austin: University of Texas Press, 1964), 28–29.

7. Captured while leading the 7th Missouri Infantry at the battle of Helena, Col. Levin M. Lewis was imprisoned on Johnson's Island until November 1864. After being exchanged he returned to his old unit (redesignated as the 16th Missouri Infantry). Just ten days before the surrender of the department, Lt. Gen. E. Kirby Smith promoted Lewis to brigadier general. Arthur M. Bergeron, "Levin M. Lewis," in *The Confederate General,* 6 vols., ed. William C. Davis (National Historical Society, 1991), 6:188–89.

8. Mary Hervey, nicknamed "Molly,"was Calvin Hervey's daughter. Barbara O. Chandler and J. Ed Howe, *History of Texarkana and Bowie and Miller Counties, Texas-Arkansas* (Texarkana, 1939), 320.

9. This is probably S. M. Frost, captain of Company A, 5th Missouri Cavalry. *CSR-Mo.,* 5th Cavalry, roll 38.

10. William A. Alston was promoted to captain in March 1863 and assigned as assistant adjutant general to Maj. Gen. John B. Magruder in the District of Texas. *Service Records of Confederate General and Staff Officers,* series M331, roll 5.

11. Capt. Edward F. Pearson of the 9th Missouri Infantry was quartermaster for Col. Charles Mitchell's 1st Missouri Brigade. *Service Records of Confederate General and Staff Officers,* series M331, roll 195.

12. John W. Lewis served at various times from 1862 as assistant adjutant general on the staffs of Brig. Gen. D. M. Frost, Brig. Gen. T. F. Drayton, Maj. Gen. Sterling Price, and finally Magruder. *Service Records of Confederate General and Staff Officers,* series M331, roll 157.

13. Thomas H. Murray was lieutenant colonel of the 11th Missouri Infantry. "Register of Officers, Parsons Division Missouri Volunteers," MHS.

14. In all likelihood McPheeters is referring to James W. Finley, a prominent planter in Hempstead County. The title of "major" may stem from Finley's militia service, or it may simply be a courtesy extended to him by McPheeters. U.S. Census, 1860, Population, Hempstead County, Arkansas.

15. At various times during the war, Capt. Stephen D. Yancey served as assistant adjutant general on the staffs of Magruder and Maj. Gen. John G. Walker. *Service Records of Confederate General and Staff Officers,* series M331, roll 275; *O.R.,* 48(2):1263.

16. Dr. Thomas Brandon was a physician and father of four living in Hempstead County. U.S. Census, 1860, Population, Hempstead County, Arkansas.

17. "Mr. Thompson" is probably Thomas H. Thompson, a plantation owner residing in Hempstead County. Ibid.

18. McPheeters is probably referring to the battle of Kinston (Mar. 8, 1865) since he had no way of knowing that the last major battle fought by the Confederate Army of Tennessee was occurring on that date in Bentonville, North Carolina

(Mar. 19–21, 1865).

19. Twenty-six-year-old Samuel Gibson of Monticello, Arkansas, was elected major of the 26th Arkansas Infantry in May 1864. *CSR-Ark.*, 26th Infantry, roll 125.

20. Following the harsh newspaper commentaries of Gov. Thomas C. Reynolds regarding Sterling Price's handling of the Missouri Expedition, the general asked for and was granted a court of inquiry to clear his name. Albert Castel, *General Sterling Price and the Civil War in the West* (Baton Rouge: Louisiana State University Press, 1968), 264–67.

21. Frank S. Reed was the junior second lieutenant for Company B, 10th Missouri Infantry. "Register of Officers, Parsons Division Missouri Volunteers," MHS.

22. This is probably 1st Lt. A. P. Saugrain, former adjutant for the 27th Arkansas (Shaler's) Infantry regiment who, in April 1865, was serving as assistant inspector general on Sterling Price's staff. *CSR-Ark.*, 27th Infantry, roll 198.

23. A resident of St. Louis, Dr. Lewis T. Pim had served as the medical director for Maj. Gen. John C. Breckinridge's Army of Middle Tennessee in November 1862 and later in 1863 as medical director of general hospitals for Gen. Braxton Bragg. Transferred to the Trans-Mississippi in August 1864, Pim was designated as assistant to Dr. John Haden, chief of the Medical Bureau of the Trans-Mississippi Department. *Service Records of Confederate General and Staff Officers*, series M331, roll 198; *O.R.*, 48:(1):1318.

24. This is probably Spring Hill resident Robert S. Brandon, the sixteen-year-old son of Dr. Thomas Brandon. U.S. Census, 1860, Population, Hempstead County, Arkansas.

11. SURRENDER

1. Robert L. Kerby, *Kirby Smith's Confederacy, The Trans-Mississippi South, 1863–1865* (New York: Columbia University Press, 1972) 412–15; Joseph H. Parks, *General Edmund Kirby Smith, CSA* (Baton Rouge: Louisiana State University Press, 1992) 456–60; Albert Castel, *General Sterling Price and the Civil War in the West* (Baton Rouge: Louisiana State University Press, 1993) 267–68; Daniel O'Flaherty, *General Jo Shelby, Undefeated Rebel* (Chapel Hill: University of North Carolina Press, 2000) 227–34; John N. Edwards, *Shelby and His Men* (Cincinnati: Miami Printing and Publishing Co., 1867) 516–20, 534–42.

2. Kerby, *Kirby Smith's Confederacy*, 415–19.

3. Kerby, *Kirby Smith's Confederacy*, 420–26; Parks, *General Edmund Kirby Smith*, 472–76; Castel, *General Sterling Price*, 270–272; Edwards, *Shelby and His Men*, 532–41.

4. Andrew Rolle, *The Lost Cause, The Confederate Exodus to Mexico* (Norman: University of Oklahoma Press, 1992) 8–18; Edwards, *Shelby and His Men*, 543–51.

5. The court of inquiry investigating Maj. Gen. Sterling Price's conduct during the Missouri Expedition convened in Shreveport on April 21, 1865. *O.R.*, 41(1):701–29.

6. This may be Capt. David C. Knox of St. Louis, who was assistant chief of subsistence for the 4th Arizona Regiment at San Antonio. *Service Records of Confederate General and Staff Officers*, series M331, roll 158, National Archives (microfilm).

7. McPheeters may have been referring to John D. Trimble, a fifty-eight-year-

old merchant at Washington, Arkansas. U.S. Census, 1860, Population, Hempstead County, Arkansas.

8. Gen. Robert E. Lee's forces and the Confederate government evacuated Richmond, Virginia, on April 2, 1865.

9. During Sterling Price's 1864 raid into Missouri, Caleb J. Perkins led Perkins's Missouri Cavalry Battalion, a largely unarmed unit in Col. Charles Tyler's brigade. After the campaign, the unit was assigned to Brig. Gen. Mosby Parsons's infantry division and designated Perkins's Sharpshooter Battalion. *O.R.,* 41(1):642; Stewart Sifakis, *Compendium of the Confederate Armies: Missouri* (New York: Facts on File, 1992), 108; "Register of Officers in Parsons Division of Missouri Volunteers," MHS.

10. Unbeknownst to McPheeters, Gen. Joseph E. Johnston would formally surrender the Army of Tennessee to Maj. Gen. William T. Sherman that day (April 26, 1865).

11. Secretary of State William Henry Seward survived the assassination attempt by Lewis Paine.

12. Capt. R. M. Littlejohn was assistant quartermaster for the 1st Arkansas (Monroe's) Cavalry attached to Brig. Gen. William L. Cabell's brigade. *Service Records of Confederate General and Staff Officers,* series M331, roll 158.

13. At the beginning of the war, Dr. R. A. Burton was surgeon for the 1st Arkansas Infantry, but by 1865 he was serving as a surgeon at the general hospital in Camden. *Service Records of Confederate General and Staff Officers,* series M331, roll 142.

14. Robert C. Newton was colonel of the 5th Arkansas Cavalry. Earlier in the war, Dr. Randolph A. Brunson, a resident of Camden, had been in charge of the post hospital at Pine Bluff, but in 1865 he was stationed at the hospital in Fulton, Arkansas. Sifakis, Stewart Sifakis, *Compendium of the Confederate Armies: Arkansas* (New York: Facts on File, 1992), 58; *Service Records of Confederate General and Staff Officers,* series M331, roll 37.

15. "Col. Thompson" may be either Col. Gideon W. Thompson of the 11th Missouri Cavlary or Lt. Col. Lee L. Thompson of the 4th Arkansas (Gordon's) Cavalry. It is also possible that McPheeters is using the term "colonel" out of respect for a prominent citizen in the area, much like he did for Calvin Hervey. If so, "Col. Thompson" may be Thomas H. Thompson, a plantation owner residing in Hempstead County. *Service Records of Confederate General and Staff Officers,* series M331, roll 247; U.S. Census, 1860, Population Hempstead County, Arkansas.

16. Lt. Gen. E. Kirby Smith ordered the court of inquiry moved from Shreveport to Washington, Arkansas, because he had intelligence that Price was plotting his arrest. The Missourian apparently believed Smith was contemplating surrendering the department and was willing to take drastic measures to prevent such a move. By relocating the court to Washington, Smith effectively removed Price and his influence from departmental headquarters. Albert Castel, *General Sterling Price and the Civil War in the West* (Baton Rouge: Louisiana State University Press, 1968), 264–70.

17. When terms of surrender were presented to General Smith on May 8, he rejected them and called a meeting of the governors of Arkansas, Louisiana, Missouri, and Texas at Marshall, Texas. Their purpose was to draft a set of liberal, more acceptable terms. Robert L. Kerby, *Kirby Smith's Confederacy: The Trans-Mississippi South, 1863–1865* (New York: Columbia University Press, 1972), 415–19.

18. Disgruntled members of Samuel McPheeters's Presbyterian congregation had

driven him from the pulpit earlier in the war, and they finally effected his departure from St. Louis altogether. Walter B. Stevens, *St. Louis: The Fourth City, 1764–1909.* (St. Louis: S. J. Clarke, 1909), 1002–3.

19. As commander of the 12th Arkansas Battalion of Sharpshooters, Maj. William F. Rapley had been captured at Vicksburg. After his exchange, he served as volunteer aide-de-camp and assistant inspector general to Maj. Gen. James F. Fagan. Sifakis, *Compendium of the Confederate Armies: Arkansas,* 92; Joseph H. Crute Jr., *Confederate Staff Officers, 1861–1865* (Powahatan, Va.: Derwent, 1982), 58.

20. Spring Hill Township resident Waddy Finley was the seventeen-year-old son of planter James W. Finley. U.S. Census, 1860, Population, Hempstead County, Arkansas.

21. Unbeknown to McPheeters, Lt. Gen. Simon Bolivar Buckner, E. Kirby Smith's chief of staff, formally surrendered the Trans-Mississippi Department in New Orleans that day.

22. Charles McLaren was an ardent Missouri secessionist who, during the early days of the war in St. Louis, had helped organize a pro-Southern militia unit known as the Minute Men. "Col. S. Chambry" was probably Samuel L. Chambliss, former lieutenant colonel of the 13th Louisiana Partisan Rangers Battalion. Louis S. Gerteis, *Civil War St. Louis* (Lawrence: University Press of Kansas, 2001), 79, 90; Arthur W. Bergeron Jr., *Guide to Louisiana Confederate Military Units* (Baton Rouge: Louisiana State University Press, 1989), 60–61.

23. In 1864 Maj. Gen. John Pope assumed command of the Federal Military Division of Missouri whose headquarters were in St. Louis. Ezra J. Warner, *Generals in Blue* (Baton Rouge: Louisiana State University Press, 1964), 376–77.

EPILOGUE

1. W. M. McPheeters, "Private Paper No. 1. Reasons for Quitting Home and Joining the Southern Army," William McPheeters Collection, MHS.

2. William McPheeters to Andrew Johnson, June 19, 1865, McPheeters Collection, MHS.

3. The Wickham mansion on Lucas Place, the first private street in St. Louis, was undamaged throughout the war. Wickham was the first friend contacted by McPheeters when he returned to the city, which holds significance when one speculates on the arrangements McPheeters must have made before he fled in June 1862. Other banished Confederates who left property behind enemy lines often secured that property and other assets by leaving them in the care of trusted friends. For example, one Memphis woman, banished by Maj. Gen. William T. Sherman, was given one day to prepare for her exile. In that brief time she placed the gold that her husband had left in her keeping in a bank lockbox. She entrusted the key to a friend, asking him to pay the taxes on their home and plantation during her absence. Elizabeth Merriwether Avery, *Recollections of Ninety-two Years* (Nashville: Tennessee Historical Commission, 1958).

4. In this letter, Mrs. Davis acknowledged the gift of $3,000 for her husband's defense fund, deposited with Lanier and Company Bankers, New York. Varina Davis to William McPheeters, Fortress Monroe, Feb. 23, 1867, McPheeters Collection, MHS.

5. Nor was the contribution from the ladies' relief fair the only purse given to

Maj. Gen. Sterling Price. His friends in St. Louis launched a drive to raise $50,000 to build a home for him and his family, but he died in September 1867 before completion of this effort. *The Missouri Republican,* Apr. 19, 1903, in scrapbook, McPheeters Collection, MHS.

6. During the course of the faculty meetings, there was no discussion whatsoever of the Civil War or of the former use of the McDowell Building. "Minutes of the Proceedings of the Faculty of the Missouri Medical College, March 16, 1868 to May 26, 1876," MLWU.

7. *Catalog of the Missouri Medical College, 1870–71,* MLWU.

8. "All Serene. The St. Louis Life Insurance Company and Its Policy Holders," *St. Louis Times,* Apr. 25, 1873; "The St. Louis Mutual," *St. Louis Times,* Apr. 27, 1873.

9. In 1878 the McPheeters' residence was listed as 3452 Pine Street; the doctor's office remained at 1000 Olive Street at the rear of the property. The Forest Park Addition was developed in 1888, bounded on the east by Kingshighway and on the west by Union Boulevard. This fashionable neighborhood was enhanced in 1890 when the Missouri Cable Railroad laid a second cable from Grand Avenue to Kingshighway. The McPheeters Pine Street home was north of Kingshighway but in the vicinity of this fashionable development. "Obituary," in scrapbook, McPheeters Collection, MHS; *Gould's St. Louis Directory, 1878;* Charles C. Savage, *Architecture of the Private Streets* (Columbia: University of Missouri Press, 1987), 42–67.

10. W W. M. McPheeters, "Matters and Things in General—A Brief Retrospect of a Half a Century" (paper presented before the St. Louis Medical Society, Dec. 15, 1894), MHS, 83–87.

11. Surrounding Sallie and William McPheeters were their family members— daughter Sally, with her husband Mead Robinson and their three children; Margaret and her husband, Albert Price, with their five children; and Fanny, their youngest daughter. The city newspapers described the family in vivid detail, and in the center of the festivities stood the proud, slender figure of the aging physician. Unidentified newpaper clipping, scrapbook, May 11, 1899, McPheeters Collection, MHS.

12. The building purchased by the St. Louis Medical Society was its first permanent home and was located at 3525 Pine Street, less than a block from McPheeters's home. R. O. Muether, M.D., "The Evolution of the St. Louis Medical Society," in Joseph A. Hardy Jr. et al., *St. Louis Medical Society Centennial Volume* (St. Louis: n.p., 1939), 15–20.

13. Menu for the banquet, program, and photographs, Menu Collection, MHS.

14. "Society Proceedings, St. Louis Medical Society, Meeting of March 25, 1905: In Memoriam—Dr. William McPheeters," *Journal of the Missouri State Medical Association* 1, no. 11 (May 1905).

INDEX

A

abolitionists, 337n24
Adams, John, 116, 356n12
Adams, Mr., 35
Adges, Mr., 201
Alabama (cruiser), 185, 367n41
Albemarle (ironclad), 364n2
Alexander, Miss, 50
Alexandria, La., 2, 290; Graham,
    Malcolm, 299; opinion of planter,
    253; Smith, Edmund Kirby, 200;
    Smith, Solomon A., 358n14;
    Szymanski, Ignatius, 350n18;
    Union forces, 121, 125, 129, 161
Allen's Bayou, 247
"All in the eye Betty Martin," 110
Alston, Benjamin, 367n33
Alston, William A., 282, 283, 285,
    294, 377n10
Alton, Ill., 19–20
Alton Military Prison, 19–20
ambulances, 324–25, 330, 372n41
American Medical Association, 9,
    317, 360n37
amputation: arms, 42, 52, 228; classifica-
    tion, 343n29; description of, 363n56;
    equipment, 132, 139, 363n56; legs,
    42, 343n32; limbs, 57, 141, 150,
    152; as medical procedure, 224,
    230, 363n56; success rate, 343n32;
    thigh, 51
Anderson, Charles D., 207, 369n9
Anderson, Mattie, 272, 278
Anderson, Mollie, 272, 278
Anderson, William L., 355n6
Anheuser-Busch, 318
Anthony House, Little Rock, Ark., 53
aristocracy of merit, xi
aristocracy of privilege, xi
Arkadelphia, Ark., 74, 122, 270; camp
    site, 67; medical laboratory, 23;

ordnance center, 347n25; Union
    forces, 301; wounded Confederate
    soldiers, 66
Arkansas: Clayton, Powell, 343n22;
    Confederate forces, 253; control
    by Union forces, 75–76; economic
    strain, 253; fall of Little Rock, Ark.,
    59–60; Federal Department of
    Arkansas, 271; Flanagin, Harris,
    347n23; Helena campaign, 38–40;
    Price, Sterling, xii; Steele, Frederick,
    157; as Union target, 57–58
Arkansas Cavalry Battalion, 355n6
Arkansas Gazette, 348n32
Arkansas Post, Ark., 31, 57
Arkansas River, 2, 28, 74, 196, 270, 290;
    capture of Union boats, 172, 179,
    211; crossing of, 34, 58–60, 63, 65,
    216–17, 241–42; encampment, 215;
    mouth of, 310; noise of cannon fire,
    182; Pine Bluff, Ark, 305
Arkansas State Penitentiary, 346n15
Arkansas True Democrat, 357n11
Arlington Heights, Va., 189
Armistead, Franck S., 72, 84, 348n36
Armstrong, Eliza, 300, 303
Army Church, 341n13
Army Medical Association: establish-
    ment by William McPheeters,
    76–77, 318; gunshot wounds,
    113–14, 120; heart demonstration,
    97; intermittent fever, 94–95;
    masturbation, 101; pneumonia,
    97; typhoid fever, 101
Army Medical Board, 360n37
Army of Middle Tennessee, 378n23
Army of Missouri, 349n41, 368n44
Army of Northern Virginia, 157, 291
Army of Tennessee: Buckner, Simon
    Bolivar, 368n2; Cockrell's Missouri
    Brigade, 355n62; defeat at

Missionary Ridge, Tenn., 76;
Granbury, Hiram, 365*n12;* Hood,
John Bell, 374*n16;* Johnston,
Joseph E., 157; last major battle
of Confederate forces, 377–78*n18;*
surrender, 291, 379*n10*
Army of the Border, 371*n36*
Army of the Cumberland, 374*n16*
Army of the Potomac, 21
Army of the West, 21
Army of Virginia, 23
Arthur (steamboat), 309
asepsis, 57, 319
Ashland, Va., 339*n54*
Ashley, Mrs. William Elliott, 261
Ashley, William Elliott, 62, 254, 346*n17*
Athens, La., *122,* 161
Atlanta, Ga., 369*n18*
Austin, Tx., *2*

B

Baer, Caleb Dorsey, 39, 40, 53, 327,
342*n18,* 344*n11*
Baird's (courier station), 110, 275
Baltimore, Md., 188–91
banishment: Anderson, Mattie, 272;
Anderson, Mollie, 272; Frost, Mrs.
Daniel Marsh, 344*n8;* McPheeters,
Sallie Buchanan (Mrs. William), xii,
272–73, 274, 333–34; McPheeters,
Samuel Brown, 17; pro-Confederate
women, 271–72; Reed, Georgia T.,
272; Snodgrass, Harriet, 71; Union
policies, xii, 47–48; Ward, Jane, 272
Banks, Nathaniel Prentiss, 119, 124–27,
137–38, 157, 357*n18,* 359*n27,*
359*n28,* 360*n32*
Bass, John J., 364*n59*
Bass, Mr., 101
Bass, Thomas Coke, 154, 249, 364*n59,*
373*n55*
Bates, Edward, 185, 367*n42*
Bates, Fleming, 281
Bates, Mr., 264, 277
Bates, Mrs. Fleming, 260
Bates County, Mo., 235
Batesville, Ark., *196,* 217, 219, *290*

Baton Rouge, La., *2, 290,* 308–9, 334
Battle of Chickamauga, 348*n33*
Battle of Helena: *See* Helena campaign
Battle of Jenkins' Ferry, 150–51, 164,
361*n42,* 362*n48,* 362*n52,* 362*n53,*
363*n54*
Battle of Mansfield, *122,* 137–38, 289,
357*n18,* 359*n28,* 359*n29*
Battle of Marks' Mill, 362*n47*
Battle of Mine Creek, 341*n14,* 352*n31,*
366*n21,* 366*n25,* 372*n37*
Battle of Pea Ridge, 29, 55
Battle of Pilot Knob, *196,* 224–25,
370*n20*
Battle of Pleasant Hill, *122,* 138–41, 292,
350*n14,* 357*n18,* 360*n32,* 360*n33*
Battle of Poison Spring, 361*n44*
Battle of Reed's Bridge, 346*n18*
Battle of Shiloh, 22, 33, 46, 56, 342*n17*
Battle of the Saline River: *See* Battle of
Jenkins' Ferry
Baxter, Dr., 293
Baxter Springs, Ks., 349*n9*
Bayou Bartholomew, *270*
Bayou Bodcaw, *74, 122,* 144, 199,
270, 274
Bayou DeView, Ark., *28, 36*
Bayou Dorcheat, *74, 122, 270,* 275
Bayou Lafourche, 359*n29*
Bayou Meto, *28,* 346*n18*
Bayou Teche, 359*n29*
Beatie, Mr., 69
Beaumont, Godfrey N., 41, 343*n27*
Beaumont, William, 3, 335*n3*
Beauregard, Pierre Gustave T., 189,
285, 359*n30*
Beech Hill, Ark., *270,* 276
Bell, Mrs. Robert Joe, 355*n7*
Bell, Robert Joe, 97, 341*n12,* 354*n55,*
355*n7*
Bell, Samuel S., 78, 327, 349*n7*
Bell, William, 46
Benton, Ark., 66, *74, 122,* 144, *196,* 214
Benton, La., *122,* 129
Benton County, Ark., 239
Bentonville, N.C., 377–78*n18*
Bermuda Hundred, 185

Berry, Mr., 228
Berthold Mansion, St. Louis, Mo., 12
Bienville Parish, La., 161
Big Black River, 222
Big Blue River, 371n34, 371n36
Big Cornie Creek, 122, 163
Big Creek, 28, 53
Bill Cush: See Quesenberry, William
Black, Judge, 53
Blacklands, 248
Black River, 196, 220–21
Black Water River, 231
Blair, Frank, 16
Blair, Montgomery, 185, 367n42
Blake, Mr., 79, 81, 93
bleeding, 110, 317, 319
Blessington, Joseph P., 360n36
blistering, 317, 319, 339n51
Blocher, William D., 170, 182, 366n23
blue mass, 41, 343n28
Blue River, 196, 246
Blunt, James G., 79, 233, 236, 349n9,
    370n27, 370n28
Blunt, Mr., 52, 53
boats: Alabama (cruiser), 185, 367n41;
    CSS Albemarle (ironclad), 364n2;
    Arthur (steamboat), 309; Clara Eames
    (steamboat), 365n13; Emma (steam-
    boat), 307; Gen. Fletcher (steamboat),
    275; USS Kersarge (sloop), 367n41;
    Lebanon (steamboat), 365n13; Mattie
    Stephens (steamboat), 309; CSS
    Missouri (ironclad), 130, 133, 358n18;
    The Nelson (steamboat), 276; New
    Uncle Sam (steamboat), 8; CSS
    Pontchartrain (gunboat), 65, 347n22;
    USS Queen City (gunboat), 367n35;
    CSS Tennessee (ironclad), 369n8;
    Twilight (steamboat), 305, 307; Tyler
    (gunboat), 33, 342n20; Woodford
    (steamboat), 46
Boggs, William Robertson, 200, 368n5
Boggy Depot, Indian Territory, 2, 196,
    243–46, 372n47, 373n55
Bois d'Arc Creek, 274, 288
Bond, John B.: correspondence with
    William McPheeters, 267–68; as

medical purveyor for District of
    Arkansas, 352n41; official correspond-
    ence with William McPheeters,
    90–92, 98, 114, 119, 130; official visit
    with William McPheeters, 116–17,
    128, 165, 175, 204, 206, 209; visit to
    Camp Bragg, 83
Bond, Mrs. John B., 117
Bonham, Tx., 89, 196, 246–48, 302,
    347n26, 373n49, 373n50, 373n52
Boon, William Carson, 248, 373n52
Boonville, Mo., 196, 229–31
Booth, John Wilkes, 296, 299
Border States: banishment, xii–xiii;
    Lincoln, Abraham, xi; political
    unrest, 10–12
Bossier Parish, La., 361n43
Boston Mountains, 240–41
Bowie County, Tx., 250
Boyd, Mr., 114–15, 118, 121, 193,
    260–61, 287, 294, 301
Boyd, Mrs., 260
Bragg, Braxton, 70–72, 78, 85, 89, 90,
    332, 378n23
brain fever, 324, 336n14
Brandon, Robert S., 289, 293–94,
    298–99, 378n24
Brandon, Sally, 294, 296, 298–99
Brandon, Thomas, 285–86, 288–89,
    293, 296–99, 377n16
Breckenridge, John C., 117, 190,
    349n10, 378n23
Brice's Crossroads, 366n30
Brinker, Arthur, 218, 369n15
Brinker, Isaac: church attendance, 248;
    dinner with William McPheeters,
    221; District of Arkansas, 341n11;
    mess arrangement with William
    McPheeters, 212; Missouri
    Expedition, 224, 229, 249; official
    correspondence with William
    McPheeters, 266; official visit with
    William McPheeters, 36, 200,
    203–4, 206; social visits, 175–76;
    visits from relatives, 232; visit with
    William McPheeters, 289; winter
    quarters, 262

Bristoe Station, Va., 350n12

Broadfoot, Charles W., 26, 100, 339–40n55

Broadwell, Moses, 130, 145

Broadwell, William A., 130, 358n17

Brookhart, Jacob F., 40, 52, 53, 85, 327, 343n21

Brooks, William H., 351n28

Brown, Mrs., 53

Brownsville, Ark., 59

Brownsville, Tx., 2

Bruce, Mrs., 100, 155, 213

Bruinsburg, Miss., 30

Brunson, Randolph A., 298, 379n14

Brush Creek, Mo., 371n36

Buchanan, George, 9

Buchanan, Mr., 92

Buchanan, Sallie: See McPheeters, Sallie Buchanan (Mrs. William)

Buckner, Simon Bolivar, 200, 292, 368n2, 380n21

Buffington, Mrs., 276

Bull Run Creek, Va., 350n12

Burbridge, John Q., 190, 368n48

Burnside, Ambrose E., 71

Burton, John B., 275, 377n6

Burton, R. A., 298, 379n13

Buster, Michael W., 261, 298, 375n22

butternut boys, xii, 31, 125

Byram's Ford, Mo., 371n34, 371n36

C

Cabell, Edward Carrington: Camp Bragg, 79, 81, 83, 85, 88–91, 93, 98–100, 104; Camp Sumter, 112, 116–17; correspondence from William McPheeters, 170, 211, 257, 262, 274, 281, 303; correspondence to William McPheeters, 119–20, 163, 173, 210; dinner with William McPheeters, 192–93, 206; District of Arkansas, 347n24; Little Rock campaign, 66, 70–71, 73; loan of servant, 300, 353n50; official correspondence with William McPheeters, 182, 200; procurement of medical supplies, 204–5; Red River campaign, 131–32,

134–36, 152; return from Little Rock, Ark., 159; social visits, 91, 100, 175–77, 181, 194; trip to Shreveport, La., 208; visit with Sallie McPheeters, 287; visit with William McPheeters, 184, 203, 288, 298, 300

Cabell, William Lewis: capture of, 237, 352n31, 372n37; destruction of Pacific Railroad, 226; 1st Arkansas (Monroe's) Cavalry, 379n12; imprisonment, 352n31; Missouri Expedition, 213; Scott, Mrs. Joseph T., 87; Sheppard, Lemuel, 374n17; skirmish with Union forces, 235, 371n34; von Phul, William, 356n13

Cache River, 28, 35

Caddo Parish, La., 359n23

Caddo River, 74, 122

Cage, Duncan C., 83, 350n19

Cairo, Ill., 23, 272, 290, 310, 333

Cake, Amos F., 52, 344n9

Caledonia, Mo., 196, 225

Calhoun, Ark., 122, 159

California, 7

California, Mo., 196, 229

Camden, Ark., 2, 74, 122, 196, 270, 290; Bond, John B., 352n41; Brunson, Randolph A., 379n14; Burton, R. A., 379n13; Cabell, Edward Carrington, 104, 119, 121, 200, 262, 265; Confederate encampment, 147–48, 152–55, 158–59, 163–95, 202–12; Cunningham, Francis D., 97, 118; Gallagher, Mr., 306; Hervey, Mrs. Calvin Monroe, 298–300; Holmes, Theophilus Hunter, 109; McPheeters, William Marcellus, 203–12, 274–75, 278–80, 303–5, 334; negro troops, 307; news accounts, 98; Price, Sterling, 90–91, 119–21; Rainey, John S. H., 302, 304, 376n31; Rainey, Mrs. John, 303–4; return of Confederate forces, 161–63; Schaumburg, Mrs. Wright C., 99–100; Snead, Thomas Lowndes, 105; Taylor, Henry Clay,

103, 112–13; transfer of division, 120–21; Union forces, 145–48; winter quarters, 76–77, 86–87; Wooten, Thomas D., 216, 225

Campbell, James Knox, 139–40, 360*n34*

Camp Bragg, *74*, 76–101, 274, 354*n54*, 354*n56*

Camp Chase, Ohio, 349*n8*

Camp Grinstead, *122*, 164–75, 365*n15*

Camp Jackson, Mo., 13

Camp Jackson Affair, 13–14, 158, 300

Camp Sumter, *74*, 111–21, *122*, 355*n4*

Camp Yell, 205

Canadian River, *196*, 243

Cane Hill, Ark., *196*, 240

Caney Creek, 36–37

Cantharis beetles, 339*n51*

Careyville, Ark., 306

Careyville Landing, Ark., 276

Carpenter, Seymour D., 225, 370*n22*

Carriage Point, Indian Territory, 247

Carroll, Miss, 26, 260, 269

Carrollton, Mo., 233, 371*n29*

Carter, Jonathan H., 133, 358*n18*

Carter, Walker R., 346*n16*

Carthage, Mo., *196*, 238

Cass County, Mo., 235–36

Casselberry, Isaac, 343*n25*

Castleberry, Isaac, 41, 42, 50

Catlett, George C., 358*n19*

Centerville, Ark., 111, *270*, 280, 303

Central Arkansas River Valley, 59

Chambers, Ben, 25, 27, 339*n50*

Chambliss, Samuel L., 380*n22*

Chambry, S., 309, 380*n22*

Champagnolle, Ark., *270*, 278–79

Chandler, John L., 180, 188, 367*n37*

Chase, Salmon P., 184, 185, 367*n42*

Chattanooga, Tenn., 71, 78, 347*n23*

Chaytor, Joseph, 355*n61*

Chaytor, Mrs. Joseph, 101, 355*n61*

Cheauto Sulphur Springs, Mo., 231

Chenowith, Benjamin D., 92, 353*n45*

Cherokee Nation, 239–40, 247, 372*n39*, 372*n44*

Chicago Times, 81, 86, 188

Chickamauga, Battle of, 348*n33*

Chickamauga, Ga., 76

Chickasaw Nation, 247

children, mortality study, 336*n14*

chloroform, 38, 94, 353*n49*, 363*n54*, 363*n56*

Choctaw Indians, 147, 361*n46*

Choctaw Nation, 242, 245–47, 372*n45*

cholera, 7, 8, 319, 336–37*n17*, 336*n14*

Chouteau, Augustine, 47

Christian Brothers Academy, 20

Christie, Robert J., 97, 354*n56*

Christopher, Mr., 78, 280

Churchill, Mrs. Thomas James: biographical data, 339*n48*; breakfast with William McPheeters, 190; command send-off, 121; dinner with William McPheeters, 88, 162, 187, 204, 283; as friend, 25, 27; medical care, 103; message to William McPheeters, 78; military ball, 355*n7*; social visits, 87, 91–92, 116–17, 165, 167–72, 177, 181, 206–8; tea with William McPheeters, 101, 174; visit with James Tappan, 163

Churchill, Thomas James: Battle of Mansfield, 137–38; Battle of Pleasant Hill, 138–41, 360*n32*, 360*n33*; Battle of Jenkins' Ferry, 150, 362*n48*; Blocher, William D., 366*n23*; in Camden, Ark., 154; capture of, 349*n8*; command send-off, 121; commendation for William McPheeters, 363*n55*; dining with friends, 135; Dunlap, W. Watkins, 352*n40*; imprisonment, 349*n8*; intended visit from William McPheeters, 81; Jandon, Benjamin A., 365*n11*; Johnson, Benjamin S., 364*n7*; Kidder, Charles E., 365*n19*; march to Camden, Ark., 143–44; medical care, 190–92, 194; Moore, Charles B., 366*n22*; official correspondence with William McPheeters, 256; official visit with William McPheeters, 208; promotion, 155; Red River campaign, 125,

127, 130, 132; report to Richard
Taylor, 136, 137, 141; request for
medical visit, 103–4; resumption of
command, 162; review of troops,
136, 166; Royston, Charles E.,
365n16; Sevier, Ambrose H.,
352n42; social visits, 169, 171–72,
177, 181, 187, 204, 206–7; tea with
William McPheeters, 101, 174;
trip to Camden, Ark., 169; trip to
Lewisville, Ark., 158; visit to hospi-
tals, 152; visit with Mrs. Snead, 144;
visit with William McPheeters,
78, 87–90, 98, 120; and William
McPheeters, 147; Wright, William
Fulton, 365n14
Cincinnati Commercial, 190
City Hospital, 316
City Hotel, Boonville, Mo., 230
City Hotel, New Orleans, La., 309
Claiborne Parish, La., 160
Clara Eames (steamboat), 365n13
Clarendon, Ark., 28, 59, 367n35
Clark, Bennett H., 77, 79–80, 81,
88, 349n6
Clark, Henry M., 141, 255, 361n38
Clark, John Bullock, 213, 227, 232,
366n21
Clark, John Bullock, Jr., 93, 99, 353n46,
353n48, 366n25, 369n13
Clark, Mrs. Henry M., 163
Clarksville, Tx., 196, 249–50
Clay, Henry, 11
Clayton, Powell, 40, 325–26, 343n22
Clear Boggy Creek, 196
Clear Lake, Ark., 322
Clemens, Samuel, 338n40
Clifford, Mr., 294
Clothing Bureau, 358n22, 377n6
Cochrane, John, 173, 366n28
Cocke, John B., 151, 362n51
Cole County, Mo., 228
Collinsburg, La., 144, 369n12
Collinsville, La., 128–29
Compton, Freeman W., 256, 374n11
Confederacy: currency, 248, 252; cur-
rency law, 180, 367n36; mail ser-

vices, 45; recognition by England
and France, 268; sympathizers,
12–20, 45–49, 271–72, 344n8
Confederate Congress, 58, 68, 96, 152,
363n57, 367n36
Confederate forces: ambulances,
324–25; Arkansas Cavalry Battalion,
355n6; Arkansas State Penitentiary,
346n15; Army of Middle Tennessee,
378n23; Army of Missouri, 349n41,
368n44; Army of Northern
Virginia, 157, 291; arrival in
Arkansas, 250; arrival in Missouri,
221; Battalion of Artillery, 170, 182;
battle at Nashville, Tenn., 258,
374n16; Battle of Chickamauga,
348n33; battle of Fort Harrison,
370n26; Battle of Jenkins' Ferry,
150–51, 362n48, 362n52, 362n53,
363n54; battle of Kennesaw
Mountain, 367n39; battle of
Kinston, 377n18; Battle of
Mansfield, 137–38, 289, 357n18,
359n28, 359n29; Battle of Marks'
Mill, 362n47; Battle of Mine Creek,
341n14, 352n31, 366n21, 366n25,
372n37; battle of Mobile Bay,
369n8; battle of Peeble's Farm,
370n26; Battle of Pilot Knob, 196,
224–25, 370n20; Battle of Pleasant
Hill, 122, 138–41, 292, 357n18,
360n32; Battle of Poison Spring,
361n44; battle of Spotsylvania
Courthouse, 365n9; battle of the
Wilderness, 364n7; battle plan,
342n16; Baxter Springs, Ks., 349n9;
Camp Bragg, 76–101, 274, 354n54,
354n56; Camp Grinstead, 164–75,
365n15; camp hygiene, 321–25;
Camp Sumter, 111–21, 355n4; capture of Union boats, 211, 365n13;
capture of Union soldiers, 218,
225–26, 229, 232; casualty rate,
362n53; cavalry, 43, 56, 59–60,
350n13; conditions in field hospitals,
57, 360n36; Consolidated Crescent
Regiment of Louisiana, 361n40;

Crescent Regiment of La., 142; crossing Arkansas River, 216–17, 241–42; crossing of Bayou DeView, Ark., 341n12; Dawson's Arkansas Infantry, 351n26, 366n27; defeat at Little Rock, Ark., 75; defeat at Missionary Ridge, Tenn., 76; defeat at Prairie Grove, Ark., 75; defeat by Union forces, 194; defeat of William T. Sherman, 184; Department of Alabama, Mississippi, and East Louisiana, 291; departure from Camp Grinstead, 175; departure from Richmond, Ark., 258; description of accommodations, 354n54; desertion, 88, 108, 110, 199, 252; destruction of CSS *Alabama* (steamer), 185, 367n41; destruction of Iron Mountain Railroad, 224; destruction of Pacific Railroad, 226, 227; destruction of supplies, 372n37; 8th Missouri Cavalry, 352n35; 8th Missouri Infantry, 350n16, 351n26, 352n39, 354n54; 11th Missouri Cavalry, 352n38, 379n15; 11th Missouri Infantry, 343n27, 377n13; encampment at Camp Bragg, 76–101; encampment at Richmond, Ark., 254–58; encampment at Washington, Ark., 259–62; encampment locations, 321–22, 324; evacuation of Little Rock, Ark., 60; evacuation of Richmond, Va., 294; execution of deserters, 88; 15th Arkansas Cavalry Battalion, 375n22; 15th Louisiana Cavalry, 364n4; 5th Arkansas Cavalry, 379n14; 5th Light Artillery Battalion, 366n23; 5th Missouri Cavalry, 375–76n27, 377n9; 5th North Carolina Cavalry, 339n54; 1st Arkansas (Crawford's) Cavalry, 368n45; 1st Arkansas (Dobbin's) Cavalry, 344n33; 1st Arkansas Infantry, 379n13; 1st Arkansas (Monroe's) Cavalry, 355n1, 372n42,

379n12; 1st Cherokee Mounted Rifles, 372n44; 1st Chickasaw Mounted Rifles, 372n45; 1st Choctaw Mounted Rifles, 372n45; 1st Engineers Battalion, 352n37; 1st Missouri Brigade, 376n28, 377n11; 1st North Carolina Junior Reserves, 339–40n55; 46th Arkansas Mounted Infantry, 373n51; 14th Missouri Cavalry, 345n12, 369n15, 369n16; 4th Arizona Regiment, 378n6; 4th Arkansas Cavalry, 379n15; 4th Confederate Engineer Troops, 340n7; 4th Louisiana Infantry Battalion, 364n6; 4th Missouri Cavalry, 355n61, 368n48, 369n13, 374n12; Greene's Regiment, 306; guerrilla raids, 76, 81, 350n13; Helena campaign, 33–34, 75, 325–27, 342n20; hospital accommodations, 322, 323, 324; Infirmary Corps, 39; losses to Union forces, 370n20; loss of ironclad gunboats, 207; march from Louisiana to Camden, Ark., 161–63; march through Arkansas, 239–40; march through Indian Territory, 241–47; march through Missouri, 221–39; march through Texas, 247–49; march to Camden, Ark., 175; march to Louisiana, 158–61; march to Missouri, 212–21; medical care of wounded soldiers, 363n56; mess arrangements, 323; militia training, 13; Mississippi, 117; Missouri Cavalry Battalion, 350n15, 375n22; Missouri Expedition, 212–50; Missouri State Guard, 13, 338n45, 348n38, 353n48, 360n35; morale, 59, 237, 291; move to Camp Sumter, 103–4; New Mexico campaign, 375n21; 19th Arkansas Infantry, 350n11, 366n27; 9th Battalion of Missouri Sharpshooters, 343n21, 344n9, 368n49, 375n24; 9th Missouri Infantry, 352n34, 353n48; number of sick, 323–24; operations against Union boats, 188; paroles, 329; police arrangements, 324; Pratt's Texas Battery, 353*n45*; pursuit of Union forces, 148–50; Red River campaign, *122*, 123–55, 157; removal of dead soldiers, 362*n52*; retreat from Little Rock, Ark., *74*, 76; retreat from Missouri, 236–50, 371*n36*; retreat from Pleasant Hill, La., 139–40; route of Churchill's infantry, *122*; rumors of victory, 96–97, 169–70, 172, 187, 191–92, 285–87, 348*n35*; sanitary conditions, 324; scarcity of water in camp, 323; 2d Arkansas Mounted Rifles, 347*n23*; 2d Indian Brigade, 361*n45*; 7th Missouri Volunteer Cavalry, 367*n37*, 371*n32*; Sharpshooter Battalion, 379*n9*; shortage of provisions, 242–43, 253; 16th Missouri Infantry, 374*n8*, 377*n7*; 16th Texas Infantry, 360*n36*, 370*n24*; 6th Missouri Cavalry, 344*n10*; 6th Missouri Infantry, 347*n26*, 366*n25*, 370*n24*; 6th Trans-Mississippi Infantry, 368*n47*; skirmishes in Virginia, 350*n12*; skirmish with Union forces, 221, 225–31, 233–39, 371*n34*, 371*n36*; success of Mosby Parsons, 350*n14*; surrender, 291, 296–97, 379*n10*; surrender of Fort Gaines, 207; surrender terms, 300; swamps, 324, 341*n12*; tent arrangements, 322–24; 10th Missouri Cavalry, 346*n14*, 372*n42*; 10th Missouri Infantry, 341*n12*, 354*n55*, 354*n56*, 378*n21*; Texas cavalry Brigade, 84, 85, 138, 142; 3d Missouri Field Artillery, 355*n1*; 13th Louisiana Partisan Rangers, 380*n22*; 30th Texas Cavalry, 373*n54*; 38th Arkansas Infantry, 350*n11*, 355*n1*, 356*n11*, 366*n26*; 34th Arkansas Infantry, 351*n28*; 39th Arkansas Infantry, 351*n26*, 362*n51*; 32d Arkansas Infantry, 343*n21*, 349*n6*, 359*n26*; 37th Arkansas Infantry, 349*n7*, 351*n26*, 356*n11*; 36th Arkansas Infantry, 343*n21*, 344*n35*, 351*n26*, 359*n26*; 33d Arkansas Infantry, 350*n11*, 355*n3*, 362*n50*, 365*n11*, 367*n40*; 33d Texas Cavalry, 376*n32*; 12th Arkansas Battalion of Sharpshooters, 380*n19*; 12th Arkansas Cavalry, 365*n15*; 12th Missouri Cavalry, 346*n14*, 370*n23*, 371*n35*; 12th Missouri Infantry, 351*n24*, 365*n18*; 20th Texas Cavalry, 364*n58*, 364*n59*, 373*n55*; 25th Arkansas Infantry, 352*n33*, 367*n33*; 21st Texas Cavalry, 353*n45*; 24th Arkansas Infantry, 350*n11*, 367*n38*; 27th Arkansas Infantry, 350*n11*, 370*n25*, 378*n22*, 380*n22*; 26th Arkansas Infantry, 359*n26*, 365*n11*, 378*n19*; as unwanted visitors, 253; use of General Hospital, 325; victories during Red River campaign, 142, 148–49, 157; victories in Alabama, 119; victories in Florida, 119; victories in Mississippi, 119, 174; victories in North Carolina, 159; victories in Virginia, 161–62, 164, 176, 179, 188–89; victory at Chattanooga, Tenn., 71–72, 78; victory at Chickamauga, Ga., 76; victory at Richmond, Va., 120; victory in Florida, 356*n16*; victory on the Potomac, 232; Walker, John George, 357–58*n13*; winter quarters, 76–101; wounded soldiers in Little Rock, Ark., 55–57; yellow flags, 40, 343*n23*; *See also* 9th Missouri Infantry; Army of Tennessee

Conrow, Aaron H., 136, 359*n24*
Consolidated Crescent Regiment of Louisiana, 361*n40*
consumption: *See* tuberculosis
convulsions, 336*n14*
Cook, Mr., 52
Cooper, Douglas Hancock, 246, 372*n45*, 372*n46*
Cooper County, Mo., 231

Copperheads, 349*n40*
Cordova, Mexico, 315
Corinth, Miss., 21
cornea, ulceration of, 79
correspondence: Alston, William A.,
294; Bond, John B., 114, 119, 130,
267, 268; Boyd, Mr., 193; brother,
79, 106, 155, 255, 265, 289; Cabell,
Edward Carrington (from), 119–20,
173, 210, 265; Cabell, Edward
Carrington (to), 163, 170, 211,
257, 262, 274, 281, 303; Churchill,
Mrs. Thomas James, 178, 189;
Churchill, Thomas James, 266;
Clark, Henry M., 255;
Cunningham, Francis D., 43,
92–93, 116, 118, 120; Graham,
Malcolm, 164, 255, 281, 299–300;
Greene, Charles, 296; Haden,
John M., 281; Harper, Richard S.,
266; Hervey, Mrs. Calvin Monroe,
299; Johnson, Andrew, 314; Jordan,
Irene, 120, 210, 303; Jordan, Mr.,
119; letter from wife, 81–82, 180,
213, 255; letter to wife during
Helena campaign, 40; letter to wife
during march from Louisiana, 163;
letter to wife during march to
Louisiana, 158; letter to wife during
Missouri Expedition, 204, 223, 226,
230, 249; letter to wife during Red
River campaign, 130, 132, 145, 155;
letter to wife during winter quarters, 262, 264; letter to wife from
Camp Bragg, 80, 85, 89, 98, 100;
letter to wife from Camp Grinstead,
165, 167; letter to wife from Camp
Sumter, 113–15; letter to wife
from encampment near Camden,
Ark., 178, 181, 188; Lonergan,
Thomas A., 255; MacLean, Lauchlan
A., 170; Marvin, Enoch M., 93;
McDowell, Joseph Nash, 274;
Mhoon, John, 297; Monroe,
Thomas, 164; niece, 69, 168, 187,
254, 255, 257; Polk, John Widener,
130, 167, 262; Polk, Trusten, 281,

282, 296, 303; Price, Sterling, 268,
303; Reynolds, Thomas Caute, 96,
99, 106, 114, 286–87; Rice, Mrs.
Dorsey, 249; Sandridge, Fanny Lu,
208; Shaler, James R., 274; sisters,
88, 89, 98, 100, 159, 164–65, 166,
208; Snead, Harriet, 165, 167; Snead,
Thomas Lowndes, 164, 195, 263,
289; Taylor, Henry Clay, 106, 118,
164, 301; Wooten, Mrs. Thomas D.,
178; Wooten, Thomas Dudley
(from), 89, 107, 164, 165, 225, 266;
Wooten, Thomas Dudley (to), 82,
105–6, 163, 167, 213, 216, 253, 262;
Yandell, David Wendell, 165
cotton, 123–25, 154–55, 172, 252, 263,
306, 358*n17*
Cotton Plant, Ark., *28, 35*
Cow Skin River, 239
Craighead County, Ark., 339*n50*
Crawford, Washington L., 255, 374*n9*
Crease, Sophy, 202
Crescent Regiment of La., 142
Crittenden, Lt., 82, 89
Crockett, Davy, 248
CSS *Alabama* (cruiser), 367*n41*
CSS *Albemarle* (ironclad), 364*n2*
CSS *Missouri* (ironclad), 130, 133, 358*n18*
CSS *Pontchartrain* (gunboat), 65, 347*n22*
CSS *Tennessee* (ironclad), 369*n8*
Cuba, 292
Cuitman, Chas. O., 23
Cullen, Matthew R., 200, 211–12, 368*n4*
Cundiff, J. H. R., 72, 348*n38*
Cunningham, Francis D.: appointment as
Medical Director of the District of
Arkansas, 342*n18;* breakfast with
William McPheeters, 92, 100–101;
correspondence with William
McPheeters, 43, 92–93, 116, 118,
120; dinner with William
McPheeters, 80; medical care of
wounded soldiers, 39; medical
inspector for the Trans-Mississippi
Department, 342*n18;* official visit
with William McPheeters, 87; social
visits, 81, 91, 97; transfer to Little

Rock, Ark., 326; transfer to Virginia, 147, 342*n18*
currency law, 180, 367*n36*
Current River, *196*
Curtis, Mr., 187
Curtis, Samuel R., 17, 371*n36*

D

Dailey, William E., 246, 372*n47*
Dahlgren, Ulrich, 357*n17*
Danley, Benjamin Franklin, 70, 348*n32*
Danley, Christopher Columbus, 348*n32*
Dardenelle, Ark., *196,* 216
Davidson, John W., 346*n18*
Davidson, Mr., 92, 100
Davies, Mr., 267
Davis, George, 85, 351*n27*
Davis, Jefferson: Confederate Congress, 96; Confederate president, 12; creation of medical department, 22; defense of Little Rock, Ark., 58; imprisonment, 315; inauguration anniversary, 109; message to forces, 168, 365*n17;* monetary gift from William McPheeters, 315; Smith, Edmund Kirby, 345*n15;* Vicksburg campaign, 30; view of Trans-Mississippi, 22; visit with William McPheeters, 315
Davis, Mrs. Jefferson, 315, 380–81*n4*
Dawson, Charles L., 366*n27*
Dawson's Arkansas Infantry, 351*n26,* 366*n27*
Dean, Eliza, 287, 300
decaying vegetable matter, 322
Delaries, Mrs., 307
Democratic Convention, 213
Democratic Party, 12
Dent, Frederick (father), 336*n7*
Dent, Frederick (son), 336*n7*
Dent, Julia: See Grant, Julia Dent (Mrs. Ulysses S.)
Department of Alabama, Mississippi, and East Louisiana, 291
Department of Kansas, 371*n30*
Department of Mississippi, 364*n60,* 376–77*n5*

Department of Mississippi and East Louisiana, 348*n31*
Department of Missouri, 15, 17, 371*n33*
Department of the Cumberland, 371*n33*
Department of the Gulf, 359*n27*
Department of West Virginia, 371*n30*
Derrick, Miss, 274, 288
Des Arc, Ark., *28, 35*
desertion, 88, 108, 199, 252
DeVall's Bluff, Ark., *28,* 53, 59, *196,* 345*n13*
diary entries: Arkadelphia, Ark., 69–70; arrival in Arkansas, 250; banishment of wife, 273–77; Battle of Mansfield, 137–38; Battle of Pilot Knob, *196,* 224–25; Battle of Pleasant Hill, 138–41; at Calvin Hervey's, 267–69, 273–74, 293–303; Camp Bragg, 70–73, 77–101, 103–11; Camp Grinstead, 164–75; Camp Sumter, 111–21; crossing Arkansas River, 216–17, 241–42; encampment at Richmond, Ark., 254–58; encampment at Washington, Ark., 259–62; encampment near Camden, Ark., 175–95; Helena campaign, 34–44; Little Rock, Ark., 24–27, 61–69; march from Louisiana to Camden, Ark., 161–63; march through Arkansas, 239–40; march through Indian Territory, 241–47; march through Missouri, 221–39; march through Texas, 247–49; march to Louisiana, 158–61; march to Missouri, 212–21; Missouri Expedition, 212–50; preparations for Missouri Expedition, 204–12; Red River campaign, 127–55; retreat from Missouri, 236–50; return to St. Louis, Mo., 292–311; stay in Helena, Ark., 50–53; trip to Shreveport, La., 199–203
Dickenson, Mr, 277
Dickinson, A. C., 89, 352*n37*
Dickinson, Mr., 280
Dick (McPheeter's servant), 109
Dickson, Mr., 295

dining invitations: Ashley, William Elliott, 254; Christopher, Mr., 78; Churchill, Thomas James, 204; Drayton, Thomas Fenwick, 92; Eakin, John R., 259; Hamilton, Edward L., 256; Hill, Nicholas S., 265; Hill, Parson, 70; Jordan, Irene, 266; Lovett, Alexander, 256; MacLean, Lauchlan A., 177; Madden, John W., 78; Smizer, George, 37; Williamson, Mrs., 256; Wilson, Dr., 262

diphtheria, 319

District of Arkansas: Armistead, Franck S., 348n36; Brinker, Isaac, 341n11; Buckner, Simon Bolivar, 368n2; Burton, John B., 377n6; Cabell, Edward Carrington, 347n24; Clark, Henry M., 361n38; Clark, John Bullock, Jr., 366n25; Danley, Benjamin Franklin, 348n32; diminishment of, 75; Dockery, Thomas Pleasant, 353n43; Dunlap, W. Watkins, 352n40; Fagan, James Fleming, 340–41n8; Hill, Nicholas S., 339n53; Hinsdale, John W., 351n22; Holmes, Theophilus Hunter, 31, 68, 118–19, 339n52; Magruder, John Bankhead, 374n7; Marmaduke, John Sappington, 341n14; Marvin, Enoch M., 341n13; Moore, Charles B., 366n22; Morgan, A. S., 369n11; Parsons, Mosby Monroe, 350n14; Price, Sterling, 58, 119, 338n45, 356n15; Shaler, James R., 370n25; shortage of provisions, 253; Sigourney, Andrew, 350n18; Slaughter, R. M., 342n18; Taylor, Henry Clay, 348n29; Tracy, Henry W., 348n30; Walker, Lucius Marsh, 347n20; Wooten, Thomas D., 147

District of Texas, 377n10

District of Western Louisiana, 125, 357–58n13, 357n18, 368n2

Dix, Dorothea, 19

Dixon, Mr. (Ark.), 144, 159

Dixon, Mr. (La.), 160

Dobbins, Archibald S., 43, 61, 344n33

Dockery, Mrs.(mother), 203

Dockery, Mrs.(wife), 203

Dockery, Thomas Pleasant, 91, 203, 304, 353n43

Dodge, Grenville M., 272, 333

Doiters, Misses, 162

Dooley's Ferry, Ark., 270, 286, 298–99

Dorne, Andrew J., 247–48, 373n49

Dover, Ark., 217

Dover, Mo., 196, 233

Drake, Dr., 212

Drayton, John Edward, 85, 351n26

Drayton, Thomas Fenwick: arrival at camp, 72; assumption of Division command, 119; church attendance, 86, 90; Drayton, John Edward, 351n26; invitation to William McPheeters, 92–93; Lewis, John W., 377n12; march to Shreveport, La., 127, 129; military ball, 355n7; move to Camp Sumter, 103; relieved of command, 130; review of troops, 100; social visits, 98, 101, 113, 119, 133; transfer to Texas, 348n39; travel to Texas, 134; visit with William McPheeters, 95, 98, 101, 112–13, 119, 133; von Phul, Benjamin, 353n46

Dred Scott case, 10, 356n10

Dryden, C. F., 85, 351n24

Duncan, Robert, 113, 135, 298, 356n11

Dunlap, W. Watkins, 89, 130, 154, 178, 194, 205, 352n40

Dutch, 226, 228

dysentery, 58, 202, 210, 215, 296

E

Eakin, John R., 259, 296, 375n18

Eakin, Mrs. (formerly Betty Erwins), 71, 259, 260, 263, 264

Early, Jubal, 368n46

8th Missouri Cavalry, 352n35

8th Missouri Infantry, 350n16, 351n26, 352n39, 354n54

Eleven Point River, *196*
11th Missouri Cavalry, 352*n38*, 379*n15*
11th Missouri Infantry, 343*n27*, 377*n13*
Eliot, William Greenleaf, 5
El Paso, Tx., *2*
emancipation, 115
Emma (steamboat), 307
empirical medical therapeutics, 317–18
Engineer Corps, 89
England, 292
Ericson, James P., 234, 371*n31*
Erwins, Betty: *See* Eakin, Mrs. (formerly
   Betty Erwins)
Ewell, Richard, 190
Ewing, Thomas, Jr., 370*n21*, 370*n22*
exile (as choice), 292

F

Fagan, James Fleming: Adams, John,
   356*n12*; Battle of Marks' Mill,
   362*n47*; Battle of Pilot Knob,
   370*n20*; brigade inspection by
   William McPheeters, 324; Cabell,
   William Lewis, 352*n31*; cavalry
   brigade, 340–41*n8*; defeat of Union
   forces, 148; District of Arkansas,
   340–41*n8*; Dockery, Thomas
   Pleasant, 353*n43*; Helena campaign,
   32, 35, 38, 342*n16*, 342*n20*; Missouri
   Expedition, 198, 213–15, 223–24,
   228, 235, 239, 244; promotion, 155;
   Rapley, William F., 380*n19*; skirmish
   with Union forces, 228, 235–37,
   371*n34*, 372*n37*; visit with William
   McPheeters, 204, 301
Falcon, Ark., 111, *270*, *274*
Fannin County, Tx., 247
Farragut, David G., 369*n8*
Fayetteville, Ark., *196*, 240, 373*n53*
Federal Arsenal, 25, 339*n49*
Federal Department of Arkansas, 271
Federal Military Division of Missouri,
   380*n23*
15th Arkansas Cavalry Battalion, 375*n22*
15th Louisiana Cavalry, 364*n4*
5th Arkansas Cavalry, 379*n14*
5th Light Artillery Battalion, 366*n23*

5th Missouri Cavalry, 375–76*n27*, 377*n9*
5th North Carolina Cavalry, 339*n54*
Finley, James W., 284, 286, 288, 293,
   298–99, 377*n14*, 380*n20*
Finley, Waddy, 298–99, 303, 304, 380*n20*
Finnegan, Joseph, 119, 356*n16*
"the fire bell in the night," 10
1st Arkansas (Crawford's) Cavalry,
   368*n45*
1st Arkansas (Dobbin's) Cavalry, 344*n33*
1st Arkansas Infantry, 379*n13*
1st Arkansas (Monroe's) Cavalry, 355*n1*,
   372*n42*, 379*n12*
1st Cherokee Mounted Rifles, 372*n44*
1st Chickasaw Mounted Rifles, 372*n45*
1st Choctaw Mounted Rifles, 372*n45*
1st Engineers Battalion, 352*n37*
1st Indiana Cavalry, 343*n25*
1st Kansas Colored Infantry, 361*n44*
1st Missouri Brigade, 376*n28*, 377*n11*
1st North Carolina Junior Reserves,
   339–40*n55*
1st U.S. Volunteers, 16
flag of truce: Cabell, Edward Carrington,
   159; Grant, Ulysses S., 329; letter
   from Sallie McPheeters, 180; letter
   to Sallie McPheeters, 181; Little
   Rock, Ark., 98, 100, 178, 181, 188,
   191, 194; Louisville, Ky., 213; mail
   services, 271; procurement of medical supplies, 41; St. Louis, Mo.,
   99–100; travel to Helena, Ark., 53
Flanagin, Harris, 66, 67, 84, 347*n23*,
   348*n34*
fleas, 175, 179
Fleming, Dr., 223
Fleming, Mrs. (formerly Mary Lee), 223
flies, 182, 184
Folsom, Isaac, 203, 369*n7*
Forney, John H., 200, 368*n3*
Forrest, Nathan Bedford, 107–8, 117,
   118, 119, 174, 356*n14*, 366*n30*
Fort Curtis, Ark., 342*n20*
Fort Davidson, Mo., 370*n20*, 370*n21*
Fort Delaware, 354*n57*
Fort Gaines, Ala., 207, 369*n8*, 369*n9*

Fort Gibson, Indian Territory, *2, 196,* 236, 241–42

Fort McCulloch, Indian Territory, *196, 246*

Fort Morgan, Ala., 369*n8,* 369*n9*

Fort Scott, Ks., *196*

Fort Smith, Ark., *2, 196,* 241–42

Fort Sumter, 331

46th Arkansas Mounted Infantry, 373*n51*

Fourche Bayou, Ark., 60

Fourgeaud, Victor J., 6–7

14th Missouri Cavalry, 345*n12,* 369*n15,* 369*n16*

4th Arizona Regiment, 378*n6*

4th Arkansas Cavalry, 379*n15*

4th Confederate Engineer Troops, 340*n7*

4th Louisiana Infantry Battalion, 364*n6*

4th Missouri Cavalry, 355*n61,* 368*n48,* 369*n13,* 374*n12*

Fowler, Samuel, 288, 374*n14*

Franklin, Mo., 226

Franklin County, Mo., 226

Frank (McPheeters' servant), 95, 158, 195, 244–45, 266, 286, 300, 353*n50*

Franz Josef, 124

Frazer, Miss, 189

Fredericktown, Mo., *196,* 222–23

Frémont, John C., 12, 173, 366*n28*

friendships: at Camp Bragg, 77–81, 83–95, 97–101; at Camp Sumter, 109, 112–14, 116–21; during Helena campaign, 37, 42–44, 50–53; Little Rock, Ark., 59, 61–62, 64, 68–71; during Red River campaign, 128–36, 144, 154; St. Louis, Mo., 4–5, 9–10, 310–11, 315

Frost, Daniel Marsh: banishment of wife, 47, 344*n8;* dinner with William McPheeters, 70; Lewis, John W., 377*n12;* Little Rock, Ark., 346*n12;* Scott, Joseph T., 351*n30;* Seay, William M., 351*n20;* tea with William McPheeters, 61; Tracy, Henry W., 348*n30;* visit with William McPheeters, 64; and William McPheeters, 67

Frost, Eliza "Lily" (Mrs. Daniel Marsh), 47, 51, 62, 344*n8*

Frost, S. M., 282, 377*n9*

Fugitive Slave Act (1850), 10

Fulton, Ark., *196,* 259, 298, 379*n14*

G

Gaines, John H., 182, 367*n38*

Gaines Creek, 244

Gaines Landing, Ark., *270,* 272, 274, 277, 280, 333

Gallagher, George A., 209, 212, 254, 262, 369*n10*

Gallagher, Mr., 306

Galveston, Tx., *2,* 285

Gamble, Hamilton Rowan, 112, 356*n10*

Gano, Richard Montgomery, 250, 373*n56*

Garrett, Mr., 154, 155, 158

Gasconade River, *196,* 227

Gause, Lucien C., 136, 170, 177–78, 343*n21,* 359*n26*

Gayoso Hotel, Memphis, Tenn., 49

Gelson, Mrs., 294

Gen. Fletcher (steamboat), 275

Georgetown, Mo., 231

Georgia, 157, 190

Germer, Mary, 338*n36*

Gettysburg address, 251

Gettysburg campaign, 42, 48, 343*n30*

Gibson, J. W. "Watt," 362*n52,* 363*n56*

Gibson, Samuel, 287, 378*n19*

Gibson, William C., 161, 364*n4*

Gilded Age, 318

Gilmer, Tx., 268

Glasgow, Mo., *196,* 231–32

Glenn, John E., 343*n21*

Goff, Dr., 223

gold prices, 182, 184, 185

Goose question, 96, 353*n51*

Graham, Fanny, 337*n18*

Graham, John, 4

Graham, Lilly, 337*n18*

Graham, Malcolm: correspondence with William McPheeters, 164, 255, 281, 299–300; dinner with William McPheeters, 184; loan from William McPheeters, 259, 265; 9th Missouri Infantry, 365*n8;* receipt of money, 300; receipt of money and clothes,

166; visit with Sallie McPheeters, 282; visit with William McPheeters, 284

Graham, Mrs. Malcolm (formerly Miss Washington), 205–7, 210, 305

Graham family, 4, 6, 9, 310–11, 337*n18*

Granbury, Hiram, 365*n12*

Granby, Mo., *196,* 238

Grand Avenue Presbyterian Church, 319

Grand Ecore, La., 126

grand rounds, 77

Granny Holmes, 31

Grant, Julia Dent (Mrs. Ulysses S.): introduction to William McPheeters, 5; marriage to Ulysses S. Grant, 336*n7;* and Sallie Buchanan McPheeters, 49–50

Grant, Ulysses S., 5; appointment as general in chief of the Union armies, 125; approach to Richmond, Va., 171; defeat by Confederate forces, 164, 172; marriage to Julia Dent, 336*n7;* Petersburg, Va., 176, 179, 181–83, 186, 188–89, 251; Red River campaign, 124, 126; Richmond, Va., 181–83, 184, 188; strategy, 157; surrender of Robert E. Lee, 295; Vicksburg campaign, 30, 41, 49, 59, 326–29

Gratiot Street Prison, 20, 47, 272, 273, 316, 333, 376–77*n5,* 376*n4*

Graveyard Hill, 342*n16,* 342*n20,* 344*n35*

Gray, Henry, 361*n40*

Grease (horse), 205, 304

Green, Charles, 131, 293, 302

Green, Mrs., 27

Green, Thomas, 139, 142, 360*n31*

Greene, Charles, 289, 296, 358*n20*

Greene, Colton, 170, 306, 365*n13,* 366*n21,* 369*n15*

Greenville, Mo., *196,* 222

Grenada, Miss., 21, 81

Greybacks, 214, 218

Grierson, Benjamin H., 117, 118, 119, 174

Grimes, Abasalom, 338*n40*

Grinstead, Hiram L., 151, 164, 362*n50*

Grisamore, Silas, 361*n40*

Groner, Mrs. (elder), 278

Groner, Mrs. (younger), 278

Gurley, Edward, 373*n54*

H

Haden, John M.: correspondence with William McPheeters, 88, 112, 281–82; dinner with William McPheeters, 131; Medical Director, 88, 91, 130–31, 352*n36;* Trans-Mississippi Department, 378*n23;* visit with William McPheeters, 92–93, 147, 154

Hadley, Mr., 304

Hainey House, Baton Rouge, La., 309

Halleck, Henry W., 15, 124, 331

Hamburg, Ark., *270,* 276–77

Hamilton, Mrs. Edward L., 256, 257

Hamilton, Edward L., 172, 256, 257, 366*n27*

Hanger, Mrs., 61

Hannah, Mr., 289

Hardin, Dr., 181

Hardin, Mrs., 181

Harding, Dr., 193, 307, 308

Harding, Mrs., 193, 308

Harper, Richard S., 266, 376*n29*

Harrelson, Mr., 35

Harris, Edwin E., *169,* 365*n20*

Harris' Ferry, Ark., 53

Harrisonburg, La., *290,* 308

Hart, Benjamin H., 85, 351*n26*

Hart, R. A., 328

Harvey, Mrs., 162

Hawthorn, Alexander, 362*n51,* 368*n47*

Haynes, John W., 327

Haynes, William H., 133, 358*n22*

Hébert, Louis, 348*n31*

Hedgepeth, Isaac N., 228, 370*n24*

Helena, Ark., *28, 290;* approach by Union forces, 59; Helena campaign, 38–40, 325–27, 341*n15,* 342*n16,* 342*n19,* 342*n20,* 377*n7;* occupation by Union forces, 29, 325–27; Rice, Mrs. Dorsey, 249; as target of Confederate forces, 29, 32–34

Helena campaign, *28*, 38–40, 325–27, 341*n15*, 342*n16*, 342*n19*, 342*n20*, 377*n7*

Hempstead, Mrs. (formerly Miss Gratiot), 264

Hempstead County, Ark.: Brandon, Thomas, 377*n16*; Finley, James W., 377*n14*; Smith, Thomas C., 375*n23*; Spring Hill, Ark., 334, 355*n4*, 356*n8*; Thompson, Thomas H., 377*n17*, 379*n15*; Washington, Ark., 57, 348*n34*

Henry, James, 60–61

Herman, Mo., 227

Herndon, Dr., 94, 97, 120

hernia, 353*n49*

hernia, strangulated, 94

Hervey, Calvin Monroe, 119, 267, 274, 280–89, 293–303, 334, 376*n30*

Hervey, Molly (Mary), 281, 283–85, 288–89, 293–94, 296, 298–99, 303, 377*n8*

Hervey, Mrs. Calvin Monroe, 267, 274, 281, 284, 286, 288, 298–300, 355*n7*

Hervey Sulky Plow, 376*n30*

Hickman, Edwin A., 67, 68, 347*n26*

High Point, Mo., 229

Hill, Mr., 35–36

Hill, Mrs. (formerly Mrs. Jim Johnson), 260

Hill, Nicholas S., 26, 154, 178, 265–66, 269, 273, 339*n53*

Hill, Parson, 70

Hindman, Thomas C., 23, 348*n32*

Hindman Hill, 342*n16*, 342*n20*

Hinsdale, John W., 84, 351*n22*

Hoke, Robert F., 364*n2*

Holliday, J. J., 162

Holly Springs, Miss., 21, 30, 49

Holmes, Theophilus Hunter: Army of Virginia, 23, 31; arrival from Arkadelphia, Ark., 72; Broadfoot, Charles W., 339–40*n55*; correspondence with William McPheeters, 43; Cunningham, Francis D., 342*n18*; defense of Little Rock, Ark., 58; description of, 31; District of Arkansas, 31, 58, 68, 339*n52*;

evacuation of Little Rock, Ark., 60; Gallagher, George A., 369*n10*; Helena campaign, 32, 34, 37, 39, 342*n20*; Hinsdale, John W., 351*n22*; Holmes, Theophilus Hunter, Jr., 339*n54*; Johnson, Jilson P., 349*n10*; meeting with Sterling Price, 90; pardon of deserter, 88; removal from command, 118–19; resignation of, 356*n15*; review of troops, 94; social visits, 100–101; Trans-Mississippi Department, 23, 31; travel to Lewisville, Ark., 113; visit from William McPheeters, 81, 91, 100–101; visits with William McPheeters, 25–26; Watkins, George C., 348*n37*

Holmes, Theophilus Hunter, Jr., 339*n54*

Home Guards, 13

Homer, La., *122*, 160, 162–63

hominy, 254

Honey Grove, Tx., *196*, 248

Hood, John Bell, 369*n18*, 374*n16*

Hooker, Joseph, 184, 367*n39*

Hooper, P. O., 23, 141, 360*n37*

Hopefield, Ark., 345*n13*

hospitals: children's hospital, 7; City Hospital, 316; conditions in field hospitals, 360*n36*; Main Street Hospital, 56; Marine Hospital, 10, 316; Quarantine Hospital, 316; Rock Hotel Hospital, 55; sanitary conditions, 56–57; Small Pox Hospital, 316; St. John's College, 55, 57; St. Louis Children's Hospital, 336*n15*; St. Louis County Insane Asylum, 316; St. Luke's Hospital, 316; use of churches as, 56, 68, 69; wartime surgery, 57, 317–18, 360*n36*

Hot Springs County, Ark., 66

Houston, Tx., *2*, 292

Hoy, Albert B., 247–48, 373*n50*

Huger, Benjamin, 131, 358*n20*

Hunter, Col., 324

Hunter, David, 234, 371*n30*

Hutchinson, E. C., 9

I

Illinois, 19–20
Illinois Creek, 239
Illinois River, *196*
Independence, Mo., *196*, 234–35,
    371n31, 371n34
Independence County, Ark., 219
Indian Battalion: *See* Missouri Cavalry
    Battalion
Indian Territory, 239–47, *361n45,
    361n46, 372–73n48, 372n45, 373n56*
Ingram, John P., 81, *350n15*
intermittent fever, 41, 94–95, *343n28*
ironclad gunboats, 68, 124, 129, 207,
    329, *358n18, 364n2, 369n8*
Iron Mountain Railroad, 224
Ironton, Mo., *196*, 224

J

Jackman, Sidney D., 81, *350n13*
Jackson, Claiborne Fox, 12, 16, *340n56*
Jackson, Col., 248
Jackson, Miss., 30, *290*, 329
Jackson, Mrs., 248
Jackson, Stonewall, *371n29*
Jackson, Tenn., 206
Jackson County, Mo., 235
Jacksonport, Ark., 24, *28*, 32, 34, 36
James River, 176, 180–81
Jandon, Benjamin A., 166, 182, 189,
    206, *365n11*
Jasper County, Mo., 238
Jayhawkers, 214, 215, 218, *370n28*
Jefferson City, Mo., 2, *196*, 227–29,
    290, 370n20
Jenkins' Ferry, Ark., *122*, 150, 154
Jennison, Charles R. "Doc," 233, 234,
    370n28
Jewell, Horace, 184, *367n40*
Johnson, Andrew, 173, 297, 299, 314
Johnson, Benjamin F., *372n42*
Johnson, Benjamin S., 141, 155, 163,
    165–68, 193, 205, 259, *364n7*
Johnson, Dr., 243
Johnson, Jesse W., *372n42*
Johnson, Jilson P., 79, 82, *349n10*
Johnson, Mary, 25–27, 34, 43, 53,
    61–62, 64

Johnson, Mrs. George R., 37–38, 53
Johnson, Mrs. R. H. (Dick), 116–17, 179
Johnson, Old Mrs.: dinner with
    William McPheeters, 128; medical
    care, 116–17, 202–3; message to
    William McPheeters, 78; visit with
    William McPheeters, 25–27, 53, 61,
    259, 267, 274, 283, 295
Johnson, Richard H. (Dick), 116, 119,
    128, 202–3, *357n11*
Johnson, Robert W., *357n11*
Johnson, Sally, 117, 128
Johnson, Walt, 26–27
Johnson's Island, Ohio, *364n60, 377n7*
Johnston, Albert Sidney, 38, *342n17*
Johnston, Joseph E.: Army of
    Tennessee, 157; battle of Kennesaw
    Mountain, *367n39;* defeat of
    William T. Sherman, 169–70, 173,
    184, 190–91; inability to provide
    relief to Vicksburg, Miss., 329;
    retreat from William T. Sherman,
    186; surrender, 291, 296, *379n10;*
    surrender terms, 299–301
Jones, A. J., *351n26*
Jones, B. M., *351n26*
Jones, Capt., 85
Jones, Dr., 258
Jones, Edward T., *351n26*
Jones, J. M. G., *351n26*
Jones, Judge, 51, 134
Jones, W. J. F., *351n26*
Jonesboro, Mo., *196*, 231
Jordan, Irene: buttons for William
    McPheeters, 120; correspondence
    with William McPheeters, 78, 120,
    210, 303; as friend, 25, 27; intended
    visit from William McPheeters,
    294; medical care for sick son,
    265–66; social visits, 116–17,
    127–28, 207–8, 259, 264; socks for
    William McPheeters, 80; visit with
    Sallie McPheeters, 286; visit with
    William McPheeters, 295
Jordan, Mr., 119
journal club, 77, 318

K

Kahte, Herman, 337*n26*
Kansas, 236
Kansas City, Mo., *2, 196*
Kates, Mrs., 25, 27
Kavanaugh, Benjamin Taylor, 77, 79, 167, 209, 349*n5*
Kavanaugh, Thomas H., 104, 105, 212, 355*n1*
Kearsarge (sloop), 367*n41*
Keatchie, La., *122,* 127, 135–36
Kelly, Joseph H., 140, 360*n35*
Kelly, Thomas G., 53, 345*n12*
Kemper College, 4
Kemps Ferry, Tx., 247
Kentucky, 17
Kerr, George W., 53, 80, 82, 307, 345*n14*
Kidd, R. A., 106, 355*n6*
Kidder, Charles E., 169, 192–93, 205, 365*n19*
Kilpatrick, Judson, 357*n17*
Kimmel, Manning M., 201, 202, 223, 268–69, 369*n6*
Kincannon, Andrew N., 40, 43, 53, 69, 327, 343*n21*
Kinderhook, Ark., 218
King, A. W., 376*n32*
King, Claudius E. R., 376*n32*
King, Dr., 268, 287, 288, 297, 298
King, Miss, 43
Kinston, La., 143
Kirby Smithdom, 76, 345*n15*
Knox, David C., 293, 378*n6*
Knox, Mr., 303
Koch, Robert, 319
Kyler, Dr., 43

L

Lacey, Ark., *270,* 277
Lacy, John McC., 85, 351*n28*
Lafayette County, Ark., 259
Lafayette County, Mo., 233
Lafore, Mrs., 246
La Fourche River, 215
L'Aigle Creek, *270,* 278
Lake Erie, 364*n60*
Lamar County, Tx., 248–49

Lamartine, Ark., 203
Lane, James H., 233, 234, 370*n28*
Langford, William B., 105, 106, 107–8, 355*n3*
L'Anguille River, *28*
Lawrence, G. W., 360*n37*
Lawrence, J. W., 22
Lawrence, Ks., *2*
Lawrence, William M., 23, 85, 88, 141, 351*n23,* 360*n37*
Laynesport, Ark., *196,* 250, 254
Lebanon (steamboat), 365*n13*
Lee, Mary: *See* Fleming, Mrs. (formerly Mary Lee)
Lee, Robert E.: Army of Northern Virginia, 157; battle of Spotsylvania Courthouse, 365*n9;* battle of the Wilderness, 364*n7;* defeat of George Meade, 72, 81, 96, 350*n12;* foray into Maryland, 33; Gettysburg campaign, 42, 343*n30;* Pennsylvania, 329; surrender, 291, 295; victories in Virginia, 85, 161–62; victories over Union forces, 173, 251
Leighton, Provost Marshal, 46
Levy, Lionel, 100, 355*n60*
Lewis, John W., 283, 305, 377*n12*
Lewis, Levin M., 280, 326, 377*n7*
Lewisville, Ark., *74, 122, 270;* Bond, John B., 90, 114, 116, 119, 128, 352*n41;* Cabell, Edward Carrington, 281, 300; Churchill, Mrs. Thomas James, 91, 121; Churchill, Thomas James, 104, 121, 158; encampment, 127–28; Folsom, Isaac, 369*n7;* Graham, Malcolm, 282, 284; headquarters, 111; Johnson, Old Mrs., 116, 202; Johnson, Richard H. (Dick), 119, 128, 202; Jordan, Irene, 116, 127–28, 286; Jordan, Mr., 119; McPheeters, William Marcellus, 283–84; Newton, Mrs., 99, 121, 193, 202, 210; Polk, Trusten, 281, 284, 299–300; Price, Sterling, 287; Slaughter, R. M., 84; Wright, Mrs., 202; Wright, William Fulton, 191; Yancey, Stephen D., 285
Lexington, Mo., *196,* 231, 233–34

Liberty, Mo., 306

Lincoln, Abraham: appointment of
Ulysses S. Grant as general in chief
of the Union armies, 125; assassination of, 296–97; call for troops, 12;
election of, 11; elections, 73, 173,
366n28; Gettysburg address, 251;
inauguration, 282; invasion of
Texas, 124; and McPheeters,
Samuel Brown, 17; reelection of,
251; resignation of cabinet members, 184, 185; rumors of death, 98;
treatment of Missouri, xi, 11–12

Lindell Hotel, St. Louis, Mo., 310, 314

Lindsay, Capt., 282

Lindsay, D. Herndon, 142, 361n39

Lindsay, Mrs., 282

Linn, Mo., 196, 227

Linton, M. L., 6–7

Lister, Joseph, 57, 319

Little Black River, 221

Little Blue River, 234, 371n31, 371n34

Littlejohn, R. M., 297, 379n12

Little Missouri River, 70, 74, 122, 270

Little Osage River, 196, 236, 372n37

Little Red River, 196, 217–18

Little River, 196, 375n20

Little Rock, Ark., 2, 28, 74, 122, 196,
290; Arkansas State Penitentiary,
346n15; Ashley, William Elliott,
346n17; Chandler, John L., 367n37;
Clothing Bureau, 358n22, 377n6;
defense of city, 58–59; description
of town, 23–24; dysentery, 58;
evacuation of city, 60, 63; fall of
city, 59–60; Federal Arsenal, 25,
339n49; flag of truce, 99; Flanagin,
Harris, 347n23; Frost, Daniel Marsh,
346n12; as "hospital city," 55;
inspection of infantry camps,
321–25; Main Street Hospital, 56;
malaria, 58; McPheeters, William
Marcellus, 34; Memphis and Little
Rock Railroad, 345n13; (mention),
86, 305; military hospital, 23;
morale, 59; pneumonia, 56; Price,
Sterling, 21; retreat of Confederate

forces, 74, 76; Rock Hotel Hospital,
55; Sisters of Mercy, 56; "southern
fevers," 58; St. John's College, 55,
57; St. John's Military Hospital,
369n7; storage of medical supplies,
23; typhoid, 58; as Union target,
57–58; wounded Confederate soldiers, 55–57

Lonergan, Thomas A., 255, 374n8

Longstreet, James, 90

Longview, Ark., 270, 277

Louisiana: Banks, Nathaniel Prentiss,
157; Confederate forces, 159–63,
253; economic strain, 253; invasion
of, 125–26

Louisville, Ky., 130, 181, 213

Lovett, Mrs. Alexander, 258

Lovett, Alexander, 256, 258, 374n10

Lower Arkansas River Valley, 57, 58

Lowry, Judge, 71

Lowry, Miss, 100

Lowry, Mr., 100, 181

Lucas, Mrs., 268

Lucas Place, St. Louis, Mo., 336n7,
380n3

lung congestion, 324

Lutt, Mrs., 230

Lynchburg, Va., 4

Lynch's Slave Pen, 20

M

MacCain, W. J., 246, 372n46

MacLean, Alex K., 171, 366n24

MacLean, Lauchlan A.: burial of, 258;
Camp Bragg, 83, 85; cavalry drill,
94; correspondence with William
McPheeters, 170; death of, 258, 262,
374n13; dinner with friends, 90; dinner with Stand Watie, 245; dinner
with William McPheeters, 177, 210;
evening with friends, 87; Price,
Sterling, 352n32; social visits, 129;
stabbing of, 257, 369n16, 374n13;
visit with William McPheeters, 113,
208; and William McPheeters, 226

MacRae, Fergus, 101, 355n62

MacRae, Mrs. Fergus, 294

Madden, John W., 78, 91, 248, 275, 373*n54*
Madison, Ark., *28*, 345*n13*
Magnolia, Ark., *122*, 145, 159, 195, 275
Magruder, John Bankhead: Alston, William A., 377*n10*; District of Arkansas, 374*n7*; host of party, 266; Kimmel, Manning M., 369*n6*; Lewis, John W., 377*n12*; passports to William McPheeters, 275; Price, Sterling, 254, 255, 259; social visits, 285; stop at Lewisville, Ark., 269; Turner, Edward P., 376*n33*; Yancey, Stephen D., 377*n15*
malaria, 317, 319, 343*n28*
Mansfield, Battle of, *122*, 137–38, 289, 357*n18*, 359*n28*, 359*n29*
Mansfield, La., *122*, 126–27, 136–37, 141–43, 147, 359*n28*
Marais de Cynges River, *196*, 236
Marie Saline Landing, Ark., *270*, 276
Marine Hospital, 10, 316
Marks' Mill, Ark., 362*n47*
Marks' Mill, Battle of, 362*n47*
Marmaduke, John Sappington: action against Union forces, 166; Battle of Pilot Knob, 370*n20*; Battle of Poison Spring, 361*n44*; Battle of Reed's Bridge, 346*n18*; Brinker, Arthur, 369*n15*; capture of, 237, 341*n14*, 372*n37*; Chenowith, Benjamin D., 353*n45*; defense of Little Rock, Ark., 59; Division of cavalry, 92, 341*n14*; duel, 64–65, 347*n20*; Dunlap, W. Watkins, 352*n40*; evacuation of Little Rock, Ark., 60; evening at Mrs. Wright's, 202; Greene, Colton, 365*n13*, 366*n21*; guerrilla raids, 76; Helena campaign, 32, 37, 38, 342*n16*, 342*n20*; Hoy, Albert B., 373*n50*; MacLean, Alex K., 366*n24*; Missouri Expedition, 198, 213–15, 219, 222–23, 225–29, 235–37; Newton, Thomas W., 366*n24*; promotion, 155; skirmish with Union forces, 229, 235–37, 371*n34*, 371*n36*, 372*n37*; Smith, Charles S., 352*n33*;

social visits, 204; visit to Camp Grinstead, 171; visit with William McPheeters, 201; von Phul, Francis, 367*n34*; Walker, Lucius Marsh, 64–65, 347*n20*, 347*n21*
Marmiton River, *196*, 372*n37*
Marshall, Mo., *196*, 232
Marshall, Tx., *2*; Haden, John M., 282; meeting of Governors, 292, 300, 379*n17*; Pim, Lewis T., 297; Reynolds, Thomas Caute, 99, 207, 286; Smith, Edmund Kirby, 292; Thomas, Joseph L., 118; Trans-Mississippi Department, 347*n25*
Marvin, Enoch M.: correspondence with William McPheeters, 93; Helena campaign, 342*n19*; help with wounded soldiers, 39, 342*n19*; medical care, 79–85; Methodist minister, 341*n13*; religious service, 36, 62, 63, 65; swimming in camp, 37; ulceration of cornea, 79; visit with William McPheeters, 38, 68, 131
masturbation, 101
Mattie Stephens (steamboat), 309
Maxey, Samuel Bell, 148, 361*n44*, 361*n45*, 361*n46*, 364*n59*
Maximillian (Mexico), 124
Maysville, Ark., *196*, 239
McClaren, Charles: *See* McLaren, Charles
McClellan, George B., 21, 171, 179, 182, 220, 369*n17*
McCluer, Mrs., 99
McCook, Daniel, 184, 367*n39*
McCoy, Arthur C., 264, 274, 375–76*n27*
McCulloch, Ben, 369*n6*
McDonald County, Mo., 239
McDowell, Joseph Nash, 4, 20, 272, 274, 316, 376–77*n5*
McDowell Medical College: first medical college, 4; reorganization as Missouri Medical College, 316; use as prison, 20, 46, 47, 272, 376–77*n5*
McGill, Dr., 279
McGregor, John F., 228, 370*n24*

McKie, B. D., 353*n45*

McLaren, Charles, 309, 380*n22*

McLean, William E., 43, 344*n34*

McMillan, H. W., 188, 368*n45*

McMurry, John H., 235, 371*n32*

McNair, Dr., 327

McNeil's Regiment of the United States Reserve Corps, 14

McPeters, Rufus, 52, 344*n10*

McPheeters, Alexander, 79, 106, 155, 255, 265, 289, 355*n5*

McPheeters, Eliza, 131

McPheeters, Fanny, 381*n11*

McPheeters, George, 18, 50, 51, 338*n36*, 344*n7*, 353*n47*

McPheeters, Jane, 88, 89

McPheeters, Kate, 88, 89

McPheeters, Lavinia, 62, 81, 98, 100, 159, 164–66, 208

McPheeters, Maggie (Margaret): church attendance, 279; family members, 18, 338*n36*, 353*n47*; fishing, 288, 298–99; horseback ride, 281, 283, 285; hunting, 289, 294, 296, 298; party, 284; photograph given to father, 114; Price, Albert, 381*n11*; reunion with father, 277; visit to plantation, 302–3

McPheeters, Sallie Buchanan (Mrs. William): arrest of, 272, 333, 376*n4*; banishment, xii–xiii, 272–73, 274, 333–34; banishment route, *270*; as Confederate sympathizer, 271–72; confiscation of household goods, 18–19; death of son, George, 50, 51; death of son, William, 19; departure from Helena, Ark., 51–52; disloyalty charges, 272, 273, 376*n4*; encounters with fellow passengers, 48–50; family members, 338*n36*, 381*n11*; fishing, 288; Gratiot Street Prison, 272, 273; in Helena, Ark., 44, 45; imprisonment, 272, 274, 333, 376–77*n5*, 376*n4*; and Julia Dent Grant, 50; letter to husband, 271. *see also* correspondence; marriage to William

McPheeters, 9; oath of allegiance, 309; photograph given to husband, 114; prominence in St. Louis society, 9–10, 315, 318–19; religious affiliation, 16; reunion with husband, William, 50–51; social standing, 10; social visits, 286; travel to Helena, Ark., 45, 47–50; visit with Edward Cabell, 287; visit with Gov. Polk, 284; visit with Irene Jordan, 286; visit with Malcolm Graham, 282; visit with Mr. Thompson, 281; visit with R. Slaughter, 281; visit with Sterling Price, 287–88; visit with Thomas Wooten, 280; wedding, 337*n18*; wedding anniversary, 300; wedding anniversary, golden, 318–19

McPheeters, Sally, 114, 277, 279, 281, 285, 293–94, 353*n47*, 381*n11*

McPheeters, Samuel Brown, 16–17, 301, 379–80*n18*

McPheeters, Sue, 69, 168, 187, 254, 255

McPheeters, W. A., 142; "Big Medicine," 361*n40*

McPheeters, William, 18, 19, 338*n36*, 344*n7*

McPheeters, William Marcellus: accompanied by Governor Polk, 233–34; ambulance repairs, 170; ambulances, 324–25, 330, 372*n41*; appointment as Chief Surgeon, 80, 132, 361*n40*; appointment as Medical Director, 204, 205; appointment as professor of Materia Medica, General and Special Therapeutics, 316; appointment to Board of Survey, 112; appointment to Medical Department of St. Louis University, 9; Arkansas scrip tobacco, 77, 118; Army Medical Association, 76–77, 94–95, 97, 101, 113–14, 120; arrangements to save house, 314, 380*n3*; arrival in Arkansas, 250; arrival in Missouri, 221; assignment as Examiner of Conscripts, 61; assignment to Churchill's Division,

132; as author and editor, 6–10; Battle of Jenkins' Ferry, 150–51, 363*n55;* Battle of Mansfield, 137–38, 289; Battle of Pilot Knob, *196,* 224–25; Battle of Pleasant Hill, 138–41, 146, 360*n33;* belief in medical progress, 318; biographical data, ix–xiii; birthday, 88; blue mass, 41; boat to Monticello, Ark., 275–76; Camden, Ark., 303–5; Camp Grinstead, 164–75; camp improvements, 78; camp inspections, 321–30; Camp Yell, 205; children's hospital, 7; and cholera epidemic, 7, 8, 317, 336–37*n17;* Christmas away from home, 92–93; City Board of Health, 10; commissioned as Confederate surgeon, 21; communion at church, 207; as Confederate objective, 197–98; confiscation of household goods, 18–19, 331; consequences (parlor game), 269; Consolidated Crescent Regiment of Louisiana, 361*n40;* construction of chimney, 83–84, 85, 90, 97; construction of stable, 89, 96; conversation with Jeff Thompson, 269; conversation with Thomas Reynolds, 215–16; cooking, 95, 96, 98; court martial of Robert Wood, 262; crossing Arkansas River, 216–17, 241–42; day of prayer, 62, 84, 136, 256; death of, 319; death of first wife, Pink Seldon, 6; death of son, George, 50, 51, 344*n7,* 353*n47;* death of son, William, 19, 331, 344*n7;* delivery to Isaac Brinker, 203; departure from Camp Bragg, 111; departure from Camp Grinstead, 175; departure from Helena, Ark., 53; departure from Richmond, Ark., 258; destruction of supplies, 237; difficulties with medical duties, 240; dinner parties, 256; dinner with George Watkins, 261; director of Marine Hospital, 10, 20; Division Hospital, 103–4,

148; dysentery, 296; eggnog, 92–93, 95, 106, 107, 258, 259; employment with insurance company, 314, 316–17; encampment at Richmond, Ark., 254–58; encampment at Washington, Ark., 259–62; encampment near Camden, Ark., 175–78; encampment near Shreveport, La., 130–35; escape from St. Louis, 19; essay on Voltaire (Carlyle), 92; establishment of Army Medical Association, 76–77, 318; establishment of free clinic, 5; evacuation from city, 66; evening with Edward Cabell, 203–4; evening with Thomas Wooten, 203–4; examination of conscripts, 61, 63–64, 67, 68; as faculty member, 6, 9–10, 316; family members, 338*n36,* 381*n11;* field infirmary, 139–40; fishing, 288; foraging for food, 243; founder of Academy of Science, 10; friendship with Sterling Price, 197; funeral, 319; furlough applicants, 84–85; guard duty, 240–45; hair cut, 131; harassment by Federal authorities, ix, xi–xii; Helena campaign, 38–40, 342*n19;* home defense, 64; honored by Medical Society of Missouri, 319; hospital arrangements, 103, 228, 230–31, 234–35, 238, 246–47, 249; hospital duties, 104–9; hostile Indians, 241; hunting, 285–86, 288–89, 293–94, 296–98; inspection of brigades, 174, 321–25; inspection of sick, 79; instructions to surgeons, 166–68, 171, 192; interactions with Union command, 40–44, 50; intermittent fever, 41; introduction to Trusten Polk, 155; inventory of Lauchlan MacLean's belongings, 259; inventory of medical supplies, 182–83; involvement in professional medical society, 3–4, 6, 9, 316–17; ironing, 85; journey to Helena, Ark., *28,* 33–38; lack of forage, 239–43; life at

Camp Bragg, 76–101, 103–11; life at Camp Sumter, 111–21; life in camp, 66–73; in Little Rock, Ark., 23–26; loan payment from Thomas Churchill, 208; loan to Malcolm Graham, 259, 265; lodging with Calvin Hervey, 267–69, 273–74, 280–89, 293–303, 334; lodging with Thomas Smith, 262–66; loss of supplies and papers, 237–38; march from Louisiana to Camden, Ark., 161–63; march in pursuit of Union forces, 148–50; march through Arkansas, 239–40; march through Indian Territory, 241–47; march through Missouri, 221–39; march through Texas, 247–49; march to Camden, Ark., 145–53, 175; march to Louisiana, 158–61; march to Mansfield, La., 137; march to Missouri, 212–21; march to Pleasant Hill, La., 138; march to Shreveport, La., 127–29, 142–44; marriage to Pink Seldon, 6; marriage to Sallie Buchanan, 9; as medical examiner for the St. Louis Mutual Insurance Company, 316; Medical Examining Board, 178, 180, 182–83, 185, 188–89, 192–93; medical inspector, 21, 321; medical practice, 3–6, 10, 24–26; medical visit to Sterling Price, 190; meeting with Chief Surgeons, 213; member of secret order, 210; mending, 80, 94, 107, 254, 258, 263, 264, 280; military ball, 109; Missouri Expedition, 212–50; *Missouri* (ironclad), 130, 133; molasses candy, 95, 98; monetary gift to Jefferson Davis, 315, 380–81*n4;* monetary gift to Sterling Price, 315–16; monthly reports, 166, 180; mortality study, 7, 336*n14;* move to Camp Sumter, 111; news of wife, 69, 86, 112, 121, 147, 206, 273, 276; night march, 231; oath of allegiance, xii, 12–13, 16–17, 19, 206, 310, 313, 332;

observation of Sabbath, 163; offer of Chief Surgeon position, 92; offer of District Field Inspector position, 120; office and residence, 337*n21,* 381*n9;* official duties, 178, 230, 232; order for shirts, 260, 264; orders to report for duty, 283; organization of infirmary, 92; organization of Medical Department, 220; parole, 307–8, 313–14, 332; personal cleanliness, 83, 112, 118, 127, 131, 145, 167, 181, 186, 214, 218; pitched quoits, 186, 187; pitching quoits, 368*n43;* pneumonia, 319; preparations for Missouri Expedition, 204–12, 210–11; principles, 16, 19, 313, 319, 332; procurement of medical supplies, 40–42, 79–80, 103–4, 132–33, 143, 204–6, 223, 232–34; prominence in St. Louis society, 4–5, 9–10, 315, 318–19; pro-Southern beliefs, 13–15, 331; protest against Union demands, 15–16; as public-health reformer, 7–10, 321; reasons for joining Confederate army, 331–32; receipt of palmetto hat, 210, 211; Red River campaign, 127–55; reflections on war, 106–7, 110, 115–16, 151, 169, 173–74, 179, 181–83; reflections on 1864, 260–61; religious affiliation, 4, 16; religious views, 186, 187, 207, 267; relinquishment of position as Chief Surgeon, 205, 206; report of battles, 145, 154; request for leave, 283–84; request for pardon, 314; request for return of Union ambulance, 328; request to be relieved from field duty, 282; retreat from Missouri, 236–50; retreat from Pleasant Hill, La., 139–40; return route to Spring Hill, Ark., *270;* return to Camden with family, 278–79; return to Little Rock, Ark., 53, 55; return to St. Louis, Mo., *290,* 292–311, 332; reunion with Thomas Wooten,

111; reunion with wife, Sallie, 50–51, 277–78; route to find family, *270;* saddle exchange with Henry Clay Taylor, 211; search for Sterling Price, 228; search for wife and family, 274–77, 334; self-treatment, 116, 317; sense of duty, 16, 19, 313, 319, 332; sewing, 85, 263; shaving, 280–81; shortage of provisions, 242–43; Spring Hill, Ark., 293–97; squirrel hunting, 254; starving horses, 242–46; "The St. Louis Massacre," 13, 158; supine inaction, 302–3; as surgeon in Confederate Army, 21, 23, 332; surgeon reports, 82, 85, 89; tax levies, 15, 19; temperament, 3–4; and Thomas Wooten, 131, 133; thoughts on surrender, 300, 302; tour of battlefield, 138–40, 151; training in medical therapeutics, 317–18; transportation of the sick, 324–25, 330; travel by boat, 305–10; travel to Richmond, Va., 21, 24, 332; trip to Camden, Ark., 91–92, 100, 165, 274–75; trip to Lewisville, Ark., 116–17, 202; trip to Shreveport, La., 194–95, 197–203; use of quinine, 41, 63, 116; use of statistical analysis, 8, 317, 336–37*n17,* 336*n14;* use of telephone, 319; vaccinations, 286; visits to hospitals, 140–42, 151, 225, 240; visit to convalescent camp, 63–64; visit to Union hospital, 234–35; visit with Dr. Paine, 220–21; visit with James Fagan, 204; visit with Mosby Monroe Parsons, 279; visit with Sterling Price, 214, 253, 255; visit with Union surgeon, 40–41, 142, 225, 234–35, 325–27; voting in election, 152; watermelon, 199, 201, 209; wedding, 337*n18;* wedding anniversary, 300; wedding anniversary, golden, 318–19; weight, 250; *See also* correspondence; dining invitations; friendships; medical care; medical

procedures; official correspondence; official visits; reading selections; social visits; thoughts of wife and family
McRae, Dandridge, 323, 342*n16*
McRae, Squire, 175
McRay, Charlotte, 337*n18*
Meade, George, 72, 81, 96, 350*n12*
medical care: Churchill, Mrs. Thomas James, 103; Churchill, Thomas James, 190–92, 194; daughter, Sally, 279; daughter of Thomas Snead, 25, 27; Gallagher, George A., 212–15; Graham, Mrs. Malcolm, 205–7; Johnson, Old Mrs., 116–17, 202–3; Kavanaugh, Thomas H., 212; MacLean, Lauchlan A., 257–58; Marvin, Enoch M., 79–85; negroes, 110, 264; Newton, Mrs., 202, 210; Price, Sterling, 55, 194–95, 198; sick soldiers, 82–83, 94–95, 104, 148–49, 215–17, 219–20, 242; sick woman, 110–11, 255; Smith, Miss, 68; Snead, Thomas Lowndes, 25–27; son of Irene Jordan, 265–66; son of Mrs. Johnson, 61; Tappan, James Camp, 94; Tappan, Mrs. James Camp, 84, 119, 120; Tracy, Henry W., 69, 72; Venable, Thomas, 262–64; wounded soldier, 257; wounded soldiers (Helena campaign), 39–44, 51–52, 325–28; wounded soldiers (Missouri Expedition), 222, 224–32, 234–35, 238–40, 244–47, 249; wounded soldiers (Red River campaign), 139–43, 150–52; Wright, Mrs. John C., 209
medical procedures: amputation, 224, 230, 343*n29;* amputation (description), 363*n56;* amputation equipment, 132, 139, 363*n56;* amputation of arm, 42, 52, 228; amputation of leg, 42, 343*n32;* amputation of limbs, 57, 141, 150, 152; amputation of thigh, 51; asepsis, 57, 319; battlefield medicine, 77; bleeding,

110, 317, 319; blistering, 317, 319, 339n51; broken limbs, 43, 229, 232, 238, 344n35; cauterization, 81, 83; chloroform, 38, 94, 353n49, 363n54, 363n56; control of disease, 319; empirical medical therapeutics, 317–18; fractures, 141; identification of fevers, 317; morphia, 38; post mortem examination of Lauchlan MacLean, 258; purging, 317; rational medical therapeutics, 317–18; resection, 230; taxis, 94, 353n49; use of gunpowder, 317; wartime surgery, 317–18; X-ray machines, 319

Medical Society of Missouri, 3, 319, 381n12

Medlock, Mr., 279

Memphis, Tenn., 196, 290; attack by Union forces, 107–8; McPheeters, William Marcellus, 303, 305, 310; medical supplies, 23; Smith, William Sooy, 356n14; steamer stop, 49; wounded Confederate soldiers, 327

Memphis and Little Rock Railroad, 345n13

Memphis Bulletin, 186

Meramec River, 196, 226

Mercantile Library Hall, St. Louis, Mo., 12

Meridian, Miss., 119, 356n14

Mexico, 124, 292, 359n24

Meyer, Mary, 338n36

Meyer, Mini, 338n36

Mhoon, John, 34, 35, 276, 278, 286, 297, 301, 340n7

Miller, Mr., 53

Minden, La., 266, 376n29

Mine Creek, Battle of, 341n14, 352n31, 366n21, 366n25, 372n37

Mine Creek, Ks., 341n14, 372n37

Mine Lamotte, Mo., 223

mint julips, 136, 162, 205, 210

Minute Men, 380n22

Missionary Ridge, Tenn., 76

Mississippi Delta, xii, 22

Mississippi River, 2, 28, 196, 270, 290; boat travel, 306, 308–10, 333; flooding, 7; Hopefield, Ark., 345n13; McCoy, Arthur C., 375–76n27; Sappington, G. W., 159; strategic importance, 29–30, 57; Union control, 49, 55, 124, 326

Missouri: as Confederate objective, 158, 161; Federal Military Division of Missouri, 380n23; Gamble, Hamilton Rowan, 356n10; Gratiot Street Prison, 20, 47, 376–77n5, 376n4; Missouri State Guard, 13, 338n45, 348n38, 353n48, 360n35; 90-day war, 11; political unrest, 10–13, 16; Polk, Trusten, 364n60; prisons, 20, 46, 47; Westminster College, 16

Missouri Cavalry Battalion, 375n22

Missouri Compromise, 11

Missouri Expedition, 212–50, 287–88

Missouri (ironclad), 130, 133, 358n18

Missouri Historical Society Archives, 313

Missouri Medical College, 316

The Missouri Republican, 376n4

Missouri River, 2, 196, 226, 227, 230, 233, 290, 370n27

Missouri State Guard, 13, 338n45, 348n38, 353n48, 360n35

Mitchell, Charles Burton, 68, 347n27

Mitchell, Charles E., 168, 365n16

Mitchell, Charles S.: 8th Missouri Infantry, 350n16; 1st Missouri Brigade, 376n28, 377n11; medical visit from William McPheeters, 82, 89, 352n39; visit with Calvin Hervey, 281, 297; visit with William McPheeters, 200, 265

Mobile, Ala., 119, 157, 174, 207, 369n8, 369n9

molasses candy, 95, 98

Monroe, La., 2, 290, 305–8, 334

Monroe, Thomas, 105, 107–8, 164, 355n2

Monroe County, Mo., 222–23

Monticello, Ark., 270, 274–75, 277, 334, 346n13, 378n19

Moore, Charles B., 170, 175, 184, 366*n22*
Moore, Col., 50
Moore, John S., 4
Moore, Joseph L., 213, 369*n13*
Moore, Parson, 80, 84–88, 90, 92–93, 100, 109, 207, 274–75
Moore, William, 354*n56*
Morgan, A. S., 207, 209, 369*n11*
Morgan, C. L., 353*n45*
Morgan, John Hunt, 373*n56*
Moro, Ark., *28, 37*
Moro Bayou, *270, 278*
Moro Creek, 228
Moro Landing, Ark., *270, 276, 278*
morphia, 38
Morris, J. R., 326
Morrison, Richard T. (Dick), 85, 87, 247, 351*n25*
Morton, Mr., 230–31
Mosley, Mr., 131, 132
Mount Holly, Ark., 173, 175
Mount Holly Cemetery, Little Rock, Ark., 56
Mount Lebanon, La., 364*n6*
Mouton, Alfred, 137, 359*n29*
Mt. Lebanon, La., *122,* 161, 162
Mt. Sterling, Mo., *196,* 227
Muddy Boggy Creek, *196*
Mulberry Church, 17
Mullin, Parson, 279
Murphy, Mr., 218, 281
Murphy, Mrs., 281
Murray, Thomas H., 283, 377*n13*
Musser, Mrs. Richard H., 93, 281
Musser, Richard H., 93, 301, 353*n48*
Myrtle Street prison, 20, 338*n40*

N

Napoleon III, 124
Nashville, Ark., 101
Nashville, Tenn., 374*n16*
Natchez, Miss., *290,* 310
Natchitoches, La., *122,* 148
Ned (Sevier's servant), 193
negroes: construction of building, 83, 98; construction of desk, 136; dissection of, 354*n56*; fight with Frank (McPheeter's servant), 158; 1st Kansas Colored Infantry, 361*n44*; Frank (McPheeters' servant), 353*n50*; help fighting fire, 90; impressment of, 354*n57*; McPheeters, Sallie Buchanan (Mrs. William), 49; medical care, 110, 264; travel by boat, 276; troops, 307; vaccinations, 286
The Nelson (steamboat), 276
Neosho, Mo., 238
Neosho River, *196*
Newman, Dr., 129
New Mexico campaign, 375*n21*
New Orleans, La., *2, 290,* 309, 334, 380*n21*
Newton, Mrs.: command send-off, 121; correspondence with William McPheeters, 193; dinner with William McPheeters, 103; as friend, 66; medical care for dysentery, 202, 210; military ball, 355*n7*; social visits, 61, 99, 101, 116, 264
Newton, Robert C., 298, 379*n14*
Newton, Thomas W., 171, 366*n24*
Newton County, Mo., 238
Newtonia, Mo., *196,* 238, 372*n38*
New Uncle Sam (steamboat), 8
Nicholson, William L., 363*n54*
19th Arkansas Infantry, 350*n11*, 366*n27*
90-day war, 11
9th Battalion of Missouri Sharpshooters, 343*n21*, 344*n9*, 368*n49*, 375*n24*
9th Missouri Infantry: Boon, William Carson, 373*n52*; Buster, Michael W., 375*n22*; Clark, John Bullock, Jr., 353*n48*; Gibson, J. W. "Watt," 362*n52*; Graham, Malcolm, 365*n8*; Harris, Edwin E., 365*n20*; Lindsay, D. Herndon, 361*n39*; Musser, Richard H., 353*n48*; Pearson, Edward F., 377*n11*; Venable, Thomas, 375*n24*; White, James D., 352*n34*
North Carolina, 12, 159, 339–40*n55*, 339*n52*, 339*n54*

Northern Subdistrict of Arkansas,
    369–70n19
Northern Subdistrict of Texas, 373n52,
    373n53
Nutt, L. M., 166, 365n12

O

oath of allegiance: Kahte, Herman,
    337n26; McPheeters, Sallie
    Buchanan (Mrs. William), 309;
    McPheeters, William Marcellus,
    12–13, 16–17, 19, 206, 310, 313,
    332; text of, 337n26
O'Fallen, Colonel, 5
official correspondence, 165, 174,
    253–56; Bond, John B., 90–92, 98,
    114, 119, 130; Brinker, Isaac, 266;
    Cabell, Edward Carrington, 182,
    200; Churchill, Thomas James, 256;
    Haden, John M., 282; Pflager,
    Henry W., 281; Pim, Lewis T.,
    297; Polk, John Widener, 296–97
official visits: bank, 264; Bond, John B.,
    116–17, 128, 165, 175, 204, 206,
    209; Brinker, Isaac, 206–7;
    Churchill, Thomas James, 208;
    Cunningham, Francis D., 87;
    division surgeons, 164–65; Hoy,
    Albert B., 247–48; Madden,
    John W., 248; Reynolds, Capt.,
    168; surgeons, 172, 185, 208–11
Ohio Railroad, 174
Ohio River, 290
Okolona, Miss., 356n14
Old Blockley Hospital, 3, 4
Old Pap: See Price, Sterling
Old Tige, 352n31
Olustee, Fla., 356n16
orchitis, 89, 352n39
Osage County, Mo., 227–28
Osage River, 196, 227–28, 290, 370n23
Otey, Miss, 50
Ouachita County, Ark., 77, 364n59
Ouachita House, Monroe, La., 307
Ouachita River, 74, 122, 196, 270, 290;
    Arkadelphia, Ark., 347n25; crossing
    of, 67, 278; encampment, 66–68;

Red River campaign, 148–49; use of
    river for travel, 275–76, 306

P

Pacific Railroad, 226, 227
Paine, Dr., 220–21
Paine, Lewis, 379n11
Palmer, Mr., 64, 65, 66
Paraclifta, Ark., 375n20
Paris, Tx., 196, 248, 250
Parker, Mr., 195
Parkman, Mr., 206
Parmer, Mr., 61
paroles, 307–8, 329, 350n18
Parsons, Dr., 152
Parsons, Homer Lee, 244–45, 364n58,
    372n43
Parsons, John Durant, 364n58
Parsons, Mosby Monroe: Baer, Caleb
    Dorsey, 342n18, 344n11; Battle of
    Jenkins' Ferry, 362n48; brigade
    inspection by William McPheeters,
    324; death of, 359n24; District of
    Arkansas, 350n14; exile to Mexico,
    292; Helena campaign, 342n16;
    march from Louisiana to Camden,
    Ark., 163; promotion, 155; Red
    River campaign, 125, 130, 132,
    143–46, 150; Reynolds, James H.,
    351n21; Seay, William M., 351n20;
    Standish, Austin M., 339n47; success
    as commander, 350n14; Tracy,
    Henry W., 348n30; visit with Irene
    Jordan, 128; visit with William
    McPheeters, 81, 121, 206, 279;
    and William McPheeters, 140
Parsons, William H., 353n45
Partisan Rangers Battalion: See 14th
    Missouri Cavalry
Pascagoula Bay, Ala., 119
Patterson, Mo., 222
Patterson, Mr., 175, 209
Payton, Mrs. D., 202
Pea Ridge, battle of, 29, 55
Pearl River, 290
Pearson, Edward F., 282, 377n11
Peers, Valentine J., 14

Pemberton, John C., 33, 329
Perkins, Caleb J., 296, 379n9
Perry, Charles, 34, 35, 91, 283
Perry County, Ark., 215
Perryville, Indian Territory, 196, 243–45
Petersburg, Va., 176, 179, 181–83, 186, 188–89, 251
Peterson, Dr., 201
Peterson, Mrs., 201
Pflager, Henry W., 187, 225, 257, 281, 368n44
Philadelphia, Penn., 3
Phillips County, Ark., 249, 341n15
phthisis, 83, 350n17; See also tuberculosis
Pickett, Col., 324
Pierce, Lt. Gov., 161
Pike, Albert, 246, 355n7, 372–73n48, 373n53
Pike, Misses, 355n7
Pilot Knob, Battle of, 196, 224–25, 370n20
Pilot Knob, Mo., 196, 224
Pim, Lewis T., 289, 297, 378n23
Pindall, Lebbeus A., 343n21, 344n9
Pine Bluff, Ark, 28, 58, 182, 277, 305, 343n22, 379n14
Pine Mountain, Ga., 367n32
Pine Street Church, 16, 17, 319
Pineville, Mo., 196, 239
Pin Indians, 239, 241
Pinnell, Ethan A., 354n54
The Planters House, 3, 319
Pleasant Hill, Battle of, 122, 138–41, 292, 357n18, 360n32, 360n33
Pleasant Hill, La., 122, 126
Pleasonton, Alfred, 370n27, 371n34, 371n36
pleurisy (with effusion), 258, 374n15
pleuro-pneumonia (with effusion), 258
Plymouth, N.C., 159, 364n2
pneumonia, 95, 97
Pocahontas, Ark., 196, 220–21
Poison Springs, Ark., 275
Poison Spring, Battle of, 361n44
Polignac, Camille Armand Jules Marie de, 139, 140, 143, 359n30
Polk, Allen J.: relation to William

McPheeters, 38; use of house as hospital, 39–40, 325–28, 341n15; and William McPheeters, 51, 53
Polk, Anna Eliza (Mrs. John Widener): arrest of, 346n13; social visits, 62, 206; visit with William McPheeters, 71, 129, 144, 155, 275
Polk, Cadwallader, 189, 368n47
Polk, James K., 347n20
Polk, John Widener: brief meeting with William McPheeters, 144; Churchill, Thomas James, 346n13; correspondence with William McPheeters, 130, 167, 262; on leave to visit family, 65; official visits, 64; social visits, 62; travel with William McPheeters, 275–77; visit with William McPheeters, 61, 63, 208, 275
Polk, Leonidas, 117, 118, 174, 177, 356n14, 367n32
Polk, Mrs., 43
Polk, Mrs. Allen: travel with Sallie McPheeters, 45, 47–48, 52; visit with Sallie McPheeters, 51
Polk, Thomas G., 135–36, 359n25
Polk, Trusten: accompanying William McPheeters, 233–34; breakfast with William McPheeters, 190; capture of, 364n60; church attendance, 248; conversation with William McPheeters, 181; correspondence with William McPheeters, 281, 282, 296, 303; dining invitations, 204, 206, 254, 256, 259; dinner with Stand Watie, 245; dinner with William McPheeters, 187; exile, 292; foraging for food, 243; governor of Missouri, 364n60; imprisonment, 364n60; introduction to William McPheeters, 155; military judge, 364n60; Missouri Expedition, 212–13, 246–49; religious service, 255, 256; retreat from Missouri, 236; ride into country, 255; service for Lauchlan MacLean, 258; social visits, 226, 260, 263–66; Trans-Mississippi

Department, 364n60; visit with
Dr. Paine, 221; visit with Sallie
McPheeters, 284; visit with Thomas
Reynolds, 217; visit with William
McPheeters, 177, 184, 207, 264–65,
283–84, 299–300; Walker, Judge,
259; Watkins, George C., 259;
winter quarters, 262
Polk County, Ark., 217
Ponder's Mill, Mo., 196, 221
Pontchartrain (gunboat), 347n22
Pope, Dr., 259
Pope, John, 310, 380n23
Pope, Mr., 250
Porter, David Dixon, 30, 124–26
Port Hudson, La., 29, 52, 290, 309, 326
Potosi, Mo., 196, 225
Powell, Beletha, 162, 364n6
Powhatan, Ark., 196, 219–20
Prairie Grove, Ark., 31
Pratt's Texas Battery, 353n45
Prentiss, Benjamin M.: former Union
commander, 59; Helena campaign,
33, 41; request for safe passage, 50
Presidential election, 242
Preston, William I., 257, 374n12
Price, Celsus, 97, 114, 299, 301, 354n53
Price, Mrs. Edwin, 232
Price, Sterling, xii; appointment of
William McPheeters as Medical
Director, 204; Arkansas infantry, 21;
arrival at Camp Sumter, 116; attendance at barbecue, 78; background,
338n45; Battle of Jenkins' Ferry,
362n48; Battle of Pilot Knob,
370n20; battle of Westport, 371n36;
bridge construction, 59; Cage,
Duncan C., 350n19; church attendance, 184; Clark, Henry M.,
361n38; commander of Missouri
forces, 21, 24, 68; correspondence
with William McPheeters, 43, 303;
court of inquiry, 287–88, 293, 299,
378n5, 378n20, 379n16; Crawford,
Washington L., 374n9; defense of
Little Rock, Ark., 58–60; departure
from Arkadelphia, Ark., 70; dining

invitations, 256, 259; dining with
friends, 88; dinner with Stand
Watie, 245; disintegration of army,
291; District of Arkansas, 58, 119,
338n45, 356n15; Dunlap, W.
Watkins, 352n40; encounter with
Union forces, 145; exile to Mexico,
292; friendship with William
McPheeters, 197; Gallagher,
George A., 369n10; Helena campaign, 31–34, 35–39, 342n16,
342n19, 342n20; inspection reports,
321–30; Kavanaugh, Benjamin
Taylor, 349n5; Kerr, George W.,
345n14; Kimmel, Manning M.,
369n6; on leave, 261–62; leave
request from William McPheeters,
283; Lewis, John W., 377n12;
MacLean, Lauchlan A., 352n32;
Magruder, John Bankhead, 254,
255, 259; Marvin, Enoch M.,
341n13; medical care, 55, 194–95,
198; meeting at headquarters, 66,
67, 154, 206; Mhoon, John, 340n7;
Missouri Expedition, 212, 214, 219,
224–26, 230, 247–49; Missouri
Expedition route, 196; monetary
gift from William McPheeters,
315–16; monetary gifts, 381n5;
Monroe, Thomas, 355n2; Morrison,
Richard T. (Dick), 351n25; orders
to report to Texas, 285; Price,
Celsus, 354n53; Red River campaign, 125, 145–54; reorganization
of command, 261; return from
Camden, Ark., 91; return from
Washington, Ark., 255; review
of troops, 92, 176; secessionist
activities, 32; Shreveport, La., 293,
301; skirmish with Union forces,
233, 238–39; Slaughter, R. M.,
342n18; Smith, Edmund Kirby,
379n16; Snead, Thomas Lowndes,
338–39n46; social visits, 87, 154,
165, 182, 190–91, 193, 206, 208–10;
Stonehill, Edward B., 351n29; surrender of army, 292; Taylor, Henry

Clay, 348n29; Taylor, Theodore T., 365n10; tea with William McPheeters, 61; Thomas, Joseph L., 349n41; Tracy, Henry W., 348n30; travel to Washington, Tx., 97; trip to Camden, Ark., 90, 119; trip to Shreveport, La., 197–203; trip to Washington, Ark., 253, 254; Tyler, John, Jr., 353–54n52; victories over Union forces, 157; visit from ladies, 71; visits from relatives, 232–33; visit with Sallie McPheeters, 287–88; visit with William McPheeters, 79, 84, 90, 95–96, 249, 261, 293, 299; von Schmelling, Wedig, 372n40; and William McPheeters, 332; Wooten, Thomas Dudley, 341n10; written attack from Thomas Reynolds, 375n19

Prince John: See Magruder, John Bankhead

Prince's Ford, Mo., 227, 370n23

Princeton, Ark., 122, 149, 153, 196, 213

prisons: Alton Military Prison, 19–20; Arkansas State Penitentiary, 346n15; Fortress Monroe, 315; Gratiot Street Prison, 20, 47, 376–77n5, 376n4; McDowell College, 20, 46, 47; Myrtle Street prison, 20, 338n40; pro-Confederate women, 271

Pryor, Richard, 112–14, 117–18, 121, 356n8

Q

Quantrill, William C., 79, 349n9

Quarantine Hospital, 316

Queen City (boat), 367n35

Quesenberry, William, 248, 373n53

quinine, 41, 63, 116, 343n28

quoits, 186, 187, 368n43

R

Radcliff, Mr., 191

Rainey, John S. H., 267, 302, 304–5, 376n31

Rainey, Mrs. John S. H., 300, 303

Raleigh, N.C., xi, 25, 98, 168, 254, 255

Raleigh Academy, 339n52

Ramsey, Mr., 52

Randal, Horace, 362n48

Randolph County, Ark., 220

Rapidan River, Va., 350n12

Rapley, William F., 301, 380n19

Rappahannock River, Va., 350n12

rational medical therapeutics, 317–18

Rayburn, Amy, 269

Rayburn, Miss, 202

Rayburn, Mr., 66

reading selections: Acts of the Apostles, 109; African travel sketches, 114, 115; Bible, 112, 118, 144, 153, 160, 165, 167, 170, 173, 176, 177, 253, 292; Carlyle, 94–95; The Convict (James), 185, 187; The Dairyman's Daughter, 82; The Dutch Republic, 119–21, 132, 147–48, 153, 159; Evidences of Christianity (Alexander), 85–86, 89, 91; Flower of the Flock, 67, 68; Grace Abounding (Bunyan), 177; Great Expectations (Dickens), 193; Great Preparation (Cummings), 168–69; Heart of Midlothian, 287; History of England (Macaulay), 25, 269, 274, 281–82, 284; The History of the French Revolution, 171; Home Influences, 104–5; Kenilworth (Scott), 289; The Last Days of Jesus (Moore), 164, 165, 168; Life of Stonewall Jackson (Daniel), 88–89; Little Dorrit (Dickens), 187–88, 192; Mary, Queen of Scots, 267–68; The Merchant of Venice (Shakespeare), 257; Miscellanies (Carlyle), 91; Moss Side, 169–70; The Mother's Reward, 105–6; Narrative (Sir Edward Seawell), 107–8, 110; Othelo (Shakespeare), 257; Phillip the Second (Prescott), 266; physiology, 96–98; Pilgrim's Progress (Bunyan), 178–79, 182; A Practical View (Wilberforce), 78; Rob Roy (Scott), 268; St. Valentine's Day, or the Fair Maid of Perth, 182, 185; Sunny Side, 173; Tongues of Fire (Arthur), 82, 84; Yankee newspapers, 113, 176

Rector, Thomas, 261, 283, 375n20

Rector, W. F., 328
Red Lake, 298–99
Red River, *2, 74, 122, 196, 270, 290;*
    Confederate forces, 75; crossing of,
    247, 250, 259; encampment, 250,
    251; fishing, 298–99; flooding, 281;
    headquarters, 111; Hervey's planta-
    tion, 268, 286, 303; marching route,
    129; march to Shreveport, La.,
    199–200; mouth, 308; as target of
    Union forces, 123–26
Red River campaign, 124–55, 157;
    Banks, Nathaniel Prentiss, 124–27,
    359*n27;* route of Churchill's
    infantry, *122;* Tappan, James
    Camp, 359*n25*
Red River County, Tx., 249
Reed, Frank S., 289, 378*n21*
Reed, Georgia T., 272
Reed's Bridge, Battle of, 346*n18*
Reeler, Miss, 297
religious services: Anderson, Dr., 311;
    Boyd, Mr., 115, 118, 294, 301; in
    camp, 255, 256; Curtis, Mr., 187;
    Davies, Mr., 267, 295; Dryden,
    C. F., 85; Episcopal church, 134,
    155, 187, 279; Jewell, Horace, 184;
    Kavanaugh, Benjamin Taylor, 77,
    167, 209; Marvin, Enoch M., 36,
    62, 63, 65; McGill, Dr., 279;
    Methodist church, 67, 69, 80, 83,
    85, 167, 181, 184, 191, 248, 287;
    Moore, Parson, 207; Mosley, Mr.,
    131; Mount Holly Church, 209;
    Patterson, Mr., 209; Presbyterian
    church, 62, 79, 115, 209; Radcliff,
    Mr., 191, 305; Synod of the
    Cumberland Presbyterian church,
    79; with Thomas Drayton, 86, 90;
    Welch, Mr., 61–62; Williamson,
    Dr., 261; Woods, Parson, 90
Reynolds, Capt., 168
Reynolds, D. W., 365*n18*
Reynolds, James H., 84, 351*n21,* 365*n18*
Reynolds, J. J., 271–72, 333
Reynolds, Mr., 293
Reynolds, Thomas Caute: Confederate

Congress, 363*n57;* conversation
    with William McPheeters, 215–16;
    correspondence with William
    McPheeters, 96, 99, 106, 114,
    286–87; Cundiff, J. H. R., 348*n38;*
    dinner with William McPheeters,
    242; exile to Mexico, 292; governor
    of Missouri, 340*n56;* meeting with
    William McPheeters, 26; visit with
    William McPheeters, 61, 70, 200,
    207–8, 210, 217; and William
    McPheeters, 226–27; written attack
    on Sterling Price, 259, 375*n19,*
    378*n20*
Rhett, Thomas G., 131, 358*n21*
Rice, Mrs. Dorsey, 44, 69, 249
Rice, Dr., 42–43, 50, 52, 61
Rice, Samuel A. (Ross), 40, 343*n24*
Richmond, Ark., *196,* 253, 254
Richmond, Mrs., 279
Richmond, Va.: attack by Union forces,
    120, 179, 356–57*n17;* Confederate
    victory, 120; Crittenden, Lt., 89;
    evacuation of, 294, 379*n8;* Grant,
    Ulysses S., 171, 181–83, 184, 188;
    Holmes, Theophilus Hunter, 118;
    Johnson, Jilson P., 349*n10;* Lee,
    Robert E., 157; McPheeters,
    William Marcellus, x, 21, 24, 332;
    Scott, Thomas W., 69; Snead,
    Thomas Lowndes, 263, 289; Tyler,
    John, Jr., 101; Union forces, 120
Richwood, Mo., *196,* 225–26
Rider, Cass, 26, 64
Riggins, George W., 130, 133, 142,
    358*n16*
Riggin's Mill, Mo., 228
Rightor Hill, 342*n16,* 342*n20*
Rio Grande River, *2*
Ripley County, Mo., 221
Ritchie, Mrs., 279
River Station, Mo., 222
Robinson, Mead, 381*n11*
Robinson, Walter C., 43, 52, 344*n35*
Rock Hotel Hospital, 55
Rockport, Ark., 66, *74, 122, 196,* 214
Rogers, Henry C., 143, 361*n41*

Rolla, Mo., *2, 196, 290*
Rose, Dr., 19
Rosecrans, William Starke, 70–72, 78, 79, 235, 370*n27,* 371*n33*
Ross, John, 241, 372*n39*
Ross, Leonard Fulton, 50, 325–26
Royston, Charles E., 168, 186, 188, 190–93, 259, 365*n16*
Royston, Grandison D., 264, 375*n26*
Ruffin, Dr., 234
Rush, Benjamin, 317
Russell, Almira, 337*n18*
Russelville, Mo., *196,* 229
Rust, Albert, 96, 353*n51*
Rutledge, Mo., 239

S

Sabine Crossroads, La., 127, 359*n28*
Sabine River, *290*
Saline County, 231–32
Saline River, *74, 122, 196, 270;* battle with Union forces, 150–51, 164, 361*n42,* 362*n48,* 362*n52,* 362*n53,* 363*n54;* crossing of, 277; encampment, 66, 232
Saline River, Battle of the: *See* Battle of Jenkins' Ferry
Salomon, Frederick, 343*n24,* 344*n34,* 362*n48*
San Antonio, Tx., *2,* 297, 378*n6*
Sandidge, Dr.: *See* Sandridge, J. M.
Sandridge, Fanny Lu, 208, 210, 211, 369*n12*
Sandridge, J. M., 144, 199, 201, 361*n43,* 369*n12*
Sandridge, Mrs. J. M., 199
Sappington, G. W., 159, 364*n3*
Saugrain, A. P., 289, 378*n22*
Savannah, Ga., 251, 263, 375*n25*
scarlet fever, 25
Schaumburg, Mrs. Wright C., 86–88, 99, 100, 351*n30*
Schaumburg, Wright C., 351*n30*
Scott, Mrs. Joseph T., 86–87, 99, 100, 287, 351*n30*
Scott, Joseph T., 99, 141, 351*n30,* 355*n59,* 360*n37*

Scott, Thomas W., 69, 348*n31*
Scurry, William Read, 151, 362*n48,* 362*n49*
Seay, William M., 84, 92, 175, 350*n20*
2d Arkansas Mounted Rifles, 347*n23*
2d Indian Brigade, 361*n45*
Sedalia, Mo., *196,* 231–32
Seddon, James A., 32
Seldon, Lt.: *See* Shelton, A.
Seldon, Pink, 4, 6
Seven Days' Battles, 21
7th Missouri Infantry, 377*n7*
7th Missouri Volunteer Cavalry, 367*n37,* 371*n32*
Sevier, Ambrose H.: church attendance, 134; Churchill, Thomas James, 352*n42;* dinner with Dr. Standish, 144; dinner with Thomas Churchill, 204; party at Thomas Snead's, 182; promotion, 155; return from Little Rock, Ark., 194; trip to Camden, Ark., 180; trip to Little Rock, Ark., 191; visit with William McPheeters, 90, 259; and William McPheeters, 162–63
Sevier, Anne Maria: *See* Churchill, Mrs. Thomas James
Sevier County, Ark., 250, 254, 374*n10,* 374*n14*
Seward, William Henry, 185, 296–97, 367*n42,* 379*n11*
Seymour, Truman, 356*n16*
Shaler, James R., 230, 274, 370*n25*
Shanks, David, 227, 370*n23,* 371*n35*
Sharp, Mr., 276
Sharpshooter Battalion, 379*n9*
Shaver, Robert G., 172, 177, 182, 366*n26*
Sheffield, Mrs., 307
Shelby, Joseph Orville: Battle of Marks' Mill, 362*n47;* capture of Union boats, 179, 367*n35;* capture of Union soldiers, 229; destruction of Iron Mountain Railroad, 224; exile, 291; guerrilla raids, 76; Iron Brigade, 347*n28,* 370*n23,* 374*n13;* McCoy, Arthur C., 375–76*n27;* mention, 68; Missouri Expedition,

198, 220, 222, 225–27, 229; skirmish with Union forces, 222, 225,
227, 233–39, 371*n34*, 371*n36*,
372*n37*; Thompson, M. Jeff,
369–70*n19*; visit with William
McPheeters, 86; Wood,
Carville H., 355*n58*
Shelton, A., 373*n51*
Sheppard, Lemuel, 258, 374*n17*
Sherman, William T.: Atlanta, Ga.,
194, 369*n18*; banishment, 380*n3*;
battle of Atlanta, 368*n50*; battle of
Kennesaw Mountain, 367*n39*; battle
of Peachtree Creek, 368*n50*; battle
with Confederate forces, 285;
Johnston, Joseph E., 169–70, 184,
186, 190–91, 379*n10*; Mississippi,
117, 119, 356*n14*; New Orleans,
La., 118; Savannah, Ga., 251, 263,
375*n25*; surrender terms, 299–300
Shields, James, 233, 371*n29*
Shiloh, Battle of, 22, 33, 46, 56, 342*n17*
Shoal Creek, 238
Shreveport, La., *2, 122, 290;* Cabell,
Edward Carrington, 208, 210, 211;
communication lines, 303–5;
courier from, 161; court of inquiry,
293, 299, 379*n16*; encampment,
159; evacuees, 305; Green, Charles,
302; march to city, 199–201;
Marvin, Enoch M., 93; newspaper
accounts, 72; Price, Sterling, 301;
Red River campaign, 121, 124–31;
Reynolds, Thomas Caute, 26;
Smith, Edmund Kirby, 31, 57; as
target of Union forces, 75; von
Phul, William, 117
Shreveport News, 375*n19*
Sibley, Henry Hopkins, 261, 375*n21*
Sibley tent, 375*n21*
Sigourney, Andrew, 83, 350*n18*
Simpson, John H., 193, 368*n49*
Simpson, Mr., 304
Sisters of Mercy, 56
16th Kansas Volunteer Cavalry, 371*n31*
16th Missouri Infantry, 374*n8, 377*n7*
16th Texas Infantry, 360*n36, 370*n24*

6th Missouri Cavalry, 344*n10*
6th Missouri Infantry, 347*n26, 366*n25,
370*n24*
6th Trans-Mississippi Infantry, 368*n47*
skirmishes: Big Blue River, *196,* 235;
Jefferson City, *196,* 228; Lexington,
196, 233; Little Blue River, *196,*
234, 371*n34*; Little Osage River,
196, 236–37; Marmiton River, *196,*
237; Mine Creek, *196;* Newtonia,
196, 238–39; Westport, *196,* 235–36
Slaughter, R. M.: Camp Bragg, 104;
Camp Sumter, 105; church
attendance, 79, 85; dining invitations, 256; dinner with William
McPheeters, 131; District of
Arkansas, 342*n18;* Helena campaign,
39, 342*n19;* hunting, 287; Little
Rock campaign, 66; medical pur-
veyor, 342*n18;* Parsons, Mosby
Monroe, 132, 134; search for
Sterling Price, 228; trip to
Lewisville, Ark., 84; visit with Mr.
Boyd, 114; visit with William
McPheeters, 135, 155, 205, 267
slavery, xi, 10–12, 115, 337*n24, 353*n51*
Slemons, William F., 364*n58, 372*n43*
small pox, 244, 319, 324; *See also*
varioloid
Small Pox Hospital, 316
Smith, A. J., 119, 126, 370*n27*
Smith, Charles S., 88, 148, 171, 217,
352*n33*
Smith, Edmund Kirby: arrival at camp,
69; Battle of Jenkins' Ferry, 362*n48;*
Boggs, William Robertson, 368*n5;*
court of inquiry, 379*n16;* day of
prayer, 256; defense of Little Rock,
Ark., 57–58; defense of Shreveport,
La., 126, 129–30; disintegration of
army, 291; Gallagher, George A.,
369*n10;* Greene, Colton, 366*n21;*
headquarters move to Houston,
Tx., 292; Holmes, Theophilus
Hunter, 356*n15;* Kirby Smithdom,
76, 345*n15;* meeting with Sterling
Price, 90; military strategy for

Missouri Expedition, 197–99;
orders to move camp, 121; policy
for seizing property, 252; Price,
Sterling, 379*n16;* Red River cam-
paign, 125, 144–50; review of
troops, 131; Schaumburg,
Wright C., 351*n30;* Shaler,
James R., 370*n25;* Smith,
Solomon A., 358*n14;* social visits,
154; and Sterling Price, 200; surren-
der terms, 292, 379*n17;* tea with
William McPheeters, 61; Trans-
Mississippi Department, 23, 75, 76,
157–58, 339*n52,* 345*n15;* victories
over Union forces, 157; visit with
William McPheeters, 53, 70, 134,
154; Wood, Robert C., 374*n13*
Smith, J. S., 337*n18*
Smith, Lt., 269
Smith, Miss, 68
Smith, Mrs. Edmund Kirby, 134
Smith, Mrs. Thomas, 191
Smith, Solomon A., 130, 358*n14,* 358*n15*
Smith, Thomas C., 71, 262–66, 375*n23*
Smith, William Sooy, 356*n14*
Smizer, George, 37, 43, 51, 52, 69
Snead, Harriet (Mrs. Thomas Lowndes):
arrest of, 346*n16;* message to
William McPheeters, 165; parole,
346*n16;* visit with William
McPheeters, 27, 53, 62, 112–14,
117, 121, 144, 155
Snead, Minnie, 25
Snead, Thomas Lowndes: aide to
Sterling Price, 338–39*n46;* child sick
with scarlet fever, 25, 27; correspond-
ence with William McPheeters, 164,
195, 289; discussions with William
McPheeters, 84, 85, 97; election to
Confederate Congress, 152,
338–39*n46,* 363*n57;* Helena campaign, 34–35, 38; medical care,
25–27; news from wife, 147; party,
182; return from furlough, 83;
Snead, Harriet (Mrs. Thomas
Lowndes), 346*n16;* social visits,
98–99, 101, 105–6; travel to Helena,

Ark., 53; trip to Shreveport, La.,
119; visit to Daniel M. Frost, 64;
visit to Parson Moore's, 87; visit
with Mrs. Snead, 114, 117
Snider, Mrs., 51
Snodgrass, Harriet, 71, 265
social visits: Alston, William A., 285;
Ashley, Mrs. William Elliott,
261; Bates, Mr., 264; Bates, Mrs.
Fleming, 260; Boyd, Mr., 260–61;
Boyd, Mrs., 260; Brinker, Isaac,
175–76, 289; Bruce, Mrs., 155;
Buster, Michael W., 261; Cabell,
Edward Carrington, 175–77, 181,
192–94, 204–6, 288, 298, 300;
Carroll, Miss, 260, 269;
Cunningham, Francis D., 81, 91,
97; Davis, Jefferson, 315; Dorne,
Andrew J., 248; Drayton, Thomas
Fenwick, 98, 101, 113, 119, 133;
Dunlap, W. Watkins, 178, 205;
Eakin, Mrs. (formerly Betty
Erwins), 260, 263; Fagan, James
Fleming, 301; Fleming, Mrs., 223;
Gause, Lucien C., 178; Gibson,
William C., 161; Graham,
Malcolm, 184; Graham, Mrs.
Malcolm, 210, 305; Hamilton,
Edward L., 172, 257; Hamilton,
Mrs. Edward L., 257; Hardin, Dr.,
181; Hardin, Mrs., 181; Harvey,
Mrs., 162; Hedgepeth, Isaac N.,
228; Hempstead, Mrs. (formerly
Miss Gratiot), 264; Hill, Mrs. (for-
merly Mrs. Jim Johnson), 260; Hill,
Nicholas S., 178, 269, 273; Holmes,
Theophilus Hunter, 100–101;
Jackson, Col., 248; Jackson, Mrs.,
248; Jandon, Benjamin A., 189;
Johnson, Benjamin S., 193;
Johnson, Old Mrs., 274, 283, 295;
Jordan, Irene, 116–17, 127–28,
207–8, 264, 295; Kidder,
Charles E., 192–93; Lovett,
Alexander, 258; Lovett, Mrs.
Alexander, 258; Lowry, Mr.,
181; Lucas, Mrs., 268; MacLean,

Lauchlan A., 208, 210; Magruder, John Bankhead, 285; Marmaduke, John Sappington, 201, 204; Marvin, Enoch M., 38, 68, 131; McGregor, John F., 228; Mhoon, John, 301; Mitchell, Charles S., 200; Newton, Mrs., 264; Nutt, L. M., 166; Polk, John Widener, 208, 275; Polk, Mrs. John Widener, 155, 206, 275; Polk, Trusten, 177, 187, 190, 204, 206–7, 264–65, 283–84, 299–300; Price, Celsus, 299; Price, Mrs. Edwin, 232; Quesenberry, William, 248; Rapley, William F., 301; Rayburn, Amy, 269; Rector, Thomas, 261; Reynolds, Thomas Caute, 61, 70, 200, 207–8, 210, 215–17; Royston, Charles E., 190–93; Royston, Grandison D., 264; Sevier, Ambrose H., 204, 259; Shaler, James R., 230; Shaver, Robert G., 172; Shelby, Joseph Orville, 86; Sibley, Henry Hopkins, 261; Slaughter, R. M., 155, 205, 267, 281; Smith, Edmund Kirby, 154, 200; Snead, Harriet, 155, 165; Snead, Thomas Lowndes, 101, 105–6; Standish, J. M., 199; Stonehill, Edward B., 86; Swindell, James H., 182, 184, 189; Tappan, James Camp, 120, 172, 173, 177–79, 191–93; Tappan, Mrs. James Camp, 155, 173, 175; Taylor, Charles M., 174, 181; Taylor, Henry Clay, 175, 184, 210, 265; Taylor, Mrs. Henry Clay, 154–55, 178, 184, 206; Taylor, Theodore T., 165, 166; Thompkins, Mrs., 181; Thompson, M. Jeff, 261; Thompson, Mr., 281; Thompson, Mrs., 268; Tracy, Henry W., 210; Turner, Edward P., 269; Von Phul, Frank, 178; Watkins, George C., 177, 190, 204, 206; Wilson, Dr., 260, 264; Wood, Robert C., 266; Wooten, Mrs. Thomas D., 204;

Wright, John C., 170, 172, 173, 175, 209; Wright, Mrs. John C., 173; Yancey, Stephen D., 285; Yandell, David Wendell, 200; *See also* Churchill, Mrs. Thomas James; Churchill, Thomas James; Price, Sterling; Wooten, Thomas Dudley

South Carolina, 201

Southern Relief Fair, 315, 381*n5*

Southern Unionists, 12

Southwest Independent, 373*n53*

Spring Creek, Ark., 37

Springfield, Mo., *2, 196*

Spring Hill, Ark., *74, 122, 270, 290;* Boyd, Mr., 193, 260; Camp Bragg, 103–4, 110–11, 117; Camp Sumter, 111–21, 355*n4;* lodging with Calvin Hervey, 264–69, 273–74, 279–89, 293–303, 334; McPheeters, William Marcellus, 293–97, 299–303; Pryor, Richard, 356*n8;* Wooten, Thomas Dudley, 261–62, 274

Spring River, *196*

Standish, Austin M., 25, 339*n47*, 359*n24*

Standish, J. M.: *See* Sandridge, J. M.

St. Charles, Ark., *28*

Steele, Frederick: Arkansas Expedition Army, 59; Battle of Jenkins' Ferry, 150–51, 361*n42*, 362*n48;* Battle of Poison Spring, 361*n44;* bridge construction, 60; command of Little Rock, Ark., 333; failure to pursue Confederate forces, 75; Little Rock campaign, 59–61; Red River campaign, 124, 142–50, 157; retreat from Camden, Ark., 148–49, 361*n42;* Union commander, 59

St. Francis River, *28, 196,* 222, *290*

St. Francis Station, Mo., 226

St. John's College, 55, 57

St. John's Military Hospital, 369*n7*

St. Joseph, Mo., 131

St. Louis, Mo., *2, 196, 290;* Academy of Science, 10; Anheuser-Busch, 318; arrival of William McPheeters, 3–4; Camp Jackson, 13; Camp Jackson Affair, 13; cholera epidemic, 7, 8,

317; City Hospital, 316; Federal prison, xii; fire, 8; 1st U.S. Volunteers, 16; immigrant population, 7–8, 11; improvements in infrastructure, 318; Kahte, Herman, 337n26; Lynch's Slave Pen, 20; Marine Hospital, 10, 316; martial law, 11–12, 16, 46, 271, 331; medical practice, ix, xi; medical schools, 4, 6, 9–10; Medical Society of Missouri, 3, 319, 381n12; Mercantile Library Hall, 12; Mississippi River flood, 7; Missouri Historical Society Archives, 313; mortality study, 7, 336n14; Myrtle Street prison, 20, 338n40; population growth, 7–8; postbellum social climate, 314–15; prisons, 20, 46, 47, 376–77n5, 376n4; pro-Confederate women, 45–47, 271–72, 344n8; prosperity of city, 10; public-health reform, 7–8; Quarantine Hospital, 316; Recorders Court, 14; return of William McPheeters, 310, 334; Scott, Mrs. Joseph T., 99; secessionist activities, 12–13, 16; shoemaking, 318; slave auction, 337n24; Small Pox Hospital, 316; source of medical supplies, 23; St. Louis Arsenal, 13; St. Louis Children's Hospital, 336n15; St. Louis County Insane Asylum, 316; St. Louis Western Dispensary, 316; St. Luke's Hospital, 316; tax levies, 15; Taylor, Daniel, 337n26; tuberculosis, 7; unemployment, 314; violence, 13–14, 16; William M. McPheeters Collection, 313

St. Louis Children's Hospital, 336n15

St. Louis County Insane Asylum, 316

St. Louis Democrat, 184

"The St. Louis Massacre," 13, 158, 300

St. Louis Medical and Surgical Journal, 6–7, 8, 10

St. Louis Medical College, 246

St. Louis Medical Society: See Medical Society of Missouri

St. Louis Mutual Insurance Company, 316

St. Louis Republican, 89, 104, 112, 176, 273, 318, 334

St. Louis University, 6, 9, 20

St. Louis Western Dispensary, 316

St. Luke's Hospital, 316

Stonehill, Edward B., 86, 89, 351n29

Stowe, Harriet Beecher, Uncle Tom's Cabin, 10

Strawberry River, 196, 219

Strickland, E., 326

Sturgis, Samuel D., 174, 366n30

Swamp Fox: See Thompson, M. Jeff

swamps, 324, 341n12

Swindell, James H.: arrest of, 193; dinner with William McPheeters, 80; medical care of wounded soldiers, 40, 53, 327; procurement of medical supplies, 41; social visits, 182, 184, 189; surgeon for 32d Arkansas Infantry, 343n21; visit to hospital, 42, 64, 151; visit with William McPheeters, 166, 169, 175

Szymanski, Ignatius, 83, 350n18

T

Tappan, James Camp: as brigade commander, 80, 350n11; brigade inspection by William McPheeters, 324; dinner with William McPheeters, 136; Grinstead, Hiram L., 362n50; medical care, 94; message to William McPheeters, 119; Mitchell, Charles E., 365n16; official visit with William McPheeters, 103; Polk, Thomas G., 359n25; resumption of command, 162; social visits, 88, 120, 163, 172, 173, 177–79, 191–93; substitute commander, 158–59; temporary command of division, 158–59; visit with William McPheeters, 120; Williams, David S., 365n11

Tappan, Mrs. James Camp: accompanying division, 159–60; dinner with William McPheeters, 136; medical care, 84, 119, 120; military ball,

355*n7;* social visits, 155, 163, 173, 175; visit with William McPheeters, 83, 90, 144

taxis, 94, 353*n49*

tax levies, 15

Taylor, Charles M.: correspondence with William McPheeters, 70; letter about Lincoln assassination, 296; medical care of wounded soldiers, 152; Trans-Mississippi Department, 23, 366*n29;* visit as Medical Inspector, 174–75; visit with William McPheeters, 112, 148, 181, 275

Taylor, Daniel, 337*n26*

Taylor, Henry Clay: church attendance, 184; correspondence with William McPheeters, 106, 113, 118, 301; dinner with William McPheeters, 79–80, 103; District of Arkansas, 348*n29;* hunting, 287; Price, Sterling, 348*n29;* saddle exchange with William McPheeters, 211; social visits, 175, 210; visit with William McPheeters, 53, 68, 86, 265

Taylor, Mrs. Henry Clay: letter from husband, 144; as officer wife, 351*n30;* review of troops, 178; social visits, 86–88, 90, 92, 100; visit with William McPheeters, 154–55, 206

Taylor, Richard: Battle of Mansfield, 359*n28;* Battle of Pleasant Hill, 360*n32;* battle with Union forces, 125–27, 136–38, 140–41, 157, 357*n18;* District of Western Louisiana, 357*n18,* 358*n13;* Mouton, Alfred, 359*n29;* reinforcements, 121, 129; surrender, 291; visit from Thomas Churchill, 136

Taylor, Theodore T., 165, 166, 202, 365*n10*

Tennessee, 21, 251

Tennessee (ironclad), 369*n8*

10th Missouri Cavalry, 346*n14,* 372*n42*

10th Missouri Infantry, 341*n12,* 354*n55,* 354*n56,* 378*n21*

Terry's Ferry, 60, 65

testes, inflammation of, 89, 352*n39*

tetanus, 227

Texarkana, Tx., 376*n30*

Texas: Confederate forces, 247–50, 253; disbandment of army, 292; drought, 252; headquarters of Edmund Kirby Smith, 292; as Union target, 75, 123–24

Texas cavalry Brigade, 84, 85, 138, 142

Texas Republican (Marshall), 375*n19*

3d Minnesota Infantry, 60

3d Missouri Field Artillery, 355*n1*

13th Louisiana Partisan Rangers, 380*n22*

30th Texas Cavalry, 373*n54*

38th Arkansas Infantry, 350*n11,* 355*n1,* 356*n11,* 366*n26*

34th Arkansas Infantry, 351*n28*

39th Arkansas Infantry, 351*n26,* 362*n51*

32d Arkansas Infantry, 343*n21,* 349*n6,* 359*n26*

37th Arkansas Infantry, 349*n7,* 351*n26,* 356*n11*

36th Arkansas Infantry, 343*n21,* 344*n35,* 351*n26,* 359*n26*

33d Arkansas Infantry, 350*n11,* 355*n3,* 362*n50,* 365*n11,* 367*n40*

33d Texas Cavalry, 376*n32*

Thomas, George H., 251, 374*n16*

Thomas, Joseph L., 73, 104, 118, 119, 135, 228, 349*n41*

Thompkins, Mr., 101

Thompkins, Mrs., 100, 181

Thompson, Col., 298–99, 379*n15*

Thompson, Gideon W., 379*n15*

Thompson, Jesse E., 104, 106, 107, 109, 113, 355*n1*

Thompson, Lee L., 379*n15*

Thompson, M. Jeff: Boonville, Mo., 229; dinner with William McPheeters, 227; Fredericktown, Mo., 223; Sedalia, Mo., 232; Shelby, Joseph Orville, 369–70*n19;* Swamp Fox, 369–70*n19;* visit with Calvin Hervey, 268–69, 283; visit with William McPheeters, 225; Washington, Ark., 261

Thompson, Mrs. Thomas H., 268, 286
Thompson, Thomas H., 281, 285–86, 288, 377*n17*, 379*n15*
thoughts of wife and family: at Calvin Hervey's, 273–74; Christmas, 1863, 92–93; encampment in Arkansas, 255, 258, 260, 263, 264; Missouri Expedition, 202, 226, 230, 241, 250; during search for wife and family, 274–76; summer of 1864, 160, 166, 168, 169, 171–74, 177, 180, 194
ticks, 160
Tidewater Virginia, xii, 22
Tilden, Mr., 52
Tishimingo County, Miss., 21
Tracy, Henry W.: arrest of, 248; crossing Arkansas River, 217; dinner with William McPheeters, 210; District of Arkansas, 348*n30*; drunk, 247; Frost, Daniel Marsh, 348*n30*; march to Boonville, Mo., 229; medical care, 69, 72; Parsons, Mosby Monroe, 348*n30*; Price, Sterling, 348*n30*; trip to town, 133; visit to Calvin Hervey's, 281; visit with William McPheeters, 80, 90
Trans-Mississippi Department: administrative organization, 22; Alston, Benjamin, 367*n33*; Arkadelphia, Ark., 347*n25*; Army Medical Board, 360*n37*; Buckner, Simon Bolivar, 368*n2*; Clothing Bureau, 358*n22*, 377*n6*; Cullen, Matthew R., 368*n4*; Cundiff, J. H. R., 348*n38*; Cunningham, Francis D., 342*n18*; defense of, 124; devastation of, 123; disintegration of, 291; economic strain, 252–53, 291; effect of Vicksburg campaign, 30; geographic area, ix, 21; Greene, Charles, 358*n20*; Haden, John M., 352*n36*; Haynes, William H., 358*n22*; help with Confederate war effort, 157–58; Hickman, Edwin A., 347*n26*; Holmes, Theophilus Hunter, 23, 339*n52*; Holmes, Theophilus Hunter, Jr., 339*n54*; Huger,

Benjamin, 358*n20*; inspection reports, 321–25; isolation of, 55, 57, 76; junkyard of the Confederate army, 22; Lawrence, W. M., 351*n23*; Levy, Lionel, 355*n60*; Marmaduke, John Sappington, 341*n14*; McDowell, Joseph Nash, 376–77*n5*; Medical Department, 22, 55; Pim, Lewis T., 378*n23*; Polk, Trusten, 364*n60*; Price, Sterling, 338*n45*; Rhett, Thomas G., 358*n21*; Sappington, G. W., 364*n3*; shortage of provisions, 253; Smith, Edmund Kirby, 23, 31, 76, 345*n15*; Smith, Solomon A., 358*n14*, 358*n15*; surrender, 302, 334, 380*n21*; surrender terms, 292; survival of, 75, 197; Taylor, Charles M., 23, 366*n29*; Taylor, Richard, 357*n18*; Turnbull, Charles J., 367*n33*; Union strategy, 157; Yandell, David Wendell, 358*n14*, 358*n15*
Trenton, Ark., 40, 41, 42, 306, 326–27
Trimble, John D., 293, 378–79*n7*
Trinity, La., 308
tuberculosis, 7, 319, 336*n14*; See also phthisis
Tulip, Ark., *122, 149*, 151–52, *196*, 213
Tupelo, Miss., 332
Turnbull, Charles J., 178–79, 367*n33*
Turner, Edward P., 269, 284, 376*n33*
12th Arkansas Battalion of Sharpshooters, 380*n19*
12th Arkansas Cavalry, 365*n15*
12th Missouri Cavalry, 346*n14*, 370*n23*, 371*n35*
12th Missouri Infantry, 351*n24*, 365*n18*
20th Texas Cavalry, 364*n58*, 364*n59*, 373*n55*
25th Arkansas Infantry, 352*n33*, 367*n33*
21st Texas Cavalry, 353*n45*
24th Arkansas Infantry, 350*n11*, 367*n38*
29th Iowa Infantry, 363*n54*
27th Arkansas Infantry, 350*n11*, 356*n11*, 370*n25*, 378*n22*, 380*n22*
26th Arkansas Infantry, 359*n26*, 365*n11*, 378*n19*
Twilight (steamboat), 305, 307

Tyler, Charles, 379*n9*
Tyler, John, Jr., 97, 98, 99, 101,
    353–54*n52*
Tyler, Tx., *2*, 347*n25*, 370*n24*
Tyler (gunboat), 33, 342*n20*
typhoid fever, 58, 101

U

ulceration of cornea, 79
Uncle Tom's Cabin (Stowe, Harriet
    Beecher), 10
Union, Mo., *196, 226*
Union command: tax levies, 15; travel
    policies, 45, 47; use of banishment,
    xii, 47–48
Union County, Ark., 163, 365*n15*
Union forces: amphibious forces,
    124–25; Arkansas Expedition Army,
    59; Arkansas State Penitentiary,
    346*n15*; assistance from Confederate
    surgeons, 363*n54*; Atlanta, Ga., 194;
    battle at Nashville, Tenn., 374*n16*;
    Battle of Chickamauga, 348*n33*;
    Battle of Jenkins' Ferry, 150–51,
    361*n42*, 362*n48*, 362*n53*, 363*n54*;
    battle of Kennesaw Mountain,
    367*n39*; Battle of Mansfield,
    137–38, 359*n28*; Battle of Mine
    Creek, 372*n37*; battle of Mobile
    Bay, 369*n8*; Battle of Pilot Knob,
    196, 224–25, 370*n20*; Battle of
    Pleasant Hill, 138–42, 360*n32*;
    Battle of Poison Spring, 361*n44*;
    battle of Spotsylvania Courthouse,
    365*n9*; battle of the Wilderness,
    364*n7*; capture by Confederate
    forces, 218, 225–26, 229, 232; cap-
    ture of Confederate boats, 369*n8*;
    capture of Confederate soldiers,
    326–27, 329; Charleston, S.C., 284;
    defeat by James Fagan, 148; defeat
    by Joseph Johnston, 184; defeat by
    Nathan B. Forrest, 174; defeat by
    Robert E. Lee, 161–62, 164, 172,
    176; defeat in Florida, 356*n16*;
    destruction of CSS *Alabama*
    (cruiser), 185, 367*n41*; destruction
    of property, 221, 233, 235, 238–39,

241; encounter with Sterling Price's
    forces, 145; final assault, 251; 1st
    Indiana Cavalry, 343*n25*; 1st Kansas
    Colored Infantry, 361*n44*;
    Gettysburg campaign, 48; guerrilla
    raids, 76; Helena campaign, 33,
    39–40, 325–27, 342–43*n20*, 342*n16*;
    Home Guards, 13; interactions with
    pro-Southern women, 45–47; iron-
    clad gunboats, 329; Kansas 5th
    Federal, 40; losses to Confederate
    forces, 119–20, 361*n44*, 362*n47*,
    364*n2*, 370*n20*; medical care of
    wounded soldiers, 363*n56*;
    Missouri's role, 11–12; morale, 159;
    negro troops, 307; offer of medical
    supplies to William McPheeters,
    327–28; Petersburg, Va., 181–83,
    188–89; raid on Hamburg, Ark.,
    276–77; raid on Richmond, Va.,
    120, 356–57*n17*; Red River
    campaign, 124; retreat back to
    Little Rock, Ark., 157; retreat by
    Ulysses S. Grant, 188–89; retreat
    from Camden, Ark., 148–49;
    Richmond, Va., 181–83, 188;
    route to Shreveport, 126–27; 7th
    Missouri Infantry, 377*n7*; 16th
    Kansas Volunteer Cavalry, 371*n31*;
    skirmish with Confederate forces,
    221, 225–31, 233–39, 371*n34*,
    371*n36*; surrender terms, 300; 3d
    Minnesota Infantry, 60; threatening
    Shreveport, La., 121, 124; 29th
    Iowa Infantry, 363*n54*; use of ban-
    ishment, 333–34; vandalism, 153,
    251; visit to Polk hospital, 325–28;
    vulnerability of, 127
University of North Carolina, Chapel
    Hill, 3, 339*n52*
University of Pennsylvania College of
    Medicine, 3, 317
U.S. Census of 1860, 338*n36*
U.S. Corps of Engineers, 7
USS *Kersarge* (sloop), 367*n41*
USS *Queen City* (gunboat), 367*n35*

V

Vallandigham, Clement Laird, 73, 79, 176–77, 349*n40*, 366*n31*
Valle, Francis, 88, 93, 352*n35*
Van Buren County, Ark., 217–18
Vance, Dr., 199, 201
Van Dorn, Earl, 369*n6*
varioloid, 217, 369*n14; See also* small pox
Venable, Thomas, 262–64, 375*n24*
Verandah Hotel, 200
Versailles, Mo., 229
Vicksburg, Miss., *290;* fall of city, 40–41, 42, 48, 326–29, 345*n15;* McPheeters, William Marcellus, 310; Price, Sterling, 21; Sherman, William T., 119; surrender terms, 329; Vicksburg campaign, 29–30, 32–33, 347*n26*
Volker, Henry, 18, 338*n36*
von Phul, Benjamin, 92, 353*n46*
von Phul, Francis, 353*n46,* 367*n34*
von Phul, Frank, 178, 248
von Phul, William, 117, 356*n13*
von Schmelling, Wedig, 372*n40*
von Snelling, Wedig, 241

W

Walker, John George, 129, 139, 143–45, 150, 357–58*n13,* 362*n48,* 362*n49,* 377*n15*
Walker, Judge, 259
Walker, Lt., 278
Walker, Lucius Marsh: Chenowith, Benjamin D., 353*n45;* death of, 65, 347*n20;* defense of Little Rock, Ark., 59; District of Arkansas, 347*n20;* Dobbins, Archibald S., 344*n33;* duel, 64–65, 347*n20;* Helena campaign, 32, 342*n16,* 342*n20;* Marmaduke, John Sappington, 64–65, 347*n20,* 347*n21;* Polk, James K., 347*n20*
Walker, Tandy, 361*n45*
Walker's Greyhounds, 357–58*n13*
Walnut Hill, Ark., *122,* 128, 201
Warburg, Edward, 328
Ward, Jane, 272, 278
Ware, Hamilton B., 35
war news, 169–74, 176–77, 179–81, 184, 188–92, 207

war prices, 128, 131, 199, 200, 293
Warren, Ark., *270,* 277, 334
Warren, Mr., 71
wartime surgery, 57, 317–18, 360*n36*
Washington, Ark., 2, *74, 122, 196, 270, 290;* Burton, R. A., 298; Cabell, Edward Carrington, 274, 287, 298; Camp Sumter, 111; court of inquiry, 379*n16;* encampment, 69–71, 259–62; 1st Missouri Brigade, 376*n28;* Jordan, Irene, 286, 294–95; Lawrence, W. M., 85; Lowry, Judge, 71; McDowell, Joseph Nash, 274; McPheeters, William Marcellus, 334; Price, Sterling, 253, 254, 287–88, 299; Rector, Thomas, 375*n20;* seat of government, 57, 348*n34;* Slaughter, R. M., 79; Thomas, Joseph L., 119; Trimble, John D., 379*n7;* Wooten, Thomas Dudley, 298
Washington, Miss: *See* Graham, Mrs. Malcolm (formerly Miss Washington)
Washington, Mo., 227
Washington, Tx., 97
Washington (Ark.) Telegraph, 58, 375*n18*
Washington City, 188
Washington County, Ark., 240
Washington County, Mo., 225
Washington University, 333
watermelon, 199, 201, 209
Watie, Stand, 245, 372*n44*
Watkins, George C.: conversation with William McPheeters, 190; dinner visit, 81, 91, 204, 206; dinner with William McPheeters, 261; Holmes, Theophilus Hunter, 348*n37;* overnight visit, 72; social visits, 101; visit with Gov. Polk, 259; visit with Mrs. Wright, 202; visit with William McPheeters, 87, 177
Watson, Cal, 134, 359*n23*
Waul, Thomas N., 362*n48*
Waverly, Mo., *196,* 233
Wayne County, Mo., 222
Wear, Hamilton B., 341*n9*
Webb, Dr., 61, 346*n14*

Webb, Frederick F., 346*n14*
Webb, William, 332, 346*n14*
Welch, Mr., 27, 61, 62
Wells, E. C., 20, 337*n18*
Welton, Louis A., 98, 354*n57*
Westminster College, Mo., 16
Westphalia, Mo., *196*, 228
Westport, Mo., *196, 235,* 371*n34*
Whigs, 12
White, James D., 88, 177, 189, 324,
   352*n34*
White Cloud (steamboat), 307–9
White Haven, 336*n7*
White River, *28, 196, 290;* capture of
   Union boats, 179, 367*n35;* Des Arc,
   Ark., 35; DeVall's Bluff, Ark.,
   345*n13;* encampment, 219; Harris
   Ferry, 53; Jacksonport, Ark., 24;
   mouth of, 310; Union gunboats,
   329–30
Whitfield House, 154
Wickham, John, 311, 314, 336*n7,*
   337*n18,* 380*n3*
Wilcox, Lt., 337*n18*
Williams, David S., 166, 178, 365*n11*
Williams' farm, 259
Williamson, Dr., 261
Williamson, Mrs., 256
Wills, J. M., 89, 352*n38*
Wilson, Dr., 260, 262, 264
Winfrey, Caleb, 235, 371*n35*
winter quarters, 76–101
Wittsburg, Ark., 369*n7*
wolves, 243, 244
women: assistance to Confederate
   forces, 56; banishment, 47–48, 271;
   as Confederate sympathizers, 45–47,
   271; display of colors, 47, 271;
   imprisonment, 271; interactions
   with Union forces, 45–47; Southern
   Relief Fair, 315, 381*n5*
Wonder County, Mo., 229
Wonder Creek, 229
Wood, Carville H., 98, 355*n58*
Wood, Mrs., 98
Wood, Robert C., 218, 257, 262, 266,
   345*n12,* 369*n16,* 374*n13*

Woodford (steamboat), 46
Woods, Parson, 90
Wooten, Mrs. Thomas D., 178, 192,
   204, 212, 286
Wooten, Thomas Dudley: appointment
   as Medical Director of the District
   of Arkansas, 147, 341*n10;* Army
   Medical Association, 97, 120;
   assignment to Parsons' Division,
   132, 134; assistance with mail, 43;
   breakfast with William McPheeters,
   298; camp inspections, 321–25;
   chief surgeon, 341*n10;* church
   attendance, 79; conversation with
   William McPheeters, 203–4;
   correspondence from William
   McPheeters, 82, 105–6, 163–64,
   167, 213, 216, 253, 262; correspondence to William McPheeters, 89,
   107, 164, 165, 225, 266; departure
   for Texas, 80; dinner with William
   McPheeters, 131, 165, 175–76, 181,
   192, 194; fishing, 288, 298–99;
   Helena campaign, 39, 342*n19;*
   hunting, 72, 285–86, 296; on leave,
   302; medical care of wounded soldiers, 39, 66, 152; medical duties,
   141; medical supplies, 133; medical
   visit to Sterling Price, 190; move to
   Camp Sumter, 104; official visit to
   brigade, 103; return from Texas, 95;
   reunion with William McPheeters,
   111; social visits, 261, 284–86;
   swimming in camp, 37; visit from
   William McPheeters, 155, 184, 187,
   212, 267–68, 274, 281–82, 294, 301;
   visit to camp, 70; visit to Fagan's
   Brigade, 78; visit to Henry Clay
   Taylor, 68; visit with Mr. Boyd,
   114; visit with Sallie McPheeters,
   280; visit with William McPheeters,
   62; and William McPheeters, 36
Worthen, Mr., 26, 27, 88
Wright, John C., 167, 170, 172, 173,
   175, 209, 365*n15*
Wright, Mrs. (Ark.), 191, 202
Wright, Mrs. John C., 173, 175, 209

Wright, Mrs. (La.), 117

Wright, William Fulton: arrival of, 167, 170; church attendance, 184; Churchill, Thomas James, 365*n14*; delivery of mess supplies, 175; home to Lewisville, Ark., 191, 202; news from town, 188; return from visit home, 178; trade of horses, 205; trip to Camden, Ark., 180, 187

X

X-ray machines, 319

Y

Yancey, Stephen D., 285, 377*n15*

Yandell, David Wendell: assistance with wounded soldiers, 141, 342*n17*; correspondence with William McPheeters, 145, 155, 165; social visit, 200; Trans-Mississippi Department, 358*n14, 358n15;* visit with William McPheeters, 130–31, 147, 154

Yates, Paul Christian, 113, 356*n11*

Yazoo River, *290*

Yell County, 215

yellow flags, 40, 343*n23*